SEVENTH EDITION

The Norton
Field Guide
to Writing
with Handbook

SEVENTH EDITION

The Norton

Field Guide to Writing

with Handbook

Richard Bullock
WRIGHT STATE UNIVERSITY

Deborah Bertsch
COLUMBUS STATE COMMUNITY COLLEGE

W. W. NORTON & COMPANY
Independent Publishers Since 1923

W. W. NORTON & COMPANY has been independent since its founding in 1923, when William Warder Norton and Mary D. Herter Norton first published lectures delivered at the People's Institute, the adult education division of New York City's Cooper Union. The firm soon expanded its program beyond the Institute, publishing books by celebrated academics from America and abroad. By mid-century, the two major pillars of Norton's publishing program—trade books and college texts—were firmly established. In the 1950s, the Norton family transferred control of the company to its employees, and today—with a staff of five hundred and hundreds of trade, college, and professional titles published each year— W. W. Norton & Company stands as the largest and oldest publishing house owned wholly by its employees.

Editor: Sarah Touborg
Project Editor: Christine D'Antonio
Developmental Editor: Claire Wallace
Associate Editor: Caroline Fairey Meese
Managing Editors, College: Kim Yi and Carla Talmadge
Production Manager: Stephen Sajdak
Media Editor: Joy Cranshaw
Associate Media Editor: Jessica Awad
Media Editorial Assistant: Felicia Jarrin
Ebook Producer: Sophia Purut
Media Producer: Lindsey Heale

Junior Media Producer: Daria Turner
Marketing Research and Strategy Director,
   Composition: Michele Dobbins
Design Director: Rubina Yeh
Book Designers: Anna Palchik, Jen Montgomery
Composition: Graphic World
Photo Editor: Ted Szczepanski
Photo Research: Dena Digilio Betz
Director of College Permissions: Megan Schindel
Permissions Clearing: Josh Garvin
Manufacturing: Transcontinental—Beauceville

Permission to use copyrighted material is included in the Credits section of this book, which begins on page C-1.

ISBN 978-1-324-08752-6

W. W. Norton & Company, Inc., 500 Fifth Avenue, New York, NY 10110
wwnorton.com
W. W. Norton & Company Ltd., 15 Carlisle St., London W1D 3BS

1 2 3 4 5 6 7 8 9 0

Preface

The Norton Field Guide to Writing began as an attempt to offer the kind of writing guides found in the best rhetorics in a format as user-friendly as the best handbooks, and on top of that, to be as flexible as possible. We wanted to create a handy guide to help college students with all their written work. Just as there are field guides for bird watchers, for gardeners, and for accountants, this would be one for writers.

In its first six editions the *Field Guide* has obviously touched a chord with many writing instructors, and it remains the best-selling college rhetoric—a success that leaves us humbled and grateful, but also determined to improve the book with each new edition. To that end, we've expanded and updated Part 1 on academic literacies, with a new chapter on using generative AI effectively and responsibly; added new student and professional examples throughout; added a new feature to the genre chapters called "More Ways to Approach"; updated advice on composing with sound; and (we hope) made numerous other improvements throughout the book. Coauthor Deborah Bertsch has created new and expanded digital resources, including new videos now cross-referenced throughout the book. But it's not just us: this new edition has also been shaped by our community of adopters and their students. Through formal and informal reviews, emails and letters, and conversations with teachers and students using the *Field Guide*, we've learned from you what you need to teach effectively and what your students need to learn.

The Norton Field Guide still aims to offer both the guidance new teachers and first-year writers need and the flexibility many experienced teachers want. In our own teaching we've seen how well explicit guides to writing work for students and novice teachers. But too often, writing textbooks provide far more information than students need or instructors can assign and as a result are bigger and more expensive than they should be. So we've tried to provide enough structure without too much detail—to give the information college writers need to know while resisting the temptation to tell them everything there is to know.

WHAT'S NEW IN THE SEVENTH EDITION

An expanded and updated Part 1, Academic Literacies, helps set students up for success from day one of their college experience, with a new chapter on using generative AI tools effectively and newly expanded chapters on reading and learning online.

A new section on honesty in Chapter 1 enhances the coverage of ethics in rhetoric by discussing the role of personal integrity in being a student and writer.

"More Ways to Approach ___" (a Literacy Narrative, a Profile, a Report, etc.) offers students choices beyond conventional essays, helping them compose in the way that works best for them. For example, in the Reporting Information chapter, students are prompted to create an infographic, a series of *TikTok* videos, or an "explainer" (Chapters 12–23).

New readings throughout for nearly every genre. As in previous editions, the *Field Guide* features authentic student writing from a range of two-year and four-year schools across the country, along with high-interest professional writing that demonstrates how the genres and processes learned in first-year writing transfer outside the classroom. Researched writing is documented in the latest MLA or APA style. Vibrant and diverse new selections include a text analysis, "What Writers Can Learn from *Goodnight Moon*"; a student argument, "Banning *ChatGPT* Will Do More Harm than Good"; and a review of *Killers of the Flower Moon* by an Osage writer in the Evaluations chapter; and many more. All new readings are asterisked in the table of contents.

Advice throughout the book guides students on using generative AI tools responsibly. The Research section, for example, includes sample AI acknowledgment statements for MLA and APA, and the Media / Design section offers suggestions for creating images with AI—and for evaluating those images for inaccuracies and biases. The ebook features an animated video modeling a student using generative AI to help probe experiences and ideas for a personal narrative.

Updated coverage of composing with sound includes advice for using voice, music, ambient sounds, and silence—and tips for creating podcasts and other audio-based texts.

A new section on hyperlinks in the Documentation chapter helps students decide whether to document sources through hyperlinks—and offers tips for doing so.

A revised chapter on personal narratives introduces the concept of a braided narrative form, featuring a student example.

New practical advice on annotation is provided in the ebook. This ebook-exclusive chapter welcomes students to the community of engaged readers, fostering belonging through a discussion of common active reading and annotation strategies, including a video tutorial for using digital annotation tools in the Norton Ebook Reader.

Sixteen new animated videos more than double the number embedded and cross-referenced in the ebook and provide more balanced coverage throughout. New topics include the use of summary as a reading comprehension tool; anticipation of counterarguments; and revision strategies, including peer review.

Fully revised InQuizitive for Writers activities incorporate updated, engaging examples throughout; include a brand-new activity on using inclusive language; and offer new comprehensive activities that cover all the Situations, Processes, and Genres topics or all the Research topics—with the option of either MLA or APA documentation questions.

The updated and expanded Norton Teaching Tools site is now more intuitively organized and easier to navigate, with new *PowerPoint* class activities for more chapters in the book, teaching suggestions and sample assignments for bringing generative AI into the classroom, and periodic updates on new and developing topics.

WAYS OF TEACHING WITH *THE NORTON FIELD GUIDE TO WRITING*

The Norton Field Guide is designed to give you both support and flexibility. It has clear assignment sequences if you want them, or you can create your own. If, for example, you assign a position paper, there's a full chapter. If you want students to use sources, you can add the appropriate research chapters. If you want them to submit a topic proposal, you can add that chapter.

If you're a new teacher, the Genres chapters offer explicit assignment sequences—and the color-coded links will remind you of detail you may want to bring in. The Norton Teaching Tools site offers advice on creating a syllabus, responding to writing, and more.

If you focus on genres, there are complete chapters on all the genres college students are often assigned. Color-coded links will help you bring in details about research or other writing strategies as you wish.

If you teach a corequisite, IRW, or stretch course, the Academic Literacies chapters offer explicit guidelines to help students write and read in academic contexts, summarize and respond to what they read, and develop academic habits of mind that will help them succeed in college.

If you teach a dual-credit course, the Norton Teaching Tools site offers advice on supporting students in various dual-enrollment contexts, including online, in high schools, and on college campuses.

If you organize your course thematically, Chapter 29 on generating ideas and text can help get students thinking about a theme. You can also assign them to do research on the theme, starting with Chapter 48 on finding sources, or perhaps with Chapter 28 on writing as inquiry. If they then write in a particular genre, there will be a chapter to guide them.

If you want students to do research, there are nine chapters on the research process, including guidelines and sample papers for MLA and APA styles.

If you teach for transfer, three chapters about fields of study help students connect what they're reading, writing, and learning in your class to other college courses. The Considering the Rhetorical Situation questions that appear throughout the book prompt students to reflect on the key concepts of audience, purpose, genre, stance, and media/design, thus helping students develop a framework for analyzing future writing tasks. Finally, the "More Ways to Approach" prompts in the Genres chapters help students develop rhetorical flexibility.

If you teach writing about writing, you might use the chapter on literacy narratives as an introduction to your course—and use the Fields section to help students research and analyze the key features of writing in particular disciplines or careers.

If you focus on modes, you'll find chapters on using narration, description, and so on as strategies for many writing purposes, and links that lead students through the process of writing an essay organized around a particular mode.

WHAT'S IN THE BOOK

The Norton Field Guide covers twelve genres often assigned in college. Much of the book is in the form of guidelines, designed to help students consider the choices they have as writers. The book is organized into nine parts:

- ✳ **ACADEMIC LITERACIES.** Chapters 1–6 focus on writing and reading in academic contexts, summarizing and responding, developing academic habits of mind, writing online, and writing with generative AI.

- ▓ **RHETORICAL SITUATIONS.** Chapters 7–11 focus on purpose, audience, genre, stance, and media and design. In addition, almost every chapter includes tips to help students focus on their rhetorical situations.

- ▲ **GENRES.** Chapters 12–23 cover twelve genres, four of them—literacy narrative, textual analysis, report, and argument—treated in greater detail.

- ● **FIELDS.** Chapters 24–26 cover the key features of major fields of study and give guidance on reading and writing in each of those fields.

- ⁘ **PROCESSES.** Chapters 27–36 offer advice for generating ideas and text, drafting, revising and rewriting, editing, proofreading, reflecting, compiling a portfolio, collaborating with others, and writing as inquiry.

- ◆ **STRATEGIES.** Chapters 37–46 cover ways of developing and organizing text—comparing, describing, taking essay exams, and so on.

- ● **RESEARCH / DOCUMENTATION.** Chapters 47–55 offer advice on how to do academic research; work with sources; quote, paraphrase, and summarize source materials; and document sources using MLA and APA styles.

- ◗ **MEDIA / DESIGN.** Chapters 56–59 give guidance on choosing the appropriate print, digital, or spoken medium; designing text; using images and sound; and giving spoken presentations.

- ★ **HANDBOOK.** At the end of the book is a handbook to help students edit what they write. The handbook is organized around the intuitive categories of sentences, language, and punctuation to make it easy to use.

HIGHLIGHTS

It's easy to use.   Menus, directories, and a glossary/index make it easy for students to find what they're looking for. Color-coded templates and documentation maps even make MLA and APA documentation easy.

It has just enough detail, with short chapters that include color-coded links sending students to more detail if they need more.

It's uniquely flexible for teachers. Short chapters can be assigned in any order—and color-coded links help draw from other chapters as need be.

It includes a user-friendly handbook, with an intuitive organization around sentences, language, and punctuation to make it easy for students to find what they need. And we go easy on the grammatical terminology, with links to the glossary for students who need detailed definitions.

RESOURCES

Like the book itself, the resources that accompany *The Norton Field Guide to Writing* are designed to provide flexibility, with a wealth of options for student learning and for new and experienced instructors alike.

Ebooks.   Included with all new Seventh Edition copies of the print book, *Norton Field Guide* ebook access can also be purchased standalone from the Norton website and can be offered through Inclusive Access programs on many campuses. The ebook's built-in highlighting and note-taking capabilities help students engage with and respond to what they read, and instructors can share notes, videos, or external links with students using the instructor annotation tool. Norton ebooks can be viewed on—and synced among—all computers and mobile devices, and they can be made available for offline reading.

Videos.   A collection of short videos—including sixteen that are new to the Seventh Edition—is available in the ebook and for streaming online. Informed by feedback from hundreds of composition instructors, topics include the writing process, rhetorical situations, specific kinds of writing, critical reading strategies, and more. Videos are now cross-referenced throughout the book—including the print format—making it easier for students to access them when they are most useful.

InQuizitive for Writers.   Included with all new copies of the *Field Guide*, InQuizitive gives students practice with writing, editing, and research in a low-stakes, feedback-driven environment. The activities are adaptive: students receive additional practice and feedback in the areas where they need more help, with links to relevant pages in the *Little Seagull Handbook* ebook. After practicing with InQuizitive, students will be better prepared to start drafting, find and evaluate sources, and edit their own writing.

Norton Teaching Tools. The Norton Teaching Tools site for *The Norton Field Guide* is your first stop when looking for creative, engaging resources to refresh your syllabus or design a new one. The Norton Teaching Tools site is searchable and can be filtered by chapter or by resource type, making it easy to find exactly what you need, download and customize it, and import it into your LMS course. Contents for the Seventh Edition include:

- A comprehensive guide to teaching first-year writing, with chapters on developing a syllabus, responding to student writing, teaching research and information literacy skills, and more

- Access to *The Norton Guide to Equity-Minded Teaching*, written by renowned teaching and learning experts, to help any instructor striving to ensure that all students—and, in particular, historically underserved students—have an equal chance for success

- A robust collection of sample writing assignments, peer review templates, and rubrics

- Thoroughly revised tips for teaching every chapter and reading in the book

- Class-activity *PowerPoints*, as well as genre flowcharts and documentation maps from the book

- A collection of sample student essays organized by genre, rhetorical mode, and field, including some that are documented and annotated.

- A collection of videos on topics including thesis statements, rhetorical situations, critical reading strategies, and commonly assigned genres

- Expanded support for assigning InQuizitive for Writers

- A collection of sample student essays organized by genre, rhetorical mode, and field, including some that are documented and annotated

- Worksheets and templates in Word and PDF formats with guidance on editing paragraphs, responding to a draft, and more

Quizzes.   Quizzes on topics not covered in InQuizitive for Writers—within the broad categories of sentences, language, punctuation/mechanics, and paragraph editing—as well as pre- and post-diagnostics for InQuizitive, can be easily imported into your LMS. Comprehension quizzes for each chapter and reading in the *Field Guide* are also available.

Plagiarism Tutorial.   Now available for integration directly into most campus learning management systems, the Plagiarism Tutorial guides students through why plagiarism matters, what counts as plagiarism, and how to avoid plagiarizing, with activities and short quizzes to assess what they've learned. Students earn 90 percent for completing the tutorial and an additional 10 percent based on their quiz performance. You can see your students' scores, how much time they spent working, and when they finished in your Class Activity Report.

Resources for Your LMS.   Easily add high-quality Norton digital resources to your online, hybrid, or lecture courses. Get started building your course with our easy-to-use integrated resources. All activities can be accessed right within your existing learning management system. Graded activities can be configured to report to the LMS course gradebook. Integration links are available for the *Norton Field Guide* ebook, InQuizitive for Writers, the *Little Seagull Handbook* ebook, the Plagiarism Tutorial, and all videos. Instructors can also add customizable quizzes to their LMS or upload additional resources from the Norton Teaching Tools site, including *PowerPoint* slides, worksheets, sample writing assignments and rubrics, peer-review templates, and model student essays. All resources can be found at digital .wwnorton.com/fieldguide7h.

Acknowledgments

As we've traveled around the country and met many of the students, teachers, and WPAs who are using *The Norton Field Guide*, we've been gratified to hear that so many find it helpful, to the point that some students tell us that they aren't going to sell it back to the bookstore when the term ends—the highest form of praise. As much as we like the positive response, though, we are especially grateful when we receive suggestions for ways the book might be improved. In this seventh edition, as we did in the sixth edition, we have tried to respond to the many good suggestions we've gotten from students, colleagues, reviewers, and editors. Thank you all, both for your kind words and for your good suggestions.

Some people need to be singled out for thanks, especially Marilyn Moller, the guiding editorial spirit of the *Field Guide* through all seven editions. When we presented Marilyn with the idea for this book, she encouraged us and helped us conceptualize it—and then taught us how to write a textbook. The quality of the *Field Guide* is due in large part to her knowledge of the field of composition, her formidable editing and writing skills, her sometimes uncanny ability to see the future of the teaching of writing—and her equally formidable, if not uncanny, stamina.

Editor Sarah Touborg guided us through this new edition with good humor and better advice. Just as developmental editor John Elliott did with the third and fourth editions, Sarah shepherded the fifth, sixth, and now seventh editions through revisions and additions with a careful hand and a clear eye for appropriate content and language. Her painstaking editing shows throughout this book, and we're grateful for her ability to make us appear to be better writers than we are.

Many others have contributed, too. Thanks to project editor Christine D'Antonio for her energy, patience, and great skill in guiding the book from manuscript to final pages. Claire Wallace brought her astute eye and keen judgment to the documentation of all the selections, while Caroline Fairey Meese managed the extensive reviewing process and took great care of the manuscript at every stage. *The Norton Field Guide* is more than just a print book, and we thank Joy Cranshaw, Felicia Jarrin, Sophia Purut, Kim Yi, and Mica Clausen for creating and producing the superb ebook and instructors' site. Anna Palchik designed the award-winning, user-friendly, and attractive interior, Pete Garceau created the beautiful new cover design, and Debra Morton Hoyt and Rubina Yeh further enhanced the design for accessibility in print and online. Stephen Sajdak transformed a scribbled-over manuscript into a finished product with extraordinary speed and precision, while Jude Grant copyedited. Megan Schindel and Josh Garvin cleared text permissions, coping efficiently with ongoing changes, and Ted Szczepanski cleared permission for the images found by Dena Digilio Betz. Michele Dobbins, Lib Triplett, Annie Stewart, Erin Brown, Heidi Balas, Emily Frankenberger, Sarah Purnell, and Ryan Schwab helped us all keep our eyes on the market. Thanks to all, and to Mike Wright, Ann Shin, and Julia Reidhead for supporting this project in the first place. Last but not least, our profound gratitude goes to the tireless Norton travelers, led so energetically by Erik Fahlgren.

Rich worked with many, many people at Wright State University who deserve thanks for their support and assistance. Jane Blakelock taught Rich most of what he knows about electronic text and writing on and for the web and assembled an impressive list of useful links for the book's website. Adrienne Cassel and Catherine Crowley read and commented on many drafts. Peggy Lindsey shared her students' work and the idea of using charts to show how various genres might be organized. Brady Allen, Deborah Bertsch, Vicki Burke, Melissa Carrion, Jimmy Chesire, Carol Cornett, Mary Doyle, Byron Crews, Deborah Crusan, Sally DeThomas, Stephanie Dickey, Scott Geisel, Karen Hayes, Chuck Holmes, Beth Klaisner, Nancy Mack, Marty Maner, Cynthia Marshall, Sarah McGinley, Kristie McKiernan, Michelle Metzner, Kristie Rowe, Bobby Rubin, Cathy Sayer, David Seitz, Caroline Simmons, Tracy Smith, Rick Strader, Mary Van Loveren, and A. J. Williams responded to drafts, submitted good models of student writing, contributed to the instructor's manual, tested the *Field Guide* in their classes, provided support, and shared with Rich some of their best teaching ideas. Henry Limouze and then Carol Loranger, chairs of the English Department, gave him room to work on this project with patience and good humor. Sandy Trimboli, Becky Traxler, and Lynn Morgan, the secretaries to the writing programs, kept him anchored. And he thanks especially the more than 300 graduate teaching assistants and 10,000 first-year students who class-tested various editions of the *Field Guide* and whose experiences helped to shape it.

Deb is grateful to Columbus State's dean of Arts and Sciences, Allysen Todd, and to current and former English Department chairs Amanda Gradisek and Robyn Lyons-Robinson, who encouraged and supported her work on the *Field Guide*; to her fellow faculty members in the English Department, who show her every day what it means to be a good teacher, writer, collaborator, and colleague; to her high school teaching partners, who helped her navigate the world of dual credit, enriching her own teaching in the process; and to her students, whose wit, work ethic, and writing regularly dazzle her. Deb is also incredibly grateful to Rich Bullock, Joy Cranshaw, Michele Dobbins, Maureen Daly Goggin, Caroline Fairey Meese, Sarah Touborg, and Lib Triplett for mentoring her—with great kindness and generosity—through her *Field Guide* work.

The Norton Field Guide has also benefited from the good advice and conversations we've had with writing teachers across the country, including (among many others) Anne Champion, Sarah Fish, and Diana Gingo at Collin College; Polina Chemishanova, Cyndi Miecznikowski, and Melissa Schaub at the University of North Carolina at Pembroke; Maureen Mathison, Susan Miller, Tom Huckin, Gae Lyn Henderson, and Sundy Watanabe at the University of Utah; Christa Albrecht-Crane, Doug Downs, and Brian Whaley at Utah Valley State College; Anne Dvorak and Anya Morrissey at Longview Community University; Jeff Andelora at Mesa Community College; Robin Calitri at Merced College; Lori Gallinger, Rose Hawkins, Jennifer Nelson, Georgia Standish, and John Ziebell at the Community College of Southern Nevada; Stuart Blythe at Indiana University–Purdue University Fort Wayne; Janice Kelly at Arizona State University; Jeanne McDonald at Waubonsee Community College; Web Newbold, Mary Clark-Upchurch, Megan Auffart, Matt Balk, Edward James Chambers, Sarah Chavez, Desiree Dighton, Ashley Ellison, Theresa Evans, Keith Heller, Ellie Isenhart, Angela Jackson-Brown, Naoko Kato, Yuanyuan Liao, Claire Lutkewitte, Yeno Matuki, Casey McArdle, Tibor Munkacsi, Dani Nier-Weber, Karen Neubauer, Craig O'Hara, Martha Payne, Sarah Sandman, and Kellie Weiss at Ball State University; Patrick Tompkins at Tyler Community College; George Kanieski and Pamela Hardman at Cuyahoga Community College; Daniela Regusa, Jeff Partridge, and Lydia Vine at Capital Community College; Elizabeth Woodworth, Auburn University–Montgomery; Stephanie Eason at Enterprise Community College; Kate Geiselman at Sinclair Community College; Ronda Leathers Dively at Southern Illinois University; Debra Knutson at Shawnee State University; Guy Shebat and Amy Flick at Youngstown State University; Martha Tolleson, Toni McMillen, and Patricia Gerecci at Collin College; Sylva Miller at Pikes Peak Community College; Dharma Hernandez at Los Angeles Unified School District; Ann Spurlock at Mississippi State University; Luke Niiler at the University of Alabama; Jeff Tix at Wharton County Junior College; Florence Bacabac at Utah Tech University; Courtney Barko at West Virginia University; and Maureen Fitzpatrick and Marianne Kunkel at Johnson County

Community College. We would like to thank Antonio Byrd at University of Missouri–Kansas City and Sarah Z. Johnson at Madison College for offering advice that helped inform the new coverage of generative AI.

Finally, we're grateful to the students whose work appears in this edition of the book—and to the instructors who helped them create such compelling writing. One of the new student-written readings published in the Seventh Edition of the *Field Guide* was nominated for the Norton Writer's Prize, and we thank Jill Talbot at University of North Texas for this nomination.

REVIEWERS

The authors and editors at W. W. Norton are grateful to the many instructors across the country whose astute feedback helped shape this new edition of the *Field Guide* and its digital resources: Hannah Abraham-Shea, Pima Community College; Kaye Adkins, Missouri Western State University; Troy Alvey, Ivy Tech Community College; Damien Augustine, San Juan College; Maggie Ayala, DeSales University; Stuart Barbier, Delta College; Cortney Barko, West Virginia University; Cindy Beck, Arkansas State University–Beebe; Dana Brewer, Weatherford College; Sarah Bruton; Fayetteville Tech Community College; Shelly Cain, Northwest Shoals Community College; Michael Courteau, Normandale Community College; Sherri Craig, Southeastern Louisiana University; Teresa Cusumano, Lehigh University; Janine Dalton, Haywood Community College; Jill Darley-Vanis, Clark College; Henry Dixon, State College of Florida Bradenton; Tara Edwards, Lone Star College–North Harris; Barbara Flinn, Youngstown State University; Janine Focht-Hansen; San Antonio College; Keith Foster, Arkansas State University–Beebe; Karen Galli, Hudson County Community College; Melisa Garcia, University of San Francisco; Paola Gemme, Arkansas Tech University; Jenna Gersie, University of Colorado Boulder; Kathryn Glanzer, Tabor College; Risa Gorelick, New Jersey Institute of Technology; Anissa Graham, University of North Alabama; Cortney Green, Central Carolina Technical College; Daniel Hamilton, University of Louisville; Heather Hoffman, Southeast Community College; Deana Hueners, Dakota State University; Elizabeth Isenkul, Tidewater Community College; Margaret A. Johnson, Langston University; Kerri Jordan, Mississippi College; Alexandra Kay, SUNY Orange; Mark Keats, Clark College; Brandon Killen, Penn State University; Alexander Lalama, Bradley University; Cheney M. Luttich, Southeast Community College; David McDevitt, California State University, Long Beach; Lora Meredith, Colorado Mountain College; Josh

Miller, Cape Fear Community College; Donna Mixon, Daytona State College; Eric Morel, University of Delaware; David Muller, The College of New Jersey; Zakaria Naiyer, Citrus College; Valarie O'Bryan, Utah Tech University; Trenton Olsen, Brigham Young University–Idaho; Diane Paul, Southeast Community College; Madison Peschock, Ocean County College; Sarah Piper, Oklahoma State University; Arnetra Pleas, Holmes Community College; Kale Riley, Southeast Community College; Adam Ruh, Western Colorado University; Jamie Sadler, Richmond Community College; Melissa Schaub, University of North Carolina at Pembroke; Stella Setka, West Los Angeles College; Nathan Shank, Oklahoma Christian University; Jennifer Smith, Weatherford College; Kyle Smith, Fayetteville State University; Kelly Stone Gamble, Southeastern Oklahoma State University; Raymond Summerville, Fayetteville State; Brittney Swanson, Santa Fe College; Laura Taggett, Lone Star College–CyFair; Jayanti Tamm, Ocean County College; Harun Thomas, Daytona State College; Jeanette Trammell, California Baptist University; Daniel Vanek, Shasta College; Vallie Lynn Watson, University of North Carolina at Wilmington and Brunswick Community College; Rachael Wiley, Pennsylvania State University; Greg Winston, Husson University; Tiffany Wong, California State University, Bakersfield.

It's customary to conclude by expressing gratitude to one's spouse and family, and for good reason. Writing and revising *The Norton Field Guide* over the past several years, we have enjoyed the loving and unconditional support of our spouses, Barb and Todd, who provide the foundation for all we do. Thank you. We couldn't have done it without you.

How to Use This Book

There's no one way to do anything, and writing is no exception. Some people need to do a lot of planning on paper; others write entire drafts in their heads. Some writers compose quickly and loosely, going back later to revise; others work on one sentence until they're satisfied with it, then move on to the next. And writers' needs vary from task to task, too: sometimes you know what you're going to write about and why, but need to figure out how to do it; other times your first job is to come up with a topic. *The Norton Field Guide* is designed to allow you to chart your own course as a writer, offering guidelines that suit your writing needs. It is organized in nine parts:

1. **ACADEMIC LITERACIES**: The chapters in this part will help you know what's expected in the reading and writing you do for academic purposes, and in summarizing and responding to what you read. One chapter even provides tips for developing habits of mind that will help you succeed in college, whatever your goals.

2. **RHETORICAL SITUATIONS**: No matter what you're writing, it will always have some purpose, audience, genre, stance, and medium and design. This part will help you consider each of these elements, as well as the particular kinds of rhetorical situations created by academic assignments.

3. **GENRES**: Use these chapters for help with specific kinds of writing, from abstracts to explorations to evaluations and more. You'll find more detailed guidance for four especially common assignments: literacy narratives, textual analyses, reports, and arguments.

4. **FIELDS**: The chapters in this part will help you apply what you're learning in this book to your other general education courses or courses in your major.

5. **PROCESSES**: These chapters offer general advice for all writing situations—from generating ideas and text to drafting, organizing, revising and rewriting, compiling a portfolio—and more.

6. **STRATEGIES**: Use the advice in this part to develop and organize your writing—to use comparison, description, dialogue, and other strategies as appropriate.

7. **RESEARCH / DOCUMENTATION** : Use this section for advice on how to do research, work with sources, and compose and document research-based texts using MLA and APA styles.

8. **MEDIA / DESIGN** : This section offers guidance in designing your work and using visuals and sound, and in deciding whether and how to deliver what you write on paper, on screen, or in person.

9. **HANDBOOK** : Look here for help with sentence-level editing.

WAYS INTO THE BOOK

The Norton Field Guide gives you the writing advice you need, along with the flexibility to write in the way that works best for you. Here are some of the ways you can find what you need in the book.

Brief menus. Inside the front cover you'll find a list of all the chapters; start here if you are looking for a chapter on a certain kind of writing or a general writing issue. Inside the back cover is a menu of all the topics covered in the **HANDBOOK** .

Complete contents. Pages xxiii–xl contain a detailed table of contents. Look here if you need to find a reading or a specific section in a chapter.

Guides to writing. If you know the kind of writing you need to do, you'll find guides to writing twelve common genres in Part 3. These guides are designed to help you through all the decisions you have to make—from coming up with a topic to editing and proofreading your final draft.

Color-coding. The parts of this book are color-coded for easy reference: light blue for **ACADEMIC LITERACIES**, orange for **RHETORICAL SITUATIONS**, green for **GENRES**, gray for **FIELDS**, lavender for **PROCESSES**, red for **STRATEGIES**, blue for **RESEARCH / DOCUMENTATION**, pink for **MEDIA / DESIGN**, and yellow for the **HANDBOOK** . You'll find a key to the colors on the front cover flap and also on each left-hand page following a part opener. When you see a word highlighted in a color, that tells you where you can find additional detail on the topic.

Glossary / index. At the back of the book is a combined glossary and index, where you'll find full definitions of key terms and topics, along with a list of the pages where everything is covered in detail.

Directories to MLA and APA documentation. A brief directory inside the back cover will lead you to guidelines on citing sources and composing a list of references or works cited. The documentation models are color-coded so you can easily see the key details.

WAYS OF GETTING STARTED

If you know your genre, simply turn to the appropriate genre chapter. There you'll find model readings, a description of the genre's Key Features, and a Guide to Writing that will help you come up with a topic, generate text, organize and write a draft, get response, revise, edit, and proofread. The genre chapters also point out places where you might need to do research, use certain writing strategies, design your text a certain way—and direct you to the exact pages in the book where you can find help doing so.

If you know your topic, you might start with some of the activities in Chapter 29, Generating Ideas and Text. From there, you might turn to Chapter 48, for help finding sources on the topic. When it comes time to narrow your topic and come up with a thesis statement, Chapter 30 can help. If you get stuck at any point, you might turn to Chapter 28, Writing as Inquiry; it provides tips that can get you beyond what you already know about your topic. If your assignment or your thesis defines your genre, turn to that chapter; if not, consult Chapter 28 for help determining the appropriate genre, and then turn to that genre chapter.

Contents

---

* New to this edition

---

* New to this edition

---

* New to this edition

∴ Part 5   Processes 321

---

* New to this edition

* New to this edition

---

* New to this edition

---

* New to this edition

SEVENTH EDITION

The Norton
Field Guide
to Writing
with Handbook

Part 1
Academic Literacies

Whenever we enter a new community—start a new job, move to a new town, join a new club—there are certain things we need to learn. The same is true upon entering the academic world. We need to be able to **READ** and **WRITE** in certain ways. We're routinely called on to **SUMMARIZE** something we've heard or read and to **RESPOND** in some way. To succeed, we need to develop certain **HABITS OF MIND**—everyday things such as asking questions and being persistent. And increasingly, we need to **WRITE AND LEARN ONLINE**—and engage responsibly with **GENERATIVE AI** as part of the process. The following chapters provide guidelines to help you develop these fundamental academic literacies—and know what's expected of you in academic communities.

Academic
Literacies

❋ academic literacies   ● fields   ◆ strategies   ● media / design

■ rhetorical situations   ⦙ processes   ● research   ★ handbook

▲ genres

1 Writing in Academic Contexts

Write an essay arguing whether genes or environment do more to determine people's intelligence. Research and write a report on the environmental effects of electricity-generating windmills and then create an infographic of your findings. Write a personal narrative in which you explore the concept of social mobility in your own life. Whatever you're studying, you're surely going to be doing a lot of writing, in classes from various disciplines—the above assignments, for example, are from psychology, environmental science, and education. Writing in college can serve many different purposes—to **ARGUE** for what you think about a topic and why, to **REPORT** on what's known about an issue, to **EXPLORE** your thinking about something you're studying, to connect a topic to your personal life—and may take the form of a written text, a visual text, a video, an online text, or a combination. In truth, there's no one thing called "academic writing," but the writing you do in college shares some features and conventions, and learning about them will help you join the academic and other conversations going on in classrooms across campus and in the world. This chapter describes what's typically expected of academic writers and the writing they do.

170–96
146–69
270–79

What's Expected of Writing in Academic Contexts

Again, making generalizations about the writing done in academic contexts is difficult, because academic writing includes so many genres and variations that depend on the academic discipline and its requirements, the course level (a course in a major, for example, likely requires different genres and more specialized vocabulary than a general education course in the same field), and the individual instructor's goals for the course and personal preferences. To complicate matters further, academic writing is constantly changing and evolving: writers reshape what's expected in both the form and content of academic writing, often using multiple genres, media, and technologies. Plus, style expectations and rules change over

61–69

time, and new tools, such as **ARTIFICIAL INTELLIGENCE** (AI), lead to new ways of conveying scholarly information. Still, some expectations hold, regardless of the genre and assignment:

Honesty. Perhaps above all else, your instructors expect that you will be honest in what you write. At the most basic level, to be honest means that you create yourself what you submit—you haven't plagiarized, you haven't bought a paper from an online mill, you haven't had an AI bot create a paper for you. But being an honest writer means more than that. When you're asked to write something as part of your course work, that assignment is intended to help you learn about the subject you're studying. Your instructor expects that you'll do your best to fulfill the assignment in the spirit in which it was assigned: you'll think, do research or explore your own life and thoughts, draft, and revise to show what you know and how you think. If you do that, you're being honest with your subject matter, your instructor, and yourself, whether you're writing an argument, a report, a narrative, or something else.

An indication of why your topic matters. You need to help your readers understand why your topic is worth exploring and why your writing is worth reading. Even if you are writing in response to an assigned topic, you can better make your point and achieve your purpose by showing your readers why your topic is important and why they should care about it. For example, in the prologue to *Our Declaration*, political philosopher Danielle Allen explains why her topic, the Declaration of Independence, is worth writing about:

> The Declaration of Independence matters because it helps us see that we cannot have freedom *without* equality. It is out of an egalitarian commitment that a people grows—a people that is capable of protecting us all collectively, and each of us individually, from domination. If the Declaration can stake a claim to freedom, it is only because it is so clear-eyed about the fact that the people's strength resides in its equality.
>
> The Declaration also conveys another lesson of paramount importance. It is this: language is one of the most potent resources each of us has for achieving our own political empowerment. The men who wrote the Declaration of Independence grasped the power of words. This reveals itself in the laborious processes by which they brought the Declaration, and their revolution, into being. It shows itself forcefully, of course, in the text's own eloquence.

By explaining that the topic matters because freedom and equality matter—and language gives us the means for empowering ourselves—Allen gives readers reason to read her careful analysis.

Evidence that you've considered your subject carefully. Whether you're composing a report, an argument, an analysis, a narrative, or some other kind of writing, you need to show that you've thought seriously about the topic and have done any necessary research. You can show that you've considered the subject carefully in various ways: citing authoritative sources, incorporating information you learned in class, using analytical techniques appropriately, reflecting on your personal experience, and/or pointing out connections among ideas.

Careful attention to style expectations. In academic contexts, you should almost always write in complete sentences, use capitalization and punctuation as recommended in a handbook or other guide, check your spelling by consulting a dictionary, proofread carefully, and avoid any abbreviations used in texting or other informal writing. Grammar conventions are important, and it's a good idea to follow them in most kinds of academic writing. If you choose not to, however, you should make clear that you are doing so intentionally, for a particular purpose.

If the assignment allows for more informal language, regional variations, or other varieties of English, be sure that mixing language varieties advances your purpose for your audience—and use italics, quotation marks, or a **SIGNAL PHRASE** to make sure your audience knows that you're making deliberate language choices. For example, in her literacy narrative "Reading, Writing, and Riding" (p. 97), Austin College student Karla Mariana Herrera Gutierrez quotes her Spanish-speaking grandmother using both quotation marks and italics: "'*Toma el autobus a la oficina y pide la pension,*' my grandmother whispers to herself as she approaches the bus stop to go to the police office for her pension."

529–32

Access the ebook for a video on voice and code-meshing.

What's Expected in Arguments

While a case can be made that all writing makes an argument, most of the time arguments take the form of essays that take a position, analyze or evaluate something, report information, or examine something from a particular perspective—or a combination. Readers of arguments usually expect them to include the following:

A response to what others have said. Whatever your topic, it's unlikely that you'll be the first one to write about it. And if, as this chapter assumes, all academic writing is part of a larger conversation, you are in a way adding your own voice to that conversation. One good way of doing that is to present your ideas as a response to what others have said about your

521–32

Access
Chapter 51
in the ebook
for a video on
incorporating
quotations.

topic—to begin by **QUOTING, PARAPHRASING, OR SUMMARIZING** what others have said and then to agree, disagree, or both.

For example, in "Come Look at the Freaks" (p. 175), an essay arguing for casting people with disabilities in theater and film productions, Wilkes University student Brianna Schunk cites an authority and then responds: "[*Extraordinary Bodies* author Rosemarie] Garland-Thompson asserts that people who have 'ordinary' (non-disabled) bodies are considered superior to those who do not, and these 'normates' have social power and authority (8). However, by considering myself an actress with a disability—an identity important to me—I assert my power. Disability is not bad, it's just different."

A clear, appropriately qualified thesis. When you write arguments in an academic context, you're usually expected to state your main point explicitly, often in a **THESIS STATEMENT**. Rohan Mehta, a high school

342–44

senior at Moravian Academy in Bethlehem, Pennsylvania, states his thesis clearly in his essay "Banning *ChatGPT* Will Do More Harm than Good" (p. 181). After noting that in high schools nationwide AI websites have been blocked by school administrators, he writes: "If educators actively engage with students about the technology's capabilities and limitations—and work with them to define new academic standards—*ChatGPT*,

343–44

and generative AI more broadly, could both democratize and revitalize K–12 education on an unprecedented scale." Often you'll need to **QUALIFY** your thesis statement to acknowledge that the subject is complicated and there may be more than one way of seeing it or exceptions to the generalization you're making about it. Here, for example, is a qualified thesis, from an essay by Olivia Mazzucato, a student at UCLA, evaluating the movie *The Lovebirds*: "Though the film's story gets convoluted, Rae and Nanjiani are able to salvage the muddy plot with their razor-sharp comedic wit and hilarious chemistry." Mazzucato makes a claim that *The Lovebirds* achieves success, while acknowledging at the beginning of the sentence that the film's plot is flawed.

Good reasons supported by evidence. You need to provide good reasons for your thesis and evidence to support those reasons. For example, Rohan Mehta offers several reasons why school administrators should guide students in appropriate uses of AI and trust them to use it rather than blocking it: AI programs can give students opportunities to sharpen their thinking as they "discuss" their writing with the program, to "verbalize the range of possibilities"; the programs can act as "an easily hoodwinked, slightly delusional tutor"; they can act as a means of learning to think critically; and, anyway, "blocking it will only send it underground." Evidence to support your reasons sometimes comes from your own experience but more often from published research and scholarship, research you do yourself, or firsthand accounts by others.

Compared with other kinds of writing, academic writing is generally expected to be more objective and less emotional. You may find *Romeo and Juliet* deeply moving or cry when you watch *A Dog's Journey*—but when you write about the play or the film for a class, you must do so using evidence from the text to support your thesis. You may find someone's ideas deeply offensive, but you should respond to them with reason rather than with emotional appeals or personal attacks.

Acknowledgment of multiple perspectives.   Debates and arguments in popular media are often framed in "pro/con" terms, as if there were only two sides to any given issue. Once you begin seriously studying a topic, though, you're likely to find that there are several sides and that each of them deserves serious consideration. In your academic writing, you need to represent fairly the range of perspectives on your topic—to explore three, four, or more positions on it as you research and write. For example, in her report "Sleepless Nights of a University Student" (p. 146), Drexel University student Renae Tingling examines sleep deprivation in several ways: through academic research, a survey of students, and a personal sleep-deprivation experiment.

A credible, authoritative stance.   If one goal of academic writing is to contribute to a larger conversation, your tone should convey your credibility and establish your authority to write about your subject. Sometimes you can achieve such a tone by stating your assertions directly, using active verbs and definitive language ("humans cause climate change")—as long as you can adequately support a strong assertion. At other times, acknowledging the limitations of your claims or findings—for example, by saying "most likely" instead of "definitely," or "the data suggest" rather than "the data prove"—can help convey not only your credibility but your respect for interpretations that differ from your own. Depending on your topic, you might also demonstrate your credibility by highlighting your personal connection to or experience with your subject. In all, your writing should send the message that you've done the research, analysis, and critical reflection to know what you're talking about. For example, here's how Brianna Schunk establishes her credibility in the first paragraph of her essay:

> When I first saw Gaten Matarazzo in the TV show *Stranger Things* and some of the first words out of his toothless little mouth were, "I have cleidocranial dysplasia," I actually cried with joy. Until then, I had never seen another human not related to my family who had cleidocranial dysplasia on television in a popular TV show. I was so shocked, I made my friend rewind the episode so I could hear him say it again. Having cleidocranial dysplasia myself, it is so much easier to be able to compare myself to Matarazzo when explaining my condition to other people, and I only wish he could have come into my life earlier. Representation—how we portray ourselves and are portrayed by others—is incredibly important to all groups of people, but especially to people with disabilities.

See Schunk's firsthand experience with her topic, her use of vivid language ("toothless little mouth," "I was so shocked"), and her strong final sentence ("Representation . . . is incredibly important to all groups of people, but especially to people with disabilities") lend her writing a confident tone. Her stance sends the message that she knows what she's talking about.

Carefully documented sources. Clearly acknowledging sources and documenting them carefully and correctly is a basic requirement of academic writing. When you use the words or ideas of others—including visuals, video, or audio—those sources must be documented in the text and in a works-cited or references list at the end. (If you're writing something that will appear online, you may also refer readers to your sources by using **HYPERLINKS** in the text; ask your instructor if you need to include a list of references or works cited as well.)

540–41 ●

◄► Access the ebook for a video on understanding academic argument.

What's Expected in Narratives and Exploratory Writing

Telling stories or writing narratives about yourself or others, playing with ideas, exploring alternatives to common genres of writing—these are also common forms of formal and informal writing found in college classrooms. While the expectations readers have for such writing may be broader and less specific than in some other academic genres, they are likely to include the following:

A clear structure. Some writers use a chronological structure, as Drexel University student Renae Tingling does in her report on inadequate sleep.

She describes her personal study of sleep deprivation, including sleeping only half as much as normal for several days: "It wasn't by chance that by the start of the first day, I had already reached my quota of embarrassing absentminded mistakes after having pressed the wrong button on the elevator and wandered into the wrong classroom." Other writers, like Columbus State Community College student Brian Diehl, take a different approach. In "Talking with Granddad" (p. 270), an essay that explores his ability to communicate with his grandfather who has dementia, Diehl includes personal narratives, a research paper, self-portraits by an artist afflicted with Alzheimer's, and an interview, but each part contributes to the whole clearly and meaningfully.

Vivid, specific details. Details are the specific features or characteristics of an object, the particulars of a topic, the sights, sounds, smells, and tastes that bring a scene to life for readers. Diehl, for instance, begins his exploration with details about his grandfather's nursing home: "I'm met with a clash of two scents: the buttery aroma of a nearby popcorn machine and that distinct 'old people' smell." Rea Karim describes her first encounter with an *American Girl* novel this way: "On the cover a quirky-looking girl with thick glasses, braided pigtails, and a checkered dress looked back at me." And Karla Mariana Herrera Gutierrez helps us understand the concept of a secondary discourse by showing us that we learn such discourses "through becoming members of social institutions, like churches, stores, community groups—and schools."

A point or indication of your text's significance. Significance most basically is an answer to the question "Why is this text important—why does it matter—to the writer? to the reader?" Sometimes the significance is stated directly, often in the conclusion. Diehl, for example, ends his exploration by reflecting on what he's learned about communicating with his grandfather: "What's needed is a repeated effort to be present with the individual, expressing joy over what they say instead of sweating over anything we could ever say." Gutierrez sprinkles indications of her narrative's significance throughout, discussing scholarly concepts and then relating them to her own family's life; at one point, she describes the potential for trouble when we encounter cultural ideas that conflict with one another and then shows how that kind of conflict played out when she asked for permission to attend a sleepover at a friend's house.

THINKING ABOUT AN ACADEMIC RHETORICAL SITUATION

As you'll learn throughout this book, all writing takes place within a particular context—a **RHETORICAL SITUATION** that includes your **PURPOSE**, **AUDIENCE**, **GENRE**, **STANCE**, and **MEDIUM/DESIGN**. Thinking critically about an academic rhetorical situation can help you make effective choices in your writing.

- *What do you see as your instructor's purpose for this assignment?* To have you demonstrate learning of some kind? To show your understanding of course material? To discuss ideas, concepts, or facts? To explore ideas and look for connections among them? Have you been given a description of what your writing should include?

- *What is your purpose as the writer, apart from fulfilling your instructor's expectations?* To persuade your audience to do or believe something? To inform them about something and help them understand it? To play with ideas and see where they lead?

- *Who is your audience?* Your instructor? Your classmates? Others? How much does the audience know about the topic? Are they in an academic field with particular conventions you need to follow?

- *What genre does the assignment require?* A narrative, a report, an exploration, an analysis, an argument, or something else? Does the assignment specify the genre? If not, can you figure out what's required from the verb or other key terms in the assignment wording? Do you get to choose your genre?

- *How can you convey a credible, authoritative stance?* By showing that you understand the larger context of your topic? By showing confidence in what you say? By stating your claims forthrightly and clearly? By acknowledging the limitations of your claims? By adopting a tone appropriate for your genre?

- *What media are available, permitted, and appropriate?* Are any required? Will you present your work as a paper document, a digital text, an oral presentation, or something else? Can you—and should you—use photos, drawings, charts, graphs, or slides or embed audio or video files?

- *What design issues need to be considered?* Should you assume that your written text must follow MLA or APA formatting guidelines? Do you need to include any visual or audio elements? How much freedom do you have to design your work?

2 Reading in Academic Contexts

We read news sites to know about the events of the day. We read textbooks to learn about history, chemistry, and other academic topics—and other academic sources to do research and develop arguments. We read posts and blogs to follow (and participate in) conversations about issues that interest us. And as writers, we read our own writing to make sure it says what we mean it to say and proofread our final drafts to make sure they say it the way we intended. In other words, we read many kinds of texts for many different purposes. This chapter offers a number of strategies for various kinds of reading you do in academic contexts.

TAKING STOCK OF YOUR READING

One way to become a better reader is to understand your reading process; if you know what you do when you read, you're in a position to decide what you need to change or improve. Consider the answers to the following questions:

- What do you read for pleasure? for work? for school? Consider all the sorts of reading you do: books, magazines, and newspapers, websites, *Facebook*, texts, blogs, product instructions.

- When you're facing a reading assignment, what do you do? Do you do certain things to get comfortable? Do you play music or seek quiet? Do you plan your reading time or set reading goals for yourself? Do you flip through or skim the text before settling down to read it, or do you start at the beginning and work through it?

- When you begin to read something for an assignment, do you make sure you understand the purpose of the assignment—why you must read this text? Do you ever ask your instructor (or whoever else assigned the reading) what its purpose is?

- How do you motivate yourself to read material you don't have any interest in? How do you deal with boredom while reading?

- Does your mind wander? If you realize that you haven't been paying attention and don't know what you just read, what do you do?
- Do you ever highlight, underline, or annotate text as you read? Do you take notes? If so, what do you mark or write down? Why?
- When you read text you don't understand, what do you do?
- As you anticipate and read an assigned text, what attitudes or feelings do you typically have? If they differ from reading to reading, why do they?
- What do you do when you've finished reading an assigned text? Write out notes? Think about what you've just read? Move on to the next task? Something else?
- How well do your reading processes work for you, both in school and otherwise? What would you like to change? What can you do to change?

The rest of this chapter offers advice and strategies that you may find helpful as you work to improve your reading skills.

READING STRATEGICALLY

Academic reading is challenging because it makes several demands on you at once. Textbooks present new vocabulary and new concepts, and picking out the main ideas can be difficult. Scholarly articles present content and arguments you need to understand, but they often assume that readers already know key concepts and vocabulary and so don't generally provide background information. As you read more texts in an academic field and begin to participate in its conversations, the reading will become easier, but in the meantime you can develop strategies that will help you read effectively.

Previewing the Text

It's usually a good idea to start by skimming a text—read the title and subtitle, any headings, the first and last paragraphs, the first sentences of all the other paragraphs. Study any illustrations and other visuals. Your goal is to get a sense of where the text is heading. At this point, don't stop to look up unfamiliar words; just mark them in some way to look up later.

Adjusting Your Reading Speed to Different Texts

Different texts require different kinds of effort. Some that are simple and straightforward can be skimmed fairly quickly. With academic texts, though, you usually need to read more slowly and carefully, matching the pace of your reading to the difficulty of the text. You'll likely need to skim the text for an overview of the basic ideas and then go back to read it closely. And then you may need to read it yet again. (But do try always to read quickly enough to focus on the meanings of sentences and paragraphs, not just individual words.) With visual texts, too, you'll often need to look at them several times, moving from gaining an overall impression to closely examining the structure, layout, and other visual features—and exploring how those features relate to any accompanying verbal text.

Looking for Organizational Cues

As you read, look for cues that signal the way the text's ideas are organized and how each part relates to the ones around it.

The introductory paragraph and thesis often offer a preview of the topics to be discussed and the order in which they will be addressed. Here, for example, is a typical thesis statement for a report: *Types of prisons in the United States include minimum and medium security, close security, maximum security, and supermax.* The report that follows should explain each type of prison in the order stated in the thesis.

Transitions help guide readers in following the direction of the writer's thinking from idea to idea. For example, "however" indicates an idea that contradicts or limits what has just been said, while "furthermore" indicates one that adds to or supports it.

Headings identify a text's major and minor sections, by means of both the headings' content and their design.

Thinking about Your Initial Response

Some readers find it helps to make brief notes about their first response to a text, noting their reaction and thinking a little about why they reacted as they did.

What are your initial reactions? Describe both your intellectual reaction and any emotional reaction, and identify places in the text that caused you to react as you did. An intellectual reaction might consist of an evaluation ("I disagree with this position because . . ."), a connection ("This idea reminds me of . . ."), or an elaboration ("Another example of this point is . . ."). An emotional reaction could include approval or disapproval ("YES!

Access the ebook for a video about reading scholarly articles.

This is exactly right!" "NO! This is so wrong!"), an expression of feeling ("This passage makes me so sad"), or one of appreciation ("This is said so beautifully"). If you had no particular reaction, note that, too.

What accounts for your reactions? Are they rooted in personal experiences? aspects of your personality? positions you hold on an issue? As much as possible, you want to keep your opinions from interfering with your understanding of what you're reading, so it's important to try to identify those opinions up front.

Dealing with Difficult Texts

Let's face it: some texts are difficult. You may have no interest in the subject matter, or lack background knowledge or vocabulary necessary for understanding the text, or simply not have a clear sense of why you have to read the text at all. Whatever the reason, reading such texts can be a challenge. Here are some tips for dealing with them:

Look for something familiar. Texts often seem difficult or boring because we don't know enough about the topic or about the larger conversation surrounding it to read them effectively. By skimming the headings, the abstract or introduction, and the conclusion, you may find something that relates to something you already know or are at least interested in—and being aware of that prior knowledge can help you see how this new material relates to it.

Look for "landmarks." Reading a challenging academic text the first time through can be like driving to an unfamiliar destination on roads you've never traveled: you don't know where you're headed, you don't recognize anything along the way, and you're not sure how long getting there will take. As you drive the route again, though, you see landmarks along the way that help you know where you're going. The same goes for reading a difficult text: sometimes you need to get through it once just to get some idea of what it's about. On the second reading, now that you have "driven the route," look for the ways that the parts of the text relate to one another, to other texts or course information, or to other knowledge you have.

Monitor your understanding. You may have had the experience of reading a text and suddenly realizing that you have no idea what you just read. Being able to monitor your reading—to sense when you aren't understanding the text and need to reread, focus your attention, look up unfamiliar terms, take some notes, or take a break—can make you a more efficient and better reader. Keep these questions in mind as you read: What is my purpose for reading this text? Am I understanding it? Does it make sense? Should I slow down, reread, annotate? skim ahead and then come back? pause to reflect?

Be persistent. Research shows that many students respond to difficult texts by assuming they're "too dumb to get it"—and quitting reading. Successful students, on the other hand, report that if they keep at a text, they will come to understand it. Some of them even see difficult texts as challenges: "I'm going to keep working on this until I make sense of it." Remember that reading is an active process, and the more you work at it the more successful you will be.

Annotating

Many readers find it helps to annotate as they read: highlighting keywords, phrases, sentences; connecting ideas with lines or symbols; writing comments or questions in the margin, on sticky notes, or using annotating or note-taking tools in ebooks; circling new words so you can look up the definitions later; noting anything that seems noteworthy or questionable. Annotating forces you to read for more than just the surface meaning. Especially when you are going to be writing about or responding to a text, annotating creates a record of things you may want to refer to.

Annotate as if you're having a conversation with the author, someone you take seriously but whose words you do not accept without question. Put your part of the conversation in the margin, asking questions, talking back: "What's this mean?" "So what?" "Says who?" "Where's evidence?" "Yes!" "Whoa!" or even ☺ or ☹ or texting shorthand like LOL or INTRSTN. If you're reading a text online, you can use a digital annotation tool like *Hypothesis* or *Diigo* to highlight portions of the text and make notes electronically—and even share your annotations with others.

What you annotate depends on your **PURPOSE** , or what you're most interested in. If you're analyzing a text that makes an explicit argument, you would probably underline the **THESIS STATEMENT** and then the **REASONS** and **EVIDENCE** that support that statement. It might help to restate those ideas in your own words in the margins—in order to understand them, you need to put them in your own words! If you're trying to identify patterns, you might highlight each pattern in a different color or mark it with a sticky note and write any questions or notes about it

■ 73–74

⁘ 342–44

◆ 402

402–9

in that color. You might annotate a visual text by circling and identifying important parts of the image.

There are some texts that you cannot annotate, like library books and some ebooks. Then you will need to use sticky notes or make notes elsewhere, and you might find it useful to keep a reading log for this purpose.

Coding

You may also find it useful to record your thoughts as you read by using a coding system—for example, using "X" to indicate passages that contradict your assumptions, or "?" for ones that puzzle you. You can make up your own coding system, of course, but you could start with this one*:

- ✔ Confirms what you thought

- X Contradicts what you thought

- ? Puzzles you

- ?? Confuses you

- ! Surprises you

- ☆ Strikes you as important

- ➜ Is new or interesting to you

You might also circle new words that you'll want to look up later and highlight or underline key phrases.

A Sample Annotated Text

Here is an excerpt from Justice: What's the Right Thing to Do?, *a book by Harvard professor Michael J. Sandel, annotated by a writer who was doing research for a report on the awarding of military medals:*

What Wounds Deserve the Purple Heart?

On some issues, questions of virtue and honor are too obvious to deny. Consider the recent debate over who should qualify for the Purple Heart. Since 1932, the U.S. military has awarded the medal to soldiers wounded or killed in battle by enemy action. In addition to the honor, the medal entitles recipients to special privileges in veterans' hospitals.

✔

Adapted from Harvey Daniels and Steven Zemelman, Subjects Matter: Every Teacher's Guide to Content-Area Reading (Heinemann, 2004).

Since the beginning of the current wars in Iraq and Afghanistan, growing numbers of veterans have been diagnosed with post-traumatic stress disorder and treated for the condition. Symptoms include recurring nightmares, severe depression, and suicide. At least three hundred thousand veterans reportedly suffer from traumatic stress or major depression. Advocates for these veterans have proposed that they, too, should qualify for the Purple Heart. Since psychological injuries can be at least as debilitating as physical ones, they argue, soldiers who suffer these wounds should receive the medal.

PTSD increasingly common among veterans.

Argument: Vets with PTSD should be eligible for PH because psych. injuries are as serious as physical.

After a Pentagon advisory group studied the question, the Pentagon announced, in 2009, that the Purple Heart would be reserved for soldiers with physical injuries. Veterans suffering from mental disorders and psychological trauma would not be eligible, even though they qualify for government-supported medical treatment and disability payments. The Pentagon offered two reasons for its decision: traumatic stress disorders are not intentionally caused by enemy action, and they are difficult to diagnose objectively.

No PH for PTSD vets? Seems unfair!

Did the Pentagon make the right decision? Taken by themselves, its reasons are unconvincing. In the Iraq War, one of the most common injuries recognized with the Purple Heart has been a punctured eardrum, caused by explosions at close range. But unlike bullets and bombs, such explosions are not a deliberate enemy tactic intended to injure or kill; they are (like traumatic stress) a damaging side effect of battlefield action. And while traumatic disorders may be more difficult to diagnose than a broken limb, the injury they inflict can be more severe and long-lasting.

Argument: PTSD is like punctured eardrums, which do get the PH.

As the wider debate about the Purple Heart revealed, the real issue is about the meaning of the medal and the virtues it honors. What, then, are the relevant virtues? Unlike other military medals, <u>the Purple Heart honors sacrifice, not bravery</u>. It requires no heroic act, only an injury inflicted by the enemy. The question is what kind of injury should count.

PH "honors sacrifice, not bravery." Injury enough. So what kind of injury?

A veteran's group called the Military Order of the Purple Heart opposed awarding the medal for psychological injuries, claiming that doing so would "debase" the honor. A spokesman for the group stated that "shedding blood" should be an essential qualification. He didn't explain why bloodless injuries shouldn't count. But Tyler E. Boudreau, a former Marine captain who favors including psychological injuries, offers a compelling analysis of the dispute. He attributes the opposition to a deep-seated attitude in the military that views post-traumatic stress as a kind of weakness. "The same culture that demands tough-mindedness also encourages skepticism toward the suggestion that the violence of war can hurt the healthiest of minds. . . . Sadly, <u>as long as</u>

Wow: one vet's group insists that for PH, soldier must bleed!

☆

our military culture bears at least a quiet contempt for the psychological wounds of war, it is unlikely those veterans will ever see a Purple Heart."

So the debate over the Purple Heart is more than a medical or clinical dispute about how to determine the veracity of injury. At the heart of the disagreement are rival conceptions of moral character and military valor. Those who insist that only bleeding wounds should count believe that post-traumatic stress reflects a weakness of character unworthy of honor. Those who believe that psychological wounds should qualify argue that veterans suffering long-term trauma and severe depression have sacrificed for their country as surely, and as honorably, as those who've lost a limb. The dispute over the Purple Heart illustrates the moral logic of Aristotle's theory of justice. We can't determine who deserves a military medal without asking what virtues the medal properly honors. And to answer that question, we have to assess competing conceptions of character and sacrifice.

Argument based on different ideas about what counts as a military virtue.

Summarizing

Writing a summary, boiling down a text to its main ideas, can help you understand it. To do so, you need to identify which ideas in the text are crucial to its meaning. Then you put those crucial ideas into your own words, creating a brief version that accurately sums up the text. Here, for example, is a summary of Sandel's analysis of the Purple Heart debate:

Access the ebook for a video on summarizing while reading.

> In "What Wounds Deserve the Purple Heart?," Harvard professor Michael J. Sandel explores the debate over eligibility for the Purple Heart, the medal given to soldiers who die or are wounded in battle. Some argue that soldiers suffering from post-traumatic stress disorder should qualify for the medal because psychological injuries are as serious as physical ones. However, the military disagrees, since PTSD injuries are not "intentionally caused by enemy action" and are hard to diagnose. Sandel observes that the dispute centers on how "character" and "sacrifice" are defined. Those who insist that soldiers must have had physical wounds to be eligible for the Purple Heart see psychological wounds as reflecting "weakness of character," while others argue that veterans with PTSD and other psychological traumas have sacrificed honorably for their country.

READING CRITICALLY AND RHETORICALLY

To read academic texts effectively, you need to look beyond the words on the page or screen to the **RHETORICAL CONTEXT** of the text and the argument it makes. Academic texts—both the ones you read and the ones you write—are parts of ongoing scholarly conversations in which

129–30 ▲

writers respond to the ideas and assertions of others in order to advance knowledge. To enter those conversations, you must first read carefully and critically to understand the rhetorical situation, the larger context within which a writer wrote, and the argument the text makes.

Considering the Rhetorical Situation

As a reader, you need to think about the message that the writer wants to articulate, including the intended audience and the writer's attitude toward that audience and the topic, as well as about the genre, medium, and design of the text.

PURPOSE   What is the writer's purpose? To entertain? inform? persuade readers to think something or take some action? What is *your* purpose for reading this text?
73–74

AUDIENCE   Who is the intended audience? Are you a member of that group? If not, should you expect that you'll need to look up unfamiliar terms or concepts or that you'll run into assumptions you don't necessarily share? How is the writer addressing the audience—as an expert addressing those less knowledgeable? as an outsider addressing insiders?
75–78

GENRE   What is the genre? Is it a report? an argument? an analysis? something else? Knowing the genre can help you to anticipate certain key features.
79–84

STANCE   Who is the writer, and what is their stance? Critical? Curious? Opinionated? Objective? Passionate? Indifferent? Something else? Knowing the stance affects the way you understand a text, whether you're inclined to agree or disagree with it, to take it seriously, and so on.
85–87

MEDIA / DESIGN   What is the medium, and how does it affect the way you read? If it's a print text, what do you know about the publisher? If it's on the web, who sponsors the site, and when was it last updated? Are there any headings, summaries, or other elements that highlight key parts of the text?
88–90

Believing and Doubting

One way to develop a response to a text is to play the believing and doubting game, sometimes called reading with and against the grain. Your goal is to **LIST** or **FREEWRITE** notes as you read, writing out as many reasons as
330
329

you can think of for believing what the writer says (reading with the grain) and then as many as you can for doubting it (reading against the grain).

First, try to look at the world through the writer's perspective. Try to understand their reasons for arguing as they do, even if you strongly disagree. Then reread the text, trying to doubt everything in it: try to find every flaw in the argument, every possible way it can be refuted—even if you totally agree with it. Developed by writing theorist Peter Elbow, the believing and doubting game helps you consider new ideas and question ideas you already have—and at the same time see where you stand in relation to the ideas in the text you're reading.

Analyzing the Argument

All texts make some kind of argument, claiming something and then offering reasons and evidence as support for any claim. As a critical reader, you need to look closely at the argument a text makes—to recognize all the claims it makes, consider the support it offers for those claims, and decide how you want to respond. What do you think, and why? Here are some questions to consider when analyzing an argument:

- *What claim is the text making?* What is the writer's main point? Is it stated as a **THESIS** or only implied? Is it limited or **QUALIFIED** somehow? If not, should it have been?

- *How is the claim supported?* What **REASONS** does the writer provide for the claim, and what **EVIDENCE** is given for the reasons? What kind of evidence is it? Facts? Statistics? Examples? Expert opinions? Images? How convincing do you find the reasons and evidence? Is there enough evidence?

- *What appeals besides logical ones are used?* Does the writer appeal to readers' **EMOTIONS**? try to establish **COMMON GROUND**? demonstrate their **CREDIBILITY** as trustworthy and knowledgeable? How successful are these appeals?

- *Are any **COUNTERARGUMENTS** acknowledged?* If so, are they presented accurately and respectfully? Does the writer concede any value to them or try to refute them? How successfully does the writer deal with them?

- *What outside sources of information does the writer cite?* What kinds of sources are they, and how credible do they seem? Are they current and authoritative? How well do they support the argument?

- *Do you detect any **FALLACIES**?* Fallacies are arguments that involve faulty reasoning. Because they often seem plausible, they can be persuasive. It is important, therefore, that you question the legitimacy of such reasoning when you run across it.

342–44

6

402

402–9

413

410–11

410–13

411–13

413–15

Considering the Larger Context

All texts are part of ongoing conversations with other texts that have dealt with the same topic. An essay arguing for an assault-weapons ban is part of an ongoing conversation on gun legislation, which is itself part of a conversation on individual rights and responsibilities. Academic texts document their sources in part to show their relationship to the ongoing scholarly conversation on a particular topic. In fact, anytime you're reading to learn, you're probably reading for some larger context. Whatever your reading goals, being aware of that larger context can help you better understand what you're reading. Here are some specific aspects of the text to pay attention to:

Who else cares about this topic? Especially when you're reading in order to learn about a topic, the texts you read will often reveal which people or groups are part of the conversation—and might be sources of further reading. For example, an essay describing the formation of Mammoth Cave in Kentucky could be of interest to geologists, cave explorers, travel writers, or tourists. If you're reading such an essay while doing research on the cave, you should consider how the audience to whom the writer is writing determines the nature of the information provided—and its suitability as a source for your research.

What conversations is this text part of? Does the text refer to any concepts or ideas that give you some sense that it's part of a larger conversation? An argument on airport security measures, for example, is part of larger conversations about government response to terrorism, the limits of freedom in a democracy, and the possibilities of using technology to detect weapons and explosives, among others.

What terms does the writer use? Do any terms or specialized language reflect the writer's allegiance to a particular group or academic discipline? If you run across words like "false consciousness," "ideology," and "hegemony," for example, you might guess that the text was written by a Marxist scholar.

What other writers or sources does the writer cite? Do the other writers have a particular academic specialty, belong to an identifiable intellectual school, share similar political leanings? If an article on politics cites Paul Krugman and Gail Collins in support of its argument, you might assume that the writer holds liberal opinions; if it cites Ross Douthat and Jennifer Rubin, the writer is likely a conservative.

READING COLLEGE TEXTBOOKS

The textbooks you're assigned to read in college courses present some special challenges. In the first place, they're assigned—your instructors require you to read them as an important part of your coursework. And that means you're likely to be tested on their contents or otherwise expected to know the information contained in them. That makes reading college textbooks a high-stakes activity, one you must take seriously. Textbooks usually cover a lot of information, much more than in a regular nonfiction book, so often their sheer size is daunting, and figuring out what you need to learn and what is good to know but not necessary can be difficult. Much of the general advice about reading in an academic context in this chapter holds true for college texts, but using certain techniques—and avoiding some common pitfalls—can help you read and study your textbooks effectively.

Useful Tips for Reading Any Textbook

- *Read actively, but don't read textbook chapters from beginning to end.* They aren't stories, even if narratives are embedded within them. Instead, preview the text, reading titles, headings, illustrations, graphs, charts, and introductions. If the text includes outlines of the chapter's contents and end of chapter summaries, pay close attention to them. Try to figure out the chapter's main idea, paying particular attention to the first sentences of each paragraph. Read section by section.

- *Pay particular attention to the study questions at the end of each chapter as you preview the text.* The kinds of questions asked will give you clues on how to read it. If a text prompts you to "explain," "define," "differentiate," "label," "describe," or "list," such words ask for understanding of terms and concepts that are not in need of interpretation—they need to be learned. If, however, the prompts ask questions like these, from a history text, then the tasks asked of you here are quite different: "What were the major events?" "What were the main crises?" "What were the primary purposes and strategies?" "How did this movement change over time?" "How did this movement transform the culture?" These sorts of questions require synthesis and interpretation. Different tasks, reflecting different teaching goals and disciplinary emphases, lead to different kinds of questions. As a result, you need to adjust your reading to reflect the differences.

- *As you read the chapter, take notes.* Use a pencil, separate notebook, or note-taking feature of your learning management system to put the main ideas into your own words. In a science course, you might create a list of important terms and their definitions; in a humanities course, entries might include significant people, texts, or events and what made them important. It's important to do the exercises and sample problems in a math textbook.

- *After reading through the chapter, try to answer any study questions provided in the text.* If you can't answer one, go back to the chapter to find the answer.

- *At the end of each section, take a moment to write a brief* **SUMMARY** *of what you just read, ideally without looking at the section.* See what you can remember, restating it in your own words.

29–40

- *Don't try to do too much in one session.* Work on a textbook assignment in chunks of twenty to thirty minutes. Then take a break and switch to a different subject.

- *When you're reviewing your reading, focus on the main ideas and concepts.* Make an **OUTLINE** from memory, and then use the textbook and your own summaries to fill it in. Next, read through your course notes and look for connections between what was said in class and what the textbook says—they sometimes differ!

335–37

Reading Ebooks

You are likely studying from one or more e-textbooks. Most of the time, ebook versions of college textbooks look and read very much like their print versions, but there are differences. Often ebooks offer features that you may find helpful:

- The table of contents may consist of links that will take you directly to the chapter or section you need.

- A search tool may help you find information anywhere in the book and provide a glossary of terms if you need definitions.

- Important terms may be linked to definitions and additional information, accessible by a single click or mouseover.

- Embedded videos may offer additional information and brief lectures by the authors or other experts.

- Built-in highlighters and comment boxes let you annotate the ebook as you would a print text.

- A text-to-speech function may let you listen to the text as an audiobook.

- Embedded self-quizzes that check your work and explain the correct answer may allow you to see how well you understand a section or chapter's contents.

READING ONSCREEN

If you're used to reading websites and social media posts, be aware that research shows we tend to read differently onscreen than we do when we read print texts: we skim and sample, often reading just a sentence or two before jumping to another site, another text. If we need to scroll the page to continue, we often don't bother. In general, we don't read as carefully as we do when reading print texts, and we're less likely to reread or take other steps if we find that we don't understand something. Here are some strategies that might help you read effectively onscreen whether you're reading a webpage, a post, or an ebook:

Adjust your reading speed and effort to your purpose. Many students use the web to get an overview of a topic and find potential sources. In that case, skimming and browsing are sensible and appropriate tactics. But if you're reading to evaluate a source, find specific information on a topic, or learn course content, you probably need to read more slowly and carefully.

Keep your purpose in mind as you read. Clicking on hyperlinks and jumping from site to site can be tempting. Resist the temptation! Making a list of specific questions you're seeking to answer can help you stay focused and on task.

Print out longer texts. Some people find reading online to be harder on their eyes than reading pages of print, and many find that they comprehend and remember information in longer texts better if they read them in print. Reading a long text is similar to walking through an unfamiliar neighborhood: we form a mental map of the text as we read and then associate the information with its location in the text, making remembering easier. Since forming such a map is more difficult when reading an electronic text, printing out texts you need to read carefully may be a good strategy.

Download material to read offline. Many ebooks let you download portions of the text to read offline, and if you're reading a webpage, you can use the Print function in your browser to save the page as a PDF. Reading the material without an internet connection can help you avoid distractions.

Take advantage of search functionality. Whether you're reading a website, an ebook, or a PDF, use Search tools to find key terms or concepts quickly. If the text you're reading doesn't have a Search icon, use the Find feature in your browser: CTRL+F (Windows) or CMD+F (Mac).

Use bookmarks. Use the bookmark function in your web browser or in your ebook to flag material you want to revisit. In some ebooks, you can customize your bookmarks by adding your own titles and notes—which can serve as a kind of study guide later.

Make the reading experience interactive. Use digital annotation tools like *Hypothesis* or *Perusall*—or use the built-in note-taking tools available in most ebooks—to take notes on your reading. Use the highlighters in ebooks to color-code key information (green for definitions, blue for examples, and so on). Interact with embedded quizzes, animations, audio, or other multimedia elements. The more you engage with your online reading material, the more you'll learn from it.

READING VISUAL TEXTS

Photos, drawings, graphs, diagrams, and charts are frequently used to help convey important information and often make powerful arguments themselves. So learning to read and interpret visual texts is just as necessary as it is for written texts.

Taking visuals seriously. Remember that visuals are texts themselves, not just decoration. When they appear as part of a written text, they may introduce information not discussed elsewhere in the text. Or they might illustrate concepts hard to grasp from words alone. In either case, it's important to pay close attention to any visuals in a written text.

Looking at any title, caption, or other written text that's part of a visual will help you understand its main idea. It might also help to think about its purpose: Why did the writer include it? What information does it add or emphasize? What argument is it making? See, for example, how a psychology textbook uses visuals to help explain two ways that information can be represented:

Analogical and Symbolic Representations

When we think about information, we use two basic types of internal representations: analogical and symbolic.

Analogical representations usually correspond to images. They have some characteristics of actual objects. Therefore, they are analogous to actual objects. For example, maps correspond to geographical layouts. Family trees depict branching relationships between relatives. A clock corresponds directly to the passage of time. **Figure 2.1a** is a drawing of a violin from a particular perspective. This drawing is an analogical representation.

Figure 2.1 Analogical versus Symbolic Representations
(a)   (b)

(a) Analogical representations, such as this picture of a violin, have some characteristics of the objects they represent.
(b) Symbolic representations, such as the word "violin," are abstract and do not have relationships to the physical qualities of objects.

By contrast, **symbolic representations** are abstract. These representations usually consist of words or ideas. They do not have relationships to physical qualities of objects in the world. The word "hamburger" is a symbolic representation that usually represents a cooked patty of beef served on a bun. The word "violin" stands for a musical instrument **(Figure 2.1b).**   —Sarah Grison and Michael Gazzaniga, *Psychology in Your Life*

The headings tell you the topic: analogical and symbolic representations. The paragraphs define the two types of representation, and the illustrations present a visual example of each type. The visuals make the information in the written text easier to understand by illustrating the differences between the two.

Reading charts and graphs. To read the information in charts and graphs, you need to look for different things depending on what type of chart or graph you're considering. A line graph, for example, usually contains certain elements: title, legend or clearly labeled parts, x axis (horizontal), y axis (vertical), and source information. Figure 2.2 shows one such graph taken from a sociology textbook.

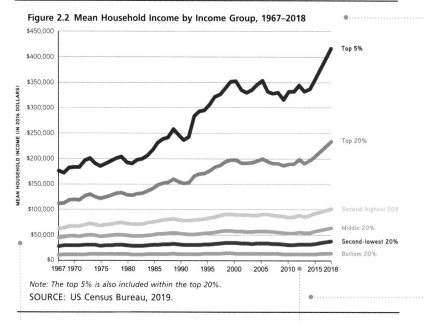

Figure 2.2 Mean Household Income by Income Group, 1967–2018

Title: Indicates the topic.

Legend or Labels: Explains the symbols used. Here, colors show the different categories, which are each clearly labeled.

Note: The top 5% is also included within the top 20%.
SOURCE: US Census Bureau, 2019.

Source: The origin of the data.

y axis: Defines the independent variable (something that doesn't change depending on other factors).

x axis: Defines the dependent variable (something that changes, depending on other factors).

Other types of charts and graphs include some of these same elements. But the specific elements vary according to the different kinds of information being presented, and some charts and graphs can be challenging to read. For example, the chart in Figure 2.3, from the same textbook, includes elements of both bar and line graphs to depict two trends at once:

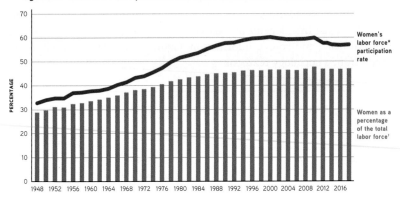

Figure 2.3 Women's Participation in the Labor Force in the United States

*Women in the labor force as a percentage of all civilian women age 16 and over.
†Women in the labor force as a percentage of the total workforce (both men and women) age 16 and over.
SOURCE: US Bureau of Labor Statistics, 2018.

the red line shows the percentage of women in the United States who were in the labor force over a sixty-eight-year period, and the blue bars show the percentage of US workers who were women during that same period. Both trends are shown in two-year increments. To make sense of this chart, you need to read the title, the y-axis legend, and the labels and their definitions carefully.

If you need more help

See Chapter 49, **EVALUATING SOURCES**, for questions to help you analyze a text's rhetorical situation. See also Chapter 29 on **GENERATING IDEAS AND TEXT**; you can adapt those methods as ways of looking at texts, especially clustering and cubing. And see also Chapter 32 on **ASSESSING YOUR OWN WRITING**, Chapter 33 on **GETTING RESPONSE AND REVISING**, and Chapter 34 on **EDITING AND PROOFREADING** if you need advice for reading your own writing.

504–14
329–39
361–64
365–71
372–82

3 Summarizing and Responding
Where Reading Meets Writing

Summarizing a text helps us see and understand its main points and to think about what it says. Responding to that text then prompts us to think about—*and say*—what we think. Together, summarizing and responding to texts is one way that we engage with the ideas of others. In a history course, you might summarize and respond to an essay arguing that Civil War photographers did not accurately capture the realities of the battle-field. In a philosophy course, you might summarize Plato's "Allegory of the Cave" and respond to its portrayal of knowledge as shadows on a wall.

And in much of the writing that you do, you'll need to cite the ideas of others, both as context for your own thinking and as evidence to support your arguments. In fact, there's probably no topic you'll write about that someone else hasn't already written about—and one way of intro-ducing what you have to say is as a response to something others have said about your topic. A good way of doing that is by summarizing what they've said, using the summary as a launching pad for what you say. This chapter offers advice for summarizing and responding, writing tasks you'll have occasion to do in many of your college classes—and provides a short guide to writing a summary and response essay, a common assignment in composition classes.

SUMMARIZING

In many of your college courses, you'll likely be asked to summarize what someone else has said. Boiling down a text to its basic ideas helps you focus on the text, figure out what the writer has said, and understand (and remember) what you're reading. In fact, summarizing is an essen-tial academic skill, a way to incorporate the ideas of others into your own writing. Following are some guidelines for summarizing effectively:

Read the text carefully. To write a good summary, you need to read the original text carefully to capture the writer's intended meaning as clearly and evenhandedly as you can. Start by **SKIMMING** the text to get a general sense of what it's saying. If some parts don't make sense, don't worry; at this point, you're reading just to get the gist. Then reread the text more slowly, **ANNOTATING** it paragraph by paragraph. If there's an explicit **THESIS** stating the main point, highlight it in some way. Then try to capture the main idea of each paragraph in a single sentence.

_____ 12 ✳

_____ 15–18 ✳
_____ 342–44 ⁝

▶ Access
Chapter 2
in the ebook
for a video on
summarizing
while reading.

State the main points concisely and accurately. Summaries of a complete text are generally between 100 and 250 words in length, so you need to choose your words carefully and to focus only on the text's main ideas. Leave out supporting evidence, anecdotes, and counterarguments unless they're crucial to understanding the text. For instance, in summarizing "You Don't Need Words to Calm a Grumpy Kid" (see p. 155), Michaeleen Doucleff's report on the importance of touch in parenting, you would omit details about the studies of how mice respond to touch.

Describe the text accurately and fairly—and using neutral language. Present the author's ideas evenhandedly and fairly; a summary isn't the place to share your opinion of what the text says. Use neutral verbs such as "states," "asserts," or "concludes," not verbs that imply praise or criticism like "proves" or "complains."

_____ 529–32 ●

Use SIGNAL PHRASES to distinguish what the author says from what you say. Introducing a statement with phrases such as "He says" or "The essay concludes" indicates explicitly that you're summarizing what the author said. When first introducing an author, you may need to say something about their credentials. For example:

> In "Our Declaration," political philosopher Danielle Allen analyzes the language of the Declaration of Independence.

> Jason Stanley, a Rutgers University philosophy professor, explains the many ways language can be used as a tool for suppression in his *New York Times* opinion piece, "The Ways of Silencing."

Later in the text, you may need to refer to the author again as you summarize specific parts of the text. These signal phrases are typically briefer: "In Stanley's view . . . ," "Allen then argues . . ."

Use quotations sparingly, if at all. You may need to **QUOTE** keywords or memorable phrases, but most or all of a summary should be written in your own words, using your own sentence structures.

523–26

    DOCUMENT any text you summarize in a works-cited or references list. A summary of a lengthy work should include **IN-TEXT DOCUMENTATION** noting the pages summarized; they aren't needed with a brief text like the one summarized below (see p. 257).

538–41
MLA 545–80
APA 597–623

An Example Summary

In "Forget about Living to 100. Let's Live Healthier Instead" (p. 257), physician and professor Dave A. Chokshi argues that the United States needs a new approach to aging that focuses not only on longevity but on quality of life, too. Citing data suggesting that the average American enjoys just one healthy birthday beyond the age of sixty-five, Chokshi proposes setting a national goal to increase Americans' "health span"—the number of years spent in good health. To achieve this goal, Chokshi recommends a broad range of actions, including increasing investments in preventive care, combating homelessness, and countering ageist stereotypes, to "re-engineer" US health and social service systems. The costs of such actions, Chokshi argues, would be offset by the social and economic contributions that healthy older adults make in families, schools, workplaces, and other settings. Overall, Chokshi stresses the need for a bold plan to change narratives and systems around aging in order to support Americans' well-being beyond the traditional US retirement age.

This summary begins with a signal phrase stating the author's name and credentials and the title of the text being summarized. The summary includes only the main ideas, in the summary writer's own words.

RESPONDING

When you summarize a text, you show that you understand its main ideas; responding to a text pushes you to engage with those ideas—and gives you the opportunity to contribute your own ideas to a larger conversation. You can respond in various ways, for instance, by taking a **POSITION** on the text's argument, by **ANALYZING THE TEXT** in some way, or by **REFLECTING** on what it says.

170–96
114–45
383–92

Deciding How to Respond

You may be assigned to write a specific kind of response—an argument or analysis, for instance—but more often than not, the nature of your response is left largely up to you. If so, you'll need to read closely and critically to understand what the text says, to get a sense of how—and how well—it does so, and to think about your own reaction to it. Only then can you decide how to respond. You can respond to what the text says (its ideas), to how it says it (the way it's written), or to where it leads your own thinking (your own personal reaction). Or you might write a response that mixes those ways of responding. You might, for example, combine a personal reaction with an examination of how the writing caused that reaction.

If you're responding to what a text says, you might agree or disagree with the author's argument, supporting your position with good reasons and evidence for your response. You might agree with parts of the argument and disagree with others. You might find that the author has ignored or downplayed some important aspect of the topic that needs to be discussed or at least acknowledged. Here are some questions to consider that can help you think about what a text says:

- What does the writer claim?
- What **REASONS** and **EVIDENCE** does the writer provide to support that claim?
- What parts of the text do you agree with? Is there anything you disagree with—and if so, why?
- Does the writer represent any views other than their own? If not, what other perspectives should be considered?
- Are there any aspects of the topic that the writer overlooks or ignores?
- If you're responding to a visual text, how do the design and any images contribute to your understanding of what the text "says"?

402
402–9

Here is a brief response to Dave A. Chokshi's "Forget about Living to 100. Let's Live Healthier Instead," one that responds to his argument:

> I agree with Dave A. Chokshi's assertion that we need a "bold" and "audacious" plan to help Americans live more years in good health, and I believe his proposal fits the bill because it shifts the narrative around

healthy aging in the United States from one of individual responsibility to one of collective responsibility. Too often, we get the message that our health rests solely on our personal habits regarding our diet, doctor's visits, or exercise activities. Those habits are important, of course, but not everyone has access to healthy food, affordable medical care, or adequate workout time or space. Chokshi acknowledges this disparity and calls for structural changes to help address it—changes like increasing public investments not only in medical care but also in affordable housing, indoor air quality, and other social and environmental components of health. However, as much as I admire the boldness of Chokshi's proposal, I don't think it's quite bold enough: his plan doesn't address the high cost of health insurance for individuals, which I believe is part of our nation's health span problem in the first place. Overall, I applaud Chokshi's proposal, but I wish he'd included universal health care as part of his audacious solution.

If you're focusing on the way a text is written, you'll consider what elements the writer uses to convey their message—facts, stories, images, and so on. You'll likely pay attention to the writer's word choices and look for any patterns that lead you to understand the text in a particular way. To think about the way a text is written, you might find some of these questions helpful:

- What is the writer's message? Is there an explicit statement of that message?

- How well has the writer communicated the message?

- How does the writer support what they say—by citing facts or statistics? by quoting experts? by noting personal experiences? Are you persuaded?

- Are there any words, phrases, or sentences that you find notable and that contribute to the text's overall effect?

- How does the text's design affect your response to it? If it's a **VISUAL TEXT**—a photo or ad, for example—how do the various parts of the text contribute to its message?

▲ 134–40

Here is a brief response to Chokshi's essay that analyzes the various ways it makes its argument:

In "Forget about Living to 100. Let's Live Healthier Instead," Dave A. Chokshi uses a range of evidence to convince readers that his proposal

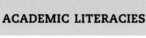
for improving health span in the United States has merit. Drawing on his personal experience as a physician, Chokshi begins with a brief anecdote about a patient whose long-term health goal is to blow out their birthday candles without coughing—a piece of evidence that puts a human face on Chokshi's topic. Next, Chokshi shares statistics about chronic health conditions and the aging population in the United States to underscore the scope of the problem he aims to address. In introducing his proposed solution, Chokshi offers evidence in the form of comparisons with other countries that have already created national health goals similar to the ones Chokshi proposes. As he outlines the details of his proposal, Chokshi refers to numerous studies and expert opinions, such as those published in the journal *Nature Aging*, to illustrate the potential benefits of his plan. Chokshi also offers specific examples—like reimagined birthday cards that portray aging in a positive light—to help readers envision the kinds of changes his proposal calls for. Together, the anecdotes, statistics, comparisons, and other types of evidence build a case for prioritizing health span over life span—and for embracing Chokshi's proposed plan.

Access the ebook for a video on responding to the views of others.

If you're reflecting on your own reaction to a text, you might focus on how your personal experiences or beliefs influenced the way you understood the text or on how it reinforced or prompted you to reassess some of those beliefs. You could also focus on how it led you to see the topic in new ways—or note questions that it's led you to wonder about. Some questions that may help you reflect on your own reaction to a text include:

- How did the text affect you personally?
- Is there anything in the text that really got your attention? If so, what?
- Do any parts of the text provoke an emotional reaction—make you laugh or cry, make you uneasy? What prompted that response?
- Does the text bring to mind any memories or past experiences? Can you see anything related to yourself and your life in the text?
- Does the text remind you of any other texts?
- Does the text support (or challenge) any of your beliefs? How?
- Has reading this text given you any new ideas or insight?

Here is a brief response to Chokshi's essay that reflects on an important personal issue:

Something that caught my attention in Dave A. Chokshi's "Forget about Living to 100. Let's Live Healthier Instead" was his mention of campaigns to combat ageist stereotypes, including a campaign for revised birthday cards that focus on celebrating aging rather than making fun of it. As a marketing major, I found this idea fascinating, and I wondered what other positive-aging campaigns might be developed. My grandfather retired a few years ago but has recently tried to reenter the workforce, in part because he misses the intellectual stimulation and social connection he enjoyed when he was working. So far, though, he's been passed over for jobs, and he feels it's due to stereotypical beliefs about older adults—for instance, the belief that older people aren't good with technology. Perhaps we need a campaign to dispel such beliefs and to help the larger public understand and value the considerable talents that people like my grandfather have to offer in the workplace. This could be part of the "new narratives about healthy aging" that Chokshi says our country needs.

WRITING A SUMMARY AND RESPONSE ESSAY

You may be assigned to write a full essay that summarizes and responds to something you've read. Following is one such essay. Beatriz Cardoso e Souza, a student at Columbus State Community College, responds to a *New York Times* column by Ben Wildavsky, "Let's Stop Pretending College Degrees Don't Matter" (see p. 170).

BEATRIZ CARDOSO E SOUZA

Let's Stop Pretending That Expensive College Degrees and Student Loans Aren't Barriers

Growing up in Brazil, with a teacher as a mother, I was taught from a young age that attending college was not a choice but a duty. Education was considered the most crucial factor in determining my future. In his article "Let's Stop Pretending College Degrees Don't Matter," author

Ben Wildavsky shares a similar point of view. Wildavsky highlights the value of a college education, arguing that recent headlines asserting the irrelevance of college degrees in today's job market are misleading and could decrease economic opportunities, especially for those who need them the most. Wildavsky cites data showing the substantial increase in earnings for college graduates compared to high school graduates, and he explains that despite a growing movement among some states and businesses to drop college-degree requirements from jobs, most supervisors and human resources professionals continue to seek candidates with college degrees. While I agree with Wildavsky that a college education can lead to better-paying jobs, the author fails to discuss how costly college can be in the United States and how student loans can negatively impact the lives of young professionals. Many graduates finish college with a negative net worth, which will limit how they can spend their earnings and shape their career paths.

Wildavsky is correct when he states that obtaining a college diploma increases the chances of getting better-paying jobs. However, he fails to recognize that attending college in the United States is expensive. Besides costly tuition, the cost of living is also high, and many students cannot keep a full-time job while enrolled in college. According to Melanie Hanson, a researcher for the Education Data Initiative, the median cost of attending a public college for four years and living on campus is $104,108. In addition, while four years is the regular period to finish a bachelor's degree, only 40.4% of students complete their bachelor's degree within that period. Most students take up to six years to graduate ("Average Cost"). In Brazil, where I first started on my college path, education is considered a citizen's right instead of a privilege. Students there have the option of attending public universities where tuition is free, and the Brazilian private colleges tend to be affordable. In Europe, too, college costs are far lower than in the United States: In Austria, tuition is free for students from European Union countries, with living costs averaging $13,350 per year. Costs in Germany, Ireland, Norway, and Sweden are similar (Collier). All of this data points to the fact that many students in the United States face financial barriers that prevent them from attending college, but Wildavsky doesn't take such barriers into consideration.

Wildavsky also does not address the student loan debt crisis and how negatively it can impact the earnings of college students. Even though I believe education is essential, I delayed enrolling in college to finish my degree after moving to the United States. I feared needing to borrow money to attend college and how it could lead to a bad credit score. Additionally, my husband already had student loan debt, which left him with a negative net worth and forced him to settle for low-wage positions when he couldn't find a good-paying job quickly enough after graduation. My husband is not the only one. According to a 2023 report from the job-networking platform *Handshake*, 70% of college seniors with student loans stated that their debt would influence the jobs they'll take after graduating, with many of them expecting to do gig work in addition to a full-time job in order to pay their expenses (Liu). Moreover, Hanson reports that every year, the debt from student loans grows by a median of $78.7 billion ("Economic Effects").

Overall, Wildavsky's argument focuses on how obtaining a college degree increases graduates' earnings, but he does not address the need for changes in the U.S. education system to make those potential earnings more accessible to more students. If college degrees in the U.S. were perceived not only as a means to financial stability but also as a right of every citizen and a tool for social change, more individuals would be able to reap the benefits of higher education. Instead of only reinforcing the importance of college degrees, perhaps Wildavsky could analyze the bigger picture and advocate for initiatives seeking to lower the cost of attending college.

Works Cited

Collier, Sabrina. "How Much Does It Cost to Study in Europe?" *Top Universities*, 15 Sept. 2022, www.topuniversities.com/student -info/student-finance/how-much-does-it-cost-study-europe.

Hanson, Melanie. "Average Cost of College & Tuition." Education Data Initiative, 18 Nov. 2023, educationdata.org/average-cost-of -college.

———. "Economic Effects of Student Loan Debt." *Education Data Initiative*, 20 Sept. 2023, educationdata.org/student -loan-debt-economic-impact.

Liu, Jennifer. "70% of College Seniors with Student Debt Say Looming Repayments Will Impact Their Career Plans." *CNBC*, 29 Aug. 2023, www.cnbc.com/2023/08/29/70percent-of-college-seniors-with-loans -say-debt-will-influence-their-career.html.

Wildavsky, Ben. "Let's Stop Pretending College Degrees Don't Matter." *The New York Times*, 21 Aug. 2023, www.nytimes. com/2023/08/21/opinion/skills-based-hiring-college-degree-job -market-wage-premium.html.

In her response, Souza both agrees and disagrees with Wildavsky's argument, using sources and personal experience to support her contention that Wildavsky ignores important contexts, like the burden of student debt. She cites five sources within the text and at the end in a works-cited section.

Key Features of Summary and Response Essays

A clearly identified author and title. Usually the author and title of the text being summarized are identified in a signal phrase in the first sentence. The author (or sometimes the title) may then be referred to in an abbreviated form if necessary in the rest of the essay: for example, "Wildavsky argues . . ." or "According to 'Let's Stop Pretending College Degrees Don't Matter,' . . ."

A concise summary of the text. The summary presents the main and supporting ideas in the text, usually in the order in which they appear. Souza, for example, reduces Wildavsky's argument to three sentences that capture Wildavsky's main points while leaving out his many examples.

An explicit response. Your essay should usually provide a concise statement (one sentence if possible) of your overall response to the text.

- *If you're responding to the argument,* you'll likely agree or disagree (or both), and so your response itself will constitute an argument, with an explicit thesis statement. Souza first agrees with Wildavsky that college degrees are important for economic mobility, but then she introduces her thesis: that student loan repayments cut into earnings for many graduates.

- *If you're analyzing the text,* you'll likely need to explain what you think the author is saying and how the text goes about conveying that message. An analysis of Wildavsky's text, for example, might focus on his use of "stepping stones" and "barriers" as metaphors to explore competing perceptions of the value of college degrees.

- *If you're responding with a reflection,* you might explore the ideas, emotions, or memories that the text evokes, the effects of its ideas on your own beliefs, or how your own personal experiences support or contradict the author's position. Souza, for example, reflects on how her and her husband's experience with his college debt complicates Wildavsky's argument.

Support for your response. Whatever your response, you need to offer reasons and evidence to support what you say.

- *If you're responding to what the text says,* you may offer facts, statistics, anecdotal evidence, and textual evidence, as Souza does. You'll also need to consider—and acknowledge—any possible counterarguments, positions other than yours.

- *If you're responding to the way the text is written,* you may identify certain patterns in the text that you think mean something, and you'll need to cite evidence from the text itself. For example, Wildavsky twice refers to the economic concept of "revealed preferences" to illustrate what he sees as the disconnect between perception and reality in job hiring.

- *If you're reflecting on your own reaction to the text,* you may connect its ideas with your own experiences or beliefs or explore how the text reinforced, challenged, or altered your beliefs. Someone who's on the fence about getting a degree, for example, might find a welcome middle ground in Wildavsky's "both/and" approach to college and career credentialing.

Ways of Organizing a Summary and Response Essay

You can organize a summary and response essay in various ways. You may want to use a simple, straightforward structure that starts out by summarizing the text and then gives the **THESIS** of your response followed by details that develop the thesis.

342–44

Summary, followed by response

Introduce the text and summarize it, usually in one paragraph. → State your thesis. → Respond to the text:
- what it says
- how it's written
- how you react
→ Conclude by summing up your response and its implications.

Or you may want to start out with the thesis and then, depending on whether your response focuses on the text's argument or its rhetorical choices, provide a paired summary of each main point or each aspect of the writing and a response to it.

Introduction and thesis, followed by point-by-point summary and response

Introduce the text and state your thesis. → Summarize the first point in the text or one of its rhetorical features and respond to it.

↓

Summarize the next point or another feature and respond to it.

↓

Continue as needed. → Conclude by summing up your response and its implications.

If you need more help

358–60
361–64
365–71
372–82
533–41

See Chapter 31 for guidelines on **DRAFTING** and Chapter 30 for help writing a thesis and coming up with a title. See Chapter 32 on **ASSESSING YOUR OWN WRITING**, Chapter 33 on **GETTING RESPONSE AND REVISING**, and Chapter 34 on **EDITING AND PROOF-READING**. See Chapter 52 on **ACKNOWLEDGING SOURCES, AVOIDING PLAGIARISM**.

4 Developing Academic Habits of Mind

A little advice from Serena Williams: "Stick to it and work hard." She wasn't just talking about tennis, and her words resonate for all of us, for everything we set out to do. And here's Michael Jordan, who tells us "Never quit!" and then goes on to issue a warning: "If you quit once, it becomes a habit." Serena Williams and Michael Jordan may be two of the greatest athletes ever, but neither of them was born a champion. They became great by working hard, hanging in there, never giving up.

They succeeded, in other words, by developing certain habits of mind that can serve us all well—and that are especially valuable when it comes to succeeding in school. This chapter is about developing *academic habits of mind.* Just as Serena Williams wasn't born with her powerful serve, none of us was born knowing how to write academic papers or ace exams. But we, too, can learn and can develop the habits we need to succeed. This chapter offers advice for developing habits of mind that writing teachers nationwide have identified as essential for college success.

Engage

We all know people who see school as a series of hoops to jump through, who seem uninvolved—and even bored. We also know people who are passionate about something—a video game, a hobby, a profession—and who invest themselves, their time, and their emotions wholeheartedly in those activities. Successful students make that investment in school. In other words, they engage with what they're studying, what they're doing, and what they're learning.

Think about your purpose for being in college. What are your goals? To get a degree? To qualify for a particular job or profession? To find intellectual stimulation? To explore life? Try to define why you are in school, both in larger terms ("to get a degree in accounting") and in terms of the specific courses you're taking ("Learning to write better will help me be a better student in general and communicate effectively at work").

Fight off boredom.   Every job, including the job of being a student, involves some tasks that are dull but need to be done. When you encounter such a task, ask yourself how it helps you reach a larger goal. Shooting a hundred free throws for practice may not seem interesting, but it can help you win games. When you're listening to a lecture or reading a textbook, take notes, highlight, and annotate; doing that forces you to pay attention and increases what you remember and learn. Trying to identify the main ideas as you listen to a lecture will help you stay focused. When you're studying, try alternating between different tasks: reading, writing, doing problem sets, drawing, and so on.

If you get distracted, figure out ways to deal with it.   It's hard to engage with what you're reading or studying when you're thinking about something else—paying a tuition bill, the last episode of *The Last of Us*, whatever. Try taking a few moments to write out what's on your mind, in a journal or somewhere else. Sometimes that simple act frees your mind to think about your work, even if it doesn't solve anything.

Raise your hand.   When you think you know the answer to a teacher's question (or when you yourself have a question), raise your hand. Most teachers appreciate students who take chances and who participate in class. At the same time, be polite: don't monopolize discussion or interrupt others when they're speaking.

Get involved.   Get to know other students; study with them; join a campus organization. People who see themselves as part of something larger, even just a study group with three or four others, engage more in what they're doing than those who try to go it alone.

Be Curious

When we're young, we're curious about everything, and we learn by asking questions (why? why *not*?) and by exploring our surroundings (digging holes, cutting up magazines, investigating attics and basements). As we get older, though, we focus on things that interest us—and may as a result start to ignore other things or even to forget how to explore. In college, you'll be asked to research, study, and write about many topics you know nothing about. Seize the opportunity. Be curious! And take a tip from Dr. Seuss: "The more that you read, the more things you will know. / The more that you learn, the more places you'll go."

Ask questions. It's tempting to stay within our comfort zones, thinking about things we know and like, listening to those whose views we tend to agree with—to say what we already believe rather than to stop and think. Resist that temptation! Take every opportunity to ask questions, to learn more about things you're already interested in, and especially to learn about things you don't (yet) know anything about. As marine biologist Sylvia Earle says, "The best scientists and explorers have the attributes of kids! They ask questions and have a sense of wonder. They have curiosity. Who, what, where, why, when, and how! They never stop asking questions, and I never stop asking questions, just like a five year old."

Listen! Pay attention to what others say, including those who you don't necessarily agree with. The words and ideas of others can challenge the way we think, prompt us to rethink what we think—and spark our curiosity: Why does X think that? What do I think—*and why?* Why do my neighbors oppose science-based reading methods? What do educators think about it? Paying attention to all sides of an argument, doing research to find out what others have said about a topic, or searching social media to see the latest postings on a trending topic are all ways you can listen in on (and engage in) conversations on important issues of all kinds.

Be Open to New Ideas

No matter where you go to school, you're going to encounter ideas and concepts and even facts that challenge your own beliefs; you're also likely to meet people whose backgrounds and ways of looking at life are very different from your own. Be open-minded, open to new ideas and to what others think and say. Consider the perspectives and arguments of others. Learning involves accepting new ideas, acknowledging the value of different perspectives, and coming to understand our own beliefs in new ways. Listen to what others say, and think before you respond.

- *Treat the ideas of others with respect,* whether you agree with them or not, and encourage others to do the same. We don't open up if we don't feel safe.

- *Try to withhold judgment.* Be willing to listen to the thoughts of others and to consider ideas that may at first seem alien or weird (or wrong). Remember that your weird is likely someone else's normal—and the reverse.

- *Look for common ground between your perspectives and those of others—* places where you can agree, even in the midst of serious disagreement.

Connect What You Know to New Knowledge

You know a lot about many different subjects, and not just the classes you took in school. You learned from playing, working, having friends, pursuing hobbies, caring for loved ones and pets, interacting with others, reading, watching TV, surfing the web—in other words, living. The best way to learn is by connecting new information and skills, like the information and skills you're being asked to learn in college, to the knowledge and skills you already have.

Start with your own knowledge. It's tempting to head to Google or Wikipedia when faced with an unfamiliar topic, but you're likely to learn it better if you start by connecting the new knowledge with the knowledge you already have.

Brainstorm what you already know about a topic. When faced with new information, take a few minutes to jot down what you already know about the subject. If nothing comes immediately to mind, try coming up with a word or phrase related to the subject for each letter of the alphabet or sketch a picture of something related to it.

Look for analogies between your knowledge and the new information or skill. An analogy is simply a comparison: "In the short story "The Yellow Wallpaper," the narrator is ill and confined to her bed. That's like when I had COVID and had to stay in bed for a week." You could then consider ways in which your experience—ill, uncomfortable, bored—matched or differed from the narrator of the story. If you're writing an argument, how is this task like the time you persuaded your math teacher to let you retake a test? How is it different?

Get an overview. When you start studying, skim the chapters in your texts before you start reading closely to get an overall sense of what you're studying and where it's heading. That overview will help you connect all the parts of the text.

Use the "novelty effect." Sometimes you encounter a word, concept, or image that is entirely new to you. You can't connect it to anything you've learned before, but the very novelty of it may burn it into your memory—and you can help cement that memory by inventing an association. For example, the first time you encounter the term "liminal," meaning "on the threshold of" or "between two states or places," you might better remember it by associating it with "limit," as in "at the limit or boundary; one foot inside my door, one foot out."

Be Flexible

Being flexible means being adaptable. In college, you'll likely face novel situations and need to find new ways to address problems, such as juggling school, work, and family; adjusting to roommates and making new friends; and figuring out how to do unfamiliar new assignments and how to take tests. You'll even have to do new kinds of writing: lab reports, reflections, literacy narratives, and many, many more; if your school writing up until this point has usually (or always) called for a five-paragraph theme, that's not going to be the case anymore.

Look for new ways to do things.   As the saying goes, "If all you have is a hammer, everything looks like a nail." Look for other tools to add to your toolbox: try solving math problems with words or by drawing, or starting a writing project by sketching out the parts.

Try not to see things as right or wrong, good or bad.   Be willing to consider alternative points of view and to withhold judgment. Often ideas or actions can only be judged in context; they may be true in some cases or in part, and you often need to understand the larger situation or take into account various perspectives. For example, you may believe that lying is wrong, but is it excusable if telling the truth will cause someone pain? You find a required reading assignment boring and useless, but why, then, did your instructor assign it?

Approach academic assignments rhetorically.   Analyze each assignment's purpose, intended audience, and the rest of its **RHETORICAL SITUATION**. Think about what's required in terms of content and format—and also about what's appropriate in terms of language and style. And what's expected in the discipline: informal language, sentence fragments, and photographs without captions might be appropriate for a sociology blog, for example, whereas a research project for a history course might have different requirements for how it's organized, formatted, and documented.

▮ 71

Be Creative

If you think that creativity is something artists have (and are born with), think again. From the young man selling homemade granola at a local farm market to the woman who puts together an eye-catching outfit from thrift-store bins, many of us are at work expressing ourselves in distinctive ways. Psychologists tell us that acting creatively opens us up to becoming more creative—and it's safe to say that doing so will make your work more productive and very likely more fun.

- *Play with ideas.* Freewrite. Make lists. Try looping, clustering, and the other ways of **GENERATING IDEAS** covered in this book. Take some time to think about the ideas you come up with.

329–39

- *Don't wait until the last minute.* Some students say they do better under the pressure of a deadline. Don't believe it! It's *always* better to give yourself time to think, to explore ideas, to "sleep on" assignments that first stump you.

- *Take risks!* Explore questions and topics that you haven't thought about before. Try out methods you haven't used previously. Challenge yourself to come up with ten ideas. Or twenty.

- *Ask questions.* And remember that there's no such thing as a dumb question.

Persist—and Seek Help

Sometimes a task can be tedious or frustrating; you may feel that you're drowning in a difficult course, can't figure out a complex problem, or can't master a tricky move in a video game. Persisting—keeping at it even when you don't think you can succeed—can make the difference between failing and succeeding. Here are some tips for getting past obstacles:

- *Don't give up.* Often the difference between successful and unsuccessful people is simply that the successful ones keep at a task. If they encounter difficulties, they try to figure out how to deal with them. That may mean looking at a task or problem in a new way, thinking about how they solved similar problems in the past, or trying different strategies. If a textbook seems hopelessly confusing, for example, try **OUTLINING** or **SUMMARIZING** the parts you don't understand.

335–37
29–31

- *Make a plan and establish a schedule,* and stick to them.

- *Break large projects into smaller goals.* Especially with assignments that call for a huge amount of work, approach it in stages: focus on getting through the next chapter, the next draft, the next whatever. It may be good to "keep your eyes on the prize," but it's usually best to take it one step at a time.

- *When you're working on several assignments, tackle the hardest ones first.* Work on them when you're fresh and your mind is clear.

- *If you don't understand something, ask for clarification.* Better to admit to confusion than to act as if you know something when you don't.

- *Ask for help when you need it.* Teachers are usually happy to help students during office hours or by appointment, before or after class, or over email. Get to know your teachers: they're there to help you.

- *Take advantage of whatever help is available* at your school's writing center or learning center and in class. An important part of being persistent is getting help when you need it.

Reflect

Pay attention to the ways you work and make decisions. Reflect on the ways you think and on how you think about the world. This kind of "metacognitive" thinking is one of the most important habits of mind, and it's one that will continue to serve you well throughout your life.

- *Figure out when you are most efficient* and do your best work—and try to schedule your work accordingly.

- *Pay attention to what you're reading and how you're doing it.* Think about why you're reading *x*, and use **READING STRATEGIES** appropriate to your purpose. If you lose the thread of an explanation or argument, figure out where you got lost and why.

❋ 11–28

- *After completing an assignment, reflect in writing* on what you did well, what problems you had, and how you solved them (or not). What would you do differently next time—or if you had more time? You'll find prompts for "Taking Stock of Your Work" at the end of Chapters 12–23 that can help.

- *Troubleshoot.* Pay attention to bumps in the road as you encounter them. Try to understand what caused the problem, what you did to solve it, how successful you were and why.

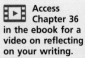
Access Chapter 36 in the ebook for a video on reflecting on your writing.

- *Try to focus on your achievements, what you can do,* rather than on what you may not be able to do or to do as well as you'd like.

Collaborate

Whether you're working in a face-to-face group, posting on an online discussion board, or exchanging drafts with a classmate for peer review, you likely spend a lot of time working with others on writing tasks. Even if you do much of your writing sitting alone at a computer, you probably get help from others at various stages in the writing process—and provide help as well. Two (or more) heads can be better than one—and learning to work well with a team is as important as anything else you'll learn in college.

Working with others face-to-face.   While informal groups can sometimes accomplish a lot, it's often better to be organized.

- *Make sure everyone is facing everyone else and is physically part of the group.* Doing that makes a real difference in the quality of the interactions—think how much better conversation works when you're sitting around a table than it does when you're sitting in a row.
- *Create a safe environment so everyone is comfortable participating.* Thoughtfulness, respect, and tact are key, since most writers (as you know) are sensitive and need to be able to trust those commenting on their work. Respond to the contributions of others as you would like others to respond to yours.
- *Set an agenda for each meeting—and pay careful attention to time.* Appoint one person as timekeeper to make sure all necessary work gets done in the available time.
- *Appoint another person to be group leader or facilitator.* That person needs to make sure everyone gets a chance to speak, no one dominates the discussion, and the group stays on task.
- *Appoint a member of the group to keep a record of the group's discussion,* jotting down the major points as they come up and afterward writing a **SUMMARY** of the discussion that the group members then approve.

29–31 *

Working with others online.   You're likely to work with one or more people online. When sharing writing or collaborating with others online in other ways, consider the following suggestions:

- As with all online communication, choose your words carefully to avoid inadvertently hurting someone's feelings. Without facial expressions, gestures, and other forms of body language and without tone of voice, your words carry all the weight.

- Remember that the AUDIENCE for what you write may well extend beyond your group. Your work might be forwarded to others, so there's no telling who else might read it.

75–78

- Decide as a group how best to deal with the logistics of exchanging drafts and comments. You can cut and paste text directly into email, send it as an attachment to a message, or post it to your class course management system site or a file-sharing site like *Dropbox* or *Google Docs*. You may need to use a combination of methods, depending on each group member's access to equipment and software. In any case, name your files carefully so that everyone knows which version to use.

- Make sure everyone has a chance to contribute. If you're using conferencing software like *Zoom* or *Microsoft Teams*, be aware that only one person at a time can speak, and those who chime in quickly can dominate the conversation, sometimes silencing quieter members of the group.

Creating group projects.   Creating a document with a team is common in business and professional work and in some academic fields as well. Here are some tips for making collaboration of this kind work well:

- Define the task as clearly as possible. Make sure everyone understands and agrees with the stated goals.

- Divide the task into parts. Decide which parts can be done by individuals, which can be done by a subgroup, and which need to be done by everyone together.

- Assign each group member certain tasks. Try to match tasks to each person's skills and interests and to divide the work equally.

- Establish a deadline for each task. Allow time for unforeseen problems before the project deadline.

- Try to accommodate everyone's style of working. Some people value discussion; others want to get right down to the writing. There's no best way to get work done; everyone needs to be conscious that their way is not the only way.

- Work for consensus—not necessarily total agreement. Everyone needs to agree that the plan to get the writing accomplished is doable and appropriate—if not exactly the way you would do the project if you were working alone.

- *Make sure everyone performs.* In some situations, your instructor may help, but in others the group itself may have to develop a way to make sure that the work gets done well and fairly. During the course of the project, it's sometimes helpful for each group member to write an assessment both of the group's work and of individual members' contributions.

Making the most of writing conferences.   Conferences with instructors or writing tutors, whether face-to-face or online, can be an especially helpful kind of collaboration. These one-on-one sessions often offer the most strongly focused assistance you can get—and truly valuable instruction. Here are some tips for making the most of conference time:

- *Be prepared.* Have at hand all necessary materials, including the draft you'll be discussing, your notes, any outlines—and, of course, any questions.

- *Be prompt.* Your instructor or tutor has set aside a block of time for you, and once that time is up, there's likely to be another student writer waiting.

- *Listen carefully, discuss your work seriously, and try not to be defensive.* Your instructor or tutor is only trying to help you produce the best piece possible. If you sense that your work is being misunderstood, explain what you're trying to say. Don't get angry! If a sympathetic reader who's trying to help can't understand what you mean, maybe you haven't conveyed your meaning well enough.

- *Take notes.* During the conference, jot down keywords and suggestions. Immediately afterward, flesh out your notes so you'll have a complete record of what was said.

- *Reflect on the conference.* Afterward, think about what you learned. What do you have to do now? Create a plan for revising or doing further work, and write out questions you will ask at your next conference or in a follow-up email or text.

Take Responsibility

In one way or another, all the habits of mind discussed above involve taking responsibility for your own actions. It may be tempting to blame others or society or bad luck for problems in your academic life, but the more you take ownership of your own learning, the more control you have over the results. Some ways you can enhance your sense of responsibility and demonstrate it include these:

- *Acknowledge that how much you learn and what grades you get depend mostly on you.* Teachers often say that they don't *give* grades, students *earn* grades—an important difference.

- *Treat school as you do a job,* one for which you must show up on time, perform tasks at a certain level of competence, and meet deadlines. In college, where your time is mostly unstructured, you have to become your own boss. So attend class regularly, follow instructions, and turn in assignments on time.

- *Get organized.* Maintain a calendar so you know what's due when. Create a schedule for your day that includes time for class, studying, working, and personal activities. Develop a system for organizing your written work and notes for each course you're taking. Learn where to find the materials you need to do your classwork.

- *Use research sources responsibly.* **QUOTE**, **PARAPHRASE**, and **SUMMA-RIZE** the work of others accurately, and **DOCUMENT** it correctly. Give appropriate credit to those whose ideas and words you are using.

521–32
538–41

5 Writing and Learning Online

Email. *Facebook. Snapchat, Instagram, Pinterest, TikTok.* Texts. Posts. It may seem as if almost all writing is done online now. In college courses, you may still be required to turn in some writing assignments on paper, but more and more writing is not only done online but submitted that way, too, through learning management systems (LMSs), email, or some other online system. You may rarely use email, but your professor may require you to do so. And many classes are being taught online, with little or no face-to-face communication between instructors and students.

Online, your instructor and classmates often cannot see or hear you—and that matters more than you might think. A puzzled look or a smile of recognition can start an important conversation in a face-to-face class, but in an online environment your audience may have only your written words to respond to. Therefore, you need to express your thoughts and feelings as clearly as you can *in writing.*

So it's useful to think about how the digital medium affects the way we write and learn—and how we can do both effectively online. This chapter provides some advice.

WRITING ONLINE

For most of us, email, texting, and other online communication tools are already parts of everyday life. But using them for academic purposes may require some careful attention. Following are some guidelines.

Email and Messaging

Much of your course-related communication will probably happen through email platforms or messaging tools, including those built into an LMS. When you're emailing or messaging with friends, you can be informal, using abbreviations, acronyms, emojis, and other shorthand ways of communicating. With your instructors or classmates you don't know well, though, you need to write more formally: in emails, use an appropriate salutation ("Dear Professor McWilliams") and craft a specific subject line; instead of writing "Question about paper," be specific: "Profile organization question." In both email messages and texts, write clearly and concisely in complete sentences; use standard capitalization and punctuation; and proofread. If you're writing about group work or a specific course, identify the course or group explicitly. If you're writing to request something—for example, to read a draft or to write a letter of recommendation—be sure to give your readers adequate time to do what you ask before any deadlines. And be careful before you hit Send—you want to be good and sure that you neither say something you'll regret later (don't send an email when you're angry—cool down and reread it!) nor include anything you don't want the whole world reading (don't put confidential or sensitive information in an email, text, or chat message).

Discussion Forums

Whether you're taking classes online or in person, you'll most likely participate in discussion forums—digital spaces where class members can discuss course material, share ideas, collaborate on projects, or get feedback on drafts. Discussion forums are usually set up through an **LMS** or through platforms like *Facebook Groups, Slack,* or *Microsoft Teams.* Typically, forums are organized by weeks or units of a course, and instructors provide prompts to which students respond via threaded conversations. Here are some tips for using discussion forums productively:

❋ 56–58

- *Review your instructor's guidelines and prompts.* Pay attention to any specific expectations for the number of posts and replies you should make, the length of your responses, and the due dates. Look for key terms in the prompts—like "describe," "compare," or "analyze"—that can help you figure out how to respond. Check for other requirements, too. Should you cite sources in your post? refer to class readings? apply course concepts?

- *Participate regularly.* The more you participate in your class forums, the more engaged you'll be in the conversations—and in the learning that accrues from them. So check the boards often, or set up notifications for new posts. And be sure to read your classmates' replies to your own posts—they might offer insights that help you think about course material in new ways or see your own work in a different light.

- *Be respectful and supportive.* Think of your classmates as your partners in a learning community, and make sure your posts and replies help create a collaborative and welcoming environment. When you reply to a peer, greet them by name. Show them that you've read their work carefully—mention details that you found especially interesting or insightful, for example. Be open to viewpoints and perspectives that differ from your own, and use a respectful tone, even if you disagree about something.

- *Engage thoughtfully with others' posts.* In responding to your class-mates' posts, try to go beyond simply agreeing with or restating their ideas. Instead, *engage* with their ideas—show them that you take their work seriously and want to move the conversation forward. You might, for example, ask probing questions, share examples from your own experiences, offer a different angle on a topic, or reflect on how your classmates' ideas connect with course material.

- *Think about medium and design.* Depending on your instructor's guide-lines, you may want to go beyond print text in your posts or replies. Most discussion forums allow you to upload or embed a variety of media types: video, audio, images, slides, links, and so on. For text-based posts, you can use design features like paragraphs, bullets, and headings to make your posts easy to read.

Blogs

Your instructor may ask you to create or contribute to a blog as part of your coursework. Blogs are websites that are maintained and updated regularly by individuals or groups who post opinions, reflections, information, and more—with writing, photos, video and audio files, and links to other sites. Blogs are an easy way to share your writing with others—and to invite response. Free blog hosting sites such as *WordPress, Wix,* or *Blogger* offer templates that let you create a blog and post to it easily, and some learning management systems include blogging capability as well.

Depending on your course and your instructor's preferences, you might use a blog as a place to respond to course readings, document your progress on a project, engage in peer review, reflect on your learning, or showcase your finished work. You might also be expected to comment on classmates' blogs—and to respond to their comments on your own blog. Be sure to think about your RHETORICAL SITUATION—especially your audience and purpose—to ensure that your tone, style, and content are appropriate.

If your blog is public, remember that anyone can read it, including potential employers; so just as with *Instagram* and other social media, you'll want to be careful about how you present yourself and avoid posting anything that others could see as offensive. (Think twice before posting when you're angry or upset.) You may want to activate privacy settings that let you restrict access to some of the content or that make your blog unsearchable by *Google* and other search tools. Also, assume that what you post in a blog is permanent: your friends, family, employer—anyone—may read a posting years in the future, even if the blog is no longer active.

LEARNING ONLINE

It's likely that much of your learning in college will happen online. At the very least, you'll access course material through an online learning platform. But you might also take fully online courses—or hybrid courses that combine in-person and online learning. Following is advice for managing such learning effectively.

Keeping Track of Files

You'll create lots of documents as a college student. In a single writing course, for example, you may write three or four drafts of four essays—that's twelve to sixteen documents. To keep track of your files, you'll need to create folders, establish consistent file names, and back up your work.

Creating folders. Create a folder for each course, and name it with the course title or number and the academic term: ENG 101 Fall 2026. Within each course folder, create a folder for each major assignment. Save your work in the appropriate folder, so you can always find it.

Naming and saving files. If you're expected to submit files electronically, your instructor may ask you to name them in a certain way. If not, devise a system that will let you easily find the files, including multiple drafts of your writing. For example, you might name your files using *Your last name + Assignment + Draft number + Date:* Jones Evaluation Draft 2 10-5-2026.docx. You'll then be able to find a particular file by looking for the assignment, the draft number, or the date. Saving all your drafts as separate files will make it easy to include them in a portfolio; also, if you lose a draft, you'll be able to use the previous one to reconstruct it.

Backing up your work. Hard drives fail, laptops and tablets get dropped, flash drives are left in public computers. Because files stored in computers can be damaged or lost, you should save your work in several places: on your computer, on a flash drive or portable hard drive, in space supplied by your school, or online. You can also ensure that an extra copy of your work exists by emailing a copy to yourself.

Finding Basic Course Information

You'll need to learn some essential information about any online courses you take:

- *The phone number for the campus help desk* or technology center. Check the hours of operation, and keep the number handy.
- *The syllabus,* list of assignments, and calendar with deadlines.
- *Where to find tutorials* for your school's learning management system and other programs you may need help with.
- *Whether the course is synchronous or asynchronous.* In a *synchronous* class, you'll spend at least some of your course time in live virtual meetings with your classmates and teacher. In an *asynchronous* class, you'll interact with your peers and instructor through discussion boards, blogs, or other tools that don't require you to be logged in at a certain time. In both formats, course materials like videos, presentation slides, lecture notes, and assignments are usually available at any time through an LMS.
- *How and when you can contact your instructor*—in person during office hours? by phone or email? through a videoconferencing platform like Zoom?—and how soon you can expect a response.
- *What file format you should use* to submit assignments—.doc, .docx, .rtf, .pdf, something else?—and how to submit them.
- *How to use the spell-check function* on your word processor or LMS.
- *How to participate in online discussions*—will you use a discussion board? a chat function in an LMS? a videoconferencing platform? something else?

Using Learning Management Systems

Whether you're in a face-to-face, hybrid, or online class, you may be asked to do some or all of your classwork online using an LMS such as *Blackboard, D2L, Moodle,* or *Canvas.* An LMS is a web-based educational tool that brings together all the course information your instructor wants you to have, along with features that allow you to participate in the class in various ways. Your school's LMS likely includes the following features that you'll be expected to use:

A course homepage contains posts from your instructor; a calendar with due dates for assignments; and links to the course syllabus, other course content, and additional features available on the site.

A discussion board enables you to communicate with classmates even if everyone isn't logged in to the board at the same time.

A chat tool allows you to engage in written conversations in real time, with all participants logged in simultaneously. In a classroom, doing this may be like texting with many others at once, so the rules for class discussion apply: be patient while waiting for a response; focus on the topic being discussed; avoid sarcasm or personal attacks.

A dropbox is a place where you submit assignments online. If your course dropbox has folders for each assignment, be sure to upload your assignment into the correct folder. Keep in mind that systems go down, so don't wait until the last minute to submit a file. It's a good idea to double-check that the file you've submitted has been uploaded; often you can simply exit the dropbox and then return to it to see that your file is where it should be.

A web conferencing platform. If your course meets partly or completely online, you may attend class through a conferencing tool built into your LMS.

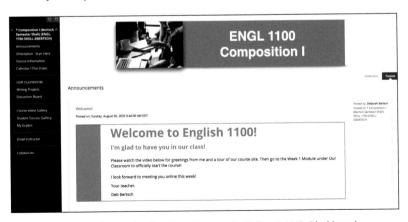

A course homepage from Columbus State Community College's LMS, *Blackboard*.

Online portfolios. Many LMSs allow you to create an online portfolio where you may post your coursework as well as photos, personal information, and links to other websites.

Additional features. An LMS may also include email; a space to keep a journal; a whiteboard for posting images, graphics, and presentations; video and audio uploading capabilities; a gradebook; a blog tool; and other features that can help you keep track of your work in a class.

Managing Challenges of Online Learning

Online classes offer a great deal of freedom and flexibility. You can work on your class almost anywhere—and often at your own pace (while still meeting deadlines, of course). Even so, online classes can present challenges, like managing your time effectively and keeping yourself motivated, disciplined, and engaged. Here are some tips for addressing those challenges and succeeding as an online learner:

- *Schedule your own "do dates."* Online classes may have only one or two due dates per week, but successful students create their own "do dates"—dates when they'll *do* the work. Try breaking the work into chunks each week and assigning yourself a specific day and time for each chunk: one day for reading the assigned texts, another day for generating ideas for a writing project, and so on. Put reminders in your phone, or ask friends or family to hold you accountable. The sense of accomplishment you get in completing one task can motivate you to move on to the next.

- *Find a good place to work, and avoid multitasking.* Having a dedicated work space can help you stay focused. Find a place that suits you best—a quiet corner in your home, a favorite booth in a cafe, a desk at your school library. Turn off notifications on your phone, and consider using a website blocker like *Freedom* or *Cold Turkey* to minimize distractions further.

- *Take breaks to increase productivity.* Working long stretches online can be exhausting. Be sure to take breaks from the work—and from the screen time. If you can, take a full day off from your course each week. And when you're in the midst of a work session, take micro breaks to help you recharge. Consider setting a timer on your phone—say twenty-five minutes of focused work, followed by a five-minute break. Then repeat the cycle, with a longer break after several work sessions. Or use a productivity app like *TomatoTimer* to schedule your focus times and your break times.

- *Connect with your classmates—and your teacher.* You might not see your online classmates in person, but you can still get to know them and draw on them for support. In online writing courses, you'll typically have lots of opportunities to interact via discussion boards, peer review, and maybe web-based meetings or break-out rooms. As you get acquainted with your peers, try to identify at least one who can be your go-to person for reminders, tips, and general help. Then check in with each other via email, text, *FaceTime*, or other tools. Take advantage of opportunities to connect with your teacher, too. Use the email, chat, or videoconferencing tools available in your LMS to reach out to your instructor whenever you need help.

- *Participate actively in online class meetings.* If your class requires real-time meetings via *Zoom*, *Google Meet*, or another platform, try to approach the online session as you would an in-person one: do your homework, write down questions for your teacher or classmates, and show up on time. During the session, keep yourself engaged and focused by taking notes, speaking during discussions, or making comments in the chat box. You might also volunteer to moderate the chat conversation and alert your teacher to important questions or comments.

Using Web Conferencing Tools

Zoom, Skype, Microsoft Teams, and *Google Meets* are all online platforms that enable groups of people to see and talk with one another. You may be in a class that meets partly or solely in a web conference session, or you may use one of these programs to meet with your classmates or instructor outside of class. Since you're on camera, consider both your own appearance and the background. Here are some additional hints for participating in an online video conference:

- *Consider adding a virtual background* instead of the room behind you. *Zoom*, for example, offers several; or you can download photos of your own.

- *Keep your microphone muted when you aren't speaking.* Background noise, coughing, even setting drink glasses on the desk during a session can distract everyone.

- *Consider recording online class sessions* and meetings (with other participants' permission) so you can review them later.

- *Make sure everyone has an opportunity to speak.* Remember that online video discussions are different from face-to-face meetings or even conference calls. In *Zoom* and other programs, only one person can speak at a time, and people who are quick to respond can sometimes drown out and silence those who need more time before responding.

- *Monitor yourself.* Because it's harder to "read the room" by gauging others' reactions (and in large online classes, figuring out who's talking may be difficult), you'll need to make sure you're not holding the floor too long, being repetitive, or going off topic.

6 Writing with Generative AI

ChatGPT. Microsoft Copilot. Google Gemini. You probably use these or other generative AI tools in your daily life, and it's likely you'll engage with them as part of your academic life, too. Maybe you'll use *ChatGPT* as a virtual tutor to help you study for a test or understand a difficult concept. Or perhaps you'll interact with AI to brainstorm research questions for a project you'll work on, find patterns in survey data you've collected, or get feedback on an essay you're writing. Generative AI can serve as a powerful aid to our academic work, but we need to use the tools responsibly and productively. That means knowing why, when, and how to use AI in academic settings—and how not to use it. This chapter provides advice for incorporating AI tools into your writing and learning process in useful and ethical ways.

THINKING ABOUT YOUR ACADEMIC CONTEXT

A central message of this book is that all writing happens within particular contexts—and those contexts shape how and what we write. The same could be said about using AI: you'll use it differently in your personal life than you will in a professional context—and differently still in academic settings. In a workplace, for example, you'll need to follow data privacy and other guidelines established by your employer. In academic contexts, you're likely to encounter a range of expectations or conditions for AI use depending on your class and your instructor's approach to AI. Here are some things to consider as you engage with AI in your college courses:

Check your instructor's policies and expectations for AI use. Probably the most important guideline for using AI is to know your instructor's stance on it. Some instructors encourage use of AI for course assignments, and some forbid it entirely. Others allow AI for some but not all assignments or activities, and many instructors have special parameters for AI use. For example, they might stipulate which AI tools you can use or ask you to follow a particular method for acknowledging and documenting AI use. So it's important to check your syllabus and assignment prompts for specific policies. Above all, you need to know that it's *never* acceptable to submit AI-produced work as your own.

Remember your role as a writer in college. One reason your college instructors ask you to write is because they know the act of writing is valuable in and of itself. Writing helps you learn course content, grapple with difficult questions and ideas, connect with others, and understand yourself and the world. Writing is, in fact, a form of thinking—and thinking critically is one of the most important goals of all college classes. As a college student, then, you're expected to engage in the practice of writing with **HONESTY** and with a focus on learning. If you offload your writing to AI, you'll shortchange yourself by limiting your thinking and learning.

At the same time, part of learning to write in academic contexts involves learning to use the resources available to you: library databases, writing center services, media production labs, and so on. Like those resources, generative AI can help support—but not replace—your own intellectual work as a college writer. AI can serve as a kind of thinking or writing partner, another resource you turn to when you need to talk through an idea or move beyond a blank screen. By taking an active role in working with AI—and by being transparent with your instructors and others about that interaction—you stay in charge of your writing and learning. The prompts on pages 63 to 67 can help you use AI in such a way.

Consider the learning objectives of your assignment. All writing assignments are designed with certain learning goals in mind, and you should consider those goals as you experiment with AI. Ask yourself: What skills or knowledge is your assignment intended to help you develop? Will using AI (if permitted) help support that development—or hinder it? If, for example, one of the goals of an assignment is to practice revision strategies, then having AI revise your draft *for* you wouldn't be appropriate. On the other hand, getting feedback on your draft from AI—and then using that feedback to revise your own work—could help you meet the learning goal.

USING AI TO SUPPORT YOUR WRITING PROCESS

Once you've considered your context for writing and have determined that AI use is appropriate, you can begin incorporating AI tools into your writing process. Be sure to follow your instructor's guidelines and to use AI in a way that assists—but doesn't replace—your own thinking, learning, and writing. After all, your teachers are interested in what *you* have to say, not in what a bot says.

Conversing with AI

One way to ensure that you're actively engaged as you work with AI is to have a dialogue with the AI tool—a back-and-forth conversation where the AI functions as a kind of stand-in for a tutor or other writing mentor. On the next several pages are sample prompts you might use to start such a dialogue at various points in your writing process. Let's begin by looking at one sample prompt. (Note that the brackets indicate places where you can supply your own words.)

> I'm going to give you a topic for [a personal narrative] I'm writing. Act as a college writing tutor and ask me questions to help me [generate ideas for detail, dialogue, description, and action that I could use in my narrative]. Ask one question at a time, wait for my response, and then ask me the next question.

Notice that the prompt is set up as a template, which you can adapt to your own **RHETORICAL SITUATION**. For example, you can change the items in brackets to fit your specific genre and purpose, like this:

🔲 71

> I'm going to give you a topic for [a profile] I'm writing. Act as a college writing tutor and ask me questions to help me [develop an interesting angle that I can focus on for my profile]. Ask one question at a time, wait for my response, and then ask me the next question.

Notice, too, that the sample prompt gives the AI tool a "role" to play: "Act as a college writing tutor." Often this helps the AI figure out what kind of help you need and what stance to take in its response to you. Here are some other things to keep in mind as you work with the prompts:

- *Continue the AI conversation beyond the initial prompt* you enter—and take charge of that conversation. Redirect the bot if it gets stuck in a loop (say something like, "Let's move on to _____"), ask for clarification ("What do you mean by _____?"), and challenge its assumptions ("But what about the idea that _____?"). If you prompt the bot for feedback on a draft and it provides only glowing commentary, push it to give you suggestions for improvement, too.

- *Try starting a new conversation* if a prompt doesn't produce useful output. In a fresh conversation, AI will likely generate a different response to the same prompt, and that new response may be more helpful. You can also try rephrasing your prompt, perhaps by providing more detail about your topic, your purpose, or what kind of assistance you need.

- *Practice to get better.* The more you interact with AI, the better you'll get at understanding how it works—and at developing useful prompts that fit your purposes.

 Access the ebook for a video on brainstorming with generative AI tools.

Prompts for help with generating ideas and text.   AI tools can help you develop topic ideas, explore what you know about a topic, or generate details and other information for a piece of writing. Be careful not to ask AI to simply generate ideas *for* you, though. Instead, ask it to assist you in developing your own ideas through prompts like these:

- Act as an encouraging writing tutor to help me generate topic ideas for [a literacy narrative—a personal story about reading, writing, or developing some other skill]. Ask me questions to help me brainstorm several potential topic ideas. Ask one question at a time, wait for my response, and then ask me the next question

- I'm writing [a report on foster care] and have done some preliminary research, but I need help narrowing the topic. Ask me questions about my research to help me narrow my focus. Ask one question at a time, and then wait for my response before moving on.

- I'm writing [a position paper arguing that the Elam Ending is bad for the sport of basketball]. Can you help me identify some arguments against my position? Ask me one question at a time to prompt my thinking about potential counterarguments.

- I'm writing [an evaluation of the television show *The Bear*]. Ask me questions about my subject and its genre to help me develop criteria on which to base my evaluation.

- I need to [create a multimedia remix of an earlier piece of writing I composed for my composition class]. Ask me questions to help me decide my main purpose and intended audience.

Prompts for help with doing research.   If you need to find scholarly or popular sources, you're often better off using a search engine or a library database than an AI tool. But if you need help with other parts of your research process—like identifying keywords, generating research questions, or analyzing field data—AI tools can help. Here are prompts you can try:

- Act as an academic librarian. I'm beginning to research the topic of [teachers staying with the same cohort of students for multiple years]. Suggest keywords I could enter into a library database to help me find sources on my topic.

- I'm interested in researching the topic of [tone indicators in online communication]. Give me some background information on the topic to help me understand it better.

- I want to develop a research question on the topic of [endangered languages]. I'm going to share the notes I took on my preliminary research. Review my notes and then suggest three possible questions to guide the rest of my research process.

- For [a report I'm writing on e-bike safety], I'm planning to interview [a parent who has concerns about letting their child use an e-bike]. Help me brainstorm questions I can ask during my interview.

- I've conducted a survey about [athletes' use of self-talk]. Suggest some strategies I could use to find patterns or themes in the responses.

- I'm writing a researched essay on [tourism and climate change]. I've found and read several sources on the topic, and I need to synthesize them. Ask me questions to help me discover patterns, themes, and connections among my sources.

Prompts for help with organizing your writing. You can use AI to help you develop a plan for organizing your writing and guiding readers through it. Often, it's helpful to specify the genre you're writing in, as the following prompts do:

- I'm writing [a proposal to change the way colleges recruit athletes]. Ask me questions to help me begin creating a thesis for [my proposal].

- I'm writing [an analysis of the novel *Night Wherever We Go*]. I'm going to share some of my notes and ideas with you. Review my material and suggest two possible outlines I might use for [my analysis].

- I'm going to share a first draft of a thesis statement for [an argument] I'm writing. Give me feedback on the following: Does the thesis make a focused and specific claim? Is it qualified appropriately? Don't revise the thesis for me. Instead, ask me questions to help me figure out how to revise it.

- I'm writing [a profile of a musician], and I'm having trouble developing a conclusion. Suggest three strategies for how I might end [my profile].

Prompts for help with drafting. Start by writing your own draft, and then use AI to get suggestions for clarifying or expanding certain parts of your draft. Prompts you might try:

- Here's a section of [a personal narrative] I'm writing. Suggest places where I [might incorporate dialogue].

- Here's [my description of a movie poster I'm analyzing for a visual analysis assignment]. Are there details I should add to help readers better understand [the poster]?

- I'm in the middle of a draft of [an exploration essay], but I'm not sure where to go next. Read my draft and ask me a question to help me figure out what direction to take.

- Read these two body paragraphs from [an argument] I'm writing. Then point out places where I might need [more evidence to support my assertions].

Prompts for help with revising. You can adapt many of the prompts in Chapter 33 to get feedback from an AI tool to help you revise. Here are some additional prompts you can try:

- Here's a draft of [an argument] I wrote. Read it from the perspective of [someone who's skeptical of my claim], and tell me what comments you'd make in response.

- Act as a nonexpert on the topic of [mathematical patterns in nature]. Then read my draft of [a report] on the topic and tell me whether a nonexpert would understand it.

- I'm going to give you a draft I wrote of [a literary analysis]. Then I'll give you my instructor's evaluation criteria. Read my draft and apply the evaluation criteria. Tell me what I'm doing well and what I could improve on.

- Here's a draft of [a movie evaluation I wrote]. Analyze my stance, pointing out the words or phrases that suggest my stance. Then tell me if my stance seems [fair and balanced].

- I'm going to give you a draft of [a visual analysis] I'm writing. Then I'm going to give you a list of the key features of the genre from my assignment prompt. Review my draft against those key features. Which features are well represented? Which are not?

Prompts for help with editing and proofreading. In addition to adapting the prompts in Chapter 34, you can try these for help with editing and proofreading:

- Here's a draft of [an academic essay] I'm writing where I want to [follow the conventions for academic English to best reach my audience]. Help me identify issues with grammar, punctuation, or spelling.
- Review my draft and suggest places where I could use more effective transitions between paragraphs or sentences.
- My peer reviewer told me the following sentence was confusing. Can you help me understand why?

Evaluating AI Output

To use AI effectively, you need to take a critical, questioning approach to its output. AI tools are trained on vast amounts of human-written text, and they use that training—along with statistical analysis—to predict what words a human would expect to see in response to a query. So a chatbot doesn't actually "understand" its output in the human sense, which means AI tools have certain limitations. For example, AI can't fully appreciate your **RHETORICAL SITUATION** as a writer. It can't discern whether its output is true or accurate; in fact, it sometimes fabricates information or just gets things wrong. And because AI was trained on human words, its output may reflect human biases or harmful stereotypes, including those based on race, gender, age, and language. For all these reasons, it's important to evaluate AI output for accuracy, fairness, and relevance to your rhetorical situation. Here are some tips for doing so:

■ 71

Verify sources. AI can sometimes make up sources, citations, and URLs, so you should search online to make sure those items exist. Note that some AI tools, like *Copilot* and *Perplexity*, access sources directly from the internet and provide source links. Still, you'll want to review all sources to ensure their content is represented accurately in the AI output.

506–11 ●

FACT-CHECK information. It's a good idea to question any claims, examples, explanations, statistics, or other material a chatbot provides, especially if it's about a topic you're not familiar with. Open a new tab in your browser to see what other reliable sites have to say about the information in question.

Use your own judgment. Ask yourself questions about the AI output: Does it match what you already know about your topic? Does it seem to privilege a particular perspective or group? Are certain voices left out? Does it make assumptions based on race, gender, age, or other factors? Does the AI tool's advice seem appropriate to your rhetorical situation and your goals for writing?

Acknowledging Your Use of AI

No matter how you use AI—to generate ideas, create an outline, get feedback on your writing—it's important to let your readers know you've used it. In a sense, your interaction with AI is a form of collaboration, and acknowledging that collaboration illustrates your integrity as a writer. Depending on your instructor's guidelines, you may need to do one or all of the following:

Show your work. Many instructors require that you "show your work" if you've used AI, usually by submitting a record of your AI conversation. You could capture the conversation by copying and pasting it into a document or by taking screenshots of the transcript. Or, if your AI tool includes a Share feature, you could generate a link to your conversation. Check with your instructor to see if they prefer a certain method for sharing your AI interactions.

MLA 551 ●
APA 602

Create an ACKNOWLEDGMENT STATEMENT. Your instructor might ask for a written description of how you used AI in your researching or writing process. That description—or acknowledgment statement—could appear within your document, in a footnote or endnote, or as an appendix. You'll probably want to mention the AI tools you used, what kinds of assistance they provided you, and how you used their output in your work—but check with your instructor for specific guidelines.

Cite AI-generated material. If you incorporate content from AI directly into your writing—by quoting, paraphrasing, or summarizing information generated by AI—you'll need to cite the AI tool as a source. Follow **MLA** or **APA** style, and use **SIGNAL PHRASES** to introduce quoted material.

MLA 580
APA 623
529–32

Reflecting on Your Use of AI

REFLECTING on your work with AI—looking back on its role in your writing process and learning from your experiences—can help you become a more responsible and productive user of AI. Here are some questions you might consider as you reflect:

383–92

- In what part(s) of your writing process was AI most useful? Generating ideas? Researching? Getting feedback? Editing? Something else? Why?
- How helpful was the AI output you received?
- Can you point to a specific place in your text where AI influenced your work? Explain.
- How did you go about checking the AI output for inaccuracies or biases?
- What challenges did you face in working with AI? How did you address them?
- Did you take an active, engaged role in your work with the AI tool? If so, give an example. If not, how could you improve in the future?
- What did you gain from using the AI tool? What might you have lost?
- What will you do differently the next time you use AI in an academic writing context?

Part 2

Rhetorical Situations

Whenever we write, whether it's a text to a friend or a toast for a wedding, an English essay or a résumé, we face some kind of rhetorical situation. We have a **PURPOSE**, a certain **AUDIENCE**, a particular **STANCE**, a **GENRE**, and a **MEDIUM** to consider—and, as often as not, a **DESIGN**. All are important elements that we need to think about carefully. The following chapters offer brief discussions of those elements of the rhetorical situation, along with questions that can help you make the choices you need to as you write. See also the **GENRE** chapters for guidelines for considering your rhetorical situation in each of these specific kinds of writing.

Access the ebook for a video introduction to rhetorical situations.

Rhetorical Situations

* academic literacies
* rhetorical situations
* genres
* fields
* processes
* strategies
* research
* media / design
* handbook

7 Purpose

All writing has a purpose. We write to explore our thoughts and emotions, to express ourselves, to entertain; we write to record words and events, to communicate with others, to try to persuade others to believe as we do or to behave in certain ways. In fact, we often have several purposes at the same time. We may write an essay in which we try to *explain* something to an audience, but at the same time we may be trying to *persuade* that audience of something. Look, for example, at this passage from an essay written by Jada Jones as a first-year student at Tulane University. In "Black Mamas' Lives Matter: The Severe Racial Disparity in Maternal Mortality Rates," Jones reports that the assumption that "the United States falls within the top twenty developed nations with the lowest maternal mortality rates" is mistaken:

> The United States has a higher maternal mortality rate than many other industrialized countries. What's even more surprising is the fact that the number of maternal deaths in the United States has only increased over the years. According to Dr. Mary-Ann Etiebet, the executive director of a program that aims to reduce maternal mortality all over the world, "the United States is ranked 46th when it comes to maternal mortality. That's behind countries like Saudi Arabia and Kazakhstan." The reality of this statement should sound alarming, because "[i]n the U.S., at least two pregnant and/or delivering women die per day. The 'near deaths' amount to 60,000 a year."
>
> If this statistic still doesn't astound you, then consider the following fact: "Black women are three to four times more likely to experience a pregnancy-related death than white women." Currently in the United States, there is an ongoing maternal death epidemic, but what's even worse are the research studies that show a large disparity in the maternal mortality rates between Black women and White women. One journalist writes that "[a]ccording to the CDC, from 2011–2013, black women experienced roughly 43.5 deaths per 100,000 live births on average, compared to 12.7 deaths for white mothers." Since then, this racial disparity has continued to increase. As a result, many Black women are pointlessly losing their lives due to the inherent racism embedded

deep within the medical care system and medical experts' failure to immediately act on and listen to Black women's medical concerns.

Jones is reporting information here, outlining how high US maternal mortality rates are and how much more likely it is that Black women will die in childbirth than will White women. She is also making an argument that this disparity must be addressed:

> To decrease the large gap in maternal deaths between these two groups, there needs to be more attention brought to this maternal epidemic, increased advocacy for the reformation of US health care, and the creation of incentive programs to give Black mothers the necessary tools to have a healthy pregnancy.

Her main purpose is to persuade readers that steps must be taken to improve maternal mortality.

Even though our purposes may be many, knowing our primary reason for writing can help us shape that writing and understand how to proceed with it. Our purpose can determine the genre we choose, our audience, even the way we design what we write.

Identify your purpose. While a piece of writing often has many purposes, a writer usually focuses on one. When you get an assignment or see a need to write, ask yourself what the primary purpose of the writing task is—to entertain? to inform? to persuade? to demonstrate your knowledge or your writing ability? What are your own goals? What are your audience's expectations, and do they affect the way you define your purpose?

Thinking about Purpose

- *What do you want your audience to do, think, or feel?* How will your readers use what you tell them?

- *What does this writing task call on you to do?* Do you need to show that you have mastered certain content or skills? Do you have an assignment that specifies a particular **STRATEGY** or **GENRE** —to compare two things, perhaps, or to argue a position?

- *What are the best ways to achieve your purpose?* What **STANCE** should you take? Should you write in a particular genre? Do you have a choice of **MEDIUM**, and does your text require any special format or **DESIGN** elements?

393
91
85–87
635

8 Audience

Who will read (or hear) what you are writing? A seemingly obvious but crucially important question. Your audience affects your writing in various ways. Consider a piece of writing as simple as a text from a mother to her son:

Pls. take chicken out to thaw and feed Annye. Remember Dr. Wong at 4.

On the surface, this brief note is a straightforward reminder to do three things. But in fact it is a complex message filled with compressed information for a specific audience. The writer (the mother) counts on the reader (her son) to know a lot that can be left unsaid. She expects that he knows that the chicken is in the freezer and needs to thaw in time to be cooked for dinner; she knows that he knows who Annye is (a pet?), what they are fed, and how much; she assumes that he knows who (and where) Dr. Wong is. She doesn't need to spell out any of that because she knows what her son knows and what he needs to know—and in her text she can be brief. She understands her audience. Think how different such a reminder would be were it written to another audience—a babysitter, perhaps, or a friend helping out while Mom is out of town.

What you write, how much you write, how you phrase it, even your choice of **GENRE** (essay, email, text, social media post, speech)—all are influenced by the audience you envision. And your audience will interpret your writing according to their own expectations and experiences, not yours.

■ 79–84

When you are a student, your audience is most often your teachers, so you need to be aware of their expectations and learn about the conventions (rules, often unstated) for writing in specific academic fields. You may make statements that seem obvious to you, not realizing that your instructors may consider them assertions that must be proved with evidence of one sort or another. Or you may write more or less formally than teachers expect. Understanding your audience's expectations—by asking outright, by reading materials in your field of study, by trial and error—is important to your success as a college writer.

This point is worth dwelling on. You're probably reading this textbook for a writing course. As a student, you'll be expected to edit and proofread your essays carefully. But if you correspond with family, friends, or coworkers using email and texts, you might not proofread your messages much (or at all)—and your readers are probably fine with that. Whatever the rhetorical situation, your writing must meet the expectations of your audience.

Identify your audience. Audiences may be defined as *known*, *multiple*, or *unknown*. *Known audiences* can include people with whom you're familiar as well as people you don't know personally but whose needs and expectations you do know. You yourself are a known, familiar audience, and you write to and for yourself often. Class notes, to-do lists, reminders, and journals are all written primarily for an audience of one: you. For that reason, they are often in shorthand, full of references and code that you alone understand.

Other known, familiar audiences include anyone you actually know—friends, relatives, teachers, classmates—and whose needs and expectations you understand. You can also know what certain readers want and need, even if you've never met them personally, if you write for them within a specific shared context. Such a known audience might include PC gamers who read cheat codes that you've posted on the internet for beating a game; you don't know those people, but you know roughly what they know about the game and what they need to know, and you know how to write about it in ways they will understand.

You often have to write for *multiple audiences*. Business memos or reports may be written initially for a supervisor, who may pass them along to others. Grant proposals may be reviewed by four to six levels of readers—each, of course, with its own expectations and perspectives. Even writing for a class might involve multiple audiences: your instructor and your classmates.

Unknown audiences can be the most difficult to address since you can't be sure what they know, what they need to know, how they'll react. Such an audience could be your downstairs neighbor, with whom you've chatted occasionally in the laundry room. How will she respond to your letter asking her to sponsor you in an upcoming charity walk? Another unknown audience—perhaps surprisingly—might be many of your instructors, who want—and expect!—you to write in ways that are new to you. While you can benefit from analyzing any audience, you need to think most carefully about those you don't know.

Thinking about Audience

- *Whom do you want to reach?* To whom are you writing (or speaking)?

- *What is your audience's background—their education and life experiences?* It may be important for you to know, for example, whether your readers attended college, fought in a war, or have young children.

- *What are their interests?* What do they like? What motivates them? What do they care about?

- *Is there any demographic information that you should keep in mind?* Consider whether race, gender, sexual orientation, disabilities, occupation, religious beliefs, economic status, and so on should affect what or how you write. For example, writers for *Men's Health*, *InStyle*, and *Out* must consider the particular interests of each magazine's readers.

- *What political circumstances may affect their reading?* What attitudes—opinions, special interests, biases—may affect the way your audience reads your piece? Are your readers conservative, liberal, or middle of the road? Politics may take many other forms as well—retirees on a fixed income may object to increased school taxes, so a letter arguing for such an increase would need to appeal to them differently than would a similar letter sent to parents of young children.

- *What does your audience already know—or believe—about your topic?* What do you need to tell them? What is the best way to do so? Those retirees who oppose school taxes already know that taxes are a burden for them; they may need to know why schools are justified in asking for more money every few years. A good way to explain this may be with a bar graph showing how property values benefit from good schools with adequate funding. Consider which **STRATEGIES** will be effective—narrative, comparison, something else?

  ◆ 393

- *What's your relationship with your audience, and how should it affect your language and tone?* Do you know them, or not? Are they friends? colleagues? mentors? adversaries? strangers? Will they likely share your **STANCE**? In general, you need to write more formally when you're addressing readers you don't know, and you may address friends and colleagues more informally than you would a boss.

  ▪ 85–87

- *What does your audience need and expect from you?* Your history professor, for example, may need to know how well you can discuss the economy of the late Middle Ages in order to assess your learning; he may expect you to write a carefully reasoned argument, drawing conclusions from various sources, with a readily identifiable thesis in the first paragraph. Your boss, on the other hand, may need an informal email that briefly lists your sales contacts for the day; she may expect that you list the contacts in the order in which you saw them, that you clearly identify each one, and that you briefly say how well each contact went. What **GENRE** is most appropriate?

- *What kind of response do you want?* Do you want readers to believe or do something? to accept as valid your information on a topic? to understand why an experience you once had still matters to you now?

- *How can you best appeal to your audience?* Is there a particular **MEDIUM** that will best reach them? Are there any **DESIGN** requirements? (Elderly readers may need larger type, for instance.)

9 Genre

Genres are kinds of writing. Letters, profiles, reports, position papers, poems, blog posts, instructions, parodies—even jokes—are genres. For example, here is the beginning of a **PROFILE** of a mechanic who repairs a specific kind of automobile:

▲ 246–56

> Her business card reads Shirley Barnes, M.D., and she's a doctor, all right—a Metropolitan Doctor. Her passion is the Nash Metropolitan, the little car produced by Austin of England for American Motors between 1954 and 1962. Barnes is a legend among southern California Met lovers—an icon, a beacon, and a font of useful knowledge and freely offered opinions.

A profile offers a written portrait of someone or something that informs and sometimes entertains, often examining its subject from a particular angle—in this case, as a mechanic who fixes old cars. While the language in this example is informal and lively ("she's a doctor, all right"), the focus is on the subject, Shirley Barnes, "M.D." If this same excerpt were presented as a poem, however, the new genre would change our reading:

> Her business card reads
> Shirley Barnes, M.D.,
> and she's a doctor, all right
> —a Metropolitan Doctor.
> Her passion is the Nash Metropolitan,
> the little car produced by Austin of England
> for American Motors between 1954 and 1962.
> Barnes is a legend
> among southern California Met lovers
> —an icon,
> a beacon,
> and a font of useful knowledge and
> freely offered opinions.

The content hasn't changed, but the different presentation invites us to read not only to learn about Shirley Barnes but also to explore the significance of the words and phrases on each line, to read for deeper meaning and greater appreciation of language. The genre thus determines how we read and how we interpret what we read.

Genres help us write by establishing features for conveying certain kinds of content. They give readers clues about what sort of information they're likely to find and so help them figure out how to read ("This article begins with an abstract, so it's probably a scholarly source" or "This must be the list of assignments for my Econ course."). At the same time, genres are flexible; writers often tweak the features or combine elements of different genres to achieve a particular purpose or connect with an audience in a particular way. Genres also change as writers' needs and available technologies change. For example, computers have enabled us to add audio and video content to texts that once could appear only on paper.

Choosing the Appropriate Genre

How do you know which genre you should choose? Often the words and phrases used in writing assignments can give you clues to the best choice. Here are typical terms used in assignments and the genres they usually call for.

93–113 ▲

LITERACY NARRATIVE If you're assigned to explore your development as a writer or reader or to describe how you came to be interested in a particular subject or career, you'll likely need to write a literacy narrative or a variation on one. Some terms that might signal a literacy narrative: "describe a learning experience," "tell how you learned," "trace your development," "write a story."

114–45 ▲
220–33

TEXTUAL ANALYSIS or **LITERARY ANALYSIS** If your assignment calls on you to look at a nonfiction text to see not only what it says but also how it works, you likely need to write a textual analysis. If the text is a short story, novel, poem, or play, you probably need to write a literary analysis. If you are analyzing a text or texts in multiple media, you might choose either genre or mix the two. Some terms that might signal that a textual or literary analysis is required: "analyze," "examine," "explicate," "read closely," "interpret."

146–69 ▲

REPORT If your task is to research a topic and then tell your audience in a balanced, neutral way what you know about it, your goal is probably to write a report. Some terms that might signal that a report is required: "define," "describe," "explain," "inform," "observe," "record," "report," "show."

POSITION PAPER or **ARGUMENT** Some terms that might signal that your instructor wants you to take a position or argue for or against something: "agree or disagree," "argue," "claim," "criticize," "defend," "justify," "position paper," "prove."

▲ 170–96

SUMMARY If your assignment is to reduce a text into a single paragraph or so, a summary is called for. Some terms that might signal that a summary is expected: "abridge," "boil down," "compress," "condense," "recap," "summarize."

✳ 29–31

EVALUATION If your instructor asks you to say whether or not you like something or whether it's a good or bad example of a category or better or worse than something else, an evaluation is likely required. Some terms that might signal that an evaluation is expected: "assess," "critique," "evaluate," "judge," "recommend," "review."

▲ 210–19

PERSONAL NARRATIVE If you're asked to explore an important moment or event in your life, you're probably being asked to write a personal narrative. Some terms that likely signal that a personal narrative is desired: "autobiography," "chronicle," "narrate," "a significant personal memory," "a story drawn from your experience."

▲ 234–45

PROFILE If your instructor assigns you the task of portraying a subject in a way that is both informative and entertaining, you're likely being asked to write a profile. Some terms that might indicate that a profile is being asked for: "angle," "describe," "dominant impression," "interview," "observe," "report on."

▲ 246–56

PROPOSAL If you're asked to offer a solution to a problem, to suggest some action—or to make a case for pursuing a certain project, a proposal is probably in order. Some terms that might indicate a proposal: "argue for [a solution or action]," "propose," "put forward," "recommend."

▲ 257–69

EXPLORATION If your assignment calls on you to think in writing about something or to play with ideas, you are likely being asked to write an exploratory essay. Some terms that may mean that an exploration is called for: "consider," "explore," "ponder," "probe," "reflect," "speculate."

▲ 270–79

REMIX If you're asked to adapt something you've written to create something new—perhaps for a new purpose, audience, or medium—a remix is probably in order. Some terms that might indicate a remix is asked for: "convert," "modify," "recast," "reimagine," "transform."

▲ 280–90

Dealing with Ambiguous Assignments

Sometimes even the key term in an assignment doesn't indicate clearly which genre is wanted, so you need to read such an assignment especially carefully. A first step might be to consider whether it's asking for a report or an argument. For example, here are two sample assignments:

> Discuss ways in which the invention of gas and incandescent lighting significantly changed people's daily lives in the nineteenth century.

> Discuss why Willy Loman in *Death of a Salesman* is, or is not, a tragic hero.

Both assignments use the word "discuss," but in very different ways. The first may simply be requesting an informative, researched report: the thesis—new forms of lighting significantly changed people's daily lives in various ways—is already given, and you may just be expected to research and explain what some of these changes were. It's also possible, though, that this assignment is asking you to make an argument about which of these changes were the most significant ones.

In contrast, "discuss" in the second assignment is much more open-ended. It does not lead to a particular thesis but is more clearly asking you to present an argument: to choose a position (Willy Loman is a tragic hero; Willy Loman is *not* a tragic hero; even, possibly, Willy Loman both *is and is not* a tragic hero) and to marshal reasons and evidence from the play to support your position. A clue that an argument is being asked for lies in the way the assignment offers a choice of paths.

Other potentially ambiguous words in assignments are "show" and "explore," both of which could lead in many directions. If after a careful reading of the entire assignment you still aren't sure what it's asking for, ask your instructor to clarify the appropriate genre or genres.

Combining Genres

210–19
246–56
257–69
146–69

Often your writing will include more than one genre. An **EVALUATION** of mining practices might include a **PROFILE** of a coal company CEO. A **PROPOSAL** to start a neighborhood watch might begin with a **REPORT** on crime in the area. In fact, genres are seldom "pure." When you write, you'll need to consider how you'll choose aspects of various genres to achieve your purpose.

Your writing situation will often call for a certain genre that is appropriate for your purpose—an argument, a proposal, a report, a textual analysis, and so forth. Additional genres then play supporting roles. Each genre must contribute to your main point: one genre may serve as the introduction, and others may be woven throughout the text in other ways, but all must address some aspect of the topic and support your central claim. When a text includes several genres, those genres need to fit together clearly and be connected in some way. **TRANSITIONS** do that, and in so doing, they help readers make their way through the text.

355–56

It's possible to mix almost any genres together. Following are some of the most commonly mixed genres and how they combine with other genres.

Personal narratives. Sometimes a personal anecdote can help support an **ARGUMENT** or enhance a **REPORT**. Stories from your personal experience can help readers understand your motivations for arguing a certain position and can enhance your credibility as a writer.

170–96
146–69

Profiles. One way to bring a **REPORT** on an abstract topic to life is to include a profile of a person, place, or event. For example, if you were writing a report for your boss on the need to hire more sales representatives, including a profile of one salesperson's typical day might drive home the point that your sales force is stretched too thin.

170–96

Textual analyses. You might need to analyze a speech or other document as part of an **ARGUMENT**, especially on a historical or political topic. For instance, you might analyze speeches by Abraham Lincoln and Jefferson Davis if you're writing about the causes of the Civil War, or an advertisement for vape pens if you're making an argument about teen smoking.

170–96

Evaluations. You might include an evaluation of something when you write a **PROPOSAL** about it. For example, if you were writing a proposal for additional student parking on your campus, you would need to evaluate the current parking facilities to discuss their inadequacy.

257–69

Thinking about Genre

- *How does your genre affect what content you can or should include?* Objective information? Researched source material? Your own opinions? Personal experience? A mix?
- *Does your genre call for any specific* **STRATEGIES**? Profiles, for example, usually include some narration; **EVALUATIONS** often require **COMPARING AND CONTRASTING**.

393
210–19
422–28

257–69
234–45
93–113
86
73–74
85–87
635
635

- *Does your genre require a certain organization?* **PROPOSALS**, for instance, usually need to show a problem exists before offering a solution. Some genres leave room for choice. **PERSONAL NARRATIVES** and **LITERACY NARRATIVES** might begin at the beginning, middle, or end of the story.

- *Does your genre affect your tone?* A **TEXTUAL ANALYSIS** or **ARGUMENT** usually calls for a different **TONE** than a personal narrative. Should your words sound serious and scholarly? brisk and to the point? objective? opinionated? Sometimes your genre affects the way you communicate your **STANCE**.

- *Does the genre require formal (or informal) language?* An email to the mother of a friend asking for a summer job in her bookstore calls for more formal language than does a text to the friend thanking them for the lead.

- *Do you have a choice of medium?* Some genres call for print; others for an electronic medium. Sometimes you have a choice: a résumé, for instance, can be printed to bring to an interview, or it may be downloaded or emailed. Some teachers want reports turned in on paper; others prefer that they be emailed or posted in the class course management system. If you're not sure what **MEDIUM** you can use, ask.

- *Does your genre have any design requirements?* Some genres call for paragraphs; others require lists. Some require certain kinds of fonts—you wouldn't use **impact** for a personal narrative, nor would you likely use chiller for an invitation to Grandma's sixty-fifth birthday party. Different genres call for different **DESIGN** elements.

10 Stance

Whenever you write, you have a certain stance, an attitude toward your topic. The way you express that stance affects the way you come across to your audience as a writer and a person. This email from a college student to his father, for example, shows a thoughtful, reasonable stance for a carefully researched argument:

> Hi Dad,
> I'll get right to the point: I'd like to buy a car. I saved over $4,500 from working this summer, and I've found three different cars that I can get for under $3,000. That'll leave me $1,400 to cover the insurance. I can park in Lot J, over behind Monte Hall, for $75 for both semesters. And I can earn gas and repair money by upping my hours at the cafeteria. It won't cost you any more, and if I have a car, you won't have to come and pick me up when I want to come home. May I buy it?
> Love,
> Michael

While such a stance can't guarantee that Dad will give permission, it's more likely to produce results than this version:

> Hi Dad,
> I'm buying a car. A guy in my Western Civ course has a cool Nissan he wants to get rid of. I've got $4,500 saved from working this summer, it's mine, and I'm going to use it to get some wheels. Mom said you'd freak out at me if I did, but I want this car and I'm getting it.
> Michael

The writer of the first email respects his reader and offers reasoned arguments and evidence of research to convince him that buying a car is an action that will benefit them both. The writer of the second, by contrast, seems impulsive, ready to buy the first car that comes along, and defiant— he's picking a fight. Each email reflects a certain stance that shows the writer as a certain kind of person dealing with a topic in a certain way and establishing a certain relationship with his audience.

Identify your stance.   What is your attitude toward your topic? Objective? Critical? Curious? Opinionated? Passionate? Indifferent? Your stance may be affected by your relationship to your **AUDIENCE**. How do you want them to see you? As a colleague sharing information? a good student showing what you can do? an advocate for a position? Often your stance is affected by your **GENRE**: for example, lab reports require an objective, unemotional stance that emphasizes the content and minimizes the writer's own attitudes. Personal narrative, by comparison, allows you to reveal your feelings about your topic. Your stance is also affected by your **PURPOSE**, as the two emails about cars show. Your stance in a piece written to entertain will likely differ from the stance you'd adopt to persuade.

75–78

91

73–74

You communicate (or downplay) your stance through your tone—through the words you use and other ways your text expresses an attitude toward your subject and audience. For example, in a comment on your friend's blog, you might use a sarcastic tone: "*The Bachelor*'s star has all the personality of a bowling ball." In an academic essay, though, you'd probably state your position with a more measured tone: "Reality TV sometimes deserves its poor reputation." Here, the qualifier "sometimes" limits the forcefulness of your claim and helps you acknowledge other viewpoints—an important feature of academic writing.

Like every other element of writing, your tone must be appropriate for your rhetorical situation.

Just as you likely alter what you say depending on whether you're speaking to a boss, an instructor, a parent, or a good friend, so you need to make similar adjustments as a writer. It's a question of appropriateness: we behave in certain ways in various social situations, and writing is a social situation. You might sign a post to a friend with "XO," but in an email to your supervisor you'll likely sign off with "Many thanks" or "Sincerely." To write well, you need to write with integrity, to say as much as possible what you wish to say; yet you also must understand that in writing, as in speaking, your stance and tone need to suit your purpose, your relationship to your audience, the way in which you wish your audience to perceive you, and your medium.

In writing as in other aspects of life, the Golden Rule applies: "Do unto audiences as you would have them do unto you." Address readers respectfully if you want them to respond to your words with respect.

Thinking about Stance

- *What is your stance, and how does it relate to your purpose for writing?* If you feel strongly about your topic and are writing an argument that tries to persuade your audience to feel the same way, your stance and your **PURPOSE** fit naturally together. But suppose you're writing about the same topic with a different purpose—to demonstrate the depth of your knowledge about the topic, for example, or your ability to consider it in a detached, objective way. You will need to adjust your stance to meet the demands of this different purpose.

  ■ 73–74

- *How should your stance be reflected in your tone?* Can your tone grow directly out of your stance, or do you need to "tone down" your attitude toward the topic or take a different tone altogether? Do you want to be seen as reasonable? angry? thoughtful? gentle? funny? ironic? If you're writing about something you want to be seen as taking very seriously, be sure that your language and even your font reflect that seriousness. Check your writing for words that reflect the tone you want to convey—and for ones that do not (and revise as necessary).

- *How is your stance likely to be received by your audience?* Your tone and especially the attitude it projects toward your **AUDIENCE** will affect how they react to the content of what you say.

  ■ 75–78

- *Should you openly discuss your stance?* Do you want or need to announce your own perspective on your topic? Will doing so help you reach your audience, or would it be better not to say directly where you're coming from?

11 Media/Design

In its broadest sense, a medium is a go-between: a way for information to be conveyed from one person to another. We communicate through many media, verbal and nonverbal: our bodies (we catch someone's eye, wave, nod); our voices (we whisper, talk, shout, groan); and various technologies, including handwriting, print, phone, radio, video, and digital media.

Each medium has unique characteristics that influence both what and how we communicate. As an example, consider this message: "I haven't told you this before, but I love you." Most of the time, we communicate such a message in person, using the medium of voice (with, presumably, help from eye contact and touch). A phone call will do, though most of us would think it a poor second choice, and a handwritten letter or note would be acceptable, if necessary. Few of us would break such news through a social media post or during a radio call-in program.

By contrast, imagine whispering the following sentence in a darkened room: "By the last decades of the nineteenth century, the territorial expansion of the United States had left almost all Native Americans confined to reservations." That sentence starts a chapter in a history textbook, and it would be strange indeed to whisper it into someone's ear. It is appropriate, however, in the textbook, in print or in an e-book, or as a quotation in an oral presentation.

As you can see, we can often choose among various media depending on our purpose and audience. In addition, we can often combine media to create **MULTIMEDIA** texts. And different media enable us to use different ways or modes of expressing meaning, from words to images to sound to hyperlinks, that can be combined in various ways.

638

No matter the medium or media, a text's design affects the way it is received and understood. A typed letter on official letterhead sends a different message than the same words handwritten on pastel stationery. Classic type sends a different message than *flowery italics*. Some genres and media (and audiences) demand **PHOTOS**, **DIAGRAMS**, or color. Some information is easier to explain—and read—in the form of a **PIE CHART** or a **BAR GRAPH** than in the form of a paragraph. Some reports and documents are so long and complex that they need to be divided into sections,

648–54

which are then best labeled with **HEADINGS**. These are some of the elements to consider when thinking about how to design what you write.

644–45

Identify your media and design needs.   Does your writing situation call for a certain medium and design? A printed essay? An oral report with visual aids? A blog? A podcast? Academic assignments often assume a particular medium and design, but if you're unsure about your options or the degree of flexibility you have, check with your instructor.

Thinking about Media

- *What medium are you using*—print? spoken? electronic? a combination?—and how does it affect the way you will create your text? A printed résumé is usually no more than one page long; an electronic résumé posted on an employer's website has no length limits. An oral presentation should contain detailed information; accompanying slides should provide only an outline.

- *How does your medium affect your organization and* **STRATEGIES***?* Long paragraphs are fine on paper but don't work well on the web. On presentation slides, phrases or keywords work better than sentences. In print, you need to define unfamiliar terms; on the web, you can sometimes just add a link to a definition found elsewhere.

393

- *How does your medium affect your language?* Some print documents require a more formal voice than spoken media; email and texting often invite greater informality.

- *How does your medium affect what modes of expression you use?* Should your text include photos, graphics, audio or video files, or links? Do you need slides, handouts, or other visuals to accompany an oral presentation?

Thinking about Design

- *What's the appropriate look for your* **RHETORICAL SITUATION***?* Should your text look serious? whimsical? personal? something else? What design elements will suit your audience, purpose, stance, genre, and medium?

71

- *What elements need to be designed?* Is there any information you would like to highlight by putting it in a box? Are there any key terms that should be boldfaced? Do you need navigation buttons? How should you indicate links?

- *What font(s) are appropriate* to your audience, purpose, stance, genre, and medium?

648–54
75–78
- *Are you including any* **VISUALS**? Should you? Will your **AUDIENCE** expect or need any? Is there any information in your text that would be easier to understand as a chart or graph? If you need to include video or audio clips, how should the links be presented?

79–84
88–90
- *Should you include headings?* Would they help you organize your materials and help readers follow the text? Does your **GENRE** or **MEDIUM** require them?

MLA 542–94
APA 595–633
- *Should you use a specific format?* MLA? APA?

Part 3

Genres

When we make a shopping list, we automatically write each item we need in a single column. When we email a friend, we begin with a salutation: "Hi, Jordan." Whether we are writing a letter, a résumé, or a proposal, we know generally what it should contain and what it should look like because we are familiar with each of those genres. Genres are kinds of writing, and texts in any given genre share goals and features—a proposal, for instance, generally starts out by identifying a problem and then suggests a certain solution. The chapters in this part provide guidelines for writing in twelve common academic genres. First come detailed chapters on four genres often assigned in writing classes—**LITERACY NARRATIVES**, **TEXTUAL ANALYSES**, **REPORTS**, and **ARGUMENTS**—followed by brief chapters on **SEVEN OTHER GENRES** and one on **REMIXES**.

Genres

* academic literacies   ⬢ fields   ◆ strategies   ● media / design
■ rhetorical situations   ⁞ processes   ● research   ★ handbook
▲ genres

12 Writing a Literacy Narrative

Narratives are stories, and we read and tell them for many different purposes. Parents read their children bedtime stories as an evening ritual. College applicants write about significant moments in their lives. In *psychology* courses, you may write a personal narrative to illustrate how individuals' stories inform the study of behavior. In *education* courses, you may share stories of your teaching experiences. And in *computer science* courses, you may write programming narratives to develop programming skills.

This chapter provides detailed guidelines for writing a specific kind of narrative: a literacy narrative. Writers of literacy narratives traditionally explore their experiences with reading or writing, but we'll broaden the definition to include experiences with various literacies, which might include learning an academic skill, a sport, an artistic technique, or something else. For example, the third narrative in this chapter explores one writer's realization that she needs "automotive literacy" to work in her parents' car repair shop. Along with this essay, this chapter includes two additional examples, the first annotated to point out the key features found in most literacy narratives.

REA KARIM
Becoming an American Girl

Rea Karim earned an associate's degree in arts and sciences at Bellevue College, where she wrote this literacy narrative. It was nominated for the Norton Writer's Prize. Karim received a BA in political science and government from UCLA in 2023.

I stood on the monument's marble steps, surveying my country's capital. Elizabeth eagerly tugged on my denim jacket. "You gotta see this!"

Attention-getting opening.

I turned around to see her smiling at the scene before us. We stood, mesmerized by the beauty of the golden hour, as the sun set over Washington, DC, in the summer of 2017. Like all the other girls surrounding me, I belonged here. I was the walking embodiment of my ancestors' hopes and dreams.

In 2005, though, I felt far from belonging. I was four years old, and I could not speak. My life was filled with words in English, Urdu, Hindi, and Bengali. These four languages painted my dining room table and added zest into my young life, but while I could understand, none of the words came out of my mouth. My mom was extremely concerned about my inability to talk but found reassurance from a linguistics professional who told us that my speaking abilities would develop late because of the diversity of voices within our household. But once I could talk, I still felt difference from the kids around me.

Here Karim describes the setting—what hindered her literacy.

I was the only child on my block whose parents came from two different South Asian countries. My dinner plate was a battle between Indian curried vegetables and the juice of Bengali kebabs. Even though I was born in Seattle, I often felt like I was from another planet, struggling to integrate into my Cascadian hometown. At the same time, I didn't feel like I fit in with the other South Asian kids I knew either. I had roots from both India and Bangladesh, and while those countries are close in proximity, their competition could stretch for miles. On top of that, my classmates introduced me to the "Indian" stereotype that all brown kids are naturally smart, good at math, and excellent students. As hard as I tried, I could not fit into that image. I was late to start speaking, and I couldn't read.

Clearly described details.

Mama would sit with me for hours trying to get me to give up TV and learn to read with her from one of the Dot books, but I didn't like Dot the dog. He was boring, and I was stubborn. Studying always seemed like a chore, and reading didn't spark the same interest in me that it did for my classmates. Kids my age were cruising through Dot and picking up Lemony Snicket, while I was still learning the difference between *p* and *q*.

5

Because of my reading level, I didn't feel smart enough to be around the students in my class. Even though I made friends, a huge part of me felt like I couldn't fit in. I didn't feel American enough to live in my predominantly white community, and I didn't feel "brown" enough to hang out with the kids of my parents' friends. Instead of socializing with my peers, I sought refuge in my elementary school library.

A key person in Karim's narrative.

The library's tall walls covered with princess and dragon murals, the dozens of birch bookshelves, and the solitude gave me comfort. Every morning, as soon as the bus parked in the roundabout, I dashed to the library's glass doors. The librarian, Ms. McEldowney, always let me in with a comforting smile. She knew I wasn't the best reader, but she still narrated the blurbs from the newly arrived books and introduced me to some of her old favorites. Usually, I snatched whatever was on display, found a quiet spot next to a shelf, and ran my fingers over the words, trying to sound them out. In that way, I started building a friendship with books. I touched the pictures on the front and back cover, imagining that I was a part of the adventures I held in my hand.

The library became my safe haven. Days quickly turned into months, and soon I could read a book without pictures. Every day I practiced running my fingers through sentences, absorbing whatever was in front of me and reading the sentences aloud. In a matter of a few months and a dozen McEldowney recommendations, I could read.

The library is a key to her literacy development.

Yet, a huge part of me could not relate to the characters in front of me. I still felt like an outsider. I lacked the courage of the main characters from my books, often feeling like a token side character. I wanted to be fearless like the boys and girls in my stories, but sometimes I felt as if a distant force was holding me back from being fearless outside of the library. I wanted to embody red, white, and blue like the heroes American history books told me about. More than anything, I wanted to belong. Even though I had found a place among these imaginary books, I desired a place in the real world around me.

The conflict in the story.

The perceptions I had about being American were all about to change one crisp fall morning during library hour when Ms. McEldowney pulled out a thick set of chapter books. Once a glistening white, their faded covers were now coated in a thick gray dust. 10

"These," she said with a enthusiastic tone, "are the American Girls."

Ms. McEldowney explained to our class that each book was about a different girl in a different period of American history. As she held each one up for us to see, I noticed that not all the girls on the covers were white. Each girl had a unique outfit, her own personality, and her own story.

Her story.

This brief paragraph emphasizes the moment's significance.

More specific details.

My friends and I rushed to the books. Among the piles, I found *Meet Molly*. On the cover a quirky-looking girl with thick glasses, braided pigtails, and a checkered dress looked back at me. I spent that evening sitting at the dining table reading about Molly's family, her friends, and the new girl from England living with her who was seeking shelter during World War II. I read about how the two girls first felt a cultural clash between them but grew to be fascinated by each other's experiences. Their struggles reminded me of the cultural differences I had with some of my friends. Instead of viewing our lives as polar opposites, I considered sharing with them some of my household's celebrations like Chaand Raat and learning more about holidays like Easter.

What started with just a book became my lifestyle. I went to the library every morning, checked out whatever American Girl book was available, and finished it by the afternoon. From the story of Addy I learned of a family's escape from slavery. From Josefina I learned about living without a mother and having the sole responsibility of raising her Mexican American family in 1824. From Kaya I learned about the impact of the settlers on the Native Americans and the struggle of holding on to what is yours. Each book shaped my perspective of what it means to be an American. I learned that life in this country isn't on one set path. Rather, our country is a mixture of different paths, and each story matters. I started to believe that my story mattered.

The significance of Karim's reading becomes clear to her.

After elementary school, I kept reading. My avid obsession with books grew from the American Girl books to Louisa May Alcott and Ta-Nehisi Coates. Once I entered high school, I pursued the passion for history that the American Girl books instilled in me and tried my hand at AP United States History, World Government, and Comparative Politics.

In the summer of 2017, I was accepted to a program that invited sixty girls from all over the country to visit Washington, DC, and learn what it takes for a woman to run for a seat in Congress. As I packed for the trip, I glanced at the old American Girl novels I had purchased, once new and now dusty like the ones I read as a child. I thought about how I spent so much of my childhood wrapped up in the stories of other girls. I realized, then, that I was ready to live my life as the main character. I kept that realization in mind when I met and grew close to the other girls in DC. They came from diverse backgrounds like me, and we shared our passions and stories with each other, each one of us the heroine. By putting myself at the center of my own story, I finally belonged.

The end refers back to the opening anecdote but deepens its significance.

As I stood at the steps of the Lincoln Memorial underneath the setting sun, I reflected on my journey to get to that moment. I had fallen in love with the roots my parents planted in Seattle, and I was a smart

South Asian American in my own way, well versed not in math, but in history. I was no longer confined to a stereotype. Instead, I embodied the brown color of my skin and belonged to the United States—on my own terms.

In this literacy narrative, Karim tells the story of how learning to read and reading American Girl novels helped her understand her identity as an American of South Asian heritage. The significance of her story lies in the role that reading played in developing her sense of who she is and where she belongs.

KARLA MARIANA HERRERA GUTIERREZ

Reading, Writing, and Riding
A Literacy Narrative

Karla Mariana Herrera Gutierrez graduated from Austin College with a triple major in English, Spanish, and public health. Her literacy narrative was nominated for the Norton Writer's Prize and is documented in MLA style.

Eight faces sleep peacefully as my grandmother surveys the bedroom and closes the door before going outside. Out on the street, the sky is shattered by the soft yellows and pinks that break through the clouds, indicating the start of a new day. My grandmother walks down the sidewalk with her hands grasping her black bag as her mind processes recent events and tries to focus on the task at hand today. *"Toma el autobus a la oficina y pide la pension,"* my grandmother whispers to herself as she approaches the bus stop to go to the police office for her pension.

It's early in the day, but slowly more and more people begin to crowd the streets of Mexico City. The sounds of people talking and the angry honking of horns envelop my grandmother as she looks frantically down the road for the bus. It's only been a few minutes, but she has no time to lose. They told her to be at the office at a certain time, and as a recent widow she does not want to make a bad impression on the people who could make it harder for her to secure the money she needs. Finally, the white and green speck she had fixated on grows closer until she sees it's the bus she has been waiting for. Adjusting her bag, she prepares to step forward but scrunches her brow in concern when the bus doesn't seem to be slowing down. I can picture my grandmother's confused look as the bus passes by without picking her up. My mother said this was my grandmother's breaking point, and she began to cry on the side of the road. "By God's grace," my mother continued, "a lady happened to pass by, and upon seeing my mother's agitated state, she offered her assistance." A simple arm signal stopped the next bus so my grandmother could get on and go to the police department.

During the following two weeks my grandmother learned to no longer fear taking the bus; she got used to traveling downtown to the police station, to the chief's office, sometimes twice in the same day. But her obstacles were only beginning. The process involved in receiving my deceased grandfather's pension was a struggle. The police were reluctant to give it to my grandmother, hoping to wear her out because they didn't care that she had to leave her children to make these trips downtown; they only worried about the money they'd lose.

I can't imagine my grandmother's will to hide her worry as she withstood the harsh glares of the police officers with her back straight and a stone face, determined to fight for what was her family's due. I can't imagine having to trust that the legal documents a stranger presented to her were a written representation of what he was telling her and not a trap that would make her lose her pension. But I can imagine my grandmother realizing then the importance of knowing how to read and write.

Similar to the collective history of the May family described in literacy scholar Deborah Brandt's article "Accumulating Literacy," my maternal grandmother's experiences provided opportunities for learning that piled up from the moment she hailed that bus. The many obstacles my grandmother faced began with the unfamiliarity of having to navigate new experiences and then intensified when she found herself at the mercy of government officials because she was illiterate. 5

The importance of literacy became apparent in my mother's household, but obtaining an education was still not a priority. My mother and her siblings learned to read and write, but none finished high school, though one of my uncles later received his GED when he moved to the United States. Literacy and education were two separate things in my mother's youth—but that changed once she moved to the United States with my father and needed to help me when I started school. My own experiences navigating two languages and two cultures expanded my literacy as reading became a key tool not only in learning school subjects but also in learning to navigate a new environment.

I started kindergarten being thrown to the sharks—that is, the English native sharks. Like the *Jaws* theme song, any English word that reached my ears quickened my heartbeat as I turned my head from side to side, hoping to identify the source of such frightening, unfamiliar sounds. I flailed around in the uncharted waters, sobbing and crying for my mother. Every morning my stomach groaned in protest at going to this institution that filled me with dread. However, I wasn't in this alone. In the afternoons I pored over my textbooks and worksheets with my mother and her English-to-Spanish dictionary by my side. Together we conquered my homework, and the sounds that had first put me in fight-or-flight mode gradually became parts of my second language.

It takes more than learning a new language to fully assimilate into a new culture, however. Literacy constitutes more than reading and writing; it also involves the ability to understand and become a part of one's environment. Linguist James Paul Gee calls our "ways of being in the world" Discourses, beginning with the "primary Discourse" we learn at home; he defines literacy as "the mastery or fluent control over a secondary Discourse," the discourse or discourses that include the social practices and behaviors that allow us to communicate effectively with others and that we learn through becoming members of social institutions, like churches, stores, community groups—and schools (6–9). For the most part, reading books about "typical" non-Hispanic households uncovered the norms of a culture I knew little about, and it also opened a place for conflict to arise when there were conflicting cultural ideas.

Such was the case after I read a book from my favorite series, Junie B. Jones. When Junie B. gets invited to a sleepover, the idea of spending the night at another person's house riveted seven-year-old me. In the book, the sleepover takes place in the giant house of Junie B.'s rich friend, Lucille; however, Junie B.'s crazy antics alter the experience of the sleepover in the way only she knows how to do (Park). I thought my dream would come true when a school friend invited me to come over to her house. I asked my mother for permission even though I was sure she was going to say yes—but I got a lecture instead. My mother refused my request and in fast-spoken Spanish listed all the horrible things that could happen to me if I went to a sleepover. Red-faced and slightly out of breath, she ended her sermon by asking me what was wrong with my bed that I felt the need to sleep in someone else's. My mother, and father, rejected some of the freedoms other kids my age had, such as staying at each other's houses or hanging out after school, because they focused on the potential dangers that could come of such activities. I didn't want to upset my parents, so I only saw my friends at school and read my books to experience what I couldn't in real life.

If reading sometimes caused conflict at home, it was my method for success at school. I was an avid reader and when the school set up a reading program, I took full advantage of it. My school hoped to present reading as a fun activity, so it promoted what was called the Star Program, which offered prizes to students for progressing in the program, with the ultimate prize a ride in a limousine. When the program ended, the twenty kids who had completed the course pressed our young, eager faces against our classroom window as the giant white limo pulled up to the front of the school building. We waited, bouncing in anxious joy, for the teachers to open the school doors and show the wonders of this marvelous car. The driver, in a black suit and sunglasses, walked to the back of the limo and opened the car's door. It could have been the glare of the blazing sun or my young, imaginative mind, but the limo seemed to come alive as we caught a glimpse of its sleek black interior. Upon being released to climb in and enjoy our prize, we felt a blast of cold air that cut against the warmth of that spring afternoon. The flash of a camera redirected our attention to our teachers, who positioned us for a picture for the school newspaper.

The Star Program focused on a ride in a limousine, but it failed to mention the bonus prize: feeling like a superstar. My eyes bulged as I took in all the features of this elegant white car as we drove away. The many buttons and compartments for food and drinks (which this ride unfortunately failed to provide) were a novelty to me. Feeling the cold leather of the seats, I traced the shape of the interior until I reached the buttons on the door. With one push the window went down, revealing to the world my awestruck face. The breeze whipped my curly hair around, but I didn't care. I can still see the wondering faces of the people in the cars next to us doing double takes when they saw the stretched car pulling up beside them. As we drove through a roundabout, I felt regal and waved a royal wave to all my subjects because I ruled the world . . . at least for the ride's thirty minutes.

In my elementary years, I thought the Star Program was the epitome of what reading could do, and that limousine ride was only a small taste of what I could achieve by reading and focusing on my academics. Many people would assume that literacy begins like this, by an educational institution, but our literacy actually begins before our time. Brandt observes that literacy "piles up," so that "many generations of literacy . . . now occupy the same social space" (652). This piling up of earlier and more recent literacies produces a "propelling effect"; as Brandt explains, "Schooling typically brings into a family's possession books, manuals, typewriters, and the like that then become the first forms of literacy that the next generation encounters" (659). My literacy began with my grandmother, but it evolved over two generations to include more than simply learning how to read and write—it also meant assimilating into a new culture. Unlike my grandmother's experience with the bus, my ride in the limousine was a marker of my assimilation. It was the first moment that I can remember when I stood out not because of my different background, but because of the reading I had accomplished in a program open to all.

Not only did reading help me assimilate into a new culture, it also helped me with learning a new language. There wasn't someone at home who could teach me how to properly speak and write English, so it was difficult for me to become fluent. While my mother did her best to help me with her English-to-Spanish dictionary, she couldn't teach me anything that wasn't a part of my homework. It was only through reading that I managed to expand my vocabulary and use the grammar rules I learned in school. By contrast, it was easier for my sister to learn English than it was for me because she had me to converse with at home. My sister's earlier comprehension of English led to her "graduating" from ESL classes in just one year, instead of the four years it took me. My sister had me as her source of English at home, and integrating this new language into our household created a culturally diverse environment that differed from the one my parents had grown up with.

In accumulating new literacies, we improve ourselves for the next generation, and what we improve is our ability to immerse ourselves in new situations because in doing so we elevate the standards of our education to reflect our experiences. But the piling up of literacies isn't an individual effort. My grandmother learned to ride the bus after receiving help from a stranger, and the legal obstacles she faced because she was illiterate pushed her to make sure that my mom and her siblings learned to read. Because my mother knew how to read, she could help me with my homework, and because I learned English, I could converse with my sister in our new language. Each generation is shaped by the collective history of people's literacies because of the opportunities we have to learn from those who came before us and to contribute to those who follow us.

Works Cited

Brandt, Deborah. "Accumulating Literacy: Writing and Learning to Write in the Twentieth Century." *College English*, vol. 57, no. 6, Oct. 1995, pp. 649–66.

Gee, James Paul. "Literacy, Discourse, and Linguistics: Introduction." *Journal of Education*, vol. 171, no. 1, 1989, pp. 5–25.

Park, Barbara. *Junie B. Jones Is a Party Animal*. Illustrated by Denise Brunkus, Scholastic, 1997.

Gutierrez traces her literacy development not just to her own life and experiences but to the literacies, or lack of them, of her mother and grandmother as well. Her references to scholarly work on literacy deepen her story and show its significance for many, not just her personally.

ANA-JAMILEH KASSFY

Automotive Literacy

In the following literacy narrative, Ana-Jamileh Kassfy describes an experience that taught her that literacy takes many forms, as well as the importance of knowing what goes on in the family business, auto repair. She wrote this essay in a college writing class at the University of Texas at El Paso and posted it on her class blog.

My father runs a well-known family-owned auto shop here in El Paso, Texas. I come from a family of five, which consists of me, two older brothers, and my parents. My father manages the place, while one of my brothers works as a mechanic in charge of most of the heavy labor and the other spends all day standing by a state inspection machine making sure the cars can run safely on the streets of El Paso. My mother works as the shop's secretary, answering the phone and handling all paperwork. I, on the other hand, was not given the option of being a part of the family business; my job is to graduate from college. And I'll gladly accept going to school and learning in place of spending my days working on cars, even though I spent a lot of time at the shop throughout my childhood.

Since I come from a family whose life revolves around cars, and since I practically lived at the auto shop until I was able to drive, you'd think that I'd understand most of the jargon a mechanic would use, right? Wrong. During my first sixteen years of life, I did manage to learn the difference between a flathead and a Torx screwdriver. I also learned what brake pads do and that a car uses many different colorful fuses. However, rather than paying attention to what was happening and what was being said around me, most of the time I chose to focus on the social aspect of the business. While everyone was running around ordering different pads, filters, and starters or explaining in precise detail why a customer needed a new engine, I preferred to sit and speak with customers and learn their life stories. Being social worked for me—until it didn't.

One day my mother couldn't come to work and decided to have me fill in for her. That was fine with me. I thought to myself, "How hard could it be to answer a phone and say, 'Good afternoon, M & J Service, how may I help you?' or to greet customers and then turn them over to my dad?"

My morning went by pretty smoothly. I thought I had my duties down to a science. I figured aside from the permanent ringing in my ear from the annoyingly loud air compressors, a few minor paper cuts, and the almost perpetual stench of gasoline and burnt oil, my day was going to fly by.

Then, around lunchtime, my dad left to pick up a part at a car 5 dealership and my brothers went out for lunch. A woman pulled up in an '01 Hyundai Elantra that was desperately in need of a new paint job and walked into the shop. The woman seemed to be in her late forties and was wearing professional clothing with green eye shadow and bright orange lipstick. Her copper-brown hair was feathered out and she wore extremely large gold earrings. And she was angry. She demanded I tell her why she was having a difficult time starting her car. As I began to dust off the file stored in my memory as "Automotive Terms I Will Never Use," I attempted to calm her down, and then I made the mistake of asking her what the problem was.

She said in a harsh tone, "My car doesn't start, your dad just replaced the spark plugs and the motor head, and now my 'blah blah blah' is making noise! I took it to my friend who's a mechanic and he told me your dad fixed the wrong part."

I took a few seconds and just stood there looking at her, trying to add up what I had learned in my life as a "mechanic" and recall what spark plugs were. But it was useless. After a few moments, I gave up. I told her that I couldn't help her, but that she was more than welcome to wait for a mechanic to return.

After giving me an unpleasant look, she proceeded to say, while waving her hands in front of me, "I want my money back! Here is my receipt. I'm taking my car elsewhere. Your dad screwed me over. I told him it was the 'blah blah blah.' Why did he take out the 'blah blah blah'? WHY CAN'T YOU HELP ME? WHY ARE YOU HERE? BLAH BLAH BLAH!"

I stood there, overwhelmed. I began to fidget and push my hair back nervously as I wished some knowledge would kick in. It seemed unbelievable, but despite growing up in a family that lived and breathed automobiles, there was nothing I could do to help her. And my sixteen years of socializing with customers hadn't even paid off because I couldn't calm her down. When I saw my dad walk in, I sighed with relief, explained the problem to him, and it was resolved. But standing in front of that woman like a deer caught in headlights was so embarrassing. Having somebody shout, "Why can't you help me?" and "Why are you here?" made me feel so ignorant.

Unfortunately, that was only the first of many occasions when 10 people have automatically expected that I know how to take apart and rebuild an engine, or perform some other auto-related task. In reality, I know as much about cars as the next person. After that incident, it became clear to me that I could be literate on very different levels. I'm an expert at running social networks like my *Twitter* feed, and I can zip through and analyze an entire novel written in Spanish, but in other subjects, like automobiles, I am completely illiterate. And when I'm expected to know them, I feel anything but competent.

A confrontation with an irate costumer forces Kassfy to realize that she could be very literate in some situations but almost illiterate in others, and that her lack of knowledge in a workplace context put her at a real disadvantage.

Key Features / Literacy Narratives

A well-told story. As with most narratives, those about literacy often set up some sort of situation that needs to be resolved. That need for resolution makes readers want to keep on reading. We want to know how Kassfy will deal with an irate customer. Some literacy narratives simply explore the role that developing literacy of some kind played at some time in someone's life, as when Karim discovered the school library and American Girl novels. And some, like Gutierrez's, explore the writer's literacy development in a larger context.

Vivid detail. Details can bring a narrative to life for readers by giving them vivid mental sensations of the sights, sounds, smells, tastes, and textures of the world in which your story takes place. The details you use when describing something can help readers picture places, people, and events; dialogue can help them hear what is being said. We grasp the importance of books for Karim as she "touched the pictures on the front and back cover." Similarly, we can picture and hear Gutierrez as a little girl who speaks only Spanish in an English-language kindergarten, "sobbing and crying for [her] mother."

Some indication of the narrative's significance. By definition, a literacy narrative tells something the writer remembers about learning to read, write, or gain competence in a specific area. In addition, the writer needs to make clear why the incident matters to them. You may reveal its significance in various ways. Kassfy comes to understand that to work in an auto repair shop, she needs to understand automotive repair terms. Gutierrez places her literacy in a tradition going back generations—and continuing with her sister's relationship with her. Karim's narrative shows that her literacy was a key to understanding her place in society.

A GUIDE TO WRITING LITERACY NARRATIVES

Choosing a Topic

In general, it's a good idea to focus on a single event that took place during a relatively brief period of time—though sometimes learning to do or understand something may take place over an extended period. In that case, several snapshots or important moments may be needed. Here are some suggestions for topics:

- any early memory about writing, reading, speaking, or another form of literacy that you recall vividly

- someone who taught you to read or write

- someone who helped you understand how to do something

- a book, video game, recording, or other text that has been significant for you in some way

- an event at school that was related to your literacy and that you found interesting, humorous, or embarrassing

- a literacy task that you found (or still find) especially difficult or challenging

- a memento that represents an important moment in your literacy development (perhaps the start of a **LITERACY PORTFOLIO**)   377–82

- the origins of your current attitudes about writing, reading, speaking, or doing something

- learning to text, learning to write an email appropriately, creating and maintaining a *Facebook* page or blog

Make a list of possible topics, and then choose one that you think will be interesting to you and to others—and that you're willing to share with others. If several seem promising, try them out on a friend or classmate. Or just choose one and see where it leads; you can switch to another if need be. If you have trouble coming up with a topic, try **FREEWRITING**, **LISTING**, **CLUSTERING**, or **LOOPING**.   329–31

 Access the ebook for a video on generating ideas for a literacy narrative.

Considering the Rhetorical Situation

PURPOSE   Why do you want to tell this story? To share a memory with others? To fulfill an assignment? To teach a   73–74 lesson? To explore your past learning? Think about the reasons for your choice and how they will shape what you write.

75–78 ■ **AUDIENCE** Are your readers likely to have had similar experiences? Would they tell similar stories? How much explaining will you have to do to help them understand your narrative? Can you assume that they will share your attitudes toward your story, or will you have to work at making them see your perspective? How much about your life are you willing to share with this audience?

85–87 ■ **STANCE** What attitude do you want to project? Affectionate? Neutral? Critical? Do you wish to be sincere? serious? humorously detached? self-critical? self-effacing? something else? How do you want your readers to see you?

88–90 ■ **MEDIA / DESIGN** Will your narrative be in print? presented orally? online? Should you use photos, tables, graphs, or video or audio clips? Is there a font that conveys the right tone? Do you need headings?

Generating Ideas and Text

Good literacy narratives share certain elements that make them interesting and compelling for readers. Remember that your goals are to tell the story as clearly and vividly as you can and to convey the meaning the incident has for you today. Start by thinking about what you already know about writing a literacy narrative. Then write out what you remember about the setting of your narrative and those involved, perhaps trying out some of the methods in the chapter on **GENERATING IDEAS AND TEXT**. You 329–39 ⁙
498–503 ● may also want to **INTERVIEW** a teacher or parent or other person who figures in your narrative.

Explore what you already know about writing a literacy narrative. Think about recent occasions when you've had to narrate a story, either orally or in writing, in school or out. Take a few moments to think about a couple of those occasions, especially ones involving your reading, writing, speaking, or learning to do something. Why and to whom were you telling these stories? How successful do you think your narratives were? What aspects of telling the story did you feel most confident about or do especially well? What could you have done better? What do you still need to learn about writing a literacy narrative?

Describe the setting. Where does your narrative take place? List the places where your story unfolds. For each place, write informally for a few minutes, **DESCRIBING** what you remember:

439–46

- *What do you see?* If you're inside, what color are the walls? What's hanging on them? What can you see out any windows? What else do you see? Books? Lined paper? Red ink? Are there people? places to sit? a desk or a table?

- *What do you hear?* A radiator hissing? Leaves rustling? The wind howling? Rain? Someone reading aloud? Shouts? Cheers? Children playing? Music? The chime of a text arriving on your phone?

- *What do you smell?* Sweat? Perfume? Incense? Food cooking?

- *How and what do you feel?* Nervous? Happy? Cold? Hot? A scratchy wool sweater? Tight shoes? Rough wood on a bench?

- *What do you taste?* Gum? Mints? Graham crackers? Juice? Coffee?

Think about the key people. Narratives include people whose actions play an important role in the story. In your literacy narrative, you are probably one of those people. A good way to develop your understanding of the people in your narrative is to write about them:

- *Describe each person in a paragraph or so.* What do the people look like? How do they dress? How do they speak? Quickly? Slowly? With an accent? Do they speak clearly, or do they mumble? Do they use any distinctive words or phrases? You might begin by describing their movements, their posture, their bearing, their facial expressions. Do they have a distinctive scent?

- *Recall (or imagine) some characteristic dialogue.* A good way to bring people to life and move a story along is with **DIALOGUE**, to let readers hear them rather than just hearing about them. Try writing six to ten lines of dialogue between two people in your narrative. If you can't remember an actual conversation, make up one that could have happened. (After all, you are telling the story, and you get to decide

447–51

how it is to be told.) Try to remember (and write down) some of the characteristic words or phrases that the people in your narrative used.

457–64 ◆

Write about "what happened." At the heart of every **NARRATIVE** is the answer to the question "What happened?" The action in a literacy narrative may be as dramatic as winning a spelling bee or as subtle as a conversation between two friends; both contain action, movement, or change that the narrative tries to capture for readers. A compelling story dramatizes the action. Try **SUMMARIZING** the action in your narrative in a paragraph—try to capture what happened. Use active and specific verbs ("pondered," "shouted," "laughed") to describe the action as vividly as possible.

529 ●

Consider the significance of the narrative. You need to make clear the ways in which any event you are writing about is significant for you now. Write a page or so about the meaning it has for you. How did it change or otherwise affect you? What aspects of your life now can you trace to that event? How might your life have been different if this event had not happened or had turned out differently? Why does this story matter to you?

Ways of Organizing a Literacy Narrative

335–37

Start by **OUTLINING** the main events in your narrative. Then think about how you want to tell the story. Don't assume that the only way to tell your story is just as it happened. That's one way—starting at the beginning of the action and continuing to the end. But you could also start in the middle—or even at the end. Karla Gutierrez, for example, could have begun her narrative by discussing her current literacy and then gone back to trace the influences of her family. Several ways of organizing a narrative follow.

Access Chapter 30 in the ebook for a video on organizing and synthesizing ideas.

Chronologically, from beginning to end

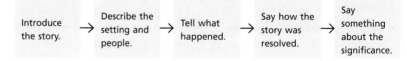

Introduce the story. → Describe the setting and people. → Tell what happened. → Say how the story was resolved. → Say something about the significance.

Beginning in the middle

Start in the middle of the action, giving enough information to let readers know what was happening. → Fill in details: setting, people, specific actions. → Make clear how the situation was resolved. → Say something about the significance.

Beginning at the end

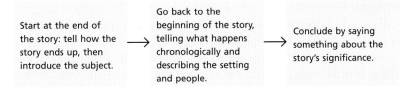

Start at the end of the story: tell how the story ends up, then introduce the subject. → Go back to the beginning of the story, telling what happens chronologically and describing the setting and people. → Conclude by saying something about the story's significance.

More Ways to Approach a Literacy Narrative

Write a series of vignettes. Instead of sharing one story, craft your literacy narrative as a collection of vignettes—brief, descriptive scenes that zoom in on important moments in your literacy development. You might weave together several vignettes that focus on different experiences with reading and writing, or you might share a series of vignettes that reveal something about other kinds of literacies you've developed, like digital literacies, financial literacies, and so on.

Write in diary or letter form. Write your literacy narrative as a set of diary entries that recount literacy memories from certain periods of your life, showing how your literacies evolved over time. Or write in the form of letters to teachers, family members, or others who influenced your literacy development—or to places or objects, like your favorite reading corner or a particular book.

650 ●

Create an INTERACTIVE TIMELINE. Highlight key events in your literacy history by making an interactive timeline. Viewers might click on different portions of the timeline to read snippets of writing you did when you were young, see covers of books that were significant to you at various times, listen to you reflect on a specific literacy memory, or engage with other media that represent your literacy history.

280–90 ▲

Remix. After you've written a draft of your literacy narrative, you might **REMIX** it: rework it into one or more of the genres above or turn it into a comic strip, a series of social media posts, a video or audio essay, or another genre or medium that fits your rhetorical situation.

Writing Out a Draft

358–60 ⁘

Once you have generated ideas and thought about how you want to organize your narrative, it's time to begin **DRAFTING**. Do this quickly—try to write a complete draft in one sitting, concentrating on getting the story on paper or screen and on putting in as much detail as you can. Some writers find it helpful to work on the beginning or ending first. Others write out the main event first and then draft the beginning and ending.

340–48 ⁘

Draft a BEGINNING. A good narrative grabs readers' attention right from the start. Here are some ways of beginning:

- *Create a question to be answered.* Karim begins her narrative at the Lincoln Memorial in Washington, DC, leading readers to wonder how this scene connects to her literacy.

- *Describe the context.* You may want to provide background information at the start of your narrative, as Gutierrez does with an anecdote about her illiterate grandmother's struggle to collect a pension.

- *Describe the setting, especially if it's important to the narrative.* Kassfy begins by describing her family's roles working in her father's auto shop.

348–52 ⁘

Draft an ENDING. Think about what you want readers to read last. An effective ending helps them understand the meaning of your narrative. Here are some possibilities:

- *End where your story ends.* It's up to you to decide where a narrative ends. Karim ends on a field trip in high school.

- *Say something about the significance of your narrative.* Gutierrez explores the meaning of her experience over several paragraphs, and Kassfy discusses her ignorance and resulting embarrassment. The trick is to touch on the narrative's significance without stating it too directly.
- *Refer back to the beginning.* Karim refers back to her trip to Washington, DC, and Gutierrez to her grandmother and the "piling up" of literacies over several generations.

Consider REWRITING. If you have time and want to explore alternatives, you might try rewriting your draft to see if a different plan or approach might work better.

370–71

Come up with a title. A good **TITLE** indicates something about the subject of your narrative—and makes readers want to take a look. Kassfy's title joins two terms—"automotive" and "literacy"—that aren't usually seen together. Gutierrez uses wordplay ("Reading, Writing, and Riding") to suggest the multiple roles literacy plays in our lives.

356–57

Considering Matters of Design
You'll probably write your narrative in paragraph form, but think about the information you're presenting and how you can design it to enhance your story and appeal to your audience.

- What would be an appropriate **FONT**? Something serious, like Times Roman? Something whimsical, like *Comic Sans*? Something else?

642–43

- Would it help your readers if you added **HEADINGS** in order to divide your narrative into shorter sections or **VIGNETTES**?

644–45
109

- Would photographs or other **VISUALS** show details better than you can describe them with words alone? If you're writing about learning to read, for example, you might scan in an image of one of the first books you read. Or if your topic is learning to write, you could include something you wrote. You could even include a video or audio recording. Would your narrative best be conveyed as a multimedia composition that combines written text, images, and video or audio?

648–54

Getting Response and Revising
The following questions can help you study your draft with a critical eye. **GETTING RESPONSE** from others is always helpful, and these questions

366–67

can guide their reading, too. Make sure they know your purpose and audience.

 Access Chapter 33 in the ebook for a video on revision strategies, including peer review.

- Do the title and first few sentences make readers want to read on? If not, how else might you begin?
- Is the sequence of events in the narrative clear? Does it flow, and are there effective transitions? Does the narrative get sidetracked at any point?
- Is anything confusing?
- Is there enough detail, and is it interesting? Will readers be able to imagine the setting? Can they picture the characters and sense what they're like? Would it help to add some dialogue so that readers can "hear" them?
- Are visuals used effectively and integrated smoothly with the written text? If there are no visuals, would using some strengthen the narrative?
- Have you made the narrative meaningful enough for readers so that they wonder and care about what will happen?
- Do you narrate any actions clearly? vividly? Does the action keep readers engaged?
- Is the significance of the narrative clear?
- Is the ending satisfying? What are readers left thinking?

The preceding questions should identify aspects of your narrative you need to work on. When it's time to **REVISE**, make sure your text appeals to your audience and achieves your purpose as successfully as possible.

367–70

Editing and Proofreading

372–75

Once you've revised your draft, follow these guidelines for **EDITING** a narrative:

457–64
355–56

- Make sure events are **NARRATED** in a clear order and include appropriate time markers, **TRANSITIONS**, and summary phrases to link the parts and show the passing of time.

HB-35

- Be careful that **VERB TENSES ARE CONSISTENT** throughout. If you start your narrative in the past tense ("he *taught* me how to use a computer"), be careful not to switch to the present ("So I *look* at him and *say* . . . ") along the way.

HB-11–12

- Check to see that **VERB TENSES** correctly indicate when an action took place. If one action took place before another action in the past, for example, you should use the past perfect tense: "I forgot to dot my i's, a mistake I *had made* many times before."

- Punctuate **DIALOGUE** correctly. Whenever someone speaks, surround the speech with quotation marks ("No way," I said). Periods and commas go inside quotation marks; exclamation points and question marks go inside if they're part of the quotation, outside if they're part of the whole sentence:

◆ 447–51

| INSIDE | Opening the door, Ms. Cordell announced, "Pop quiz!" |
| OUTSIDE | It wasn't my intention to announce "I hate to read"! |

- **PROOFREAD** your finished narrative carefully before turning it in.

⁖ 375–76

Taking Stock of Your Work

Take stock of what you've written by considering these questions:

▶ **Access Chapter 36** in the ebook for a video on reflecting on your writing.

- How did you go about coming up with ideas and generating text? Did you try freewriting, looping, mapping, something else? Which activities were most productive for you?
- How effectively did you use dialogue, description, or other narrative strategies in your writing?
- Did you use photographs or other visual or audio elements? If so, what did they add? If not, why not?
- Did you take any risks with your writing, or did you experiment in some way? Was the experiment a success? a failure? What can you learn from it?
- How did others' responses influence your writing?
- What did you learn about reading, writing, or other literacies as you worked on your piece? How might you use this learning in the future?
- Overall, what did you do well in this piece? What could still be improved? What would you do differently next time?

If you need more help

See also **PERSONAL NARRATIVES** (Chapter 19), a kind of narrative that focuses more generally on a significant event from your past, and **EXPLORATIONS** (Chapter 22), a kind of essay for thinking about a topic in writing. See Chapter 35 if you are required to submit your literacy narrative as part of a writing **PORTFOLIO**.

▲ 234–45
270–79

⁖ 377–82

13 Analyzing Texts

Both *HuffPost* and *National Review* cover the same events, but each one interprets them differently. All toothpaste ads claim to make teeth "the whitest." The Environmental Protection Agency is a guardian of America's air, water, and soil—or an unconstitutional impediment to economic growth, depending on which politician is speaking. Those are but three examples that demonstrate why we need to be careful, analytical readers of magazines, newspapers, blogs, websites, ads, political documents, even textbooks.

Text is commonly thought of as words, as a piece of writing. In the academic world, however, text can include not only writing but images— photographs, illustrations, videos, films—and even sculptures, buildings, and music and other sounds. And many texts combine words, images, and sounds. We are constantly bombarded with texts: on the web, in print, on signs and billboards, even on our clothing. Not only does text convey information, but it also influences how and what we think. We need to read, then, to understand what texts say, how they say it, and how they try to persuade or influence what we think.

Because understanding how texts say what they say and achieve their effects is so crucial, assignments in many disciplines ask you to analyze texts. You may be asked to analyze candidates' speeches in a *political science* course or to analyze the imagery in a poem for a *literature* class. In a *statistics* course, you might analyze a set of data—a numerical text—to discern patterns and trends.

This chapter offers detailed guidelines for writing an essay that closely examines a text both for what it says and for how it does so, with the goal of demonstrating for readers how—and how well—the text achieves its effects. We'll begin with three examples, the first annotated to point out the key features found in most textual analyses.

PAT FINN

The Architecture of Inequality
On Bong Joon-ho's Parasite

Pat Finn teaches English at Tenafly High School in New Jersey. He writes regularly for Architizer, an online resource for architects, where this essay appeared.

In Bong Joon-ho's Academy Award–winning film *Parasite*, architecture isn't silent, it speaks. Again and again, the built environment indicates where people fit into the social hierarchy—or if there is a place for them at all.

The film opens in the apartment of the Kim family, the movie's protagonists. This is a semi-basement apartment, or *banjiha*, a common type of working-class residence in South Korea. "It really reflects the psyche of the Kim family," Bong told Rachel Wallace for *Architectural Digest*. "You're still half overground, so there's this hope and this sense that you still have access to sunlight and you haven't completely fallen to the basement yet. It's this weird mixture of hope and this fear that you can fall even lower."

From the first shot of the film, the viewer can see that this is an improvised living situation, a space where nothing ever feels settled. As the opening credits flash across the screen, the camera lingers over socks hanging from a light fixture that is being used as a makeshift drying rack.

A clear thesis.

The meaning behind the design is explained in a quote by the filmmaker.

Clear description of the apartment and how the family lives in it.

An early rendering of the Kim family's semi-basement apartment.

Park So-dam, left, and Choi Woo-shik play the two children of the Kim family.

In the next shot, we see the two youngest members of the Kim family, siblings Ki-jung and Ki-woo, frantically scanning the apartment with their phones, searching for an unsecured wi-fi signal they can connect to. They eventually find service in the strange bathroom, in which the toilet is elevated on a tiled platform. Now, it seems, the bathroom will become a new communal space where the family will hang out and browse the internet.

The way the Kim family lives in their space, improvising as necessary, reflects the way they exist economically. Without stable jobs, the Kim family is forced to constantly hustle, make adjustments, and find new ways to make money. If they slow down, even for a second, it might prevent them from making ends meet.

The Kims' stressful lifestyle is emblematic of the so-called "gig economy" that has emerged in recent years. In his now-classic 2009 book *Capitalist Realism*, the late theorist and blogger Mark Fisher argued that the proliferation of "gig" work in the twenty-first century has taken a serious psychological toll on workers worldwide. "To

5

The family's life is analyzed with support from a scholarly source.

The Kim family's most recent "gig" is folding pizza boxes.

function effectively as a component of just-in-time production you must develop a capacity to respond to unforeseen events, you must learn to live in conditions of total instability, or 'precarity,' as the ugly neologism has it," Fisher explained. "Periods of work alternate with periods of unemployment. Typically, you find yourself employed in a series of short-term jobs, unable to plan for the future" (38).

This passage, like many others in the book, could have been written about the Kims.

In *Parasite*, the crucial difference between the experience of the working class and the upper class is not opulence but stability. The only other living space that features prominently in the film is a gleaming modern estate enclosed by concrete walls. It belongs to the Park family, for whom the Kims' college-age son, Ki-woo, goes to work as an English tutor. (With fabricated credentials, of course; like his other family members, Ki-woo is adept at hustling, or doing what he needs to survive.)

Much has been written about the Parks' gorgeous house, which is said in the film to have been designed by a famous architect named Namgoong Hyeonja. The space is so convincing that many viewers of the film assumed it was a real house, an architectural marvel. However, it is actually a series of sets designed by Lee Ha Jun, the film's production designer.

"Bong left it all to me in terms of its architectural style," Lee 10 explained in an interview with *Dezeen*. "He showed me a simple floor plan which he sketched whilst writing the script." Instead of sticking

The residence of the wealthy Park family is said to have been built by a famous architect. This is an early rendering developed by production designer Lee Ha Jun.

The illustrations and photos replace written descriptions of the set.

The sets were designed to convey "great space arrangement," according to production designer Lee Ha Jun.

to one architectural style, Lee took inspiration from multiple homes that had a minimalist design. The key element he wanted to capture was "great space arrangement."

The fact that the Parks' house was supposedly designed by a famous architect is a significant detail. As soon as Ki-woo steps into the house, he is leaving the chaotic and improvisatory space of working-class Seoul and entering planned, architectural space. Here, light fixtures do not double as drying racks and bathrooms aren't used for surfing the web. In contrast, every detail of the Parks' house speaks to the logic of its overall design.

Analysis of the significance of the home, contrasted with the apartment.

This is a living space that has carved out its niche in the social order. It asserts its right to exist.

In *Parasite*, secrets lurk even in spaces that appear meticulously logical in their design.

However, the seeming stability of the Park household ultimately proves to be an illusion. The shocking ending of the film illustrates that dark secrets lurk in every house, even ones with open floor plans. It also shows that class tensions can only be tamped down for so long. If inequality persists, and workers continue to be unable to take control of their lives, something is eventually going to crack.

Clear interpretation of the significance of the two dwellings.

Works Cited

Fisher, Mark. *Capitalist Realism: Is There No Alternative?* Zero Books, 2009.

Lee Ha Jun. "*Parasite* House Designed from 'Simple Floor Plan' Sketched by Bong Joon-ho." Interview by Bridget Cogley. *Dezeen*, 16 Apr. 2020, www.dezeen.com/2020/04/16/parasite -film-set-design-interview-lee-ha-jun-bong-joon-ho.

Parasite. Directed by Bong Joon-ho, Barunson E and A, 2019.

Wallace, Rachel. "Inside the House from Bong Joon-ho's *Parasite*." *Architectural Digest,* 31 Oct. 2019, www.architecturaldigest.com /story/bong-joon-ho-parasite-movie-set-design-interview.

Finn's analysis of the film centers on the two main sets—one family's squalid apartment and another family's lovely home. He compares and contrasts the two dwellings but, interestingly, does not reveal the feature of the house that leads to the "shocking ending of the film."

DANIELLE ALLEN

Our Declaration

Danielle Allen is a political theorist, teaches at Harvard University, and directs the Allen Lab for Democracy Renovation. This analysis is a chapter from her book Our Declaration: A Reading of the Declaration of Independence in Defense of Equality.

There's something quite startling about the phrase "We hold these truths to be self-evident." Perhaps it can be made visible most easily with a comparison.

The Catholic Church, too, is committed to a set of truths. At every mass priest and parishioners together recite a list of their beliefs called the *Credo*. One version, called the Apostles' Creed, starts like this: "I believe in God, the Father almighty, creator of heaven and earth. I believe in Jesus Christ, his only son and Lord." Each section begins with the words "I believe," and that's why this recitation is called the *Credo*. Latin, "credo" simply means "I believe."

The Declaration launches its list of truths altogether differently. Jefferson and his colleagues do not say, "I believe," or even "we believe," that all men are created equal. Instead, they say, "We hold these truths to be self-evident," and then they give us a set of either three or five truths, depending on how you count.

What's the difference between "We believe" and "We hold these truths to be self-evident"? In the Catholic *Credo*, when one says, "I believe," the basis for that belief is God's revealed word. In contrast, when Jefferson and his colleagues say, "We hold these truths to be self-evident," they are claiming to know the truths thanks to their own powers of perception and reasoning. These truths are self-evident, and so humans can grasp and hold them without any external or divine assistance.

In order to understand what "We hold these truths to be self-evident" 5 really means, then, it is important to know what "self-evident" means.

Sometimes people take it to mean that we can instantly understand an idea, but that's not really right. It's true that sometimes the idea of self-evidence is used for things that we simply perceive. For instance, when I look out my window I immediately perceive that the world includes things like trees and flowers. If outside my window there are many different kinds of tree—hickory and maple and oak, for instance—when I look at them, I nonetheless rapidly perceive that they are all the same kind of thing. That many different kinds of a particular sort of growing thing are all trees is self-evident. We can call this self-evidence from sense perception.

The immediacy of perception, though, is not the same as instantly understanding an idea. And, in fact, to call a proposition self-evident is not at all to say that you will instantly get it. It means instead that if you look into the proposition, if you entertain it, if you reflect upon it, you will inevitably come to affirm it. All the evidence that you need in order to believe the proposition exists within the proposition itself.

This second kind of self-evidence comes not from perception but from logic and how language works.

For instance, we define a chair as an object with a seat and some structure of legs to hold that seat up; and the artifact serves the purpose of having someone sit on it. Then, if I say that a chair is for sitting on, I am expressing a self-evident truth based only on the definition of a chair. Of course a chair is for sitting on! That is how I've defined the word, after all. That's a pretty trivial example of self-evidence. If that were all there were to the idea of self-evidence, it wouldn't be very interesting.

So here is where matters get more interesting: one can string 10 together more than one kind of self-evident proposition—let's call them "premises"—in order to lead to a new piece of knowledge, a conclusion, which will also count as self-evident, since it has been deduced from a few basic self-evident premises.

Aristotle called this method of stringing together valid premises to yield a self-evident conclusion, a syllogism. . . . Here is a basic example:

FIRST PREMISE: Bill Gates is a human being.
SECOND PREMISE: All human beings are mortal.
CONCLUSION: Bill Gates is mortal.

This is a bit like math. We can use a Venn diagram to show how the syllogism works. Venn diagrams represent sets of things and how they overlap, and the argument of a syllogism can be thought of as expressing facts about sets and their members. Bill Gates is in the set of human beings. And the set of human beings is entirely contained within the set of mortals. It follows that Bill Gates is in the set of mortals. The validity of this syllogism becomes self-evident when those facts are represented as in this Venn diagram:

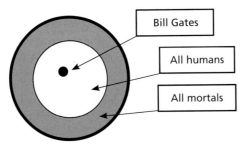

Now, in this syllogism, our two premises are both self-evident truths based on sense perception. We know Bill Gates is a human being by looking at and listening to him. As to the idea that human beings are mortal, we know that human beings die by seeing it happen all around us and never seeing a counterexample. Then we take these two premises, each self-evident through sense perception, and generate a third self-evident proposition, in this case a conclusion, through deduction. From the two premises, we can deduce the certain conclusion that Bill Gates will die.

The Declaration introduces a similar kind of argument when it says, "We hold these truths to be self-evident." At first glance, it looks as if we just have three separate self-evident truths. But if we look closer, we notice that our truths also represent an argument with two premises, which are true from sense perception, and a conclusion that is deduced from them.

Here's how it works.

After the Declaration says, "We hold these truths to be self-evident," the text proceeds to identify three truths: one about human beings, one about government, and one about revolution. The truth about human beings, though, is a three-part truth.

It is self-evidently true:

> that all men are created equal, that they are endowed by their Creator with certain unalienable Rights, that among these are Life, Liberty and the pursuit of Happiness.

How do these three claims make a single truth? Human beings are equal in all acquiring the same rights at the moment of their creation. From the moment of their emergence as living beings, human beings seek to survive, to be free from domination, and to be happy. This is something we simply observe about human beings. For that matter, we observe it about other animals, too. For instance, I've never seen a cat that didn't want to survive, to be free, and to be happy.

Then, with the next truth, we come to the difference between human beings and animals. The Declaration says, it is self-evidently true

> —That to secure these rights, Governments are instituted among Men, deriving their just powers from the consent of the governed.

This is a truly salient point. The signers are saying that, in contrast to the animal kingdom, the world of human beings is indeed full of kingdoms and other kinds of governments. The so-called animal

15

kingdom is a kingdom only metaphorically. There are no governments among animals. Animals have social hierarchies, and they have their own methods for seeking their survival, freedom, and happiness, but human beings use politics. Human beings display self-conscious thought about social organization, and politics is the activity that flows from that self-consciousness about power. Again, this is simply a matter of observation. From the beginning of time to the present day, human beings have formed governments. Human beings have done this just as regularly as birds build nests.

Then the Declaration puts these first two truths together. Since human beings seek their own survival, freedom, and happiness, and since they have a special tool for doing so—namely, the ability to form governments—it makes sense for them to stick with any particular version of that tool, any particular government, only if it's doing the work it's been built to do.

Compare it to a bird with a nest. What's the point of a bird's staying in a nest if it turns out that the nest has been built out of material inimical or poisonous to the bird? What's the use, in other words, of having a government, if it doesn't serve the purposes of protecting life, liberty, and the pursuit of happiness for which governments are set up in the first place?

The Declaration puts it this way: It is self-evidently true

> —That whenever any Form of Government becomes destructive of these ends, it is the Right of the People to alter or to abolish it, and to institute new Government, laying its foundation on such principles and organizing its powers in such form, as to them shall seem most likely to effect their Safety and Happiness.

From the facts, first, that people are simply wired, as are all animals, to seek their survival, freedom, and happiness, and, second, that human beings use governments as their central instrument for protecting their life, liberty, and pursuit of happiness, we can deduce that people have a right to change governments that aren't working for them.

This makes an argument that goes like this:

PREMISE 1: All people have rights to life, liberty, and the pursuit of happiness.

PREMISE 2: Properly constituted government is necessary to their securing these rights.

CONCLUSION: All people have a right to a properly constituted government.

In fact, a philosopher would say that a premise is missing from that 25
argument and that the full formally valid syllogism would look like this:

PREMISE 1:   All people have rights to life, liberty, and the pursuit of happiness.

PREMISE 2:   Properly constituted government is necessary to their securing these rights.

PREMISE 3:   [All people have a right to whatever is necessary to secure what they have a right to.]

CONCLUSION: All people have a right to a properly constituted government.

Politicians often craft maxims simply by dropping out pieces of their argument. With the missing premise inserted, the Declaration's truths fit together almost like the pieces of a mathematical equation; we intuitively feel the puzzle pieces snap together. That is how self-evidence should feel.

Allen's analysis focuses on the Declaration's second sentence, unpacking its logic through a careful examination of its key term, "self-evident," and explaining how the rest of the sentence forms a syllogism that "snaps together." She looks carefully at every word, restricting her analysis here to a very brief part of the text—but provides insights that illuminate the whole document.

AIMEE BENDER

What Writers Can Learn from Goodnight Moon

Aimee Bender is a novelist and fiction writer who teaches creative writing at the University of Southern California. This essay appeared in the New York Times "Draft" series on the art and craft of writing.

I gave birth to twins a little more than a year ago, and at the baby showers we received many books: colorful board books, big illustrated books, collections of Sandra Boynton and nursery rhymes and Dr. Seuss, but none multiple times except this one: a board book *Goodnight Moon*, a flimsy *Goodnight Moon*, a large lap book *Goodnight Moon*, and an anthology by the book's author, Margaret Wise Brown. Of course, I thought. It's that one that says good night a lot. I figured I'd read it before, just a story of going around the room saying good night to stuff, and I thought it was popular as a gift because it's so appropriate for bedtime and everybody wants babies to sleep.

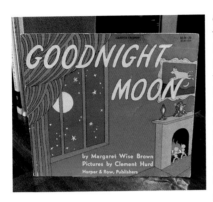

But, when I first sat down with the babies, on the bed, nestled into pillows, beginning a sleep routine as recommended by their doctor, I pulled out the big lap book and read it aloud, and by Page 2, it was clear to me that for whatever reason, I had never read this one before. The babies listened in their sleepy baby way, and as the pages turned, I felt a growing excitement—a *literary* excitement. Not what I expected from this moment. But I was struck and stunned, as I have been before, by a classic sneaking up on me and, in an instant, earning yet again another fan.

It also seemed to me to be an immediately useful writing tool.

Goodnight Moon does two things right away: It sets up a world and then it subverts its own rules even as it follows them. It works like a sonata of sorts, but, like a good version of the form, it does not follow a wholly predictable structure. Many children's books do, particularly for this age, as kids love repetition and the books supply it. They often end as we expect, with a circling back to the start, and a fun twist. This is satisfying but it can be forgettable. Kids—people—also love depth and surprise, and *Goodnight Moon* offers both. Here's what I think it does that is so radical and illuminating for writers of all kinds, poets and fiction writers and more.

First, Brown sets up her terms. We look around the room and learn about it and "meet" all the items in question. The language is direct and clear and the rhythm is just right. The telephone, which we never revisit, is aurally perfect. "In the great green room / There was a telephone / And a red balloon."

After we meet the old lady whispering "hush," there is a pause built into the page turn, and the movement begins officially. The title kicks into play. We begin with "Goodnight room" and the pacing slows: the words are fewer, or at least they seem fewer. The cello, I'd say, begins. But even though we are now revisiting the items we've met, we meet new things too, right away. We hadn't greeted the moon earlier, but here it is. Not only that, but Brown allows us to hear of two moons, the

5

real and the virtual, and not to worry about any varied rhyming scheme. When I Googled "Goodnight Moon masterpiece," I came upon a blog post by a reader who was irritated by the moon / moon repetition I had loved. Because they are such different moons! But that post was a reminder of the gentle risk Brown takes there. After the moons, we go through the whole room and our love of repetition is satisfied and we can track the little mouse and see the lights dimming in the illustrations. The page turns are beautifully paced and quite slow.

What a surprise, then, to find that there is a blank page with "Goodnight nobody" out of nowhere, sharing a spread with "Goodnight mush." What a surprise, then, that the story does not end with the old lady whispering "hush" but goes out the window into the night.

Most picture books would close with that old lady—that's the balanced choice. But we see the stars and feel the air—we've been sure we're staying in but now we're floating out. Why? And then back in for the ending of "Goodnight noises everywhere." This, the last page? At first, I looked for another page—why end here? Isn't it a little abrupt? But (after a few more readings), isn't it also the way for us to close our eyes metaphorically with the bunny and be in that state right before slipping off to sleep, that magical drifting moment after floating out with the stars and the air, when we only hear noises and next is sleep? The story has moved so close to the bunny as to become an experiential mirror of his drift and fall. How much deeper and more elegant that is than the neat symmetry we might expect.

For writers, this is all such a useful reminder. Yes, move around in a structure. But also float out of that structure. "Goodnight nobody" is an author's inspired moment that is inexplicable and moving and creates an unknown that lingers. How wonderful that this oddly compassionate moment, where even nobody gets a good night, shows up in the picture book that is the most popular! There is no template, ever. When writing, how do we allow those moments of impulse, of surprise? How do we not censor that kind of leap? (I'd argue for following tangents—for not feeling bound to the topic at hand.) And when to end a story or poem or novel or essay? It's one of the most common questions at readings: "How do you know when it's done?"

How did Brown know? On some level, it had to have been a felt ending, a note she hit that must have seemed right and took confidence and daring to pull off. The reader has time to linger with that end and accept it—it's not the obvious closing note of the music, it's not the fully resolved major chord. But she trusted it. How something ends is so much about a writer training her own instinct and her own sense of that note.

The babies are 14 months old now and I've already read the book probably a hundred times—but these unexpected choices of hers are the ones that keep my interest. I think I have a whole lot of rounds of the book to go, but I feel sure I will never crack open the meaning of "Goodnight nobody," and moments like that make rereading a genuine joy.

Bender walks us through Goodnight Moon, *first by defining the expectations of the genre of children's picture books, and then showing how the author uses surprise—playing with our expectations and even thwarting them—to demonstrate the value of "moving around in a structure" rather than adhering strictly to it.*

Key Features / Textual Analysis

A summary or description of the text. Your readers may not know the text you are analyzing, so you need to include it or tell them about it before you analyze it. Allen's text, the Declaration of Independence, is well known, so she assumes that her readers already know its first sentences. Texts that are not so well known require a more detailed summary or description. For example, Finn provides just enough information on *Parasite's* plot that readers can see how the sets fit into it.

Attention to the context. Texts don't exist in isolation: they are influenced by and contribute to ongoing conversations, controversies, debates, and cultural trends. To fully engage a particular text, you need to understand its larger context. Finn relates the film's characters and sets to contrasts between social classes, and Bender describes snuggling with her babies as she reads.

A clear interpretation or judgment. Your goal in analyzing a text is to lead readers through careful examination of the text to some kind of interpretation or reasoned judgment, sometimes announced clearly in a thesis statement. When you interpret something, you explain what you think it means, as Allen does when she carefully constructs the logical argument underlying the Declaration of Independence. Bender praises *Goodnight Moon* as "an immediately useful writing tool."

Reasonable support for your conclusions. Written analysis of a text is generally supported by evidence from the text itself and sometimes from other sources as well. The writer might support their interpretation by quoting words or passages from a verbal text or referring to images in a visual text. Allen, for example, interprets the term "self-evident" by referring to formal logic, Venn diagrams, and the Catholic Credo. Finn offers photos of the sets and quotations from the director and set designer to support his argument. Bender offers many quotes and paraphrases from *Goodnight Moon*. Note that the support you offer for your interpretation need only be "reasonable"—there is never only one way to interpret something.

A GUIDE TO WRITING TEXTUAL ANALYSES

Choosing a Text to Analyze

Most of the time, you will be assigned a text or a type of text to analyze: a poem in a literature class, the work of a political philosopher in a political science class, a speech in a history or communications course, a painting or sculpture in an art class, a piece of music in a music theory course. If you must choose a text to analyze, look for one that suits the demands of the assignment—one that is neither too large or complex to analyze thoroughly (a Dickens novel or a Beethoven symphony is probably too big) nor too brief or limited to generate sufficient material (a ten-second TV news brief or a paragraph from *Braiding Sweetgrass* would probably be too small). You might also choose to analyze three or four texts by examining elements common to all. Be sure you understand what the assignment asks you to do, and ask your instructor for clarification if you're not sure.

Considering the Rhetorical Situation

73–74	**PURPOSE**	Why are you analyzing this text? To demonstrate that you understand it? To show how its argument works—or doesn't? Or are you using the text as a way to make some other point?
75–78	**AUDIENCE**	Are your readers likely to know your text? How much detail will you need to supply?
85–87	**STANCE**	What interests you (or not) about your text? Why? What do you know or believe about it, and how will your own beliefs affect your analysis?
88–90	**MEDIA/DESIGN**	Will your analysis appear in print? on the web? How will your medium affect your analysis? If you are analyzing a visual text, you will probably need to include an image of it.

Generating Ideas and Text

In analyzing a written text, your goal is to understand what it says, how it works, and what it means. To do so, you may find it helpful to follow a certain sequence: read, respond, summarize, analyze, and draw conclusions from your analysis.

Read to see what the text says.   Start by reading carefully, to get a sense of what it says. This means first skimming to **PREVIEW THE TEXT**, rereading for the main ideas, then questioning and **ANNOTATING**.

❋ 12
15–18
13–14

Consider your **INITIAL RESPONSE**. Once you have a sense of what the text says, what do you think? What's your reaction to the argument, the tone, the language, the images? Do you find the text difficult? puzzling? Do you agree with what the writer says? disagree? agree *and* disagree? Your reaction to a text can color your analysis, so start by thinking about how you react—and why. Consider both your intellectual and any emotional reactions. Identify places in the text that trigger or account for those reactions. If you think that you have no particular reaction or response, try to articulate why. Whatever your response, think about what accounts for it.

Next, consolidate your understanding of the text by **SUMMARIZING** what it says in your own words. You may find it helpful to **OUTLINE** its main ideas. For instance, Allen carefully maps out the parts of the syllogism at the heart of her analysis.

● 529
⁝ 335–37

Access Chapter 2 in the ebook for a video on summarizing.

Decide what you want to analyze.   Having read the text carefully, think about what you find most interesting or intriguing and why. What about the argument interests you? Its logic? Its attempt to create an emotional response? Its reliance on the writer's credibility or reputation? Its use of design to achieve its aims? Its context? The experience of reading it? Does the text's language, imagery, or structure intrigue you? Or does something else? You might begin your analysis by exploring what attracted your notice.

Think about the larger context.   All texts are part of larger conversations with other texts that have dealt with the same topic. An essay arguing for handgun trigger locks is part of an ongoing conversation about gun regulation, which is itself part of a conversation on individual rights and responsibilities. Academic texts include documentation in part to weave in voices from the conversation. And, in fact, anytime you're reading to learn, you're probably reading for some larger context. Whatever your reading goals, being aware of that larger context can help you better understand what you're reading. Here are some specific aspects of the text to pay attention to:

- **Who else cares about this topic?** Especially when you're reading in order to learn about a topic, the texts you read will often reveal which people or groups are part of the conversation—and might be sources of further reading. For example, an essay describing the formation of the Grand Canyon could be of interest to geologists, environmentalists, Native Americans, travel writers, or tourists. If you're reading such an essay while doing research on the canyon, you should consider how the audience being addressed determines the nature of the information provided—and its suitability as a source for your research.

- **Ideas.** Does the text refer to any concepts or ideas that give you some sense that it's part of a larger conversation? An argument on airport security measures, for example, is part of larger conversations about government response to terrorism, the limits of freedom in a democracy, and the possibilities of using technology to detect weapons and explosives, among others.

- **Terms.** Is there any terminology or specialized language that reflects the writer's allegiance to a particular group or academic discipline? If you run across words like "false consciousness," "ideology," and "hegemony," for example, you might guess the text was written by a Marxist scholar.

- **Citations.** Whom does the writer cite? Do the other writers have a particular academic specialty, belong to an identifiable intellectual school, share similar political leanings? If an article on politics cites Michael Moore and Maureen Dowd in support of its argument, you might assume the writer holds liberal opinions; if it cites Ben Shapiro and Sean Hannity, the writer is likely a conservative.

Write a brief paragraph describing the larger context surrounding the text and how that context affects your understanding of the text.

Consider what you know about the writer. What you know about the person who created a text can influence your understanding of it. Their **CREDENTIALS**, other work, reputation, stance, and beliefs are all useful windows into understanding a text. You may need to conduct an online search to find information on the writer. Then write a sentence or two summarizing what you know about the writer and how that information affects your understanding of the text.

505

Study how the text works. Written texts are made up of various components, including words, sentences, paragraphs, headings, lists, punctuation — and sometimes images as well. Look for patterns in the way these components are used and try to decide what those patterns reveal about the text. How do they affect its message?

Outline to determine what a text says and does. A helpful way to think about a text's structure is by outlining it, paragraph by paragraph or section by section. If you're interested in analyzing its ideas, look at what each paragraph *says*; if, however, you're concerned with how the ideas are presented, pay attention to what each paragraph *does*.

- *What it says.* Write a sentence that identifies what each paragraph says. Once you've done that for the whole text, look for patterns in the topics the writer addresses. Pay attention to the order in which the topics are presented. Also look for gaps — ideas the writer has left unsaid or assumed. Such paragraph-by-paragraph outlining of the content can help you see how the writer has arranged ideas and how that arrangement builds an argument or develops a topic. Here, for example, is an outline of the first several paragraphs of Bender's analysis of *Goodnight Moon*. The numbers in the left column refer to the essay's paragraphs.

  1 As a new mother, she and her twins were given many books, including several copies of *Goodnight Moon*.
  2 Upon reading the book for the first time, she was surprised by the book.
  3 She also realized that writers could learn much from it.
  4 *Goodnight Moon* has a structure that isn't predictable, and though children like predictability and repetition, they also like to be surprised — and this book offers both predictability and surprise.
  5 The book begins by setting the stage — the room with several objects.

- *What it does.* Identify the function of each paragraph. Starting with the first paragraph, ask, What does this paragraph do? Does it introduce a topic? provide background for a topic to some? describe something? define something? entice me to read further? something else? What does the second paragraph do? the third? As you go through the text, you may identify groups of paragraphs that have a single purpose.

Here is a functional outline of Bender's first five paragraphs; again, the numbers on the left refer to the paragraphs.

1   Provides the context for the analysis

2   Describes the author's initial reaction to the book

3   Describes her realization of the book's importance—and uses a single-sentence paragraph to emphasize the realization

4   Offers an overview of the book and the typical structure of such books

5   Begins the analysis by describing the content and language of the first several pages

Analyze the argument.   Every text makes an argument and provides some kind of support for it. An important part of understanding any text is to recognize its argument—what the writer wants the audience to believe, feel, or do. Here are some questions you'll want to consider when you analyze an argument:

342–43

- *What is the claim?*   What is the main point the writer is trying to make? Is there a clearly stated **THESIS**, or is the thesis merely implied? Is it appropriately qualified?

402
402–9

- *What support does the writer offer for the claim?*   What **REASONS** are given to support the claim? What **EVIDENCE** backs up those reasons? Facts? Statistics? Examples? Testimonials by authorities? Anecdotes or stories? Are the reasons and evidence appropriate, plausible, and sufficient? Are you convinced by them? If not, why not?

413
399–409
410–11
410–13

- *How does the writer appeal to readers?*   Do they appeal to your **EMOTIONS**? rely on **LOGIC**? try to establish **COMMON GROUND**? demonstrate **CREDIBILITY**?

411

- *How evenhandedly does the writer present the argument?*   Is there any mention of **COUNTERARGUMENTS**? If so, how does the writer deal with them? By refuting them? By acknowledging them and responding to them reasonably? Does the writer treat other arguments respectfully? dismissively?

413–15

- *Does the writer use any logical **FALLACIES**?*   Are the arguments or beliefs of others distorted or exaggerated? Is the logic faulty?

- *What authorities or other sources of outside information does the writer use?* How are they used? How credible are they? Are they in any way biased or otherwise unreliable? Are they current?

- *How does the writer address you as the reader?* Does the writer assume that readers know something about what is being discussed? Does their language include you or exclude you? (Hint: If you see the word "we," do you feel included?) Do you sense that you and the writer share any beliefs or attitudes? If the writer is not writing to you, what audience is the target? How do you know?

Then write a brief paragraph summarizing the argument the text makes and the main way the writer argues it, along with your reactions to or questions about that argument.

Identify patterns.   Look for notable patterns in the text—recurring words and their synonyms, as well as repeated phrases, metaphors and other images, and types of sentences. Some readers find it helps to highlight patterns in various colors. Does the author repeatedly rely on any particular writing strategies: **NARRATION**? **COMPARISON**? Something else?

◆ 457–64

422–28

Another kind of pattern that might be important to consider is the kind of evidence the text provides. Is it more opinion than facts? nothing but statistics? If many sources are cited, is the information presented in any patterns—as **QUOTATIONS**? **PARAPHRASES**? **SUMMARIES**? Are there repeated references to certain experts or sources?

● 521–32

In visual texts, look for patterns of color, shape, and line. What's in the foreground, and what's in the background? What's completely visible, partly visible, or hidden? In both verbal and visual texts, look for omissions and anomalies: What isn't there that you would expect to find? Is there anything that doesn't really fit in?

If you discover patterns, then you need to consider what, if anything, they mean in terms of what the writer is saying. What do they reveal about the writer's underlying premises and beliefs? What do they tell you about the writer's strategies for persuading readers to accept the truth of what they are saying?

See how color-coding an essay by *New York Times* columnist William Safire on the meaning of the Gettysburg Address reveals several patterns in the language Safire uses. In this excerpt from the essay, which was published just before the first anniversary of the September 11, 2001, terrorist attacks, Safire develops his analysis through several patterns. Religious references are colored yellow; references to a "national spirit," green;

references to life, death, and rebirth, blue; and places where Safire directly addresses the reader, gray.

> But the selection of this poetic political sermon as the oratorical centerpiece of our observance need not be only an exercise. . . . Now, as then, a national spirit rose from the ashes of destruction.
>
> Here is how to listen to Lincoln's all-too-familiar speech with new ears.
>
> In those 266 words, you will hear the word *dedicate* five times. . . .
>
> Those five pillars of dedication rested on a fundament of religious metaphor. From a president not known for his piety—indeed, often criticized for his supposed lack of faith—came a speech rooted in the theme of national resurrection. The speech is grounded in conception, birth, death, and rebirth.
>
> Consider the barrage of images of birth in the opening sentence. . . .
>
> Finally, the nation's spirit rises from this scene of death: "that this nation, under God, shall have a new birth of freedom." Conception, birth, death, rebirth. The nation, purified in this fiery trial of war, is resurrected. Through the sacrifice of its sons, the sundered nation would be reborn as one. . . .
>
> Do not listen on Sept. 11 only to Lincoln's famous words and comforting cadences. Think about how Lincoln's message encompasses but goes beyond paying "fitting and proper" respect to the dead and the bereaved. His sermon at Gettysburg reminds "us the living" of our "unfinished work" and "the great task remaining before us"—to resolve that this generation's response to the deaths of thousands of our people leads to "a new birth of freedom."

The color coding helps us see patterns in Safire's language, just as Safire reveals patterns in Lincoln's words. He offers an interpretation of Lincoln's address as a "poetic political sermon," and the words he uses throughout support that interpretation. At the end, he repeats the assertion that Lincoln's address is a sermon, inviting us to consider it differently. Safire's repeated commands ("Consider," "Do not listen," "Think about") offer additional insight into how he wishes to position himself in relation to his readers.

Analyzing Visual Texts

Access the ebook for a video on analyzing a text with both written and visual elements.

In analyzing a visual text, your goal is to understand its intended effect on viewers as well as its actual effect, the ways it creates that effect, and its relationship to other texts. If the visual text accompanies a written one, you need to understand how the texts work together to convey a message or make an argument.

Describe the text. Your first job is to examine the image carefully. Focus on specific details; given the increasing use of *Photoshop* and other digital image manipulation tools, you can usually assume that every detail in the image is intentional. Ask yourself these questions:

- What kind of image is it? Does it stand alone, or is it part of a group? Are there typical features of this kind of image that it includes—or lacks?

- What does the image show? What stands out? What is in the background? Are some parts of the image grouped together or connected? Are any set apart from one another?

- As you look at the image, does the content seem far away, close up, or in between? Are you level with it, looking down from above, or looking up from below? What is the effect of your viewing position?

- Does the image tell or suggest a story about what has happened or is about to happen?

- Does the image allude to or refer to anything else? For example, the Starbucks logo features the image of a Siren, a mythical being who lured sailors to their doom.

Explore your response. Images, particularly those in advertisements, are often trying to persuade us to buy something or to feel, think, or behave a certain way. News photographs and online videos also try to evoke EMOTIONAL RESPONSES, from horror over murdered innocents to amusement at cute kittens. Think about your response:

◆ 413

- How does the image make you feel? What emotional response, if any, does the image make you feel? Sympathy? Concern? Anger? Happiness? Contentment? Something else?

- What does the image lead you to think about? What connections does it have to things in your life, in the news, in your knowledge of the world?

- Do the image and any accompanying words seem to be trying to persuade you to think or do something? Do they do so directly, such as by pointing out the virtues of a product (Chevrolet Equinox: "So long, gas stations")? Or indirectly, by setting a tone or establishing a mood (many perfume ads, like this one for Ariana Grande's Cloud Pink: "Optimistic. Confident. Uplifting")?

91 ▲

• Does the **GENRE** affect your response? For example, do you expect to laugh at a comic? feel empathy with victims of a tragedy in a photo accompanying a news story? find a satirical editorial cartoon offensive?

Consider the context. Like written texts, visual texts are part of larger conversations with other texts that have dealt with the same topic or used similar imagery. This editorial cartoon on climate change, for example, is part of an ongoing conversation about how quickly we must act on climate change:

Consider what you know about the artist or sponsor. Editorial cartoons, like the one above, are usually signed, and information about the artist and their other work is usually readily available on the web. Many commercials and advertisements, however, are created by ad agencies, so the organization or company that sponsored or posted the image should be identified and researched. How does that information affect your understanding of the text?

Decide on a focus for your analysis. What do you find most interesting about the text, and why? Its details and the way they work together (or not)? The argument it makes? The way it uses images to appeal to its audience? The emotional response it evokes? The way any words and images work together to deliver a message? These are just some ways of thinking about a visual text, ones that can help you find a focus.

However you choose to focus your analysis, it should be limited in scope so that you can zero in on the details of the visual you're analyzing. Here, for example, is an excerpt from an essay from 2014 by an art historian responding to a statement made by former president Barack Obama that manufacturing skills may be worth more than a degree in art history:

> *"I promise you, folks can make a lot more potentially with skilled manufacturing or the trades than they might with an art history degree."* President Barack Obama
>
> Charged with interrogating this quote from the president, I Google "Obama art history." I click on the first result, a video from CNN, in which the quote is introduced by a gray-haired man in a dark and serious suit, standing in front of a bank of monitors in a digitally created nonspace. The camera cuts from this man to President Obama, who stands in shirtsleeves, his tie slightly loosened. His undershirt is visible through his buttondown under the intense light from what I assume is the work-day sun.
>
> Behind him is a crowd of men and women in more casual clothing, some wearing sweatshirts that have the name of a union printed across them. Their presence creates a spectrum of skin tones. Each person was clearly vetted for visual effect, as were the president's and the newscaster's costumes, the size of their flag lapel pins, the shape of the microphones they speak into, and the angle of the light on their faces. The president makes the comment in question, immediately declares his love for art history, and says that he doesn't want to get a bunch of angry emails from art historians. The crowd behind him laughs and the clip cuts off abruptly.
>
> A click away, I find a digitized copy of a handwritten note from President Obama, apologizing to an angry art history professor who emailed him to complain about his comments. The card on which the note is written is plain, undecorated save for two lines of text printed in a conservative, serif font in a shade of blue that is just on the vibrant side of navy—THE WHITE HOUSE—and under it in smaller letters, WASHINGTON. Its tasteful, minimal aesthetic pulls double duty, meant to convey both populist efficiency (note the absence of gold gilding) and stern superiority (you know where Washington is, right?). It sets

up a productive contrast with the friendliness of the president's own handwriting, particularly his looping signature, soft on the outside with a strong slash through the middle.

Like the video of the president's speech, it is a screen-scale tour de force of political imagecraft, certainly produced with the full knowledge that it would be digitized and go viral, at least among a particular demographic.

—Joel Parsons, "Richness in the Eye of the Beholder"

Parsons begins by describing the images—Obama's clothing, the people standing behind him, the letterhead on his note card, his "looping signature"—followed by an analysis of how every aspect of the video and the note card was "certainly produced with the full knowledge that it would be digitized and go viral." Notice as well that Parsons's analysis focuses more on the visual aspects of the video and note card than on what was said or written. And in a part of his essay not shown here, he notes that his analysis is grounded in "tools . . . he learned in a first-year art history course"—a not-so-subtle response to what President Obama said.

Barack Obama speaking at a General Electric plant in Waukesha, Wisconsin, 2014.

THE WHITE HOUSE

WASHINGTON

Ann —

Let me apologize for my off-the-cuff remarks. I was making a point about the job market, not the value of art history. As it so happens, art history was one of my favorite subjects in high school, and it has helped me take in a great deal of joy in my life that

I might otherwise have missed.

So please pass on my apology for the glib remark to the entire department, and understand that I was trying to encourage young people who may not be predisposed to a four year college experience to be open to technical training that can lead them to an honorable career.

Sincerely,

Obama's apology note to Ann Johns, art history professor at the University of Texas at Austin.

399–416

Access Chapter 30 in the ebook for a video on thesis statements in analyses.

342–44

Coming Up with a Thesis

When you analyze a text, you are basically **ARGUING** that the text should be read or seen in a certain way. Once you've studied the text thoroughly, you need to identify your analytical goal: Do you want to show that the text has a certain meaning? uses certain techniques to achieve its purposes? tries to influence its audience in particular ways? relates to some larger context in some significant manner? should be taken seriously—or not? something else? Come up with a tentative **THESIS** to guide your thinking and analyzing—but be aware that your thesis may change as you continue to work.

Ways of Organizing a Textual Analysis

Examine the information you have to see how it supports or complicates your thesis. Look for clusters of related information that you can use to structure an **OUTLINE**. Your analysis might be structured in at least two ways. You might, as Bender does, discuss patterns, elements, or themes that run through the text. Alternatively, you might analyze each text or section of text separately, as Allen does. Following are graphic representations of some ways of organizing a textual analysis:

335–57

Access Chapter 30 in the ebook for a video on organizing and synthesizing ideas.

Thematically

Introduce your analysis:
• Summarize or describe the text.
• Provide needed context.
• Outline your method or focus.
State your thesis.
→
Analyze the text:
• Identify a theme or pattern.
• Use examples from the text and appropriate contexts as evidence.
Continue as needed.
→
Conclude: Explain what your analysis reveals about the text.

Part by part, or text by text

Introduce your analysis:
• Summarize or describe the text.
• Provide needed context.
• Outline your method or focus.
State your thesis.
→
Analyze first section of text.
↓
Analyze next section of text.
↓
Continue as needed.
→
Conclude: Explain what your analysis reveals about the text.

Spatially, as the text is likely to be experienced by viewers

Introduce your analysis:
- Summarize or describe the text.
- Provide needed context.
- Outline your method or focus. State your thesis.

→ Analyze the most prominent part of the text or the part viewers see first.

↓

Continue the analysis in the order the text is experienced:
- top to bottom
- left to right
- center to edges
- foreground to background
- what becomes visible as text is scrolled, video is played, or images are seen in succession

→ Conclude: Explain what your analysis reveals about the text.

More Ways to Approach a Text Analysis

Create an annotated analysis. Instead of writing a conventional essay, use the comment feature in your word processing program or LMS to create annotations alongside the text you're analyzing that contain the elements of your analysis. You might precede the annotated text with your introduction and follow it with your conclusion.

Make a video analysis. Record a video of yourself talking through your analysis. Show key passages or images from the text you're analyzing, and perhaps include video clips, photos, or other materials that provide context for the text and your analysis of it.

Design a workshop. Plan a workshop in which you present your analysis and engage others in a discussion of it. You might begin by providing an overview of your thesis and key points—and then invite participants to analyze specific passages or elements of the text based on your claims. Prepare activities and discussion questions to guide participants through the workshop.

Remix. After you've written a draft of your analysis, you might **REMIX** it: create an infographic that provides a visual representation of it, reshape it into an oral presentation with slides, or create a podcast that folds your analysis into the experience of reading, listening to, or viewing the text.

▲ 280–90

 Access Chapter 23 in the ebook for a video on creating a remix.

Writing Out a Draft

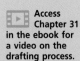 Access Chapter 31 in the ebook for a video on the drafting process.

In drafting your analysis, your goal should be to integrate the various parts into a smoothly flowing, logically organized essay. However, it's easy to get bogged down in the details. Consider writing one section of the analysis first, then another and another, until you've drafted the entire middle; then draft your beginning and ending. Alternatively, start by summarizing the text and moving from there to your analysis and then to your ending. However you do it, you need to support your analysis with evidence: from the text itself (as Finn's analysis of the "text" of a film does), or from **RESEARCH** on the larger context of the text (as Allen does), or by exploring the expectations you have as you read and how they are met or not (as Bender does). You might also compare the text you are analyzing to another text.

471

340–48

Draft a BEGINNING. The beginning of an essay that analyzes a text generally has several tasks: to introduce or summarize the text for your readers, to offer any necessary information on the larger context, and to present your thesis.

- *Summarize or describe the text.* If the text is one your readers don't know, you need to **SUMMARIZE** or **DESCRIBE** it early on to show that you understand it fully, as Finn describes the Kim family apartment and the Parks' house.

529
439–46 ◆

- *Show the text.* If you're analyzing a visual text online, consider starting off with an image, a video, or a link to it or something similar, as Finn does by including several illustrations of the sets and photos of scenes from the film.

- *Provide a context for your analysis.* If there is a larger context that is significant for your analysis, you might mention it in your introduction. Allen does this by comparing the Declaration's statement about self-evident truths to the statements of belief in the Apostles' Creed of the Catholic Church. Bender provides a personal context, the birth of her two babies.

342–44

- *State your* **THESIS**. Finn begins by asserting that in *Parasite* "the built environment indicates where people fit into the social hierarchy—or if there is a place for them at all."

Draft an ENDING. Think about what you want your readers to take away from your analysis, and end by getting them to focus on those thoughts.

348–52

- *Restate your thesis—and say why it matters.* Finn, for example, begins by asserting that *Parasite*'s sets show "where people fit into the social hierarchy" and ends by discussing the dangers of "class tensions" and inequality.

- *Explain what your analysis reveals.* Your analysis should tell your readers something about the way the text works or about what it means or says. Allen, for example, concludes by noting that "the Declaration's truths fit together almost like the pieces of a mathematical equation; we intuitively feel the puzzle pieces snap together. That is how self-evidence should feel." Bender offers thoughts about how *Goodnight Moon*'s author trusted her instincts when deciding how to end the book—and then Bender returns to reading it to her babies.

Access Chapter 30 in the ebook for a video on introductions and conclusions.

Come up with a TITLE. A good title indicates something about the subject of your analysis—and makes readers want to see what you have to say about it. Finn's title provides a preview of his thesis that the architecture seen in *Parasite* reflects the social inequality at the core of the film, while Clark's title straightforwardly announces his topic.

356–57

Consider REWRITING. If you have time and want to explore alternatives, you might try rewriting your draft to see if a different plan or approach might work better.

370–71

Considering Matters of Design

- If you cite written text as evidence, be sure to set long quotations and **DOCUMENTATION** according to the style you're using.

538–41

- If your essay is lengthy, consider whether **HEADINGS** would make your analysis easier for readers to follow.

644–45

- If you're analyzing a visual text, include a copy of the image and a caption identifying it.

- If you're submitting your essay electronically, provide links to whatever text you are analyzing.

Getting Response and Revising

365–67

The following questions can help you and others study your draft with a critical eye. Make sure that anyone you ask to read and **RESPOND** to your text knows your purpose and audience.

Access Chapter 33 in the ebook for a video on revision strategies, including peer review.

- Is the beginning effective? Does it make a reader want to continue?
- Does the introduction provide an overview of your analysis? Is your thesis clear?
- Is the text described or summarized clearly and sufficiently?
- Is the analysis well organized and easy to follow? Do the parts fit together coherently? Does it read like an essay rather than a collection of separate bits of analysis?
- Does each part of the analysis relate to and support the thesis?
- Is anything confusing or in need of more explanation?
- Are all quotations accurate and correctly documented?
- Is it clear how the analysis leads to the interpretation? Is there adequate evidence to support the interpretation?
- Does the ending make clear what your analysis shows?

367–70

Then it's time to **REVISE**. Make sure your text appeals to your audience and think hard about whether it will achieve your purpose.

Editing and Proofreading

Once you've revised your draft, edit carefully:

342–44

- Is your **THESIS** clearly stated?

521–32
538–41

- Check all **QUOTATIONS**, **PARAPHRASES**, and **SUMMARIES** for accuracy and form. Be sure that each has the required **DOCUMENTATION**.

355–56

- Make sure that your analysis flows clearly from one point to the next and that you use **TRANSITIONS** to help readers move through your text.

375–76

- **PROOFREAD** your finished analysis carefully before turning it in.

Taking Stock of Your Work

Take stock of what you've written and learned by considering these questions:

- What reading strategies did you use as you analyzed your text—annotating? coding? something else? Which strategies were most helpful?

- What writing strategies did you use to analyze your text—defining? comparing? others? Which ones helped you the most?

- Did you provide enough evidence to support your analysis? Can you point to a place in your text where you did an especially good job of providing evidence?

- Did you include any visuals, and if so, what did they add? Could you have shown the same thing with words?

- What did you learn from providing feedback on your peers' work? How did that learning affect your own writing?

- What kinds of analytical writing, if any, have you done in the past? How does your current work compare?

- Was anything new to you about this kind of writing? If so, how did you adapt to the task?

- Are you pleased with your analysis? What did it teach you about the text you analyzed? If you were to write another text analysis, what would you do differently?

 Access Chapter 36 in the ebook for a video on reflecting on your writing.

If you need more help

See Chapter 31 for guidelines on **DRAFTING**, Chapter 32 for **ASSESSING YOUR OWN WRITING**, Chapter 33 for **GETTING RESPONSE AND REVISING**, and Chapter 34 for **EDITING AND PROOFREADING**. See Chapter 35 if you are required to submit your analysis in a writing **PORTFOLIO**. See Chapter 58 for help using **VISUALS**.

359–60
361–64
365–71
372–76
377–82
647–58

14 Reporting Information

Many kinds of writing report information. Newspapers report on local and world events; textbooks give information about biology, history, writing; websites provide information about products (jcrew.com), people (billieeilish .com), institutions (smithsonian.org). We write out a lot of information ourselves, from a note we post on our door saying we've gone to choir practice to a text we send telling a friend where to meet us for dinner and how to get there.

College assignments often call for reporting information as well. In a *history* class, you may be assigned to report what you've learned about the state of US relations with Japan just before the bombing of Pearl Harbor. A *biology* course may require you to report the effects of an experiment in which plants are deprived of sunlight for different periods of time. In a *nursing* class, you may have to report the changes in a patient's symptoms after the administration of a particular drug.

This chapter focuses on reports that are written to inform readers about a particular topic. Very often this kind of writing calls for some kind of research: you need to know your subject in order to report on it! When you write to report information, you are the expert. We'll begin with three examples, the first annotated to show the key features found in most reports.

RENAE TINGLING
Sleepless Nights of a University Student

In the following report, Drexel University student Renae Tingling explains how inadequate sleep can affect college students' performance. Her essay, which is documented in MLA style, originally appeared in the 33rd, an anthology of student writing published by Drexel Publishing Group.

When can we say we've had "enough" sleep? Does the amount of sleep someone gets in a night make a difference? Is getting enough sleep even worth it? According to Newton's first law of motion, a body in

Introduces topic.

motion will stay in motion unless acted upon by an opposing external force. The human body experiences this opposing force in the form of tiredness, slowly approaching as our day comes to an end. For most college students, every day is jam-packed with an infinite number of responsibilities, ranging from exam preparation and homework assignments to managing student organizations and completing chores. Many students find themselves trapped in a cycle of work and activities with rest on the back burner.

As a first-year student, I took on a list of new and exciting ventures during my first week. As the weeks progressed, the announcement of midterms marked the end of the adjustment period. I found myself adding more tasks to my to-do list than I was marking off, while time ran shorter by the day. Surrendering a portion of my sleeping hours to my work was unavoidable. Even though I felt satisfied to have completed my assignments, the lack of sleep did not go unnoticed by my body. My body's demand for compensation resulted in my waking up at some ungodly hour the following Saturday afternoon. This hadn't been common practice for me before college, making me wonder if the same could be said for other students. Is this something that most college students perpetually struggle with? If so, why? How does this kind of schedule affect their lives as students, if at all? It's best if we start by figuring out what the big deal is about sleep.

Sleep is indeed a big deal. It plays a crucial role in an individual's overall health and wellness. A good and consistent quantity and quality of sleep can help with the regulation of physiological processes (Kabrita and Hajjar-Muça 190), such as cardiovascular activity and glucose regulation (Cheng et al. 270). For students, sleep is in some ways like our very own pot of gold. It is essential for effective processing of information (Kabrita and Hajjar-Muça 190), memorization, and proper immune function (Carter et al. 315). As David Dinges, a professor of psychology and chief of the sleep and chronobiology division in the department of psychiatry at the University of Pennsylvania School of Medicine, notes:

> We know, for example, that sleep is critical for waking cognition—that is, for the ability to think clearly, to be vigilant and alert, and sustain attention. We also know that memories are consolidated during sleep, and that sleep serves a key role in emotional regulation. (qtd. in Worley 758)

So, what exactly is a good quality of sleep? Some would argue that it's almost entirely subjective. Some students find taking short and frequent naps is an effective way of getting all their hours in, while others

Offers a personal connection to the topic.

Tingling frames her thesis as questions her report will answer.

Accurate, well-researched information.

Synthesis of information from several sources.

Sleep processes explained.

couldn't disagree more. According to Dinges, for the average person, the target should be "ideally somewhere between seven to seven and a half hours" of uninterrupted sleep (qtd. in Worley 759). The National Sleep Foundation recommends that young adults get a total of seven to nine hours of sleep with no fewer than six and no more than ten. Anything below six hours and you've reached the danger zone (Suni). Sleep deficiency can have a severe and lasting impact on a student's academic performance. Poor sleep quality can also greatly impact our decision-making process (Pilcher et al.).

Ask any university student and they would probably agree that sleep is a privilege. Countless factors at play during a student's academic journey can heavily disrupt their sleep schedule. Habitual procrastination is a major cause of increased stress among university students (Sirois), which may result in health issues such as insomnia (difficulty falling and/or staying asleep). Drinking too much coffee can be a problem. A study conducted by two Turkish dieticians finds that though consumption of most caffeinated beverages had no correlation to poor quality of sleep, coffee was the exception: students with poor sleep quality consumed a notably larger amount of coffee than those with good sleep quality (Suna and Ayaz S132). Prolonged internet usage and cigarette smoking are other behavioral factors that can eat away at students' precious hours of sleep. This brings into question those factors that exist beyond the control of the student—and to determine those factors, who better to ask than the students themselves?

A total of thirty-three students participated in a survey I conducted, ranging from freshman to pre-junior year. The questionnaire collected information pertaining to participants' class level, sleep patterns, and factors that may disrupt their sleep schedule and how those factors affect them academically. Most students (eighty percent) reported sleeping for the recommended number of hours (seven to nine) either a few times or not at all. Behavioral influences, like prolonged internet usage and late-night studying for upcoming exams, were common reasons for losing sleep. As for external influences, many students reported that disruptive roommates and outside noise hindered them from sleeping. Some students also pointed out that trying to complete assignments before their fast-approaching deadlines caused heavy stress and prevented them from getting more hours of sleep. Very few placed the blame on social activities. With habitual and external factors such as these, it is understandable that low quality of sleep can lead to poor academic performance (Carter et al. 315). Consequently, many students found it difficult to be attentive and involved during lectures (eighty-seven percent), successfully complete an exam (fifty-six percent), and maintain their involvement in student organizations (sixty-five percent)

Causes of sleep difficulties outlined.

Tingling includes her own research study to give another perspective on the topic.

5

after a night of little or no sleep. Approximately half of the participants reported that they rely or have relied on medication and/or caffeinated beverages to feel alert during the day.

At this point I decided to try an experiment: for three days I would only allow myself half my normal hours of sleep to see how my mind and body would react. About halfway through my experiment, I didn't mind the thought of having a cup of coffee myself.

The author reports on a third kind of research, a self-study.

I'll admit, getting out of bed at 5:00 a.m. was a bit of a challenge, especially after sleeping for a total of four and a half hours. It wasn't by chance that by the start of the first day, I had already reached my quota of embarrassing absentminded mistakes after having pressed the wrong button on the elevator and wandered into the wrong classroom. This unusual behavior was due to the effect that lack of sleep had on my level of self-control and alertness (Pilcher et al.). This can greatly throw off a person's decision-making process—as it did mine.

By the second day, getting half a night's worth of sleep took a greater toll on me. Most of the day's lectures managed to slip right past me. Too often to count, I found myself opening eyes I hadn't even realized were closed. What little attention span I had left went to counting down the minutes until the end of each class session. Now, we can all agree that conducting an experiment like this during the exam period would not be the wisest thing to do. Knowing this, I was prepared to add this to my list of mistakes. Funnily enough, my lack of sleep did not have its way with the quiz I took that day. In that moment, the effects of my sleep deprivation seemingly vanished. It was as though my brain ensured that I was able to place all my efforts into not failing math. Sadly, those effects came back sometime afterward and with a vengeance. I became so demotivated to do just about anything afterward that even having dinner with friends seemed like too much. I was completely against the idea of preparing for upcoming lectures and exams and used how tired I felt as an excuse. This response drives home the notion that sleep deprivation can have serious psychological impacts and weaken our ability to concentrate on academic material (Kabrita and Hajjar-Muça 190).

She clearly describes the process of sleep deprivation as she experienced it.

Oddly enough, I felt a lot less tired on the third day. Though I still felt somewhat tired, it was as if my body was getting used to the lack of sleep. At the end of the day my experiment came to a close, allowing me a well-deserved night's rest. What took me by surprise was how exhausted I felt the following morning after a full eight hours of rest. I initially expected to feel rested, having given myself the chance to get the recommended amount of sleep. But I felt as I had on the first morning of the experiment, even though I had double the amount of sleep. Thankfully, a few days of seven to eight hours of sleep was enough to get me back on track. I was able to focus on discussions during lectures and was more motivated to attend club meetings and study with friends for whatever the next exam would be. It was surprising to discover just how greatly each day was affected by the amount of sleep I got several nights before. It wasn't too hard for me to imagine the damaging effects that poor sleep habits would have over time.

Sleep is a beautiful thing; my experiment is a testament to this. Many of us see it as the easiest and most convenient thing to sacrifice on our journey to academic success. How ironic is it that, as we continue to undermine its significance, sleep can potentially determine whether we achieve that success. It should be mentioned that students often find themselves in situations where valuable hours of sleep are stolen from them by circumstances beyond their control. Whether deliberate or unintentional, lost sleep can take a lot more from us than we bargained for. If I had to summarize what I took from my research, it would be that we as students have fallen for the misconception that less sleep is the only way to stay on top of everything. As a result, we tend to make everything a priority except ourselves. We place getting those extra hours of studying above resting the brain that has to take the exam the following day. At the end of the day, the benefits of a good night's rest are limitless, so ask yourself this: Do I get enough sleep?

Conclusion: A summary of the research and its implication for Tingling's audience, college students.

Works Cited

Carter, Briana, et al. "An Analysis of the Sleep Quality of Undergraduate Students." *College Student Journal*, vol. 50, no. 3, 2017, pp. 315–22. *Gale Academic Onefile*, go.galegroup.com.

Cheng, Shu Hui, et al. "A Study on the Sleep Quality of Incoming University Students." *Psychiatry Research*, vol. 197, Feb. 2012, pp. 270–74.

Kabrita, Colette S., and Theresa A. Hajjar-Muça. "Sex-Specific Sleep Patterns among University Students in Lebanon: Impact on Depression and Academic Performance." *Nature and Science of Sleep*, vol. 8, 2016, pp. 189–96. *DovePress*, https://doi.org/10.2147/NSS.S104383.

Pilcher, June J., et al. "Interactions between Sleep Habits and Self-Control." *Frontiers in Human Neuroscience*, vol. 9, 11 May 2015, www.frontiersin.org/articles/10.3389/fnhum.2015.00284/full.

Sirois, F. M., et al. "Is Procrastination Related to Sleep Quality? Testing an Application of the Procrastination–Health Model." *Cogent Psychology*, vol. 2, 2015. *Taylor and Francis Online*, https://doi.org/10.1080/23311908.2015.1074776.

Suna, G., and A. Ayaz. "Relationship between Caffeinated Beverages and Sleep Quality in University Students." *Clinical Nutrition*, vol. 37, Sept. 2018, pp. S131–132. *ScienceDirect*, https://doi .org/10.1016/j.clnu.2018.06.1492. Supplement 1.

Suni, Eric. "How Much Sleep Do We Really Need?" *SleepFoundation .org*, 10 Mar. 2021, www.sleepfoundation.org/how-sleep-works /how-much-sleep-do-we-really-need.

Worley, Susan L. "The Extraordinary Importance of Sleep: The Detrimental Effects of Inadequate Sleep on Health and Public Safety Drive an Explosion of Sleep Research." *Pharmacy and Therapeutics: A Peer-Reviewed Journal for Managed Care and Hospital Formulary Management*, vol. 43, no. 12, 2018, pp. 758–63. *PubMed Central,* pubmed.ncbi.nlm.nih.gov/30559589.

Tingling's report draws on published research, her own survey research, and informal research using personal experience to provide a multifaceted view of the effects of inadequate sleep on college students' performance.

FRANKIE SCHEMBRI
Edible Magic

In the following report, written for a first-year writing class at Massachusetts Institute of Technology, Frankie Schembri explains the science behind how popcorn pops. Originally published in Angles 2016: Selected Essays from Introductory Writing Subjects at MIT, *this report is documented in APA style.*

Life is studded with little pockets of magic. These are the moments with mysterious emergent qualities, when the whole is greater than the sum of the parts, when one plus one somehow equals three. Such magic is even better when it comes in edible form.

When an unassuming little kernel of corn meets hot oil, it is transformed. It is elevated with an unmistakable "pop!" into a fluffy cloud of goodness ready to be dressed with butter, caramel, or whatever your heart desires.

This magic is called popcorn.

Popcorn exploded in popularity in the early 20th century but surprisingly only made it into movie theaters with the advent of sound films, or "talkies," in 1927. Silent films catered to a smaller, more exclusive clientele and owners worried that the sound of the snack being munched would detract from the experience (Geiling, 2013).

By the 1940s, popcorn had become an inextricable part of going ⁵ to the movies, and from then on, over half of the popcorn consumed yearly in America was eaten at movie theaters (Geiling, 2013). Fast-forward some 70 years and the relationship remains unbreakable. Step into any movie theater lobby across America and your senses are bombarded with the unmistakable scent of salt and butter.

Popcorn snuck into the American household in the 1960s with Jiffy Pop, a self-contained stovetop popper including kernels, oil, and even the pan, and it flourished with the popularity of microwave ovens in the 1970s (Smith, 1999, p. 124). Popcorn cultivated an important relationship with microwaves in the latter half of the 20th century, important enough that popcorn was eventually given the rare honor of its own designated microwave button (Smith, 1999, p. 127).

"But how?" you might ask. How do these ordinary kernels magically spring to life with a little heat and oil, enchanting kids and grown-ups alike?

Like most acts of magic, popcorn's "pop" can be understood with a little science.

Botanically speaking, popcorn is a type of maize, the only domesticated subgroup in the genus *Zea*, a group of plants in the grass family. The different types of maize are classified based on their kernel's size, shape, and composition (Smith, 1999, p. 6).

Corn kernels have three main structural components. First, there ¹⁰ is the germ (from the Latin *germen*, meaning seed or sprout), a small pocket of genetic material that is essentially a baby corn plant waiting to grow. The germ is surrounded by the endosperm (the Greek *endon*, within, and *sperma*, seed), a larger parcel of water mixed with soft and hard starch granules that make up most of the kernel's weight and would provide food for the corn plant if it were to sprout. Finally, the germ-endosperm complex is surrounded by the pericarp (from the Greek *peri*, around, and *karpos*, fruit), the hard shell that winds up stuck between your molars after you enjoy a bag of popcorn (Ghose, 2015).

Popcorn kernels are unique in that they are relatively small, they have endosperms containing a larger number of hard starch granules, and their pericarps are hard and impermeable, essentially sealing off the contents of the kernel from the outside environment. These characteristics have endowed popcorn kernels with the ability to pop (Ghose, 2015).

In an attempt to better understand the physics of popcorn, aeronautical engineer Emmanuel Virot and physicist Alexandre Ponomarenko, who seem to have also fallen under popcorn's spell (judging by the language of their published report), experimented with the temperature at which a kernel pops. As Virot and Ponomarenko (2015) explained, when heat is applied to the kernels via hot oil on a stovetop or in a microwave, the temperature of the kernels begins to rise accordingly. Most affected by this increase in heat is the water stored between the starch granules in the endosperm. Much like a bubbling pot of water brought to a boil, the water in the kernel begins to change from liquid into gas.

While liquid water is content to stay put, gaseous water in the form of steam craves space to move, but the hard shell of the pericarp effectively keeps the water trapped inside the kernel. As a result, the kernel acts like a tiny steamer and the starch granules inside are cooked into a gooey mass. As the mass gets hotter and hotter, the steam presses harder and harder on the inside surface of the kernel's shell like the hands of a million tiny creatures trapped inside a bubble (Virot & Ponomarenko, 2015).

The tension is palpable. The kernel begins to shake with anticipation. It rocks back and forth, back and forth, faster and faster, and faster still. Then finally . . . pop! The bubble bursts, the lid flies off the pot, and fireworks explode as the hard shell of the pericarp cracks and the steam breaks free from its kernel prison. The starchy goop also bubbles out into the world, where it meets cold, fresh air and rapidly hardens into spongy cloudlike shapes. Just like that, in just one-fifteenth of a second, a new piece of popcorn is born (Virot & Ponomarenko, 2015).

Virot and Ponomarenko (2015) determined that the temperature at which kernels typically pop is 180 °C. The pair also determined that the resulting popped kernel can be up to 40 times its un-popped volume, although usually the kernel's radius merely doubles.

But what propels the kernel, with what Virot and Ponomarenko (2015) called "all the grace of a seasoned gymnast," into the air as it pops? When the pericarp fractures, it does so in only one place first, giving some of the steam and starchy goop a head start on escaping. The starch released first extends to create a leg of sorts, off of which the rest of the kernel springboards, launching it somersaulting into the air like an Olympic gymnast. Popcorn jumps typically only reach a height of a few centimeters, but still manage to create endless entertainment for the hungry viewer.

Where does the "pop" sound come from? Arguably the most important part of the whole experience, popcorn's characteristic noise is not, contrary to popular belief, the sound of the kernel's shell breaking open. The popping sound is created by the release of trapped water vapor resonating in the kernel, similar to how, when removed, a champagne cork makes a popping sound that resonates in the glass bottle (Virot & Ponomarenko, 2015).

Making popcorn hardly seems like an opportunity to learn about physics, but the kernels' unique transformation illustrates some principles of thermodynamics, biomechanics, and acoustics, as the properties of different materials dictate how they respond to pressure and heat.

Life is studded with little pockets of magic. From the enticing smell during a night at the movies to the rising staccato sound of a bag coming to life in your microwave, popcorn is magic-meets-science in its most delicious form. And it always leaves you hungry for more.

References

Geiling, N. (2013, October 3). Why do we eat popcorn at the movies? *Smithsonian.* https://www.smithsonianmag.com/arts-culture/why-do-we-eat-popcorn-at-the-movies-475063/

Ghose, T. (2015, February 10). *The secret acrobatics of popcorn revealed.* Live Science. https://www.livescience.com/49768-mechanics-of-popcorn.html

Smith, A. (1999). *Popped culture: A social history of popcorn in America.* University of South Carolina Press.

Virot, E., & Ponomarenko, A. (2015). Popcorn: Critical temperature, jump and sound. *Journal of the Royal Society Interface, 12*(104). https://doi.org/10.1098/rsif.2014.1247

Schembri introduces her subject by placing it in a cultural context of the movies, Jiffy Pop, and microwave popcorn. She then distinguishes popcorn from other varieties of corn or maize and goes on to describe what happens when popcorn kernels are heated, pop, and fly into the air. To explore her subject from these various perspectives, she draws on scientific, historical, and popular sources.

MICHAELEEN DOUCLEFF

You Don't Need Words to Calm a Grumpy Kid.
Parents around the World Use a Magic Touch.

Michaeleen Doucleff is a correspondent for National Public Radio's Science Desk and the author of the book Hunt, Gather, Parent: What Ancient Cultures Can Teach Us about the Lost Art of Raising Happy, Helpful Little Humans. *A version of the following essay appeared on the NPR website.*

When it comes to settling down young children, parenting advice focuses mostly on one tool: What to say.

If the toddler starts to have a tantrum, say *this*. If a child can't go to sleep, say *that*. And if you wind up yelling in the process, well, there's even a script for how to apologize.

But all around the world, many parents turn to *another* tool to soothe a crying child and settle them to slumber. And it's totally silent.

Instead of talking, many parents touch their child. But it's not just any type of touch. Oh no! This touch occurs at a particular speed and with a particular pressure.

After decades of research, neuroscientists are beginning to under- 5 stand how our skin senses this specific type of touch and how that sensation lights up regions of the brain to alter our emotions.

Turns out, our skin contains nerves especially equipped to detect a gentle, stroking caress. And these nerves are part of a system inside our skin devoted to triggering the warm, calm and peaceful feeling you have when you're with people who love you.

How to Give *Piojito*

In Korea, parents call this type of touch *yakson*. In Taiwan, they say 秀秀 (xiù xiù). In India: "we have different languages in different parts of the country, but in Delhi, it's called *malish*," says Dr. Sarika Chaturvedi, who studies infant massage practices at Dr. D. Y. Patil Vidyapeeth College in Pune. "This type of touch is so ingrained in our culture. It's all about avoiding frustrations in the child and enhancing the pleasurable connection."

But in Latin America, parents may just have the best name of all: *Piojitos*, which literally means "little lice."

"If I wanted to go to sleep as a child, I would go cuddle with my

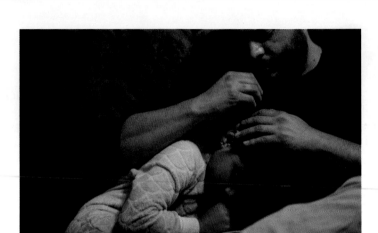

Jose Grajeda and daughter, Victoria. "If I wanted to go to sleep as a child, I would go cuddle with my mom and she would give me *piojito*," he says—Spanish for "little lice."

mom and she would give me *piojito*," says Joe Grajeda, age 40, who was born in northern Mexico and now lives in Alpine, Texas, with his three young children (Joe owns a coffee shop in Alpine and is a good friend of mine).

"Now I love giving my children *piojito*," Grajeda says, smiling 10 brightly. "My sons like to sit there and just kind of enjoy the moment. Victoria—my daughter—loves it when she's ready to go to sleep."

With *piojito* and other types of soothing caresses, the key is not to go too fast or too slow. And don't press too deeply. "You scratch someone's back, or their head, with the tip of your fingers. And you do it very lightly and softly," Grajeda explains. "You want to make the skin kind of crawl a little bit." The late Peruvian linguist Martha Hildebrandt described *piojito* as "gently scratching the scalp of a child as if he were being relieved of the itching of imaginary lice"—hence the name. ("Martha Hildebrandt").

In other words, you want to give the child a bit of the goosebumps. "We call it chicken skin in Mexico," Grajeda says, chuckling. "I love *piojito*. I ask my mom now—and my kids—to give me *piojito* now. I think it's my language of love."

How a Gentle Caress Affects the Nerves

When you give a child *piojito*, the gentle stroking turns on special nerves, in the hairy parts of our skin, called C-tactile fibers. So yes, that includes your head, back and arms.

These nerves are tuned to detect a specific speed of caressing, says Ishmail Abdus-Saboor, a neurobiologist at Columbia University. "If you rush across the skin surface too quickly, a person may actually perceive the touch as aversive," he says.

All mammals have these special neurons. And all mammalian par- [15] ents use a stroking touch or licking with their young offspring, Abdus-Saboor says. "There's evidence these neurons also respond to maybe even warmth as well," he explains. "So these neurons have the ability to detect social cues between two mammals as they caress, touch and embrace one another, such as a mother with her offspring."

Of course, human parents have been doing this type of touching "forever," Abdus-Saboor says. "This rubbing and stroking is something that we do almost innately with children. And I think it's because our system is wired to tap into this network [in the brain] that provides soothing and relief."

For some kids with autism spectrum disorder, this type of touch might not feel good, Abdus-Saboor notes, and may even feel bad. "A cardinal symptom of autism is hypersensitivity to sensory stimuli, like auditory and tactile stimuli," he says. "The relationship between touch and reward can be greatly altered."

Back in February [2023], Abdus-Saboor and his colleagues published a landmark paper in the journal *Cell* showing how activation of these special neurons, in mice, lights up the dopamine pathway in their brains (Elias et al.). This pathway motivates animals to seek out the touch again—to seek out togetherness, cuddles or grooming.

"These nerves basically have a dedicated, neuronal highway to the brains' reward centers," Abdus-Saboor says. "So why would you wire a system like this? Well, you know, turning on these neurons is so impor- tant for social encounters, relationships, bonding, mating, soothing, calming and stress relief."

In people, activating C-tactile fibers not only feels good (Pawling et [20] al.), it reduces the perception of pain in adults and babies and lowers their heart beat rate, studies have found (Gursul et al.). There's evidence that activation of these nerves may also trigger the release of naturally occurring opioids in people's brains, such as endorphins.

"These endorphins relax you and cause you to feel at peace with the world," says psychologist Robin Dunbar at Oxford University. And they help to bond or connect you to the parent who's caressing you. "They make you feel very trusting with the individuals doing the gentle stroking."

Neuroscientist Helena Wasling isn't convinced by the studies linking caressing to endorphins. But she thinks, rather, this type of touch is criti- cal for helping children feel safe and as if their bodily needs are met.

"Being touched is just a basic need, like having dinner when you are hungry. You need to have this touch in order for you to reach a good, steady state in your body. You need it so you can feel safe enough to go out and explore the world," says Wasling, who has studied the neuroscience of touch for more than a decade and now is a physiotherapist at Sahlgrenska University Hospital in Gothenburg, Sweden.

The Dawn of the Anti-touch Era

During the end of the 19th century, many European pediatricians actually advised parents *not* to touch their children because they said it would weaken them and make them dependent. This idea hit a fever pitch in the 1920s when the psychologist John B. Watson wrote a parenting book, "even though he knew basically nothing about parenting," as Wasling points out. In the book, Watson advises mothers to stay away, physically, from children: "He describes how you could give them a pat on the head if they did something really special, but when you greet them in the morning, you could give them a handshake," Wasling says.

Watson thought that lovingly caressing children—as parents all 25 over the world have done for thousands of years—would prevent them from becoming independent, self-sufficient adults. By touching, parents would be "building up a human being totally unable to cope with the world it must later live in" (44).

Watson believed that by not touching young children and toddlers, parents teach them to be independent at an early age, Wasling explains.

"But then it turns out that the opposite is actually true," Wasling says. "Children who get a lot of touch, support and closeness from their parents are actually the ones that dare to go out and explore, as they grow up, because they have a basic safety that they can rely on. They have a solid foundation."

It Works on Grown-Ups Too

And of course, *piojito* and all types of gentle caresses can soothe and relax adults, just as much as they do children, says Dunbar.

"We receive this type of touch when we're sitting in the chair at the hairdressers. And people come out of the hairdressers humming and feeling like they're on top of the world because of their new hair setting," Dunbar says, laughing. "But I tell them cheekily, 'It's not your new hair setting that makes you feel that way. It's the endorphins released in your brain while your hairdresser massaged your scalp for an hour.'"

Works Cited

Abdus-Saboor, Ishmail. Interview with the author. 29 Sept. 2023.

Chaturvedi, Sarika. Interview with the author. 3 Oct. 2023.

Dunbar, Robin. Interview with the author. 29 Sept. 2023.

Elias, Leah J., et al. "Touch Neurons Underlying Dopaminergic Pleasurable Touch and Sexual Receptivity." *Cell*, vol. 186, no. 3, 23 Jan. 2023, pp. 577–90, https://doi.org/10.1016/j .cell.2022.12.034.

Grajeda, Joe. Interview with the author. 3 Oct. 2023.

Gursul, Deniz, et al. "Stroking Modulates Noxious-Evoked Brain Activity in Human Infants." *Current Biology*, vol. 28, no. 24, 17 Dec. 2018, https://doi.org/10.1016/j.cub.2018.11.014.

"Martha Hildebrandt: El Significado de 'Hacer Piojito.'" *El Comercio* [Lima], 19 Aug. 2014, elcomercio.pe/opinion/habla-culta/martha -hildebrandt-significado-piojito-353837-noticia/?ref=ecr.

Pawling, Ralph, et al. "C-tactile Afferent Stimulating Touch Carries a Positive Affective Value." *PLOS ONE*, vol. 12, no. 3, 10 Mar. 2017, https://doi.org/10.1371/journal.pone.0173457.

Wasling, Helena. Interview with the author. 3 Oct. 2023.

Watson, John B. *Psychological Care of Infant and Child.* W. W. Norton, 1928.

Doucleff reports on scientific research that confirms what parents across cultures have known for years: that a certain kind of gentle, rhythmic touch calms children, decreases their sense of pain, and helps them bond with their parents. Using examples of soothing touch across cultures, along with neurobiological explanations of how our bodies respond to touch, Doucleff explores the significance of caresses and cuddles for children and adults alike.

Key Features / Reports

A tightly focused topic. The goal of this kind of writing is to inform readers about something without digressing—and without, in general, bringing in the writer's own opinions. All three examples focus on a particular topic—sleep deprivation, popping popcorn, and parental touch—and present information about the topics evenhandedly.

Accurate, well-researched information. Reports usually require research. The kind of research depends on the topic. Sometimes internet research will suffice, though reports done for college courses may require library research to locate scholarly sources—Tingling, for example, uses various sources available through her university library's databases, and Schembri uses a mix of scholarly and popular sources. Other topics may require or benefit from field research—interviews, observations, surveys, and so on. In addition to doing library and online research, for example, Doucleff interviewed a parent and several scientists, and Tingling conducted a survey of students.

A synthesis of ideas.   Reports seldom rely on a single source of information. Rather, they draw on several sources, making connections among the facts and ideas found in them. For example, Schembri combines information from a magazine article and a book to provide a brief history of the growth of popcorn's popularity in the United States. Doucleff integrates interview quotes, scientific research, cross-cultural examples, and historical comparisons to explain how a specific type of touch supports children's emotional, social, and physical well-being.

Various writing strategies.   Presenting information usually requires various organizing patterns—defining, comparing, classifying, explaining processes, analyzing causes and effects, and so on. Schembri explains the process governing popcorn popping and classifies different kinds of maize. Doucleff describes the speed and pressure required for giving "*piojito*" and other kinds of soothing touch, and Tingling traces the effects of inadequate sleep on college students' performance.

Clear definitions.   Reports need to provide clear definitions of any key terms that their audience may not know. Schembri defines several components of corn kernels, including the germ, endosperm, and pericarp. Tingling includes a definition of "waking cognition."

Appropriate design.   Reports often combine paragraphs with information presented in lists, tables, diagrams, and other illustrations. When you're presenting information, you need to think carefully about how to design it—numerical data, for instance, can be easier to understand and remember in a table than in a paragraph. Often a photograph can bring a subject to life, as does the photo on page 156, which accompanies Doucleff's article. Online reports offer the possibility of video and audio clips as well as links to source materials and more detailed information.

A GUIDE TO WRITING REPORTS

Choosing a Topic

Whether you get to choose your topic or are working with an assigned one, see if you can approach the topic from an angle that interests you.

If you get to choose. What interests you? What do you wish you knew more about? The possible topics for informational reports are limitless, but the topics that you're most likely to write well on are those that engage you. They may be academic in nature or reflect your personal interests or both. If you're not sure where to begin, here are some places to start:

- an intriguing technology: driverless cars, machine learning, tooth whiteners
- sports: soccer, snowboarding, ultimate Frisbee, slacklining.
- an important world event: the Israel-Hamas war, the fall of Rome, the COVID-19 pandemic
- a historical period: the African diaspora, the Middle Ages, the Ming dynasty, the Great Depression
- a common object: hoodies, gel pens, mascara, Post-it notes, PopSockets
- a significant environmental issue: melting Arctic ice, deer overpopulation, mercury and the fish supply
- the arts: rap, outsider art, the Crystal Bridges Museum of American Art, Savion Glover, Mary Cassatt

LIST a few possibilities, and then choose one that you'd like to know more about—and that your audience might find interesting, too. You might start out by phrasing your topic as a question that your research will attempt to answer. For example:

330

How is *ChatGPT* different from *Claude AI*?

How was the Great Pyramid constructed?

What kind of training do football referees receive?

If your topic is assigned. If your assignment is broad—"Explain some aspect of the US government"—try focusing on a more limited topic within the larger topic: federalism, majority rule, political parties, states' rights. Even if an assignment seems to offer little flexibility—"Explain the physics of roller coasters"—your task is to decide how to research the topic, and sometimes even narrow topics can be shaped to fit your own interests and those of your audience.

Considering the Rhetorical Situation

73–74 ■ **PURPOSE**   Why are you presenting this information? To teach readers about the subject? To demonstrate your research and writing skills? For some other reason?

75–78 ■ **AUDIENCE**   Who will read this report? What do they already know about the topic? What background information do they need in order to understand it? Will you need to define any terms? What do they want or need to know about the topic? Why should they care about it? How can you attract their interest?

85–87 ■ **STANCE**   What is your own attitude toward your subject? What interests you most about it? What about it seems important?

88–90 ■ **MEDIA/DESIGN**   What medium are you using? What is the best way to present the information? Will it all be in paragraph form, or is there information that is best presented as a chart, table, or infographic? Do you need headings? Would diagrams, photographs, or other illustrations help you explain the information?

Generating Ideas and Text

Thoughtfully written reports share certain features that make them useful and interesting to readers. Remember that your goal is to present information clearly and accurately. Start by exploring your topic.

Explore what you already know about your topic. Write out whatever you know or want to know about your topic, perhaps by **FREEWRITING**, 329 **LISTING**, or **CLUSTERING**. Why are you interested in this topic? What 330
332

questions do you have about it? Such questions can help you decide what you'd like to focus on and how you need to direct your research efforts.

Narrow your topic. To write a good report, you need to narrow your focus—and to narrow your focus, you need to know a fair amount about your subject. If you are assigned to write on a subject like biodiversity, for example, you need to know what it is, what the key issues are, and so on. If you do, you can simply list or brainstorm possibilities, choose one, and start your research. If you don't know much about the subject, though, you need to do some research to discover focused, workable topics. This research may shape your thinking and change your focus. Start with **SOURCES** that can give you a general sense of the subject, such as a *Wikipedia* entry, a magazine article, a website, perhaps an interview with an expert. Your goal at this point is simply to find out what issues your topic might include and then to focus your efforts on an aspect of the topic you will be able to cover.

Access the ebook for a video on narrowing your topic.

482–503

Come up with a tentative thesis. Once you narrow your topic, write out a statement that explains what you plan to report or explain. A strong **THESIS** is potentially interesting (to you and your readers) and limits your topic enough to make it manageable. Schembri phrases her thesis as a question: "How do these ordinary kernels magically spring to life with a little heat and oil?" Doucleff describes the "silent" tool that parents across cultures have used for generations but that scientists are just now beginning to understand and then offers this thesis: "Turns out, our skin contains nerves especially equipped to detect a gentle, stroking caress. And these nerves are part of a system inside our skin devoted to triggering the warm, calm, and peaceful feeling you have when you're with people who love you." At this point, however, you need only a tentative thesis that will help focus any research you do.

342–44

Access Chapter 30 in the ebook for a video on thesis statements in reports.

Do any necessary research, and revise your thesis. To focus your research efforts, **OUTLINE** the aspects of your topic that you expect to discuss. Identify any aspects that require additional research, and develop a research plan. Expect to revise your outline as you do your research, since more information will be available for some aspects of your topic than others, some may prove irrelevant to your topic, and some may turn out to be more than you need. You'll need to revisit your tentative thesis once you've done any research, to finalize your statement.

335–37

Access Chapter 30 in the ebook for a video on organizing and synthesizing ideas.

Ways of Organizing a Report

Reports can be organized in various ways. Here are three common organizational structures:

Reports on topics that are unfamiliar to readers

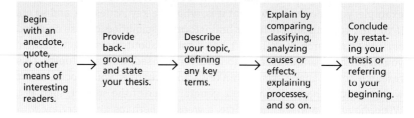

Begin with an anecdote, quote, or other means of interesting readers. → Provide background, and state your thesis. → Describe your topic, defining any key terms. → Explain by comparing, classifying, analyzing causes or effects, explaining processes, and so on. → Conclude by restating your thesis or referring to your beginning.

Reports on events or procedures

Introduce the topic; provide any necessary background information; state your thesis. → Narrate the first event or procedure. ↓ Narrate the second event or procedure. ↓ Narrate the third event or procedure. ↓ Repeat as necessary. → Conclude by telling the outcome of the event or the procedure, or stating its implications.

Reports that compare and contrast

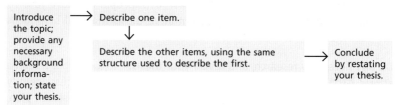

Introduce the topic; provide any necessary background information; state your thesis. → Describe one item. ↓ Describe the other items, using the same structure used to describe the first. → Conclude by restating your thesis.

Many reports use a combination of organizational structures; don't be afraid to use whatever method of organization best suits your material and your purpose.

More Ways to Approach a Report

Create an explainer. Instead of writing a conventional essay, write an explainer—a kind of report that uses a question-and-answer structure to explain a topic in a conversational way, usually focusing on what readers unfamiliar with the topic would want to know most. An explainer version of Doucleff's article, for example, might be organized around questions like these: "What's the big deal about a simple touch?" "What kind of touch works best?" "Do all kids respond the same way?" For examples of explainers, you can search "explainer" on the *New York Times* or the *Guardian* websites.

Create a comic or infographic. Often the best way to explain something is to use a combination of words and pictures. You might draw a series of comics panels to explain the various parts of something or show how your topic changes over time, or you could create an infographic to help you simplify a complicated subject using words, images, charts, and graphs.

Write a narrative. Sometimes the best way to explain a topic is to tell a story about it: how it works, how it came about, what made it possible. You might discuss a scientific discovery by telling the story of how the scientists involved figured it out, or report on the debates leading up to an important piece of legislation, or explain how engineers made an invention work.

Remix. After you've written a draft of your report, you might **REMIX** it: create a fact sheet that distills the key information into bite-size chunks, make a series of *TikTok* videos to explain important findings, or share the report content as a webinar. If your report focuses on historical events or geographical information, you could create an interactive timeline or map to help your audience explore significant dates or places.

▲ 280–90

Access Chapter 23 in the ebook for a video on creating a remix.

Writing Out a Draft

Once you have generated ideas and thought about how you want to organize your report, it's time to start **DRAFTING**. Do this quickly—try to write a complete draft in one sitting, concentrating on getting the report on paper or screen and on putting in as much detail as you can.

358–60

Writing that reports information often calls for certain writing strategies. The report on popcorn, for example, **EXPLAINS THE PROCESS**

◆ 452–56

of popping, whereas the report on touch describes the psychological and physiological benefits of receiving gentle caresses. When you're reporting on a topic your readers aren't familiar with, you may wish to **COMPARE** it with something more familiar; you can find useful advice on these and other writing strategies in Part 6 of this book.

422–28 ◆

Draft a BEGINNING. Essays that report information often need to begin in a way that will get your audience interested in the topic. Here are a few ways of beginning:

340–48 ⁛

- *Simply state your thesis.* Opening with a thesis works well when you can assume your readers have enough familiarity with your topic that you don't need to give much detailed background information.

- *Begin by providing a context for your report.* Tingling starts her report on sleep deprivation by describing college students' busy lives, which often cause them to get inadequate sleep.

- *Start with something that will provoke readers' interest.* Doucleff's report opens with an intriguing idea: that there's an effective alternative to the traditional parenting advice for soothing a fussy or restless child.

- *Begin with an illustrative example.* Schembri evokes the childhood wonder of popping corn before exploring its history and physics.

Draft an ENDING. Think about what you want your readers to read last. An effective ending leaves them thinking about your topic.

348–52 ⁛

- *Summarize your main points.* This is a practical way to end when you've presented several key points you want readers to remember. Tingling ends this way, summarizing the results of her research.

- *Point out the implications of your report.* Tingling ends by noting that lost sleep can have greater effects than simply sleepiness: it "can take a lot more from us than we bargained for."

- *Frame your report by referring to its introduction.* Schembri returns to her introductory evocation of popcorn as "little pockets of magic," and Doucleff ends by pointing out that the same technique she refers to in her opening can help soothe adults, too.

- *Tell what happened.* If you are reporting on an event, you could conclude by telling how it turns out.

Access Chapter 30 in the ebook for a video on introductions and conclusions.

Come up with a title. You'll want a title that tells readers something about your subject—and makes them want to know more. Tingling's title,

"Sleepless Nights of a University Student," clearly indicates what's to come in her report. Doucleff suggests that her essay will reveal "a magic touch" for helping children settle down. See the chapter on **ORGANIZING YOUR WRITING AND GUIDING YOUR READERS** for tips on coming up with titles that are informative and enticing enough to make readers wish to read on.

340–57

Considering Matters of Design

You'll probably write the main text of your report in paragraph form, but think about what kind of information you're presenting and how you can design and format it to make it as easy as possible for your readers to understand. You might ask yourself these questions:

- What is an appropriate **FONT**? A font like Times New Roman that is easy to read in print? A font like Arial or Verdana that is visually appealing on-screen? Something else?

642–43

- Would it help your readers if you divided your report into shorter sections and added **HEADINGS**?

644–45

- Is there any information that would be easier to follow in a **LIST**?

643–44

- Could any of your information be summarized in a **TABLE** or **FIGURE**?

650

- Do you have any data that readers would more easily understand in the form of a bar **GRAPH**, line graph, or pie chart?

650

- Would **ILLUSTRATIONS** (diagrams, photos, drawings, and so on), video or audio clips, or links help you explain anything in your report?

648–54

Getting Response and Revising

The following questions can help you study your draft with a critical eye. **GETTING RESPONSE** from others is always helpful, and these questions can guide their reading, too. Make sure they know your purpose and audience.

366–67

- Do the title and opening sentences get readers' interest? If not, how might they do so?
- What information does this text provide, and for what purpose?
- Does the introduction explain why this information is being presented? Does it place the topic in a larger context?
- Are all key terms defined that need to be?

Access Chapter 33 in the ebook for a video on revision strategies, including peer review.

- Do you have any questions? Where might more explanation or an example help you understand something better?

- Is any information presented visually, with a chart, graph, table, drawing, or photograph? If so, is it clear how the illustration relates to the written text? Is there any text that would be more easily understood if it were presented visually?

- Is any information presented through digital media, such as hyperlinks, video clips, or audio files? If so, is the relation of these elements to the written text made clear? Would any aspect of the report be clearer if presented using such elements?

- Does the organization help make sense of the information? Does the text include description, comparison, or any other writing strategies? Does the topic or rhetorical situation call for any particular strategies that should be added?

529–32 ●
- If the report cites any sources, are they quoted, paraphrased, or summarized effectively (and with appropriate documentation)? Is information from sources introduced with **SIGNAL PHRASES**?

- Does the report end in a satisfying way? What are readers left thinking?

These questions should identify aspects of your report you need to work 367–70 on. When it's time to **REVISE**, make sure your report appeals to your audience and achieves your purpose as successfully as possible. If you have 370–71 time and want to explore alternatives, you might try **REWRITING** your draft to see if a different plan or approach might work better.

Editing and Proofreading

372–75 Once you've revised your draft, follow these guidelines for **EDITING** a report:

- Check your use of key terms. Repeating key words is acceptable in reports; using synonyms for unfamiliar words may confuse readers, while the repetition of key words or the use of clearly identified HB-25–31 ★ **PRONOUNS** for them can be genuinely helpful.

355–56 - Check to be sure you have **TRANSITIONS** where you need them.

644–45 ● - If you have included **HEADINGS**, make sure they're parallel in structure and consistent in design.

648–54 ● - Make sure that any photos or other **VISUALS** have captions, that charts and graphs have headings—and that all are referred to in the main text. Use white space as necessary to separate sections of your report and to highlight graphic elements.

- Check any **DOCUMENTATION** to see that it follows the appropriate style.

● 538–41

- **PROOFREAD** and spell-check your report carefully.

⋰ 375–76

Taking Stock of Your Work

Take stock of what you've written by considering these questions:

Access Chapter 36 in the ebook for a video on reflecting on your writing.

- How well did you convey the information? Is it complete enough for your audience's needs?

- What writing strategies (for example, defining, comparing, classifying) did you rely on, and how did they help you achieve your purpose?

- What element of your rhetorical situation (purpose, audience, genre, stance, media/design) was the easiest to figure out for this writing project? What element was the hardest to figure out? Why?

- How did you go about researching the information for this piece?

- How did you go about drafting this piece? For example, did you write out an outline or plan? Do something else? How could you make the drafting process more productive in the future?

- How well did you synthesize information from your sources? Can you point to a specific place in your text where you did an especially good job of making connections among the facts and ideas in your sources?

- Did you use tables, graphs, diagrams, photographs, illustrations, or other graphics? If so, what did they add to the piece? If not, can you think of such elements you might have used?

- What did you do to keep yourself engaged with your writing task? If you weren't engaged, how could you improve in the future?

- What did you learn about yourself as a writer through your work on this project? How can you apply that learning to future writing tasks?

If you need more help

See Chapter 35 if you are required to submit your report in a writing **PORTFOLIO**. See also Chapter 20 on **PROFILES**, a report based on firsthand research.

⋰ 377–82
▲ 246–56

15 Arguing a Position

Everything we say or do presents some kind of argument, takes some kind of position. Often we take overt positions: "Everyone in the United States is entitled to affordable health care." "The university needs to offer more language courses." "Photoshopped images should carry disclosure notices." But arguments can be less direct and specific as well—for example, empty chairs that honor fallen veterans and COVID-19 victims or a yellow smiley face, which might be said to argue for a good day.

Access Chapter 1 in the ebook for a video on understanding academic argument.

In college course work, you are constantly called on to argue positions: in an *English* class, you may argue for a certain interpretation of a poem; in a *business* course, you may argue for the merits of a flat tax; in a *linguistics* class, you may argue that English is now a global language. All those positions are arguable—people of goodwill can agree or disagree with them and present reasons and evidence to support their positions.

This chapter provides guidelines for writing an essay that argues a position. We'll begin with three examples, the first one annotated to point out key features of this kind of writing.

BEN WILDAVSKY

Let's Stop Pretending College Degrees Don't Matter

Ben Wildavsky is the author of The Career Arts: Making the Most of College, Credentials, and Connections. *A version of this opinion piece originally appeared in the* New York Times.

Wildavsky provides context for the argument.

It would be easy to believe, from scanning the headlines, that a college degree is becoming increasingly irrelevant in a fast-evolving job market.

Fourteen states, including 10 in the past year alone, have dropped degree requirements for many state jobs (Whissemore; Guber and Wolfson). The trend is gathering steam at many high-profile businesses, notably tech firms like IBM and Accenture (Lohr). All this comes as college enrollment has dropped, with an assist from a tight job market and worries about student debt (Whitford).

In a world marked by continued racial disparities in employment and economic well-being (Bowdler and Harris), there is a growing outcry that expensive college degrees represent a barrier rather than a steppingstone. The argument goes: Many talented people, including disadvantaged minorities, may possess the skills needed for many white-collar roles without holding the formal credentials listed as prerequisites ("Paper Ceiling").

The basic counterargument is presented: people can't get jobs because they don't have degrees.

These advocates, who can be found on the left and the right, mean well. Nonetheless, a look at the data suggests the skills-based hiring movement may actually amount to little more than populist virtue signaling. The evidence so far suggests that the movement may do little to expand economic opportunity. What's worse, it sends a degree-skeptical message that risks hurting rather than helping those who would benefit most from pursuing an education beyond high school.

Thesis: There is no merit in the argument against college and it hurts students.

As always, it's useful to look at what economists call "revealed preferences"—or what people do, regardless of what they say.

The economic advantage of getting a college degree remains at just about an all-time high when compared with the average earnings of Americans with only a high-school diploma. In recent years, a typical college graduate earned a median wage premium of more than $30,000, or almost 75 percent more than those who had completed just high school, a 2019 New York Fed analysis found (Abel and Dietz).

Introduces the first reason and supporting evidence: focus on people's actions.

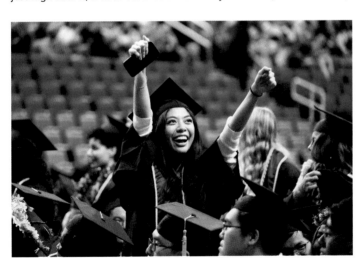

In April 2022, a major study by the Society for Human Resource Management, or S.H.R.M., found that 71 percent of executives said that some alternative credentials are equivalent to a bachelor's degree. But only 58 percent of supervisors (most likely beneath those executives on the organization chart) concurred, a figure that fell to 36 percent for human resources professionals, or those typically closest to hiring decisions ("Rise").

In another experiment by S.H.R.M., hiring managers and human resources professionals evaluated hypothetical job applicants with traditional degrees more highly than those with alternative credentials, particularly when the job ad used strict degree requirements. This was the case even when the latter were viewed as more likely to have the technical skills needed for the job ("Making").

Another study often cited as evidence of declining employer interest in college degrees doesn't fully capture what's happening. The Burning Glass Institute's "Emerging Degree Reset" report from last year pointed to a decline in degree requirements for middle-skill jobs in particular (Fuller 5–6). But the analysis was based on online job postings, not actual hiring decisions (Lohr). A later data analysis found that in some key respects, "employers are hiring more (not less) college grads" (Levanon).

What about all the Silicon Valley firms so often associated with the "death of the degree" narrative? Here, too, revealed preferences are, well, revealing.   10

Degree requirements in formal job listings remain in the 70 to 90 percent range at blue-chip firms like Google, Apple and Intel. Even much-hyped alternative-credential programs—like the online Grow with Google certificates, which offer professional training in high-demand tech fields such as cybersecurity and digital support—aren't designed to get certificate holders hired at Google (Fuller 14).

There is a reason college graduates earn so much more, and it isn't just because they've got an extra piece of paper. The huge growth in the wage premium for college degrees reflects not state bureaucracies or corporate H.R. policies, but century-long economic changes that generate more jobs requiring the abilities and knowledge acquired in college.

The broad education and targeted skills that college graduates usually obtain prepare them for career success. That includes analytical and communications abilities, tailored preparation in popular subjects like business, nursing and computer science, or liberal arts majors that have significant long-term benefits. When undergrads are also able to develop their social capital to build professional networks, so much the better (D'Agostino). It's a category error to treat college degrees like dubious occupational licenses that have become barriers to entry in certain fields.

Evidence in favor of attending college is presented.

Refutes a study cited by opponents of college.

Introduces a second reason: tech firms are not driving the move away from college.

Evidence: Most tech companies seek college graduates.

Introduces a third reason: the skills, knowledge, and social savvy developed in college makes better employees.

College degree alternatives may still play a worthwhile role for some students. For all the benefits that accrue to earning traditional two- and four-year degrees, large populations of learners need something different. Tailored, short-term, skills-based programs and credentials in everything from data science to graphic design should be widely accessible—and they should be simple to acquire and reacquire over a lifetime, to meet changing needs. Whenever possible, students should be able to combine them, over time, into two- or four-year degrees. Remember, much of the growth in skills-based credentials seems to be coming from people who already have degrees and want to supplement them with additional skills. They're taking a "both/and" approach to get ahead, not giving up on degrees altogether (Gallagher 3–6).

Acknowledgment that there is some merit in the other side's argument.

We often hear that the strong preference for degrees isn't fair to 15 the majority of Americans who didn't go to college. But that majority is falling fast, and the percentage of college-educated American adults is pushing 50 percent when associate degrees are included ("Census Bureau"). And while the percentage of Black and Latino college graduates is significantly lower, it is far higher than a few decades earlier. In fact, in 1960, only 41 percent of Americans had completed high school. It might have been plausible then to argue that plenty of dropouts had great talents and were unfairly penalized by high school diploma requirements. But it would have been badly misguided to oppose efforts to vastly improve high school graduation rates, which stand at 91 percent today ("Table 104.10").

A fourth reason: that many people don't go to college is no reason to argue that they shouldn't.

College degree requirements aren't sacred. But they reflect the unmistakable reality that higher education helps people do well.

A brief but forceful conclusion: college helps people have better lives.

Works Cited

Abel, Jaison R., and Richard Deitz. "Despite Rising Costs, College Is Still a Good Investment." *Liberty Street Economics*, Federal Reserve Bank of New York, 5 June 2019, libertystreeteconomics.newyorkfed .org/2019/06/despite-rising-costs-college-is-still-a-good-investment/.

Bowdler, Janis, and Benjamin Harris. "Racial Inequality in the United States." *U.S. Department of the Treasury*, 21 July 2022, home.treasury .gov/news/featured-stories/racial-inequality-in-the-united-states.

"Census Bureau Releases New Educational Attainment Data." *United States Census Bureau*, 24 Feb. 2022, www.census.gov/newsroom /press-releases/2022/educational-attainment.html.

D'Agostino, Susan. "Leveling the Playing Field for Social Capital." *Inside Higher Ed*, 4 Aug. 2022, www.insidehighered.com/news/2022/08/05 /how-colleges-can-level-playing-field-social-capital.

Fuller, Joseph B., et al. *The Emerging Degree Reset*. The Burning Glass Institute, 2022. https://static1.squarespace.com/static/6197797102be715f55c0e0a1/t /6202bda7f1ceee7b0e9b7e2f/1644346798760/The+Emerging+Degree+Reset +%2822.02%29Final.pdf.

Gallagher, Sean R. *Educational Credentials Come of Age: A Survey on the Use and Value of Educational Credentials in Hiring.* Northeastern University Center for the Future of Higher Education and Talent Strategy, Dec. 2018, cps.northeastern.edu/wp-content /uploads/2021/03/Educational_Credentials_Come_of_Age_2018.pdf.

Guber, Stacey, and Jonathan Wolfson. "Help Wanted: No Degree Necessary." *The Wall Street Journal*, 19 June 2023, www.wsj .com/articles/help-wanted-no-degree-necessary-georgia-florida -skills-based-hiring-1e294181.

Levanon, Gad. "It turns out that employers are hiring more (not less) college grads. . . ." *LinkedIn*, 2023, www.linkedin.com/posts/gad -levanon-3b9b933_hiring-education-collegedegree-activity -7010971318510604289-y65Z?utm_source=share&utm _medium=member_ios.

Lohr, Steve. "A 4-Year Degree Isn't Quite the Job Requirement It Used to Be." *The New York Times*, 8 Apr. 2022, www.nytimes .com/2022/04/08/business/hiring-without-college-degree.html.

Making Alternative Credentials Work: A New Strategy for HR Professionals. SHRM, www.shrm.org/content/dam/en/shrm/about/ press-room/Making-Alternative-Credentials-Work-A-New-Strategy -for-HR-Professionals.pdf. Accessed 20 July 2023.

"The Paper Ceiling: A Labor Market Out of Balance." *Stars,* Opportunity Work / Ad Council, www.tearthepaperceiling.org/the-paper-ceiling. Accessed 19 July 2023.

The Rise of Alternative Credentials in Hiring. SHRM, www.shrm.org /about/press-room/shrm-report-survey-finds-rise-alternative -credentials-hiring. Accessed 21 July 2023.

"Table 104.10: Rates of High School Completion and Bachelor's Degree Attainment among Persons Age 25 and Over, by Race/Ethnicity and Sex: Selected Years, 1910 through 2021." *Digest of Education Statistics*, National Center for Education Statistics, 2021, nces.ed.gov/ programs/digest/d21/tables/dt21_104.10.asp.

Whissemore, Tabitha. "House Panel Examines Skills-Based Hiring." *Community College Daily*, American Association of Community Colleges, 12 Dec. 2023. www.ccdaily.com/2023/06/skills-based -hiring-expands-diversifies-talent-pool-and-opportunities/.

Whitford, Emma. "College Enrollments Decline for Third Straight Year amid Strong Job Market, Student Debt Fears." *Forbes*, 20 Oct. 2022, www.forbes.com/sites/emmawhitford/2022/10/20/college -enrollments-decline-for-third-straight-year-amid-strong -job-market-student-debt-fears/?sh=5aba821d1043.

Wildavsky offers a wealth of reasons and evidence to show that attending college is beneficial and that arguments that college degrees are irrelevant are mistaken. The extensive list of works cited helps build the credibility of his argument.

BRIANNA SCHUNK

Come Look at the Freaks
Examining and Advocating for Disability Theatre

In this essay, Wilkes University student Brianna Schunk argues that our culture should support disability theatre in various ways. Schunk's essay was nominated for the Norton Writer's Prize, and it is documented in MLA style.

When I first saw Gaten Matarazzo in the TV show *Stranger Things* and some of the first words out of his toothless little mouth were, "I have cleidocranial dysplasia" ("Chapter One" 00:35:21), I actually cried with joy. Until then, I had never seen another human not related to my family who had cleidocranial dysplasia on television in a popular TV show. I was so shocked, I made my friend rewind the episode so I could hear him say it again. Having cleidocranial dysplasia myself, it is so much easier to be able to compare myself to Matarazzo when explaining my condition to other people, and I only wish he could have come into my life earlier. Representation—how we portray ourselves and are portrayed by others—is incredibly important to all groups of people, but especially to people with disabilities.

Disability, until recently, has rarely been studied through the lens of culture. Up until the last fifty years, disability was studied in the fields of medicine and science by doctors and surgeons. However, the world has recently begun to publish works not related to science and medicine, and this study of the true experience of disability is called *disability culture*. Disability culture has taken root in many fields, such as fiction, nonfiction, the analysis of stories, sociological studies of the disability experience, and visual, musical, and theatre arts. Champions like Rosemarie Garland-Thomson have brought disability culture to a wider audience. In her book *Extraordinary Bodies*, Garland-Thomson uses the lens of feminist critique as well as comparison to the study of race and gender to explain disability culture in America. Her publications are regarded as some of the earliest works on the emerging field of disability culture. *Disability* refers to an incredibly wide spectrum of things, ranging from physical conditions to unseeable mental illnesses and cognitive impairment, but all are part of disability culture. Using studies and reports like Garland-Thomson's, we can share our experiences of being disabled with both able-bodied and disabled people.

Disability theatre is about making theatre for and with people with disabilities, and it is an important topic to me because I am an actor with a disability. Cleidocranial dysplasia affects me physically but is not immediately noticeable and manifests in less visible ways, such as hearing loss in my left ear and years of corrective orthodontic surgery. Throughout most of my life I didn't even consider myself disabled because my disability does not affect my life as much as some other people's disabilities affect theirs. In addition, people around me discouraged me from considering myself disabled, likely because the idea of disability is so stigmatizing. This stems from the power difference found between people with disabilities and people without. Garland-Thomson asserts that people who have "ordinary" (non-disabled) bodies are considered superior to those who do not, and these "normates" have social power and authority (8). However, by considering myself an actress with a disability—an identity important to me—I assert my power. Disability is not bad, it's just different. In the same way able-bodied people are different from one another, so people with disabilities are different from one another and from people who are able-bodied. However, people advocate less for people with disabilities than for any other minority group, and especially so in the theatre and entertainment world. As Lennard Davis notes in a *HuffPost* article, many people turn a blind eye when an able-bodied actor portrays a disabled person, but if anyone does blackface today it is widely acknowledged to be racist.

Many people in the field of disability theatre think it is acceptable for able-bodied actors to portray people with disabilities. This is a strange gray area for two main reasons. One, there are often not enough actors with disabilities available to play the roles; and two, sometimes the character needs to go through a period of time when they are not disabled, such as the story of Stephen Hawking (a role played by able-bodied actor Eddie Redmayne), whose disability developed as he grew older—a situation that has no definite solution. Unfortunately, "the current reality is that non-disabled actors get to play whatever roles they want whereas disabled actors don't" (Davis). That there aren't enough disabled actors stems from a vicious cycle identified by disability scholar Carrie Sandahl, who observes that most theatre departments are inaccessible to people with disabilities. They are often denied admission to acting programs because educators are not willing to work with them or the programs do not have the means to accommodate them (255). Also, many training programs can be a challenge to people with disabilities. Sandahl notes that the origin of the "neutral" body in many acting techniques stems from the study of body normalcy (261). Bodies were considered "damaged physically and emotionally from the process of living, and those bodies capable of cure are suitable actors"—disabled bodies could not be "cured" and therefore could not be actors (262). These limitations then lead to fewer actors with disabilities in the professional world. And directors are not willing to work with or adapt stories for actors with disabilities, thinking "their impairments would detract from the playwright's or director's intent for a nondisabled character" (255).

We can get to the root of the problem by recognizing and eliminating disability stereotypes. Marilyn Dahl's essay "The Role of the Media in Promoting Images of Disability" explores common metaphors surrounding people with disabilities, such as villains who are marked as evil because of a missing body part or victims who are completely helpless and dependent on others. However, Dahl's essay also highlights how news reports do the same thing in creating fantastic stories out of the lives of people with disabilities, creating what Dahl calls "heroes by hype." Jack Nelson has also done research into stereotyped characters, even going so far as to categorize them: the "supercrip," the disabled villain, the burden, the misfit, and the victim. However, Nelson gives examples of a few positive representations as well, such as Nemo and his "lucky fin" in the children's animated movie *Finding Nemo*. Nelson stresses that "what most people with disabilities ask is that they [should] be portrayed as real people with real problems that often are not connected to their disability" (289).

Some actors and directors worry that in casting people with disabilities in disabled roles they face "typecasting" them, an idea that stems from years of stereotyping characters with disabilities. When people deny actors with disabilities opportunities to expand their repertoire and play parts traditionally played by able-bodied actors, they close their minds to creating a whole new level of theatre. Having someone with a disability play a typically able-bodied role can add much depth to the character and to the story and can bring to life the character's journey and problems through the medium of the human body. For example, when I was in a local production of the musical *Side Show*, a story about a pair of conjoined twins on the freak show circuit who later achieved vaudeville and film performance fame, I played one of the "World's Tiniest Cossacks," among other ensemble roles. I resonated deeply with my character, because even though I do not have dwarfism, my short stature relates to my disability, and I took to playing a "freak" easily because my condition leads me to entertain people. Playing a character who makes a living by entertaining people with their different body structure was easy, because I drew on my real-life experience. It wasn't the best thing that we didn't have actors with dwarfism to play that part, but at least there was a disabled actor playing the part—a part that honored disability. In the same way that our having actual twin sisters play the main characters added a whole new level of connection between the sisters in our production, so I felt that my playing the part of a disabled character created a whole new connection to the show for myself and for the audience.

People with disabilities originally had a connection to disability theatre through the world of freak shows. Freak shows "challenged the boundaries of the individual" (Garland-Thomson 59) to audiences by presenting bodies different from their own. Those shows were among the early origins of the celebration of disability culture. They also provided a place for people to "identify with nonconformity" (Garland-Thomson 68)—specifically, people wounded and missing limbs from war. When the shows gradually shut down in the mid-twentieth century, people with disabilities couldn't find jobs to sustain themselves because the people who took away their celebration of bodily difference refused to hire them to work anywhere else. They found some work in the developing film industry, in films such as Tod Browning's 1932 movie *Freaks*. It features a cast of actors with disabilities, including people with dwarfism, a pair of conjoined twins, and "pinheads," or actors with microcephaly.

This movie, in addition to providing jobs and representation to actors with disabilities, also challenged traditional stereotypes about people with disabilities. As the movie progresses and one sees the freaks going about their daily lives, one comes to root for them and value their lives and ambitions as humans, not as freaks or disabled characters. The script even recognizes this, with the characters calling out the ableism of one able-bodied woman in the movie by saying, "Cleopatra ain't one of us. Why, we're just filthy things to her" (*Freaks* 00:25:21–23). Nowadays, we have countless organizations and forms of media that celebrate disability. Derrick Vanmeter, a theatre professor at Clayton State University, lists several organizations, such as Full Radius Dance, which puts on dance shows with people in wheelchairs, and That Uppity Theatre Company, which introduces artists with disabilities in their work *The DisAbility Project*. The Star Wars movies portray people losing limbs—becoming disabled—without any accompanying storylines or stereotypes, instead tying their disabilities to the overarching theme of keeping the universe in balance, which video blogger Hank Green of the vlogbrothers channel

Ali Stroker as Ado Annie in the 2019 Broadway revival of *Oklahoma!*

summarizes as "when someone cuts someone's hand off in *Star Wars* . . . they're gonna get their hand chopped off too" ("13 Severed Hands" 00:01:21–26). Even musicals such as *Sideshow, Next to Normal* (a story about a woman with bipolar disorder), and Deaf West's production of *Spring Awakening* create stories using characters with disabilities and support them as humans with desires and goals. In 2019, actor Ali Stroker, who played Ado Annie in the Broadway revival of the classic musical *Oklahoma!*, became the first person who uses a wheelchair to win a Tony award, proving actors with disabilities can excel in starring roles created for able-bodied characters.

I encourage other people with disabilities to do theatre and see theatre and seek out opportunities to participate in theatre, and I encourage everyone to support us in our endeavors and to support disability theatre on a whole. Directors: Cast more disabled actors; open up your shows to a completely different take by using an actor with a disability. Choose to perform more shows about people with disabilities, and honor those roles with actors who truly know the disabled experience, not just able-bodied actors who can fake a limp. Theatre is the place for everyone to express themselves and tell their stories, and we as a theatre community need to honor all people. As a performer with a skeletal condition, my whole life is technically disability theatre. I am evidence that these two worlds can work together, and I want to show that to the world. No one can stop me from doing what I love to do, and I hope I can extend this confidence and belief to every other human that I meet. We can all be brilliant.

Works Cited

"Chapter One." *Stranger Things*, season 1, episode 1, 21 Laps Entertainment / Monkey Massacre, 2016. *Netflix*, www .netflix.com.

Dahl, Marilyn. "The Role of the Media in Promoting Images of Disability: Disability as Metaphor: The Evil Crip." *Canadian Journal of Communication*, vol. 18, no. 1, 1993. *ProQuest Central*, https://doi.org/10.22230/cjc.1993v18n1a718.

Davis, Lennard J. "Let Actors with Disabilities Play Characters with Disabilities." *HuffPost*, 6 Dec. 2017, www.huffpost.com/entry /let-actors-with-disabilit_b_380266.

Freaks. Directed by Tod Browning, Metro-Goldwyn Mayer, 1932.

Garland-Thomson, Rosemarie. *Extraordinary Bodies: Figuring Physical Disability in American Culture and Literature*. Columbia UP, 1997.

Nelson, Jack A. "Invisible No Longer: Images of Disability in the Media." *Images That Injure: Pictorial Stereotypes in the Media*, edited by Susan Dente Ross and Paul Martin Lester, 3rd ed., Praeger, 2011, pp. 274–91.

Sandahl, Carrie. "The Tyranny of Neutral: Disability and Actor Training." *Bodies in Commotion: Disability and Performance*, edited by Sandahl and Philip Auslander, U of Michigan P, 2005, pp. 255–67.

"13 Severed Hands!" *YouTube*, uploaded by vlogbrothers, 30 Sept. 2009, youtube.com/watch?v=lDlqwbMCBg4.

Vanmeter, Derrick. "Disability and Theatre: Access for All." Southeastern Theatre Conference, 3 Mar. 2017, Hilton Hotel, Lexington, Kentucky.

Schunk argues that actors with disabilities should be cast in the roles of characters with disabilities—and in roles of nondisabled characters as well. To make her argument, she draws on recent scholarship on disability culture and her own experiences.

ROHAN MEHTA

Banning ChatGPT Will Do More Harm than Good

Rohan Mehta wrote this argument as a high school senior at Moravian Academy in Bethlehem, Pennsylvania.

The release of *ChatGPT* has sent shock waves through the halls of higher education. Universities have rushed to release guidelines on how it can be used in the classroom. Professors have taken to social media to share a spectrum of AI policies. And students—whether or not they'll admit it—have cautiously experimented with the idea of allowing it to play a part in their academic work.

But the notion of a measured response to the emergence of this powerful chatbot seems to have barely penetrated the world of K–12 education. Instead of transparent, well-defined expectations, high schoolers across the country have been confronted with a silent coup of blocked AI websites. (At least in my case, the entirety of openai.com has been blocked, not just chat.openai.com. Kind of annoying if I want to access the fine-tuning docs.)

That's a shame. If educators actively engage with students about the technology's capabilities and limitations—and work with them to define new academic standards—*ChatGPT*, and generative AI more broadly, could both democratize and revitalize K–12 education on an unprecedented scale.

A bold claim, I know. But after a few months of putting generative AI to the test (a nerdy case of senioritis, if you will), I'm optimistic. Exhibit A? College applications.

Few things are as mentally draining as applying to college, and as I slaved away at my supplemental essays, the promise of using *ChatGPT* as a real-time editor was attractive—partly as a potential productivity boost, but mostly as a distraction.

I had *ChatGPT* carefully review my cloying use of semicolons and grade my writing on a 0–10 scale (the results were erratic and maddening) and even role-play as an admissions counselor. Its advice was fundamentally incompatible with the creative demands of the modern college essay, and I mostly ignored it. But the very act of discussing my writing "out loud," albeit with a machine, helped me figure out what I wanted to say next. Using *ChatGPT* to verbalize the range of possibilities—from the scale of words to paragraphs—strengthened my own thinking. And I've experienced something similar across every domain

5

I've applied it to, from generating fifth-grader-level explanations of the French pluperfect to deciphering the Latin names of human muscles. (The most impressive thing I have seen *ChatGPT* do is revise one of my essays. In it, I discussed two global political figures, but concealed their identities through personification. To "make my essay a 10/10" and "increase clarity," *ChatGPT* filled in their names. The fact that it has emergent abilities like this blew my mind!)

All this adds up to a simple but profound fact: anyone with an internet connection now has a personal tutor, without the costs associated with private tutoring. Sure, an easily hoodwinked, slightly delusional tutor, but a tutor nonetheless. The impact of this is hard to overstate, and it is as relevant in large public school classrooms where students struggle to receive individual attention as it is in underserved and impoverished communities without sufficient educational infrastructure. As the psychologist Benjamin Bloom demonstrated in the early 1980s, one-on-one instruction until mastery allowed almost all students to outperform the class average by two standard deviations ("about 90% . . . attained the level . . . reached by only the highest 20%") (4).

ChatGPT certainly can't replicate human interaction, but even its staunchest critics have to admit its potential usefulness in learning is a step in the right direction. Maybe only 1% of students will use it in this way, and maybe it's only half as effective as a human tutor, but even with these lowball numbers, its potential for democratizing educational access is enormous. I would even go so far as to say that if *ChatGPT* had existed during the pandemic, many fewer students would have fallen behind.

Of course, those decrying *ChatGPT* as the end of critical thinking would likely protest that the bot will only exacerbate the lazy academic habits students might have formed over the course of the pandemic. I have enough experience with the tips and tricks we high schoolers employ on a regular basis to know that this is a valid concern — one that shouldn't be brushed off by casting *ChatGPT* as just the latest in a long line of technological revolutions in the classroom, from the calculator to the internet.

That said, *ChatGPT* has just as much potential in the classroom as 10 it does for improving individual educational outcomes. English teachers could use it to rephrase the notoriously confusing answer keys to AP test questions, to help students prepare more effectively. They could provide each student with an essay antithetical to the one they turned in, and have them pick apart these contrary arguments in a future draft. No human teacher could spend the time or energy needed to explain pages upon pages of lengthy reading comprehension questions or compose hundreds of five-page essays, but a chatbot can.

Educators can even lean into *ChatGPT's* tendency to falsify, misattribute, and straight-out lie as a way of teaching students about disinformation. Imagine using *ChatGPT* to pen essays that conceal subtle logical fallacies or propose scientific explanations that are almost, but not quite, correct. Learning to discriminate between these convincing mistakes and the correct answer is the very pinnacle of critical thinking, and this new breed of academic assignment will prepare students for a world fraught with everything from politically correct censorship to deepfakes.

There are certainly less optimistic visions for the future. But the only way we avoid them—the only way this technology gets normalized and regulated alongside its similarly disruptive forebears—is with more discussion, more guidance, and more understanding. And it's not as if there's no time to catch up. *ChatGPT* won't be acing AP English classes anytime soon ("Cheating"), and with the recent release of GPT-4, we are already seeing an explosion of ed-tech companies that reduce the effort and expertise needed for teachers and students to operate the bot.

So here's my pitch to those in power. Regardless of the specific policy you choose to employ at your school, unblock and unban. The path forward starts by trusting students to experiment with the tool, and guiding them through how, when, and where it can be used. You don't need to restructure your whole curriculum around it, but blocking it will only send it underground. That will lead to confusion and misinterpretation in the best of cases, and misuse and abuse in the worst.

ChatGPT is only the beginning. There are simply too many generative AI tools to try to block them all, and doing so sends the wrong message. What we need is a direct discourse between students, teachers, and administrators. I'm lucky enough to be at a school that has taken the first steps in this direction, and it's my hope that many more will follow suit.

Works Cited

Bloom, Benjamin S. "The 2 Sigma Problem: The Search for Methods of Group Instruction as Effective as One-to-One Tutoring." *Educational Researcher*, vol. 13, no. 6, June–Jul. 1984, pp. 4–16. *JSTOR*, www.jstor.org/stable/1175554.

"Cheating with ChatGPT: Can OpenAI's Chatbot Pass AP Lit?" *YouTube*, uploaded by The Wall Street Journal, 21 Dec. 2022, www.youtube.com/wastch?v=l01biyMZjEo&t=3s.

Mehta argues that AI bots can assist students in improving their learning and writing, so schools should not indiscriminately ban them on school computers. His argument relies on both personal experience with ChatGPT and research into the effectiveness of tutors on student learning.

Key Features / Arguments

A clear and arguable position. At the heart of every argument is a claim with which people may reasonably disagree. Some claims are not arguable because they're completely subjective, matters of taste or opinion ("I hate sauerkraut"), because they are a matter of fact ("The first *Star Wars* movie came out in 1977"), or because they are based on belief or faith ("There is life after death"). To be arguable, a position must reflect one of at least two points of view, making reasoned argument necessary: guns should (or should not) be regulated; selling human organs should be legal (or illegal). In college writing, you will often argue not that a position is correct but that it is plausible—that it is reasonable, supportable, and worthy of being taken seriously.

Necessary background information. Sometimes we need to provide some background on a topic we are arguing so that readers can understand what is being argued. Wildavsky describes the trend of dropping of degree requirements; Schunk defines disability theater.

Good reasons. By itself, a position does not make an argument; the argument comes when a writer offers reasons to back up the position. There are many kinds of good reasons. Mehta sees AI as a way to improve educational outcomes, including teaching students to spot disinformation. Schunk offers several reasons why actors with disabilities should get more parts: using nondisabled actors in roles of characters with disabilities is discriminatory; if there is a shortage of actors with disabilities, it derives from barriers to participation of those actors; and stereotypes limit the roles available to actors with disabilities.

Convincing evidence. Once you've given reasons for your position, you then need to offer evidence for your reasons: facts, statistics, expert testimony, anecdotal evidence, case studies, textual evidence. All three arguments use a mix of these types of evidence. Wildavsky cites several studies to show that employers value applicants with college bachelor's degrees. Both Schunk and Mehta cite anecdotes from their own experience to support their arguments.

Appeals to readers' values. Effective arguers try to appeal to readers' values and emotions. Schunk appeals to readers' sense of fairness in describing how disabled actors are treated differently from actors who are not disabled, and Mehta sees AI tutoring as a way for students in "underserved and impoverished communities" to improve their learning—another issue of fairness. These values are deeply held and may be seen as common ground we share with one another.

A trustworthy tone. Arguments can stand or fall on the way readers perceive the writer. Very simply, readers need to trust the person who's making the argument. One way of winning this trust is by demonstrating that you know what you're talking about. Wildavsky offers plenty of evidence to show he's done his research on the benefits of college—and he does so in a self-assured tone. There are many other ways of establishing yourself (and your argument) as trustworthy—by showing that you have some experience with your subject, that you're fair, and of course that you're honest.

Careful consideration of other positions. No matter how reasonable and careful we are in arguing our positions, others may disagree or offer counterarguments. We need to consider those other views and to acknowledge and, if possible, refute them in our written arguments. Wildavsky, for example, carefully summarizes the arguments against requiring college degrees for employment and acknowledges that some learners need other paths to appropriate job credentials.

Access
Chapter 3
in the ebook
for a video on
responding to the
views of others.

A GUIDE TO WRITING ARGUMENTS

Choosing a Topic

A fully developed argument requires significant work and time, so choosing a topic in which you're interested is very important. Students often find that widely debated topics such as "animal rights" or "abortion" can be difficult to write on because they don't feel any personal connection to them. Better topics include those that

- interest you right now
- are focused, but not too narrowly
- have some personal connection to your life

One useful way to **GENERATE IDEAS** for a topic that meets those three criteria is to explore your own roles in life.

329–39

330

Start with your roles in life. Make four columns with the headings "Personal," "Family," "Public," and "School." Then **LIST** the roles you play that relate to each heading. Here is a list one student wrote:

Personal	Family	Public	School
gamer	son	voter	college student
dog owner	younger	homeless-shelter	work-study employee
old-car owner	brother	volunteer	dorm resident
male	grandson	American	primary-education major
White		resident of Texas	
middle class			

Access the ebook for a video on the importance of choosing a topic that matters.

Identify issues that interest you. Think, then, about issues or controversies that may concern you as a member of one or more of those groups. For instance, as a primary-education major, this student cares about the controversy over whether teachers' jobs should be focused on preparing kids for high-stakes standardized tests. As a college student, he cares about the costs of a college education. Issues that stem from these subjects could include the following: Should student progress be measured by standardized tests? Should college be considered a public good and be free?

Pick four or five of the roles you list. In five or ten minutes, identify issues that concern or affect you as a person who inhabits each of those roles. It might help to word each issue as a question starting with "Should."

Frame your topic as a problem. Most position papers address issues that are subjects of ongoing debate—their solutions aren't easy, and people disagree on which ones are best. Posing your topic as a problem can help you think about the topic, find an issue that's suitable to write about, and find a clear focus for your essay.

For example, if you wanted to write an argument on the lack of student parking at your school, you could frame your topic as one of several problems: What causes the parking shortage? Why are the university's parking garages and lots limited in their capacity? What might alleviate the shortage?

Choose one issue to write about. Remember that the issue should be interesting to you and have some connection to your life. It is a tentative choice; if you find later that you have trouble writing about it, simply go back to your list of roles or issues and choose another.

Considering the Rhetorical Situation

PURPOSE   Do you want to persuade your audience to do something? Change their minds? Consider alternative
views? Accept your position as plausible—see that you
have thought carefully about an issue and researched
it appropriately?

73–74

AUDIENCE   Who is your intended audience? What do they likely
know and believe about this issue? How personal is it
for them? To what extent are they likely to agree or
disagree with you—and with one another? Why? What
common ground can you find with them?

75–78

STANCE   What's your attitude toward your topic, and why? How
do you want your audience to perceive your attitude?
How do you want your audience to perceive you? As
an authority on your topic? As someone much like
them? As calm? reasonable? impassioned or angry?
something else?

85–87

MEDIA/DESIGN   What media will you use, and how do your media
affect your argument? Does your print or online argument call for photos or charts? If you're giving an oral
presentation, should you put your reasons and support
on slides? If you're writing electronically, should you
include audio or video evidence or links to counterarguments or your sources?

88–90

Generating Ideas and Text

Most essays that successfully argue a position share certain features that
make them interesting and persuasive. Remember that your goal is to stake
out a position and convince your readers that it is plausible.

Explore what you already know about the issue.   Write out whatever you
know about the issue by **FREEWRITING** or as a **LIST** or **OUTLINE**. Why are
you interested in this topic? What is your position on it at this point, and
why? What aspect do you think you'd like to focus on? Where do you need
to focus your research efforts? This activity can help you discover what
more you need to learn. Chances are you'll need to learn a lot more about
the issue before you even decide what position to take.

329
330
335–37

Do some research. At this point, try to get an overview. Start with one or two general sources of information that will give you a sense of the issue from various perspectives. Using your university library's resources can help you avoid excessively biased or partisan sources and can provide access to news sources that may otherwise be hidden behind a paywall. For some issues, you may need to **INTERVIEW** an expert. For example, one student who wanted to write about chemical abuse of animals at 4-H competitions interviewed an experienced show competitor. Use your overview source to find out the main questions raised about your issue and to get some idea about the various ways in which you might argue it.

498–500

Explore the issue strategically. Most issues may be argued from many different perspectives. You'll probably have some sense of the different views that exist on your issue, but you should explore multiple perspectives before deciding on your position. The following methods can help you explore issues:

429–39

- As a matter of **DEFINITION**. What is it? How should it be defined? How can "organic" or "genetically modified food" be defined? How do proponents of organic food define it—and how do they define "genetically modified food"? How do advocates of "genetically modified food" define it—and how do they define "organic food"? Considering such definitions is one way to identify different perspectives on the topic.

417–21

- As a matter of **CLASSIFICATION**. Can the issue be divided into categories? Are there different kinds of, or different ways of, producing organic foods and genetically modified foods? Do different categories suggest particular positions or perhaps a way of supporting a certain position? Are there other ways of categorizing foods?

422–38

- As a matter of **COMPARISON**. Is one subject being considered better than another? Is organic food healthier or safer than genetically modified food? Is genetically modified food healthier or safer than organic? Is the answer somewhere in the middle?

452–56

- As a matter of **PROCESS**. Should somebody do something? What? Should people buy and eat more organic food? More genetically modified food? Should they buy and eat some of each?

Reconsider whether the issue can be argued. Is this issue worth discussing? Why is it important to you and to others? What difference will it make if one position or another prevails? Is it **ARGUABLE**? At this point, you want to be sure that your topic is worth arguing about.

399–416

Draft a thesis.   Having explored the possibilities, decide your position, and write it out as a complete sentence. For example:

Access the ebook for a video on developing an argumentative thesis statement.

> Parents should be required to have their children vaccinated.
>
> Pod-based coffeemakers should be banned.
>
> Genetically modified foods should not be permitted in the United States.

Qualify your thesis.   Rather than taking a strict pro or con position, in most cases you'll want to **QUALIFY YOUR POSITION** — in certain circumstances, with certain conditions, with these limitations, and so on. This is not to say that we should settle, give in, sell out; rather, it is to say that our position may not be the only "correct" one and that other positions may be valid as well. **QUALIFYING YOUR THESIS** also makes your topic manageable by limiting it. For example:

400–401

342–44

> Parents should be required to have their children vaccinated, with only medical exemptions allowed.
>
> Pod-based coffeemakers should be banned unless the pods are recyclable.
>
> Genetically modified foods should not be permitted in the United States if a link between genetically modified organisms and resistance to antibiotics is proven.

Come up with good reasons.   Once you have a thesis, you need to come up with sound **REASONS** to convince your readers that it's plausible. Write out your position, and then list several reasons. For instance, if your thesis is that pod-based coffeemakers should be banned, two of your reasons might be:

402

> The pods cannot be recycled.
>
> Other methods of making coffee are more environmentally sound.

Think about which reasons are best for your purposes. Which seem the most persuasive? Which are most likely to be accepted by your audience? Which seem to matter the most now? If your list of reasons is short or you think you'll have trouble developing them enough to write an appropriate essay, this is a good time to rethink your topic — before you've invested too much time in it.

Develop support for your reasons. Next you have to come up with

402–9 ◆

EVIDENCE to support your reasons: facts, statistics, examples, testimony by authorities and experts, anecdotal evidence, scenarios, case studies and observation, and textual evidence. For some topics, you may want or need to use evidence in visual form like photos, graphs, and charts; online, you could also use video or audio evidence and links to evidence in other websites.

What counts as evidence varies across audiences. Statistical evidence may be required in certain disciplines but not in others; anecdotes may be accepted as evidence in some courses but not in engineering. Some audiences will be persuaded by emotional appeals while others will not. For example, if you argue that foods produced from genetically modified organisms (GMOs) should be allowed to be sold because they're safe, you could support that reason with *facts*: GMOs are tested thoroughly by three separate US government agencies. Or you could support it with *statistics*: a study of 29 years of data on livestock fed GMO feed found that GMO-fed cattle had no adverse health effects on people who ate them. *Expert testimony* might include R. E. Goodman of the Department of Food Science and Technology at the University of Nebraska–Lincoln, who writes that "there is an absence of proof of harm to consumers from commercially available GMOs."

Identify other positions.   Now think about positions other than yours and the reasons people are likely to give for those positions. Be careful to represent their points of view as accurately and fairly as you can. Then decide whether you need to acknowledge or to refute each position.

Acknowledging other positions.   Some positions can't be refuted but are

411 ◆

too important to ignore, so you need to **ACKNOWLEDGE** concerns and objections they raise to show that you've considered other perspectives. For example, in an essay arguing that vacations are necessary to maintain good health, medical writer Alina Tugend acknowledges that "in some cases, these trips—particularly with entire families in tow—can be stressful in their own way. The joys of a holiday can also include lugging around a ridiculous amount of paraphernalia, jet-lagged children sobbing on airplanes, hotels that looked wonderful on the Web but are in reality next to a construction site." Tugend's acknowledgment moderates her position and makes her argument appear more reasonable.

Refuting other positions.   State the position as clearly and as fairly as

412–13 ◆

you can, and then **REFUTE** it by showing why you believe it is wrong. Perhaps the reasoning is faulty or the supporting evidence inadequate. Acknowledge the merits of the position, if any, but emphasize its shortcomings. Avoid logical **FALLACIES** such as attacking the person holding the position or bringing up a competing position that no one seriously entertains.

◆ 413–15

Ways of Organizing an Argument

Readers need to be able to follow the reasoning of your argument from beginning to end; your task is to lead them from point to point as you build your case. Sometimes you'll want to give all the reasons for your argument first, followed by discussion of any other positions. Alternatively, you might discuss each reason and any opposing arguments together.

Access Chapter 30 in the ebook for a video on organizing and synthesizing ideas.

Reasons to support your argument, followed by opposing arguments

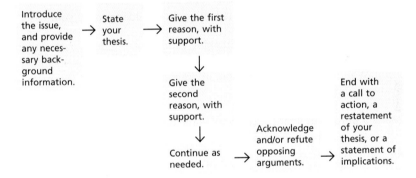

Reason/opposing argument, reason/opposing argument

Consider carefully the order in which you discuss your reasons. Usually what comes last makes the strongest impression on readers and what comes in the middle the least impression, so you might want to put your most important or strongest reasons first and last.

More Ways to Approach an Argument

Write an editorial or letter to the editor. Choose a specific publication and write your argument for its audience, taking into account what they already understand about your topic and what their likely position on it will be.

Write a social media post. Write your argument for *Facebook*, *Instagram*, or *YouTube*. Consider what you can—and cannot—say in the space available to you and what other media you might include to make your case.

Create a podcast. Explore how making your argument orally, rather than in writing, would change what you say or include and how you can best say it. Who might you ask to record an interview? How might you include evidence from sources?

Make a parody or spoof. Sometimes the best way to make an argument is to turn it into a parody, to make your audience laugh while still understanding your point of view.

280–90 ▲ **Remix.** After you've written a draft of your argument, you might **REMIX** it: rework it into one or more of the genres above or turn it into a visual argument or infographic.

Writing Out a Draft

Once you have generated ideas, done some research, and thought about 358–60 ⁘ how you want to organize your argument, it's time to start **DRAFTING**. Your goal in the initial draft is to develop your argument—you can fill in support and transitions as you revise. You may want to write your first draft in one sitting, so that you can develop your reasoning from beginning to end. Or you may write the main argument first and the introduction and conclusion after you've drafted the body of the essay; many writers find that beginning and ending an essay are the hardest 340–52 ⁘ tasks they face. Here is some advice on how you might **BEGIN AND END** your argument:

Draft a beginning. There are various ways to begin an argument essay, depending on your audience and purpose. Here are a few suggestions:

- *Offer background information.* You may need to give your readers information to help them understand your position. Wildavsky describes a trend of dropping degree requirements among tech companies and state governments.

- *Begin with an anecdote.* Schunk starts by describing the first time she saw on television an actor who had the same disability that she has.

- *Define a key term.* You may need to show how you're using certain keywords. Schunk describes "disability culture," "disability theatre," and "cleidocranial dysplasia" as she develops her argument against disability stereotypes in theater.

- *Explain the context for your position.* All arguments are part of a larger, ongoing conversation, so you might begin by showing how your position fits into the arguments others have made. Mehta contrasts the reaction to AI chatbots by universities to the way K–12 educators are reacting.

- *Begin with something that will get readers' attention.* Wildavsky leads off with a surprising statement—that it's easy to conclude that "a college degree is becoming increasingly irrelevant."

Draft an ending. Your conclusion is the chance to wrap up your argument in such a way that readers will remember what you've said. Here are a few ways of concluding an argument essay:

- *Summarize your main points.* Especially when you've presented a complex argument, it can help readers to **SUMMARIZE** your main point. Schunk sums up her argument by stating, "Theatre is the place for everyone to express themselves and tell their stories, and we as a theatre community need to honor all people."

- *Call for action.* Mehta does this by calling for schools to "unblock and unban" ChatGPT and other AI tools. Schunk calls for theater and film directors to cast more actors with disabilities.

- *Frame your argument by referring to the introduction.* Wildavsky returns to the question of whether or not college is irrelevant by asserting that "higher education helps people do well."

● 529 _____

Access Chapter 30 in the ebook for a video on introductions and conclusions.

Come up with a title. Most often you'll want your title to tell readers something about your topic—and to make them want to read on. Mehta straightforwardly summarizes his argument: "Banning *ChatGPT* Will Do More Harm than Good." Schunk's "Come Look at the Freaks: Examining and Advocating for Disability Theatre" offers a shocking suggestion—and then a subtitle phrased in scholarly language. Wildavsky's title, "Let's Stop Pretending College Degrees Don't Matter," entices us to find out why they may not matter—and who says so. See the chapter on **ORGANIZING YOUR WRITING AND GUIDING YOUR READER** for more advice on composing a strong title.

340–57

Considering Matters of Design

You'll probably write the main text of your argument in paragraph form, but think about what kind of information you're presenting and how you can design it to make your argument as easy as possible for your readers to understand. Think also about whether any visual or audio elements would be more persuasive than written words.

642–43

- What would be an appropriate **FONT**? Something serious like Times Roman? Something traditional like Courier? Something else?

644–45

- Would it help your readers if you divided your argument into shorter sections and added **HEADINGS**?

643–44

- If you're making several points, would they be easier to follow if you set them off in a **LIST**?

650
648–54

- Do you have any supporting evidence that would be easier to understand in the form of a **BAR GRAPH**, **LINE GRAPH**, or **PIE CHART**?

- Would **VISUALS**—photos, diagrams, or drawings—add support for your argument? Online, would video, audio, or links help?

Getting Response and Revising

365–71

At this point you need to look at your draft closely, and if possible, **GET RESPONSE** from others as well. Following are some questions for looking at an argument with a critical eye.

- Is there sufficient background or context?
- Have you defined terms to avoid misunderstandings?
- Is the thesis clear and appropriately qualified?

- Are the reasons plausible?
- Is there enough evidence to support these reasons? Will readers accept the evidence as valid and sufficient?
- Can readers follow the steps in your reasoning?
- Have you considered potential objections or other positions? Are there any others that should be addressed?
- Have you cited enough sources, and are these sources credible?
- Are source materials documented carefully and completely, with in-text citations and a works-cited or references section or, when writing online, with links to each source?
- Are any visuals or links that are included used effectively and integrated smoothly with the rest of the text? If there are no visuals or links, would using some strengthen the argument?

Access Chapter 33 in the ebook for a video on revision strategies, including peer review.

Next it's time to **REVISE**, to make sure your argument offers convincing evidence, appeals to readers' values, and achieves your purpose. If you have time and want to explore alternatives, you might try **REWRITING** or **REMIX-ING** your draft to see if a different plan or approach might work better.

367–70

370–71

280–90

Editing and Proofreading

Once you've revised your draft, follow these guidelines for **EDITING** an argument:

372–75

- Check to see that your tone is appropriate and consistent throughout, reflects your **STANCE** accurately, and enhances the argument you're making.

85–87

- Be sure readers will be able to follow the argument; check to see you've provided **TRANSITIONS** and summary statements where necessary.
- Make sure you've smoothly integrated **QUOTATIONS**, **PARAPHRASES**, and **SUMMARIES** from source material into your writing and **DOCU-MENTED** them accurately.

355–56

521–32

538–41

- Make sure that **VISUALS** have captions and that charts and graphs have headings—and that all are referred to in the main text.

648–54

- If you're writing online, make sure all your links work.
- **PROOFREAD** and spell-check your essay carefully.

375–76

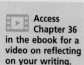
Access Chapter 36 in the ebook for a video on reflecting on your writing.

Taking Stock of Your Work

Take stock of what you've written by considering these questions:

- How did you go about researching your topic? What would you do differently next time?

- Did your stance change as you researched and wrote your argument? Why or why not?

- What types of evidence did you use in your argument—facts? statistics? expert testimony? something else? Why did you choose those types of evidence?

- How did feedback from peers, teachers, tutors, or others influence your writing?

- In what ways were you open to other perspectives as you worked on your argument?

- If you were going to revise this argument for a different audience (say, a letter to an online forum or a newspaper), what changes would you need to make?

- What was most meaningful to you about this piece or about your experience of writing it?

If you need more help

377–82
114–45
210–19
257–69

See Chapter 35 if you are required to submit your argument as part of a writing **PORTFOLIO**. See also Chapter 13 on **ANALYZING TEXTS**, Chapter 17 on **EVALUATIONS**, and Chapter 21 on **PROPOSALS** for advice on writing those specific types of arguments.

16 Annotated Bibliographies and Reviews of Scholarly Literature

When we do research, we may consult annotated bibliographies to evaluate potential sources and literature reviews when we need an overview of the important research ("literature") on a topic. In some courses, you may be asked to create annotated bibliographies or literature reviews to demonstrate that you have researched your topic thoroughly. This chapter offers advice on writing both.

ANNOTATED BIBLIOGRAPHIES

Annotated bibliographies describe, give publication information for, and sometimes evaluate each work on a list of sources. There are two kinds of annotations, *descriptive* and *evaluative*; both may be brief, consisting only of phrases, or more formal, consisting of sentences and paragraphs. Sometimes an annotated bibliography is introduced by a short statement explaining its scope.

Descriptive annotations simply summarize the contents of each work, without comment or evaluation, like the examples in the following excerpt from a bibliography of print and video sources that the author, Sean Kelliher, proposed using in a research paper for an Introduction to Music Studies class at the University of Denver.

SEAN KELLIHER

Tunesmith Terror Techniques
Identifying Patterns in the Music of Horror Video Games: An Annotated Bibliography

Ludomusicology, the study of music in video games, is a relatively new field in musicology that faces unique obstacles, like the lack of a standardized analytical method. My research paper will use the affect, literacy, and interaction (ALI) model proposed by musicologist Isabella van Elferen, along with techniques suggested by Tim Summers, a teaching fellow at the University of London, to analyze various video games in the horror genre. Along with using analysis of other games as sources, this paper will compare the compositional techniques used to identify patterns that do or do not show up.

Elferen, Isabella van. "Analysing Game Musical Immersion: The ALI Model." *Ludomusicology Approaches to Video Game Music*, edited by Michiel Kamp et al., Equinox Publishing, 2016, pp. 32–52.

> Dr. Isabella van Elferen, a musicologist who is currently a professor at Kingston University London, has written many papers about horror music in media, specifically gothic horror. This essay proposes a method of analyzing video game music, the ALI model, based on how immersive the music is. The ALI model stands for affect, literacy, and interaction. Affect is the emotional response from the player, literacy is the use of common musical tropes to communicate with the player, and interaction is how the player's action affects the music of the game. Elferen then goes on to give examples of her analysis of *Dead Space 2* and *Amnesia* with the ALI model, a consistent, thorough form of analysis. Unlike the other analysis methods in this bibliography, the ALI model focuses on the effect on the player rather than the musical mechanics of the game.

Merriner, Ashley. *Aural Abjections and Dancing Dystopias: Sonic Signifiers in Video Game Horror*. 2017. U of Oregon, MA thesis.

> Ashley Merriner has a Master of Arts degree in musicology from the University of Oregon, focusing on popular music studies. This paper seeks to answer the question "What does fear sound like?" by analyzing two games, *Silent Hill* and *Bioshock*. Merriner relies on film theory to analyze and compare these two games. This thesis is an example of a thorough analysis of a horror game.

"Let's Play: Layers of Fear [Full Release] - Part 1 - A Beautiful Canvas [Twitch Facecam]." *YouTube*, uploaded by ChristopherOdd, 21 Feb. 2016, www.youtube.com/watch?v=M095GUg_5Yk.

> Christopher Odd is a longtime YouTuber who live streams video games and then uploads the unedited video onto *YouTube*. This is a video of Odd playing through the first few hours of *Layers of Fear*, a gothic video game, with a video of himself in the corner. Tim Summers suggests adding videos of other players' playthroughs as sources for analyzing video game music. One player's experience of a video game may not be the same as another's, so it is good to have another person's playthrough so that one can catch things that may not have happened during their own playthrough. Also, since video games are an interactive real-time experience, it will be much easier to use a rewindable video to analyze the music and the effect it has on the player.

Roberts, Rebecca. "Fear of the Unknown: Music and Sound Design in Psychological Horror Games." *Music in Video Games: Studying Play*, edited by K. J. Donnelly et al., Routledge, 2014.

> Roberts received her master's in musicology from the University of Southampton, focusing on video game music. In this essay, Roberts talks about how music is an important part of horror video games and how music and sound design enhance certain aspects of the game. Roberts gives examples of the way music intensifies events in specific video games. Unlike the other analyses, this is more of a general overview of music in horror games.

These annotations are purely descriptive; the author expresses none of their own opinions. The bibliography entries are documented in MLA style.

Evaluative annotations offer opinions on a source as well as describe it. They are often helpful in assessing how useful a source will be for your own writing. The following evaluative annotations are from a bibliography by Kelly Green, a student at Arizona State University. Following her instructor's directions, she labeled each required part of her annotation — summary, degree of advocacy, credibility, and reliability.

KELLY GREEN

Researching Hunger and Poverty

Abramsky, Sasha. "The Other America, 2012: Confronting the Poverty Epidemic." *The Nation*, vol. 294, no. 20, 25 Apr. 2012, www.thenation.com/article/archive/other-america-2012-confronting-poverty-epidemic/.

> The author presents the image of American poverty in 2012 with examples from various families living in poverty. The author explores the conditions that make up the new recession and suggests that people in America notice the scale of the issue and take action to solve it [Summary]. The author advocates poverty reform and shows bias toward the interests of low-income families. He acknowledges other perspectives on the issue respectfully [Degree of Advocacy]. Abramsky is a freelance journalist with experience in several magazines and newspapers. He has written several books on the topic of poverty [Credibility]. *The Nation* is one of the oldest-running magazines in the United States and contains opinions on politics and culture [Reliability].

Ambler, Marjane. "Sustaining Our Home, Determining Our Destiny." *Tribal College Journal*, vol. 13, no. 3, spring 2002, www.tribalcollegejournal.org/sustaining-home-determining-destiny/.

> The author examines the causes of poverty on Native American reservations, the factors that lead to solutions to Native American poverty, and the ways in which tribal colleges have helped improve life on reservations [Summary]. The author is strongly biased toward Native American interests and advocates that effective solutions to poverty originate within the reservations, especially in tribal colleges and universities [Degree of Advocacy]. Marjane Ambler was an editor for the *Tribal College Journal* for nine years and worked in national park service for nearly a decade [Credibility]. This article was published in 2002 in the *Tribal College Journal*, a national magazine published by the American Indian Higher Education Consortium [Reliability].

These annotations not only summarize the sources in detail but also evaluate their bias, or "degree of advocacy"; credibility; and reliability.

Key Features / Annotated Bibliographies

A statement of scope. Sometimes you need or are asked to provide a brief introductory statement to explain what you're covering. The author of the bibliography on music in video games introduces it with a brief paragraph establishing its context and purpose.

Complete bibliographic information. Annotations should provide all the information about each source using one documentation system (MLA, APA, or another one) so that you, your readers, or other researchers will be able to find the source easily. It's a good idea to include sources' URLs or **PERMALINKS** to make accessing online sources easier.

● 496

A concise description of the work. A useful annotation describes each item as carefully and objectively as possible, giving accurate information and showing that you understand the source. These qualities will help build authority—for you as a writer and for your annotations.

Relevant commentary. If you write an evaluative bibliography, your comments should be relevant to your purpose and audience. The best way to achieve relevance is to consider what questions a potential reader might have about each source: What are the main points of the source? What is its argument? How even-handed or biased is it? How current and reliable is it? What are the author's credentials? Will the source be helpful for your project?

Consistent presentation. All annotations should follow a consistent pattern: if one is written in complete sentences, they should all be. Each annotation in the video game music bibliography, for example, begins with a sentence describing the author's credentials.

A BRIEF GUIDE TO WRITING ANNOTATED BIBLIOGRAPHIES

Considering the Rhetorical Situation

PURPOSE Will your bibliography need to demonstrate the depth or breadth of your research? Will your readers actually

■ 75–78

track down and use your sources? Do you need or want to convince readers that your sources are good?

75–78 ■ **AUDIENCE** For whom are you compiling this bibliography? What does your audience need to know about each source?

85–87 ■ **STANCE** Are you presenting yourself as an objective describer or evaluator? Or are you expressing a particular point of view toward the sources you evaluate?

88–90 ■ **MEDIA/DESIGN** If you are publishing the bibliography electronically, will you provide links from each annotation to the source itself? Online or offline, should you distinguish the bibliographic information from the annotation by using a different font?

Generating Ideas and Text

Decide what sources to include. You may be tempted to include in a bibliography every source you find or look at. A better strategy is to include only those sources that you or your readers may find potentially useful in researching your topic. For an academic bibliography, consider the qualities in the list below. Some of these qualities should not rule a source in or out; they simply raise issues you need to think about.

- *Appropriateness.* Is this source relevant to your topic? Is it a primary source or a secondary source? Is it aimed at an appropriate audience? General or specialized? Elementary, advanced, or somewhere in between?

- *Credibility.* Is the author reputable? Is the publication, publishing company, or sponsor of the site reputable? Do the ideas more or less agree with those in other sources you've read?

- *Balance.* Does the source present enough evidence for its assertions? Does it show any particular bias? Does it present opposing arguments fairly?

- *Timeliness.* Is the source recent enough? Does it reflect current thinking or research about the subject?

482–503 ● If you need help **FINDING SOURCES**, see Chapter 48.

Compile a list of works to annotate. Give the sources themselves in whatever documentation style is required; see the guidelines for **MLA** and **APA** styles in Chapters 54 and 55.

MLA 542–94 ●
APA 595–633

Determine what kind of bibliography you need to write. Will your bibliography be descriptive or evaluative? Will your annotations be in the form of phrases? complete sentences? paragraphs? The form will shape your reading and note taking. If you're writing a descriptive bibliography, your reading goal will be just to understand and capture the writer's message as clearly as possible. If you're writing an evaluative bibliography, you will also need to assess the source as you read in order to include your own opinions of it.

Read carefully. To write an annotation, you must understand the source's argument; but when writing an annotated bibliography as part of a topic proposal for a research project, you may have neither the time nor the need to read the whole text. Here's a way of quickly determining whether a source is likely to serve your needs:

- Check the publisher or sponsor (university press? scholarly journal? popular magazine? website sponsored by a reputable organization?).
- Read the preface (of a book), abstract (of a scholarly article), introduction (of an article in a nonscholarly magazine or a website).
- Skim the table of contents or the headings.
- Read the parts that relate specifically to your topic.

Research the writer, if necessary. If you are required to indicate the writer's credentials, you may need to do additional research. You may find information by typing the writer's name into a search engine or looking up the writer in *Gale Literature: Contemporary Authors*. In any case, information about the writer should take up no more than one sentence in your annotation.

Summarize the work in a sentence or two. DESCRIBE it as objectively as possible: even if you're writing an evaluative annotation, you can evaluate the central point of a work better by stating it clearly first. *If you're writing a descriptive annotation, you're done.*

439–46

Establish criteria for evaluating sources. If you're EVALUATING SOURCES for a project, you'll need to evaluate them in terms of their usefulness for your project, their STANCE, and their overall credibility.

504–14

85–87

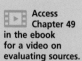

Access Chapter 49 in the ebook for a video on evaluating sources.

Write a brief evaluation of the source. If you can generalize about the worth of the entire work, fine. You may find, however, that some parts are useful while others are not, and what you write should reflect that mix.

Be consistent—in content, sentence structure, and format.

- *Content.* Try to provide about the same amount of information for each entry. If you're evaluating, don't evaluate some sources and just describe others.

- *Sentence structure.* Use the same style throughout—complete sentences, brief phrases, or a mix.

642–43 ●

- *Format.* Use one documentation style throughout; use a consistent FONT for each element in each entry—for example, italicize or underline all book titles.

Ways of Organizing an Annotated Bibliography

Access Chapter 30 in the ebook for a video on organizing and synthesizing ideas.

Depending on their purpose, annotated bibliographies may or may not include an introduction. Most annotated bibliographies cover a single topic and so are organized alphabetically by author's or editor's last name. When a work lacks a named author, alphabetize it by the first important word in its title. Consult the documentation system you're using for additional details about alphabetizing works appropriately.

Single-category bibliography

State scope. → List first alphabetical entry, and annotate it. → List second alphabetical entry, and annotate it. → Continue listing and annotating. → List final alphabetical entry, and annotate it.

Sometimes an annotated bibliography needs to be organized into several subject areas (or genres, periods, or some other category); if so, the entries are listed alphabetically within each category. For example, a bibliography about terrorism breaks down into subject categories such as "Global Terrorism" and "Weapons of Mass Destruction."

Multicategory bibliography

More Ways to Approach an Annotated Bibliography

Design a visual bibliography.   Make a poster, infographic, or concept map to represent and categorize your annotations in a visual way. Use icons, images, or color coding to represent each category of annotations and help your readers understand connections among your sources.

Create a collection of social media posts.   Compose each annotation as a separate post on *LinkedIn*, *TikTok*, *Instagram*, or another platform, making sure to tailor your posts to the particular platform and its rhetorical situation. Share the key idea from each source, along with your own evaluative comments—and perhaps provide a link to the source itself. Develop a hashtag to create continuity among your posts, and encourage your followers to engage by reposting, sharing, or replying to your work.

Make a podcast series.   Develop a catchy title for your podcast series, along with an intro segment that explains the scope and purpose of your bibliography. Then devote each episode to a discussion of one of your sources. Comment on the source in a conversational style, and perhaps invite a guest who can contribute to the discussion.

Remix.   After you've written a draft of your annotated bibliography, you might **REMIX** it: rework it into one or more of the genres above or turn it into a slide presentation, an oral presentation, or another genre or medium that fits your rhetorical situation.

▲ 280–90

Taking Stock of Your Work

Access Chapter 36 in the ebook for a video on reflecting on your writing.

Take stock of what you've written by considering these questions:

- Did curiosity about your topic play a role in your research and writing? If so, how?
- What previous experience did you have with research? In what ways, if any, did you draw on that experience for your annotated bibliography?
- How did you go about researching the entries in this bibliography? What databases or other tools did you use? How did you decide on keywords for your search?
- How did you approach sources that were difficult to understand? What reading strategies did you use to make sense of them?
- How did you decide which sources to include in your bibliography and which ones to leave out?
- Did you cite sources accurately?
- Overall, what was challenging about writing an annotated bibliography? What was rewarding?

REVIEWS OF SCHOLARLY LITERATURE

Reviews of scholarly literature describe and evaluate important research ("literature") available on a topic. In writing a literature review, your goal is to give an overview of the literature on a topic. You do that by discussing the literature that is most relevant to your topic and your purposes, providing clear and accurate summaries of appropriate source material, and describing relationships among facts and concepts. Here is a brief excerpt from a literature review that describes scholarship in zombie movies; it was written by a student at the University of Mary Washington.

CAMERON CARROLL

Zombie Film Scholarship
A Review of the Literature

Zombies are the shambling undead creatures that attack in hordes and strike terror into the hearts of moviegoers with their mindless aggression. Monsters on the big screen fascinate American audiences and scholars alike as representations of cultural fears and reflections of public perceptions, and they have done so since they first shuffled into theaters. The walking dead first haunted cinemas in 1932 with the release of *White Zombie* and have gone through cycles of popularity both at the box office and in scholarly debate. Without a doubt, the height of zombie scholarship began in the mid-2000s with only shallow mentions made in horror analyses before then. Only the English discipline gave the zombie credit as a subject worthy of study. As author and English professor Kyle Bishop wrote in 2010, "The zombie phenomenon has yet to be plumbed to its depths by the academic and literary markets."[1] Although significant zombie research has only surfaced in the 2000s, a valiant effort is currently being made to explore zombie symbolism and its historical and cultural context across nontraditional scholarly fields, such as anthropology, psychology, sociology, and philosophy.

. . .

Zombies, as creatures that waver between living and dead, necessarily bring forth questions on the nature of being and thus also fall into the realm of philosophy as seen in *Zombies, Vampires, and Philosophy: New Life for the Undead* published in 2010 and edited by Richard Greene and K. Silem Mohammed, professors of philosophy and English, respectively. Philosophers in the study of zombies seek to answer such questions as, is it better to be undead or dead? Richard Greene argues that since death is a state of nonexistence and Undeath is at least a primal existence, the question comes down to the classic "to be, or not to be?" For him, Undeath is the only option for a state of being, since death is nonexistence. Existence in any form is inherently better than utterly ceasing to be.[16] Greene's philosophy colleague, William Larkin, counters that zombies are driven to actions seen as evil and mindless, both states that humans do not usually choose. He cites how zombie films repeatedly depict survivors who ask their friends and family to kill them should it appear that they will turn into zombies, so desperate are they to avoid Undeath.[17] Simon Clark, a writer with a master's degree in Fine Arts, discusses morality in relation to zombies: if zombies are nonmoral and whether or not they are the freest creatures because of their lack of morality. Clark writes that they become ultimately free in their modern incarnations from turn-of-the-millennium cinema.[18] Zombies break through barriers that survivors put up to keep them confined and are so primal that they cannot be held accountable for their actions, making them truly liberated. A fictional creature encourages real discussions in philosophical debate, demonstrating yet another area that inspires scholars to reexamine their own field because of zombies.

. . .

The message to take away from zombie scholarship is that what it represents is evolutionary and infinitely debatable, but the victory for zombie studies is that zombies are being studied at all. After decades of being underrepresented in horror scholarship, zombies are finally getting their due as a cultural icon, complete with varying opinions and interpretations. Scholarly debate proves that the zombie is a valid resource for understanding American culture and worthy of the enthusiastic pursuit of interdepartmental scholarship. As shown within the scholarly works above, the debate over the meaning of the living dead is quite lively, indeed.

Notes

1. Kyle William Bishop, *American Zombie Gothic: The Rise and Fall (and Rise) of the Walking Dead in Popular Culture* (Jefferson, NC: McFarland, 2010), 7.

. . .

16. Richard Greene and K. Silem Mohammed, eds., *Zombies, Vampires, and Philosophy: New Life for the Undead* (Chicago: Open Court, 2010), 13.

17. Greene and Mohammed, 20.

18. Greene and Mohammed, 208.

Carroll begins by establishing a context for her discussion and then focuses on her topic, the scholarship of zombies in film. In her review, she discusses the history of zombie scholarship in general and then in psychology, social trends, fiction, and, in this excerpt, philosophy. A history major, she follows Chicago style; in addition to the notes, she included a bibliography listing all her sources, including the two noted here.

Key Features / Reviews of Scholarly Literature

Careful, thorough research.　A review of scholarly literature demands that you research all the major literature on the topic—or at least the major literature available to you, given the time you have.

Accurate, objective summaries of the relevant literature.　Readers expect a literature review to objectively summarize the main ideas or conclusions of the texts reviewed.

Critical evaluation of the literature.　A literature review offers considered selection of the most important, relevant, and useful sources of information on its topic, so you must evaluate each source to decide whether it should be included and then to determine how it advances understanding of the topic.

SYNTHESIS **of the scholarship.** A literature review differs from an annotated bibliography in that the review identifies key concepts, similarities, and differences within the body of literature, showing how the sources relate to one another by method, study findings, themes, main ideas, or something else.

● 515–20

A clear focus. Because a literature review provides an overview of your topic's main issues and explains the main concepts underlying your research, it must be carefully organized and clearly focused on your specific topic.

Taking Stock of Your Work

Take stock of what you've written by considering these questions:

 Access Chapter 36 in the ebook for a video on reflecting on your writing.

- Did curiosity about your topic play a role in your research and writing? If so, how?

- What previous experience did you have with research? In what ways, if any, did you draw on that experience for your literature review?

- How did you approach sources that were difficult to understand? What reading strategies did you use to make sense of them?

- What helped you the most in finding, keeping track of, and evaluating the scholarship? What can you do next time to make the process more efficient and productive?

- How did you decide which sources to include in your literature review and which ones to leave out?

- What led you to group related sources together as you did?

- How did you go about synthesizing similar sources?

- Overall, what was challenging about writing a literature review? What was rewarding?

If you need more help

See Chapter 31 for guidelines on **DRAFTING**, Chapter 32 for **ASSESSING YOUR OWN WRITING**, Chapter 33 for **GETTING RESPONSE AND REVISING**, and Chapter 34 for **EDITING AND PROOFREADING**. See Chapter 35 if you are required to submit your bibliography in a writing **PORTFOLIO**.

⁘ 358–60
361–64
365–71
372–76
377–82

17 Evaluations

TechSpot reviews computer gaming equipment. The *Princeton Review* and *U.S. News & World Report* evaluate colleges and universities. You probably consult such sources to make decisions, and you probably evaluate things all the time—when you recommend a film (or not) or a teacher (ditto). An evaluation is basically a judgment; you judge something according to certain criteria, supporting your judgment with reasons and evidence. You need to give your reasons for evaluating it as you do because often your evaluation will affect your audience's actions: they must see this movie, needn't bother with this book, should be sure to have the Caesar salad at this restaurant, and so on.

Techspot aggregates reviews of electronics from across the web and *Amazon*.

In college courses, students in *literature, film, drama,* and *art* classes may be assigned to evaluate poems, fiction, movies, plays, and artwork, and those in *business* and *political science* classes may be asked to evaluate advertising or political campaigns or plans for business or public-policy initiatives. In a review that follows, written for *Slate,* movie fan and Osage Nation member Joel Robinson offers his evaluation of the film *Killers of the Flower Moon.*

JOEL ROBINSON

Killers of the Flower Moon *Is Not the Story an Osage Would Have Told. You Should Still See It.*

I've always been so proud to be Osage. I'm thankful that I have a father that instilled that identity in me from a young age, as well as a non-Indigenous mother who has always reinforced it. But being Indigenous comes with a heavy load. All too often, it feels that we're carrying on our ancestors' Sisyphean task of struggling to become more visible and have our issues heard by non-Indigenous communities.

So when I heard years ago that this story I had grown up hearing was being adapted into a feature film and that none other than Martin Scorsese was directing it, I was knocked off my feet. I also had conflicting thoughts. On one hand, this was an opportunity for us to have our history told like never before. On the other, it was being done by an outsider who hadn't grown up with it like we had.

In 2021 those nerves were somewhat quieted. That year, I decided that I wanted to get more involved with my tribe and be given a name. My recent ancestors chose not to follow traditional naming practices (an effect of colonization), so finding my family's clan has required a ton of work that I'm still undertaking. But because our Wahzhazhe Cultural Center was busy with this film, they were hardly able to handle any other requests for a long time. Knowing that Scorsese and his crew were making use of them and many other resources on the rez began to ease my concerns and gave me hope that we would be properly represented. And represented we were.

Before I saw *Killers of the Flower Moon,* I spoke with Jim Gray, a former chief of the Osage Nation. In our conversation, he told me that he's never seen a film immerse itself in a culture like this one did with ours. Having now seen it, I have to wholeheartedly agree. Language was taught by our teachers, including Christopher Cote, who gave a wonderful interview after he saw the film at the Los Angeles premiere (Chuba). The costumes were made by Osage artists. Everything feels authentic to the time period.

As far as the story itself goes, I do not think that this is how an [5] Osage would've told it. From all I've read about Scorsese and Leonardo DiCaprio initiating a shift in the story's focus to center the Osage perspective rather than that of Tom White and the then-named Bureau of Investigation, I was hopeful that we would experience this tragedy through Mollie Burkhart (played sensationally by Lily Gladstone), the real-life Osage woman whose family was the target of one of the schemes of William Hale (Robert De Niro). Instead, the filmmakers opted to follow her white husband, convicted murderer Ernest Burkhart (DiCaprio). While I am disappointed in this choice, I do think that viewing the plot through the lens of Ernest grants the non-Osage audience the opportunity to gain more knowledge and understanding of the murderous scheme as the movie goes on.

Like Christopher said, I think it would take an Osage to make this film from the perspective of an Osage person. The problem is that, as Gladstone has said, no one is giving an Osage filmmaker Scorsese money to tell our story right now (Zilko). I hope that as more and more Indigenous filmmakers are given opportunities, an Osage will have the chance to adapt Charles H. Red Corn's novel *A Pipe for February*. The book tells the story of the Reign of Terror from the perspective of someone that lived through it, and I think it serves as a necessary companion to David Grann's more journalistic *Killers of the Flower Moon*.

As I was watching the film, I kept wondering how Scorsese would end it. After all, there's no white savior here. We were not saved by what is now known as the FBI. Our people got through this by relying on one another. Many cases weren't investigated, much less solved. It's hard to put an end to a chapter that's still present. To me, the finale just might be perfect. It elicited every single emotion I've ever felt when learning about the Reign of Terror. It made me so angry, so sad, and so disillusioned with our country's justice system. It also serves as a painful reminder of how stories centered on nonwhite groups are often told. The affected population is all too frequently granted a mere footnote in their own story in favor of making sure the "good guys" are glorified for "saving the day," regardless of historical accuracy (Stein).

Additionally, I feel that this scene turns the camera both inward and onto the audience simultaneously. (Slight spoilers ahead.) The all-white cast of what seems to be a radio program delivers this story of depravity not only to an in-studio audience of the same demographic, but also to the (presumably) predominantly white audience in the movie theater. The message from Scorsese? To my mind, it's that he knows that he and the viewers are and have always been complicit in these atrocities. It's now up to the audience whether they understand and accept their culpability.

There's been so much made of the run time of this movie, but I wholeheartedly encourage you to see it. It doesn't fly by per se, but it does maintain a good pace that I never found tedious. There's a lot to tell here—my ancestors lived through more than a decade of this. A length of three and a half hours is more than justified. Besides, the masterful performances by everyone involved help to keep you locked in.

It's important to me that you, the non-Osage reader of this article, know that this is merely a chapter in Osage history. While the effects of the Reign of Terror still live with us today, we do not live as victims. We are a proud, resilient people and our tribe is a thriving nation. I know that for many of you, this will be your first exposure to our people. I do hope it's not the last.

It's also important that you know that we are not the only tribe with a story like this. While this one is specific to my tribe, all tribes have their own dark histories that deserve to be told. I'm hopeful that this film will prove again to the powers that be that there is an audience for Indigenous-focused stories, and I hope that this can be a catalyst for other tribes to have their stories told.

For any non-Indigenous person seeing this film and encountering this history for the first time, I encourage you to be angry. I think it's a very healthy emotion to feel when learning about an event like this. This is a depiction of greed, racism, and an attempted extermination of a people, after all. But rather than sitting and wrestling with that anger internally, I hope that you can turn it into a drive to get engaged. Indigenous communities still have many issues that affect us today. I hope you use your anger to help us fight for visibility and for change.

Finally, I leave you with this: As the opportunity for Native peoples to have a voice in the entertainment space increases, more stories will come to light. Although some people will be content to plug their ears or bury their heads in the sand, that doesn't change history. No matter what you want to believe, you cannot understand the formation of the United States as we know it today without first reckoning with and understanding the sins it was formed through.

Works Cited

Chuba, Kirsten. "Osage Consultant Admits to Complicated Feelings over *Killers of the Flower Moon*: 'This Film Isn't Made for an Osage Audience.'" *The Hollywood Reporter*, 17 Oct. 2023, www .hollywoodreporter.com/movies/movie-news/killers-of-the-flower -moon-osage-consultant-mixed-feelings-1235620231/.

Gray, Jim. Personal communication with the author. 20 Sept. 2023.

Killers of the Flower Moon. Directed by Martin Scorsese, Apple Studios, 2023.

Red Corn, Charles H. *A Pipe for February*. U of Oklahoma P, 2005.

Stein, Ellin. "What's Fact and What's Fiction in *Killers of the Flower Moon*." *Slate*, 20 Oct. 2023, slate.com/culture/2023/10/killers -flower-moon-movie-true-story-osage.html.

Zilko, Christian. "Lily Gladstone Tempers Optimism about Native American Progress in Hollywood: 'Nobody Is Going to Hand an Osage Filmmaker $200 Million.'" *IndieWire*, 23 Sept. 2023, www .indiewire.com/news/general-news/lily-gladstone-nobody-would -hand-osage-filmmaker-200-million-1234908271/.

Robinson begins his evaluation by explaining his personal context as an Osage, which strongly influences his choice of criteria and judgment of the film. These criteria include the authenticity of the film's portrayal of the Osage and the historical events, the way the story was told, and the reasons for the film's length and its ending.

Key Features / Evaluations

A concise description of the subject. You should include just enough information to let readers who may not be familiar with your subject understand what it is; the goal is to evaluate, not summarize. Depending on your topic and medium, some of this information may be in visual or audio form. Robinson, for example, might have included a brief summary of the plot of *Killers of the Flower Moon* in his first paragraphs: "The film tells the true story of the murders of several members of the Osage Nation in the 1920s by white settlers after oil was found on the tribe's lands." Since he writes as an Osage, though, he focuses less on the plot, which he "had grown up hearing," and more on the film's cultural significance.

Clearly defined criteria. You need to determine clear criteria as the basis for your judgment. In reviews or other evaluations written for a broad audience, you can integrate the criteria into the discussion as reasons for your assessment. In more formal evaluations, you may need to announce your criteria explicitly. Robinson evaluates the film based on its accurate portrayal of Osage culture and language, the perspective from which the story is told, and the honesty of the events' portrayal.

A knowledgeable discussion of the subject. To evaluate something credibly, you need to show that you know it yourself and that you understand its context. Robinson not only discusses the film in detail, but he also cites several Osage and other sources to support his evaluation.

A balanced and fair assessment. An evaluation is centered on a judgment. While Robinson states that the film's point of view disappoints him, he concedes that its perspective may help non-Osage viewers understand the events portrayed; he also finds the film's length to be "more than justified" by those events. It is important that any judgment be balanced and fair. Seldom is something all good or all bad. A fair evaluation need not be all positive or all negative; it may acknowledge both strengths and weaknesses. For example, a movie's soundtrack may be wonderful while the plot is not.

Well-supported reasons. You need to argue for your judgment, providing reasons and evidence that might include visual and audio as well as verbal material. Robinson gives several reasons for his positive assessment of

Killers: the significance of the events, the actors' "masterful performances," its accurate portrayal of Osage culture. He supports these reasons with several examples from the film.

A BRIEF GUIDE TO WRITING EVALUATIONS

Choosing Something to Evaluate

 Access Chapter 14 in the ebook for a video on narrowing your topic.

You can more effectively evaluate a limited subject than a broad one: review certain dishes at a local restaurant rather than the entire menu; review one film or scene rather than all the films by Alfred Hitchcock or all seventy-three *Game of Thrones* episodes. The more specific and focused your subject, the better you can write about it.

Considering the Rhetorical Situation

73–74 **PURPOSE**   Are you writing to affect your audience's opinion of a subject? to help others decide what to see, do, or buy? to demonstrate your expertise in a field?

75–78 **AUDIENCE**   To whom are you writing? What will your audience already know about the subject? What will they expect to learn from your evaluation of it? Are they likely to agree with you or not?

85–87 **STANCE**   What is your attitude toward the subject, and how will you show that you have evaluated it fairly and appropriately? Think about the tone you want to use: Should it be reasonable? passionate? critical?

88–90 **MEDIA/DESIGN**   How will you deliver your evaluation? In print? Electronically? As a speech? Can you show images or audio or video clips? If you're submitting your text for publication, are there any format requirements?

Generating Ideas and Text

329 **Explore what you already know.**   **FREEWRITE** to answer the following questions: What do you know about this subject or subjects like it? What are your initial or gut feelings, and why do you feel as you do? How does this subject reflect or affect your basic values or beliefs? How have others evaluated subjects like this?

Identify criteria.   Make a list of criteria you think should be used to evaluate your subject. Think about which criteria will likely be important to your **AUDIENCE**. You might find **CUBING** and **QUESTIONING** to be useful processes for thinking about your criteria.

75–78
332
332–33

Evaluate your subject.   Study your subject closely to determine to what extent it meets each of your criteria. You may want to list your criteria and take notes related to each one, or you may develop a rating scale for each criterion to help stay focused on it. Come up with a tentative judgment.

Compare your subject with others.   Often, evaluating something involves **COMPARING AND CONTRASTING** it with similar things. We judge movies in comparison with the other movies we've seen and french fries with the other fries we've tasted. Sometimes those comparisons can be made informally. For other evaluations, you may have to do research—to try on several pairs of jeans before buying any, for example—to see how your subject compares.

422–28

State your judgment as a tentative thesis statement.   Your **THESIS** statement should be one that addresses both pros and cons. "*Hawaii Five-O* is fun to watch despite its stilted dialogue." "Of the five sport-utility vehicles tested, the Toyota 4Runner emerged as the best in comfort, power, and durability, though not in styling or cargo capacity." Both of these examples offer a judgment but qualify it according to the writer's criteria.

342–44

Anticipate other opinions.   I think Quinta Brunson is a brilliant writer and actor whose TV show *Abbott Elementary* is first-rate. You think Brunson is a terrible actor whose show is unwatchable. How can I write a review of her series that you will at least consider? One way is by **ACKNOWLEDGING OTHER VIEWPOINTS**—and **REFUTING** those opinions as best I can. I may not persuade you to watch Brunson's show, but I can at least demonstrate that by certain criteria she should be appreciated. You may need to **RESEARCH** how others have evaluated your subject.

411
412–13

471

Identify and support your reasons.   Write out all the **REASONS** you can think of that will convince your audience to accept your judgment. Review your list to identify the most convincing or important reasons. Then review how well your subject meets your criteria, and decide how best to **SUPPORT** your reasons: through examples, authoritative opinions, statistics, visual or audio evidence, or something else.

402

402–9

Access Chapter 30 in the ebook for a video on organizing and synthesizing ideas.

Ways of Organizing an Evaluation

Evaluations are usually organized in one of two ways. One way is to introduce what's being evaluated, followed by your judgment, discussing your criteria along the way. This is a useful strategy if your audience may not be familiar with your subject.

Start with your subject

Describe what you're evaluating. → State your judgment. → Provide reasons and evidence, discussing criteria as you apply them. → Acknowledge objections or other opinions. → Restate your overall judgment.

You might also start by identifying your criteria and then follow with a discussion of how well your subject meets those criteria. This strategy foregrounds the process by which you reached your conclusions.

Start with your criteria

Identify criteria for evaluation. → Describe what you're evaluating. → Evaluate it against each of your criteria, one at a time, adding potential objections or other opinions in relation to each criterion. → State your overall judgment.

More Ways to Approach an Evaluation

Evaluate something unusual or offbeat. If you have the opportunity, look for something to evaluate that others might find novel or interesting: your university's financial aid form, the covers of your textbooks, your campus's walking paths. If something has been designed and created in any medium, you can evaluate it.

Evaluate an experience. Sometimes relating an experience—how it feels to live through an event that unfolds in time—can be a powerful way to evaluate it: a boring lecture, a video game, a dentist's appointment, a television mystery, a concert. All create expectations that are or aren't fulfilled, which also function as criteria for how we evaluate our experience.

Create a podcast or blog. You might include not only your writing but also video or audio interviews, links to clips of films or television shows, and other information to show the reasons and evidence behind your evaluation. If you're evaluating a building, public space, or an object or machine, you might create a video showing how well the space or machine meets (or doesn't meet) your criteria. How well does it work? do what it's intended to do?

Remix. After you've written a draft of your evaluation, you might **REMIX** it: rework it into one of the genres above or turn it into an infographic, webpage, or other medium that fits your rhetorical situation.

▲ 280–90

Taking Stock of Your Work

Take stock of what you've written by considering these questions:

Access Chapter 36 in the ebook for a video on reflecting on your writing.

- How did you decide on your stance for your evaluation? How well does your evaluation communicate that stance?

- How did you develop criteria for your evaluation?

- In working on this piece, did you use a process or strategy you've used before? If so, what was it? How well did it work? What new strategies or processes do you want to try in the future?

- What academic habits of mind—like creativity, flexibility, persistence, or another habit—did you need in order to write this evaluation? What specific examples can you give?

- How satisfied are you with your writing? What would you do differently next time?

If you need more help

See Chapter 31 for guidelines on **DRAFTING**, Chapter 32 for **ASSESSING YOUR OWN WRITING**, Chapter 33 for **GETTING RESPONSE AND REVISING**, and Chapter 34 for **EDITING AND PROOFREADING**. See Chapter 35 if you are required to submit your evaluation in a writing **PORTFOLIO**.

358–60
361–64
365–71
372–76
377–82

18 Literary Analyses

Literary analyses are essays that examine literary texts closely to understand their messages, interpret their meanings, appreciate their techniques, or understand their historical or social contexts. Such texts traditionally include novels, short stories, poems, and plays but may also include films, TV shows, videogames, music, and comics. You might read Gwendolyn Brooks's poem "We Real Cool" and notice how she uses slang to get across her message. You could explore the distinctive point of view in Ambrose Bierce's story "An Occurrence at Owl Creek Bridge." Or you could point out the differences between Stephen King's *The Shining* and Stanley Kubrick's screenplay based on that novel. In all these cases, you use specific analytical techniques to go below the surface of the work to deepen your understanding of how it works and what it means.

You may be assigned to analyze works of literature in courses in *English, film, drama,* and many other subjects. Here are two poems by American poets Richard Blanco, a Cuban American poet who teaches at Florida International University, and Langston Hughes, a poet and novelist who was part of the Harlem Renaissance in the 1920s and 1930s, followed by a student's analysis of the poems for a literature course at Emory University.

 RICHARD BLANCO
Complaint of El Río Grande

I was meant for all things to meet:
to make the clouds pause in the mirror
of my waters, to be home to fallen rain
that finds its way to me, to turn eons
of loveless rock into lovesick pebbles
and carry them as humble gifts back
to the sea which brings life back to me.

5

I felt the sun flare, praised each star
flocked about the moon long before
you did. I've breathed air you'll never   10
breathe, listened to songbirds before
you could speak their names, before
you dug your oars in me, before you
created the gods that created you.

Then countries—your invention—maps   15
jigsawing the world into colored shapes
caged in bold lines to say: you're here,
not there, you're this, not that, to say:
yellow isn't red, red isn't black, black is
not white, to say: *mine*, not *ours*, to say   20
war, and believe life's worth is relative.

You named me big river, drew me—blue,
thick to divide, to say: *spic* and *Yankee*,
to say: *wetback* and *gringo*. You split me
in two—half of me *us*, the rest *them*. But   25
I wasn't meant to drown children, hear
mothers' cries, never meant to be your
geography: a line, a border, a murderer.

I was meant for all things to meet:
the mirrored clouds and sun's tingle,   30
birdsongs and the quiet moon, the wind
and its dust, the rush of mountain rain—
and us. Blood that runs in you is water
flowing in me, both life, the truth we
know we know: be one in one another.   35

LANGSTON HUGHES
The Negro Speaks of River

I've known rivers:
I've known rivers ancient as the world and older than
the flow of human blood in human veins.

My soul has grown deep like the rivers.

I bathed in the Euphrates when dawns were young.
I built my hut near the Congo and it lulled me to sleep.   5
I looked upon the Nile and raised the pyramids above it.
I heard the singing of the Mississippi when Abe Lincoln
went down to New Orleans, and I've seen its muddy
bosom turn all golden in the sunset.

I've known rivers:
Ancient, dusky rivers.

My soul has grown deep like the rivers.   10

KRITHIKA SHRINIVAS
Blanco and Hughes
Rivers and Identity

Throughout the course of human history, rivers have been essential in shaping the emergence and development of complex human civilizations. Rivers are a main source of drinking water, and they have also been crucial for cultivating agriculture and for fishing. However, in both Richard Blanco's poem "Complaint of El Río Grande" and Langston Hughes's poem "The Negro Speaks of Rivers," the symbol of the river transcends its traditional associations as the poets delve into more abstract elements of the human experience, such as pride, race, and identity. Blanco is a modern-day poet, while Hughes wrote during the Harlem Renaissance in the 1920s, but their poems both present compelling narratives about the intersection of rivers and discrimination of various kinds, depicting rivers as agents of change. Both Blanco and Hughes use the river as a symbol to make points about unity and division, and both weave in real rivers and geographical boundaries, but their interpretation of the river symbol varies when they speak of oppression in their respective eras.

In Blanco's "Complaint of El Río Grande," the river symbolizes the harmony of nature and how it is being obstructed to further mankind's selfish agendas. Blanco first uses the river symbol when describing its interactions with other elements of nature. The river is a "home to fallen rain" (line 3), and serves to "turn eons/of loveless rock into lovesick pebbles" (4–5). This imagery creates a somber mood, illustrating how nature can be fragmented and distraught. However, the river is personified as a unifier and healer, bringing the natural world together in order to establish harmony. The river takes the rain that has "fallen," a word choice suggesting aimlessness and apathy, and provides it with an identity greater than that of a raindrop by welcoming it into a bigger body of water; it molds the rock—typically associated with ruggedness—and transforms it into a smoother pebble, illustrating its healing ability. The river's personification as a unifier transcends its ties with nature and ventures into the realm of humankind: "Blood that runs in you is water/flowing in me" (33–34). Blood symbolizes life, and this line shows the river's viewpoint that all of life should be treated equally, as nature is all the same in essence.

However, Blanco suggests that the river is unable to continue promoting unity and healing the natural world because of mankind's exploitation of it, evident in the words "you dug your oars in me" (13). This line employs an accusatory tone, using the sharpness of the word "dug" to illustrate the action of boating, in order to highlight the manipulation that the river had to endure at the hands of mankind. The oar is a phallic symbol that cuts through the surface of the river, indicating man's exploitation of the river as they row the boat. This idea of mankind's imposition on nature and overall destructive tendencies is furthered in the line "never meant to be your/geography: a line, a border, a murderer" (27–28). While the first stanza uses abstract images to highlight the ethereal qualities of the river, the introduction of mankind reduces the river to a mere border, demonstrating a sharp contrast between the river's original role as a healer and man's manipulation of it. Rather than allowing it to be a free-flowing body of water, mankind has placed limitations on the river, oppressing its original identity for their own benefit.

While Blanco's poem explores the river as a symbol of unity that has been manipulated by humankind, in Hughes's poem, "The Negro Speaks of Rivers," the river symbol is used to explore pride and race, ideas that are deeply rooted in identity. The river is introduced when the speaker acknowledges their familiarity with rivers, claiming to have known rivers "older than the flow of human blood in human veins" (Hughes, line 2). In a way reminiscent of Blanco's poem, these lines represent the duality of rivers and their association with blood—like veins, rivers wind around on their landscape and hold a substance, water, the way veins hold blood. This idea communicates that rivers are more than mere water, serving as a symbol of one's heritage, identity, and roots. Additionally, as blood is a symbol of life, this shows the endurance of the African people, connecting back to Langston Hughes's own heritage. The blood has flowed from ancient times, generation to generation before reaching the speaker. Through such images, Hughes demonstrates that the speaker has great pride in their heritage and race.

Hughes continues to discuss the symbol of the river when the speaker states, "My soul has grown deep like the rivers" (3). Rivers require extensive time to grow and gain depth; a soul that is compared to rivers is one that has had to face the wear and tear of time in order to grow. This illustrates the strife and struggles that the African American community has had to endure over the course of a history marred by slavery and oppression. Near the end of the poem, Hughes reiterates the speaker's familiarity with rivers, this time noting their "dusky" quality (9), in order to demonstrate the history of turmoil and suffering. Blanco's and Hughes's poems both convey the connection that rivers have to a person's identity. However, Blanco depicts the river symbol as a victim of humanity, whereas Hughes's poem portrays the river in a more empowering manner, showing its involvement in race and identity.

Although Blanco's and Hughes's poems differ in their interpretation of the river symbol, they both refer to real rivers and geographical divisions to delve into the theme of oppression. In "Complaint of El Río Grande," Blanco demonstrates the oppression that mankind inflicts on nature and other people when he refers to "maps/jigsawing the world" (15–16). Reminiscent of the colonization of the Americas by European settlers, the word "jigsawing" is particularly striking, showing a parallel between the disjointed nature of puzzle pieces and the act of colonization. While the speaker—the river—yearns for the idealistic world of the past where there were no geographic boundaries, humankind is depicted as having fragmented a world that was once whole and harmonious. The words "*spic* and *Yankee*, / . . . *wetback* and *gringo*" (23–24) refer to the tensions between the United States and Mexico, and the divisions that mankind has imposed between groups of people, oppressing some while empowering others.

The idea of oppression is also described in Hughes's "The Negro Speaks of Rivers" through references to real rivers and locations, which

5

convey broader ideas of history and identity. The poem begins by referencing rivers in places that were cradles of early civilization. Hughes takes the reader on a journey, narrating how the speaker "bathed in the Euphrates" (4) and "built [their] hut near the Congo" (5). Both lines illustrate the speaker's deeply rooted connection to their place of origin as they immerse themselves in its early history. The speaker says that the Congo River "lulled [them] to sleep" (5), showing how the speaker finds comfort when looking back on their heritage. This personification of the river in this poem is similar to the personification of the river in Blanco's poem, where the river is also depicted as a source of solace and tranquility.

Hughes shifts from these scenic images to pointing out a power dynamic where the speaker "raised the pyramids/above [the Nile]" (6); this shows the sense of autonomy that the ancestors of the speaker and other African Americans had in Africa before their history was marred by slavery and oppression. However, it is clear that the speaker refuses to lose hope for a future free of oppression for their people, as is demonstrated when the speaker says of the Mississippi River, "I've seen its muddy bosom turn all golden in the sunset" (7). This conveys that although the water is currently murky—a sign that the oppression has not left—a better future is still possible, indicated by the word "golden," which suggests hope.

"Complaint of El Río Grande" and "The Negro Speaks of Rivers" use the symbol of the river in ways that transcend its traditional associations, delving into ideas that are deeply relevant to the human experience. Both writers use the river as a way of considering the divisions and discrimination present in their own time periods. By using differing interpretations of the river and weaving in real-world rivers and geographical divisions, the writers establish how multifaceted the symbol is, gesturing at the idea that there is hope for a better future, but that humanity is also marred by an oppression that is still present today.

Works Cited

Blanco, Richard. "Complaint of El Río Grande." *Richard Blanco*, www.richard-blanco.com/book/how-to-love-a-country /complaint-of-el-rio-grande/. Accessed 9 Oct. 2019.

Hughes, Langston. "The Negro Speaks of Rivers." *Poetry Foundation*, https://www.poetryfoundation.org/poems/44428/the-negro -speaks-of-rivers. Accessed 9 Oct. 2019.

Shrinivas focuses her analysis on specific words and phrases used by each poet to compare and contrast their treatments of rivers as symbols of both natural and human traits.

Key Features / Literary Analyses

An arguable thesis. A literary analysis is a form of argument; you are arguing that your analysis of a literary work is valid. Your thesis, then, should be arguable, as Shrinivas's is: "Both Blanco and Hughes use the river as a symbol to make points about unity and division, and both weave in real rivers and geographical boundaries, but their interpretation of the river symbol varies when they speak of oppression in their respective eras." A mere summary—"The two poets write about rivers"—would not be arguable and therefore would not be a good thesis.

Careful attention to the language of the text. The key to analyzing a text is looking carefully at the language, which is the foundation of its meaning. Specific words, images, metaphors—these are where analysis begins. You may also bring in contextual information, such as cultural, historical, or biographical facts, or you may refer to similar texts. But the words, phrases, and sentences that make up the text you are analyzing are your primary source when dealing with texts. That's what literature teachers mean by "close reading": reading with the assumption that every word of a text is meaningful.

Attention to patterns or themes. Literary analyses are usually built on evidence of meaningful patterns or themes within a text or among several texts. These patterns and themes reveal meaning. Shrinivas notes that both poems address oppression of minorities and contrasts Blanco's river's rejection of the role imposed on it ("I wasn't meant . . . to be your geography: a line, a border, a murderer") with Hughes's identification of rivers with his heritage ("I've known rivers: / Ancient, dusky rivers. / My soul has grown deep like the rivers.").

A clear interpretation. A literary analysis demonstrates the plausibility of its thesis by using evidence from the text and, sometimes, relevant contextual evidence to explain how the language and patterns found there support a particular interpretation. When you write a literary analysis, you show readers one way the text may be read and understood; that is your interpretation.

MLA style. Literary analyses usually follow MLA style. Shrinivas's essay includes a works-cited list and refers to line numbers using MLA style.

A BRIEF GUIDE TO WRITING LITERARY ANALYSES

Considering the Rhetorical Situation

PURPOSE
What do you need to do? Show that you have examined the text carefully? Offer your own interpretation? Demonstrate a particular analytical technique? Or some combination? If you're responding to an assignment, does it specify what you need to do?

73–74

AUDIENCE
What do you need to do to convince your readers that your interpretation is plausible and based on sound analysis? Can you assume that readers are already familiar with the text you are analyzing, or do you need to tell them about it?

75–78

STANCE
How can you see your subject through interested, curious eyes—and then step back in order to see what your observations might mean?

85–87

MEDIA/DESIGN
Will your analysis focus on an essentially verbal text or one that has significant visual content, such as a graphic novel? Will you need to show visual elements in your analysis? Will it be delivered in a print, spoken, or electronic medium? Are you required to follow MLA or some other style?

88–90

Generating Ideas and Text

Look at your assignment. Does it specify a particular kind of analysis? Does it ask you to consider a particular theme? To use any specific critical approaches? Look for any terms that tell you what to do, words like "analyze," "compare," "interpret," and so on.

Study the text with a critical eye. When we read a literary work, we often come away with a reaction to it: we like it, we hate it, it made us cry or laugh, it perplexed us. That may be a good starting point for a literary analysis, but to write about literature you need to go beyond initial reactions, to think about how the text works: What does it *say*, and what does it *do*? What elements make up this text? How do those elements work together or fail to work together? Does this text lead you to think or feel a certain way? How does it fit into a particular context (of history, culture, technology, genre, and so on)?

Choose a method for analyzing the text.   There are various ways to analyze your subject. Three common focuses are on the text itself, on your own experience reading it, and on other cultural, historical, or literary contexts.

- *The text itself.* Trace the development and expression of themes, characters, and language through the work. How do they help create the overall meaning, tone, or effect for which you're arguing? To do this, you might look at the text as a whole, something you can understand from all angles at once. You could also pick out parts from the beginning, middle, and end as needed to make your case, **DEFINING** key terms, **DESCRIBING** characters and settings, and **NARRATING** key scenes. You might focus on one text or examine the same themes in several different works. For example, Shrinivas's essay about two poems by Blanco and Hughes offers a text-based analysis that looks at their differing ways of using rivers as symbols.

429–38
439–46
457–64

- *Your own response as a reader.* Explore the way the text affects you or develops meanings as you read through it from beginning to end. By doing such a close reading, you're slowing down the process to notice how one element of the text leads you to expect something, confirming earlier suspicions or surprises. You build your analysis on your experience of reading the text—as if you were pretending to drive somewhere for the first time, though in reality you know the way intimately. By closely examining the language of the text as you experience it, you explore how it leads you to a set of responses, both intellectual and emotional. If you were responding in this way to the Blanco poem, you might discuss how the meaning of the first line of the poem, "I was meant for all things to meet," changes as the poem moves from its description of the natural world to the world of man and its many diversions.

136

- *Context.* Analyze the text as part of some larger **CONTEXT** —as part of a certain time or place in history or as an expression of a certain culture (how does this text relate to the time and place of its creation?), as one of many other texts like it, a representative of a genre (how is this text like or unlike others of its kind? how does it use, play with, or flout the conventions of the genre?). A context-based approach to the Hughes poem might look at the ways he was influenced by the poets and musicians of the Harlem Renaissance of the 1920s and 1930s.

Read the work more than once. Reading literature, watching films, or listening to speeches is like driving to a new destination: the first time you go, you need to concentrate on getting there; on subsequent trips, you can see other aspects—the scenery, the curve of the road, other possible routes—that you couldn't pay attention to earlier. When you experience a piece of literature for the first time, you usually focus on the story, the plot, the overall meaning. By experiencing it repeatedly, you can see how its effects are achieved, what the pieces are and how they fit together, where different patterns emerge, how the author crafted the work.

To analyze a literary work, then, plan to read it more than once, with the assumption that every part of the text is there for a reason. Focus on details, even on a single detail that shows up more than once: Why is it there? What can it mean? How does it affect our experience of reading or studying the text? Also, look for anomalies, details that *don't* fit the patterns: Why are they part of the text? What can they mean? How do they affect the experience of the text? See the **READING IN ACADEMIC CONTEXTS** chapter for several different methods for reading a text.

✳ 11–28

Compose a strong thesis. The **THESIS** of a literary analysis should be specific, limited, and open to potential disagreement. In addition, it should be analytical, not evaluative: avoid thesis statements that make overall judgments, such as a reviewer might do: "Virginia Woolf's *The Waves* is a failed experiment in narrative" or "No one has equaled the achievement of *The Lego Movie*." Rather, offer a way of seeing the text: "The choice presented in Robert Frost's 'The Road Not Taken' ultimately makes no difference"; "The plot of *The Lego Movie* reflects contemporary American media culture."

⁝ 342–44

▶ **Access Chapter 30** in the ebook for a video on thesis statements in analyses.

Read the text carefully. When you analyze a text, you need to find specific, brief passages that support your interpretation. Then you should interpret those passages in terms of their language, their context, or your reaction to them as a reader. To find such passages, you must read the text closely, questioning it as you go, asking, for example:

- What language provides evidence to support your thesis?
- What does each word (phrase, passage) mean exactly?

- Why does the writer choose *this* language, *these* words? What are the implications or connotations of the language? If the language is dense or difficult, why might the writer have written it that way?

426–27
- What images, **SIMILES**, or **METAPHORS** are used? What is their effect on the meaning?

- What patterns of language, imagery, or plot do you see? If something is repeated, what significance does the repetition have?

- How does each word, phrase, or passage relate to what precedes and follows it?

- How does the experience of reading the text affect its meaning?

136
- What words, phrases, or passages connect to a larger **CONTEXT**? What language demonstrates that this work reflects or is affected by that context?

- How do these various elements of language, image, and pattern support your interpretation?

422–28
Your analysis should focus on analyzing and interpreting your subject, not simply summarizing or paraphrasing it. Many literary analyses also use the strategy of **COMPARING** two or more works.

Find evidence to support your interpretation. The parts of the text you examine in your close reading become the evidence you use to support your interpretation. Some think that we're all entitled to our own opinions about literature. And indeed we are. But when writing a literary analysis, we're entitled only to our own *well-supported* and *well-argued* opinions. When you 399–416 analyze a text, you must treat it like any other **ARGUMENT**: you need to discuss how the text creates an effect or expresses a theme, and then you 402–9 have to show **EVIDENCE** from the text—significant plot or structural elements; important characters; patterns of language, imagery, or action—to back up your argument.

Pay attention to matters of style. Literary analyses have certain conventions for using pronouns and verbs.

- In informal papers, it's OK to use the first person: "I believe Frost's narrator has little basis for claiming that one road is 'less traveled.'" In more formal essays, make assertions directly; claim authority to make statements about the text: "Frost's narrator has no basis for claiming that one road is 'less traveled.'"

- Discuss textual features in the **PRESENT TENSE** even if quotations from the text are in another tense: "When Nick finds Gatsby's body floating in the pool, he says very little about it: 'the laden mattress moved irregularly down the pool.'" Describe the historical context of the setting in the **PAST TENSE**: "In the 1920s, such estates as Gatsby's were rare."

★ HB-11–12

★ HB-11–12

Cite and document sources appropriately. Use **MLA** citation and documentation style unless told otherwise. Format **QUOTATIONS** properly, and use **SIGNAL PHRASES** to introduce quoted material.

● MLA 542–94
523–26
529–32

Think about format and design. Brief essays do not require **HEADINGS**; text divisions are usually marked by **TRANSITIONS** between paragraphs. In longer papers, though, headings can be helpful.

● 644–45
⁝ 355–56

Organizing a Literary Analysis
Of a single text

Access Chapter 30 in the ebook for a video on organizing and synthesizing ideas.

Comparing two texts

More Ways to Approach a Literary Analysis

Create a podcast. How does reading aloud the literary work or an excerpt from it change your interpretation of the work? Are there interviews with the author or recordings of the author reading the work? You might compare your own reading with those of others.

Write a parody. Play with your analysis by creating a spoof of the literary work, your analysis of it, or both. You might even write a performance review of the author and the work.

Remix. After you've written a draft of your literary analysis, you might **REMIX** it: rework it into one or more of the genres above or turn it into an infographic, a comic book, or blog post.

280–90 ▲

Taking Stock of Your Work

Take stock of what you've written by considering these questions:

Access Chapter 36 in the ebook for a video on reflecting on your writing.

- How did you go about analyzing the text? Did you focus on the text itself? your own response? the larger context? something else? Why?

- How did you come up with your thesis? Did you need to revise, expand, or narrow it?

- Did you provide enough evidence from the text or its context to support your analysis?

- How did your audience affect the language and tone you used in your piece?

- Did you try anything new in your writing process for this piece? A new way of generating ideas and text? A new way of drafting or revising? Something else? If so, what was the result?

- How did you plan and manage your time for this project? How well did you stick to your plan? If changes were needed, how did you adapt?

- What did you learn about yourself as a reader through your work on this piece? How can you apply that learning to future reading tasks?

- Are you pleased with your analysis? What did it teach you about the text you analyzed? Did it make you want to read more works by the same author?

If you need more help

See Chapter 31 for guidelines on **DRAFTING**, Chapter 32 for **ASSESSING YOUR OWN WRITING**, Chapter 33 for **GETTING RESPONSE AND REVISING**, and Chapter 34 for **EDITING AND PROOFREADING**. See Chapter 35 if you are required to submit your analysis in a writing **PORTFOLIO**.

358–60
361–64
365–71
372–76
377–82

19 Personal Narratives

We write personal narratives to explore our past—about shopping for a party dress with Grandma, or driving a car for the first time, or breaking up with our first love. Personal narratives focus on events and people and places that are important to us. We usually have two goals when we write a narrative: to capture important moments and to convey something about their significance for us. You may be asked to write personal narratives in *psychology*, *education*, and *English* courses. The following example, written by Ryan McLendon for a writing course at the University of North Texas, was nominated for the 2022 Norton Writer's Prize.

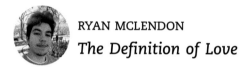

RYAN MCLENDON
The Definition of Love

When her teacher asks, "What does love mean to you?," Viviana grins with a mouth full of piano keys and rasps in her big-girl voice that *love* is Bubba using his pocketknife to cut strawberries because he hasn't had a chance to do the dishes yet.

She gets sent home with a note I find when I'm digging through her backpack for her homework folder:

We are concerned about your child's definition of love.

My little sister is in kindergarten. ("Not little," she'd correct me with all the authority of a girl twice her size. Not little, I'd agree.) I know her as a girl who can spot a spider from across the living room with a glance and safely transport it outside without so much as a trembling finger. Her teachers know her as a girl who makes bird calls in class and crawls under tables when she's bored.

Last week's note about the bird calls hadn't gone over well with our grandmother, Nina.   5

I tuck the note in my pocket and tell myself Nina doesn't need to see it.

My fifteen-year-old brother has a smile like a cartoon. It's a direct result of hours spent singing along to *Beetlejuice*, the musical; the high notes, the low notes, and the dramatic speak-singing of a theater kid floats through the wall connecting our bedrooms.

"You could use a buddy. Don't you want a pal? Yes I do! Yes I do!"

I knock on his open door to ask him to quiet down a little so I can concentrate on finishing an essay—because even when visiting home for the holidays, I never get a break from college classes. There's no reply, so I crack open the door. He's standing hunched over his desk, doing a stupid little back-and-forth with his too-thin hips and speak-singing as he methodically slots his newest Lego kit together. The box had advertised "a dozen hours of fun!" Chris distills the massive *Jurassic World* kit into 180 minutes of him with his headphones on, forgetting the world exists.

I forget my essay in favor of sitting on the crumpled blue comforter 10 at the foot of his bed and throwing his dwindling pile of Legos at the ceiling as *Beetlejuice* blasts from the speaker of his phone, his head-phones set precariously on the corner of his desk.

Before we came to live with our grandmother, our mother had rules: music is meant to be shared, and bugs are always a good luck charm. Roly-polies, butterflies, ladybugs. Dragonflies, in the case of Chris, who was born on the thirteenth and who knows better than to utter the name Macbeth. According to *Google*, dragonflies like water lilies. But we live in south Texas, an hour from the gulf, and water lilies are hard to care for. So, my sister grabs the easy-to-care-for spider lily instead.

"It has nothing to do with Chris," Nicolette tells me on the back porch when I joke that she's trying to ward away her brother's bad luck. Her too-large T-shirt brushes the ground from where she's crouched over the lip of the pot, water pail tipped at a methodical 45-degree angle. She glares up at me, hands never wavering. "I'm proving I can keep something alive."

"I never doubted you," I tell her. She scoffs.

"Yeah, but Nina did."

My siblings and I are half siblings: different dads, same mom. 15

When our mom died, her mother, Nina, came out of retirement to open her home to us. But she's old. I don't think she knew what she was getting into. How much energy it takes to raise four kids eleven years apart. She tires easily, and the air thickens with her moods. Chokes. So on her bad days, I take over bedtime reading.

Viviana chooses the book—books with pictures of woodland creatures, and faeries, and sad things that get better, because she can't bear when they don't get better. I tuck her into my side and do my silliest voices and watch her curious fingers brush over the paintings before I turn the page.

By the middle of the first chapter, Nicolette sits at the foot of the bed, one foot dangling lazily over the side with the other curled loosely beneath her. "I can't concentrate on my debate homework when you're so loud and obnoxious." A freshman in high school on her University Scholastic League debate team. Top of her class. Her frown would fit cleanly in a room full of lawyers.

"Then you can go use my desk," I offer.

She shrugs, flips her shiny hair over her shoulder, and doesn't move. 20

By the beginning of the second chapter, Chris stands at the foot of the bed, hands for horns and cross-eyed as he acts out the characters, never quite in time with my narration, but never more than a sentence behind.

On Nina's good days, I'll leave my room for a study snack and find Viviana with her favorite sparkling tiara balanced precariously on her pigtails, her plastic princess shoes sending her into a tizzy on the tile as she twirls around the living room. On the TV, Mirabel from *Encanto* is lamenting her luck. Between one peal of laughter and the next, Viviana never quite sings in time, but she's never more than a beat behind, and grinning all the same. She clutches Chris's foam *Minecraft* sword in one sinewy outstretched arm, and her laughter twists into a howling shriek when I barely avoid being smacked on my way out of the kitchen.

My car is a 2008 seven-seater with a CD player and no Bluetooth features. For a while after I got it—after we freed it from Mom's garage, and I took on the long and horrible process of cleaning it out—it was just me, my siblings, and the *Now That's What I Call Music!* hits from the early 2000s that came in Mom's CD holder—the ones I couldn't throw out. Mostly, we listened to it to and from school. Nicolette for debate competitions, and Chris for theater.

Chris's first major role in theater was in *The Tell-Tale Heart* by Edgar Allan Poe. On stage, he looked sharper, smothered in gaudy makeup, expressive mouth spasming around his words. He's my brother, and I'm biased, but he wiped every kid clean that night.

When I think of Poe, I think of ravens, and so under the too-harsh 25 stage lights, he became a bird.

When I pick up Chris from his theater rehearsals after school, my car becomes a birdcage, housing a flutter of hands and odd noises. Like a wild raven, some days he brings me odds and ends he found abandoned in the nooks and crannies he shimmies into. One day, it was an aux cord he pawned from a friend for a Coke.

Chris hits the DISC/AUX button and hooks the aux up to the stereo, his other hand reaching for my phone in the cup holder. He puts in my password and pulls up a musical we both like, the rapid speak-singing of his day never slowing.

Nicolette's bus arrives before Chris's rehearsals let out. I wait in the driveway for the yellow taxi from hell to turn the corner and spit her out. She claims she isn't a theater kid, but she has her lines memorized to muscle memory:

"Hey, Nicki. How was your day?"

"Fine." 30

"Really? What did you learn?"

"Literally nothing at all."

Her sunflower shoes scuff the driveway, her jacket kissing the ground as she makes her way into the house, heading straight for the pantry. I start up the coffee maker and push aside the bowls to find Nicolette's cactus mug.

The pot clicks on with a groan, hissing displeasure at the watery mess I make, coffee as bitter as it can be brewed because that's how she likes it. I pull out a fresh carton of creamer and use my teeth to open the seal. The script begins again as Nina turns the corner into the kitchen.

"How was your day, Nicolette?" Nina asks. 35

"Fine."

"Well, good. I'm glad to hear it."

The script ends. I pour a little creamer in Nicolette's coffee. She takes the carton from my hands and pours a little in mine.

Viviana struggles with numbers. We all did when we were her age.

Nina doesn't get *why* she struggles. 40

"Y'all did just fine. Your mom sent me your test scores. She was always so proud. So what's wrong with her?"

Add up all the variables, and there's a difference: Mom taught Nicolette, Chris, and me how to work with numbers. How to wrangle them into something sensible. Something musical. She'd use flashcards with bugs and flowers, her voice soft as she guided us through the frustration that always felt so big for such little bodies.

Nina threw those cards away. Said they were old, and no good, and that Viviana wouldn't need them. (I try not to hold it against her. She didn't want any reminder of the daughter she lost. The mother we lost before she had a chance to show Viviana how to work with numbers.)

So when Viviana struggles with her frustration, I sit her down with M&Ms. M&M&M&Ms—a few extra M's to make her giggle. I place the M&Ms in her hands and watch her curl her marker-coated fingers into fists, her frustration crumbling with the candy shells.

I tell her, "Count the M&Ms as you crush them." And she does. 45

When I have bad days, I go home and teach the kids how to defend themselves. How to sideswipe with scissors. I tell Nicolette, "Put down your homework and pay attention to me. This is how you choke out a man twice your size."

I don't realize how big she's gotten until the silver trinkets on her charm bracelet carve into my neck. I tell her to squeeze harder so I could feel how badly it would hurt someone else. Chris bites his nails from the sideline and tells her to take her bracelet off. His bitten hands lurch for her, for *me*, when Nicolette jumps off the floor to use her weight as leverage, trusting me to catch the both of us or trusting she's tough enough to break our fall. The trinkets drag across my windpipe and leave angry red divots in my throat.

I tell her, "Again. Do it again." And she does.

One day, Nina walks into my room and catches me pulling out a splinter in my palm with my teeth.

"What are you doing?"

"I've got a splinter." 50

"Stop that."

Her knobby knuckles are an iron shackle on my wrist as she leads me into her bathroom. She grabs a pair of tweezers and turns on the faucet. "Stick it under that," she says, so I shove my hand under the water. A minute later, steady fingers made for a needle and thread remove the splinter from my damp palm.

She places the tweezers in my hand.

"I taught your mom how to do that, too."

Competitions are what Nicolette lives for. Everything is a game: rock-paper-scissors for aux cord privileges in my car (Chris gets shotgun as the second oldest); an origami bird contest, even though Chris has been folding for years, because Nicolette would rather die than be shown up by her brother; a contest of strengths: Who can stir the Rice Krispies pot for the longest before their arms give out?

When I walk into my room and find Nicolette passed out at my desk, it becomes a competition: How quietly can I remove a blanket from the top shelf of my closet; how tightly can I tuck the blanket around her shoulders before she stirs; how much of her homework can I tug from under her cheek so that she won't see the drool on it?

When I was little—God knows how small, but small enough for skinned knees to be the end of the world—Mom taught me how to remove splinters. She showed me how to pucker the skin, soften the wound, and gently remove the woodchip.

It's one of the few things I don't think I've ever taught my siblings how to do. It's a small piece of our mom I'm not ready to give back just yet.

I don't tell Nina I know how. Maybe I should have.

Instead, when Chris or Nicolette or Viviana get a splinter, I take them into a bathroom and show them how to tear it out with their teeth.

Nicolette's spider lily *flourished*.

Chris is wearing his Beetlejuice grin when he waves his spindly arms at me from across the aisle at Ross, snatching my attention away from the rack of jeans I'd been halfheartedly staring at. He found a short-sleeved space-themed button-up chock-full of galaxies. The shirt was huge on his narrow shoulders. Far too impractical to justify buying.

I told Nina I wanted it and slipped it on one of the empty hangers in his closet after the wash.

The shirt sits over the back of his chair as he's building his newest Lego kit. I toss his Legos at the ceiling and pretend I'm not paying attention when he skips "Dead Mom" on the *Beetlejuice* soundtrack.

Instead, I make it a game of how far I can tug his shirt off the back   65
of the chair before he swats at me, and I think about the note from Viviana's teacher. The one I never answered.

Chris catches me in the act when one of the buttons catches on the top of the chair. He laughs and throws a Lego at me. I think about the definition of love.

McLendon braids together a number of short, descriptive scenes—often called vignettes—to create a compelling portrait of a family navigating loss. Through vivid detail and imagery, he brings the four siblings to life for readers, helping us understand their struggles, joys, and ways of expressing love for each other. McLendon uses design elements—white space and lines across the page—to visually distinguish one vignette from another.

Key Features / Personal Narratives

A compelling story. Your narrative should be interesting, to yourself and others. It need not be about a world-shaking event, but your topic—and how you write about it—should interest your readers. At the center of most good stories stands a conflict or question to be resolved. The most compelling narratives feature some sort of situation or problem that needs resolution. That need for resolution is another name for suspense. It's what makes us want to keep reading. McLendon's opening scene, which focuses on a teacher's note home—"We are concerned about your child's definition of love"—creates a kind of suspense for readers, making us eager to know how the family will respond.

Vivid details. Details bring a narrative to life by giving readers mental images of the sights, sounds, smells, tastes, and textures of the world in which your story takes place. The goal is to show as well as tell, to take readers there. When McLendon's sister Viviana "grins with a mouth full of piano keys and rasps in her big girl voice," we can see her youthful, beaming smile and hear her effort to sound older. A narrative is more than simply a report of what happened; it uses vivid details and dialogue to bring the events of the past to life, much as memorable fiction brings to life events that the writer makes up or embellishes. Depending on your topic and medium, you may want to provide some of the details in audio or visual form.

Clear significance. Memories of the past are filtered through our view from the present: we pick out some moments in our lives as significant, some as more important or vivid than others. Over time, our interpretations change, and our memories themselves change.

A well-constructed narrative conveys something about the significance of its subject. As a writer, you need to reveal something about what the incident means to you. You don't, however, want to simply announce the significance as if you're tacking on the moral of the story. McLendon suggests that he's contemplating a definition of love based on small, everyday acts that hold a family together: reading bedtime stories in silly voices, teaching a sibling to count with M&Ms, sharing an afternoon coffee ritual, building Legos. He doesn't, however, come right out and say that's why the stories he shares are so important to him.

A BRIEF GUIDE TO WRITING PERSONAL NARRATIVES

Choosing a Topic to Write About

You might focus your narrative on a single event, or you might braid together several related events or storylines, as McLendon does with his vignettes. Either way, you can get started by **LISTING** several events or incidents from your past that you consider significant in some way. They do not have to be earthshaking; indeed, they may involve a quiet moment that only you see as important—a brief encounter with a remarkable person, a visit to a special place, a memorable achievement (or failure), something that makes you laugh whenever you think about it. Writing about events that happened at least a few years ago is often easier than writing about recent events because you can more easily step back and see those events with a clear perspective. To choose the event or series of events that you will write about, consider how well you can recall what happened, how interesting it will be to readers, and whether you want to share it with an audience.

330

 Access Chapter 6 in the ebook for a video on brainstorming with generative AI.

Considering the Rhetorical Situation

73–74 ■

PURPOSE   What is the importance of the memory or memories you are trying to convey? How will this story help you understand yourself and your readers understand you, as you were then and as you are now?

75–78 ■

AUDIENCE   Who are your readers? Why will they care about your narrative? What do you want them to think of you after reading it? How can you help them understand your experience?

85–87 ■

STANCE   What impression do you want to give, and how can your words contribute to that impression? What tone do you want to project? Sincere? Serious? Humorous? Detached? Self-critical?

88–90 ■

MEDIA/DESIGN   Will your narrative be a print document? a speech? Will it be posted on a website? Can you include photographs, audio or video clips, or other visual texts? If you're composing in a braided form, how will you help readers visually navigate the different scenes or storylines of your vignettes? Will you insert typographical elements—like blank spaces or a series of asterisks—between sections? use icons or images to distinguish one section from another? use headings or font changes? something else?

Generating Ideas and Text

332–33 ⁖

Think about what happened.   Take a few minutes to write out an account of the incident or series of incidents: **WHAT** happened, **WHERE** it took place, **WHO** else was involved, what was said, how you feel about it, and so on. Can you identify any tension or conflict that will make for a compelling story? If not, you might want to rethink your topic.

Access Chapter 15 in the ebook for a video on the importance of choosing a topic that matters.

Consider the significance.   Why do you still remember this event or series of events? What effect has it had on your life? What makes you want to tell someone else about it? Does it say anything about you? What about it might interest someone else? If you have trouble answering these questions, you should probably find another topic. But in general, once you have defined the significance, you can be sure you have a story to tell—and a reason for telling it.

Think about the details. The best personal narratives connect with readers by giving them a sense of what it was like to be there, leading them to experience in words and images what the writer experienced in life. Spend some time **DESCRIBING** the incident or series of incidents, writing what you see, hear, smell, touch, and taste when you envision it. Do you have any photos or memorabilia or other **VISUAL** materials you might include in your narrative? Try writing out **DIALOGUE**, things that were said (or, if you can't recall exactly, things that might have been said). Look at what you come up with—is there detail enough to bring the scenes to life? anything that might be called vivid? If you don't have enough detail, you might reconsider whether you recall enough about the topic to write about it. If you have trouble coming up with plenty of detail, try **FREEWRITING**, **LISTING**, or **LOOPING**.

◆ 439–46

● 648–54
◆ 447–51

329
330
331

Ways of Organizing Personal Narratives
Tell about the event from beginning to end

Start by telling about the earliest incidents. → Tell about other incidents, one by one, in the order they occurred. → Explain the significance of the event.

Access Chapter 30 in the ebook for a video on organizing and synthesizing ideas.

Start at the end and tell how the event came about

Start by telling what happened overall. → Tell about earlier incidents, introducing key people and describing key places. → Explain the significance of the event.

Braid multiple vignettes together

Start by telling about one scene or storyline, describing key people and places. → Share another scene or storyline, describing key people and places. → Return to an earlier scene or storyline to continue the narrative. → Continue as needed, making sure each section relates thematically to others. → Explain the significance of the collection of vignettes.

More Ways to Approach a Personal Narrative

Write a letter. Instead of writing a conventional essay, write your narrative in letter form. You might write to a family member, a friend, a mentor, or even to a place or object—like your childhood home or a cherished keepsake.

Create a photo, video, or audio essay. Make a photo essay by arranging a series of photos in a sequence that tells your story, adding captions or other text to provide context and help readers follow the narrative. Create a video essay by combining still or moving images with voice-over, on-screen words, or music to share your story. Make an audio essay by recording yourself as you narrate your story, changing the pacing and tone of your voice to match the action—and perhaps adding music or ambient sounds to set a scene or create a mood.

Design an interactive webpage. Create a webpage that lets users move through your story in a nonlinear way. Perhaps include a clickable map that shows where your story takes place, an image gallery that viewers swipe through to see photographs related to the story, a draggable timeline of the story's events, or other multimedia elements.

280–90 ▲

Remix. After you've written a draft of your personal narrative, you might **REMIX** it: rework it into one or more of the genres above or turn it into a graphic memoir, a series of social media posts, a script for a play, or another genre or medium that fits your rhetorical situation.

Taking Stock of Your Work

Take stock of what you've written by considering these questions:

Access Chapter 36 in the ebook for a video on reflecting on your writing.

- How did you decide on your topic and determine the conflict or question to be resolved in your narrative?

- How effectively did you use dialogue, description, or other narrative strategies in your work?

- Did you use photographs or other visual or audio elements? What did they add? Can you think of such elements you might have used?

- How did you go about revising your work? How effective do you think your revisions were?
- What previous writing experiences, if any, did you draw on in writing your narrative? Did those experiences help you or hinder you?
- How much did you reflect on your story and what it means to you—and might mean to others?
- What was your most important achievement in this piece? What's the best part of this narrative? Why?

If you need more help

See Chapter 31 for guidelines on **DRAFTING**, Chapter 32 for **ASSESSING YOUR OWN WRITING**, Chapter 33 for **GETTING RESPONSE AND REVISING**, and Chapter 34 for **EDITING AND PROOFREADING**. See Chapter 35 if you are required to submit your personal narrative in a writing **PORTFOLIO**.

358–60
361–64
365–71
372–76
377–82

20 Profiles

Profiles are written portraits—of people, places, events, or other things. We find profiles of celebrities, travel destinations, and offbeat festivals in magazines and newspapers, on radio and TV, on the web, and through various social media. A profile presents a subject in an entertaining way that conveys its significance, showing us something or someone that we may not have known existed or that we see every day but don't know much about. In college *journalism* classes, students learn to create profiles using words and, in many cases, photos and video as well. Here's a profile of a poetry busker—someone who writes or performs poetry on the spot in public spaces, usually for tips. Written by Duquesne University student Katia Faroun, the profile appeared in 2021 in *Off the Bluff Magazine*, a publication of the university's media department.

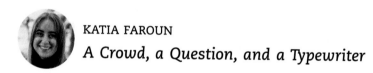

KATIA FAROUN

A Crowd, a Question, and a Typewriter

In a crowd of people, he's the only one sitting down. He speaks in dings and clickety-clacks. After meeting him, people may walk away elated, hopeful, or in tears—but always with a piece of paper in hand.

Meet poet Taylor Garling.

Wherever people are, that's where Taylor's at. Whether it be at Pittsburgh's Strip District, Market Square, or the Bloomfield Saturday Market, Taylor is there with his 1978 Olympia SM8 typewriter, waiting to render strangers in verse.

On Saturdays, Taylor hits the market. Donning a pork pie hat, he sets up his desk and loads paper into his typewriter as shoppers fill the area. People approach him—either curious about his setup or drawn by his signs advertising "Poetry!?" or "Poetry Store"—and ask for a poem. A few minutes later, they return for the final product, and Taylor has them determine the worth of his poem. As they walk away, Taylor is

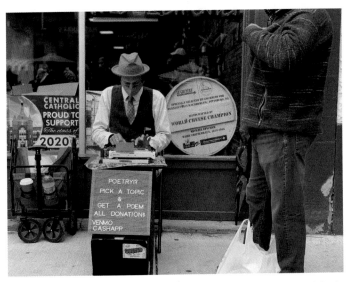

Taylor types up a poem for a customer outside of Pennsylvania Macaroni Co. in the Strip District.

comforted by the fact that some way or another, he's impacted their day for the better.

"Sometimes I feel like a bartender in a way," Taylor says, "because you have someone give you a really heavy topic, and you write them a poem, and they get a really nice sense of comfort from it."

The poem-writing process is nothing traditional for Taylor. There's no formula, no recipe to follow—he just goes by his mood and what he feels like writing that day. When he meets someone who's interested in a poem, he tries to get a read on them—their vibe, their intentions—and starts asking questions.

"It's really a lot of questions—asking the right ones, and listening," Taylor says. "Really listening intently."

The first poem Taylor ever gifted was for a man going through relationship issues. He asked for a poem that would give him hope—one about love and its challenges. The man gave him $10 for the poem, and as Taylor ended the night with conversations in his mind and cash in his pocket, he knew this was for him.

"I went to the bathroom and I counted up my money, and I had like a hundred bucks in a span of five hours, and so I was like, 'Okay, this is what I wanna do,'" Taylor says.

Originally from the West Coast, Taylor lives a nomadic lifestyle. 10 Young and tired of clocking in and out of restaurant jobs, Taylor left his home state of Washington at nineteen and began hitchhiking around California.

"I was just kinda fed up with the normal ways of society," Taylor says.

Taylor likes to go with the flow. He's worked in Idaho and sailed along the coast of Washington with some friends, and he made his way to Pittsburgh at the start of summer 2020. Sometimes he picks up jobs, but for the past year, writing has been his main source of income—and he likes it that way.

"The appeal of being my own boss, doing my own hours—it's kinda like everyone's little dream job in some respects, being able to do what they like to do," Taylor says.

Poetry wasn't always Taylor's thing. He started playing the guitar at thirteen and found a passion for songwriting. He would write poems here and there, but it wasn't until he started poetry busking—or writing poems on the street for donations—that his affinity for poetry took off.

"It kinda just fell into my niche of something I was already doing 15 for a while," Taylor says.

Even then, he doesn't always get requests specifically for poems. He's written lists, letters, wedding vows—even poetic resignation notices. The topics of his poems range from odes to deceased loved ones and ill friends, to lighthearted stories about relationships or weed. He's even written some spells and incantations.

One of the heavier poems he's written was for the memorial of a mother's dead son. Another was a letter to the family of someone with terminal cancer. Something about Taylor's demeanor makes people comfortable enough to share their stories of loss and heartbreak and request that he render their pain into art.

His favorite thing to write about? Love. Though his tattoos and cigarettes may suggest otherwise, Taylor's a softie, and the theme of love fills most of his poetry.

One of Taylor's favorites is a poem he wrote for a guy in Texas. He asked Taylor for a poem about being scared to fall in love—a feeling Taylor empathized with because of his own personal experiences. Upon receiving the poem, the man started to cry.

These kinds of moments are special for Taylor. He's empathetic: he 20 loves to give hugs to people after writing for them, and the knowledge that he's helped make someone's day better is what he likes most about writing poems for strangers.

"I'm just glad I'm able to be a conduit, I guess, to help those people out," Taylor says. "That's always a nice feeling."

Taylor started poetry busking in the fall of 2019, when a friend encouraged him to try it out. He's outgoing and kind to others, and his mom, Julie Garling, sees it as the perfect way for those two qualities to come together.

"It's something he can do to give back or to help them through a situation. He's always been sensitive to other people's feelings and always looked out for the underdog," Julie says.

As a mother, it's made Julie proud to see Taylor become a considerate, sensitive, and empathetic person. Though she has yet to receive a poem of her own from her son, she loves to see his heart go out to the people he meets.

"Those moments when I see him helping others and being kind 25 are the moments I'm proudest of," Julie says.

Taylor's affinity for typing poetry has inspired his friends as well. Garrett Miller has known Taylor since 2012 and thinks of him as a brother. A few months after Taylor started poetry busking, he encouraged Garrett to do the same, and helped him find a passion during a difficult time in Garrett's life.

"He sat down with me, and he just put his typewriter in front of me and was like, 'Type me something.' And I typed something, and I made him cry," Garrett says.

Taylor and Garrett spent time traveling along the West Coast and into Texas busking along various "bar strips," or streets lined with bars and restaurants. They write together, drink together, and have serious conversations about the challenges of life. Two creative minds, they often inspire each other, and each friend's writing style has influenced the other's.

"When we didn't have people getting poems from us, we were always bouncing ideas off of each other and swapping stories of our past that we didn't even remember sometimes," Garrett says.

The joy of poetry busking only lasted for a few months before the 30 pandemic hit. For Taylor, it impacted everything: foot traffic, interactions with strangers, even his presentation. He'd usually set up his table and have some incense burning, but it's not the same feeling when people are concerned about contracting a deadly virus.

"You can't really give hugs to people that are crying after you write them a poem," Taylor says.

Not only did the pandemic affect the flow of traffic, it disrupted Taylor's writing momentum as well.

"I felt like I was on fire. I felt like I was really getting into it," Taylor says. "I had the sense that I was really getting the motors turning, and then all that happened, and now it's like a total standstill."

He's been able to attend some events over the summer, such as open-air markets, where the area is less crowded but people are still around. But it's nothing like months past, where he'd sit outside on busy streets during the weekends and catch large groups of people.

When the pandemic started, Taylor tried to adapt to the changing 35 circumstances. He began mailing out poems and has kept his *Instagram* active with photos of his newest works, typed on brightly colored paper.

Still, it's not the same.

"Doing it in person, it's a lot easier for the magic to happen. Over the internet, it's not as potent," Taylor says.

Faroun's profile focuses on a relatively unusual type of street performer—a poet who writes on demand for strangers. Using details—like the specific make and model of Garling's vintage typewriter—along with descriptions of people's reactions to the poems Garling writes for them, Faroun brings the poetry busker and his work to life for readers.

Key Features / Profiles

An interesting subject. The subject may be something unusual, or it may be something ordinary shown in an intriguing way. You might profile an interesting person (like the street poet), a place (like a company that makes paper straws), an event (like the rescue of a sea turtle), or an object (like a rare automobile).

Any necessary background. A profile usually includes just enough information to let readers know something about the subject's larger context. Faroun tells us about Garling's nomadic past—hitchhiking in California, working stints in Idaho and Texas—to explain how Garling ended up in Pittsburgh, but she leaves out other details about his history that don't matter for this profile.

An interesting angle. A good profile captures its subject from a particular angle. Sometimes finding an angle will be fairly easy because your topic—like making a living writing poetry for strangers—is offbeat enough to be interesting in and of itself. Other topics, though, may require you to find a particular aspect that you can focus on. For example, a profile of a person might focus on the important work the person does or a challenging hobby they pursue; it would likely ignore aspects of the person's life that don't relate to that angle.

A firsthand account. Whether you're writing about a person, place, object, or event, you need to spend time observing and interacting with your subject. With a person, interacting means watching and conversing. Journalists tell us that "following the guy around," getting your subject to do something and talk about it at the same time, yields excellent material for a profile. When one writer met Theodor Geisel (Dr. Seuss) before profiling him, she asked him not only to talk about his characters but also to draw one—resulting in an illustration for her profile. With a place, object, or event, interacting may mean visiting and participating, although sometimes you may gather even more information by playing the role of the silent observer.

Engaging details. You need to include details that bring your subject to life. These may include *specific information* ("Whether it be at Pittsburgh's Strip District, Market Square, or the Bloomfield Saturday Market, Taylor is there with his 1978 Olympia SM8 typewriter"); *sensory images* ("Donning a pork pie hat, he sets up his desk and loads paper into his typewriter as shoppers fill the area"); *figurative language* ("He speaks in dings and clickety-clacks"); *dialogue* ("'Sometimes I feel like a bartender in a way,' Taylor says, 'because you have someone give you a really heavy topic, and you write them a poem, and they get a really nice sense of comfort from it'"); and *anecdotes* (A man "asked Taylor for a poem about being scared to fall in love. . . . Upon receiving the poem, the man started to cry."). Choose details that show rather than tell—that let your audience see and hear your subject rather than merely read an abstract description of it. Sometimes you may let them see and hear it literally, by including *photographs* or *video and audio clips*. And be sure all the details create some *dominant impression* of your subject: the impression that we get out of this profile, for example, is of a compassionate, creative young man who has a talent for connecting with others through the words he writes for them.

A BRIEF GUIDE TO WRITING PROFILES

Choosing a Suitable Subject

A person, a place, an object, an event—whatever you choose, make sure it's something that arouses your curiosity and that you're not too familiar with. Knowing your subject too well can blind you to interesting details. **LIST** five to ten interesting subjects that you can experience firsthand. Obviously, you can't profile a person who won't be interviewed or a place or activity that can't be observed. So before you commit to a topic, make sure you'll be able to carry out firsthand research.

330 ⋱

Considering the Rhetorical Situation

73–74 ■

PURPOSE   Why are you writing the profile? What angle will best achieve your purpose? How can you inform and engage your audience?

75–78 ■

AUDIENCE   Who is your audience? How familiar are they with your subject? What expectations of your profile might they have? What background information or definitions do you need to provide? How interested will they be—and how can you capture and hold their interest?

85–87 ■

STANCE   What view of your subject do you expect to present? Sympathetic? Critical? Sarcastic? Will you strive for a carefully balanced perspective?

88–90 ■

MEDIA/DESIGN   Will your profile be a print document? an electronic document? an oral presentation? Can (and should) you include images or any other visuals? Will it be recorded as an audio file or a multimodal text?

Generating Ideas and Text

Explore what you already know about your subject.   Why do you find this subject interesting? What do you know about it now? What do you expect to find out about it from your research? What preconceived ideas about or emotional reactions to this subject do you have? Why do you have them? It may be helpful to try some of the activities in the chapter on **GENERATING IDEAS AND TEXT**.

329–39 ⋱

Visit your subject.   If you're writing about an amusement park, go there; if you're profiling the man who runs the carousel, make an appointment to meet and interview him. And perhaps interview others who can provide insight into your subject, as Faroun did by talking with the street poet's mother and friend. Get to know your subject—if you profile the owner of a local BBQ place, sample the ribs! Take photos or videos if there's anything you might want to show visually in your profile. Find helpful hints for **OBSERVING** and **INTERVIEWING** in the chapter on finding sources.

498–500
500–503

If you're planning to interview someone, prepare questions. Faroun likely asked Garling questions like these: "What led you to becoming a street poet?" "What are some of the most memorable topics you've been asked to write about?" She probably asked Garling's mother questions about the personality traits that make her son good at his craft and asked his friend how Garling inspired him to try poetry busking himself. See the **INTERVIEWING** guidelines in Chapter 48 for help with planning good questions and conducting interviews.

500–503

Do additional research. You may be able to write a profile based entirely on your field research. You may, though, need to do some library or web **RESEARCH** as well, to deepen your understanding, get a different perspective, or fill in gaps. Often the people you interview can help you find sources of additional information; so can the sponsors of events and those in charge of places. To learn more about a city park, for instance, contact the government office that maintains it. Download any good photos of your subject that you find online, both to refer to as you write and to illustrate your profile.

471

Analyze your findings. Look for patterns, images, recurring ideas or phrases, and engaging details. Look for contrasts or discrepancies: between a subject's words and actions, between the appearance of a place and what goes on there, between your expectations and your research findings. Faroun probably expected to meet someone who enjoys writing poetry—but may not have anticipated how much Garling enjoys building connections with the people he writes for. You may find the advice in the **READING IN ACADEMIC CONTEXTS** chapter helpful here.

11–28

Come up with an angle. What's most memorable about your subject? What most interests you? What will interest your audience? Faroun focuses on the rewards of life as a street poet—and on the challenges that emerged for Garling as a result of the COVID-19 pandemic. Sometimes you'll know your angle from the start; other times you'll need to look further into your topic. You might try **CLUSTERING**, **CUBING**, **FREEWRITING**, and **LOOPING** to help you see your topic from many different angles.

330–31
332
329
331

439–46

422–28

447–51

Note details that support your angle. Use your angle to focus your research and generate text. Try **DESCRIBING** your subject as clearly as you can, **COMPARING** your subject with other subjects of its sort, writing **DIALOGUE** that captures your subject. Faroun, for instance, tells us how Garling's customers walk away "elated, hopeful, or in tears," and she quotes Garling comparing himself to a bartender who helps people through tough times—thus illustrating the rewards of his work. Faroun also describes the ways Garling tries to adapt to the challenges of the pandemic, including by mailing his poems and showcasing photos of them "typed on brightly colored paper" on *Instagram*. Engaging details will bring your subject to life for your audience. Together, these details should create a dominant impression of your subject.

Ways of Organizing a Profile

457–65

One common way to organize a profile is by **NARRATING**. For example, if you're profiling a chess championship, you may write about it chronologically, creating suspense as you move from start to finish.

Access Chapter 30 in the ebook for a video on organizing and synthesizing ideas.

As a narrative

| Introduce your subject and your angle on it; provide any necessary background. | → | Tell about various incidents or characteristics, one by one, that bring your subject to life. | → | Conclude by stating your overall impression — with an anecdote, a quote, a summary comment, or some other ending. |

439–47

Sometimes you may organize a profile by **DESCRIBING** —a person or a place, for instance.

As a description

| Introduce your subject and your angle on it, providing any necessary background. | → | Present details that create some dominant impression of your subject:
• sensory details
• examples
• dialogue
• anecdotes
• *and so on* | → | State your overall impression, offering a final anecdote or quote or finishing a description begun earlier. |

More Ways to Approach a Profile

Write a "day in the life" profile. Create a portrait of one day (or morning or afternoon) in the life of your subject. If you're profiling a person, shadow them for a while. If you're profiling an event or a place, spend a stretch of time watching how activities unfold. Then recount the experience chronologically with narration and description, focusing on the events and interactions that best capture a particular slice of life.

Write an "as told to" profile. Write your profile in first person from the perspective of your profile subject, drawing on the words they've told you. Begin by recording and transcribing an in-depth interview or set of interviews with the person. Then use the transcript to craft the profile, choosing the most compelling parts and organizing and editing the material to create a cohesive whole. Collaborate closely with your profile subject throughout the process—share drafts with them and get feedback to make sure you're representing them accurately. And be sure to indicate somewhere in your profile that the words were spoken to you by your subject. For example, if Katia Faroun had written her profile in this manner, she might have included "as told to Katia Faroun" under the title, or she might have added some other note at the beginning or end of the piece. You can find versions of this type of profile at the *Humans of New York* website.

Create a digital exhibit. Use a website builder to create an online exhibit of your profile subject. You might include an interactive timeline that highlights important events in the life of a person you're profiling, a clickable map that shows the layout of a place you're profiling, an image gallery that displays photographs of your subject, or exhibit "rooms" where users can engage with video or audio clips of your subject.

Remix. After you've written a draft of your profile, you might **REMIX** it: rework it into one or more of the genres above or turn it into a mini documentary, a podcast, a Q&A article, or another genre or medium that fits your rhetorical situation.

▲ 280–90

Access Chapter 36 in the ebook for a video on reflecting on your writing.

Taking Stock of Your Work

Take stock of what you've written by considering these questions:

- How did you go about choosing a subject—and an angle on that subject?

- What strategies did you use for the beginning and ending of your profile? How did you decide on those strategies?

- What design or media choices did you make? Why did you make them, and how effective were they?

- In what ways did you reflect on your writing as you worked on it? How did the act of reflecting help you in your writing?

- What setbacks did you face as you worked on your writing? How did you overcome them and persist as a writer?

- How did you use concepts or methods you learned elsewhere (in other classes, for example) as you worked on your profile?

- What were your writing goals for yourself in this piece? How well did you achieve them? How could you improve in the future?

If you need more help

358–60
361–64
365–71
372–76
377–82

See Chapter 31 for guidelines on **DRAFTING**, Chapter 32 for **ASSESSING YOUR OWN WRITING**, Chapter 33 for **GETTING RESPONSE AND REVISING**, and Chapter 34 for **EDITING AND PROOFREADING**. See Chapter 35 if you are required to submit your profile in a writing **PORTFOLIO**.

21 Proposals

Proposals are part of our personal lives: lovers propose marriage, friends propose sharing dinner and a movie, you offer to pay half the cost of a car and insurance if your parents will pay the other half. Proposals are also part of our academic and professional lives: Student leaders lobby for lights on bike paths. Musicians, artists, writers, and educators apply for grants. Researchers in all fields of the humanities, social sciences, sciences, and technology seek funding for their projects. In business, contractors bid on building projects, and companies and freelancers solicit work from potential clients. These are all examples of proposals, ideas put forward for consideration that say, "Here is a solution to a problem" or "This is what ought to be done." For example, here's a proposal for increasing Americans' "health span"—the number of years spent living in good health. The author, Dave A. Chokshi, is a physician at Bellevue Hospital in New York City and a professor at the City College of New York. A version of Chokshi's proposal originally appeared in the *New York Times*.

DAVE A. CHOKSHI

Forget about Living to 100. Let's Live Healthier Instead.

When I ask my patients about their long-term health goals, they seldom say they want to live to be 100. Instead they talk about aging with independence and dignity, being free from aches and pains or having the strength to play with their grandchildren. "I'd just like to blow out the candles on my birthday cake without coughing," a 60-something patient suffering from emphysema told me.

Yet our national dialogue around aging doesn't reflect this basic reality about what people value in their lives.

Our country is long overdue for an audacious health goal. The average life span in the United States is about 1.5 times what it was a century ago (Dattani et al.), a stunning achievement. Equally stunning is that life expectancy is now stagnating (Chokshi, "Life Expectancy"), a revelation that has mostly been met with a collective shrug.

The Census Bureau predicts that by 2034, there will be more people in the United States age 65 or older than under 18, for the first time in history ("Older People"). Increasingly people are suffering from addiction, other chronic diseases and injuries, even at younger ages ("Chronic Diseases"). Our current state of politics, mired in narrow debates about who does and does not deserve health insurance, is not up to meeting these challenges (Chokshi, "Pandemic"). We need a fresh approach to talking about health before we can improve it.

A new health moonshot should not just be oriented around increasing life spans but should focus, too, on what's referred to as health span—the years people can expect to live in good health (Olshansky). As President John F. Kennedy said decades ago: "It is not enough for a great nation merely to have added new years to life. Our objective must also be to add new life to those years" ("Special Message").   5

Let's start with what already matters to each of us: healthy birthdays. When we are younger, many of us take for granted having our faculties intact with the passing years. But as we age, every birthday spent flourishing versus feeling frail becomes an increasingly precious experience.

Peer nations have already taken steps to center health span in their policies. Singapore, with a longer average life span and an even more rapidly aging society than the United States, committed in its national health reforms last year "to prevent or delay the onset of ill health" (*White Paper*). Britain has set an explicit goal of increasing healthy life expectancy by five years by 2035 (*Understanding*). And in Japan, local programs already invest in initiatives to help older adults share their skills and wisdom across generations, such as teaching youths how to cook, make art and garden, with benefits for young and old alike (Venkataraman).

Yet in the United States, we do not rigorously measure and report health span as we do life expectancy. Best estimates indicate that the average American can expect to celebrate only a single birthday in good health after the traditional retirement age of 65. Meanwhile, Singapore, Britain and Japan (along with Canada, Costa Rica and Chile) already report average health spans of at least 70 years ("Healthy Life Expectancy").

Healthy life expectancy (HALE) at age 60 (years) for both sexes				
Countries	*2019*	*2015*	*2010*	*2000*
Canada	19.0	18.8	18.6	17.3
Chile	18.4	18.0	17.2	16.4
Costa Rica	18.7	18.6	18.0	16.9
Japan	20.4	20.0	19.7	18.7
Singapore	20.0	19.5	18.8	16.6
United Kingdom	18.3	17.9	17.8	16.3
United States	16.4	16.5	16.5	15.7

Source: World Health Organization.

A bold but common-sense national goal would be to add a decade of healthy birthdays after retirement age. Achieving a target health span of 75 years would push us to think about health equity, given the lower healthy life expectancies for certain groups, such as Native Americans, Black Americans and low-income Americans (Davis et al.).

Measuring health span, however, must go hand in hand with re-engineering our health and social systems. Doubling our national investment in primary care—to at least 10 cents of every dollar spent on health services—would make our medical infrastructure more proactive (McCauley). We would be more effective at catching and treating diseases earlier and centering patient care on trusted relationships built over time. Increased access to primary care would mean that medical innovations offering hope for reversing diabetes or curing hepatitis could be made more available to those who would benefit from them (Chokshi, "Ask a Doctor"; Roy et al.).

Rebalancing national health expenditures toward primary care should be part of a broader shift toward disease prevention. For instance, President Biden's cancer moonshot has emphasized the importance of reducing tobacco use and getting more people vaccinated against human papillomavirus to prevent new diagnoses of cancer ("President"). The National Institutes of Health could build on these efforts by advancing the science of healthy longevity and developing better ways to stall cognitive and physical decline, particularly by facilitating behavioral changes like reducing sedentary time (Kennedy et al.).

The quest to improve health span should integrate mental and emotional health. Health departments have tackled smoking, infectious diseases and blood pressure—often resulting in remarkable gains in life expectancy. Extending health span would require taking on other major causes of morbidity, too, such as anxiety and loneliness (Chokshi and Stine). A lack of social connection can increase the risk of depression and dementia, often leading to a vicious cycle of illness and isolation (*Our Epidemic*). The role of public health must be to interrupt those vicious cycles and seed virtuous ones, particularly for emotional support and connection (Chokshi, "Vicious and Virtuous Cycles").

Adding a decade of healthy birthdays to Americans' lives would also require us to reckon with issues beyond health care. When I take care of patients experiencing homelessness, who have a markedly lower healthy life expectancy than average ("Homelessness"), I measure their blood pressure and check their bloodwork as I do for any other patient. But the most definitive treatment for any issues they may be experiencing is not medicine or surgery; it's housing. One of my patients who struggled for years to give up cigarettes quit smoking the day he moved into his new apartment. When I asked him what changed, he had a laconic answer: "Less stress and more sleep." It was a recipe for better health I wish I could prescribe to everyone.

Housing costs money, of course, as do other basic needs, such as healthy food and quality education. But they should be seen as investments for the economic benefits of extending health span. One study published in the journal *Nature Aging* in 2021 estimated that improving health spans and increasing the average life span by one year would be worth $725 billion annually (Scott et al.).

A better quality of life in older age could provide cascading returns for society. "As we age, we gain knowledge and expertise, along with the intellectual and cognitive abilities to decide if something matters," Linda P. Fried, a geriatrician and the dean of the Columbia Mailman School of Public Health, has said (qtd. in "Aging Redefined").

But unlocking this longevity dividend would require new narratives about healthy aging ("Global Roadmap"). Older Americans already contribute to society through working, caring for grandchildren, volunteering and civic participation. Social infrastructure could be further adapted around older age as a latent natural resource, waiting for us to tap it in ways that build purpose and connection (Chokshi and Jennings). Schools could host youth mentoring programs. Employers could create additional part-time or flexible work opportunities (Davis et al.). Even smaller campaigns that combat ageist stereotypes, like reimagining birthday cards to ditch denigrating jokes in favor of celebratory pride ("Anti-ageist Birthday Card Project"), could change these narratives. "Great stories take time," reads one, depicting a stylish woman in sunglasses with flowing white hair.

In Spanish, the word for retirement is "jubilación." Its English cognate matches what I most wish for my parents after a half-century of working: that their birthdays are not just healthy but jubilant, too. For my patient with emphysema, a dockworker originally from South America, our primary care team has painstakingly helped get his symptoms under better control. But to truly thrive, he would also need a more dignified place to live, larger public investments in indoor air quality and stronger social connections to supplant screen time. All of these seem like tall orders until I reflect on the boldness it took for him to immigrate across a continent and carve out a life for his family in the United States, like so many of our forebears. It's that boldness our nation would have to channel to make a moonshot for health span a reality. It wouldn't happen in weeks, months or even the next couple of years—but then again, great stories take time.

Works Cited

"Aging Redefined." *Columbia Mailman School of Public Health*, 12 Dec. 2022, https://www.publichealth.columbia.edu/news/aging-redefined.

"Anti-ageist Birthday Card Project." *Changing the Narrative*, changingthenarrativeco.org/anti-ageist-birthday-cards/. Accessed 1 Sept. 2023.

Chokshi, Dave A. "Ask a Doctor: Is It Possible to Reverse My Diabetes?" *The Washington Post*, 17 Apr. 2023, www.washingtonpost.com/wellness/2023/04/17/diabetes-reverse-weight-loss/.

———. "Life Expectancy Is Falling. Here's How to Change That." *The New York Times*, 31 Aug. 2022, www.nytimes.com/2022/08/31/opinion/us-life-expectancy.html.

———. "The Pandemic Cracked the Door Open to Universal Health Care. Here's How We Could Still Get There." *Salon*, 16 Apr. 2023, www.salon.com/2023/04/16/the-cracked-the-door-open-to-universal-health-care-heres-how-we-could-make-it-real/.

———. "Vicious and Virtuous Cycles in Health." *JAMA Health Forum*, vol. 4, no. 2, 2023, https://doi:10.1001/jamahealthforum.2023.0505.

Chokshi, Dave A., and Christopher C. Jennings. "Latent Natural Resources for Health." *JAMA Forum Archive*, 2 Nov. 2017, jamanetwork.com/channels/health-forum/fullarticle/2760196.

Chokshi, Dave A., and Nicholas Stine. "Milestones on the Path to Population Health." *Health Affairs*, 11 Apr. 2016, www.healthaffairs.org/content/forefront/milestones-path-population-health.

"Chronic Diseases in America." *Centers for Disease Control and Prevention*, www.cdc.gov/chronicdisease/resources/infographic/chronic-diseases.htm. Accessed 1 Sept. 2023.

Dattani, Saloni, et al. "Life Expectancy." *Our World in Data*, ourworldindata.org/life-expectancy. Accessed 5 Sept. 2023.

Davis, Andy, et al. "How Employers Can Spark a Movement to Help Us Live Longer and Healthier Lives." *Deloitte Insights*, 20 June 2023, www2.deloitte.com/us/en/insights/industry/health-care/employers-aging-and-health.html.

"The Global Roadmap for Healthy Longevity." *National Academy of Medicine*, nam.edu/initiatives/grand-challenge-healthy-longevity/global-roadmap-for-healthy-longevity/. Accessed 6 Sept. 2023.

"Healthy Life Expectancy (HALE)." *World Health Organization*, apps.who.int/gho/data/view.main.HALEXv. Accessed 6 Sept. 2023.

"Homelessness Makes You Sick." *Health Care for the Homeless*, www.hchmd.org/homelessness-makes-you-sick. Accessed 14 Sept. 2023.

Kennedy, Brian K., et al. "Geroscience: Linking Aging to Chronic Disease." *Cell*, vol. 159, no. 4, 2014, pp. 709–13, https://doi.org/10.1016/j.cell.2014.10.039.

McCauley, Linda, et al., editors. *Implementing High-Quality Primary Care: Rebuilding the Foundation of Health Care*. National Academies Press, 2021, https://doi.org/10.17226/25983.

"Older People Projected to Outnumber Children for First Time in U.S. History." *United States Census Bureau*, 13 Mar. 2018, www.census.gov/newsroom/press-releases/2018/cb18-41-population-projections.html.

Olshansky, S. Jay. "From Lifespan to Healthspan." *JAMA*, vol. 320, no. 13, 2018, pp. 1323–24, https://doi.org/10.1001/jama.2018.12621.

Our Epidemic of Loneliness and Isolation: The U.S. Surgeon General's Advisory on the Healing Effects of Social Connection and Community. Office of the U.S. Surgeon General, 2023, www.hhs.gov/sites/default/files/surgeon-general-social-connection-advisory.pdf.

"The President and First Lady's Cancer Moonshot." *The White House*, www.whitehouse.gov/cancermoonshot/#objectives. Accessed 12 Sept. 2023.

Roy, Viktor, et al. "Making Hepatitis C a Rare Disease in the United States." *Health Affairs*, 15 June 2016, www.healthaffairs.org/content/forefront/making-hepatitis-c-rare-disease-united-states.

Scott, Andrew J., et al. "The Economic Value of Targeting Aging." *Nature Aging*, vol. 1, Jul. 2021, pp. 616–23, https://doi.org/10.1038/s43587-021-00080-0.

"Special Message to the Congress on the Needs of the Nation's
Senior Citizens." *The American Presidency Project*, 21 Feb. 1963,
www.presidency.ucsb.edu/documents/special-message-the
-congress-the-needs-the-nations-senior-citizens.
Understanding the Drivers of Healthy Life Expectancy: Report. Office
for Health Improvement and Disparities, 1 June 2023, www
.gov.uk/government/publications/understanding-the-drivers-of
-healthy-life-expectancy/understanding-the-drivers-of-healthy
-life-expectancy-report.
White Paper on Healthier SG. Healthier SG / Forward SG, 21 Sept.
2022, file.go.gov.sg/healthiersg-whitepaper-pdf.pdf.
Venkataraman, Bina. "Japan Can Teach the World a Better Way to
Age." *The Washington Post*, 15 Aug. 2023, www.washingtonpost
.com/opinions/2023/08/15/japan-elderly-care-dignity-respect/.

This proposal clearly defines the problem—that most Americans enjoy only one birthday in good health beyond the age of 65—and offers a solution: to set a new national goal to add a decade of healthy life after retirement. The author provides arguments and evidence from research and personal experience to show why his solution would work.

Key Features / Proposals

A well-defined problem. Some problems are self-evident and relatively simple, and you would not need much persuasive power to make people act—as with the problem "This university discards too much paper." While some people might see nothing wrong with throwing paper away, most are likely to agree that recycling is a good thing. Other issues are controversial: some people see them as problems while others do not, such as this one: "Motorcycle riders who do not wear helmets risk serious injury and raise health-care costs for everyone." Some motorcyclists believe that wearing or not wearing a helmet should be a personal choice; you would have to present arguments to convince your readers that not wearing a helmet is indeed a problem needing a solution. Any written proposal must establish at the outset that there is a problem—and that it's serious enough to require a solution. For some topics, visual or audio evidence of the problem may be helpful.

A recommended solution. Once you have defined the problem, you need to describe the solution you're suggesting and to explain it in enough detail for readers to understand what you are proposing. Again, photographs, diagrams, or other visuals may help. Sometimes you might suggest several solutions, weigh their merits, and choose the best one.

A convincing argument for your proposed solution. You need to convince readers that your solution is feasible—and that it is the best way to solve the problem. Sometimes you'll want to explain in detail how your proposed solution would work. Chokshi, for example, outlines several steps for implementing his proposal, including increasing investments in preventive care, advancing the science of longevity, and addressing homelessness and ageism.

 Access Chapter 15 in the ebook for a video on anticipating counterarguments.

A response to anticipated questions. You may need to consider any questions readers may have about your proposal—and to show how its advantages outweigh any disadvantages, as Chokshi does when he argues that the economic, social, and civic benefits that accrue from improved health span will outweigh the costs of implementing his plan.

A call to action. The goal of a proposal is to persuade readers to accept your proposed solution. This solution may include asking readers to take action.

An appropriate tone. Since you're trying to persuade readers to act, your tone is important—readers will always react better to a reasonable, respectful presentation than to anger or self-righteousness.

A BRIEF GUIDE TO WRITING PROPOSALS

Deciding on a Topic

Choose a problem that can be solved. Complex, large problems, such as poverty, hunger, or terrorism, usually require complex, large solutions. Most of the time, focusing on a smaller problem or a limited aspect of a large problem will yield a more manageable proposal. Rather than tackling the problem of world poverty, for example, think about the problem faced by people in your community who have lost jobs and need help until they find employment.

Considering the Rhetorical Situation

PURPOSE　　　Do you have a stake in a particular solution, or do you simply want to eliminate the problem by whatever solution might be adopted?

73–74

AUDIENCE　　Do your readers share your view of the problem as a serious one needing a solution? Are they likely to be open to possible solutions or resistant? Do they have the authority to carry out a proposed solution?

75–78

STANCE　　　How can you show your audience that your proposal is reasonable and should be taken seriously? How can you demonstrate your own authority and credibility?

85–87

MEDIA/DESIGN　How will you deliver your proposal? In print? Electronically? As a speech? Would visuals, or video or audio clips, help support your proposal?

88–90

Generating Ideas and Text

Explore potential solutions to the problem. Many problems can be solved in more than one way, and you need to show your readers that you've examined several potential solutions. You may develop solutions on your own; more often, though, you'll need to do **RESEARCH** to see how others have solved—or tried to solve—similar problems. Don't settle on a single solution too quickly—you'll need to **COMPARE** the advantages and disadvantages of several solutions in order to argue convincingly for one.

471

422–28

Decide on the most desirable solution(s). One solution may be head and shoulders above others—but it's important to be open to rejecting all the possible solutions on your list and starting over if you need to, or to combining two or more potential solutions in order to come up with an acceptable fix.

Think about why your solution is the best one. Why did you choose your solution? Why will it work better than others? What has to be done to enact it? What will it cost? What makes you think it can be done? Writing out answers to these questions will help you argue for your solution: to show that you have carefully and objectively outlined a problem, analyzed the potential solutions, weighed their merits, and determined the reasons the solution you propose is the best.

Access
Chapter 30
in the ebook
for a video on
organizing and
synthesizing ideas.

Ways of Organizing a Proposal

You can organize a proposal in various ways, but always you will begin by establishing that there is a problem. You may then identify several possible solutions before recommending one of them or a combination of several. Sometimes, however, you might discuss only a single solution.

Several possible solutions

Introduce and explain the problem. → Identify possible solutions, and consider their pros and cons one by one. → Propose a solution, and give reasons why it is best. → Call for action, or reiterate your proposed action.

A single solution

Introduce and explain the problem. → Explain the proposed solution. → Give reasons why it is the best solution. → Call for action, or reiterate your proposal.

↓

Anticipate and answer questions.

More Ways to Approach a Proposal

Create a series of blog posts.   One post might explain the problem you seek to address, perhaps sharing personal stories to illustrate the issue. Another post might describe your solution in detail, and still another might address readers' questions about the proposal. A final post could inspire readers to take a specific action to help bring your proposal to fruition.

Create a social media campaign.   Present your proposal in short segments through *TikTok, YouTube, Instagram, LinkedIn,* or another platform. Perhaps use video or audio to share the story of someone affected by the problem your proposal addresses. Use charts or other graphics to outline your solution. Develop interactive polls to solicit your audience's response to your proposal, and create a hashtag to "brand" your campaign and build community.

Write a script for a public forum on your topic.   Imagine sharing your proposal at a town hall meeting, a conference, or some other public forum. Write a script for your presentation, and prepare answers for questions you anticipate your audience asking. Perhaps create slides to accompany your talk.

Remix.   After you've written a draft of your proposal, you might **REMIX** it: rework it into one or more of the genres above or turn it into an infographic, podcast, webpage, fundraising letter, or another genre or medium that fits your rhetorical situation.

▲ 280–90

Taking Stock of Your Work

Take stock of what you've written by considering these questions:

Access Chapter 36 in the ebook for a video on reflecting on your writing.

- How did you determine your audience for this piece?
- How did you decide on and limit your topic?
- How did you determine the best solution to the problem you defined?
- What writing strategies did you use to guide your reader through your text? How effectively did you use them?
- What editing and proofreading processes did you use, and how effective were they?
- Based on your experiences with this piece, what academic habit of mind—for example, being flexible, creative, and so on—do you want to work on as you tackle your next writing project?
- What did you learn about writing as you wrote your proposal? How might you use that learning as you write in other contexts now or in the future?
- What did you do well in this piece? What could still be improved? What would you do differently next time?

TOPIC PROPOSALS

Instructors often ask students to write topic proposals to ensure that their topics are appropriate or manageable. Some instructors may also ask for an **ANNOTATED BIBLIOGRAPHY** showing that appropriate sources of information are available—more evidence that the project can be carried out. Here a student proposes a topic for an assignment in a writing course in which she has been asked to take a position on a global issue.

197–206 ▲

CATHERINE THOMS

Social Media and Data Privacy

The relationship between social media and data privacy is an issue that has recently risen to the forefront of many social media users' concerns. While we have been posting and sharing online, major companies like *Facebook* and *Google* have been silently collecting information about our personal lives and leaving that data vulnerable to potentially harmful exposure. As someone who has had their private information compromised multiple times by large-scale data breaches, I feel compelled to share my research on the dangers of such security breaches and how they can happen.

In this paper, I will argue that it is crucial for consumers to be aware of the ways in which social media platforms can gain access to consumers' private data and what those platforms can do with that data. In March 2018, it was revealed that 87 million *Facebook* profiles were exposed to manipulation by the political consulting firm Cambridge Analytica during the 2016 presidential election. I will use this scandal as an example of how the unlawful exposure of personal data can have far-reaching effects on external world events, and I plan to analyze how this scandal has functioned as a global catalyst for further scrutiny into the privacy mechanisms of social media.

I will concentrate on the specific ways personal data may be misused. Although sharing thoughts and pictures on social media may not seem like anything to think twice about, many people don't realize just how much is at stake should enough of that personal data fall into the wrong hands. Much of my research will be done on specific social media applications such as *Facebook* and *Google Analytics*, as that is where the heart of the issue resides and where consumers can learn the most about their personal data exposure and protection.

Thoms defines and narrows her topic (from data breaches to the specific ways consumers' data may be misused), discusses her interest, outlines her argument, and discusses her research strategy. Her goal is to convince her instructor that she has a realistic writing project and a clear plan.

Key Features / Topic Proposals

A concise discussion of the subject. Topic proposals generally open with a brief discussion of the subject, outlining any important areas of controversy or debate associated with it and clarifying the extent of the writer's current knowledge of it. In its first two paragraphs, Thoms's proposal includes a concise statement of the topic she wishes to address.

A clear statement of your intended focus. State what aspect of the topic you intend to write on as clearly as you can, narrowing your focus appropriately. Thoms does so by stating her intended topic—data breaches— and then showing how she will focus on the specific ways consumers' data may be misused.

A rationale for choosing the topic. Tell your instructor why this topic interests you and why you want to write about it. Thoms both states what made her interested in her topic and hints at a practical reason for choosing it: plenty of information is available.

Mention of resources. To show your instructor that you can achieve your goal, you need to identify the available research materials.

If you need more help

See Chapter 31 for guidelines on **DRAFTING**, Chapter 32 for **ASSESSING YOUR OWN WRITING**, Chapter 33 for **GETTING RESPONSE AND REVISING**, and Chapter 34 for **EDITING AND PROOFREADING**. See Chapter 35 if you are required to submit your proposal in a writing **PORTFOLIO**.

358–60
361–64
365–71
372–76
377–82

22 Explorations

Sometimes we write essays just to think about something—to play with an idea, develop a thought, explore possible solutions to a problem, or even to figure out what the problem is. Exploratory essays are our attempt to think something through by writing about it and to share our thinking—or the progression of our understanding—with others. In college, you might be asked in courses across the curriculum to write formal or informal exploratory essays, journals, design reports, or learning log entries. Have a look at one example of an exploratory essay written for a first-year composition class at Columbus State Community College. The author, Brian Diehl, was a high school student taking college courses when he wrote his exploration.

BRIAN DIEHL

Talking with Granddad

An overcast sky chokes the usual radiant light of summer on this Sunday afternoon—an ironic backdrop to the sign in front of me, which reads "Sunrise on the Scioto." Upon entering the nursing home's lobby, I'm met with a clash of two scents: the buttery aroma of a nearby popcorn machine and that distinct "old people" smell. The latter always seems to outlast its opponent and seeps into my nostrils around every corner of the building. I make sure to grab a few hard candies before taking an elevator up to the third floor.

Knock, knock, knock.

No answer. Peeking into the doorway, I see a man slouched in his bed absorbing the sounds of a televised college football game.

"Hey Granddad, it's me!" A slow turn allows him to see the boy now in front of him. "You know who I am, right?"

He stares blankly.

"I'm Brian, your grandson!"

The scruff around his face rises, revealing a smile of recognition. ". . . Yes," he responds.

5

"How've you been holding up?" I ask. The drone of the TV fills the silence. "Hey, I have a girlfriend now! Would you like to see her?"

I bring the image on my phone closer to him. After some scrutiny, he exclaims, "Well, I'll be damned!"

"Has Grandma stopped by recently?"   10

". . . Well, I'll be damned!"

He repeats this phrase after every question I ask. After a while, I lightly wrap my arms around his motionless body, and we part ways.

For the longest time, there has been no medical phenomenon more intriguing to me than dementia. One may be familiar with Alzheimer's disease, the most common type of dementia characterized by plaques and tangles that spread throughout the brain, destroying tissue and eventually affecting memory, language, and other neurological functions ("Dementia"). When my grandfather showed signs of Alzheimer's in its early stages, I found myself struggling in my attempts to talk with him; my words sometimes seemed to bounce off a brick wall. Knowing that my other grandparents could be at risk of dementia as well, I wondered: How could I communicate more effectively with family members who may exhibit memory loss in the future?

Of course, communication is a two-way street, so before I could explore verbal tactics on my end, I decided to first gain an understanding of how people with dementia might express their mental state—how *they* try to communicate their experiences and perceptions. This is when I came across the story of artist William Utermohlen, who was diagnosed with Alzheimer's in 1995. As a way of understanding the disease, the artist chose to paint himself. On the next page is a series of Utermohlen's self-portraits, revealing changes in his perception of himself over time.

Comparing the 1996 portrait to the one drawn pre-diagnosis, we   15
can notice an immediate disappearance of details such as hair texture and facial shadows. Utermohlen's unicolor portrayal of himself inside a green framework reflects neurologist Bruce Miller's comments on artistic creativity among people with brain diseases: "Alzheimer's affects the right parietal lobe in particular, which is important for visualizing something internally and then putting it onto a canvas. The art becomes more abstract, the images are blurrier and vague, more surrealistic" (qtd. in Grady). This surrealism becomes more apparent in the next portrait, where the eyes are positioned far too low, the forehead and ear are enlarged, and the frown of the artist becomes more solemn. The true erasure of identity begins in the 1998 portrait, revealing a fragmented Utermohlen with his most melancholic facial expression yet. Perhaps the most devastating work is the fifth portrait; other than an oval serving as the bare structure of a human head, there is hardly a distinguishable

A collage showing details from William Utermohlen's self-portraits. The first (top left) was made in 1967, and the rest were made following his diagnosis of Alzheimer's disease: the top middle in 1996, the top right in 1997, and the bottom row, from left to right, in 1998, 1999, and 2000.

facial feature contained in the canvas. The final portrait—with its pencil scratches, eraser smudges, and incompleteness—suggests a dramatic alteration of Utermohlen's sense of self. What can perhaps be represented by this artist's works are the combined voices of those just like him—those who cannot verbalize their reality. As heartbreaking as Utermohlen's portraits are, they offer caregivers and others a bridge toward understanding dementia from the perspective of those who experience it.

After gaining insight into the possible mental state of someone with dementia, I sought to find concrete methods of verbal communication that could best meet the needs of individuals with Alzheimer's. I came across a study published in the *Journal of Speech, Language, and Hearing Research* conducted by Jeff Small and colleagues, who set out to evaluate the effectiveness of ten common strategies for communicating with people with Alzheimer's. As part of the study, the researchers audio-recorded twenty-two couples—individuals with Alzheimer's and their spouses—as the couples engaged in everyday tasks like setting the table, getting an item upon request, and using the telephone. The success of each communication strategy was measured by the number of communication breakdowns that occurred after its usage. Small and colleagues report that "eliminating distractions, speaking in simple sentences, and employing yes/no questions" resulted in fewer breakdowns (364). On the other hand, using a slower rate of speech caused an increase in the number of breakdowns. This study suggests the viability of some verbal techniques over others, but I was still left with a burning question: Doesn't communication effectiveness ultimately depend on what personally works for the individual with Alzheimer's?

At this point, I decided to reach out to somebody who could shed light on my question: my grandmother, Andrea Diehl. Being the embodiment of positivity that she is, her continual presence by my grandfather's side at the nursing home was one of the greatest factors that helped keep him stable. Below is a portion of our interview that highlights their communication dynamic in the midst of his dementia.

> **Brian:** Did you make any changes to your communication with Granddad during his state of dementia? If so, what methods worked for you?
>
> **Andrea:** Anything that worked for me was something that was familiar already to him, something that *he* wanted to say. I always made sure he was smiling. Anything that I knew was going to please him was the object of my time with him. I would give him a hot chocolate and give him a little hug, and then when I put a marshmallow in that hot chocolate, he would smile! There were many things that I tried to do to keep him above board and happy. There were many little tricks like that. I wanted him to have the memories that were still living in both of our minds.
>
> **Brian:** In what ways did Grandpa communicate with you?
>
> **Andrea:** He would reminisce about old times. For example, we had taken seven cruises on one cruise line, and we would relive those because he remembered those! He would ask, "Do you remember that meal we had? Do you remember when I found just the right things to make the drink I wanted to make?" He could remember those things and then ask me if I remembered them! It was a joy, every minute.

Reflecting on my grandmother's experiences, it becomes clear that one does not need to be a master of psychological techniques in order to properly approach communication with a person affected by dementia.

What's needed is a repeated effort to be present with the individual, expressing joy over what *they* say instead of sweating over anything *we* could ever say. Even if one were to find a golden strategy that makes conversation a breeze, its use alone will never mitigate the frustration of identity loss portrayed so vividly by Utermohlen. Instead, the most important action one can take is a demonstration of love. Ranging from hugs to marshmallow drops, small acts of kindness honor the humanity of the person with Alzheimer's. It is the enjoyment of their company that fosters communication. It is relationship, not repetition, that gives way to a signal of understanding, even if that signal is as simple as a smile.

Looking back on my initial visit with my grandfather, I knew that he processed every word I said. Those shining blue eyes and unwavering smile told me that he fully knew of my presence, but he was unable to express that awareness in my world. I like to think that my grandfather's mind found an entire universe overflowing with worlds unique to him, each planet representing a blissful memory of a life full of love.

Did dementia ever take his universe away? No.   20

Well, I'll be damned!

Works Cited

"Dementia." *The Gale Encyclopedia of Psychology*, edited by Jacqueline L. Longe, 3rd ed., Gale, 2016. *Credo Reference*, search.credoreference.com/content/entry/galegp/dementia/0.

Diehl, Andrea. Interview with author. 11 Nov. 2020.

Grady, Denise. "Self-Portraits Chronicle a Descent into Alzheimer's." *The New York Times*, 24 Oct. 2006, www.nytimes.com/2006/10/24 /health/24alzh.html.

Small, Jeff A., et al. "Effectiveness of Communication Strategies Used by Caregivers of Persons with Alzheimer's Disease during Activities of Daily Living." *Journal of Speech, Language, and Hearing Research*, vol. 46, no. 2, Apr. 2003, pp. 353–67. *EBSCOhost*, https://doi.org/10.1044/1092-4388(2003/028).

Diehl's challenges in conversing with a grandparent with Alzheimer's disease spur him to explore ways to communicate effectively with people with dementia. Through his exploration, Diehl ponders the merits of several communication strategies, including those recommended by experts and those used by his own grandmother.

Key Features / Explorations

A topic that intrigues you. An exploratory essay has a dual purpose: to ponder something you find interesting or puzzling, and to share your thoughts with an audience. Your topic may be anything that interests you. You might write about someone you've never met and are curious about, an object or occurrence that makes you think, a problem you need to solve—or one you need to define. Your goal is to explore the meaning that the person, object, event, or problem has for you in a way that will interest others. One way to do that is by making connections between your personal experience and more general ones that readers may share. Diehl writes about his interactions with his own grandfather, but in so doing he raises questions and offers insights about how others communicate with people affected by dementia.

Some kind of structure.   An exploratory essay can be structured in many ways, but it needs to *be* structured. It may seem to wander, but all its paths and ideas should relate, one way or another. The challenge is to keep your readers' interest as you explore your topic and to leave readers satisfied that the journey was pleasurable, interesting, and profitable. Often doing this requires **COMBINING GENRES**. For example, Diehl begins with a narrative that includes snippets of dialogue, moves into a visual analysis of a series of self-portraits, summarizes a study of communication strategies, and then recounts an interview with his grandmother. He ends by proposing that demonstrating love for a person with dementia is more important than using any particular strategy for communication.

82–83

Specific details.   You'll need to provide specific details to help readers understand and connect with your subject, especially if it's an abstract or unfamiliar one. Diehl notes how his grandfather is "slouched in his bed absorbing the sounds of a televised college football game" and how the "scruff around his face rises, revealing a smile of recognition." Later, Diehl captures an anecdote from his grandmother to help bring her relationship with her husband to life: "'I always made sure he was smiling. Anything that I knew was going to please him was the object of my time with him. I would give him a hot chocolate and give him a little hug, and then when I put a marshmallow in that hot chocolate, he would smile!'" In addition to details and anecdotes, exploratory essays may include researched information, as Diehl's does when it mentions a study of communication strategies among couples affected by Alzheimer's. In some cases, photographs or other visuals—like the self-portraits Diehl analyzes—help provide examples as well as set a certain tone for an exploration.

A questioning, speculative tone.   In an exploratory essay, you are working toward answers, not providing them neatly organized and ready for consumption. So your tone is usually tentative and open, demonstrating a willingness to entertain, accept, and reject various ideas as your essay progresses from beginning to end. Often this tone is achieved by asking questions, like Diehl does: "Knowing that my other grandparents could be at risk of dementia as well, I wondered: How could I communicate more effectively with family members who may exhibit memory loss in the future?" "This study suggests the viability of some verbal techniques over others, but I was still left with a burning question: Doesn't communication effectiveness ultimately depend on what personally works for the individual with Alzheimer's?"

A BRIEF GUIDE TO WRITING EXPLORATIONS

Deciding on a Topic

Choose a subject you want or need to explore. Write a list of things that you think about, wonder about, find puzzling or annoying. They may be big things—life, relationships—or little things—quirks of certain people's behavior, curious objects, everyday events. Try clustering one or more of those things, or begin by freewriting to see what comes to mind as you write. If you need to define and solve a problem, try googling the topic to see what others have said about it and how you might think about it—and to see what potential solutions have already been proposed.

Considering the Rhetorical Situation

73–74 ■	**PURPOSE**	What's your goal in writing this essay? To explore a topic that interests you? To work through an issue or problem that concerns you? To provoke readers to think about something? What aspects of your subject do you want to ponder and reflect on?
75–78 ■	**AUDIENCE**	Who is the audience? How familiar are they with your subject? How will you introduce it in a way that will interest them? Even if your primary audience is yourself, how will you help readers understand your thinking?
85–87 ■	**STANCE**	What is your attitude toward the topic you plan to explore—questioning? playful? critical? curious? something else?

MEDIA/DESIGN   Will your essay be a print document? an oral presentation? Will it be posted on a website or a blog? Would it help to include any visuals or video or audio files?

88–90

Generating Ideas and Text

Explore your subject in detail.   Exploratory essays often include descriptive details. Diehl, for example, describes Utermohlen's self-portraits as he speculates about their meaning and effect: "This surrealism becomes more apparent in the next portrait, where the eyes are positioned far too low, the forehead and ear are enlarged, and the frown of the artist becomes more solemn." Diehl also compares and contrasts the portraits, pointing out the changes between the pre-diagnosis portrait and those that follow. You may also make your point by defining, narrating, even classifying. Virtually any organizing pattern will help you explore your subject.

Back away.   Ask yourself why your subject matters: Why is it important or intriguing or significant? You may try listing or outlining possibilities, or you may want to start drafting to see where the first round of writing takes your thinking. Your goal is to think on-screen (or on paper) about your subject, to play with its possibilities.

Think about how to keep readers with you.   Explorations may seem loose or unstructured, but they must be carefully crafted so that readers can follow your train of thought. It's a good idea to sketch out a rough thesis to help focus your thoughts. You might not include the thesis in the essay itself, but every part of the essay should in some way relate to it. If Diehl's essay has a thesis, it's this: "One does not need to be a master of psychological techniques in order to properly approach communication with a person affected by dementia. What's needed is a repeated effort to be present with the individual, expressing joy over what *they* say instead of sweating over anything *we* could ever say."

Ways of Organizing an Exploratory Essay

Exploratory essays may be organized in many ways because they mimic the way we think, associating one idea with another in ways that make sense but do not necessarily form a "logical" progression. In general, you might consider organizing an exploration using this overall strategy.

 Access Chapter 30 in the ebook for a video on organizing and synthesizing ideas.

Synthesize your insights

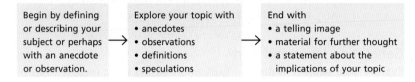

Begin by defining or describing your subject or perhaps with an anecdote or observation. → Explore your topic with
- anecdotes
- observations
- definitions
- speculations
→ End with
- a telling image
- material for further thought
- a statement about the implications of your topic

Share anecdotes to create an overall impression

Introduce your subject. → Offer an anecdote or idea related to your subject. → Offer another anecdote or idea. → Continue as needed, making sure each anecdote or idea relates to the others. → End with thoughts, questions, or implications of the ideas and their relationships.

Ponder solutions to a problem

Introduce your subject and define the problem. → Offer one potential solution, including its pros and cons. → Describe another potential solution, including its pros and cons. → Continue outlining potential solutions as needed. → End by weighing the merits of each one and settling on a tentative best solution (though it may not be perfect).

More Ways to Approach an Exploration

Write in journal or letter form.   Write your exploration in the form of journal entries that chronicle your process of pondering your topic over days or weeks. Or write in the form of letters, emails, or postcards to someone who's interested in your topic and your inquiry into it.

Create a blog or podcast series.   Your initial post or episode might introduce your topic and explain why you're interested in exploring it, perhaps posing an intriguing question that will give readers or listeners a reason to follow your series. Other posts or episodes could reveal your discoveries and reflections incrementally, with the final one synthesizing your findings and insights and perhaps posing further questions. For a blog series, you could integrate images, videos, and other media relevant to your exploration; for a podcast, you could add background music, sound effects, ambient sounds, or discussions with guests.

Remix. After you've written a draft of your exploration, you might **REMIX** it: rework it into one or more of the genres above or turn it into a series of social media posts, a collection of **VIGNETTES**, an op-ed, or another genre or medium that fits your rhetorical situation.

▲ 280–90

▲ 109

Taking Stock of Your Work

Take stock of what you've written by considering these questions:

Access Chapter 36 in the ebook for a video on reflecting on your writing.

- How did you decide on your topic?

- Why did you organize your piece as you did?

- Describe your revision process for this piece. What worked, and what didn't work? Did you learn anything new—about your topic, about yourself, about something else—as you revised your piece?

- Did you use visual elements (photographs, diagrams, drawings), audio elements, or links? If so, what did they add? If not, what might you have used?

- How did curiosity play a role in the writing of your exploration? Can you point to a specific part of your text that illustrates your curiosity about your topic?

- What have you learned about your writing ability from writing this piece? What do you need to work on in the future?

- What was most rewarding about your work on this piece?

If you need more help

See Chapter 31 for guidelines on **DRAFTING**, Chapter 32 for **ASSESSING YOUR OWN WRITING**, Chapter 33 for **GETTING RESPONSE AND REVISING**, and Chapter 34 for **EDITING AND PROOFREADING**.

358–60
361–64
365–71
372–76

23 Remixes

Just as musicians alter existing tracks to create new ones, writers sometimes "remix" or refashion their writing for new contexts. A mechanical engineer uses elements of her technical report about a new engine part to write instructions for the machinists who assemble the part. A historian turns his scholarly article on slavery and disability into a podcast episode for the general public. A sociology student transforms her essay on food insecurity into an infographic to persuade her college administration to start a food pantry. In each case, the writer modifies all or part of their earlier work for a new purpose, audience, genre, stance, or medium.

In college courses across the curriculum, you might be asked to do the same—for example, by writing a researched report for a class assignment and then sharing your work through a multimedia presentation for your classmates or others. For a capstone project in your major, you might be asked to return to some earlier writing you've done, reimagining or extending it for a new purpose.

This chapter offers suggestions for creating remixes—texts that grow out of and "play on" earlier texts you've composed. Let's start by looking at an example: a profile originally published in a university alumni magazine that gets remixed into two different videos for the university's website.

Original Text: A Print Profile

"Rare Earth," a profile that inspired two remixes, traces Dr. Rattan Lal's path from refugee to premier soil scientist. Following is an excerpt from the piece, which appeared in the *Ohio State Alumni Magazine*. The author, Todd Jones, is a senior writer for the magazine.

TODD JONES
Rare Earth

The thin man in the Ohio State ballcap hunches down near his home garden, in the backyard with the two buckeye trees. He's holding a clump of dirt. "No, no. Not dirt," he says. "This is soil. Soil is not the same as dirt. Soil is a living entity. That's the part we must understand."

His hands are cupped, as if holding a baby bird. He gazes in admiration, points to roots and a worm. He tells us a tablespoon of soil contains billions of microorganisms. "Soil is one. Indivisible. Interconnected," he says. "Soil is the basis of all terrestrial life. Every living thing on the planet depends on it, and yet this material is underappreciated and unrecognized."

His face is wrinkled and weathered, a testament to years spent researching in the fields, forging wisdom about our place in the world. "We belong to nature. We belong to soil," he says. "Therefore, we have a duty and obligation to soil." He has researched soil for five decades on five continents, traveling to 106 countries to spread a message: that we must "make an investment to restore [soil]. You always want to leave something behind," the concept underlying regenerative agriculture. But more work must be done to spread understanding about the critical role of soil in the health of the planet. "That challenge," he says, "is my motivator, my driving force."

Lal surveys an Ohio cornfield.

Thomson Reuters has long listed Dr. Rattan Lal, Ohio State Distinguished University Professor of Soil Science, among the top 1 percent of the most frequently cited agricultural researchers in the world. In 2007, Lal was recognized for his contributions to the Intergovernmental Panel on Climate Change, which shared the 2007 Nobel Peace Prize with former U.S. vice president Al Gore. In 2019, Lal was awarded the Japan Prize, one of the most prestigious honors in science and technology. That same year, he won the Alumni Medalist Award, the highest honor bestowed by The Ohio State University Alumni Association.

Such status suggests that Lal deserves a gilded lair, but he sits behind an ordinary metal desk in a painted cinder-block room measuring 9 feet by 12 feet. "My office is fine," Lal says. "The office is in proportion to your contributions."

His modesty also masks a fierce inner drive. Three heart attacks 5 have not slowed him, and praise from international peers has not inflated him. He has more speeches to give, papers to write, conference calls to join, classes to teach, research to conduct, and students to mentor. "This is who he is," says Sukhvarsha Sharma, his wife of 48 years. "He has very high expectations of himself. He wants to make a difference in the environment, and through that, make a difference in peoples' lives."

There are times when Lal looks like a symphony conductor as he speaks, his voice accompanied by slowly moving hands, as if words about soil were notes in a musical sonnet. In those moments, your eyes might fall on an ancient symbol in faded blue ink on the back of Lal's right hand. He thinks he was about 8 years old when a stranger on a bicycle came to his school in India offering cheap tattoos. The boy couldn't resist. Nearly seven decades later, he regrets his choice. "I would not get it done now," Lal says. "But a small decision about a tattoo, that's very little in importance. Decisions about soil are very, very important. Those are decisions that influence other people's lives and have very long-lasting impact."

The impact is intensifying because the world's population is projected to increase nearly 50 percent in the next 80 years—an ominous forecast that Lal tells Ohio State students on a summer afternoon while lecturing in an Introduction to Soil Science class. Humanity, Lal warns, is facing a dire necessity to advance food security by protecting finite, fragile soil resources. "Agriculture and soil are, can be, and must be a solution," he says, clasping and shaking his hands for emphasis.

In that moment, you could see Lal's tattoo, an ink version of the symbol for om, considered the most sacred of mantras in his Hindu religion. Through the word's three distinct sounds—"a-u-m"—the speaker is meant to understand the essence of the universe: Everything is connected. Om is the sound of Lal's life.

"There's just kind of an equanimity, a sense of mental peace, about him," says Ellen Maas, one of Lal's current doctoral students. "His manner is not one that is focused on himself. He just cares so deeply about humanity and the planet. He finds an inner strength in caring about things bigger than himself."

Lal's family experience shaped his worldview. The youngest of three, 10 he was raised by his father after his mother died of an illness when Lal was 3 months old. When India was partitioned to form Pakistan in 1947, his family fled as refugees to the Indian village of Rajaund, about 120 miles northwest of New Delhi. They left a 9-acre farm and settled on one totaling only 1.5 acres, a change that marked Lal with a different tattoo, just as permanent but invisible.

"It taught me that the land is very precious," Lal says. "You cannot let it waste. Your life depends on it. Our land was so small, but it was not a unique situation. There are right now in the world about 600 million farm families that have less than 2 acres. In a way, what I do and what I think relates back to those people and my experience."

Lal helped grow rice, wheat, cotton, and sugarcane on his family farm. But unlike his siblings, he also was sent to school by his father. The child felt chosen, obligated to make good on a privileged opportunity. In 1959, his diligence and excellent grades met Ohio State in serendipity: he enrolled at the Government Agricultural College and Research Institute (which became Punjab Agricultural University his senior year). Ohio State had helped establish the institute only four years earlier. "One of the professors, Dr. [Dev Raj] Bhumbla, had just returned with a PhD from Ohio State, and he started teaching a soil class," Lal says. "I was in that class. My best subject was botany, but he told me to go into soil science. In fact, he recommended my name to faculty at Ohio State to be a student there."

In 1965, Lal boarded a plane for the first time and traveled alone 7,300 miles to pursue his doctorate. He brought along an insatiable hunger to succeed. At Punjab Agricultural University, he had run 4 miles—

yes, run them—to school from home every day, studied by the light of a kerosene lamp, sometimes held up by his grandmother. He found an agricultural book in the library so essential that he spent two months hand-copying it to have his own edition. "Nothing can be achieved without the strongest possible desire to achieve it," Lal says.

His desire and degree mixed to fuel a career trek around the globe. Ohio State connections landed him research jobs, first in Sydney, Australia, for a year, and then in Nigeria, where the Rockefeller Foundation asked him to set up a soil science laboratory at the International Institute of Tropical

Lal holds his undergraduate diploma from Punjab Agricultural University.

Agriculture. Lal and his wife—only a year into their arranged marriage—went in spite of a bloody civil war. They stayed 18 years, even as three Nigerian governments were toppled by coups. "Once, I was at the house of a general," Lal says. "He had invited me to come talk about suggestions to control soil erosion. Two days later, he was hanged and his family shot. People have said if I was there when they came, I would not be here today."

One moment can make a difference. So can one person. This is 15 why he accepts invitations to speak about soil, whether the audience is filled with heads of power or young burgeoning minds. "The students are ambassadors of Ohio State," Lal says. "They represent us. They carry on the work that we do."

There are twenty-two students in this day's class. Lal speaks to them without notes, standing next to a podium, hand in pocket. His tone is measured, but his message linking soil management to the nourishment of humankind is urgent. "The story has to be told in a language that farmers and policymakers understand and can relate to. That's critical," Lal says. "That's going to take education. We have to change opinions in a humble way. That falls on your generation."

Remix 1: A Video Profile

Eventually, the writer and photographer of "Rare Earth" collaborated with others to remix the article into a video profile. The remix uses recorded footage to showcase Dr. Lal in action as he and his students assess the results of no-till farming. Below are a few frames from the video; you can view the complete video in the Norton ebook or at digital.wwnorton.com/fieldguide7h.

(gentle music)

and what practices can be shown are not sustainable

And we're gonna quantify the total fresh weight

If we can do no-till and we can have better yields

Remix 2: An Explainer Video

The original profile piece was remixed into yet another video, this time a motion-graphics video that explains the science behind regenerative agriculture. Below are some frames from the full video, available in the Norton ebook or at digital.wwnorton.com/fieldguide7h.

All three texts remix parts of the others, but each has a different purpose, audience, and medium/design. The print article is designed for magazine subscribers and aims to profile Dr. Lal's personal and professional achievements as an alumnus of the university. The video profile is produced for the web and provides a firsthand look at Dr. Lal's work in agriculture, while the explainer video helps viewers understand a crucial concept in Dr. Lal's research. Together the remixes offer a fuller picture of the scientist and his contributions to his field.

Key Features / Remixes

A connection to the original subject. A remix always hearkens back to the original subject in some way. Sometimes the connection is obvious— Dr. Lal takes center stage in both the video profile and the print profile, though each profile shares a different aspect of his story. Other times, just a fragment of the original subject inspires the remix. For example, the science behind Dr. Lal's work is mentioned only briefly in the print article but becomes the sole focus of the explainer video.

A modification of the earlier work. By definition, a remix involves change. Something in the writing situation changes—like the writer's purpose or audience—and that change requires other modifications as well. The writer might need to work within a new medium, or adopt a different stance, or write in a new genre to get their message across most effectively. When the creators of the "Rare Earth" article needed to explain the complex concept of regenerative agriculture, they determined that a visual medium would better suit their purpose than a print-based one.

Attention to genre and media/design expectations. Often remixes require a change in genre or a change in medium (or both), and effective remixes meet audience expectations for the new genre or medium. The profile video of Dr. Lal, for example, uses background music, on-screen titles, and clips of recorded footage— all of which are typical features of a profile (genre) delivered through a video (medium).

SOME TYPICAL WAYS OF REMIXING

Your writing situation—especially your purpose and audience—will determine the type of remix you might create. Following, though, are some common ways of remixing texts for new genres or media.

234–45 ▲   **Personal narratives.** With their vivid details and scenes, **PERSONAL NARRATIVES** lend themselves to visual remixes as photo montages, graphic memoirs, comic strips, and digital stories. You might also repurpose parts of a narrative into a new genre—for example, by sharing an anecdote to support a point in an argument.

246–56 ▲   **Profiles.** A print **PROFILE** that showcases an interesting person, place, or event might get remixed into a mini documentary or a podcast to bring the subject to life even more fully for an audience. You could also incorporate a profile into another genre—like a report—to make an abstract concept more concrete.

170–96 ▲   **Arguments.** With their focus on making and supporting claims, **ARGUMENTS** are often remixed as newspaper op-eds, public service announcements (PSAs) for radio or television, or print or online petitions. With instructor permission, you might remix an argument you've written on gun control for your first-year writing class into a proposal for your public health class.

Proposals. A written **PROPOSAL** might morph into a slide show for a presentation and then into a fund-raising letter to secure financial support for a proposed project. In your college classes, you might repurpose parts of a topic proposal for a report, an argument, or some other genre you're asked to write—as long as your instructors approve.

▲ 257–69

Reports. Research findings from **REPORTS** often get remixed into infographics, poster presentations, timelines, and listicles (articles presented in list form). In college courses, you might remix a report you've written into an oral presentation to your class.

▲ 146–69

In creating a remix as part of your college coursework, be sure to follow your school's academic integrity policies. Most policies forbid students from reusing or resubmitting their previous work without instructor permission. If you plan to remix something you've created for one class into a project for another class, get approval from *both* instructors beforehand.

A BRIEF GUIDE TO CREATING REMIXES

Determining What Will Change in Your Remix

When you compose a remix, you're not starting from scratch—you already have a general topic and a text to work from. Still, you need to determine how your remix will be different from your earlier work.

A good place to start is to think about what has changed in your writing situation. Has your instructor asked you to prepare a *Prezi* version of an academic essay you've written for your course? If so, the media/design elements of your rhetorical situation have changed. Or maybe you've written a report for a class assignment, and now you want to inspire a particular group of people to take action on your topic. In this case, your purpose and audience have changed. Usually, a change in one element of the rhetorical situation affects the others, so it's important to carefully consider all those elements as you plan your remix.

Access the ebook for a video on creating a remix.

Considering the Rhetorical Situation

PURPOSE   Why are you creating the remix? To share the same message from your earlier work through a different genre or medium? To make a new point about your topic? To explain a concept from your earlier work? To

■ 73–74

reach a different audience? To reach the same audience in a new way? To persuade or inform or entertain?

75–78 **AUDIENCE**   Who will read, view, or listen to your remix? Are they the same audience as before? a different audience? Why should they care about your message? What will they already know? How can you engage their interest?

79–84 **GENRE**   Will you work within a new genre or the same one as earlier? Will you mix multiple genres? Which genres would work best for your purpose and audience? What expectations will your audience have for genre?

85–87 **STANCE**   Will your stance in the remix be the same as or different from your earlier stance? What is your relationship with your audience? Are you an equal, a student, an interested or concerned outsider, something else? What tone is appropriate—objective, impassioned, respectful, informal, something else?

88–90 **MEDIA / DESIGN**   Will you work within a new medium or the same one as earlier? What medium would be most appropriate for your audience and purpose? Will you use multiple media, combining sounds, visuals, words, movement? What expectations will your audience have for design and format? What steps can you take to make your 641–42 composition **ACCESSIBLE** to diverse audiences?

Generating Ideas and Text

Return to your earlier work.   Remember, you're not starting from a blank slate. You can go back to your earlier work to decide what to keep, delete, change, or add as you create your remix. Are there key ideas you want to be sure to include in your remix? Will you need to condense some information from your earlier work? explore a new angle on your topic? reframe an argument? conduct more research? find or create images or sounds? Try **FREEWRITING**, **LISTING**, or **CLUSTERING** to figure out what 329
330
330–31 you can use from your earlier work and what you'll need to reimagine or create anew.

If you're remixing for a new genre, examine sample texts in your chosen genre. Whether you're creating a brochure, a business plan, an infographic, or something else, find samples that you think are effective. Then study the genre features: What do you notice about the use of headings, bullets, photos, and other **DESIGN** elements? What do you notice about the formality of the language, the lengths of sentences and paragraphs, the **TONE**? How is source information documented? How are **VISUALS** or sounds acknowledged or cited? Consider how you'll make use of the genre features in your own remixed composition.

■ 88–90

■ 86
● 648–54

If you're remixing for a new medium, consider your capabilities and your options. Maybe you want to create a website, a video, a podcast, or some other digital text, but you don't have access to the tools you need or you're not skilled in using them. Your school might have a multimedia support center or other resources to help you get started. Another option: with your instructor's permission, you could perhaps create a "pre-production" document instead of a full-fledged multimedia piece. For example, you might make a mock-up of a website in a *Microsoft Word* document. Or you might write a script for a podcast or create a detailed **STORYBOARD** for a video.

⁂ 333–34

Remember, too, that online tools and templates can make composing with sound and visuals easier. Some tools you might consider using (with a free trial) include:

For brochures, advertisements, posters
Adobe Express, Canva

For infographics
Venngage, Piktochart, Canva

For interactive line charts
StorylineJS

For interactive timelines
Tiki-Toki, TimelineJS

For photo montages
Fotor

For picture books
Storybird, StoryJumper

For podcasts
Podbean

For slide presentations
Prezi, Canva

For comics, storyboards, graphic novels
Pixton

For videos
Animoto, Powtoon

For virtual reality stories
SceneVR

For websites
Adobe Express, Google Sites, Weebly, Wix

For free music and sound effects
Free Music Archive, Orange Free Sounds

For free images
Pexels, Pixabay

Ways of Organizing a Remix

Your organizational strategy will depend on your genre and medium, and you may be able to consult the relevant genre chapter as a guide. If appropriate, you might also consider creating a simple **STORYBOARD** to plan out a sequence of text and images for your remix.

333–34

Taking Stock of Your Work

Take stock of what you've created by considering these questions:

Access Chapter 36 in the ebook for a video on reflecting on your writing.

- What elements of your rhetorical situation changed as you moved from your original work to your remix—your purpose? audience? genre? stance? medium? In what specific ways does your remixed composition respond to those changes?

- What part of the composing process was most enjoyable as you worked on your remix? Why?

- What technological, logistical, design, or other challenges did you face in creating your remix, and how did you address them?

- What previous composing experiences (print-based and multimedia ones), if any, did you draw on in creating your remix? Did those experiences help you or hinder you?

- What resources did you use to complete your remix? How did those resources help you, and how might you use them in future composing situations?

- What new things did you learn about your topic in the process of remixing your earlier work?

- What new things did you learn about composing? about genres, media, and other elements of rhetorical situations?

- What are you most proud of in this piece?

If you need more help

52–60
637–39
640–46
647–58
383–92
377–82

See Chapter 5 for guidelines on **WRITING AND LEARNING ONLINE**, Chapter 56 for **CHOOSING MEDIA**, Chapter 57 for **DESIGNING TEXT**, and Chapter 58 for **USING VISUALS, INCORPORATING SOUND**. If you're required to write a formal **REFLECTION** to accompany your remix, see Chapter 36, and see Chapter 35 for guidelines on compiling a **PORTFOLIO**.

Part 4
Fields

When we study at a college or university, we take courses in many academic fields of study, or disciplines, in the humanities, social sciences, the sciences, and various career-oriented fields. Each field of study has its own methods of doing research and communicating, requiring us to learn how to **READ** and **WRITE** in the ways appropriate to that field. The chapters that follow offer advice on how to adapt your reading and writing to the demands of various fields of study.

Fields

* academic literacies   ⬡ fields   ◆ strategies   ⬭ media / design
■ rhetorical situations   ⦙ processes   ● research   ★ handbook
▲ genres

24 Fields of Study

Most colleges and universities are organized around fields of study, often referred to as *disciplines*, that share ways of seeing the universe, doing research, and presenting information—each through a different lens. For example, historians and economists differ in the ways they examine human behavior; biologists and physicists differ in the ways they study the natural world. The various majors that colleges and universities offer invite you to learn to see the world in their distinctive ways and join professions that use distinctive skills. Marketing majors, for example, learn ways of influencing human behavior; education majors learn ways of teaching students; and music majors learn the intricacies of playing an instrument or singing. As you immerse yourself in a major, you come to see the world with a particular perspective.

Academic Fields and General Education

Your general education courses have a different goal: to prepare you for the demands of living in a complex and changing world—a world in which you'll need to use your ability to understand a wide range of facts, theories, and concepts to interact with a wide variety of people, work in various jobs, and make important decisions. In other words, these courses are designed to teach you how to learn and think. They are also helpful if you're not sure what you'd like to major in, because you can sample courses in various disciplines to help you decide. In your first couple of years, you will likely take general education courses in the following subject areas:

- the humanities, which include the arts, communications, history, literature, music, philosophy, and religion
- the social sciences, which may include anthropology, economics, political science, geography, psychology, and sociology
- the sciences, which usually include such disciplines as astronomy, biology, chemistry, geology, mathematics, and physics

It's important to note that these lists are far from comprehensive; schools differ in the courses and majors they offer, so some schools may offer courses in fields that aren't on any of these lists—and some of these courses might not be available at your school. You may also take courses in career-oriented fields such as education, business, engineering, and nursing.

Studying, Reading, and Writing in Academic Fields

Each field focuses on the study of particular subjects and issues. In *psychology*, you study the human mind—what it is and why we behave as we do. In *sociology*, you study the way society shapes our actions. In *biology*, you study life itself, from bacteria and fungi to organisms interacting with their environment. In *history*, you study the past to understand the present. In *nursing*, you study best ways of providing patient care within the health-care system. In *engineering*, you learn how to solve technical problems and design engineering systems.

Each field also examines the world through a distinctive lens, using its own methods to study and analyze those subjects. For example, scientists test hypotheses with experiments designed to prove or disprove their accuracy; sociologists study groups by using statistical evidence; and historians examine diaries, speeches, or photographs from the past. In addition, disciplines develop technical terms and ways of using language that allow scholars to understand one another—but that can be hard to understand. For example, consider the word "significant." When people say that something is *significant* in day-to-day conversation, they usually mean that it's important, a big deal; in statistics, though, a *significant* result is one that is probably true—but it may or may not be important.

Disciplines also present information using methods standard in that discipline. In *business* courses, you're likely to read case studies of specific companies and write business cases and other communications. In *education* courses, you'll read and write lesson plans; in *science* courses, you'll read and write laboratory reports; in *English* courses, you'll read fiction, poetry, and plays and write literary analyses. In each, you'll present information in ways used in conversations among scholars in the discipline. And that means that you may need to adapt your reading and writing to the genres, concepts, and methods of the various academic fields you encounter.

Thinking about Reading and Writing in the Fields

- What reading assignments do you have in your other courses?
- What makes them easy or hard to read? What helps you read them?
- Do you enjoy reading some genres or subjects more than others? Why?
- What writing assignments do you have in your other courses?
- Do you alter or adjust your writing processes in different courses? Why or why not?
- What makes writing in some courses hard or easy?
- Do you enjoy writing in certain genres or on certain topics? Why?

25 Reading across Fields of Study

We read shopping lists differently from graphic novels and operating instructions differently from poems. For that matter, we read novels and poems differently—and go about reading textbooks differently still. Just as we write using various processes—generating ideas and text, drafting, getting responses and revising, editing, and proofreading—we vary our reading processes from task to task. We will likely read a mathematics textbook differently from a case study in nursing, and read a speech by Abraham Lincoln in a history course differently from the way we'd read it in a rhetoric course. This chapter offers advice on how to engage with texts in a variety of fields.

Considering the Rhetorical Situation

A good way to approach reading in academic fields is to treat reading as a process that you adapt to the demands of each new situation. Instead of diving in and focusing your reading on the details of the content, it's often useful to take some time to consider the text's purpose, your purpose, the audience, the author, the author's stance, the genre, and the medium and design. This information can help you decide how to get the most out of the text.

- *The text's* **PURPOSE**. When was the text written, and why? Is it a textbook? a classic work that lays out concepts that have become fundamental to the field? a work proposing a new way of looking at an issue?

- *Your purpose as a reader.* Why are you reading this text? To study for a test? To find sources for a research project? To learn about something on your own?

- *The* **AUDIENCE**. For whom was the text written? Students like you? Scholars in the field? Interested nonspecialists? Readers who lived at some point in the past or in a particular location? What facts

73–74

75–78

and concepts does the text assume its readers already know and understand?

- *The author.* Who wrote what you are reading? Does knowing the author's identity matter? Is the author reliable and credible? For example, is the author a respected scholar? Is the author known for a particular point of view?

- *The author's* **STANCE**. What is the author's stance toward the subject? toward the reader? Approving? Hostile? Critical? Passionate? What elements of the text reveal the author's stance?

  85–87

- *The* **GENRE**. What is the text's genre? How was it meant to be read? Is that how you're reading it? What are the genre's key features? Knowing the key features of the genre can help you understand the text's content as you read and predict the text's organization.

  79–84

- *The* **MEDIUM** *and* **DESIGN**. The medium and design of a text affect how you must read it. You may need to read a textbook differently from an article found on the internet, for example. An online textbook may require different commenting and note-taking strategies from a print text. Understanding the limitations and the advantages of a particular genre, medium, and design will help you get the most out of your reading.

  88–90

Advice for Reading across Fields of Study

Becoming knowledgeable in a field of study requires learning its specialized ways of thinking, writing, and reading, including the terminology specific to the field and the kinds of texts the field is likely to produce and study. However, there is some general advice that can help you as you begin to read the kinds of texts you're likely to encounter in college.

Pay attention to vocabulary. All disciplines require that you learn their vocabulary, which includes not only concepts and facts but also the names of important figures in the field and what they represent. Scholars typically write for other scholars in the same field, so they may assume that readers understand these terms and references and refer to them without explanation—and even "popular" writing often makes the same assumption. You'll find that much of the work in all your courses consists of learning terms and concepts. So it's important to take good notes in lectures, writing down terms your instructor emphasizes as they are defined or, if they aren't, writing them down to look up later. Your textbooks introduce and define key terms and often include a glossary in the back that provides definitions.

In addition, be aware that disciplinary vocabularies use different kinds of words. In the sciences, the language is likely very technical, with many terms based on Greek and Latin roots (for example, the Greek prefix *gastr-* forms "gastropod" [snail], "gastric" [stomach], and "gastroscopy" [examination of the abdomen and stomach]). In the humanities, the vocabulary often alludes to complex concepts. Consider, for example, these sentences from *The Swerve*, a book by literary historian Stephen Greenblatt:

> The household, the kinship network, the guild, the corporation—these were the building blocks of personhood. Independence and self-reliance had no cultural purchase.

Almost every term—"household," "guild," "personhood," and "cultural purchase," to name a few—carries a wealth of information that must be understood. While understanding the scientific terms requires a good dictionary, these particular terms require an encyclopedia—or the knowledge gained by much reading.

Consider the author—or not. In some disciplines, it's important to know who wrote a text, while in others the identity or **STANCE** of the author is considered irrelevant. Historians, for example, need to know who the author of a text is, and the perspective that author brings to the text is central to reading history. Literary scholars may try not to consider the author at all, focusing solely on a close reading of the text itself. Scientists may consider the author's identity or the school or lab where the author works to decide whether or not to read a text. Mathematicians resolutely ignore the author, focusing solely on the information in the text itself. So to make sense of a text in a discipline, you need to find out how that discipline sees the role of the author.

85–87 ■

Identify key ideas and make comparisons. Whatever the discipline, look for the main ideas its texts present. Rather than highlight or underline them, write out the key ideas in your own words. As you read texts on the same subject, you may want to develop a matrix to help you **COMPARE AND CONTRAST** as well as **SYNTHESIZE** the main ideas. The following chart, adapted from one developed by two librarians, presents the main ideas in two sources and then synthesizes the two versions. This example

422–28 ◆
515–20 ●

synthesizes one main idea found in each of two articles on how social media affect political participation among youths and then, in the third column, synthesizes those ideas:

Source #1: Skorik, M. M. "Youth Engagement in Singapore"	Source #2: Ahmad, K. "Social Media and Youth Participatory Politics"	Synthesis: Main Ideas
Summary of 1st main idea: Singapore's government has consistently applied controls on traditional media outlets but has left social media outlets untouched and unregulated.	**Summary of 1st main idea:** Online participation in political campaigns and issues was almost five times greater than traditional participation. Researchers concluded that this "could provide the participant with anonymity, in turn less vulnerability to political vengeance."	**Synthesis of 1st main ideas:** Government control and censorship of mainstream media has caused protesters to look for alternative communication tools.
Summary of 2nd main idea:	**Summary of 2nd main idea:**	**Synthesis of 2nd main ideas:**
Summary of 3rd main idea:	**Summary of 3rd main idea:**	**Synthesis of 3rd main ideas:**

Adapted from Michelle Chiles and Emily Brown, "Literature Review." Bristol Community College, Fall River, MA, 2015. Unpublished *PowerPoint*.

More main ideas can be summarized and synthesized in the rows below; add as many as needed.

You might also get into the habit of skimming the list of works cited or references at the end of articles and books. As you do so, you'll begin to see who the most important people are in the discipline and what counts as evidence.

Build a map of the discipline. To make sense of a new idea, you need to have some way of fitting it into what you already know. Reading in an unfamiliar discipline can be hard because you likely won't have a sense of where the information in the text fits into the conversations of the discipline, its history, or your goals—what you'd like to know or do in this field. It's useful to visualize the discipline so that you can place readings into the appropriate context. Possible ways of organizing a discipline follow.

Draw a word map. Using your textbook and perhaps some online sources as guides, draw an overview of the field. Here's one for psychology:

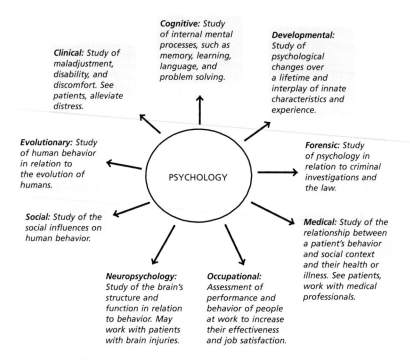

Cognitive: Study of internal mental processes, such as memory, learning, language, and problem solving.

Clinical: Study of maladjustment, disability, and discomfort. See patients, alleviate distress.

Developmental: Study of psychological changes over a lifetime and interplay of innate characteristics and experience.

Evolutionary: Study of human behavior in relation to the evolution of humans.

PSYCHOLOGY

Forensic: Study of psychology in relation to criminal investigations and the law.

Social: Study of the social influences on human behavior.

Medical: Study of the relationship between a patient's behavior and social context and their health or illness. See patients, work with medical professionals.

Neuropsychology: Study of the brain's structure and function in relation to behavior. May work with patients with brain injuries.

Occupational: Assessment of performance and behavior of people at work to increase their effectiveness and job satisfaction.

Create a timeline. Sometimes it's helpful to understand how a discipline developed over time, how its research methods or emphases came to be, so you can place its texts and key developments within that history. On the next page, for example, is a timeline of the behaviorist approach in psychology.

Write a conversation among researchers. To better understand the similarities and differences among various schools of thought within a discipline, choose some of the most prominent proponents of each school and write a fictional conversation among them, outlining where they agree and disagree and where they published or disseminated their theories and findings. Here, for instance, is a snippet of a dialogue that might have

Timeline of the behaviorist approach, 1900–2000

1900

1901: Ivan Pavlov teaches dogs to salivate in response to a bell, demonstrating classical conditioning.

1920: John Watson shows that classical conditioning works with people through Little Albert experiment.

1920

1924: Mary Cover Jones shows how behavioral therapy can cure phobias.

1940

1938: B. F. Skinner publishes *The Behavior of Organisms* on operant behavior.

1948: B. F. Skinner shows that pigeons can become "superstitious."

1960

1961: Albert Bandura shows that aggressive behavior can be learned.

1968: Teodoro Ayllon and Nathan Azrin create a token economy in a psychiatric hospital.

1980

1984: David McCormick and Richard Thompson show the role of the cerebellum in classical conditioning.

1991: Russell Richardson and Mahlon DeLong show the role of neurons in operant conditioning.

2000

taken place between developmental psychologist Jean Piaget and behavioral psychologist B. F. Skinner:

> **Piaget:** Children learn by adapting to conflicts between what they already know and challenges to that knowledge.
> **Skinner:** Bosh! We can't know what's in someone's mind; we have to focus on their behavior.
> **Piaget:** If a child sees something that doesn't match her preconceptions, she learns from it and through her behavior assimilates the new information into her thinking.
> **Skinner:** But if we reinforce a certain behavior by rewarding it, the child will do it more, and if we ignore it, the behavior will stop. It doesn't matter what, if anything, the child is thinking.

Tips for Reading in Various Fields of Study

Though groups of disciplines (the sciences, the arts and humanities, and so on) within each field share many similarities, each discipline has features unique to it. While you should expect to read difficult texts in any field several times, taking notes in your own words rather than highlighting or underlining, you need to be aware that reading, say, a biology text likely requires different reading techniques than a history text would. Here are some tips that can help you read effectively in various disciplines.

The humanities

- Much of the scholarship in the humanities is based on texts of one sort or another—the Constitution, the Bible, Toni Morrison's novels, Mozart's piano concertos, Georgia O'Keeffe's paintings. When reading in the humanities, then, be aware of the differences between reading **PRIMARY SOURCES** like those and **SECONDARY SOURCES** (commentaries, analyses, evaluations, and interpretations of primary sources).

482–83

- When reading a primary source, you may need to ask questions like these: What kind of document is this? Who created it? When and where was the source produced? Who was it intended for? What is its historical context? Why did the creator of the source create it? How was it received at the time of its creation? Has that reception changed?

- Read primary sources carefully and expect to reread them, perhaps several times. The way a text is organized, its sentence structure, its wording, and its imagery can all contribute to its overall message, and that's true of documents like the Declaration of Independence, the Torah, and Descartes's *Principles of Philosophy*.

- Similarly, plan to reread secondary sources. The argument of interpretations, analyses, or critical works requires close attention to their logic and use of evidence.

- Reading secondary sources requires that you examine them with a critical eye. The questions on page 512 can help you understand the source and evaluate its accuracy, perspective or angle, and usefulness for your own work.

- Remember that in the humanities, "criticism" doesn't necessarily mean looking for flaws and errors. Rather, it's another term for analyzing or evaluating.

- Some key terms you need to know in order to read texts in the humanities include: "analogy," "allusion," "argument," "deductive reasoning," "inductive reasoning," "irony," "metaphor," "natural law," "natural rights," "political rights," "premise." If you don't understand the meaning of any of these terms, be sure to look up their definitions.

The social sciences

- As you read in the social sciences, you need to pay attention to the hypotheses, claims, reasons, and evidence presented in the texts. Are they persuasive? How do they compare or contrast with other arguments?

- Be sure you understand what a theory in the social sciences is: a way of organizing information to help enhance our understanding of behavior, events, phenomena, or issues. For example, in sociology, social exchange theory assumes that we behave according to our sense of whether we'll be rewarded or punished by those with whom we interact. Remember that a theory is not an unsupported opinion but rather a coherent, logical frame for understanding and describing.

- Many articles include a **LITERATURE REVIEW** that summarizes and critiques previous work on the topic. Since scholarly work always grows out of the work of others, authors need to connect their work to articles and books previously published on the topic. Many literature reviews discuss limitations and problems in previous studies, ultimately identifying missing elements or gaps in them (often identified with words like "but," "however," and "although"), leading to a rationale for why this new work is needed.
▲ 206–9

- The "Discussion" and "Conclusion" sections (which are sometimes combined into a single section) explain and interpret the results of a study in the context of the previous literature, note any limitations in the current study, and recommend future research to address those limitations. In other words, these sections discuss what the author thinks the study means. As you read, consider possible flaws or omissions in the author's thinking as well as in the research design; for example, the study is too broad, the research question is poorly defined, or the study doesn't address its significance—the "so what?" question. Your insights could lead you to a better understanding of the topic—or to a research project of your own.

- Some key terms you need to know in order to read texts in the social sciences include "adaptation," "aggregate," "alienation," "capital," "class system," "deviance," "interest," "markets," "motivation," "norm," "power," "schema," "supply and demand," and "value." If you don't understand the meaning of any of these terms, be sure to look up their definitions.

The sciences

- Remember that scientific texts are not collections of established facts. They make claims and argue for them, using reasons and evidence to support those arguments. Scientific texts report the results of studies and experiments and are written by scientists for an audience of other scientists in the same field. These texts are different from science writing, which is often a form of nonfiction sometimes written by scientists, journalists, or other writers and aimed at general audiences to inform about scientific topics.

- If you're examining potential sources for a research project, read selectively: use articles' **ABSTRACTS** to decide whether an article is likely to be useful for your project, and skim the text to find the information relating to your needs. Many scientific articles follow a structure nicknamed IMRaD (Introduction, Methods, Results, and Discussion), so you may need to read only the sections of the article that discuss what you're looking for.

- Pay attention to the sample size—the number of units of whatever is being studied that are included in the study (a larger sample size is generally better than a smaller one)—and error bars in graphs, which show the uncertainty in the findings of the study being described.

- Scientists often make their arguments through visuals as much as through words, so read images, graphs, and charts as carefully as you would the words in the text.

- Some key terms you need to know in order to read texts in the sciences include "skepticism," "data," "evidence/observation," "hypothesis," "variables," "biodiversity," "falsifiability," "theory," "evolution," "experimentation," "population," "qualitative," "quantitative," "repeatability," "empirical," "paradigm," "rational/agnostic," "cosmos." If you don't understand the meaning of any of these terms, be sure to look up their definitions.

Mathematics texts: A special case. Math texts can be especially challenging for several reasons. Mathematics courses build on one another, so the texts in each course assume that you know certain concepts; they may also assume that you understand the ways mathematicians talk about math and the terms they use. Many math textbooks seem to jump right into the topic, providing little background beyond a definition of the first term to be used. And math texts are written largely focused on symbols and abstract

Glossary

concepts expressed less in words than in formulas, proofs, and exercises. For those reasons, reading math texts requires some different strategies:

- Start by looking not at the text but at your course syllabus and notes to figure out what you should be learning from it. Then skim the chapter to get an overview of the content.
- Take notes as you read, putting definitions, explanations, and theorems into your own words.
- Spend the bulk of your time on the examples, working through them and trying to put their main ideas into your own words. Work each one out on your own without looking at the solution.
- Work through the end-of-chapter problems to test your understanding. But do so methodically: Read the entire problem. Draw a picture or diagram to help visualize the problem. Read it again, identifying the most important information; be sure you understand what the problem is asking for. Then decide on a method for solving it, and come up with an answer. If you get stuck, think about how you'd deal with this information if it weren't a math problem. In that case, how would you go about solving it? Finally, reread the problem, and ask yourself if you've answered the question that was asked.
- Plan to move slowly through the text; this kind of reading takes time and patience!
- When you don't understand something and can't figure it out, ask your instructor or visit your school's math help center. Often, a conversation with someone who understands what you're struggling with is the most effective—and efficient—way to learn it.

A Note on Career-Focused Fields

In general, the advice here for reading texts in general-education courses holds for reading in every major, including career-oriented disciplines, such as business administration, nursing, teaching, and education. At the same time, it's worth paying attention to the ways of thinking and the priorities of every field as you read in them. Here are a few examples:

Both business administration and education focus on processes. In business, much reading discusses how businesspeople do things, manage workers, set up systems, follow best accounting practices, and the like; in education, your reading will likely focus on how to write lesson plans, how to present information appropriately, and so on. Drawing flowcharts and diagrams of processes can help you understand the steps involved and help you remember them.

Engineers solve problems. So when reading engineering texts, look for relationships among concepts and ideas, and think about ways those concepts can be used to solve complex problems. Pay close attention to charts, graphs, diagrams, and visuals, as they often pack considerable information into a single image. When reading a graph, for example, consider not only the data as presented but also relationships in the data, and look for inferences and predictions you can make from the data presented.

Engineering and nursing texts contain a lot of information, much of which you won't need right away, so don't try to master every fact or procedure. Instead, read the chapter introductions, summaries, and questions, and skim, looking for the answers to the questions. You might also review a study guide for the NCLEX nursing licensing exam or the NCEES PE exam in engineering and focus your reading on the subject areas the exam focuses on. In general, work to understand the concepts you need rather than trying to memorize an avalanche of information; look for patterns in the information and how concepts are interrelated.

26 Writing in Academic Fields of Study

In a *literature* course, you're asked to write an analysis of a short story. In a *biology* course, you must complete several lab reports. In a *management* course, you may create a detailed business plan. In fact, just about every course you take in college will require writing, and to write successfully, you'll need to understand the rhetorical situation of your writing in the course—and in the larger field of study. That understanding will come in time, especially as you begin writing in your major. For now, this chapter offers help in determining the general expectations of writing done in various academic fields of study.

Considering the Rhetorical Situation

To write in academic fields, you need to use the same processes and strategies you're asked to use in your writing classes, including analyzing the RHETORICAL SITUATION in which you're writing. These questions can help:

71

PURPOSE

73–74

Why do people in this discipline write? To share scholarship and research findings? persuade? teach or provide guidance? show learning or mastery? track progress? propose solutions or plans of action? explore ideas or the self? earn grants or other rewards? something else?

AUDIENCE

75–78

To whom do people in this discipline write? To colleagues and other scholars? students? managers? employees? customers? clients? granting agencies? the public? others? What do they already know about the discipline and the topic? What specialized terms or concepts do they understand, and which ones need to be defined or explained? How much evidence or support is required, and what kinds (empirical data, research findings, logical analysis, personal testimony, something else) will they accept?

79–84 **GENRE** What genres—reports, analyses, arguments, instructions, case studies, résumés, to name only a few—are typically used in this discipline? Are they organized in a certain way, and do they contain specific kinds of information? How much flexibility or room for innovation and creativity is allowed? What counts as evidence or support for assertions, and how is it cited (in citations in the text, in footnotes, in a works-cited page, informally in the text, or in some other way)?

85–87 **STANCE** What attitude is considered appropriate in this discipline? Objective? Unemotional? Critical? Passionate? Should you write as a conscientious student, showing what you can do? an instructor of others? an advocate for a position? someone exploring an idea? something else? Does the discipline require a certain tone? formal or informal language? Can you include your personal perspective and write using "I"? Should you write only in the third person and use passive voice?

88–90 **MEDIA/DESIGN** What media are typically used in this discipline? Print? Spoken? Electronic? A combination? Are certain design elements expected? to be avoided? Are visuals commonly used? What kinds—charts, graphs, photos, drawings, video or audio clips, or something else? In which genres? How much design freedom do you have?

Writing in Academic Fields of Study

Generalizing about the requirements of writing in academic disciplines is tricky; what constitutes a discipline is sometimes unclear, and universities group academic fields together in various ways. For example, in some universities psychology is considered a science, while in others it's a social science. Economics is sometimes part of a college of business administration, sometimes in a college of arts and sciences. In addition, the writing required in, say, history differs from that required in English literature, though both are considered parts of the humanities.

Furthermore, certain genres of writing, like *case studies* and *research reports*, can share the same name but have very different organizational structures and content, depending on the discipline in which they're used. For example, research reports in psychology and the natural sciences include a review of relevant scholarly literature in the introduction; in reports in sociology and other social sciences, the literature review is a separate section. A case study in business identifies a problem or issue in an organization; provides background information; includes a section, "Alternatives," that discusses possible solutions to the problem and why they were rejected; outlines and argues for a proposed solution; and proposes specific strategies for achieving the proposed solution. A case study in nursing, on the other hand, includes three sections: patient status, which gives an overview of the patient's condition and treatment; the nurse's assessment of the patient's symptoms and their possible causes; and a plan for helping the patient improve. The guide below offers general advice on how to write in broad academic disciplines, but as the differences between two disciplines' expectations for case studies show, it's always wise to ask all your professors for guidance on writing for their particular fields.

Writing in the Arts and Humanities

The arts and humanities focus on human culture and the expressions of the human mind, and the purpose of writing in these fields is to explore and analyze aspects of the human experience across time and sometimes to create original works of literature, music, and art. The methods used in these disciplines include careful reading, critical analysis, historical research, interpretation, questioning, synthesis, and imitation. Courses in the arts and humanities typically include fine arts, architecture, music, dance, theater, film, photography, literature, history, classical and modern languages, linguistics, and philosophy.

Writing in the arts and humanities generally serves a broad audience that includes professors and scholars, other students, the general public, and oneself. Genres may include **ANNOTATED BIBLIOGRAPHIES**, **ANALYSES**, **ARGUMENTS**, essays, **EVALUATIONS**, **JOURNALS**, **PERSONAL NARRATIVES**, **REPORTS**, **PRESENTATIONS**, **PROPOSALS**, **REFLECTIONS**, and **LITERATURE REVIEWS**, as well as fiction and poetry. Support is often based on textual and observational evidence and personal insight, though in some fields empirical evidence and data are also valued. Writers in the arts and humanities tend to use modifiers (such as "arguably" or "perhaps") to acknowledge that their insights and conclusions are interpretive, not definitive. Documentation is usually done in **MLA** or Chicago style. Elements of style favored in writing in the arts and humanities may include

197–206

114–45

170–96

210–19

337–38

234–45

146–69

659–69

257–69

383–92

206–9

MLA 542–94

the use of "I"; the active voice; an informal vocabulary, if appropriate; and vivid language.

A Sample of Writing in History:
A Researched Essay

Identifies a problem in current understanding of a historical event.

Offers a narrative of a past event.

Demonstrates familiarity with relevant sources.

Offers a strong thesis.

Clear, engaging writing style.

The Pueblo Revolt of 1680 was one of the most significant yet mis-represented events in the history of American Indians. After three generations of being oppressed by Spanish rule, the Pueblo Indians throughout the southwest region of North America banded together, organizing a widespread rebellion in the blistering summer heat of 1680 and successfully liberating themselves from their oppressors by springtime. When examining the causes of the revolt, the lack of authentic Pueblo voices within the written records challenges the valid-ity of the available sources and makes one wonder if we will ever know what went on through the eyes of the Pueblo. Although in the traditional narrative, the Spaniards are regarded as missionaries sent by God to "save" the "barbaric" Pueblos, the event, if seen from the Pueblo perspective, can be understood as a violent retaliation by the Pueblo against the Spanish oppression. The Pueblo uprisings, from burning down churches to the violent deaths of Catholic friars, reveal spiritual abuse as the major cause of the revolt. Moreover, without texts writ-ten by the Pueblo, their architecture and spatial organization provide valuable insight into the causes of the revolt era and help to overcome the veneer of Spanish colonialism.

Adapted from "Letting the Unspoken Speak: A Reexamination of the Pueblo Revolt of 1680," by E. McHugh, which appeared in the Armstrong Undergraduate Journal of History.

Typical organization of arts and humanities essays.   Typical essays in the arts and humanities include these elements:

Introduction containing an argumentative thesis that is appropriately qualified or limited → An argument with support: reasons, evidence, examples, comparisons, and sometimes counterarguments → Conclusion that restates or refines thesis and raises questions and implications → List of works cited, usually in MLA or Chicago format

Writing in Science and Mathematics

The sciences include biology, chemistry, geology, earth sciences, and physics. Mathematics may include statistics and logic as well. All these fields aim to increase our knowledge of the physical and natural world and its phenomena through observation, experiment, logic, and computation.

Scientists and mathematicians typically write **ABSTRACTS**, **LITERATURE REVIEWS**, **REPORTS**, **ARGUMENTS**, poster **PRESENTATIONS**, **PROPOSALS**, and **LAB REPORTS** for audiences that may include other researchers, granting agencies, teachers, students, and the general public. Support in the sciences most often consists of repeatable empirical evidence; in mathematics, careful reasoning and the posing and solving of problems; in both, careful attention to the work of previous researchers. The writing in these fields focuses on the subject of the study, not the researcher, so most often the passive voice is used. Source material is paraphrased and summarized and cited in CSE or **APA** style.

Glossary
▲ 206–9
146–69
170–96
● 659–69
▲ 257–69
◆ 317-18

● APA 595–633

A Sample of Scientific Writing:
A Scientific Proposal in Biology

Planarians, flatworms widely known for their incredible regenerative capabilities, are able to restore an entire organism from even a small fragment of tissue. This ability to regenerate is attributed solely to neoblasts, pluripotent adult stem cells located throughout the parenchyma of the animal (Newmark & Sanchez Alvarado, 2002). Neoblasts are stimulated to migrate and proliferate in times of injury (Guedelhoefer & Sanchez Alvarado, 2012). Lethally irradiated planarians (devoid of stem cells and therefore unable to regenerate) can restore regenerative capability through transplantation of a single neoblast from a healthy planarian (Wagner et al., 2011). Many studies have concluded that the population of neoblasts is not homogenous (Scimone et al., 2014), and there are different responses to different injury types. Wenemoser and Reddien (2012) observed a body-wide increase in mitotic activity, such as cell division and migration, with any injury.

Careful reference to previous sentence.

Passive voice, third person.

Specialized disciplinary vocabulary.

Sources paraphrased and summarized.

Adapted from "Identifying Genes Involved in Suppression of Tumor Formation in the Planarian Schmidetea mediterranea," by E. Dorsten, which appeared in the student journal Best Integrated Writing.

Typical organization of research reports in the sciences. Typical reports in the sciences include elements that follow the IMRaD structure: Introduction, Methods, Results, and Discussion. They also include an abstract and a list of references.

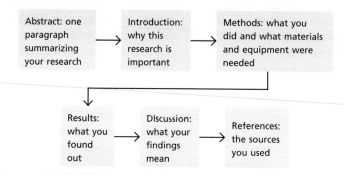

Abstract: one paragraph summarizing your research → Introduction: why this research is important → Methods: what you did and what materials and equipment were needed

Results: what you found out → Discussion: what your findings mean → References: the sources you used

Writing in the Social Sciences

Anthropology, archaeology, criminal justice, cultural studies, gender studies, geography, psychology, political science, and sociology are considered social sciences because they all explore human behavior and society using observation, experimentation, questionnaires, and interviews.

Social scientists typically write for fellow scholars, teachers, students, and the general public. They may write in several genres: **ABSTRACTS**, **ANNOTATED BIBLIOGRAPHIES**, **ANALYSES**, **ARGUMENTS**, case studies, ethnographies, **LITERATURE OR RESEARCH REVIEWS**, **REPORTS**, **SUMMARIES**, and **PRESENTATIONS**. Claims are typically supported by empirical evidence, fieldwork done in natural settings, observation, and interviews. Writers in these fields strive for an objective tone, often using the passive voice. Sources may be cited in **APA** or Chicago style.

A Sample of Writing in the Social Sciences: A Research Report

Traditional economic theory states that a minimum wage above the marginal product of labor will lead to increased unemployment. . . . This paper aims to look at a different but related question, namely, whether or not a minimum wage makes a population happier. Since

Objective tone.

people would arguably be happier if they could make enough money to cover their costs of living and less happy if the unemployment rate rose, the answer to such a question could help determine which effect ○·············· *Research question.* is the dominant force and if an overall increase in the minimum wage is a good policy for society. Although scant research has been done ○·············· *Specialized language.* on a minimum wage's effect on happiness, one could assume that research done on the size of the positive and negative effects of minimum wages could indicate whether or not it would leave a population happier. Therefore, I begin by reviewing relevant economic theory and ○·············· *Literature review.* research on the effects of a minimum wage increase to provide background information and describe what related questions have been approached and answered. I then describe the data and method used ○·············· *Empirical method.* to answer this question, followed by the interpretation of such results *Analysis and* as well as the implications. ○·············· *evaluation of results.*

Adapted from *"The Effect of Minimum Wages on Happiness,"* by J. Nizamoff, which appeared in the student journal Beyond Politics.

Typical organization of a research report in the social sciences. Typical research reports in social science courses might include the following elements, though the order and names of the elements may differ from discipline to discipline. For example, in psychology, the literature review is part of the introduction, not a separate section as shown here.

Writing in Business

The focus of the academic discipline of business is business-management principles and their application, and the purpose of writing in business is often to motivate readers to make a decision and then act on it. The primary methods used include problem solving, planning, and experiential learning, or learning by doing. Courses typically taught include finance, economics, human resources, marketing, operations management, and accounting.

The audiences for writing in business usually include colleagues, employees in other departments, supervisors, managers, clients, customers, and other stakeholders—often several at the same time as a text moves through an organization. Genres may include memos, emails, letters, case studies, executive summaries, **RÉSUMÉS**, business plans, **REPORTS**, and **ANALYSES**. Support usually takes the form of facts and figures, examples, narratives, and expert testimony, and documentation is usually done in **APA** or Chicago style. Elements of style favored in business writing include these features: the main point is presented early; the language is simple, direct, and positive; and the active voice is used in most cases.

A Sample of Writing in Business: A Business Plan Executive Summary

Financial Projections

Precise numbers, confidently stated.

Based on the size of our market and our defined market area, our sales projections for the first year are $340,000. We project a growth rate of 10% per year for the first three years.

Clear, direct writing, free of jargon and hedging.

The salary for each of the co-owners will be $40,000. On start up we will have six trained staff to provide pet services and expect to hire four more this year once financing is secured. To begin with, co-owner Pat Simpson will be scheduling appointments and coordinating services, but we plan to hire a full-time receptionist this year as well.

Positive tone.

Already we have service commitments from over 40 clients and plan to aggressively build our client base through newspaper, website, social media, and direct mail advertising. The loving on-site professional care that Pet Grandma Inc. will provide is sure to appeal to cat and dog owners throughout the West Vancouver area.

Adapted from "Business Plan Executive Summary Sample," by S. Ward, which appeared on the personal finance website The Balance.

Typical organization of business plans. A common assignment in business courses is a business plan. Business plans typically include these sections:

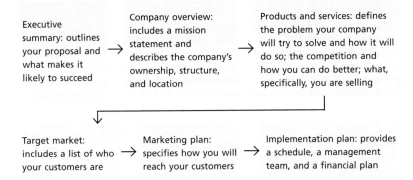

Executive summary: outlines your proposal and what makes it likely to succeed → Company overview: includes a mission statement and describes the company's ownership, structure, and location → Products and services: defines the problem your company will try to solve and how it will do so; the competition and how you can do better; what, specifically, you are selling

Target market: includes a list of who your customers are → Marketing plan: specifies how you will reach your customers → Implementation plan: provides a schedule, a management team, and a financial plan

Writing in Education

The focus of study in education is how people learn and how to teach effectively. Its primary methods include observation, problem solving, and practice teaching. Courses typically center on teaching methods, the philosophy of education, educational measurement and assessment, educational psychology, and instructional technology, among others.

Educators typically write for audiences that include their students, parents, other teachers, administrators, and the public. Genres may include lesson plans, **SUMMARIES**, **REPORTS**, **ANNOTATED BIBLIOGRAPHIES**, **PORTFOLIOS**, and **REFLECTIONS**. Support for claims may include facts, statistics, test scores, personal narratives, observations, and case studies. Sources are documented in **APA** style. Clarity and correctness are important in writing in education; "I" may be used in reflective writing and informal communication, while in formal writing the third person is preferred.

29–40
146–69
197–206
377–82
383–93
APA 595–633

A Sample of Writing in Education: A Teaching Philosophy Statement

My Image of the Child:

I believe that the student should be at the center of the instructional process. I have an image of children as strong and capable beings. The

Sections labeled with headings.

Argument is constructed to show teaching priorities.

classroom is a place where the teacher serves as a facilitator and guide as the students construct their own understanding of the world around them. Although it is the teacher's role to plan lessons and evaluate students' progress, it is of the utmost importance to always take the children and their own unique needs into consideration. For my second field experience, I was placed at Margaret Manson Elementary. Their school motto is that "the children come first." When children are the priority in teaching, an amazing amount of learning can take place. I believe in creating opportunities for students to develop to their fullest potential while developing and expanding their horizons and world-views. In order to accomplish this, there must be a welcoming, positive environment that is open and honest. When students feel comfortable at school they will surely be more engaged and responsive to class activities. I also consider it essential to be passionate and enthusiastic about learning so that the students can have a most relevant and meaningful experience.

As a reflective piece, "I" is appropriate.

Discusses both teaching and personal qualities.

Writing carefully crafted and proof-read.

Adapted from "Statement of Teaching Philosophy," by K. Tams, which was part of Kelly Tams's Teaching Portfolio at McGill University.

Typical organization of lesson plans in education. Frequent assignments in education courses are lesson plans, which typically include these elements:

Learning objectives: what you want students to learn and how the lesson connects to course goals → Introduction for students: how you will introduce the lesson to your students → Sequence of activities: what you want students to do, in what order, and how you will move them from one activity to the next → Conclusion: how you will wrap up the lesson → Assessment plan: how you will assess both students' work and the success of the lesson

Writing in Engineering and Technology

In the fields of engineering and technology, the focus is how to create and maintain useful structures, systems, processes, and machines. Engineers and technicians define problems as well as solve them, weigh various alternatives, and test possible solutions before presenting them to clients. This is a broad set of disciplines that may include civil, computer, electrical, mechanical, and structural engineering; computer science; and various technology specialties, such as HVAC and automotive technology.

Engineers and technicians typically write for their peers and team members, their clients, and the public. Writing tasks may include **ABSTRACTS**, **EVALUATIONS**, instructions, **LITERATURE REVIEWS**, memos, **PROPOSALS**, **REPORTS**, and **SUMMARIES**. Support usually includes data, examples, mathematical and logical reasoning, and experimental results, and sources are usually cited in **APA** format. Engineers and technicians value writing that includes logical ordering of ideas and precise language. Tables, charts, figures, illustrations, and headings and subheadings within the writing—all ways of quickly and efficiently conveying information—are also valued.

A Sample of Writing in Engineering: A Research Report

2. MATERIALS AND METHODS •··· *Headings used.*

To begin testing, an ATV test bed was designed (see Figure 1). To secure •······· *Charts, graphs, and photos included.*
the machine, a loose rope was attached to the front of the machine and
then to the testing platform. An additional rope was then attached at •······· *Precise description of procedure.*
a 90° angle to the front of the machine to act as the lifting force. The
test bed platform could be raised to a maximum of 60°, which simulated
hills or steep terrain. Each test was started at 0° and then increased by
increments of 10 (angles were determined by a digital level attached to
platform). Once the machine was at the appropriate angle, a lift force •······· *Technical language used for precision.*
was applied to observe turnover weight. Once the machine's tires lifted
off of the platform, the scale was read to determine the amount of
weight. Each machine was tested from front to rear and side to side.

Adapted from "Analysis of All Terrain Vehicle Crash Mechanisms," by S. Tanner, M. Aitken, and J. N. Warnock, which appeared in the Journal of Undergraduate Research in Bioengineering.

Typical organization of lab reports in engineering. Lab reports, a typical assignment in engineering classes, usually include the IMRaD elements, along with an abstract and a list of references. This format may vary depending on the engineering field and the requirements of the experiment or task.

| Introduction: why this research is important | → | Methods: what you did and what equipment was needed | → | Results of the experiment or task: what you found | → | Discussion of those results: what they mean | → | References: the sources you used |

Writing in Health Sciences and Nursing

Health sciences and nursing is a broad set of fields that may include nursing, anatomy, physiology, nutrition, and pharmacology as well as athletic training, exercise science, physical or occupational therapy, and speech pathology. Consequently, the methods used are also broad and varied, and they may include study of theories and techniques, observation, role-playing, and experiential learning.

Writing in these fields may include **ABSTRACTS**, **ANNOTATED BIBLIOGRA-PHIES**, **ARGUMENTS**, case studies, instructions, **PERSONAL NARRATIVES**, **REPORTS**, **REFLECTIONS**, **LITERATURE OR RESEARCH REVIEWS**, **SUMMARIES**, and charts **DESCRIBING** patients' conditions and care. The audiences for this writing may include other patient care providers, clinic and hospital administrators and staff, insurance companies, and patients or clients. Support for assertions typically includes scholarly research, observation, and description, and high value is placed on accurate information and detail. Other aspects of this writing include a preference for writing in the third person, paraphrased source information, and the use of headings and subheadings. Sources are usually cited in **APA** format.

A Sample of Writing in Nursing: A Case Study

Careful description of patient's condition.

Detailed observation using precise terms.

Ms. D is a morbidly obese 67 year old female, 240 lbs, 5'2" with type II diabetes mellitus. She was transferred from a nursing home to the hospital for pneumonia, but also suffers from congestive heart disease, sleep apnea, psoriasis, and osteoarthritis. She has a weak but productive cough with tonsil suction, and she was on breathing treatments

Patient status.

with albuterol. Her skin is very dry and thin with several lesions and yeast infections, and the deep folds of her lower abdomen bled during the bed bath. She did not want to wear her breathing mask at night and refused to get out of bed. She cried when encouraged to use the bathroom or to move her legs. She expressed great fear of returning to the nursing home.

Behavior as well as medical conditions taken into account.

   From the outset, we realized that Ms. D needed care beyond physical therapy and treatment for pneumonia; we realized that her obesity and refusal to participate in her health care expressed important patterns of her life. Morbid obesity does not happen overnight; it is a progressive pattern associated with activity levels, diet, and self-care practices, as well as other possible physiological and psychosocial dimensions. Johnson's (1980) Behavioral System Model, which outlines seven behavioral subsystems, was helpful in providing a perspective of the complexity of Ms. D's health needs. We also assessed that Ms. D lacked confidence in taking care of herself (reflecting the *achievement subsystem*) and lacked a sense of family support from her two sons (*affiliative subsystem*). Her fear of returning to the nursing home coupled with her need for ongoing care challenged her sense of interdependency as addressed in Johnson's *dependency subsystem*.

Patient assessment.

Use of paraphrased scholarly source to aid assessment.

Adapted from "Esthetic Knowing with a Hospitalized Morbidly Obese Patient," by R. Brinkley, K. Ricker, and K. Tuomey, which appeared in the Journal of Undergraduate Nursing Scholarship.

Typical organization of case studies in health sciences and nursing.   Case studies, typical assignments in these fields, usually include the following elements:

Patient status: symptoms, lab findings, history, doctor's orders, how much help the patient needs $\rightarrow$ Assessment: why the patient is being cared for; origins of current situation; when symptoms started, how the patient has been treated, the expected outcome $\rightarrow$ Care plan: what has been done, how current care is working, how care might be improved

Part 5
Processes

To create anything, we generally break the work down into a series of steps. We follow a recipe (or the directions on a box) to bake a cake; we break a song down into different parts and the music into various chords to arrange a piece of music. So it is when we write. We rely on various processes to get from a blank screen or page to a finished product. The chapters that follow offer advice on some of these processes—including **WRITING AS INQUIRY**, **GENERATING IDEAS**, **DRAFTING**, **GETTING RESPONSE**, **EDITING**, **COMPILING A PORTFOLIO**, and more.

Processes

✷ academic literacies   ⬢ fields   ◆ strategies   ⬤ media / design
◼ rhetorical situations   ⁞ processes   ⬤ research   ★ handbook
▲ genres

27 Processes of Writing

Many people think that good writers can just sit down in front of a screen or piece of paper and create a finished piece of writing. After all, in the movies, newspaper reporters pound out stories that then appear on the front page; novelists crank out hundreds of pages without breaking a sweat. That kind of talent for getting it right the first time happens on occasion, or for formulaic writing like business memos. Most of the time, though, we write the way we learn to draw, play piano, drive a car, or bake a cake: by working, practicing, making mistakes, and changing what we do as a result. In a way, because we usually need to generate ideas, draft, revise, and edit what we write, we learn to write every time we write.

You may have learned in school about a writing process that looks something like this: prewrite, outline, draft, revise, edit—five steps, to be done in order. That's the way the chapters in this book look, too; but that ordering is somewhat misleading. Sometimes we have to do considerable research before we can begin to figure out what we need to say. Sometimes we have to revise several times, getting responses from others between drafts. Sometimes we reach a certain point in our writing and realize that we need to stop, abandon the work in progress, and start over. And sometimes we can knock out a draft quickly, revising and editing as we go.

In other words, the processes writers use can vary from text to text, genre to genre, task to task. What is easy to describe as a set of lockstep activities:

research $\longrightarrow$ generate ideas $\longrightarrow$ write a draft $\longrightarrow$ get response $\longrightarrow$ revise $\longrightarrow$ edit

often looks more like this:

And it will differ from text to text, assignment to assignment. As writer and writing teacher Donald M. Murray once wrote, "Any process is legitimate if it produces an effective text."

Still, it's good to know the various processes you can use to create an effective text. The chapters that follow can help you understand writing as a way of learning; give you ways to generate ideas and text; offer advice on organizing, drafting, revising, and editing your writing; help you assess your own writing and get response from others; compile your writing into a portfolio; and reflect on your writing and learning.

28 Writing as Inquiry

Sometimes we write to say what we think. Other times, however, we write in order to figure out what we think. Much of the writing you do in college will be the latter. Even as you learn to write, you will be writing to learn. This chapter is about writing with a spirit of inquiry—approaching writing projects with curiosity, moving beyond the familiar, keeping your eyes open, tackling issues that don't have easy answers. It's about starting with questions and going from there—and taking risks. As Mark Twain once said, "Sail away from the safe harbor. . . . Explore. Dream. Discover." This chapter offers strategies for doing just that with your writing.

Starting with Questions

The most important thing is to start with questions—with what you *don't* know rather than with what you *do* know. Your goal is to learn about your subject and then to learn more. If you're writing about a topic you know well, you want to expand on what you already know. In academic writing, interesting topics arise from important questions, issues, and problems that are already being discussed. As a writer, you need to find out what's being said about your topic and then see your writing as a way of entering that larger conversation.

So start with questions, and don't expect to find easy answers. If there were easy answers, there would be no reason for discussion—or for you to write. For purposes of inquiry, the best questions can't be answered by looking in a reference book or searching online. Instead, they are ones that help you explore what you think—and why. As it happens, many of the strategies in this book can help you ask questions of this kind. Following are some questions to get you started.

How can it be DEFINED?   What is it, and what does it do? Look it up in a ◆ 429–38 dictionary; check *Wikipedia*. Remember, though, that these are only starting points. How *else* can it be defined? What more is there to know about it? If your topic is being debated, chances are that its very definition is subject to debate. If, for instance, you're writing about marriage, how you define marriage will affect how you approach the topic.

439–47 **How can it be DESCRIBED?**   What details should you include? From what vantage point should you describe your topic? If, for example, your topic is the physiological effects of running a marathon, what are those effects—on the lungs, heart muscles, nerves, brain, and so on? How will you describe the physical experience of running more than twenty-six miles from the runner's point of view?

452–56 **How can it be EXPLAINED?**   What does it do? How does it work? If you're investigating the use of performance-enhancing drugs by athletes, for example, what exactly are the effects of these drugs? What makes them dangerous—and are they always dangerous or only under certain conditions? Why are they illegal—and should they be illegal?

422–28 **What can it be COMPARED with?**   Again using performance-enhancing drugs by athletes as an example, how does taking such supplements compare with wearing high-tech footwear or uniforms? Does such a comparison make you see taking steroids or other performance-enhancing drugs in a new light?

395–38 **What may have CAUSED it? What might be its EFFECTS?**   Who or what does it affect? What causes cerebral palsy in children, for example? What are its symptoms? If children with cerebral palsy are not treated, what might be the consequences?

417–21 **How can it be CLASSIFIED?**   Is it a topic or issue that can be placed into categories of similar topics or issues? What categories can it be placed into? Are there legal and illegal performance-enhancing supplements (human growth hormone and steroids, for instance), and what's the difference? Are some safe and others less safe? Classifying your topic in this way can help you consider its complexities.

114–45 **How can it be ANALYZED?**   What parts can the topic be divided into? For example, if you're exploring the health effects of cell phone use, you might ask these questions: What evidence, if any, suggests that cell phone radiation causes cancer? Are any cancers associated with cell phone use? What do medical experts and phone manufacturers say? How can cell phone users reduce their risk, if there is any?

How can it be interpreted? What does it really mean? How do you interpret it, and how does your interpretation differ from those of other writers? What evidence supports your interpretation, and what argues against it? Imagine you're exploring the topic of sports injuries among young women. Do these injuries reflect a larger cultural preoccupation with competition? anatomical differences between male and female bodies? something else?

What expectations does it raise? What will happen next? What makes you think so? If this happens, how will it affect those involved? For instance, will the governing bodies of professional sports require more testing of athletes' blood, urine, and hair than they do now? Will such tests be unfair to athletes taking drugs for legitimate medical needs?

What are the different POSITIONS on it? What controversies or disagreements exist, and what evidence is offered for the various positions? What else might be said? Are there any groups or individuals who seem especially authoritative? If so, you might want to explore what they have said.

170–96

What are your own feelings about it? What interests you about the topic? How much do you already know about it? For example, if you're an athlete, how do you feel about competing against others who may have taken performance-enhancing supplements? If a friend has problems with drugs, do those problems affect your thinking about drugs in sports? How do you react to what others say about the topic? What else do you want to find out?

Are there other ways to think about it? Is what seems true in this case also true in others? How can you apply this subject in another situation? Will what works in another situation also work here? What do you have to do to adapt it? Imagine you're writing about traffic fatalities. If replacing stop signs with roundabouts or traffic circles reduced traffic fatalities in England, could doing so also reduce accidents in the United States?

You can also start with the journalist's **QUESTIONS**: *Who? What? When? Where? Why? How?* Asking questions from these various perspectives can help you deepen your understanding of your topic by leading you to see it from many angles.

332–33

Keeping a Journal

337–38

One way to get into the habit of using writing as a tool for inquiry is to keep a **JOURNAL**. You can use a journal to record your observations, reactions, whatever you wish. Some writers find journals especially useful places to articulate questions or speculations. You may be assigned by teachers to do certain work in a journal, but in general you can use a journal to write for yourself. Note your ideas, speculate, digress — go wherever your thoughts lead you.

Keeping a Blog

54–55

You may also wish to explore issues or other ideas online in the form of a **BLOG**. Most blogs have a comments section that allows others to read and respond to what you write, leading to potentially fruitful discussions. You can also include links to other websites, helping you connect various strands of thought and research. The blogs of others, along with online discussion forums and groups, may also be useful sources of opinion on your topic, but keep in mind that they probably aren't authoritative research sources. There are a number of search engines that can help you find blog posts related to specific topics, including blogsearchengine.org and *Blogarama*. You can create your own blog on sites such as *Blogger*, *Wix*, *Svbtle*, or *WordPress*.

29 Generating Ideas and Text

All good writing revolves around ideas. Whether you're writing a job-application letter, a sonnet, or an essay, you'll always spend time and effort generating ideas. Some writers can come up with a topic, put their thoughts in order, and flesh out their arguments in their heads; but most of us need to write out our ideas, play with them, tease them out, and examine them from some distance and from multiple perspectives. This chapter offers activities that can help you do just that. *Freewriting, looping, listing, clustering,* and *talking* can help you explore what you already know about a subject; *cubing, questioning,* and *using visuals* nudge you to consider a subject in new ways; and *outlining, letter writing, journal keeping,* and *discovery drafting* offer ways to generate a text.

Freewriting

An informal method of exploring a subject by writing about it, freewriting ("writing freely") can help you generate ideas and come up with materials for your draft. Here's how to do it:

1. Write as quickly as you can without stopping for 5 to 10 minutes (or until you fill a screen or page).

2. If you have a subject to explore, write it at the top and then start writing about it; but if you stray, don't worry—just keep writing. If you don't have a subject yet, just start writing and don't stop until the time is up. If you can't think of anything to say, write that ("I can't think of anything to say") again and again until you do—and you will!

3. Once the time is up, read over what you've written, and underline or highlight passages that interest you.

4. Write some more, starting with one of those underlined or highlighted passages as your new topic. Repeat the process until you've come up with a usable topic.

Looping

Looping is a more focused version of freewriting; it can help you explore what you already know about a subject. You stop, reflect on what you've written, and then write again, developing your understanding in the process. Looping is good for clarifying your knowledge and understanding of a subject and finding a focus. Here's what to do:

1. Write for 5 to 10 minutes on whatever you know about your subject. This is your first loop.

2. Read over what you wrote, and then write a single sentence summarizing the most important or interesting idea. You might try completing one of these sentences: "I guess what I was trying to say was . . ." or "What surprises me most in reading what I wrote is . . ." This will be the start of another loop.

3. Write again for 5 to 10 minutes, using your summary sentence as your beginning and your focus. Again, read what you've written, and then write a sentence capturing the most important idea—in a third loop.

Keep going until you have enough understanding of your topic to be able to decide on a tentative focus—something you can write about.

Listing

Some writers find it useful to keep lists of ideas that occur to them while they're thinking about a topic. Follow these steps:

1. Write a list of potential ideas about a topic. Don't try to limit your list—include anything that interests you.

2. Look for relationships among the items on your list: What patterns do you see? If other ideas occur to you, add them to the list.

3. Arrange the items in an order that makes sense for your purpose and can serve as the beginning of an outline for your writing.

Clustering or Mapping Ideas

Clustering (also called "idea mapping," "mind mapping," or "concept mapping") is a way of generating and connecting ideas visually. It's useful for seeing how various ideas relate to one another and for developing sub-topics. You can create a cluster with pencil and paper or use an online mapping tool like *Coggle*, *Bubbl.us*, or *MindMup*. Either way, the technique is simple:

1. Write your topic in the middle of a page or computer screen.

2. Write ideas relating to that topic around it, and connect them to the central idea with lines or shapes.

3. Write down examples, facts, or other details relating to each idea, and join them to connecting topics.

4. Keep going until you can't think of anything else relating to your topic.

You should end up with various ideas about your topic, and the clusters will enable you to see how they relate to one another. In the example cluster on the topic of "soft drinks" below, note how some ideas link not only to the main topic or related topics but also to other ideas.

Talking

Sometimes it's helpful to generate ideas by talking rather than writing. You might talk about your topic with a classmate, a teacher, a tutor, a friend—or even just talk out loud to yourself. If you do, be sure to take notes during or after talking, or use a voice-recording app to capture the conversation. You can also use free transcription apps, like *Otter* or *Rev*, to generate a print version of the conversation. Also, video conferencing apps like *Zoom*, *Microsoft Teams*, and *Google Meet* include transcription options. Another option, if permitted by your instructor, is to talk through your ideas with an **AI** tool like *ChatGPT*. Be sure to ask the AI tool to help you explore your own ideas—not to generate ideas for you.

61–69

Cubing

A cube has six sides. You can examine a topic as you might a cube, looking at it in these six ways:

439–46
- **DESCRIBE** it. What's its color? shape? age? size? What's it made of?

422–28
- **COMPARE** it to something else. What is it similar to or different from?

417–21
- Associate it with other things. What does it remind you of? What connections does it have to other things? How would you **CLASSIFY** it?

114–45
- **ANALYZE** it. How is it made? Where did it come from? Where is it going? How are its parts related?

- Apply it. What is it used for? What can be done with it?

170–96
- **ARGUE** for or against it. Choose a position relating to your subject, and defend it.

Questioning

It's always useful to ask questions. One way is to start with *What? Who? When? Where? How?* and *Why?* A particular method of exploring a topic is to ask questions as if the topic were a play. This method is especially useful for exploring literature, history, the arts, and the social sciences. Ask these questions:

- *What?* What happens? How is it similar to or different from other actions?

- *Who?* Who are the actors? Who are the participants, and who are the spectators? How do the actors affect the action, and how are they affected by it?

- *When?* When does the action take place? How often does it happen?

What happens before, after, or at the same time? Would it be different at another time? Does the time have historical significance?

- **Where?** What is the setting? What is the situation, and what makes it significant?

- **How?** How does the action occur? What are the steps in the process? What techniques are required? What equipment is needed?

- **Why?** Why did this happen? What are the actors' motives? What end does the action serve?

Using Visuals

Some writers use visuals—photographs, presentation slides, drawings—as tools for sparking or capturing ideas or for thinking about a topic in a new way. Here are some suggestions for doing so:

- Search for images related to your topic on a stock photo site like *Pixabay* or *Pexels*—or prompt an AI tool like *DALL-E* to create images for you. Then freewrite about the images you find. What do the images make you think of? Do they help you see your topic in a different light? Do they suggest details you hadn't considered?

    Here's an example of how a stock image helped one student generate ideas for a personal narrative about memories of her grandmother raising chickens and selling eggs.

 Freewrite: This picture is beautiful, the way the eggs are almost glowing in the basket. It makes me think of bounty—of having more than enough. Maybe that's part of the significance of my story? I didn't realize it when I was young, but Grandma sold the eggs to make her own money—to afford "extras" and to have some financial freedom apart from Grandpa. And then there was all the bounty she left us in stories and memories and recipes. Maybe I can play on this theme somehow in my writing?

- Make a *PowerPoint* or *Keynote* slide about your topic. Choose keywords for headings and subheadings, find images or icons for each, and experiment with different arrangements of the material. Doing so might help you make new connections or associations among your ideas.

- Do what filmmakers and animators do when developing a new project: create a storyboard—a scene-by-scene plan of what the final product might look like. You could draw scenes by hand (stick figures are fine!) or use stock or AI-generated images to represent each scene or section of your draft. Search for storyboard templates online to get started.

Below is an example storyboard for the student narrative mentioned earlier. Created with a template and stock images from the graphic design app *Canva*, the storyboard helped the student generate memories and details and then organize them before drafting.

Storyboard: "Egg Money" Narrative

SCENE #1
I feed the chickens while Grandma gathers the eggs, placing them gently in the pockets of her tattered apron.

SCENE #2
Grandma shows me how to separate an egg, whisking out the last drop of egg white with her finger. "No use wasting," she says. Later, after we make our egg deliveries, we'll come home to Grandma's angel food cake.

SCENE #3
Grandma and I place the eggs in cartons and wrap each in newspaper and twine.

SCENE #4
We load up the old wheelbarrow with egg cartons and set out to deliver our goods to Grandma's customers.

SCENE #5
After the egg deliveries, Grandma records every transaction in her cash ledger. I sit next to her, eating my angel food cake.

SCENE #6
Going through Grandma's attic as an adult, I find her recipe books, her county-fair ribbons, her cash ledgers documenting forty years' worth of chicken raising and egg selling.

Using Genre Features

Genres typically include particular kinds of information and organize it in particular ways. One way to generate ideas and text, then, is to identify the key features of the genre in which you're writing and use them to guide you as you write. Of course, you may alter the genre's features or combine two or more genres in order to achieve your purpose, but the overall shape and content of the genre can give you a way to develop and organize your ideas and research.

Outlining

You may create an *informal outline* by simply listing your ideas and numbering them in the order in which you want to write about them. You might prefer to make a *working outline*, to show the hierarchy of relationships among your ideas. While still informal, a working outline distinguishes your main ideas and your support, often through simple indentation:

Background and context
First main idea
    Supporting evidence or detail
    Supporting evidence or detail

Second main idea
    Supporting evidence or detail
    Supporting evidence or detail

A *formal outline* shows the hierarchy of your ideas through a system of indenting, numbering, and lettering. Remember that when you divide a point into more specific subpoints, you should have at least two of them—you can't divide something into only one part. Also, try to keep items at each level parallel in structure. Formal outlines work this way:

Thesis statement
Background and context
    I. First reason
        A. Supporting evidence
            1. Detail of evidence
            2. Detail of evidence
        B. Supporting evidence
    II. Another reason

MLA 584–94

Here is a formal outline of the first part of an **MLA** research report by Jackson Parell, "Free at Last, Free at Last: Civil War Memory and Civil Rights Rhetoric," that shows how he organized it:

I. Introduction: How 1960s civil rights leaders used Lincoln's rhetoric to advance racial equality

II. Many Americans did not see racial issues and slavery as causes of the Civil War
   A. Histories focused on the bravery and valor of the soldiers
   B. Slavery as the war's cause was downplayed or ignored
   C. Martin Luther King Jr. focused on the war's cause

III. King worked to persuade President Kennedy to outlaw segregation
   A. King drafted a second Emancipation Proclamation
   B. When that effort failed, King planned a March on Washington

Writing out a formal outline can be helpful when you're dealing with a complex subject; as you revise your drafts, though, be flexible and ready to change your outline as your understanding of your topic develops.

Another way to outline is to use an online organizing tool like *Trello*, *Jira*, or *Wrike*. These tools let you create a digital bulletin board to which you post "lists" and "cards." Below is an example *Trello* board that outlines Jackson Parell's research report. Each color-coded "card" represents a supporting detail for the main point listed at the top of a column of cards.

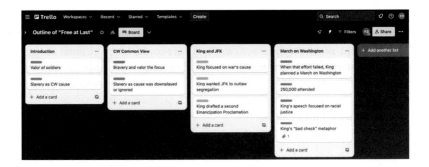

You can drag cards to different lists, depending on where the cards fit best. You can expand a card to jot down notes, save website links, and add attachments, as in the following example, which includes notes and links to the source of King's speech.

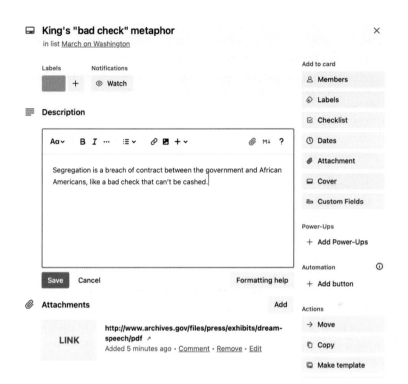

Letter Writing

Sometimes the prospect of writing a report or an essay can be intimi-dating. You may find that simply explaining your topic to someone will help you get started. In that case, write a letter or an email or a text to someone you know—your best friend, a parent or grandparent, a sibling—in which you discuss your subject. Explain it in terms that your reader can understand. Use the unsent letter to rehearse your topic; make it a kind of rough draft that you can then revise and develop to suit your actual audience.

Keeping a Journal

Some writers find that writing in a journal helps them generate ideas. Making note of your ideas, thoughts, feelings, or the events of your day can provide a wealth of topics, and a journal can also be a good place to explore what you think and why you think as you do.

Journals are private—you are the only audience—so you can feel free to write whatever comes to mind. And you can do more than write. If you choose a paper journal, doodle or draw in it, and keep clippings or scraps of paper between the pages; if you keep your journal on a computer, copy and paste interesting images or text you find online. Whatever form your journal takes, feel free to play with its contents, and don't worry about errors or grammar. The goal is to generate ideas; let yourself wander without censoring yourself or fretting that your writing is incorrect or incomplete or incoherent. That's OK.

One measure of the success of journaling and other personal writing is length: journal entries, **FREEWRITING**, **LISTING**, **CUBING**, and other types of informal writing are like warm-up exercises to limber you up and get you thinking. If you don't give them enough time and space, they may not do what you want them to. Often, students' best insights appear at the end of their journal entries. Had they stopped before that point, they would never have had those good ideas.

After you've written several journal entries, one way to study the ideas in them is to highlight useful patterns in different colors. For example, journal entries usually include some questioning and speculating, as well as summarizing and paraphrasing. Try color-coding each of these, sentence by sentence, phrase by phrase: yellow for summaries or paraphrases, green for questions, blue for speculations. Do any colors dominate? If, for example, your entries are mostly yellow, you may be restating the course content or quoting from the textbook too much and perhaps need to ask more questions. If you're generating ideas for an essay, you might assign colors to ideas or themes to see which ones are the most promising.

Discovery Drafting

Some writers do best by jumping in and writing. Here are the steps to take if you're ready to write a preliminary **DRAFT**:

1. Write your draft quickly, in one sitting if possible.

329
330
332

358–60

2. Assume that you are writing to discover what you want to say and how you need to say it—and that you will make substantial revisions in a later part of the process.

3. Don't worry about grammatical or factual correctness—if you can't think of a word, leave a blank space to fill in later. If you're unsure of a date or spelling, put a question mark in parentheses as a reminder to check it later. Just write.

If you need more help

See each of the **GENRE** chapters for specific strategies for generating text in each genre.

▲ 91

30 Organizing Your Writing, Guiding Your Readers

Traffic lights, street signs, and lines on the road help drivers find their way. Readers need similar guidance —to know, for example, whether they're reading a report or an argument, evaluation, or proposal. They also need to know what to expect: What will the report be about? What perspective will it offer? What will this paragraph cover? What about the next one? How do the two paragraphs relate to each other—and to the rest of the essay?

When you write, then, you need to organize your ideas and provide cues to help your readers navigate your text and understand the points you're trying to make. This chapter offers advice on organizing your writing and guiding your readers through it by organizing the text and its paragraphs; creating strong thesis statements, clear topic sentences, and helpful beginnings and titles; ending appropriately; and tying ideas together with transitions. See also the **GENRE** chapters for advice on organizing texts in specific genres.

91 ▲

Outlining

335–37 ⸪

At some point as writers develop their ideas and collect their information, they often create an **OUTLINE** as a plan for drafting a text. You may create an *informal outline* by simply listing your ideas and numbering them in the order in which you want to write about them. You might prefer to make a *working outline* to show the hierarchy of relationships among your ideas. Or you might need to create a *formal outline*, which shows the hierarchy of your ideas through a system of indenting, numbering, and lettering. And you might use an online organizing tool. If your instructor allows, you might use an **AI** tool like *ChatGPT* to help you construct an outline based on notes and ideas you provide.

Access the ebook for a video on organizing and synthesizing ideas.

61–69 ✳

Beginning

Whenever we pick up something to read, we generally start by looking at the first few words or sentences to see if they grab our attention, and based on them, we decide whether to keep reading. Beginnings, then, are important—both for attracting readers and for giving them some information about what's to come. How you begin depends on your **RHETORICAL SITUATION**, especially your purpose and audience. Academic audiences generally expect a text's introduction to establish context, explaining how the text fits into some larger conversation, addresses certain questions, or explores an aspect of the subject. Most introductions also offer a brief description of the text's content, often in the form of a thesis statement. The following opening paragraph of a report on cyberloafing—that is, using an employer's internet access to do non-work-related tasks—does all of this:

■ 71

> Increased technological advances and widespread internet access have revolutionized the workplace. But all this innovation has come with at least one questionable stowaway: cyberloafing—the act of browsing the internet for personal use while at work. It's becoming essential for organizations to understand cyberloafing: what it is, which factors lead employees to do it, and how it affects productivity. At its worst, cyberloafing can jeopardize an organization's information security, so awareness about cyberloafing is essential to both employees and employers in order to prevent its most negative consequences.
>
> —Rocia Celeste Mejia Avila,
> "Cyberloafing: Distraction or Motivation?"

If you're writing for a nonacademic audience or genre—for a newspaper or a website, for example—your introduction may need to entice your readers to read on by connecting your text to their interests through shared experiences, anecdotes, or some other attention-getting device. Historian Heather Cox Richardson, writing an online newsletter about the Gettysburg Address, connects the date—the day her audience would read it—to Lincoln's address. She provides a historical context for the speech and then introduces her topic, the unexpected nature of Lincoln's words:

> Access the ebook for a video on introductions and conclusions.

> For three hot days, from July 1 to July 3, 1863, more than 150,000 soldiers from the armies of the United States of America and the Confederate States of America slashed at each other in the hills and through the fields around Gettysburg, Pennsylvania.
>   When the battered armies limped out of town after the brutal battle, they left scattered behind them more than seven thousand corpses in a town with fewer than 2,500 inhabitants. With the heat of a summer sun beating down, the townspeople had to get the dead soldiers into

the ground as quickly as they possibly could, marking the hasty graves with nothing more than pencil on wooden boards.

A local lawyer, David Wills, who had huddled in his cellar with his family and their neighbors during the battle, called for the creation of a national cemetery in the town, where the bodies of the United States soldiers who had died in the battle could be interred with dignity. Officials agreed, and Wills and an organizing committee planned an elaborate dedication ceremony to be held a few weeks after workers began moving remains into the new national cemetery.

They invited state governors, members of Congress, and cabinet members to attend. To deliver the keynote address, they asked prominent orator Edward Everett, who wanted to do such extensive research into the battle that they had to move the ceremony to November 19, a later date than they had first contemplated.

And, almost as an afterthought, they asked President Lincoln to make a few appropriate remarks. While they probably thought he would not attend, or that if he came he would simply mouth a few platitudes and sit down, President Lincoln had something different in mind.

—Heather Cox Richardson,
"Letters from an American,"

Thesis Statements

A thesis identifies the topic of a text along with the claim being made about it. A strong thesis helps readers understand an essay. Working to create a sharp thesis can help you focus both your thinking and your writing. Here are four steps for moving from a topic to a thesis statement:

1. **State your topic as a question.**   You may have an idea for a topic, such as "gasoline prices," "analysis of 'real women' ad campaigns," or "famine." Those may be good topics, but they're not thesis statements, primarily because none of them actually makes a statement. One way to begin moving from topic to thesis statement is to turn your topic into a question:

   What causes fluctuations in gasoline prices?

   Are ads picturing "real women" who aren't models effective?

   What can be done to prevent famine in Burkina Faso?

2. **Then turn your question into a position.**   A thesis statement is an assertion—it takes a stand or makes a claim. Whether you're writing

Access the ebook for a video on thesis statements across genres.

a report or an argument, you are saying, "This is the way I see . . ." or "My research shows . . ." or "This is what I believe about . . ." Your thesis statement announces your position on the question you're raising about the topic, so a relatively easy way of establishing a thesis is to answer your own question:

Gasoline prices fluctuate for several reasons.

Ads picturing "real women" instead of models are effective because most women can easily identify with them.

The threat of famine in Burkina Faso could be avoided if certain measures are taken.

3. **Narrow your thesis.** A honed thesis is specific, guiding you as you write and showing readers exactly what your essay will cover. The preceding thesis statements need to be qualified and focused—they should be made more specific. For example:

Gasoline prices fluctuate because of production procedures, consumer demand, international politics, and oil companies' policies.

Dove's "Campaign for Self-Esteem" works because consumers can identify with the women's bodies and admire their confidence in displaying them.

The current threat of famine in Burkina Faso could be avoided if the government and humanitarian organizations increase the availability of water, provide shipments of food, and supply medical and nutrition assistance.

A good way to narrow a thesis is to ask **QUESTIONS** about it: *Why* do gasoline prices fluctuate? *How* could the Burkina Faso famine have been avoided? The answers will help you craft a narrow, focused thesis.

332–33

4. **Qualify your thesis.** Sometimes you want to make a strong argument and state your thesis bluntly. Often, however, you need to acknowledge that your assertions may be challenged or may not be unconditionally true. In those cases, consider limiting the scope of your thesis by adding to it such terms as "may," "probably," "apparently," "very likely," "sometimes," and "often."

Gasoline prices *very likely* fluctuate because of production procedures, consumer demand, international politics, and oil companies' policies.

Dove's ad campaign featuring "real women" *may* work because consumers can identify with the women's bodies and admire their confidence in displaying them.

The current threat of famine in Burkina Faso could *probably* be avoided if the government and humanitarian organizations increase the availability of water, provide shipments of food, and supply medical and nutrition assistance.

Thesis statements are typically positioned at or near the end of a text's introduction, to let readers know at the outset what is being claimed and what the text will be aiming to prove. A thesis doesn't necessarily forecast your organization, which may be more complex than the thesis itself. For example, Notre Dame University student Sarah Dzubay's essay, "An Outbreak of the Irrational," contains this thesis statement:

> The movement to opt out of vaccinations is irrational and dangerous because individuals advocating for their right to exercise their personal freedom are looking in the wrong places for justification and ignoring the threat they present to society as a whole.

The essay that follows this thesis statement includes discussions of herd immunity; a socioeconomic profile of parents who choose not to have their children vaccinated; outlines of the rationales those parents use to justify their choice, which include fear of autism, fear of causing other health problems, and political and ethical values; and a conclusion that parents who refuse to have their children vaccinated are being unreasonable and selfish. The paper delivers what the thesis promises but includes important information not mentioned in the thesis itself.

More Ways of Beginning

Explain the larger context of your topic.   Most essays are part of an ongoing conversation, so you might begin by outlining the context of the subject to which your writing responds. An essay exploring the "emotional climate" of the United States after Barack Obama became president begins by describing the national moods during some of his predecessors' administrations:

> Every president plays a symbolic, almost mythological role that's hard to talk about, much less quantify — it's like trying to grab a ball of mercury. I'm not referring to using the bully pulpit to shape the national agenda but to the way that the president, as America's most inescapably

powerful figure, colors the emotional climate of the country. John Kennedy and Ronald Reagan did this affirmatively, expressing ideals that shaped the whole culture. Setting a buoyant tone, they didn't just change movies, music, and television; they changed attitudes. Other presidents did the same, only unpleasantly. Richard Nixon created a mood of angry paranoia, Jimmy Carter one of dreary defeatism, and George W. Bush, especially in that seemingly endless second term, managed to do both at once.

— John Powers, "Dreams from My President"

Forecast your organization. You might begin by briefly summarizing the way in which you will organize your text. The following example from a scholarly paper on the role of immigrants in the US labor market offers background on the subject and describes the points that the writer's analysis will discuss:

Debates about illegal immigration, border security, skill levels of workers, unemployment, job growth and competition, and entrepreneurship all rely, to some extent, on perceptions of immigrants' role in the U.S. labor market. These views are often shaped as much by politics and emotion as by facts.

To better frame these debates, this short analysis provides data on immigrants in the labor force at the current time of slowed immigration, high unemployment, and low job growth and highlights eight industries where immigrants are especially vital. How large a share of the labor force are they and how does that vary by particular industry? How do immigrants compare to native-born workers in their educational attainment and occupational profiles?

The answers matter because our economy is dependent on immigrant labor now and for the future. The U.S. population is aging rapidly as the baby boom cohort enters old age and retirement. As a result, the labor force will increasingly depend upon immigrants and their children to replace current workers and fill new jobs. This analysis puts a spotlight on immigrant workers to examine their basic trends in the labor force and how these workers fit into specific industries and occupations of interest.

— Audrey Singer,
"Immigrant Workers in the U.S. Labor Force"

Offer background information. If your readers may not know as much as you do about your topic, giving them information to help them understand your position can be important, as journalist David Guterson does in an essay on the Mall of America:

> Last April, on a visit to the new Mall of America near Minneapolis, I carried with me the public-relations press kit provided for the benefit of reporters. It included an assortment of "fun facts" about the mall: 140,000 hot dogs sold each week, 10,000 permanent jobs, 44 escalators and 17 elevators, 12,750 parking places, 13,300 short tons of steel, $1 million in cash disbursed weekly from 8 automatic-teller machines. Opened in the summer of 1992, the mall was built on the 78-acre site of the former Metropolitan Stadium, a five-minute drive from the Minneapolis–St. Paul International Airport. With 4.2 million square feet of floor space—including twenty-two times the retail footage of the average American shopping center—the Mall of America was "the largest fully enclosed combination retail and family entertainment-complex in the United States."
>
> —David Guterson,
> "Enclosed. Encyclopedic. Endured. One Week at the Mall of America"

Visuals can also help provide context. For example, Guterson's essay on the Mall of America might have included a photo like the one below to convey the size of the structure.

A roller coaster in the Mall of America.

Define key terms or concepts.   The success of an argument often hinges on how key terms are **DEFINED**. You may wish to provide definitions up front—as an advocacy website, *Health Care without Harm*, does in a report on the hazards of fragrances in health-care facilities:

♦ 429–38

> To many people, the word "fragrance" means something that smells nice, such as perfume. We don't often stop to think that scents are chemicals. Fragrance chemicals are organic compounds that volatilize, or vaporize into the air—that's why we can smell them. They are added to products to give them a scent or to mask the odor of other ingredients. The volatile organic chemicals (VOCs) emitted by fragrance products can contribute to poor indoor air quality (IAQ) and are associated with a variety of adverse health effects.
>
> —"Fragrances," *Health Care without Harm*

Connect your subject to your readers' interests or values.   You'll always want to establish **COMMON GROUND** with your readers, and sometimes you may wish to do so immediately, in your introduction, as in this example:

♦ 410–11

> We all want to feel safe. Most Americans lock their doors at night, lock their cars in parking lots, try to park near buildings or under lights, and wear seat belts. Many invest in expensive security systems, carry pepper spray or a stun gun, keep guns in their homes, or take self-defense classes. Obviously, safety and security are important issues in American life.
>
> —Andy McDonie, "Airport Security: What Price Safety?"

Access Chapter 15 in the ebook for a video on the importance of choosing a topic that matters.

Start with something that will provoke readers' interest.   Writer and columnist Anna Quindlen opens an essay on feminism with the following eye-opening assertion:

> Let's use the F word here. People say it's inappropriate, offensive, that it puts people off. But it seems to me it's the best way to begin, when it's simultaneously devalued and invaluable.
> Feminist. Feminist, feminist, feminist.
>
> —Anna Quindlen, "Still Needing the F Word"

Start with an anecdote.   Sometimes a brief **NARRATIVE** helps bring a topic to life for readers. See, for example, how an essay on student loans and their effects on individuals and society begins:

♦ 457–64

Rodney Spangler first enrolled at the University of North Texas in 2001. There, he pursued a degree in what the school now calls "integrative studies," focusing on history, philosophy, and criminal justice. Rodney also worked full time, and so attended UNT off and on until 2007. For every semester of classes, Spangler took out student loans. When he left—without a degree—he estimates that he had about $30,000 in outstanding student debt.

—Charles Fain Lehman,
"The Student Loan Trap: When Debt Delays Life"

Ask a question. Instead of opening with a thesis statement, you might open with a question about the topic your text will explore, as this study of the status of women in science does:

Are women's minds different from men's minds? In spite of the women's movement, the age-old debate centering around this question continues. We are surrounded by evidence of de facto differences between men's and women's intellects—in the problems that interest them, in the ways they try to solve those problems, and in the professions they choose. Even though it has become fashionable to view such differences as environmental in origin, the temptation to seek an explanation in terms of innate differences remains a powerful one.

—Evelyn Fox Keller, "Women in Science: A Social Analysis"

Jump right in. Occasionally you may wish to start as close to the key action as possible. See how one writer jumps right in when opening his profile of a blues concert:

Long Tongue, the Blues Merchant, strolls onstage. His guitar rides sidesaddle against his hip. The drummer slides onto the tripod seat behind the drums, adjusts the high-hat cymbal, and runs a quick, off-beat tattoo on the tom-tom, then relaxes. The bass player plugs into the amplifier, checks the settings on the control panel, and nods his okay. Three horn players stand off to one side, clustered, lurking like brilliant sorcerer-wizards waiting to do magic with their musical instruments.

—Jerome Washington, "The Blues Merchant"

Ending

Endings are important because they're the last words readers read. How you end a text will depend in part on your **RHETORICAL SITUATION**. You may end by wrapping up loose ends, or you may wish to give readers

71

something to think about. Some endings do both, as Nicholas Kristof's does in arguing that guns should be regulated in the same way cars are. In the first of two paragraphs, Kristof acknowledges that his proposals aren't a cure-all for gun violence but notes that thousands of lives would be saved. In the second, he sums up his entire argument:

> These steps won't eliminate gun deaths any more than seatbelts eliminate auto deaths. But if a combination of measures could reduce the toll by one-third, that would be 10,000 lives saved every year.
> A century ago, we reacted to deaths and injuries from unregulated vehicles by imposing sensible safety measures that have saved hundreds of thousands of lives a year. Why can't we ask politicians to be just as rational about guns?
>
> —Nicholas Kristof, "Our Blind Spot about Guns"

Kristof's final question provides readers with food for thought and challenges legislators either to come up with "sensible safety measures" or to provide reasons why they can't or won't.

Ways of Ending

Restate your main point. Sometimes you'll simply **SUMMARIZE** your central idea, as in this example from an essay arguing that people have no "inner" self and that they should be judged by their actions alone:

★ HB-43

> The inner man is a fantasy. If it helps you to identify with one, by all means, do so; preserve it, cherish it, embrace it, but do not present it to others for evaluation or consideration, for excuse or exculpation, or, for that matter, for punishment or disapproval.
> Like any fantasy, it serves your purposes alone. It has no standing in the real world which we share with each other. Those character traits, those attitudes, that behavior—that strange and alien stuff sticking out all over you—*that's the real you!*
>
> —Willard Gaylin, "What You See Is the Real You"

Discuss the implications of your argument. The following conclusion of an essay on the development of Post-it notes leads readers to consider how failure sometimes leads to innovation:

> Post-it notes provide but one example of a technological artifact that has evolved from a perceived failure of existing artifacts to function without frustrating. Again, it is not that form follows function but,

rather, that the form of one thing follows from the failure of another thing to function as we would like. Whether it be bookmarks that fail to stay in place or taped-on notes that fail to leave a once-nice surface clean and intact, their failure and perceived failure is what leads to the true evolution of artifacts. That the perception of failure may take centuries to develop, as in the case of loose bookmarks, does not reduce the importance of the principle in shaping our world.

—Henry Petroski, "Little Things Can Mean a Lot"

End with an anecdote. If you take this approach, you might finish a 457–64 ◆ NARRATIVE that was begun earlier in your text or add one that illustrates the point you're making. See how Sarah Vowell uses a story to end an essay on students' need to examine news reporting critically:

I looked at Joanne McGlynn's syllabus for her media studies course, the one she handed out at the beginning of the year, stating the goals of the class. By the end of the year, she hoped her students would be better able to challenge everything from novels to newscasts, that they would come to identify just who is telling a story and how that person's point of view affects the story being told. I'm going to go out on a limb here and say that this lesson has been learned. In fact, just recently, a student came up to McGlynn and told her something all teachers dream of hearing. The girl told the teacher that she was listening to the radio, singing along with her favorite song, and halfway through the sing-along she stopped and asked herself, "What am I singing? What do these words mean? What are they trying to tell me?" And then, this young citizen of the republic jokingly complained, "I can't even turn on the radio without thinking anymore."

—Sarah Vowell, "Democracy and Things Like That"

Refer to the beginning. One way to bring closure to a text is to bring up something discussed in the beginning; often the reference adds to or even changes the original meaning. For example, Amy Tan opens an essay on her Chinese mother's English by establishing herself as a writer and lover of language who uses many versions of English in her writing:

I am not a scholar of English or literature. I cannot give you much more than personal opinions on the English language and its variations in this country or others.

I am a writer. And by that definition, I am someone who has always loved language. I am fascinated by language in daily life. I spend a great deal of my time thinking about the power of language—the way it can evoke an emotion, a visual image, a complex idea, or a simple truth. Language is the tool of my trade. And I use them all—all the Englishes I grew up with.

At the end of her essay, Tan repeats this phrase, but now she describes language not in terms of its power to evoke emotions, images, and ideas but in its power to evoke "the essence" of her mother. When she began to write fiction, she says,

> [I] decided I should envision a reader for the stories I would write. And the reader I decided upon was my mother, because these were stories about mothers. So with this reader in mind—and in fact she did read my early drafts—I began to write stories using all the Englishes I grew up with: the English I spoke to my mother, which for lack of a better term might be described as "simple"; the English she used with me, which for lack of a better term might be described as "broken"; my translation of her Chinese, which could certainly be described as "watered down"; and what I imagined to be her translation of her Chinese if she could speak in perfect English, her internal language, and for that I sought to preserve the essence, but neither an English nor a Chinese structure. I wanted to capture what language ability tests can never reveal: her intent, her passion, her imagery, the rhythms of her speech and the nature of her thoughts.
>
> —Amy Tan, "Mother Tongue"

Note how Tan not only repeats "all the Englishes I grew up with" but also provides parallel lists of what those Englishes can do for her: "evoke an emotion, a visual image, a complex idea, or a simple truth" on the one hand, and on the other, capture her mother's "intent, her passion, her imagery, the rhythms of her speech and the nature of her thoughts."

Propose some action.   This strategy is used in the following conclusion of a report on the consequences of binge drinking among college students:

> The scope of the problem makes immediate results of any interventions highly unlikely. Colleges need to be committed to large-scale and long-term behavior-change strategies, including referral of alcohol abusers to appropriate treatment. Frequent binge drinkers on college campuses are similar to other alcohol abusers elsewhere in their tendency to deny that they have a problem. Indeed, their youth, the visibility of others who drink the same way, and the shelter of the college community may make them less likely to recognize the problem. In addition to addressing the health problems of alcohol abusers, a major effort should

address the large group of students who are not binge drinkers on campus who are adversely affected by the alcohol-related behavior of binge drinkers.

—Henry Wechsler et al.,
"Health and Behavioral Consequences of Binge Drinking in College: A National Survey of Students at 140 Campuses"

Paragraphs

Paragraphs are groups of sentences (and sometimes a single sentence) that relate to one main idea. Paragraphs in some of your textbooks may contain several hundred words, while paragraphs in news articles often contain just a single sentence or even, occasionally, a phrase. In English, we show paragraphs by indenting the first word; this is one way that the white space of a text conveys meaning. In fact, we sometimes use white space to create emphasis, especially with very brief paragraphs.

This one, for instance.

In academic writing, paragraphs usually contain a topic sentence that defines the main idea. Then the paragraph is developed by presenting examples or using defining, narrating, classifying, and other writing **STRATEGIES**. Following is advice on writing topic sentences and organizing paragraphs.

393 ◆

Topic Sentences

Just as a thesis statement announces the topic and position of an essay, a topic sentence states the subject and focus of a paragraph. Good paragraphs focus on a single point, which is summarized in a topic sentence. Usually, but not always, the topic sentence begins the paragraph:

> *Graduating from high school or college is an exciting, occasionally even traumatic event.* Your identity changes as you move from being a high school teenager to a university student or a worker; your connection to home loosens as you attend school elsewhere, move to a place of your own, or simply exercise your right to stay out later. You suddenly find yourself doing different things, thinking different thoughts, fretting about different matters. As recent high school graduate T. J. Devoe puts it, "I wasn't really scared, but having this vast range of opportunity

made me uneasy. I didn't know *what* was gonna happen." Jenny Petrow, in describing her first year out of college, observes, "It's a tough year. It was for all my friends."

—Sydney Lewis, *Help Wanted: Tales from the First Job Front*

Sometimes the topic sentence may come at the end of the paragraph or even at the end of the preceding paragraph, depending on the way the paragraphs relate to one another. At other times, a topic sentence will summarize or restate a point made in the previous paragraph, helping readers understand what they've just read as they move on to the next point. See how linguist Deborah Tannen does this in the first paragraphs of an article on differences in men's and women's conversational styles:

I was addressing a small gathering in a suburban Virginia living room—a women's group that had invited men to join them. Throughout the evening, one man had been particularly talkative, frequently offering ideas and anecdotes, while his wife sat silently beside him on the couch. Toward the end of the evening, I commented that women frequently complain that their husbands don't talk to them. This man quickly concurred. He gestured toward his wife and said, "She's the talker in our family." The room burst into laughter; the man looked puzzled and hurt. "It's true," he explained. "When I come home from work I have nothing to say. If she didn't keep the conversation going, we'd spend the whole evening in silence."

This episode crystallizes the irony that although American men tend to talk more than women in public situations, they often talk less at home. And this pattern is wreaking havoc with marriage.

—Deborah Tannen, "Sex, Lies, and Conversation: Why Is It So Hard for Men and Women to Talk to Each Other?"

Access the ebook for a video on topic sentences.

Supporting Sentences

Of course, simply stating the topic of a paragraph isn't enough; you need to support your main point with evidence to prove that your idea or claim is worth considering. Such **EVIDENCE** might include reasons, facts, statistics, quotations or citations from authorities, anecdotes, textual evidence, observations, and examples. For example, in the following paragraph,

◆ 402–9

Access the ebook for a video on supporting sentences in paragraphs.

HB-65–67

linguist Dennis Baron uses quotations and examples to make his point that **"THEY"** as a singular pronoun ("Everyone forgets *their* passwords," rather than "*his or her*" or merely "*his*") has been in use for a long time:

> Faced with the onslaught of coined pronouns in the 1880s, singular *they* began to seem less and less objectionable, and more observers recognized the old but much-maligned singular *they* as the people's choice. For example, a writer in 1884 recommended *they* as an interim solution to be used while experts pondered *thon* and *lin*. According to another writer, C. K. Maddox, there was no need for invented pronouns because *they* has been singular "for ages" in the writing of standard authors like Dickens. Maddox criticized experts who withheld their approval: "Our grammarians and dictionary makers are very conservative and often positively stupid" for rejecting a term "so natural to the genius of our language that hardly one in a hundred has noticed it as an intrusion."
>
> —Dennis Baron, *What's Your Pronoun? Beyond* He *and* She

The topic sentence begins the paragraph, and then information from two different sources—a paraphrase of one writer's solution and a quotation from another—provides support for the assertion made in the topic sentence.

Paragraph Length and Number

The simplest answers to the questions "How long should my paragraphs be?" and "How many paragraphs should my essays contain?" are: "as long as you need" and "as many as you need." In other words, the length and number of paragraphs in a text depend on your content, on what you need to say. Generally, your paragraphs should signal that groups of sentences are related in meaning and should help readers make those connections. For those reasons, too many brief paragraphs may make a text hard to read because each sentence stands alone, unrelated to the surrounding sentences, while long paragraphs or an essay of a single, very long paragraph forces readers to try to group related ideas together themselves. In other words, the number of paragraphs and the number of sentences within a paragraph depend on the message you're trying to convey—not on some formula or arbitrary number. Here are some reasons to begin a new paragraph:

- to introduce a new subject or idea
- to emphasize an idea
- to give readers a needed pause
- to signal a new speaker when writing dialogue

Transitions

Transitions help readers move from thought to thought—from sentence to sentence, paragraph to paragraph. You're likely to use a number of transitions as you draft; when **EDITING**, you should make a point of checking transitions. Here are some common ones:

372–76

Causes and effects

accordingly
as a result
because
consequently
hence
so
then
therefore
thus

Changes in direction or expectations

although
but
even though
however
in contrast
instead
nevertheless
nonetheless
on the contrary
on the one hand . . .
    on the other hand
still
yet

Comparisons

also
in the same way
like
likewise
similarly

Examples

for example
for instance
indeed
in fact
such as

Sequences or similarities

again
also
and
and then
besides
finally
first, . . . second,
    . . . third, etc.
furthermore
last
moreover
next
too

Summary or conclusion

as a result
as we have seen
finally
in a word
in any event
in brief
in conclusion
in other words
in short
in the end
in the final analysis
in the whole
therefore
thus
to summarize

Time relations

after
as soon as
at first
at the same time
before
eventually
finally
immediately
later
meanwhile
next
simultaneously
so far
soon
then
thereafter

Access the ebook for a video on transitions.

Transitions can also help readers move from paragraph to paragraph and, by summing up the previous paragraph's main point, show how the paragraphs are connected. A common way to summarize is to use phrases like "this _____" and "such _____." Here's an example from an anthropologist's study of American college students:

> When I asked students in interviews whether they felt they had a "community" at AnyU, most said yes. But what they meant by community were these personal networks of friends that some referred to as "my homeys." It was these small, ego-centered groups that were the backbone of most students' social experience in the university.
>
> On a daily basis these personal networks were easily recognizable within the dorm and on campus. "Where are you now?" says the cell phone caller walking back to the dorm from class. "I'm on my way home, so ask Jeffrey and Mark to come, and I'll meet you at my room at 8." Such conversations are everywhere.
>
> —Rebekah Nathan, *My Freshman Year*

"these personal networks" ties the second paragraph to the preceding one.

"Such conversations" sums up the example as a single concept.

Titles

A title serves various purposes, naming a text and providing clues to the content. It also helps readers decide whether they want to read further, so it's worth your while to come up with a title that attracts interest. Some titles include subtitles. You generally have considerable freedom in choosing a title, but you'll always want to consider the **RHETORICAL SITUATION** to be sure your title serves your purpose and appeals to the audience you want to reach.

Some titles simply announce the subject of the text:

"Black Men and Public Space"

"Turn the National Mall into a Wildflower Meadow"

"Why Colleges Shower Their Students with A's"

"Does Texting Affect Writing?"

Some titles provoke readers or otherwise entice them to read:

"Come Look at the Freaks"

"Thank God for the Atom Bomb"

"Just How Dishonest Are Most Students?"

Sometimes writers add a subtitle to explain or illuminate the title:

"Did It Feel Good? An Analysis of *Promising Young Woman*"

"It's in Our Genes: The Biological Basis of Human Mating Behavior"

"From Realism to Virtual Reality: Images of America's Wars"

Sometimes when you're starting to write, you'll think of a title that helps you generate ideas and write. More often, though, a title is one of the last things you'll write, when you know what you've written and can craft a suitable name for your text.

31 Drafting

At some point, you need to write out a draft. By the time you begin drafting, you've probably written quite a bit—in the form of notes, lists, outlines, and other kinds of informal writing. This chapter offers some hints on how to write a draft—and reminds you that as you draft, you may well need to get more information, rethink some aspect of your work, or follow new ideas that occur to you as you write.

Establishing a Schedule with Deadlines

Don't wait until the last minute to write. Computers crash, printers jam. Life intervenes in unpredictable ways. You increase your chances of success immensely by setting and meeting deadlines: research done by ____; rough draft done by ____; revisions done by ____; final draft edited, proofread, and submitted by ____. How much time you need varies with each writing task; but trying to compress everything into twenty-four or forty-eight hours before the deadline is asking for trouble.

Getting Comfortable

When are you at your best? When do you have your best ideas? For major writing projects, consider establishing a schedule that lets you write when you stand the best chance of doing good work. Schedule breaks for exercise and snacks. Find a place to write—a place where there's a good surface on which to spread out your materials, good lighting, a comfortable chair, and the right tools (computer, pen, paper) for the job. Often, however, we must make do: you may have to do your drafting in a busy computer lab or classroom. The trick is to make yourself as comfortable as you can manage. Sort out what you *need* from what you *prefer*.

Starting to Write

All of the above advice notwithstanding, don't worry so much about the trappings of your writing situation that you don't get around to writing. Write. Start by **FREEWRITING**, start with a first sentence, start with awful writing that you know you'll discard later—but write. That's what gets you warmed up and going.

Write quickly in spurts.   Write quickly with the goal of generating a complete draft, or a complete section of a longer draft, in one sitting. If you need to stop in the middle, make some notes about where you were headed when you stopped so that you can easily pick up your train of thought when you begin again.

Break down your writing task into small segments.   Big projects can be intimidating. But you can always write one section or, if need be, one paragraph or even a single sentence—and then another and another. It's a little like dieting. If I think I need to lose twenty pounds, I get discouraged and head for the doughnuts; but if I decide that I'll lose one pound and I lose it, well, I'll lose another—*that* I can do.

Expect surprises.   Writing is a form of thinking; the words you write lead you down certain roads and away from others. You may end up somewhere you didn't anticipate. Sometimes that can be a good thing—but sometimes you can write yourself into a dead end or out onto a tangent. Just know that this is natural, part of every writer's experience, and it's OK to double back or follow a new path that opens up before you.

Expect to write more than one draft.   A first sentence, first page, or first draft represents your attempt to organize into words your thoughts, ideas, feelings, research findings, and more. It's likely that some of that first try will not achieve your goals. That's OK—having writing on-screen or on paper that you can change, add to, and cut means you're part of the way there. As you revise, you can fill in gaps and improve your writing and thinking.

> Access the ebook for a video on the drafting process.

Dealing with Writer's Block

You may sit down to write but find that you can't—nothing occurs to you; your mind is blank. Don't panic; here are some ways to get started writing again:

- Think of the assignment as a problem to be solved. Try to capture that problem in a single sentence: "How do I explain the context for my topic?" "What is the best way to organize my argument?" "What am I trying to do in the conclusion?"

- Start early and break the writing task into small segments drafted over several days. Waiting until the night before an assignment is due can create panic—and writer's block.

- Stop trying: take a walk, take a shower, do something else. Come back in a half hour, refreshed.

329
331
330
- Open a new document on your computer or get a fresh piece of paper and **FREEWRITE**, or try **LOOPING** or **LISTING**. What are you trying to say? Just let whatever comes come—you may write yourself out of your box.

- If you usually write on your computer, turn it off, get out paper and pencil, and write by hand.

330–31
- Try a graphic approach: try **CLUSTERING**, or draw a chart of what you want to say; draw a picture or a comic strip; doodle.

471
- Do some **RESEARCH** on your topic to see what others have said about it.

332
365–71
- **TALK** to someone about what you are trying to do. If there's a writing center at your school, talk to a tutor: **GET RESPONSE**. If there's no one to talk to, then talk to yourself. It's the act of talking—using your mouth instead of your hands—that can free you up.

If you need more help

329–39
361–64
365–71
See Chapter 29 on **GENERATING IDEAS AND TEXT** if you find you need more material. And once you have a draft, see Chapter 32 on **ASSESSING YOUR OWN WRITING** and Chapter 33 on **GETTING RESPONSE AND REVISING** for help evaluating your draft.

32 Assessing Your Own Writing

In school and out, our work is continually assessed by others. Teachers judge whether our writing meets their expectations; supervisors decide whether we merit raises or promotions; even friends and relatives size up in various ways the things we do. As writers, we need to assess our own work—to step back and see it with a critical eye. By developing standards of our own and being conscious of the standards others use, we can assess—and shape—our writing, making sure it does what we want it to do. This chapter will help you assess your own written work.

What we write for others must stand on its own because we usually aren't present when it is read—we rarely get to explain to readers why we did what we did and what it means. So we need to make our writing as effective as we can before we submit, post, display, or publish it. It's a good idea to assess your writing in two stages, first considering how well it meets the needs of your particular rhetorical situation, then studying the text itself to check its focus, argument, organization, and clarity. Sometimes some simple questions can get you started:

What works?
What still needs work?
Where do I need to say more (or less)?

Considering the Rhetorical Situation

PURPOSE   What is your purpose for writing? If you have multiple purposes, list them, and then note which ones are the most important. How well does your draft achieve your purpose(s)? If you're writing for an assignment, what are its requirements, and does your draft meet those requirements? 73–74

AUDIENCE   To whom are you writing? What do those readers need and expect, as far as you can tell? Does your draft 75–78 answer their needs? Do you define any terms and explain any concepts they won't know?

79–84 **GENRE** What is the genre, and what are the key features of that genre? Does your draft include each of those features? If not, is there a good reason?

85–87 **STANCE** Is your attitude toward your topic and your audience clear? Does your language project the personality and tone that you want?

88–90 **MEDIA / DESIGN** What medium (print? spoken? electronic?) or combination of media is your text intended for, and how well does your writing suit it? How well does the design of the text suit your purpose and audience? Does it meet any requirements of the genre or of the assignment, if you're writing for one?

Examining the Text Itself

Look carefully at your text to see how well it says what you want it to say. Start with its focus, and then examine its support, organization, and clarity, in that order. If your writing lacks focus, the revising you'll do to sharpen the focus is likely to change everything else; if it needs more support, the organization may well change.

Consider your focus. Your writing should have a clear point, and every part of the writing should support that point. Here are some questions that can help you see if your draft is adequately focused:

- What is your main point? Even if it's not stated directly, you should be able to summarize it for yourself in a single sentence.

- If your genre calls for a thesis, is it narrow or broad enough to suit the needs and expectations of your audience?

340–48 - How does the **BEGINNING** focus attention on your thesis or main point?

- Does each paragraph support or develop that point? Do any paragraphs or sentences stray from your focus?

348–52 - Does the **ENDING** leave readers thinking about your main point? Is there another way of concluding the essay that would sharpen your focus?

Consider the support you provide. Your writing needs to give readers enough information to understand your points and see the logic of your thinking. How much information is enough will vary according to your audience. If they already know a lot about your subject or are likely to agree with your point of view, you may need to give less detail. If, however, they are unfamiliar with your topic or are skeptical about your views, you will probably need to provide much more.

- If your text makes an argument, what **REASONS** and **EVIDENCE** do you give to support your thesis? Where might more information be helpful? If you're writing online, could you provide links to it? 402
402–9
- What key terms and concepts do you **DEFINE**? Are there any other terms your readers might need to have explained? Could you do so by providing links? 429–38
- Where might you include more **DESCRIPTION** or other detail? 439–46
- Do you make any **COMPARISONS**? Especially if your readers won't be familiar with your topic, it can help to compare it with something more familiar. 422–28
- If you include **NARRATIVE**, how is it relevant to your point? 457–64
- See Part 6 for other useful **STRATEGIES**. 393

Consider the organization. As a writer, you need to lead readers through your text, carefully structuring your material so that they will be able to follow your ideas.

- Analyze the structure by **OUTLINING** it. An informal outline will do since you mainly need to see the parts, not the details. 335–37
- Is your text complete? Does your genre or assignment require an **ABSTRACT**, a **WORKS-CITED LIST**, an **ACKNOWLEDGMENT STATEMENT**, or any other elements? Glossary
MLA 552–80
MLA 551
APA 601
- What **TRANSITIONS** help readers move from idea to idea and paragraph to paragraph? Do you need to add more? 355–56
- If there are no **HEADINGS**, would adding them help orient readers? 644–45

Check for clarity. Nothing else matters if readers can't understand what you write. Following are some questions that can help you see whether your meaning is clear and your text is easy to read:

- Does your **TITLE** announce the subject of your text and give some sense of what you have to say? If not, would a more direct title give readers a better sense of your topic? 356–57

- If your writing requires a thesis, do you state it directly? If not, will readers easily understand your main point? Try stating your thesis outright, and see if it makes your ideas easier to follow.

340–48
348–52

- Does your **BEGINNING** tell readers what they need to understand your text, and does your **ENDING** help them make sense of what they've just read?

355–56

- How does each paragraph relate to the ones before and after? Are those relationships clear—or do you need to add **TRANSITIONS**?

- Do you vary your sentences? If all the sentences are roughly the same length or follow the same subject-verb-object pattern, your text probably lacks any clear emphasis and might even be difficult to read.

648–54

- Are **VISUALS** clearly labeled, positioned near the text they relate to, and referred to clearly in the text?

521–32

- If you introduce materials from other sources, have you clearly distinguished **QUOTED**, **PARAPHRASED**, or **SUMMARIZED** ideas from your own?

429–38

- Do you **DEFINE** all the words that your readers may not know?

- Does your punctuation make your writing more clear or less? Incorrect punctuation can make writing difficult to follow or, worse, change the meaning from what you intended. As a best-selling punctuation manual reminds us, there's a considerable difference between "eats, shoots, and leaves" and "eats shoots and leaves."

383–92

You may be asked to go into greater detail in an essay-length **REFLECTION** on your writing. If so, these questions may give you a good starting point.

Assessing a Body of Your Work

If you're required to submit a portfolio of your writing as part of a class, you'll likely need to write a reflective letter or essay that introduces the portfolio's contents, describes the processes you used to create them, and assess the writing in your portfolio. See Chapter 32 for detailed advice

361–64
377–82

on **ASSESSING YOUR WRITING** and Chapter 35 for advice on compiling a **PORTFOLIO**.

33 Getting Response and Revising

If we want to learn to play a song on the guitar, we play it over and over again until we get it right. If we play basketball or baseball, we likely spend hours shooting foul shots or practicing a swing. Writing works the same way. Making meaning clear can be tricky, and you should plan on revising and, if need be, rewriting in order to get it right. When we speak with someone face-to-face or on the phone or text a friend, we can get immediate response and restate or adjust our message if we've been misunderstood. In most other situations when we write, that immediate response is missing, so we need to seek out responses from readers to help us revise. This chapter includes a list of guidelines for those readers to consider, along with various strategies for subsequent revising and rewriting.

Giving and Getting Peer Response

When you meet with other students in pairs or small groups to respond to one another's work, in class or online, you have the opportunity to get feedback on your work from several readers who can help you plan revisions. At the same time, you learn from reading others' work how they approached the writing task—you're not writing in a vacuum. Some students wonder why class time is being taken up by peer response, assuming that their instructor's opinion is the only one that counts, but seeing the work of others and learning how others see your work can help you improve the clarity and depth of your writing. The key to responding effectively is to be as specific in your response as possible and avoid being either too harsh or too complimentary. These guidelines can help:

- Read your peer review partner's draft first from beginning to end as an interested reader, trying to understand the information and ideas. Don't look for problems. In fact, a good rule of thumb is this: read your partner's drafts in the same spirit that you want yours to be read.

- Before starting a second reading, ask your partner what questions they have about the draft or if you should focus on a particular aspect or part of the draft.

- As you read the draft again, take notes on a separate sheet of paper or save your comments to a different file. Your notes might include positive comments ("I like the way you . . ."), negative comments ("This sentence seems out of place"; "_____ doesn't seem like the best word to use"), and questions ("I'm not sure what you mean by _____"; "Would this paragraph work better on p. 2?").

- When you can, do more than identify issues. Offer suggestions or possible alternatives.

- When it's your draft's turn to be discussed, read or listen carefully to your partner's responses, take notes, and ask for clarification if necessary. Do not take issue with your partner's responses or argue over them; even if you're sure that what you wrote is perfectly clear, it's worth taking a second look if your partner has had trouble understanding it.

Getting Effective Response

Ask your readers to consider some of the specific elements in the list below, but don't restrict them to those elements. Caution: if a reader says nothing about any of these elements, don't be too quick to assume that you needn't think about them yourself.

356–57

- What did you think when you first saw the **TITLE**? Is it interesting? informative? appropriate? Will it attract other readers' attention?

340–48

- Does the **BEGINNING** grab your attention? If so, how does it do so? Does it give enough information about the topic? offer necessary background information? How else might the piece begin?

342–44

- Is there a clear **THESIS**, if the genre or assignment calls for one? What is it?

411–22

- Is there sufficient **SUPPORT** for the thesis? Is there anywhere you'd like to have more detail? Is the supporting material sufficiently

538–41

    DOCUMENTED?

340–57

- Does the text have a clear pattern of **ORGANIZATION**? Does each part relate to the thesis or main idea? Does each part follow from the one preceding it? Was the text easy to follow? How might the organization be improved?

- Is the **ENDING** satisfying? What did it leave you thinking? How else might the piece end?

348–52

- Can you tell the writer's **STANCE** or attitude toward the subject and audience? What words convey that attitude? Is it consistent throughout?

85–87

- How well does the text meet the needs and expectations of its **AUDIENCE**? Where might readers need more information, guidance, or clarification? How well does it achieve its **PURPOSE**? Does every part of the text help achieve the purpose? Could anything be cut? Should anything be added? Does the text meet the requirements of its **GENRE**? Should anything be added, deleted, or changed to meet those requirements?

75–78
73–74

79–84

- Do any terms need **DEFINING**? Would examples, additional detail, **EXPLANATIONS**, **DIALOGUE**, or some other strategies help you understand the draft?

429–38
452–56
447–51

- Are **CHARTS**, **GRAPHS**, or **TABLES** clear and readable? If there are no **VISUALS**, should there be?

650
648–54

- Are sentences complete and grammatical? Are **TRANSITIONS** helpful or needed? Is the punctuation correct?

355–56

- Can any words or phrases be sharpened? Are verbs mostly active? Is language that refers to others appropriate? Are all words spelled correctly?

If permitted by your instructor, you might also get a response to your writing from an **AI** tool like *ChatGPT*. You could use many of the preceding questions as prompts to start a conversation with the AI tool.

61–69

Revising

Once you have studied your draft with a critical eye and, if possible, gotten responses from other readers, it's time to revise. Major changes may be necessary, and you may need to generate new material or do some rewriting. But assume that your draft is good raw material that you can revise to achieve your purposes. Revision should take place on several levels, from global (whole-text issues) to particular (the details). Work on your draft in that order, starting with the elements that are global in nature and gradually moving to smaller, more particular aspects. This allows you to use your time most efficiently and take care of bigger issues first. In fact, as you deal with the larger aspects of your writing, many of the smaller ones will be taken care of along the way.

358

Give yourself time to revise. When you have a due date, set **DEADLINES** for yourself that will give you time—preferably several days, but as much as your schedule permits—to work on the text before it has to be delivered. Also, get some distance. Often when you're immersed in a project, you can't see the big picture because you're so busy creating it. If you can, get away from your writing for a while and think about something else. When you return to it, you're more likely to see it with fresh eyes. If there's not enough time to put a draft away for several days or more, even letting it sit overnight or for a few hours can help.

As you revise, assume that nothing is sacred. Bring a critical eye to all parts of a draft, not only to those parts your reviewers point out. Content, organization, sentence patterns, individual words—all are subject to improvement. Be aware that a change in one part of the text may require changes in other parts.

At the same time, don't waste energy struggling with writing that simply doesn't work; you can always discard it. Look for the parts of your draft that *do* work—the parts that match your purpose and say what you want to say. Focus your efforts on those bright spots, expanding and developing them.

362
73–74

335–37

Revise to sharpen your FOCUS. If your draft includes a thesis, make sure it matches your **PURPOSE** as you now understand it. Read each paragraph to ensure that it contributes to your main point; you may find it helpful to **OUTLINE** your draft to help you see all the parts. One way to do this is to highlight one sentence in each paragraph that expresses the paragraph's main idea. Then copy and paste the highlighted sentences into a new document. Does one state the thesis of the entire essay? Do the rest relate to the thesis? Are they in the best order? If not, you need to either modify the parts of the draft that don't advance your main idea or revise your thesis to reflect your draft's focus and to rearrange your points so they advance your discussion more effectively.

340–52

Read your **BEGINNING AND ENDING** carefully; make sure that the first paragraphs introduce your topic and provide any needed contextual information and that the final paragraphs provide a satisfying conclusion.

363

Revise to strengthen the argument. If readers find some of your claims unconvincing, you need to provide more information or more **SUPPORT**. You may have to define terms you've assumed they will understand, offer additional examples, or provide more detail by describing, explaining processes, adding dialogue, or using some other **STRATEGIES**. Make sure you

393

show as well as tell—and don't forget that you might need to do so literally, with visuals like photos, graphs, or charts. You might try freewriting, clustering, or other ways of **GENERATING IDEAS AND TEXT**. If you have to provide additional evidence, you might need to do additional **RESEARCH**.

329–39
471

Revise to improve the ORGANIZATION.   If you've outlined your draft, it helps to number each paragraph and make sure each one follows from the one before. If anything seems out of place, move it—or if necessary, cut it completely. Check to see if you've included appropriate **TRANSITIONS** or **HEADINGS** to help readers move through the text, and add them as needed. Check to make sure your text meets readers' expectations of the **GENRE** you're writing in.

340–57

355–56
644–45

79–84

Revise for CLARITY.   Be sure readers will be able to understand what you're saying. Look closely at your **TITLE** to be sure it gives a sense of what the text is about and at your **THESIS**, if you state one directly: Will readers recognize your main point? If you don't state a thesis directly, consider whether you should. Provide any necessary background information, and **DEFINE** any key terms. Make sure you've integrated any **QUOTATIONS**, **PARAPHRASES**, or **SUMMARIES** into your text smoothly. Are all paragraphs **FOCUSED** around one main point? Do the sentences in each paragraph contribute to that point? Finally, consider whether there are any data that would be more clearly presented in a **CHART**, **TABLE**, or **GRAPH**.

363–64
356–57
342–44

429–38
521–32
362

650

One way to test whether your text is clear is to switch audiences: write what you're trying to express as if you were talking to an eight-year-old. Your final draft probably won't be written that way, but the act of explaining your ideas to a young audience or readers who know nothing about your topic can help you discover any points that may be unclear.

Revise VISUALS.   Make sure images are located as close as possible to the discussion to which they relate and that the information in each visual is explained in your text. Each image should be numbered and have a title or caption that identifies it and explains its significance, and you should provide **ALTERNATIVE TEXT** for each image in a digital text. Each part of a **CHART**, **GRAPH**, or **TABLE** should be clearly labeled to show what it represents. If you didn't create the image yourself, make sure to cite its source, and if you're posting your work online, obtain permission from the copyright owner.

648–54

Glossary
650

Read and reread—and reread. Take some advice from writing theorist Donald Murray:

> Nonwriters confront a writing problem and look away from the text to rules and principles and textbooks and handbooks and models. Writers look at the text, knowing that the text itself will reveal what needs to be done and what should not yet be done or may never be done. The writer reads and rereads and rereads, standing far back and reading quickly from a distance, moving in close and reading slowly line by line, reading again and again, knowing that the answers to all writing problems lie within the evolving text.
>
> —Donald Murray, *A Writer Teaches Writing*

Rewriting

Some writers find it useful to try rewriting a draft in various ways or from various perspectives just to explore possibilities. Try it! If you find that your original plan works best for your purpose, fine. But you may find that another way will work better. Especially if you're not completely satisfied with your draft, consider the following ways of rewriting. Experiment with your rhetorical situation:

- Rewrite your draft from different points of view—through the eyes of different people, perhaps, or through the eyes of an animal or even from the perspective of an object. See how the text changes (in the information it presents, its perspective, its voice).

75–78
- Rewrite for a different **AUDIENCE**. How might an email detailing a recent car accident be written to a friend, an insurance agent, a parent?

86
- Rewrite in a different **TONE**. If the first draft was written in formal academic prose, rewrite it more informally.

79–84
88–90
- Rewrite the draft in a different **GENRE** or **MEDIUM**. Rewrite an essay as a letter, story, poem, speech, comic strip, *PowerPoint* presentation. Which genre and medium work best to reach your intended audience and achieve your purpose?

Ways of rewriting a narrative

447–51
- Rewrite one scene completely in **DIALOGUE**.
- Start at the end of the story and work back to the beginning, or start in the middle and fill in the beginning as you work toward the end.

Ways of rewriting a textual analysis

- **COMPARE** the text you're analyzing with another text (which may be in a completely different genre—film, TV, song lyrics, computer game, poetry, fiction, whatever).

  ◆ 422–28

- Write a parody of the text you're analyzing. Be as silly and as funny as you can while maintaining the structure of the original text. Alternatively, write a parody of your analysis, using evidence from the text to support an outrageous analysis.

Ways of rewriting a report

- Rewrite for a different **AUDIENCE**. For example, explain a concept to your grandparents; describe the subject of a profile to a visitor from another planet, a different time, or a different culture.

  ■ 75–78

- Be silly. Rewrite the draft as if for *The Onion* or a Dave Chappelle skit, or rewrite it as if it were written by Bart Simpson.

Ways of rewriting an argument

- Rewrite taking another **POSITION**. Argue as forcefully for that position as you did for your actual one, acknowledging and refuting your original position. Alternatively, write a rebuttal to your first draft from the perspective of someone with different beliefs.

  ▲ 170–96

- Rewrite your draft as a **STORY** —make it real in the lives of specific individuals. (For example, if you were writing about abortion rights, you could write a story about a young pregnant woman trying to decide what she believes and what to do.) Or rewrite the argument as a fable or parable.

  ◆ 457–65

- Rewrite the draft as a letter responding to a hostile reader, trying at least to make them understand what you have to say.

- Rewrite the draft as an angry letter to someone or as a table-thumping dinner-with-the-relatives discussion. Write from the most extreme position possible.

- Write an **ANALYSIS** of the topic of your argument in which you identify, as carefully and as neutrally as possible, the various positions people hold on the issue.

  ▲ 114–45

Once you've rewritten a draft in any of these ways, see whether there's anything you can use. Read each draft, considering how it might help you achieve your purpose, reach your audience, and convey your stance. Revise your actual draft to incorporate anything you think will make the text more effective, whether it's other genres or a different perspective.

Access the ebook for a video on revision strategies, including peer review.

34 Editing and Proofreading

No matter what you write, you need to communicate in ways that are appropriate to your rhetorical situation. When you text your friends, for example, you might use minimal punctuation, incomplete sentences, and mainly lowercase letters—and your friends won't bat an eye. But if you write a job application letter and résumé, your readers may expect clear, error-free writing in the belief that careful attention to editing—to grammar, punctuation, language, and formality—indicates similar care in the work you'll do on the job. Most college instructors expect this kind of attention to editing and proofreading in formal assignments like research papers. This chapter offers strategies for editing and proofreading your writing carefully.

Editing

Editing is the stage where you work on the details of your paragraphs, sentences, words, and punctuation to make your writing as clear, precise, and appropriate as possible. Your goal is not to achieve "perfection" (whatever that may be) so much as to make your writing as effective as possible for your particular purpose and audience. Consult a good writing handbook for detailed advice, but use the following guidelines to help you check the paragraphs, sentences, and words in your draft. With your instructor's permission, you might also use these guidelines to prompt an **AI** tool for help with editing and proofreading.

61–69 ✳

Editing paragraphs

352–53 ⦂

- Does each paragraph focus on one point? Does it have a **TOPIC SENTENCE** that announces that point, and if so, where is it located? If it's not the first sentence, should it be? If there's no clear topic sentence, should there be one?

- Does every sentence relate to the main point of the paragraph? If any sentences do not, should they be deleted, moved, or revised?

393 ◆

- Is there enough detail to develop the paragraph's main point? How is the point developed—with narrative? definition? some other **STRATEGY**?

- Where have you placed the most important information—at the beginning? at the end? in the middle? The most emphatic spot is at the end, so in general that's where to put information you want readers to remember. The second most emphatic spot is at the beginning.

- Are any paragraphs especially long or short? Consider breaking long paragraphs if there's a logical place to do so—maybe an extended example should be in its own paragraph, for instance. If you have paragraphs of only a sentence or two, see if you can add to them or combine them with another paragraph, unless you're using a brief paragraph to provide emphasis.

- Check the way your paragraphs fit together. Does each one follow smoothly from the one before? Do you need to add any **TRANSITIONS**?

  355–56

- Do the **BEGINNING** paragraphs catch readers' attention? In what other ways might you begin your text?

  340–48

- Do the final paragraphs provide a satisfactory **ENDING**? How else might you conclude your text?

  348–52

Editing sentences

- Is each sentence complete? Does it have someone or something (the subject) performing some sort of action or expressing a state of being (the verb)? Does each sentence begin with a capital letter and end with a period, question mark, or exclamation point?

- Check your use of the **PASSIVE VOICE**. Although there are some rhetorical situations in which the passive voice ("The prince was killed by a rival") is more appropriate than the active voice ("A rival killed the prince") because you want to emphasize an action rather than who performed it, you'll do well to edit it out unless you have a good reason for using it.

  Glossary

- Check for **PARALLELISM**. Items in a list or series should be parallel in form—all nouns ("lions," "tigers," "bears"), all verbs ("hopped," "skipped," "jumped"), all clauses ("he came, he saw, he conquered"), and so on.

  Glossary

- Do many of your sentences begin with "it" or "there"? Too often these words make writing wordy and vague or even conceal needed information. Why write "There are reasons we voted for him" when you can say "We had reasons to vote for him"?

355–56

- Are your sentences varied? If they all start with the subject or are the same length, your writing might be dull and maybe even hard to read. Try varying your sentence openings by adding **TRANSITIONS**, introductory phrases, or clauses. Vary sentence lengths by adding detail to some or by combining some sentences.

- Make sure you've used commas correctly. Is there a comma after each introductory element? ("After the lead singer quit, the group nearly disbanded. However, they then produced a string of hits.") Do commas set off nonrestrictive elements—parts that aren't needed to understand the sentence? ("The books I read in middle school, like the Harry Potter series, became longer and more challenging.") Are compound sentences connected with a comma? ("I'll eat broccoli steamed, but I prefer it roasted.")

Editing words

- Are you sure of the meaning of every word? Use a dictionary; be sure to look up words whose meanings you're not sure about. And remember your audience—do you use any terms they'll need to have defined?

- Is any of your language too general or vague? Why write that you competed in a race, for example, if you could say you ran the 4×200 relay?

86

- What about the **TONE**? If your stance is serious (or humorous or critical or something else), make sure that your words all convey that attitude.

Glossary

- Do any pronouns have vague or unclear **ANTECEDENTS**? If you use "he" or "they" or "it" or "these," will readers know whom or what the words refer to?

Glossary

- Have you used any **CLICHÉS** —expressions that are used so frequently that they're no longer fresh? "Live and let live," avoiding something "like the plague," and similar expressions are so predictable that your writing will almost always be better off without them.

- Be careful with language that refers to others. Make sure that your words do not stereotype any individual or group. Mention age, gender, race, religion, sexual orientation, and so on only if they are relevant to your subject. When referring to an ethnic group, make every effort to use the terms members of the group prefer. Also, whenever possible, refer to people by the **PRONOUNS** they use for themselves. If you don't know their pronouns and you need to refer to them with pronouns, it's best to ask. If you can't ask or don't think you should, your best alternative is to use the singular "they."

Glossary

- Edit out language that might be considered sexist. Have you used words like "manpower" or "policemen" to refer to people who may be female? If so, substitute less gendered words such as "personnel" or "police officers." Do your words reflect any gender stereotypes—for example, that all engineers are male or all nurses female? If you mention someone's gender, is it even necessary? If not, eliminate the unneeded words.

- How many of your verbs are forms of "be" and "do"? If you rely too much on these words, try replacing them with more specific verbs. Why write "She did a proposal for" when you could say "She proposed"?

- Do you ever confuse "its" and "it's"? Use "it's" when you mean "it is" or "it has." Use "its" when you mean "belonging to it."

Proofreading

Proofreading is the final stage of the writing process, when you check for misspelled words, mixed-up fonts, missing pages, and so on. It's the time to pay extra attention to detail. Most readers will excuse an occasional error, but by and large, academic readers and many employers are an intolerant bunch: too many errors will lead them to declare your writing—and maybe your thinking—flawed. There goes your credibility. So careful proofreading helps ensure that your message is taken as seriously as you want it to be.

Throughout your schooling, you've been told *not* to read individual words on the page but instead to read fluently for meaning. Proofreading demands the opposite: you must slow down your reading so that you can see every word, every punctuation mark.

- Use your computer's grammar checker and spelling checker, but only as a first step, and know that they're not very reliable. Computer programs, even those based on AI, may flag (or fail to flag) errors—or "misread" what you intended to say with your writing. If you were to write, "My brother was diagnosed with a leaning disorder," "leaning" wouldn't be flagged as misspelled because it's a word (and might even be a disorder), even though it's the wrong word in that sentence.

- To keep your eyes from jumping ahead, place a ruler or piece of paper under each line as you read. (This can work onscreen as well as on paper.) Use your finger or a pencil as a pointer.

- Some writers find it helpful to read the text one sentence at a time, beginning with the last sentence and working backward.

- Temporarily change the font or size of your text as you proofread; doing so can help you notice problems you may have overlooked.

- Read the text out loud to yourself—or better, to others, who may *hear* problems you can't see. Alternatively, have someone else read your text aloud while you follow along on the screen or page—or have *Google Translate* or another text-to-speech tool read your work aloud to you.

- Ask someone else to read your text. The more important the writing is, the more important this step is.

- If you need to submit a printed text and find a mistake after you've printed it out but are unable to print out a corrected version, make the change as neatly as possible in pencil or pen.

Access the ebook for a video on editing and proofreading strategies.

35 Compiling a Portfolio

Artists maintain portfolios of their work to show gallery owners, collec-
tors, and other potential buyers. Money managers work with investment
portfolios of stocks, bonds, mutual funds, and other products. And often as
part of a writing class, student writers compile portfolios of their work. As
with a portfolio of paintings or drawings, a portfolio of writing includes a
writer's best work and, sometimes, preliminary and revised drafts of that
work, along with a statement by the writer articulating why they consider
it good. The "why" is as important as the work, for it provides you with an
occasion for assessing your overall strengths and weaknesses as a writer.
This chapter offers guidelines to help you compile both a *writing portfolio*
and a *literacy portfolio*, a project that writing students are sometimes asked
to complete as part of a literacy narrative.

Considering the Rhetorical Situation

As with the writing you put in a portfolio, the portfolio itself is generally
intended for a particular audience but could serve a number of different
purposes. It's useful, then, to consider these and the other elements of your
rhetorical situation when you begin to compile a portfolio.

PURPOSE	Why are you creating this portfolio? To show your learning? To create a record of your writing? As the basis for a grade in a course? To organize your research? To explore your literacy? For something else?	▓ 73–74
AUDIENCE	Who will read your portfolio? What will your readers expect it to contain? How can you help them understand the context or occasion for each piece of writing you include?	▓ 75–78
GENRE	What genres of writing should the portfolio contain? Do you want to demonstrate your ability to write one particular type of writing or in a variety of genres? Will your introduction to or assessment of the portfolio be in the form of a letter or an essay?	▓ 79–84

85–87 ■

STANCE How do you want to portray yourself in this portfolio? What items should you include to create this impression? What stance do you want to take in your written assessment of its contents? Thoughtful? Enthusiastic? Something else?

88–90 ■

MEDIA/DESIGN Will your portfolio be in print? Or will it be electronic? Will it include multiple media? Whichever medium you use, how can you help readers navigate its contents? What design elements will be most appropriate to your purpose and medium?

A WRITING PORTFOLIO

What to Include

A portfolio developed for a writing course typically contains examples of your best work in that course, including any notes, outlines, preliminary drafts, and so on, along with your own assessment of your performance in the course. You might include any of the following items:

- freewriting, outlines, and other work you did to generate ideas
- drafts, rough and revised
- in-class writing assignments
- source material—copies of articles and online sources, observation notes, interview transcripts, and other evidence of your research
- tests and quizzes
- responses to your drafts

61–69 ✳

- records of interactions with **AI** tools, if AI use is permitted by your instructor
- conference notes, error logs, lecture notes, and other course materials
- electronic material, including visuals, blogs, and multimedia texts
- reflections on your work

What you include will vary depending on what your instructor asks for. You may be asked to include three or four of your best papers or everything you've written. You may also be asked to show work in several different genres. In any case, you'll usually need to choose, and to do that you'll need to have criteria for making your choices. Don't base your decision solely on grades (unless grades are one criterion); your portfolio should reflect *your* assessment of your work, not your instructor's. What do you think is your best work? your most interesting work? your most ambitious work? Whatever criteria you use, *you* are the judge.

Organizing a Portfolio

If you set up a way to organize your writing at the start of the course, you'll be able to keep track of it throughout the course, making your job at term's end much easier. Remember that your portfolio presents you as a writer, presumably at your best. It should be neat, well organized, and easy to navigate. Your instructor may provide explicit guidelines for organizing your portfolio. If not, here are some suggestions.

Paper portfolios. Choose something to gather your work in. You might use a two-pocket folder, a three-ring binder, or a file folder, or you may need a box, basket, or some other container to accommodate bulky or odd-shaped items.

Label everything. Label each piece at the top of the first page, specifying the assignment, the draft, and the date: "Proposal, Draft 1, 9/12/25"; "Text Analysis, Final Draft, 10/10/25"; "Portfolio Self-Assessment, Final Draft, 11/11/25"; and so on. Write this information neatly on the page, or put it on a Post-it note. For each assignment, arrange your materials chronologically, with your earliest material (freewriting, for example) on the bottom, and each successive item (source materials, say, then your outline, then your first draft, and so on) on top of the last, ending with your final draft on top. That way, readers can see how your writing changed from draft to draft.

Electronic portfolios. You might also create an electronic portfolio, or e-portfolio. E-portfolios typically consist of a network of **LINKED** documents that might include not only your writing and reflections on that writing but also sources, writing, and art you did for other courses or for your own enjoyment; audio and video clips; and other resources. Tools that can help you create an e-portfolio include:

657

- *Courseware.* Your school may use a learning platform, such as *Blackboard*, *Canvas*, or *Moodle*, that allows you to create an e-portfolio of your work.

- *Online tools.* Several websites, including *Weebly* and *Wix*, offer free tools to help you create a preformatted e-portfolio. For example, *Google Sites* provides templates you can use to build an e-portfolio, uploading documents, images, and videos from your computer.

- *Blogging tools.* You can create an e-portfolio using a blogging platform, like *Tumblr* or *WordPress*, which allows you to upload files and create a network of linked pages. Readers can then comment on your e-portfolio, just as they might on your blog entries.

It's also possible to create an electronic portfolio using word processing, spreadsheet, or presentation software. The programs available for your use and the requirements for publishing your portfolio vary from school to school and instructor to instructor; ask your instructor or your school's help desk for assistance (and see Chapter 5 on **WRITING AND LEARNING ONLINE** for general guidance).

52–60

Assessing Your Writing Portfolio

An important part of your portfolio is your written self-assessment of your work. This is an opportunity to assess your work with a critical eye and to think about what you're most proud of, what you most enjoyed doing, what you want to improve. It's your chance to think about and say what you've learned during the class. Some instructors may ask you to write out your assessment in essay form, as an additional sample of your writing; others will want you to put it in letter form, which usually allows for a more relaxed and personal tone. See Chapter 32 for detailed advice on **ASSESSING YOUR WRITING** and Chapter 36 for advice on composing a formal **REFLECTION**.

361–64
383–92

A LITERACY PORTFOLIO

As a writing student, you may be asked to think back to the time when you first learned to read and write or to remember significant books or other texts you've read, and perhaps to put together a portfolio that chronicles your development as a reader and writer. You may also be asked to put together a literacy portfolio to accompany a **LITERACY NARRATIVE**.

93–113

What you include in such a portfolio will vary depending on what you've kept over the years and what your family has kept. You may have all your favorite books, stories you dictated to a preschool teacher, notebooks in which you practiced writing the alphabet. Or you may have almost nothing. What you have or don't have is unimportant in the end: what's important is that you gather what you can and arrange it in a way that shows how you think about your development and growth as a literate person. What have your experiences been with reading and writing? What's your earliest memory of learning to write? If you love to read, what led you to love it? Who was most responsible for shaping your writing ability? Those are some of the questions you'll ask if you write a literacy narrative. You might also compile a literacy portfolio as a way to generate ideas and text for that assignment.

What to Include

- school papers
- drawings and doodles from preschool
- favorite books
- photographs you've taken
- drawings
- poems
- letters
- journals and diaries
- lists
- reading records or logs
- electronic texts you've created
- marriage vows
- speeches you've given
- awards you've received
- workplace writing

Organizing a Literacy Portfolio

You may wish to organize your material chronologically, but there are other methods of organization to consider as well. For example, you might group items according to where they were written (at home, at school, at work), by genre (stories, poems, essays, letters, notes), or even by purpose (pleasure, school, work, church, and so on). Arrange your portfolio in the way that best conveys who you are as a literate person. Label each item you include, perhaps with a Post-it note, to identify what it is, when it was written or read, and why you've included it in your portfolio. Or you might create an e-portfolio, scanning print items to include in it along with electronic items.

Reflecting on Your Literacy Portfolio

- Why did you choose each item?
- Is anything missing? Are there any other important materials that should be here?
- Why is the portfolio organized as it is?
- What does the portfolio show about your development as a reader and writer?
- What patterns do you see? Are there any common themes you've read or written about? any techniques you rely on? any notable changes over time?
- What are the most significant items, and why?

36 Reflecting on Your Writing

Reflecting on experiences—looking back on them to understand and learn from them—is an important part of our work, school, and personal lives. Employees reflect on their job performance as they develop goals for the future. Students reflect on their coursework and extracurricular activities as they prepare applications for scholarships or internships. Lots of people reflect on their daily lives in diaries or journals. And writers reflect on their writing—they look back on their work and consider what they've learned, what they've accomplished, and how they can use their new knowledge and experience in future writing situations. But reflection isn't just an activity that writers engage in *after* they've finished writing. It's also a powerful tool for thinking and learning throughout the writing process. This chapter gives advice for making the most of that tool.

Access the ebook for a video on reflecting on your writing.

REFLECTING WHILE WRITING

When teachers ask you to reflect during your writing process, they're asking you to pause, step back, and pay attention to what you're doing and thinking as you write. This activity (sometimes called "**METACOGNITION**") can help you solve problems in your writing, adjust or adapt your strategies, and make decisions about how to move forward.

47–48

Following are questions you can ask yourself in order to prompt reflection at several points in your writing process. You might record your reflections in a process log, or talk through them with someone else, or just mull them over in your mind.

- *Reflecting as you approach a new writing assignment or task.* Have you encountered a similar assignment or task in the past? If so, what processes or strategies worked for you then, and how might you adapt them for your new writing situation now? What goals can you set for yourself? What problems might you encounter, and what resources can help you solve them?

- *Reflecting as you generate ideas and compose a draft.* What's the most intriguing idea you've generated? the most puzzling or surprising? What connections do you see among ideas? What do you like about your draft so far?

- *Reflecting as you participate in peer review.* Which comments from your peers are most helpful? Which comments do you think you'll ignore, and why? What did you learn from reviewing your classmates' drafts, and how can you apply that learning to your own draft?

- *Reflecting as you revise and edit.* What feedback did your teacher provide on your previous work, and can you apply that feedback to your current writing situation? What revision strategies have worked for you in the past, and can you use or adapt them now? What resources can you draw on for help with editing and proofreading?

REFLECTING AFTER WRITING

You may be asked to write a formal reflection on your work—perhaps after completing a writing project, after compiling a portfolio, or at the end of a course. Formal reflection assignments go by many names: portfolio cover letters, reflective self-assessments, companion pieces, statements of goals and choices, and others. Regardless of the name, reflection-after-writing assignments typically ask you to share insights about your work and the process you used to create it—and to support your insights with evidence. Considering your rhetorical situation will help you make decisions about how to approach your particular reflection task.

Considering the Rhetorical Situation

73–74 ■ **PURPOSE**   Why are you writing your reflection? To examine your growth and development as a writer over time? To assess your achievement of course learning goals? To consider how you might use your new knowledge in future writing contexts? Are you reflecting on just one piece of writing or on a body of work?

75–78 ■ **AUDIENCE**   Who will read your reflection, and what's your relationship to your reader? Is your course instructor your primary reader? Does your audience include other instructors or external evaluators whom you may not know? Will you need to introduce or contextualize the writing you're reflecting on? What examples or evidence of your learning will your readers most want to see?

GENRE   Has a genre been assigned to you? If so, what are the key features of the genre, and how can you use them in your reflection? Can you choose a genre? If so, what will you choose—a letter, a literacy narrative, a textual analysis, something else? What expectations will your audience have for your chosen genre?

79–84

STANCE   How will you portray yourself in your reflection—as introspective? curious? self-critical? What stance will you take toward the work you're reflecting on— objective? evaluative? analytical? What tone will you use—relaxed and conversational? serious and formal?

85–87

MEDIA/DESIGN   What medium will best suit your purpose and audience? A print document? An electronic text like a blog post, a video diary, or a podcast? Will visuals be helpful? Does your audience expect, or your instructor require, a certain format or type of documentation?

88–90

Generating Insights for Your Reflection

If you've responded to the "Taking Stock of Your Work" prompts in Chapters 12 through 23, you can return to those responses as a starting point to generate insights for an essay-length reflection. The following activities might also help you develop ideas and text.

Take an inventory of your writing.   List everything you wrote for your course or for a particular project—freewrites, peer reviews, notes, drafts, revisions, and so on. Then gather as much of the material as you can, and read it carefully. Pretend you're looking at your writing as an outsider, and try **ANNOTATING** or **CODING** it: notice the strengths and weaknesses of individual pieces of writing; pay attention to the language, organization, and other choices you made; note whether your writing changed over time. In other words, *study* your own writing—be curious about it! Take notes so you can harness insights from your inventory.

15–18

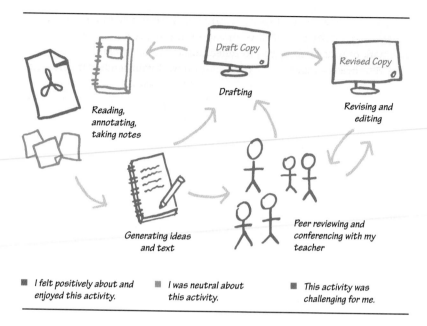

Draft Copy

Drafting

Revised Copy

Reading,
annotating,
taking notes

Revising and
editing

Generating ideas
and text

Peer reviewing and
conferencing with my
teacher

■ I felt positively about and
enjoyed this activity.

■ I was neutral about
this activity.

■ This activity was
challenging for me.

Create a map or flowchart of your current writing process. Think about a writing project you recently completed, and make a visual representation of the process you engaged in to create the work. Begin by listing the writing tools you used, the spaces where you worked, the types of tasks you completed—anything you remember about your writing process. Then represent those items with stick figures, symbols, or something else. Use arrows to show how you moved from one point in your writing process to another, and perhaps mark the times when you struggled and the times when you felt productive. When you finish your map, ask yourself what it reveals: Which parts of your writing process were most and least enjoyable? What would you change about your process if you could? What insights can you gain about what you do when you write—and what you might do better in the future? The sample map above represents one writer's process for a research assignment.*

Think of words, phrases, or images that capture your experiences as a writer. Start by listing key activities or concepts that guided your work: maybe **REVISING** was especially important to your writing process,

367–70

---

* Adapted from Tim Lockridge and Derek Van Ittersum, *Writing Workflows: Beyond Word Processing.*

75–78
41–51

or **AUDIENCE** awareness was something you worked hard to develop. Maybe a particular **ACADEMIC HABIT OF MIND**—like openness or curiosity—was a hallmark of your work. Think, too, about other words or phrases that represent your lived experiences as a writer—like the name of the café where you did your best writing, or the tool (blue notebook, *Google Docs*) that you relied on to get your work done, or the mantra that got you through your course. Freewrite about what those key words or phrases mean to you in the context of your writing and learning.

You might even use images to help brainstorm ideas for your reflection, as student Jennifer Martinez did for a writing class at Columbus State Community College in the example on the next page.

Providing Support for Your Reflection

Once you've generated insights about your writing and learning, the next step is to find evidence to support and illustrate those insights. Fortunately, you'll have a wealth of material to draw on—your own writing, your interactions with classmates, and more. In fact, you can mine your entire course experience for evidence to support your reflective insights. Some types of evidence you might use in your reflection include:

Examples and anecdotes. Recall some memories from your course experience—a time when you exhibited a particular habit of mind, for example, or when you solved a problem in your writing, or when you helped a peer re-see their work. Describe the specific instance, or narrate the story behind it.

Textual evidence. Consider all the texts that make up your learning experience: drafts and revisions, peer-review comments, discussion board posts, written feedback from your teacher, and so on. All those texts provide fodder to support the insights you share in your reflection. For example, if you want to illustrate your revising skills, you might quote a passage from an early draft of a writing project and compare it to a revised passage from a later draft. If you want to support a claim about your rhetorical knowledge, you might quote from your writing to highlight particular language choices you made to meet readers' needs. To illustrate your openness to others' ideas, you could quote a comment a peer reviewer made, and then explain how you used that comment to rethink something in your own writing. To show your evolving self-awareness as a writer, you could quote from the "Taking Stock" responses you wrote throughout the course.

Jennifer's Reflection Brainstorming

This whole semester I struggled with **SELF-DOUBT** and overwhelming anxiety at times. Slowly I was able to overcome some of these issues by trusting the writing process and just knowing that I will get through it. I have learned to give myself more time by starting earlier so I am able to work through those moments and to also take breaks when I start to feel the anxiety creep in.

Before this class I would have dreaded the thought of writing a **JOURNAL** entry. Once writing became a normal routine, I started looking forward to our journal entries. I even decided I'm going to buy my mom a daily writing prompt book. You can't be wrong with a journal; it's just your thoughts and your feelings.

One of the most helpful lessons I received from this class was a more positive attitude toward the things I struggle with. After we watched the video on **GROWTH MINDSET** at the beginning of this semester, something clicked and I started looking at all of my struggles a little differently; I understood that the struggles were helping to make me smarter. Once I accepted that my brain was like a muscle and that I should treat it that way, it was easier for me to work through rough times in my writing.

Statistics. Some students enjoy collecting and interpreting data about their writing processes and products. You might use the Compare feature in *Word* to tabulate the number of changes you made from one draft to the next. You might do a search through your process work to see how many times the word "genre" or "audience" or some other key term appeared. You might look for themes in your peer reviewers' comments and tabulate, for example, the percentage of comments related to focus or organization or editing. You might then use the numerical data as support for a particular insight you want to share or a claim you want to make in your reflection.

Visuals. Sometimes visual evidence can help support your reflective insights and claims. You might use photographs of notes, drafts, sketches, and storyboards to support an insight about your writing process. You might create a graph or chart to illustrate numerical data you've generated about your own writing, if you're using such data. You might develop a **WORD CLOUD**—a visual representation of words in a text—to highlight key themes in your writing. Remember that visuals almost never speak for themselves, so you'll need to explain them in your reflection. For example, if you include a graph, you might say something like, "The graph in figure 1 depicts how many times my peer reviewers and instructor mentioned key elements—like thesis, organization, or editing—in response to each of my essays."

● 485–88

Ways of Organizing a Reflection

The organization of your reflection will depend on your genre, and you may be able to consult the organizational diagrams in the genre chapters of this book for help. Some common genres used for reflections include letters, **LITERACY NARRATIVES**, **TEXTUAL ANALYSES**, **EXPLORATIONS**, and **REPORTS**.

▲ 93–113
114–45
270–79
146–69

A Sample Reflection

In the letter that follows, Nathaniel J. Cooney reflects on the strengths and weaknesses of the writing he produced in his first-year composition class at Wright State University.

2 June 2025

Dear Reader,

It is my hope that in reading this letter you will gain an under-standing of the projects contained in this portfolio. I enclose three works that I have submitted for an introductory writing class at Wright State University, English 102, Writing in Academic Dis-course: an informative report, an argument paper, and a remix project based largely on the content of the argument paper. I selected the topics of these works for two reasons: First, they address issues that I believe to be relevant in terms of both the intended audience (peers and instructors of the course) and the times when they were published. Second, they speak to issues that are important to me personally. Below I present general descrip-tions of the works, along with my review of their strengths and weaknesses.

My purpose in writing the informative report "Higher Standards in Education Are Taking Their Toll on Students" was to present a subject in a factual manner and to support it with well-documented research. My intent was not to argue a point. However, because I chose a narrowly focused topic and chose information to support a thesis, the report tends to favor one side of the issue over the other. Because as a student I have a personal stake in the changing standards in the formal education system, I chose to research recent changes in higher education and their effects on students. Specifically, I examine students' struggles to reach a standard that seems to be moving further and further beyond their grasp.

I believe that this paper could be improved in two areas. The first is a bias that I think exists because I am a student present-ing information from the point of view of a student. It is my hope, however, that my inclusion of unbiased sources lessens this problem somewhat and, furthermore, that it presents the reader with a fair and accurate collection of facts and examples that supports the thesis. My second area of concern is the over-all balance in the paper between outside sources supporting my own thoughts and outside sources supporting opposing points of view. Rereading the paper, I notice many places where I may have worked too hard to include sources that support my ideas.

The second paper, "Protecting Animals That Serve," is an argument intended not only to take a clear position on an issue but also to argue for that position and convince the reader that it is a valid one. That issue is the need for legislation guaranteeing that certain rights of service animals be protected. I am blind and use a guide dog. Thus, this issue is especially important to me. During the few months that I have had him, my guide dog has already encoun-tered a number of situations where intentional or negligent treat-ment by others has put him in danger. At the time I was writing the paper, a bill was being written in the Ohio House of Represen-tatives that, if passed, would protect service animals and establish consequences for those who violated the law. The purpose of the paper, therefore, was to present the reader with information about service animals, establish the need for the legislation in Ohio and nationwide, and argue for passage of such legislation.

I think that the best parts of my argument are the introduction and the conclusion. In particular, I think that the conclusion does a good job of not only bringing together the various points but also convey-ing the significance of the issue for me and for others. In contrast, I think that the area most in need of further attention is the body of the paper. While I think the content is strong, I believe the overall organization could be improved. The connections between ideas are unclear in places, particularly in the section that acknowledges oppos-ing viewpoints. This may be due in part to the fact that I had difficulty understanding the reasoning behind the opposing argument.

The argument paper served as a starting point for the remix project, for which the assignment was to revise one paper written for this class in a different genre. My remix project consists of a poster and a brochure. As it was for the argument paper, my primary goal was to convince my audience of the importance of a particular issue and viewpoint—specifically, to convince my audience to support House Bill 369, the bill introduced in the Ohio legislature that would create laws to protect the rights of service animals in the state.

Perhaps both the greatest strength and the greatest weakness of the remix project is my use of graphics. Because of my blindness, I was limited in my use of some graphics. Nevertheless, the pictures were carefully selected to capture the attention of readers and, in part, to appeal to their emotions as they viewed and reflected on the material.

I put a great deal of time, effort, and personal reflection into each project. While I am hesitant to say that they are finished and while I am dissatisfied with some of the finer points, I am satisfied with the overall outcome of this collection of works. Viewing it as a collection, I am also reminded that writing is an evolving process and that even if these works never become exactly what I envisioned them to be, they stand as reflections of my thoughts at a particular time in my life. In that respect, they need not be anything but what they already are, because what they are is a product of who I was when I wrote them. I hope that you find the papers interesting and informative and that as you read them, you, too, may realize their significance.

Respectfully,

Nathaniel J. Cooney

Nathaniel J. Cooney

Enclosures (3)

Cooney describes each of the works he includes in his portfolio and considers their strengths and weaknesses, citing examples from his texts to support his assessment and reflection.

Part 6
Strategies

Whenever we write, we draw on many different strategies to articulate what we have to say. We may **DEFINE** key terms, **DESCRIBE** people or places, and **EXPLAIN** how something is done. We may **COMPARE** one thing to another. Sometimes we may choose a pertinent story to **NARRATE**, and we may even want to include some **DIALOGUE**. The chapters that follow offer advice on how to use these and **OTHER BASIC STRATEGIES** for developing and organizing the texts you write.

Strategies

☀ academic literacies   ⬣ fields   ◆ strategies   ● media / design
■ rhetorical situations   ⁝ processes   ● research   ★ handbook
▲ genres

37 Analyzing Causes and Effects

Analyzing causes helps us think about why something happened, whereas thinking about effects helps us consider what might happen. When we hear a noise in the night, we want to know what caused it. Children poke sticks into holes to see what will happen. Researchers try to understand the causes of diseases. Writers often have occasion to consider causes or effects as part of a larger topic or sometimes as a main focus: in a **PROPOSAL**, we might consider the effects of reducing tuition or the causes of recent tuition increases; in a **PERSONAL NARRATIVE**, we might explore why the person we were meeting for coffee failed to show up.

257–69
234–45

Usually we can only speculate about *probable* causes or *likely* effects. In writing about causes and effects, then, we are generally **ARGUING** for those we consider plausible, not proven. This chapter will help you analyze causes and effects in writing—and to do so in a way that suits your rhetorical situation.

399–416

Determining Plausible Causes and Effects

What causes ozone depletion? sleeplessness? obesity? And what are their effects? Those are of course large, complex topics, but whenever you have reason to ask why something happened or what could happen, there will likely be several possible causes and just as many predictable effects. There may be obvious causes, though often they will be less important than others that are harder to recognize. (Eating too much may be an obvious cause of being overweight, but *why* people eat too much has several less obvious causes: portion size, advertising, lifestyle, and psychological disorders are only a few possibilities.) Similarly, short-term effects are often less important than long-term ones. (A stomachache may be an effect of eating too much candy, but the chemical imbalance that can result from consuming too much sugar is a much more serious effect.)

LISTING, **CLUSTERING**, and **OUTLINING** are useful processes for analyzing causes. And at times you might need to do some **RESEARCH** to identify possible causes or effects and to find evidence to support your analysis. When you've identified potential causes and effects, you need to analyze

330
330–31
335–37
471

73–74
75–78

them. Which causes and effects are primary? Which seem to be secondary? Which are most relevant to your **PURPOSE** and are likely to convince your **AUDIENCE**? You will probably have to choose from several possible causes and effects for your analysis because you won't want or need to include all of them.

Arguing for Causes or Effects

399–416 ◆

Once you've identified several possible causes or predictable effects, you need to **ARGUE** that some are more plausible than others. You must provide convincing support for your argument because you usually cannot *prove* that x causes y or that y will be caused by z; you can only show, with good reasons and appropriate evidence, that x is *likely* to cause y or that y will *likely* follow from z. See, for example, how an essay on the psychological basis for risk-taking speculates about two potential causes for the popularity of extreme sports:

> Studies now indicate that the inclination to take high risks may be hardwired into the brain, intimately linked to arousal and pleasure mechanisms, and may offer such a thrill that it functions like an addiction. The tendency probably affects one in five people, mostly young males, and declines with age. It may ensure our survival, even spur our evolution as individuals and as a species. Risk taking probably bestowed a crucial evolutionary advantage, inciting the fighting and foraging of the hunter-gatherer. . . .
>
> As psychologist Salvadore Maddi, PhD, of the University of California at Davis warns, "High-risk takers may have a hard time deriving meaning and purpose from everyday life." Indeed, this peculiar form of dissatisfaction could help explain the explosion of high-risk sports in America and other postindustrial Western nations. In unstable cultures, such as those at war or suffering poverty, people rarely seek out additional thrills. But in a rich and safety-obsessed country like America, land of guardrails, seat belts, and personal-injury lawsuits, everyday life may have become too safe, predictable, and boring for those programmed for risk taking.
>
> —Paul Roberts, "Risk"

Roberts suggests that genetics is one likely cause of extreme sports and that an American obsession with safety is perhaps a cause of their growing popularity. Notice, however, that he presents these as likely or possible, not certain, by choosing his words carefully: "studies now *indicate*"; "the inclination to take high risks *may* be hardwired"; "[r]isk taking *probably* bestowed a crucial evolutionary advantage"; "this . . . dissatisfaction *could help* explain." Like Roberts, you'll almost always need to qualify what you say about causes and effects—to say that something *could explain* (rather than saying it "explains") or that it *suggests* (rather than "shows"). Causes and effects can seldom be proved definitively, so it's important to acknowledge that your argument is not the last word on the subject.

Ways of Organizing an Analysis of Causes and Effects

Your analysis of causes and effects may be part of a proposal or some other genre of writing, or you may write a text whose central purpose is to analyze causes or speculate about effects. While there are many ways to organize an analysis of causes and effects, three common ways are to state a cause and then discuss its effects, to state an effect and then discuss its causes, and to identify a chain of causes and effects.

Identify a cause and then discuss its effects.   If you were writing about climate change, you might first show that many scientists fear it will have several effects, including more violent storms, the extinction of various kinds of plants, and elevated sea levels.

Identify an effect and then trace its causes.   If you were writing about school violence, for example, you might argue that it is a result of sloppy dress, informal teacher-student relationships, low academic standards, and disregard for rules.

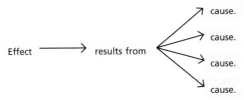

Identify a chain of causes and effects.   You may sometimes discuss a chain of causes and effects. If you were writing about the right to privacy, for example, you might consider the case of Megan's law. A convicted child molester raped and murdered a girl named Megan; the crime caused

New Jersey legislators to pass the so-called Megan's law (an effect), which requires that convicted sex offenders be publicly identified. As more states enacted versions of Megan's law, concern developed for the rights of those who are identified—the effect became a cause of further effects.

First cause → leads to → first effect, → which leads to → next effect. → Continue the chain as need be.

Considering the Rhetorical Situation

As a writer or speaker, it's important to think about the message you want to articulate, the audience you want to reach, and the larger context you are writing in.

73–74 ■ **PURPOSE**　　Your main purpose may be to analyze the causes and effects of something. But sometimes you'll have another goal that calls for such analysis—a business report, for example, might need to explain what caused a decline in sales.

75–78 ■ **AUDIENCE**　　Who is your intended audience, and how will analyzing causes help you reach them? Do you need to tell them why some event happened or what effects resulted?

79–84 ■ **GENRE**　　Does your genre require you to analyze causes? Proposals, for example, often need to consider the effects of a proposed solution.

85–87 ■ **STANCE**　　What is your stance, and could analyzing causes or effects show that stance? Could it help demonstrate your seriousness or show that your conclusions are reasonable?

88–90 ■ **MEDIA/DESIGN**　　You can rely on words to analyze causes, but sometimes a visual will help readers *see* how causes lead to effects.

If you need more help

321 ⁝ See also the **PROCESSES** chapters for help with generating ideas, drafting, and so on if you need to write an entire text whose purpose is to analyze causes or speculate about effects.

38 Arguing

Basketball fans argue about who's better, LeBron James or Steph Curry. Political candidates argue that they have the most experience or best judgment. A toilet paper ad argues that "you deserve a little luxury in your life, and so does your bottom." As you likely realize, we are surrounded by arguments, and much of the work you do as a college student requires you to read and write arguments. When you write a **LITERARY ANALYSIS**, for instance, you argue for a particular interpretation. In a **PROPOSAL**, you argue for a particular solution to a problem. Even a **PROFILE** argues that a subject should be seen in a certain way. This chapter offers advice on some of the key elements of making an argument, from developing an arguable thesis and identifying good reasons and evidence that supports those reasons to building common ground and dealing with viewpoints other than your own.

▲ 220–33
257–69
246–56

Reasons for Arguing

We argue for many reasons, and they often overlap: to convince others that our position on a subject is reasonable, to influence the way they think about a subject, to persuade them to change their point of view or take some sort of action. In fact, many composition scholars and teachers believe that all writing makes an argument.

As a student, you'll be called on to make arguments continually: when you participate in class discussions, when you take an essay exam, when you post a comment to an online discussion or a blog. In all these instances, you're adding your opinions to some larger conversation, arguing for what you believe — and why.

▶ Access Chapter 1 in the ebook for a video on understanding academic argument.

Arguing Logically: Claims, Reasons, and Evidence

The basic building blocks of argument are claims, reasons, and evidence that supports those reasons. Using these building blocks, we can construct a strong logical argument, also known as *logos*.

Claims. Good arguments are based on arguable claims—statements that reasonable people may disagree about. Certain kinds of statements cannot be argued:

- *Verifiable statements of fact.* Most of the time, there's no point in arguing about facts like "the earth is round" or "George H. W. Bush was America's forty-first president." Such statements contain no controversy, no potential opposition—and so no interest for an audience. However, you might argue about the basis of a fact. For example, until recently it was a fact that our solar system had nine planets; but when further discoveries led to a change in the definition of "planet," Pluto no longer qualified.

- *Issues of faith or belief.* By definition, matters of faith cannot be proven or refuted. If you believe in reincarnation or don't believe there is an afterlife, there's no way I can convince you otherwise. However, in a philosophy or religion course you may be asked to argue, for example, whether or not the universe must have a cause.

- *Matters of simple opinion or personal taste.* If you think cargo pants are ugly, no amount of arguing will convince you to think otherwise. If you've downloaded every Taylor Swift album and think she's the greatest singer ever, you won't convince your Nirvana-loving parents to like her, too. If matters of taste are based on identifiable criteria, though, they may be argued in an **EVALUATION**, where "Tom Cruise is a terrible actor" is more than just your opinion—it's an assertion you can support with evidence.

210–19 ▲

You may begin with an opinion: "I think wearing a helmet makes riding a bike more dangerous, not less." As it stands, that statement can't be considered a claim—it needs to be made more reasonable and informed. To do that, you might reframe it as a question—"Do bike riders who wear helmets get injured more often than those who don't?"—that may be answered as you do research and start to write. Your opinion or question should lead you to an arguable claim, however, one that could be challenged by another thoughtful person. In this case, for example, your research might lead you to a focused, qualified claim: "Contrary to common sense, wearing a helmet while riding a bicycle increases the chances of injury, at least to adult riders."

Qualifying a claim. According to an old saying, there are two sides to every story. Much of the time, though, arguments don't sort themselves neatly into two sides, pro and con. No matter what your topic, your argument will rarely be a simple matter of being for or against; in most cases, you'll want to qualify your claim—that it is true in certain circumstances, with certain conditions, with these limitations, and so on. Qualifying your claim shows that you're reasonable and also makes your topic more manageable by limiting it. The following questions can help you qualify your claim:

- *Can it be true in some circumstances or at some times but not others?* For example: "Freedom of speech should generally be unrestricted, but individuals can sue for slander or libel."

- *Can it be true only with certain conditions?* For instance: "Cell phones and computer monitors should be recycled, but only by licensed, domestic recyclers."

- *Can it be true for some groups or individuals but not others?* For example: "Intermittent fasting can lead to weight loss and other health benefits for many people, but some people—including athletes, older adults, and those with certain health conditions—should avoid the practice."

SOME WORDS FOR QUALIFYING A CLAIM

sometimes	nearly	it seems/seemingly
rarely	usually	some
in some cases	more or less	perhaps
often	for the most part	possibly
routinely	in many cases	in most cases

Drafting a thesis statement. Once your claim is focused and appropriately qualified, it can form the core of your essay's **THESIS STATEMENT**, which announces your position and forecasts the path your argument will follow. For example, here is the opening paragraph of an essay by the then–executive director of the National Congress of American Indians arguing that the remains of Native Americans should be treated with the same respect given to others. The author outlines the context of her argument and then presents her thesis (here, in italics):

 342–44

Access Chapter 15 in the ebook for a video on developing an argumentative thesis statement.

> What if museums, universities and government agencies could put your dead relatives on display or keep them in boxes to be cut up and otherwise studied? What if you believed that the spirits of the dead could not rest until their human remains were placed in a sacred area? The ordinary American would say there ought to be a law—and there is, for ordinary Americans. *The problem for American Indians is that there are too many laws of the kind that make us the archeological*

property of the United States and too few of the kind that protect us from such insults.

> —Suzan Shown Harjo, "Last Rites for Indian Dead: Treating Remains Like Artifacts Is Intolerable"

Reasons. Your claim must be supported by reasons that your audience will accept. A reason can usually be linked to a claim with the word "because":

CLAIM	+	BECAUSE	+	REASON
College students should strive to graduate		because		they will earn far more over their lifetimes than those who do not

Keep in mind that you likely have a further reason, a rule or principle that underlies the reason you link directly to your claim. In this argument, the underlying reason is that graduating from college leads to a boost in lifetime income because employers value college graduates. If your audience doesn't accept that principle, you may have to back it up with further reasons or evidence.

To come up with good reasons, start by stating your position and then answering the question "Why?"

> **CLAIM:** College students should strive to graduate. *Why?*
>
> **REASON:** (Because) They will earn far more over their lifetimes than those who do not. *Why?*
>
> **UNDERLYING REASON:** The economy values college graduates and pays them more.

As you can see, this exercise can continue indefinitely as the underlying reasons grow more and more general and abstract. You can do the same with other positions:

> **CLAIM:** Smoking should be banned. *Why?*
>
> **REASON:** (Because) It is harmful to smokers and also to nonsmokers.
>
> **UNDERLYING REASON:** People should be protected from harmful substances.

Evidence. Evidence to support your reasons can come from various sources. In fact, you may need to use several kinds of evidence to persuade your audience that your claim is true. Some of the most common types of evidence include facts, statistics, examples, authorities, anecdotes, scenarios, case studies, textual evidence, and visuals.

Facts are ideas that are proven to be true. Facts can include observations or scholarly research (your own or someone else's), but they need to be accepted as true. If your audience accepts the facts you present, they can be powerful means of persuasion. For example, an essay on the problems faced by people who lose their senses of smell and taste offers these facts to demonstrate the seriousness of this loss:

> Smell is intimately tied to both taste and appetite, and anosmia often robs people of the pleasure of eating. But the sudden absence also may have a profound impact on mood and quality of life.
>
> Studies have linked anosmia to social isolation and anhedonia, an inability to feel pleasure, as well as a strange sense of detachment and isolation. Memories and emotions are intricately tied to smell, and the olfactory system plays an important though largely unrecognized role in emotional well-being, said Dr. Sandeep Robert Datta, an associate professor of neurobiology at Harvard Medical School.
>
> —Roni Caryn Rabin,
> "Some Covid Survivors Haunted by Loss of Smell and Taste"

Rabin quotes a specialist, which gives her facts credibility; citing the studies she refers to would provide even greater credibility.

Statistics are numerical data, usually produced through research, surveys, or polls. Statistics should be relevant to your argument, as current as possible, accurate, and obtained from a reliable source. An argument advocating that Americans should eat less meat presents these data to support the writer's contention that we eat far too much of it:

> Americans are downing close to 200 pounds of meat, poultry, and fish per capita per year (dairy and eggs are separate, and hardly insignificant), an increase of 50 pounds per person from 50 years ago. We each consume something like 110 grams of protein a day, about twice the federal government's recommended allowance; of that, about 75 grams come from animal protein. (The recommended level is itself considered by many dietary experts to be higher than it needs to be.) It's likely that most of us would do just fine on around 30 grams of protein a day, virtually all of it from plant sources.
>
> —Mark Bittman, "Rethinking the Meat-Guzzler"

Bittman's statistics demonstrate the extent to which Americans have increased their meat consumption over the last half century, the proportion of our diets that comes from meat, and, by comparison, how much protein our bodies require—and summarize the heart of his argument in stark numeric terms.

Examples are specific instances that illustrate general statements. In a book on life after dark in Europe, a historian offers several examples to demonstrate his point that 300 years ago, night—without artificial lighting—was treacherous:

> Even sure-footed natives on a dark night could misjudge the lay of the land, stumbling into a ditch or off a precipice. In Aberdeenshire, a fifteen-year-old girl died in 1739 after straying from her customary path through a churchyard and tumbling into a newly dug grave. The Yorkshireman Arthur Jessop, returning from a neighbor's home on a cold December evening, fell into a stone pit after losing his bearings.
>
> —A. Roger Ekirch, *At Day's Close: Night in Times Past*

Ekirch illustrates his point and makes it come alive for readers by citing two specific individuals' fates.

Authorities are experts on your subject. To be useful, authorities must be reputable, trustworthy, and qualified to address the subject. You should carefully **EVALUATE** any authorities you consult to be sure they have the credentials necessary for readers to take them seriously. When citing experts, you should clearly identify them and the origins of their authority in a **SIGNAL PHRASE**, as does the author of an argument that deforested land can be reclaimed:

504–14

529–39

> Reed Funk, professor of plant biology at Rutgers University, believes that the vast areas of deforested land can be used to grow millions of genetically improved trees for food, mostly nuts, and for fuel. Funk sees nuts used to supplement meat as a source of high-quality protein in developing-country diets.
>
> —Lester R. Brown, *Plan B 2.0: Rescuing a Planet under Stress and a Civilization in Trouble*

Access Chapter 51 in the ebook for a video on introducing and explaining quotations.

Brown cites Funk, an expert on plant biology, to support his argument that humans need to rethink the global economy in order to create a sustainable world. Without the information on Funk's credentials, though, readers would have no reason to take his proposal seriously.

Anecdotes are brief **NARRATIVES** that your audience will find believable and that contribute directly to your argument. Anecdotes may come from your personal experience or the experiences of others. In an essay arguing that community colleges shouldn't drop the word "community" from their name, journalist Anna Clark opens with an anecdote about her parents' experiences with community college:

◆ 457–64

▶ **Access the ebook for a video on using personal stories in academic writing.**

> My parents took turns going to college. While raising three kids, my father lost his left big toe in an accident at a tool-and-die shop and Mom babysat dozens of neighborhood rugrats. We didn't have enough. The kitchen cabinets were too bare. So, Dad signed up for classes at Lake Michigan College, the local two-year school formerly known as Benton Harbor Community College.
>
> With his hands cupping his chin at a lamplit table, he softly read aloud from his textbooks; for years, his murmuring carried down the hallway to my bedroom, like a lullaby. When I was 11, he earned his bachelor's degree through an extension program hosted by LMC and got a job at Whirlpool Corporation. Then it was Mom's turn. She did her homework alongside my siblings and I at the kitchen table. The same year I graduated high school, she earned her associate's degree, on her way to her own B.A. My mother and I posed in front of the fireplace, each in cap and gown, grinning for the camera, for each other, for wherever it was we were headed next.
>
> —Anna Clark, "Why We Need to Keep the 'Community' in Community Colleges"

Clark uses this anecdote to illustrate one of the main points of her argument: that community colleges are cornerstones of the local community and "deserve to be taken on their own terms."

Scenarios are hypothetical situations. Like anecdotes, "what if?" scenarios can help you describe the possible effects of particular actions or offer new ways of looking at a particular state of affairs. For example, a mathematician presents this lighthearted scenario about Santa Claus in a tongue-in-cheek argument that Christmas is (almost) pure magic:

> Let's assume that Santa only visits those who are children in the eyes of the law, that is, those under the age of 18. There are roughly 2 billion such individuals in the world. However, Santa started his annual activities long before diversity and equal opportunity became issues, and as a result he doesn't handle Muslim, Hindu, Jewish and Buddhist children. That reduces his workload significantly to a mere

15% of the total, namely 378 million. However, the crucial figure is not the number of children but the number of homes Santa has to visit. According to the most recent census data, the average size of a family in the world is 3.5 children per household. Thus, Santa has to visit 108,000,000 individual homes. (Of course, as everyone knows, Santa only visits good children, but we can surely assume that, on an average, at least one child of the 3.5 in each home meets that criterion.)

—Keith Devlin, "The Mathematics of Christmas"

Devlin uses this scenario, part of his mathematical analysis of Santa's yearly task, to help demonstrate that Christmas is indeed magical—because if you do the math, it's clear that Santa's task is physically impossible.

Case studies and observations feature detailed reporting about a subject. Case studies are in-depth, systematic examinations of an occasion, a person, or a group. For example, in arguing that class differences exist in the United States, sociologist Gregory Mantsios presents studies of three "typical" Americans to show "enormous class differences" in their lifestyles.

Observations offer detailed descriptions of a subject. Here's an observation of the emergence of a desert stream that flows only at night:

At about 5:30 water came out of the ground. It did not spew up, but slowly escaped into the surrounding sand and small rocks. The wet circle grew until water became visible. Then it bubbled out like a small fountain and the creek began.

— Craig Childs, *The Secret Knowledge of Water*

Childs presents this and other observations in a book that argues (among other things) that even in harsh, arid deserts, water exists, and knowing where to find it can mean the difference between life and death.

521–32 *Textual evidence* includes **QUOTATIONS**, **PARAPHRASES**, and **SUMMARIES**. Usually, the relevance of textual evidence must be stated directly, as excerpts from a text may carry several potential meanings. For example, here is an excerpt from a student essay analyzing the function of the raft in *Huckleberry Finn* as "a platform on which the resolution of conflicts is made possible":

[T]he scenes where Jim and Huck are in consensus on the raft contain the moments in which they are most relaxed. For instance, in chapter 12 of the novel, Huck, after escaping capture from Jackson's Island, calls the rafting life "solemn" and articulates their experience as living "pretty high" (Twain 75–76). Likewise, subsequent to escaping the unresolved feud between the Grangerfords and Shepherdsons in chapter 18, Huck is unquestionably at ease on the raft: "I was powerful glad to get away from the feuds. . . . We said there warn't no home like a raft, after all. Other places do seem so cramped up and smothery, but a raft don't. You feel mighty free and easy and comfortable on a raft" (134).

—Dave Nichols, "'Less All Be Friends': Rafts as Negotiating Platforms in Twain's *Huckleberry Finn*"

Huck's own words support Nichols's claim that he can relax on a raft. Nichols strengthens his claim by quoting evidence from two separate pages, suggesting that Huck's opinion of rafts pervades the novel.

Visuals can be a useful way of presenting evidence. Remember, though, that charts, graphs, photos, drawings, and other **VISUAL TEXTS** seldom speak for themselves and thus must be explained in your text. For example, the image below is a photograph of a poster carried by demonstrators at the 2008 Beijing Summer Olympics, protesting China's treatment of Tibetans. If you were to use this photo in an essay, you would need to explain that the poster combines the image of a protester standing before a tank during the 1989 Tiananmen Square uprising with the Olympic logo, making clear to your readers that the protesters are likening China's treatment of Tibetans to its brutal actions in the past. Similarly, you could use the image on the next page to make an argument about the burdens American teachers carry.

648–54

Choosing appropriate evidence. The kinds of evidence you provide to support your argument depend on your **RHETORICAL SITUATION**. If your purpose is, for example, to convince readers to accept the need for a proposed solution, you'd be likely to include facts, statistics, and anecdotes. If you're writing for an academic audience, you'd be less likely to rely on anecdotes, preferring authorities, textual evidence, statistics, and case studies instead. And even within academic communities, different disciplines and genres may focus primarily on different kinds of evidence. If you're not sure what counts as appropriate evidence, ask your instructor for guidance.

■ 71

Arguing with a Hostile Audience

Academic arguments are often presented to an audience that is presumed to be open-minded and fair, and the goal of such arguments is to demonstrate that your position is plausible and reasonable. Sometimes, though, your goal is to change people's minds, to try to get them to see some issue differently. That can be more of a challenge, because your audience likely has good reasons for thinking as they do, or their views reflect their basic values, and they may well feel defensive, angry, or threatened when you challenge them. These situations call for different argumentative strategies, such as Rogerian argument.

Rogerian argument. This method of presenting an argument is based on the work of psychologist Carl Rogers. The method assumes that common ground—areas of shared values or beliefs—exists between people who disagree. If they can find that common ground, they're more likely to come to some agreement or compromise position.

Since the goal of a Rogerian argument is to find compromise, it is organized differently than a traditional argument. First you must show that you understand your opponents' position, and then you offer your own position. Here's how a typical Rogerian argument is organized; be aware that each section may require several paragraphs:

Introduction. Here you introduce the issue, acknowledging the various sides of the controversy and being as fair as you can.

Describe the opposing view. In this section, you try to capture the opposing view as accurately and as neutrally as you can. There may be circumstances when that view might be valid, and you should include them, too. Your goal here is to show that you understand the opposing view, and why your readers hold that view, convincingly enough that they will agree that it's accurate. By doing so, you establish your credibility and honest desire to understand those whose views differ from yours.

342–44

State your THESIS and support it.   Now it's time to outline your position and defend it with reasons and evidence. As with a traditional argument, your goal here is to show that you have thought carefully about your position and researched it thoroughly. As with all arguing, your **TONE** should show your openness to ideas and avoid sounding as if you and you alone know the truth about the issue or that you are intellectually or morally superior to your opponent.

86 ■

Conclude.   In your concluding section, you bring together the two perspectives you've just outlined to show how, while your opponent's views have merit, your position deals with the issue or solves the problem in a better way—or how a compromise position, somewhere in the middle, allows both sides to benefit.

You may find value in using Rogerian techniques in traditional arguments, including seeking common ground, describing issues and positions in neutral terms, and addressing those with opposing views respectfully and with goodwill.

Convincing Readers You're Trustworthy

For your argument to be convincing, you have to establish your own credibility with readers (also known as *ethos*)—to demonstrate your knowledge about the topic, to show that you and your readers share some common ground, and to show yourself to be evenhanded in the way you present your argument.

Building common ground.   One important element of gaining readers' trust involves identifying some common ground, some values you and your audience share. For example, to introduce a book arguing for the compatibility of science and religion, author Chet Raymo offers some common memories:

> Like most children, I was raised on miracles. Cows that jump over the moon; a jolly fat man that visits every house in the world in a single night; mice and ducks that talk; little engines that huff and puff and say, "I think I can"; geese that lay golden eggs. This lively exercise of credulity on the part of children is good practice for what follows—for

believing in the miracle stories of traditional religion, yes, but also for the practice of poetry or science.

—Chet Raymo, *Skeptics and True Believers: The Exhilarating Connection between Science and Religion*

Raymo presents childhood stories and myths that are part of many people's shared experiences to help his readers find a connection between two realms that are often seen as opposed.

Acknowledging, accommodating, and refuting other viewpoints. To show that you have carefully considered the viewpoints of others, including those who may agree or disagree with you, it's important to incorporate those viewpoints into your argument by acknowledging, accommodating, or refuting them.

Acknowledging. One essential part of establishing your credibility is to acknowledge that there are viewpoints different from yours and to represent them fairly and accurately. Rather than weakening your argument, acknowledging possible objections to your position shows that you've thought about and researched your topic thoroughly. For example, in an essay about his experience growing up homosexual, writer Andrew Sullivan admits that not every young gay man or woman has the same experience:

> I should add that many young lesbians and homosexuals seem to have had a much easier time of it. For many, the question of sexual identity was not a critical factor in their life choices or vocation, or even a factor at all.
>
> —Andrew Sullivan, "What Is a Homosexual?"

In response to a reasonable objection, Sullivan qualifies his assertions, making his own stance appear to be reasonable.

Accommodating. You may be tempted to ignore views you don't agree with, but in fact it's important to demonstrate that you're aware of them and have considered them carefully. You may find yourself conceding that opposing views have some merit and qualifying your claim or even making them part of your own argument. See, for example, how a philosopher arguing that torture is sometimes "not merely permissible but morally mandatory" addresses a major objection to his position:

Access Chapter 3 in the ebook for a video on responding to the views of others.

The most powerful argument against using torture as a punishment or to secure confessions is that such practices disregard the rights of the individual. Well, if the individual is all that important—and he is—it is correspondingly important to protect the rights of individuals threatened by terrorists. If life is so valuable that it must never be taken, the lives of the innocents must be saved even at the price of hurting the one who endangers them.

—Michael Levin, "The Case for Torture"

Levin acknowledges his critics' argument that the individual is indeed important; but he then asserts that if the life of one person is important, the lives of many people must be even more important. In effect, he uses an opposing argument to advance his own.

Refuting.   Often you may need to refute other arguments and make a case for why you believe they are wrong. Are the values underlying the argument questionable? Is the reasoning flawed? Is the evidence inadequate or faulty? For example, an essay arguing that colleges and universities need to do a better job of supporting students with disabilities includes this refutation:

Access Chapter 15 in the ebook for a video on anticipating counterarguments.

Although schools may claim that they provide sufficient support, there are several instances where a lack of federal oversight lets students fall through the cracks. For instance, note-taking services are relatively common accommodations, but many students report difficulty receiving notes from peer note-takers at all (Scott, 2019). When students do receive notes, they often are incomplete or inaccessible. For example, on one memorable occasion, I saw notes submitted in illegible neon purple cursive handwriting. In other words, schools may be fully complying with the law, and yet student needs are not adequately met. Administrators can also find loopholes in the law, such as refusing to provide accommodations or dismissing the need to renovate inaccessible buildings by exaggerating the burden it will create—on the institution.

—Yael Lenga, "Disability in Higher Education: Building Access and Building Futures"

Lenga bases her refutation on examples and personal experiences showing that students with disabilities don't always receive appropriate or effective accommodations, even when schools comply with federal disability rights laws.

When you incorporate differing viewpoints, be careful to avoid the **FALLACIES** of attacking the person making the argument or refuting

413–15 ◆

a competing position that no one seriously entertains. It's also important that you not distort or exaggerate opposing viewpoints. If *your* argument is to be persuasive, other arguments should be represented fairly.

Appealing to Readers' Emotions

Logic and facts, even when presented by someone who seems reasonable and trustworthy, may not be enough to persuade readers. Many successful arguments include an emotional component that appeals to readers' hearts as well as to their minds. Advertising often works by appealing to its audience's emotions, as in this paragraph from a Volvo ad:

> Choosing a car is about the comfort and safety of your passengers, most especially your children. That's why we ensure Volvo's safety research examines how we can make our cars safer for everyone who travels in them—from adults to teenagers, children to babies. Even those who aren't even born yet.
>
> —*Volvo.com*

This ad plays on the fear that children—or a pregnant mother—may be injured or killed in an automobile accident.

Keep in mind that emotional appeals, also known as *pathos*, can make readers feel as though they're being manipulated and, consequently, less likely to accept an argument. For most kinds of academic writing, use emotional appeals sparingly.

Checking for Fallacies

Fallacies are arguments that involve faulty reasoning. It's important to avoid fallacies in your writing because they often seem plausible but are usually unfair or inaccurate and make reasonable discussion difficult. Here are some of the most common fallacies:

- **Ad hominem** arguments attack someone's character rather than address the issues. ("Ad hominem" is Latin for "to the man.") It's an especially common fallacy in political discourse and elsewhere: "Jack Turner has no business talking about the way we run things in this city. He's just another liberal snowflake." Whether or not Turner is a "liberal snowflake" has no bearing on the worth of his argument about "the way we run things in this city"; insulting one's opponents isn't an argument against their positions. A variation, the "you too" or "whataboutism" fallacy, results when someone responds to criticism by accusing the attacker of hypocrisy but not answering the criticism itself: "You say I'm lying, but what about your use of a company car to take a family vacation?"

- *Bandwagon appeals* argue that because others think or do something, we should, too. For example, an advertisement for a breakfast cereal claims that it is "America's favorite cereal." It assumes that readers want to be part of the group and implies that an opinion that's popular must be correct.

- *Begging the question* is a circular argument. It assumes as a given what is trying to be proved, essentially asserting that A is true because A is true. Consider this statement: "Affirmative action can never be fair or just because you cannot remedy one injustice by committing another." This statement begs the question because in trying to prove that affirmative action is unjust, it assumes that it is an injustice.

- *Either-or* arguments, also called *false dilemmas*, are oversimplifications that assert there can be only two possible positions on a complex issue. For example, "Those who oppose our actions in this war are enemies of freedom" inaccurately assumes that if someone opposes the war in question, they oppose freedom. In fact, people might have many other reasons for opposing the war.

- *False analogies* compare things that resemble each other in some ways but not in the most important respects—for example, "Trees pollute the air just as much as cars and trucks do." Although it's true that plants emit hydrocarbons, and hydrocarbons are a component of smog, plants also produce oxygen, whereas motor vehicles emit gases that combine with hydrocarbons to form smog. Vehicles pollute the air; trees provide the air that vehicles' emissions pollute.

- *Faulty causality,* also known as *post hoc, ergo propter hoc* (Latin for "after this, therefore because of this"), assumes that because one event followed another, the first event caused the second—for example, "Legalizing same-sex marriage in Sweden led to a decline in the marriage rate of opposite-sex couples." The statement contains no evidence to show that the first event caused the second.

- *Straw man* arguments misrepresent an opposing position to make it sound ridiculous or extreme and thus easy to refute, rather than dealing with the actual position. For example, if someone argues that funding for supplemental nutrition assistance should be cut, a straw man response would be "You want the poor to starve," transforming a proposal to cut a specific program into an exaggerated argument that the proposer hasn't made.

- *Hasty generalizations* are conclusions based on insufficient or inappropriately qualified evidence. This summary of a research study is a good example: "Twenty randomly chosen residents of Brooklyn, New York, were asked whether they found graffiti tags offensive; fourteen said yes, five said no, and one had no opinion. Therefore, 70 percent of Brooklyn residents find tagging offensive." In Brooklyn, a part of New York City with a population of over 2 million, twenty residents is far too small a group from which to draw meaningful conclusions. To be able to generalize, the researcher would have had to survey a much greater percentage of Brooklyn's population.

- *Slippery slope* arguments assert that one event will inevitably lead to another, often cataclysmic event without presenting evidence that such a chain of causes and effects will in fact take place. Here's an example: "If the state legislature passes this 2 percent tax increase, it won't be long before all the corporations in the state move to other states and leave thousands unemployed." According to this argument, if taxes are raised, the state's economy will be ruined—not a likely scenario, given the size of the proposed increase.

Considering the Rhetorical Situation

To argue effectively, it's important to think about the message you want to articulate, the audience you want to persuade, the effect of your stance, and the larger context you are writing in.

PURPOSE
What do you want your audience to do? To think a certain way? To take a certain action? To change their minds? To consider alternative views to their current ones? To accept your position as plausible? To see that you have thought carefully about an issue and researched it appropriately?

73–74

AUDIENCE
Who is your intended audience? What do they likely know and believe about your topic? How personal is it for them? To what extent are they likely to agree or disagree with you? Why? What common ground can you find with them? How should you incorporate other viewpoints they might have? What kinds of evidence are they likely to accept?

75–78

GENRE   What genre will help you achieve your purpose? A
position paper? An evaluation? A review? A proposal?
An analysis?

STANCE   What's your attitude toward your topic, and why?
What strategies will help you to convey that stance?
How do you want your audience to perceive you? As
an authority on your topic? As someone much like
them? As calm? reasonable? impassioned or angry?
something else?

MEDIA / DESIGN   What media will you use, and how will your choice of
media affect your argument? If you're writing on paper,
does your argument call for photos or charts? If you're
giving an oral presentation, should you put your reasons
and support on slides? If you're writing online, should
you add links to sites representing other positions or
containing evidence that supports your position?

If you need more help

See also Chapter 15 for advice on writing an **ARGUMENT** essay. And see other appropriate
GENRE chapters and all the **PROCESSES** chapters for guidelines on drafting, revising, and
so on for help writing an essay that includes arguments.

39 Classifying and Dividing

Classification and division are ways of organizing information: various items may be classified according to their similarities, or a single topic may be divided into parts. We might classify different kinds of flowers as annuals or perennials, for example, and classify the perennials further as daylilies, irises, roses, and peonies. We might also divide a garden into distinct areas: for herbs, flowers, and vegetables.

Writers often use classification and division as ways of developing and organizing material. This book, for instance, classifies comparison, definition, description, and several other common ways of thinking and writing as strategies. It divides the information it provides about writing into eight parts: "Rhetorical Situations," "Genres," and so on. Each part further divides its material into various chapters. Even if you never write a book, you will have occasion to classify and divide material in **ANNOTATED BIBLIOGRAPHIES**, essays **ANALYZING TEXTS**, and other kinds of writing. This chapter offers advice for classifying and dividing information for various purposes—and in a way that suits your own rhetorical situation.

▲ 197–206
114–45

Classifying

When we classify something, we group it with similar things. A linguist would classify French, Spanish, and Italian as Romance languages, for example—and Russian, Polish, and Bulgarian as Slavic languages. In a phony news story from the *Onion* about a church bake sale, the writer classifies the activities observed there as examples of the seven deadly sins:

> GADSDEN, AL—The seven deadly sins—avarice, sloth, envy, lust, gluttony, pride, and wrath—were all committed Sunday during the twice-annual bake sale at St. Mary's of the Immaculate Conception Church.
>
> —"All Seven Deadly Sins Committed at Church Bake Sale,"
> *Onion*

The article goes on to categorize the participants' behavior in terms of the sins, describing one parishioner who commits the sin of pride by bragging about her cookies and others who commit the sin of envy by resenting the popularity of the prideful parishioner's baked goods (the eating of which leads to the sin of gluttony). In all, the article humorously notes, "347 individual acts of sin were committed at the bake sale," and every one of them can be classified as one of the seven deadly sins.

Dividing

As a writing strategy, division is a way of breaking something into parts—and a way of making the information easy for readers to follow and understand. See how this example about children's ways of nagging divides their tactics into seven categories:

> James U. McNeal, a professor of marketing at Texas A&M University, is considered America's leading authority on marketing to children. In his book *Kids as Customers* (1992), McNeal provides marketers with a thorough analysis of "children's requesting styles and appeals." He [divides] juvenile nagging tactics into seven major categories. A *pleading* nag is one accompanied by repetitions of words like "please" or "mom, mom, mom." A *persistent* nag involves constant requests for the coveted product and may include the phrase "I'm gonna ask just one more time." *Forceful* nags are extremely pushy and may include subtle threats, like "Well, then, I'll go and ask Dad." *Demonstrative* nags are the most high risk, often characterized by full-blown tantrums in public places, breath holding, tears, a refusal to leave the store. *Sugar-coated* nags promise affection in return for a purchase and may rely on seemingly heartfelt declarations, like "You're the best dad in the world." *Threatening* nags are youthful forms of blackmail, vows of eternal hatred and of running away if something isn't bought. *Pity* nags claim the child will be heartbroken, teased, or socially stunted if the parent refuses to buy a certain item. "All of these appeals and styles may be used in combination," McNeal's research has discovered, "but kids tend to stick to one or two of each that prove most effective . . . for their own parents."
>
> —Eric Schlosser, *Fast Food Nation:*
> *The Dark Side of the All-American Meal*

Here the writer announces the division scheme of "seven major categories." Then he names each tactic and describes how it works. Notice the italics: each tactic is italicized, making it easy to recognize and follow. Take away the italics, and the divisions would be less visible.

Creating Clear and Distinct Categories

When you classify or divide, it's important to create clear and distinct categories. If you're writing about music, you might divide it on the basis of the genre (hip-hop, rock, classical, gospel), artist (male or female, group or solo), or instruments (violins, trumpets, bongos, guitars). These categories must be distinct so that no information overlaps or fits into more than one category, and they must include every member of the group you're discussing. The simpler the criteria for selecting the categories, the better. The nagging categories in the example from *Fast Food Nation* are based on only one criterion: a child's nagging behavior.

Sometimes you may want to highlight your categories visually to make them easier to follow. Eric Schlosser does that by italicizing each category: the *pleading* nag, the *persistent* nag, the *forceful* nag, and so on. Other **DESIGN** elements—bulleted lists, pie charts, tables, images—might also prove useful.

640–46

Sometimes you might show categories visually, as in the following chart. The differences among the six apple varieties pictured are visible at a glance, and the chart next to the photos shows the best uses for each variety—and its level of tartness.

	EATING	BAKING	COOKING	
Red Delicious	✔	✔		LESS TART
Honeycrisp	✔	✔	✔	
Red Rome		✔	✔	
Braeburn	✔		✔	
McIntosh	✔	✔	✔	MORE TART

All photos © New York Apple Association.

The photographs allow us to see the differences among the varieties at a glance. Although the varieties shown here are arranged according to the tartness of their flavor, they could have been arranged in other ways, too—for example, alphabetically or by shape or size.

For another example, see how *The World of Caffeine* authors Bennett Alan Weinberg and Bonnie K. Bealer use a two-column list to show what they say are the differing cultural connotations of coffee and tea:

Coffee Aspect	Tea Aspect
Male	Female
Boisterous	Decorous
Indulgence	Temperance
Hardheaded	Romantic
Topology	Geometry
Heidegger	Carnap
Beethoven	Mozart
Libertarian	Statist
Promiscuous	Pure

—Bennett Alan Weinberg and Bonnie K. Bealer,
The World of Caffeine

Considering the Rhetorical Situation

As a writer or speaker, it's important to think about the message you want to articulate, the audience you want to reach, and the larger context you are writing in.

73–74 ◼ **PURPOSE** Your purpose for writing will affect how you classify or divide information. Weinberg and Bealer classify coffee as "boisterous" and tea as "decorous" to help readers understand the cultural styles the two beverages represent, whereas J. Crew might divide sweaters into cashmere, wool, and cotton to help shoppers find and buy clothing from its website.

75–78 ◼ **AUDIENCE** Who do you want to reach, and will classifying or dividing your material help them follow your discussion?

GENRE   Does your genre call for you to categorize or divide information? A long report might need to be divided into sections, for instance.

79–84

STANCE   Your stance may affect the way you classify information. Weinberg and Bealer's classification of coffee as "Beethoven" and tea as "Mozart" reflects a stance that focuses on cultural analysis (and assumes an audience familiar with the difference between the two composers). If the authors were botanists, they might categorize the two beverages in terms of their biological origins ("seed based" and "leaf based").

85–87

MEDIA/DESIGN   You can classify or divide in paragraph form, but sometimes a pie chart or list will show the categories better.

88–90

If you need more help

See also **CLUSTERING**, **CUBING**, and **LOOPING**, three methods of generating ideas discussed in Chapter 29 that can be especially helpful for classifying material. And see all the **PROCESSES** chapters for guidelines on drafting, revising, and so on if you need to write a classification essay.

330–31
332
331
321

40 Comparing and Contrasting

Comparing things looks at their similarities; contrasting them focuses on their differences. It's a kind of thinking that comes naturally and that we do constantly—for example, comparing Houston with Dallas, iPhones with Androids, or three paintings by Renoir. And once we start comparing, we generally find ourselves contrasting—Houston and Dallas have differences as well as similarities.

257–69

210–19

As a student, you'll often be asked to compare and contrast paintings or poems or other things. As a writer, you'll have cause to compare and contrast in most kinds of writing. In a **PROPOSAL**, for instance, you'll need to compare your solution with other possible solutions; or in an **EVALUATION**, such as a movie review, you might contrast the film you're reviewing with some other film. This chapter offers advice on ways of comparing and contrasting things for various writing purposes and for your own rhetorical situations.

Most of the time, we compare obviously similar things: laptops we might purchase, three competing political candidates, two versions of a film. Occasionally, however, we might compare things that are less obviously similar. See how John McMurtry, a former football player, compares football with war in an essay arguing that the attraction football holds for spectators is based in part on its potential for violence and injury:

> The family resemblance between football and war is, indeed, striking. Their languages are similar: "field general," "long bomb," "blitz," "take a shot," "front line," "pursuit," "good hit," "the draft," and so on. Their principles and practices are alike: mass hysteria, the art of intimidation, absolute command and total obedience, territorial aggression, censorship, inflated insignia and propaganda, blackboard maneuvers and strategies, drills, uniforms, marching bands, and training camps. And the virtues they celebrate are almost identical: hyperaggressiveness, coolness under fire, and suicidal bravery.
>
> —John McMurtry, "Kill 'Em! Crush 'Em! Eat 'Em Raw!"

McMurtry's comparison helps focus readers' attention on what he's arguing about football in part because it's somewhat unexpected. But the more unlikely the comparison, the more you might be accused of comparing apples and oranges. It's important, therefore, that the things we compare be *legitimately* compared—as is the case in the following comparison of the health of the world's richest and poorest people:

> World Health Organization (WHO) data [from 2006] indicate that roughly 1.2 billion people are undernourished, underweight, and often hungry. At the same time, roughly 1.2 billion people are overnourished and overweight, most of them suffering from excessive caloric intake and exercise deprivation. So while 1 billion people worry whether they will eat, another billion should worry about eating too much.
>
> Disease patterns also reflect the widening gap. The billion poorest suffer mostly from infectious diseases—malaria, tuberculosis, dysentery, and AIDS. Malnutrition leaves infants and small children even more vulnerable to such infectious diseases. Unsafe drinking water takes a heavier toll on those with hunger-weakened immune systems, resulting in millions of fatalities each year. In contrast, among the billion at the top of the global economic scale, it is diseases related to aging and lifestyle excesses, including obesity, smoking, diets rich in fat and sugar, and exercise deprivation, that cause most deaths.
>
> —Lester R. Brown, *Plan B 2.0: Rescuing a Planet under Stress and a Civilization in Trouble*

While the two groups of roughly a billion people each undoubtedly have similarities, this selection from a book arguing for global action on the environment focuses on the stark contrasts.

Two Ways of Comparing and Contrasting

Comparisons and contrasts may be organized in two basic ways: block and point by point.

The block method.   One way is to discuss separately each item you're comparing, giving all the information about one item and then all the information about the next item. A report on Americans' changing perception of the value of college, for example, compares perceptions from the early 2010s with perceptions a decade later, using one paragraph for each time period:

> A decade or so ago, Americans were feeling pretty positive about higher education. Public-opinion polls in the early 2010s all told the same story.

In one survey, 86 percent of college graduates said that college had been a good investment; in another, 74 percent of young adults said a college education was "very important"; in a third, 60 percent of Americans said that colleges and universities were having a positive impact on the country. Ninety-six percent of parents who identified as Democrats said they expected their kids to attend college—only to be outdone by Republican parents, 99 percent of whom said they expected their kids to go to college. . . .

A decade later, Americans' feelings about higher education have turned sharply negative. The percentage of young adults who said that a college degree is very important fell to 41 percent from 74 percent. Only about a third of Americans now say they have a lot of confidence in higher education. Among young Americans in Generation Z, 45 percent say that a high school diploma is all you need today to "ensure financial security." And in contrast to the college-focused parents of a decade ago, now almost half of American parents say they'd prefer that their children not enroll in a four-year college.

—Paul Tough, "Americans Are Losing Faith in the Value of College. Whose Fault Is That?"

The point-by-point method. The other way to compare things is to focus on specific points of comparison. In this paragraph, humorist David Sedaris compares his childhood with his partner's, discussing corresponding aspects of the childhoods one at a time:

Certain events are parallel, but compared with Hugh's, my childhood was unspeakably dull. When I was seven years old, my family moved to North Carolina. When he was seven years old, Hugh's family moved to the Congo. We had a collie and a house cat. They had a monkey and two horses named Charlie Brown and Satan. I threw stones at stop signs. Hugh threw stones at crocodiles. The verbs are the same, but he definitely wins the prize when it comes to nouns and objects. An eventful day for my mother might have involved a trip to the dry cleaner or a conversation with the potato-chip deliveryman. Asked one ordinary Congo afternoon what she'd done with her day, Hugh's mother answered that she and a fellow member of the Ladies' Club had visited a leper colony on the outskirts of Kinshasa.

—David Sedaris, "Remembering My Childhood on the Continent of Africa"

Using Graphs and Images to Present Comparisons

Some comparisons can be easier to understand if they're presented visually, as a **CHART**, **GRAPH**, or **ILLUSTRATION**. For example, the following bar graph, from the US Bureau of Labor Statistics, compares median weekly earnings and unemployment rates by education level in 2022. It would be possible to write out this information in a paragraph—but it's much easier to understand it this way:

648–54

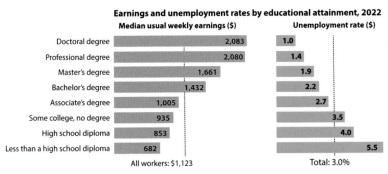

Earnings and unemployment rates by educational attainment, 2022

	Median usual weekly earnings ($)	Unemployment rate ($)
Doctoral degree	2,083	1.0
Professional degree	2,080	1.4
Master's degree	1,661	1.9
Bachelor's degree	1,432	2.2
Associate's degree	1,005	2.7
Some college, no degree	935	3.5
High school diploma	853	4.0
Less than a high school diploma	682	5.5
	All workers: $1,123	Total: 3.0%

Source: US Bureau of Labor Statistics, Current Population Survey, 2022.

Sometimes photographs can make a comparison. The two photos below show a portion of the Lahaina Historic District before and after the Maui wildfires in 2023.

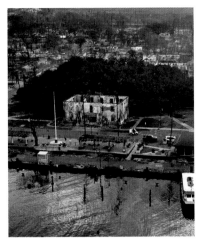

Central Lahaina, Hawaii, before the 2023 wildfires (left) and after (right).

Using Figurative Language to Make Comparisons

Another way to make comparisons is with figurative language: words and phrases used in a nonliteral way to help readers see a point. Three kinds of figurative language that make comparisons are similes, metaphors, and analogies. When Robert Burns wrote that his love was "like a red, red rose," he was comparing his love with a rose and evoking an image—in this case, a simile—that helps us understand his feelings for her. A simile makes a comparison using "like" or "as." In the following example, from an article in the food section of the *New York Times*, a restaurant critic uses several similes (underlined) to help us visualize an unusual food dish:

> Once upon a time, possibly at a lodge in Wyoming, possibly at a butcher shop in Maurice, Louisiana, or maybe even at a plantation in South Carolina, an enterprising cook decided to take a boned chicken, a boned duck, and a boned turkey, stuff them one inside the other <u>like Russian dolls</u>, and roast them. He called his masterpiece turducken. . . .
>
> A well-prepared turducken is a marvelous treat, a free-form poultry terrine layered with flavorful stuffing and moistened with duck fat. When it's assembled, it looks <u>like a turkey</u> and it roasts <u>like a turkey</u>, but when you go to carve it, you can slice through it <u>like a loaf of bread</u>. In each slice you get a little bit of everything: white meat from the breast, dark meat from the legs, duck, carrots, bits of sausage, bread, herbs, juices, and chicken, too.
>
> —Amanda Hesser,
> "Turkey Finds Its Inner Duck (and Chicken)"

Metaphors make comparisons without such connecting words as "like" or "as." See how desert ecologist Craig Childs uses a metaphor to help us understand the nature of water during a flood in the Grand Canyon:

> Water splashed off the desert and ran all over the surface, looking for the quickest way down. It was too swift for the ground to absorb. When water flows like this, it will not be clean tap water. It will be <u>a gravy of debris</u>, snatching everything it finds.
>
> —Craig Childs, *The Secret Knowledge of Water*

Calling the water "a gravy of debris" allows us to see the murky liquid as it streams through the canyon.

Analogies are extended similes or metaphors that compare something unfamiliar with something more familiar. Arguing that corporations should not patent parts of DNA whose function isn't yet clear, a genetics professor uses the familiar image of a library to explain an unfamiliar concept:

> It's like having a library of books and randomly tearing pages out. You may know which books the pages came from but that doesn't tell you much about them.
>
> —Peter Goodfellow, quoted in John Vidal and
> John Carvel, "Lambs to the Gene Market"

Sometimes analogies are used for humorous effect as well as to make a point, as in this passage from a critique of history textbooks:

> Another history text—this one for fifth grade—begins with the story of how Henry B. Gonzalez, who is a member of Congress from Texas, learned about his own nationality. When he was ten years old, his teacher told him he was an American because he was born in the United States. His grandmother, however, said, "The cat was born in the oven. Does that make him bread?"
>
> —Frances FitzGerald, *America Revised:
> History Schoolbooks in the Twentieth Century*

The grandmother's question illustrates how an intentionally ridiculous analogy can be a source of humor—and can make a point memorably.

Considering the Rhetorical Situation

As a writer or speaker, it's important to think about the message you want to articulate, the audience you want to reach, and the larger context you are writing in.

PURPOSE   Sometimes your main purpose for writing will be to compare two or more things. Other times, you may want to compare several things for some other purpose—to compare your views with those of others in an argument essay or to compare one text with another as you analyze them.

■ 73–74

▶ Access
Chapter 30
in the ebook
for a video on
comparison
and contrast
in supporting
sentences.

◼ **AUDIENCE**   Who is your audience, and will comparing your topic with a more familiar one help them to follow your discussion?

◼ **GENRE**   Does your genre require you to compare something? Evaluations often include comparisons—one book to another in a review, or ten different cell phones in *Consumer Reports*.

◼ **STANCE**   Your stance may affect any comparisons you make. How you compare two things—evenhandedly, or clearly favoring one over the other, for example—will reflect your stance.

◼ **MEDIA/DESIGN**   Some things you'll want to compare with words alone (lines from two poems, for instance), but sometimes you may wish to make comparisons visually (two images juxtaposed on a page, or several numbers plotted on a line graph).

If you need more help

⁚

See **LOOPING** and **CUBING**, two methods of generating ideas discussed in Chapter 29 that can be especially helpful for comparing and contrasting. If you're writing an essay whose purpose is to compare two or more things, see also the **PROCESSES** chapters for help with drafting, revising, and so on.

41 Defining

Defining something says what it is—and what it is not. A terrier, for example, is a kind of dog. A fox terrier is a small dog now generally kept as a pet but once used by hunters to dig for foxes. Happiness is a pink frosted doughnut, at least according to Homer Simpson. All of those are definitions. As writers, we need to define any terms our readers may not know. And sometimes you'll want to stipulate your own definition of a word in order to set the terms of an **ARGUMENT**—as Homer Simpson does with a definition that's not found in any dictionary. This chapter details strategies for using definitions in your writing to suit your own rhetorical situations.

◆ 399–416

Formal Definitions

Sometimes to make sure readers understand you, you'll need to provide a formal definition. If you are using a technical term that readers are unlikely to know or if you are using a term in a specific way, you should say then and there what the word means. The word "mutual," for example, has several meanings: it can mean "shared" or "reciprocal," as when two people have mutual interests or have mutual respect. It can mean having the "same relationship toward one another," as when two people are mutual enemies. And it can refer to a type of organization in which profits, losses, and expenses are shared by the organization's members—a common form of insurance in which policyholders pay into a common fund that is used to pay insurance claims. (Examples might include companies like Mutual of Omaha and Liberty Mutual Insurance.)

The first two meanings are commonly understood and probably require no definition. But if you were to use "mutual" in the third sense, it might need to be defined, depending on your audience. A general audience would probably need the definition; an audience from the insurance industry would not. A website that gives basic financial advice to an audience of non-specialists, for instance, offers a specific definition of the term "mutual fund":

> *Mutual funds* are financial intermediaries. They are companies set up to receive your money and then, having received it, to make investments with the money.
>
> —Bill Barker, "A Grand, Comprehensive Overview to Mutual Funds Investing"

But even writers in specialized fields routinely provide formal definitions to make sure their readers understand the way they're using certain words. See how two writers define the word "stock" as it pertains to their respective (and very different) fields:

> Stocks are the basis for sauces and soups and important flavoring agents for braises. Admittedly, stock making is time consuming, but the extra effort yields great dividends.
>
> —Tom Colicchio, *Think Like a Chef*

> Want to own part of a business without having to show up at its office every day? Or ever? Stock is the vehicle of choice for those who do. Dating back to the Dutch mutual stock corporations of the sixteenth century, the modern stock market exists as a way for entrepreneurs to finance businesses using money collected from investors. In return for ponying up the dough to finance the company, the investor becomes a part owner of the company. That ownership is represented by stock—specialized financial "securities," or financial instruments, that are "secured" by a claim on the assets and profits of a company.
>
> —"Investing Basics: Stocks," *Motley Fool*

To write a formal definition

- Use words that readers are likely to be familiar with.
- Don't use the word being defined in the definition.
- Begin with the word being defined; include the general category to which the term belongs and the attributes that make it different from the others in that category, as in the following table:

Term	General Category	Distinguishing Attributes
"Stock" is	a specialized financial "security"	that is "secured" by a claim.
"Photosynthesis" is	a process	by which plants use sunlight to create energy.
"Astronomers" are	scientists	who study celestial objects and phenomena.
"Emma Stone,"	an actor,	has been featured in several films, including *Cruella* and *Poor Things*.

Note that the category and distinguishing attributes cannot be stated too broadly; if they were, the definition would be too vague to be useful. It wouldn't be helpful in most circumstances, for example, to say, "Emma Stone is a woman who has acted" or "Photosynthesis is something having to do with plants."

Extended Definitions

Sometimes it's useful to provide a more detailed definition. Extended definitions may be several sentences long or several paragraphs long and may include pictures or diagrams. Sometimes an entire essay is devoted to defining a difficult or important concept. Here is one writer's extended definition of "soul food":

> I've been eating soul food all my life and cooking it my whole career. I don't just know soul food. Soul food is *in* my soul. . . .
>
> By definition, soul food refers to the dishes of the Cotton Belt of Georgia, Mississippi, and Alabama that traveled out to the rest of the country during the Great Migration. (The term itself came around the middle of the twentieth century.) You know what travels well? Fried chicken. Mac and cheese. Delicious, but not what anyone's meant to eat every day. I'm here to redefine soul food, to reclaim it.
>
> Soul food is the true food of African-Americans.
>
> The roots of our cooking are in West Africa. And from there, the American South, from the slave ports along the eastern coast to the

southern border. We relied on seasonal vegetables, beans, and grains, with meat on rare occasions. Let's be clear: those were horrible times of suffering under the most unspeakable evil. I don't want to romanticize any of it. Not even the food. Remember, we didn't get to choose what we ate. But we made the most delicious dishes from what little we had. And what we cooked for the slave owners effectively became what we know as "American" food today.

—Carla Hall, *Carla Hall's Soul Food*

That definition includes a description of the basic features of soul food, examples of it, and the origin of the term. We can assume that it's written for a general audience, one that doesn't know much about soul food.

Abstract concepts often require extended definitions because by nature they are more complicated to define. There are many ways of writing an extended definition, depending in part on the term being defined and on the writer's audience and purpose. The following examples show some of the methods that can be used for composing extended definitions of "democracy."

Explore the word's origins. Where did the word come from? When did it first come into use? In the following example, from an essay considering what democracy means in the twenty-first century, the writer started by looking at the word's first known use in English. Though it's from an essay written for a first-year writing course and thus for a fairly general audience, it's a definition that might pique any audience's interest:

According to the *Oxford English Dictionary*, the term *democracy* first appeared in English in a thirteenth-century translation of Aristotle's works—specifically, in his *Politics*, where he stated that the "underlying principle of democracy is freedom" and that "it is customary to say that only in democracies do men have a share in freedom, for that is what every democracy makes its aim." By the sixteenth century, the word was used much as it is now. One writer in 1586, for instance, defined it in this way: "where free and poore men being the greater number, are lords of the estate."

—Susanna Mejía, "What Does Democracy Mean Now?"

Norman Rockwell's 1943 painting *Freedom of Speech* presents a visual definition of democracy: a citizen stands to speak at a public meeting while his fellow citizens listen attentively.

Here's another example, this one written for a scholarly audience, from an essay about women, participation, democracy, and the information age:

> The very word *citizenship* carries with it a connotation of place, a "citizen" being, literally, the inhabitant of a city. Over the years the word has, of course, accumulated a number of associated meanings . . . and the word has come to stand in for such concepts as participation, equality, and democracy. The fact that the concept of locality is deeply embedded in the word *citizen* suggests that it is also fundamental to our current understanding of these other, more apparently abstract words.
>
> In Western thought, the concepts of citizenship, equality, and democracy are closely interlinked and can be traced back to a common source, in Athens in the fifth century BCE. Perhaps it is no accident that it was the same culture which also gave us, in its theater, the concept of the unity of time and space. The Greek city-state has been represented for centuries as the ideal model of democracy, with free and equal access for all citizens to decision making. Leaving aside, for the moment, the question of who was included, and who excluded from this notion of citizenship, we can see that the sense of place is fundamental to this model. Entitlement to participate in the democratic process is circumscribed by geography; it is the inhabitants of the geographical entity of the city-state, precisely defined and bounded, who have the rights to citizenship. Those who are not defined as inhabitants of that specific city-state are explicitly excluded, although, of course, they may have the right to citizenship elsewhere.
>
> —Ursula Huws, "Women, Participation, and
> Democracy in the Information Society"

Provide details.   What are its characteristics? What is it made of? See how a historian explores the basic characteristics of democracy in a book written for an audience of historians:

> As a historian I am naturally disposed to be satisfied with the meaning which, in the history of politics, men have commonly attributed to the word—a meaning, needless to say, which derives partly from the experience and partly from the aspirations of mankind. So regarded, the term *democracy* refers primarily to a form of government, and it has always meant government by the many as opposed to government by the one—government by the people as opposed to government by

a tyrant, a dictator, or an absolute monarch. . . . Since the Greeks first used the term, the essential test of democratic government has always been this: the source of political authority must be and remain in the people and not in the ruler. A democratic government has always meant one in which the citizens, or a sufficient number of them to represent more or less effectively the common will, freely act from time to time, and according to established forms, to appoint or recall the magistrates and to enact or revoke the laws by which the community is governed.

—Carl Becker, *Modern Democracy*

Compare it with other words. How is this concept like other similar things? How does it differ? What is it *not* like? **COMPARE AND CONTRAST** it. See how a political science textbook defines a *majoritarian democracy* by comparing its characteristics with those of a *consensual democracy*:

◆ 422–28

A majoritarian democracy is one

1. having only two major political parties, not many

2. having an electoral system that requires a bare majority to elect one clear winner in an election, as opposed to a proportional electoral system that distributes seats to political parties according to the rough share of votes received in the election

3. a strong executive (president or prime minister) and cabinet that together are largely independent of the legislature when it comes to exercising the executive's constitutional duties, in contrast to an executive and cabinet that are politically controlled by the parties in the legislature and therefore unable to exercise much influence when proposing policy initiatives.

—Benjamin Ginsberg, Theodore J. Lowi, and Margaret Weir, *We the People: An Introduction to American Politics*

And here's an example in which democracy is contrasted with various other forms of governments of the past:

Caesar's power derived from a popular mandate, conveyed through established republican forms, but that did not make his government any the less a dictatorship. Napoleon called his government a democratic republic, but no one, least of all Napoleon himself, doubted that he had destroyed the last vestiges of the democratic republic.

—Carl Becker, *Modern Democracy*

Give examples. See how the essayist E. B. White defines democracy by giving some everyday examples of considerate behavior, humility, and civic participation—all things he suggests constitute democracy:

> It is the line that forms on the right. It is the don't in "don't shove." It is the hole in the stuffed shirt through which the sawdust slowly trickles; it is the dent in the high hat. Democracy is the recurrent suspicion that more than half of the people are right more than half of the time. . . . Democracy is a letter to the editor.
>
> —E. B. White, "Democracy"

White's definition is elegant because he uses examples that his readers will know. His characteristics— metaphors, really—define democracy not as a conceptual way of governing but as an everyday part of American life.

417–21 ◆ **Classify it.** Often it's useful to divide or **CLASSIFY** a term. The ways in which democracy unfolds are complex enough to warrant entire textbooks, of course; but the following definition, from a political science textbook, divides democracy into two kinds, representative and direct:

> A system of government that gives citizens a regular opportunity to elect the top government officials is usually called a representative democracy or republic. A system that permits citizens to vote directly on laws and policies is often called a direct democracy. At the national level, America is a representative democracy in which citizens select government officials but do not vote on legislation. Some states, however, have provisions for direct legislation through popular referendum. For example, California voters in 1995 decided to bar undocumented immigrants from receiving some state services.
>
> —Benjamin Ginsberg, Theodore J. Lowi, and Margaret Weir, *We the People: An Introduction to American Politics*

Stipulative Definitions

Sometimes a writer will stipulate a certain definition, essentially saying, "This is how I'm defining x." Such definitions are not usually found in a dictionary—and at the same time are central to the argument the writer is making. Here is one example, from an essay by Toni Morrison. Describing a scene from a film in which a newly arrived Greek immigrant, working as a shoe shiner in Grand Central Terminal, chases away an African American competitor, Morrison calls the scene an example of "race talk," a concept she then goes on to define:

> This is race talk, the explicit insertion into everyday life of racial signs and symbols that have no meaning other than pressing African Americans to the lowest level of the racial hierarchy. Popular culture, shaped by film, theater, advertising, the press, television, and literature, is heavily engaged in race talk. It participates freely in this most enduring and efficient rite of passage into American culture: negative appraisals of the native-born black population. Only when the lesson of racial estrangement is learned is assimilation complete. Whatever the lived experience of immigrants with African Americans—pleasant, beneficial, or bruising—the rhetorical experience renders blacks as noncitizens, already discredited outlaws.
>
> All immigrants fight for jobs and space, and who is there to fight but those who have both? As in the fishing ground struggle between Texas and Vietnamese shrimpers, they displace what and whom they can. Although U.S. history is awash in labor battles, political fights and property wars among all religious and ethnic groups, their struggles are persistently framed as struggles between recent arrivals and blacks. In race talk the move into mainstream America always means buying into the notion of American blacks as the real aliens. Whatever the ethnicity or nationality of the immigrant, his nemesis is understood to be African American.
>
> —Toni Morrison, "On the Backs of Blacks"

The following example is from a book review of Nancy L. Rosenblum's *Membership and Morals: The Personal Uses of Pluralism in America*, published in the *American Prospect*, a magazine for readers interested in political analysis. In it a Stanford law professor outlines a definition of "the democracy of everyday life":

> Democracy, in this understanding of it, means simply treating people as equals, disregarding social standing, avoiding attitudes of either deference or superiority, making allowances for others' weaknesses, and resisting the temptation to respond to perceived slights. It also means protesting everyday instances of arbitrariness and unfairness—from the rudeness of the bakery clerk to the sexism of the car dealer or the racism of those who vandalize the home of the first black neighbors on the block.
>
> —Kathleen M. Sullivan, "Defining Democracy Down"

Considering the Rhetorical Situation

As a writer or speaker, it's important to think about the message you want to articulate, the audience you want to reach, and the larger context you are writing in.

73–74 ■ **PURPOSE**   Your purpose for writing will affect any definitions you include. Would writing an extended definition help you explain something? Would stipulating definitions of key terms help you shape an argument? Could an off-beat definition help you entertain your readers?

75–78 ■ **AUDIENCE**   What audience do you want to reach, and are there any terms your readers are unlikely to know (and therefore need to be defined)? Are there terms they might understand differently from the way you're defining them?

79–84 ■ **GENRE**   Does your genre require you to define terms? Chances are that if you're reporting information you'll need to define some terms, and some arguments rest on the way you define key terms.

85–87 ■ **STANCE**   What is your stance, and do you need to define key terms to show that stance clearly? How you define "fetus," for example, is likely to reveal your stance on abortion.

88–90 ■ **MEDIA/DESIGN**   Your medium will affect the form your definitions take. In a print text, you'll need to define terms in your text; if you're giving a speech or presentation, you might also provide images of important terms and their definitions. In an electronic text, you may be able to define terms by linking to an online dictionary definition.

If you need more help

321 ⁂ See also the **PROCESSES** chapters for help with generating ideas, drafting, revising, and so on if you are writing a whole essay dedicated to defining a term or concept.

42 Describing

When we describe something, we indicate what it looks like—and sometimes how it sounds, feels, smells, and tastes. Descriptive details are a way of showing rather than telling, of helping readers see (or hear, smell, and so on) what we're writing about—that the sky is blue, that Miss Havisham is wearing an old yellowed wedding gown, that the chemicals in the beaker have reacted and smell like rotten eggs. You'll have occasion to describe things in most of the writing you do—from describing a favorite hat in a **PERSONAL NARRATIVE** to detailing a chemical reaction in a lab report. This chapter will help you work with description—and, in particular, help you think about the use of *detail*, about *objectivity and subjectivity*, about *vantage point*, about creating a clear *dominant impression*, and about using description to fit your rhetorical situation.

▲ 234–45

Detail

The goal of using details is to be as specific as possible, providing information that will help your audience imagine the subject or make sense of it. See, for example, how Nancy Mairs, an author with multiple sclerosis, describes the disease in clear, specific terms:

> During its course, which is unpredictable and uncontrollable, one may lose vision, hearing, speech, the ability to walk, control of bladder and/or bowels, strength in any or all extremities, sensitivity to touch, vibration, and/or pain, potency, coordination of movements—the list of possibilities is lengthy and, yes, horrifying. One may also lose one's sense of humor. That's the easiest to lose and the hardest to survive without.
>
> In the past ten years, I have sustained some of these losses. Characteristic of MS are sudden attacks, called exacerbations, followed by remissions, and these I have not had. Instead, my disease has been slowly progressive. My left leg is now so weak that I walk with the aid of a brace and a cane, and for distances I use an Amigo, a variation on the electric wheelchair that looks rather like an electrified kiddie car. I no

longer have much use of my left hand. Now my right side is weakening as well. I still have the blurred spot in my right eye. Overall, though, I've been lucky so far.

—Nancy Mairs, "On Being a Cripple"

Mairs's gruesome list demonstrates, through *specific details*, how the disease affects sufferers generally and her in particular. We know far more after reading this text than we do from the following more general description, from a National Multiple Sclerosis Society brochure:

Multiple sclerosis is a chronic, unpredictable disease of the central nervous system (the brain, optic nerves, and spinal cord). It is thought to be an autoimmune disorder. This means the immune system incorrectly attacks the person's healthy tissue.

MS can cause blurred vision, loss of balance, poor coordination, slurred speech, tremors, numbness, extreme fatigue, problems with memory and concentration, paralysis, and blindness. These problems may be permanent, or they may come and go.

—National Multiple Sclerosis Society, *Just the Facts*

Specific details are also more effective than labels, which give little meaningful information. Instead of saying that someone is a "loser" or "really smart," it's better to give details so that readers can understand the reasons behind the label: What does this person *do* or *say* that makes them deserve this label? See, for example, how the writer of a memoir focused on his pet snake describes the way his snake, Woohoo, and he interacted:

He wound around my wrist, hung in the air, pulled himself up and into the arm of my shirt, through which he slithered until he decided on another opening, the neck, from which his head emerged, and then his forked tongue, darting out, shaking, tasting and retreating into his mouth. I gave his cold blood my heat and flexed hello to his constrictions. My fingers followed the grain of his scales down his undulating length, which grew to four feet from ten inches as the years passed, its colors freshly radiant after every shedding.

—Paul McAdory, "Snakes"

The writer might simply have said, "The snake moved around under my shirt." Instead, he shows the snake as it moves from place to place ("He wound around my wrist, hung in the air, pulled himself up and into the arm of my shirt") and describes his own physical reaction ("I . . . flexed hello to his constrictions," "My fingers followed the grain of his scales")—all details that create a far more vivid description.

Sensory details help readers imagine sounds, odors, tastes, and physical sensations in addition to sights. In the following example, writer Scott Russell Sanders recalls sawing wood as a child. Note how visual details, odors, and even the physical sense of being picked up by his father mingle to form a vivid scene:

> As the saw teeth bit down, the wood released its smell, each kind with its own fragrance, oak or walnut or cherry or pine—usually pine because it was the softest, easiest for a child to work. No matter how weathered and gray the board, no matter how warped and cracked, inside there was this smell waiting, as of something freshly baked. I gathered every smidgen of sawdust and stored it away in coffee cans, which I kept in a drawer of the workbench. When I did not feel like hammering nails I would dump my sawdust on the concrete floor of the garage and landscape it into highways and farms and towns, running miniature cars and trucks along miniature roads. Looming as huge as a colossus, my father worked over and around me, now and again bending down to inspect my work, careful not to trample my creations. It was a landscape that smelled dizzyingly of wood. Even after a bath my skin would carry the smell, and so would my father's hair, when he lifted me for a bedtime hug.
>
> —Scott Russell Sanders, *The Paradise of Bombs*

Whenever you describe something, you'll select from many possible details you might use. Simply put, to exhaust all the details available to describe something is impossible—and would exhaust your readers as well. To focus your description, you'll need to determine the kinds of details appropriate for your subject. They will vary, depending on your **PURPOSE**. See, for example, how the details might differ in four different genres:

73–74

- For a **PERSONAL NARRATIVE** *about an event*, you might choose details that are significant for you, that evoke the sights, sounds, and other sensations that give personal meaning to the event.

234–45

- For a **VISUAL ANALYSIS**, you'll probably choose details that contribute to the effectiveness the image has in delivering a message—or to the impact the image has on its audience.

134–39

---

*See the ebook at digital.wwnorton.com/fieldguide7h for a chapter on Résumés and Job Letters.

246–56

- *For a* **PROFILE**, you're likely to select details that will reinforce the dominant impression you want to give, that portray the event from the perspective you want readers to see.

- *For a lab report*, you should give certain specifics — what equipment was used, what procedures were followed, what exactly were the results.

Deciding on a focus for your description can help you see it better, as you'll look for details that contribute to that focus.

Objectivity and Subjectivity

Descriptions can be written with objectivity, with subjectivity, or with a mixture of both. Objective descriptions attempt to be uncolored by personal opinion or emotion. Police reports and much news writing aim to describe events objectively; scientific writing strives for objectivity in describing laboratory procedures and results. See, for example, the following objective account of what happened at the World Trade Center on September 11, 2001:

> ### World Trade Center Disaster — Tuesday, September 11, 2001
>
> On Tuesday, September 11, 2001, at 8:45 a.m. New York local time, One World Trade Center, the north tower, was hit by a hijacked 767 commercial jet airplane loaded with fuel for a transcontinental flight. Two World Trade Center, the south tower, was hit by a similar hijacked jet eighteen minutes later, at 9:03 a.m. (In separate but related attacks, the Pentagon building near Washington, D.C., was hit by a hijacked 757 at 9:43 a.m., and at 10:10 a.m. a fourth hijacked jetliner crashed in Pennsylvania.) The south tower, WTC 2, which had been hit second, was the first to suffer a complete structural collapse, at 10:05 a.m., 62 minutes after being hit itself, 80 minutes after the first impact. The north tower, WTC 1, then also collapsed, at 10:29 a.m., 104 minutes after being hit. WTC 7, a substantial forty-seven-story office building in its own right, built in 1987, was damaged by the collapsing towers, caught fire, and later in the afternoon also totally collapsed.
>
> — "World Trade Center," *GreatBuildings.com*

Subjective descriptions, in contrast, allow the writer's opinions and emotions to come through. A house can be described as comfortable, with a lived-in look, or as run-down and in need of a paint job and a new roof. Here's a subjective description of the planes striking the World Trade Center, as told by a woman watching from a nearby building:

Incredulously, while looking out [the] window at the damage and carnage the first plane had inflicted, I saw the second plane abruptly come into my right field of vision and deliberately, with shimmering intention, thunder full-force into the south tower. It was so close, so low, so huge and fast, so intent on its target that I swear to you, I swear to you, I felt the vengeance and rage emanating from the plane.

—Debra Fontaine, "Witnessing"

Vantage Point

Sometimes you'll want or need to describe something from a certain vantage point. Where you locate yourself in relation to what you're describing will determine what you can perceive (and so describe) and what you can't. You may describe your subject from a *stationary vantage point*, from which you (and your readers) see your subject from one angle only, as if you were a camera. This description of one of three photographs that captured a woman's death records only what the camera saw from one angle at one particular moment:

The first showed some people on a fire escape—a fireman, a woman and a child. The fireman had a nice strong jaw and looked very brave. The woman was holding the child. Smoke was pouring from the building behind them. A rescue ladder was approaching, just a few feet away, and the fireman had one arm around the woman and one arm reaching out toward the ladder.

—Nora Ephron, "The Boston Photographs"

By contrast, this description of a drive to an Italian villa uses a *moving vantage point*; the writer recounts what he saw as he passed through a gate in a city wall, moving from city to country:

La Pietra—"the stone"—is situated one mile from the Porta San Gallo, an entry to the Old City of Florence. You drive there along the Via Bolognese, twisting past modern apartment blocks, until you come to a gate, which swings open—and there you are, at the upper end of a long lane of cypresses facing a great ocher palazzo; with olive groves spreading out on both sides over an expanse of fifty-seven acres. There's something almost comically wonderful about the effect: here, the city, with its winding avenue; there, on the other side of a wall, the country, fertile and gray green.

—James Traub, "Italian Hours"

The description of quarries in the following section uses *multiple vantage points* to capture the quarries from many perspectives.

Dominant Impression

With any description, your aim is to create some dominant impression—the overall feeling that the individual details add up to. The dominant impression may be implied, growing out of the details themselves. For example, Scott Russell Sanders's memory of the smell of sawdust creates a dominant impression of warmth and comfort: the "fragrance . . . as of something freshly baked," sawdust "stored . . . away in coffee cans," a young boy "lifted . . . for a bedtime hug." Sometimes, though, a writer will state the dominant impression directly, in addition to creating it with details. In an essay about Indiana limestone quarries, Sanders makes the dominant impression clear from the start: "They are battlefields."

> The quarries will not be domesticated. They are not backyard pools; they are battlefields. Each quarry is an arena where violent struggles have taken place between machines and planet, between human ingenuity and brute resisting stone, between mind and matter. Waste rock litters the floor and brim like rubble in a bombed city. The ragged pits might have been the basements of vanished skyscrapers. Stones weighing tens of tons lean against one another at precarious angles, as if they have been thrown there by some gigantic strength and have not yet finished falling. Wrecked machinery hulks in the weeds, grimly rusting, the cogs and wheels, twisted rails, battered engine housings, trackless bulldozers and burst boilers like junk from an armored regiment. Everywhere the ledges are scarred from drills, as if from an artillery barrage or machine-gun strafing. Stumbling onto one of these abandoned quarries and gazing at the ruins, you might be left wondering who had won the battle, men or stone.
>
> —Scott Russell Sanders, *The Paradise of Bombs*

The rest of his description, full of more figurative language ("like rubble in a bombed city," "like junk from an armored regiment," "as if from an artillery barrage or machine-gun strafing") reinforces the direct "they are battlefields" statement.

The orange sunset and expanse of sky and water in this Michigan tourism ad create a dominant impression of spaciousness and warmth, while the text invites readers to visit a Michigan beach and enjoy watching the sun set rather than watching television.

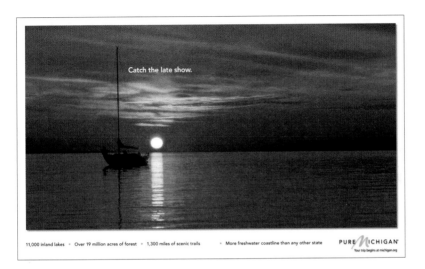

Catch the late show.

11,000 inland lakes · Over 19 million acres of forest · 1,300 miles of scenic trails · More freshwater coastline than any other state   PURE MICHIGAN
Your trip begins at michigan.org

Organizing Descriptions

You can organize descriptions in many ways. When your description is primarily visual, you'll probably organize it spatially: from left to right, top to bottom, outside to inside. One variation on this approach is to begin with the most significant or noteworthy feature and move outward from that center, as Ephron does in describing a photo. Or you may create a chronological description of objects as you move past or through them in space, as Traub does in his description of his drive. You might even pile up details to create a dominant impression, as Sanders and Mairs do, especially if your description draws on senses besides vision.

Considering the Rhetorical Situation

As a writer or speaker, it's important to think about the message you want to articulate, the audience you want to reach, and the larger context you are writing in.

PURPOSE Your purpose may affect the way you use description. If you're arguing that a government should intervene in another country's civil war, for example, describing the anguish of refugees from that war could make your argument more persuasive. If you're analyzing a painting, you will likely need to describe it.

■ 73–74

▶ Access Chapter 30 in the ebook for a video on description in supporting sentences.

75–78 **AUDIENCE** Who is your audience, and will they need detailed description to understand the points you wish to make?

79–84 **GENRE** Does your genre require description? A lab report generally calls for you to describe materials and results; a personal narrative about Grandma should probably describe her—her smile, her favorite outfit, her apple pie.

85–87 **STANCE** The way you describe things can help you convey your stance. For example, the details you choose can show you to be objective (or not), careful or casual.

88–90 **MEDIA/DESIGN** Your medium will affect the form your description can take. In a print or spoken text, you'll likely rely on words, though you may also include visuals. In an electronic text, you can easily provide links to visuals as well as audio clips and so may need fewer words of your own.

If you need more help

329
332
330
321

See also **FREEWRITING**, **CUBING**, and **LISTING**, three methods of generating ideas that can be especially helpful for developing detailed descriptions. Sometimes you may be assigned to write a whole essay describing something: see the **PROCESSES** chapters for help with drafting, revising, and so on.

43 Using Dialogue

Dialogue is a way of including people's own words in a text, letting readers hear those people's voices—not just what you say about them. **PERSONAL NARRATIVES** and **PROFILES** often include dialogue, and many other genres do as well: **LITERARY ANALYSES** often quote dialogue from the texts they analyze, and essays **ARGUING A POSITION** might quote an authoritative source as support for a claim. This chapter provides brief guidelines for the conventions of paragraphing and punctuating dialogue and offers some good examples of how you can use dialogue most effectively to suit your own rhetorical situations.

▲ 234–45
246–56
220–33
170–96

Why Add Dialogue?

Dialogue is a way of bringing in voices other than your own, of showing people and scenes rather than just telling about them. It can add color and texture to your writing, making it memorable. Most important, however, dialogue should be more than just colorful or interesting. It needs to contribute to your rhetorical purpose, to support the point you're making. See how dialogue is used in the following excerpt from a magazine profile of the Mall of America, how it gives us a sense of the place that the journalist's own words could not provide:

> Two pubescent girls in retainers and braces sat beside me sipping coffees topped with whipped cream and chocolate sprinkles, their shopping bags gathered tightly around their legs, their eyes fixed on the passing crowds. They came, they said, from Shakopee—"It's nowhere," one of them explained. The megamall, she added, was "a buzz at first, but now it seems pretty normal. 'Cept my parents are like Twenty Questions every time I want to come here. 'Specially since the shooting."
>
> On a Sunday night, she elaborated, three people had been wounded when shots were fired in a dispute over a San Jose Sharks jacket. "In the *mall*," her friend reminded me. "Right here at megamall. A shooting."
>
> "It's like nowhere's safe," the first added.
>
> —David Guterson, "Enclosed. Encyclopedic. Endured. One Week at the Mall of America"

Of course, it was the writer who decided whom and what to quote, and Guterson deliberately chose words that capture the young shoppers' speech patterns, quoting fragments ("In the *mall*. . . . Right here at megamall. A shooting"), slang ("a buzz at first," "my parents are like Twenty Questions"), even contractions ("'Cept," "'Specially").

Integrating Dialogue into Your Writing

There are certain conventions for punctuating and paragraphing dialogue:

- *Punctuating.* Enclose each speaker's words in quotation marks, and put any end punctuation—periods, question marks, and exclamation marks—inside the closing quotation mark. Whether you're transcribing words you heard or making them up, you'll sometimes need to add punctuation to reflect the rhythm and sound of the speech. In the last sentence of the example below, see how Chang-Rae Lee adds a comma after "Well" and italicizes "practice" to show intonation—and attitude.

- *Paragraphing.* When you're writing dialogue that includes more than one speaker, start a new paragraph each time the speaker changes.

529–32
- *Signal phrases.* Sometimes you'll need to introduce dialogue with SIGNAL PHRASES —"I said," "she asked," and so on—to make clear who is speaking. At times, however, the speaker will be clear enough, and you won't need any signal phrases.

Here is a conversation between a mother and her son that illustrates each of the conventions for punctuating and paragraphing dialogue:

"Whom do I talk to?" she said. She would mostly speak to me in Korean, and I would answer back in English.
  "The bank manager, who else?"
  "What do I say?"
  "Whatever you want to say."
  "Don't speak to me like that!" she cried.
  "It's just that you should be able to do it yourself," I said.
  "You know how I feel about this!"
  "Well, maybe then you should consider it *practice*," I answered lightly, using the Korean word to make sure she understood.

—Chang-Rae Lee, "Coming Home Again"

Interviews

Interviews are a kind of dialogue, with different conventions for punctuation. When you're transcribing an interview, give each speaker's name each time they speak, starting a new line but not indenting, and do not use quotation marks. Here's an excerpt from an interview that graduate student Emma Peters conducted with Brenda Ouattara, a recent two-year college graduate, while researching how the COVID-19 pandemic affected college education and online learning.

Emma Peters: What school did you go to, and what year were you in when the pandemic started?

Brenda Ouattara: I attended LaGuardia Community College in Queens, and it was during my first year there. I was only on campus for a few months before COVID, so I actually finished almost my whole two-year college experience online instead of in person.

Peters: Did you take online classes before the pandemic? How were they different?

Ouattara: I was in hybrid classes before, where we'd meet once a week in person and the rest was online. The online classes during the pandemic were more challenging—it felt like they had more work. Because, in my opinion, the professors felt like we were going to be missing out on the full experience of their class, so they would give us more work. And we also had to learn how to manage doing online courses, and how to figure out and navigate the websites.

Peters: What do you think is lost with an online learning experience that you might have had if you were in person?

Ouattara: The experience of meeting new students, meeting your actual professors, just being face-to-face to get the help that you need . . . and having the opportunities to have student fairs or any other events. All of those things were just not happening for us. I feel like it was hard for some students to really be motivated at home. I know a few of my friends actually just decided to take the semesters off. I kept going, but I wasn't as motivated to after a while because it's online, so it's not as exciting as walking in the buildings and meeting people and going straight to your professors for help.

Peters: What do you think are the benefits of online classes?

Ouattara: It's a little bit easier to manage with your personal life. You can have a regular work schedule and then come home and do assignments. But when you're in person you have to be physically in a classroom. It was definitely a benefit being able to set my own schedule.

Peters: How did being online affect your relationship with your professors?

Ouattara: The communication was different—you had to speak through email and online calls, and sometimes it was harder to get a fast response. Some professors were also struggling to use online resources, and sometimes I would ask them a question and they would ask me a question—and we were helping each other out. [Laughs]

Peters: Do you think anything will change permanently going forward after the pandemic?

Ouattara: I don't think it will go back to exactly how it was before, even though many colleges are trying. I feel like I've spent two years doing online learning and now it would almost be out of my comfort zone to go back to in-person classes—this is normal for me now, you know? But everyone is different.

In preparing the interview transcript for publication, Peters had to add punctuation, which of course was not part of the oral conversation, and probably deleted pauses and verbal expressions such as "um" and "uh." At the same time, she kept informal interjections ("you know?") and included expressions of emotion ("Laughs") to maintain the oral flavor of the interview and reflect Ouattara's voice. More tips on interviewing may be found in Chapter 48.

Considering the Rhetorical Situation

As a writer or speaker, it's important to think about the message you want to articulate, the audience you want to reach, and the larger context of your writing.

73–74 ▪	**PURPOSE**	Your purpose will affect any use of dialogue. Dialogue can help bring a profile to life and make it memorable. Interviews with experts or firsthand witnesses can add credibility to a report or argument.
75–78 ▪	**AUDIENCE**	Whom do you want to reach, and will dialogue help? Sometimes actual dialogue can help readers hear human voices behind facts or reason.
79–84 ▪	**GENRE**	Does your genre require dialogue? If you're evaluating or analyzing a literary work, for instance, you may

wish to include dialogue from that work. If you're writing a profile of a person or event, dialogue can help you bring your subject to life. Similarly, an interview with an expert can add credibility to a report or argument.

STANCE　What is your stance, and can dialogue help you communicate that stance? For example, excerpts of an interview may enable you to challenge someone's views and make your own views clear.

85–87

MEDIA/DESIGN　Your medium will affect the way you present dialogue. In a print text, you'll present dialogue through written words. In an oral or electronic text, you might include actual recorded dialogue.

88–90

If you need more help

See also the guidelines on **INTERVIEWING EXPERTS** for advice on setting up and recording interviews and those on **QUOTING**, **PARAPHRASING**, and **SUMMARIZING** for help with deciding how to integrate dialogue into your text.

499–503
521–32

44 Explaining Processes

When you explain a process, you tell how something is (or was) done—how a bill becomes a law, how an embryo develops; or you tell someone how to do something—how to throw a curve ball, how to write a personal narrative. This chapter focuses on those two kinds of explanations, offering examples and guidelines for explaining a process in a way that works for your rhetorical situation.

Explaining a Process Clearly

Whether the process is simple or complex, you'll need to identify its key stages or steps and explain them one by one, in order. The sequence matters because it enables readers to follow your explanation; it is especially important when you're explaining a process that others are going to follow. Most often you'll explain a process chronologically, from start to finish. **TRANSITIONS** —words like "first," "next," "then," and so on—are often necessary, therefore, to show readers how the stages of a process relate to one another and to indicate time sequences. Finally, you'll find that verbs matter; they indicate the actions that take place at each stage of the process.

355–56

Explaining How Something Is Done

All processes consist of steps, and when you explain how something is done, you describe each step, generally in order, from first to last. Here, for example, is an explanation of how french fries are made, from an essay published in the *New Yorker*:

> Fast-food French fries are made from a baking potato like an Idaho russet, or any other variety that is mealy, or starchy, rather than waxy. The potatoes are harvested, cured, washed, peeled, sliced, and then blanched—cooked enough so that the insides have a fluffy texture but not so much that the fry gets soft and breaks. Blanching is followed by drying, and drying by a thirty-second deep fry, to give the potatoes a crisp shell. Then the fries are frozen until the moment of service, when they are deep-fried again, this time for somewhere

around three minutes. Depending on the fast-food chain involved, there are other steps interspersed in this process. McDonald's fries, for example, are briefly dipped in a sugar solution, which gives them their golden-brown color; Burger King fries are dipped in a starch batter, which is what gives those fries their distinctive hard shell and audible crunch. But the result is similar. The potato that is first harvested in the field is roughly 80 percent water. The process of creating a French fry consists, essentially, of removing as much of that water as possible—through blanching, drying, and deep-frying—and replacing it with fat.

—Malcolm Gladwell, "The Trouble with Fries"

Gladwell clearly explains the process of making french fries, showing us the specific steps—how the potatoes "are harvested, cured, washed, peeled, sliced," and so on—and using clear transitions—"followed by," "then," "until," "when"—and action verbs to show the sequence. His last sentence makes his stance clear, pointing out that the process of creating a french fry consists of removing as much of a potato's water as possible "and replacing it with fat."

Explaining How to Do Something

In explaining how to do something, you are giving instruction so that others can follow the process themselves. See how cookbook author Amanda Hesser explains the process of making french fries. She starts by listing the ingredients and then describes the steps:

4 large long Idaho potatoes
Peanut oil
Kosher or coarse sea salt

1. Peel the potatoes. Place in a bowl, cover with water, and refrigerate for 8 hours.

2. Slice the potatoes lengthwise into ¼-inch-thick sticks. Place in a bowl, cover with water, and refrigerate for 8 hours more.

3. Drain the potato sticks and lay out on dish towels to dry. Be sure they are completely dry before frying.

4. Heat 2 inches of oil to 300 degrees in a large deep pot with a frying basket and a deep-frying thermometer clipped to the side. Add just enough potatoes to cover the bottom of the frying basket and cook until slightly limp, 1½ to 2 minutes; do not brown. Lift the basket and drain the fries, then transfer the potatoes to a wire

rack set over a baking sheet and separate the sticks. Repeat with the remaining potatoes.

5. Increase the heat to 375 degrees. Again add the potatoes in batches to the oil and fry until chestnut brown on the edges and crisp. Drain and transfer to a bowl lined with paper towels. Immediately season with salt, tossing to coat.

—Amanda Hesser, "French Fries"

Hesser's explanation leaves out no details, giving a clear sequence of steps and descriptive verbs that tell us exactly what to do: "Peel," "Slice," "Heat," and so on. After she gives the recipe, she offers variations, including adding a slice of bacon to the oil "for a light pork flavor" or adding some herb leaves into the oil and then serving the fries "with the crisped herbs."

Explaining a Process Visually

648–54

Some processes are best explained **VISUALLY**, with diagrams or photographs. The next page provides an example of how a blogger explains one process of shaping dough into a bagel—giving the details in words and then showing us in photos how to do it.

Considering the Rhetorical Situation

As always, it's important to think about the message you want to articulate, the audience you want to reach, and the larger context you're writing in.

73–74

PURPOSE   Your purpose for writing will affect the way you explain a process. If you're arguing that we should avoid eating fast food, you might explain the process by which chicken nuggets are made. But to give information about how to fry chicken, you would explain the process quite differently.

75–78

AUDIENCE   Whom are you trying to reach, and will you need to provide any special background information or to interest them in the process before you explain it?

Gently press dough to deflate it a bit and divide into 6 equal portions.

Roll each portion into a rope about ½ inch in diameter.

Wrap the dough around your hand like this.

Seal the ends together by rolling back and forth on the counter a few times.

Place bagels on a lined sheet pan. Allow to rise, uncovered.

—Patricia Reitz, *ButterYum*

Photos by Patricia Reitz (butteryum.org).

79–84 ■

GENRE Does your genre require you to explain a process? In a lab report, for example, you'll need to explain processes used in the experiment. You might want to explain a process in a profile of an activity or in a proposal for a solution.

85–87 ■

STANCE If you're giving practical directions for doing something, you'll want to take a straightforward "do this, and then do that" perspective. If you're writing to entertain, try taking a clever or amusing stance.

88–90 ■

MEDIA / DESIGN Your medium will affect the way you explain a process. In a print text, you can use both words and images. On the web, you may have the option of showing a video of the process as well.

If you need more help

246–56 ▲
457–64 ◆

321 ⁑

See also **PROFILES** if you are writing about an activity that needs to be explained. See **NARRATING** for more advice on organizing an explanation chronologically. Sometimes you may be assigned to write a whole essay or report that explains a process; see **PROCESSES** for help with drafting, revising, and so on.

45 Narrating

Narratives are stories. As a writing strategy, a good narrative can lend support to most kinds of writing—in a **POSITION PAPER** arguing for Title IX compliance, for example, you might include a brief narrative about an Olympic sprinter who might never have had an opportunity to compete on a track-and-field team without Title IX. Or you can bring a **PROFILE** of a favorite coach to life with an anecdote about a pep talk they once gave before a championship track meet. Whatever your larger writing purpose, it's important to make sure that any narratives you add support that purpose—they should not be inserted simply to tell an interesting story. You'll also need to compose them carefully—to put them in a clear *sequence*, include *pertinent detail*, and make sure they are appropriate to your particular rhetorical situation.

▲ 170–96

▲ 246–56

> Access Chapter 38 in the ebook for a video on using personal stories in academic writing.

Sequencing

When we write a narrative, we arrange events in a particular sequence. Writers typically sequence narratives in chronological order, reverse chronological order, or as a flashback.

Use chronological order. Often you may tell the story chronologically, starting at the beginning of an event and working through to the end, as Maya Angelou does in this brief narrative from an essay about her high school graduation:

> The school band struck up a march and all classes filed in as had been rehearsed. We stood in front of our seats, as assigned, and on a signal from the choir director, we sat. No sooner had this been accomplished than the band started to play the national anthem. We rose again and sang the song, after which we recited the pledge of allegiance. We remained standing for a brief minute before the choir director and the principal signaled to us, rather desperately I thought, to take our seats.
>
> —Maya Angelou, "Graduation"

Use reverse chronological order.　You may also begin with the final action and work back to the first, as Aldo Leopold does in this narrative about cutting down a tree:

> Now our saw bites into the 1890s, called gay by those whose eyes turn cityward rather than landward. We cut 1899, when the last passenger pigeon collided with a charge of shot near Babcock, two counties to the north; we cut 1898, when a dry fall, followed by a snowless winter, froze the soil seven feet deep and killed the apple trees; 1897, another drouth year, when another forestry commission came into being; 1896, when 25,000 prairie chickens were shipped to market from the village of Spooner alone; 1895, another year of fires; 1894, another drouth year; and 1893, the year of "the Bluebird Storm," when a March blizzard reduced the migrating bluebirds to near zero.
>
> —Aldo Leopold, *A Sand County Almanac*

Glossary

RÉSUMÉS* are one genre where we generally use reverse chronological order, listing the most recent jobs or degrees first and then working backward. Notice, too, that we usually write these as narratives—telling what we have done rather than just naming positions we have held:

Sept. 2024–present	*Student worker*, Department of Information Management, Central State University, Wilberforce, OH. Compile data and format reports using Excel, Word, and university database.
June–Sept. 2024	*Intern*, QuestPro Corporation, West Louisville, KY. Assisted in development of software.
Sept. 2022–June 2024	*Bagger*, Ace Groceries, Elba, KY. Bagged customers' purchases.

Use a flashback.　You can sometimes put a flashback in the middle of a narrative, to tell about an incident that illuminates the larger narrative. Terry Tempest Williams does this in an essay about the startling incidence of breast cancer in her family: she recalls a dinnertime conversation with her father right after her mother's death from cancer, when she learned for the first time what caused all the cancer in her family:

---

*See the ebook at digital.wwnorton.com/fieldguide7h for a chapter on Résumés and Job Letters.

Over dessert, I shared a recurring dream of mine. I told my father that for years, as long as I could remember, I saw this flash of light in the night in the desert. That this image had so permeated my being, I could not venture south without seeing it again, on the horizon, illuminating buttes and mesas.

"You did see it," he said.

"Saw what?" I asked, a bit tentative.

"The bomb. The cloud. We were driving home from Riverside, California. You were sitting on your mother's lap. She was pregnant. In fact, I remember the date, September 7, 1957. We had just gotten out of the Service. We were driving north, past Las Vegas. It was an hour or so before dawn, when this explosion went off. We not only heard it, but felt it. I thought the oil tanker in front of us had blown up. We pulled over and suddenly, rising from the desert floor, we saw it, clearly, this golden-stemmed cloud, the mushroom. The sky seemed to vibrate with an eerie pink glow. Within a few minutes, a light ash was raining on the car."

I stared at my father. This was new information to me.

—Terry Tempest Williams,
"The Clan of the One-Breasted Women"

Williams could have simply announced this information as a fact—but see how much more powerful it is when told in narrative form.

Use time markers. Time markers help readers follow a sequence of events. The most obvious time markers are those that simply label the time, as the narrative entries in a diary, journal, or log might. For example, here is the final part of the narrative kept in a diary by a doomed Antarctic explorer:

WEDNESDAY, MARCH 21: Got within eleven miles of depot. Monday night; had to lay up all yesterday in severe blizzard. Today forlorn hope, Wilson and Bowers going to depot for fuel.

MARCH 22 and 23: Blizzard bad as ever—Wilson and Bowers unable to start—tomorrow last chance—no fuel and only one or two [days] of food left—must be near the end. Have decided it shall be natural— we shall march for the depot with or without our effects and die in our tracks.

THURSDAY, MARCH 29: Since the 21st we have had a continuous gale from W.S.W. and S.W. We had fuel to make two cups of tea apiece and bare food for two days on the 20th. Every day we have been ready to start for our depot eleven miles away, but outside the door of the tent it remains a scene of whirling drift. I do not think we can hope for any better things now. We shall stick it out to the end, but we are getting weaker, of course, and the end cannot be far. It seems a pity, but I do not think I can write more. . . .

Last Entry: For God's sake look after our people.

—Robert F. Scott, *Scott's Last Expedition: The Journals*

More often you will integrate time markers into the prose itself, as is done in this narrative about a woman preparing and delivering meals to workers at a cotton gin:

> She made her plans meticulously and in secret. <u>One early evening</u> to see if she was ready, she placed stones in two five-gallon pails and carried them three miles to the cotton gin. She rested a little, and then, discarding some rocks, she walked in the darkness to the sawmill five miles farther along the dirt road. <u>On her way back</u> to her little house and her babies, she dumped the remaining rocks along the path.
>
> <u>That same night</u> she worked into the early hours boiling chicken and frying ham. She made dough and filled the rolled-out pastry with meat. <u>At last</u> she went to sleep.
>
> <u>The next morning</u> she left her house carrying the meat pies, lard, an iron brazier, and coals for a fire. <u>Just before lunch</u> she appeared in an empty lot behind the cotton gin. <u>As the dinner noon bell rang</u>, she dropped the savors into boiling fat, and the aroma rose and floated over to the workers who spilled out of the gin, covered with white lint, looking like specters.

> —Maya Angelou,
> *Wouldn't Take Nothing for My Journey Now*

Use transitions. Another way to help readers follow a narrative is with **TRANSITIONS**, words like "first," "then," "meanwhile," "at last," and so on. See how the following paragraphs from Langston Hughes's classic essay about meeting Jesus use transitions (and time markers) to advance the action:

355–56 ⁂

> <u>Suddenly</u> the whole room broke into a sea of shouting, <u>as</u> they saw me rise. Waves of rejoicing swept the place. Women leaped in the air. My aunt threw her arms around me. The minister took me by the hand and led me to the platform.
>
> <u>When</u> things quieted down, in a hushed silence, punctuated by a few ecstatic "Amens," all the new young lambs were blessed in the name of God. <u>Then</u> joyous singing filled the room. <u>That night</u>, for the first time in my life but one for I was a big boy twelve years old—I cried.

> —Langston Hughes, "Salvation"

Including Pertinent Detail

When you include a narrative in your writing, you must decide which details you need—and which ones you don't. For example, you don't want to include so much detail that the narrative distracts the reader from the larger text. You must also decide whether you should include any background, to set the stage for the narrative. The amount of detail you include depends on your audience and purpose: How much detail does your audience need? How much detail do you need to make your meaning clear? In an essay on the suspicion African American men often face when walking at night, a journalist deliberately presents a story without setting the stage at all:

> My first victim was a woman—white, well dressed, probably in her late twenties. I came upon her late one evening on a deserted street in Hyde Park, a relatively affluent neighborhood in an otherwise mean, impoverished section of Chicago. As I swung onto the avenue behind her, there seemed to be a discreet, uninflammatory distance between us. Not so. She cast back a worried glance. To her, the youngish black man—a broad six feet two inches with a beard and billowing hair, both hands shoved into the pockets of a bulky military jacket—seemed menacingly close. After a few more quick glimpses, she picked up her pace and was soon running in earnest. Within seconds she disappeared into a cross street.
>
> —Brent Staples, "Black Men and Public Space"

Words like "victim" and phrases like "came upon her" lead us to assume the narrator is scary and perhaps dangerous. We don't know why he is walking on the deserted street because he hasn't told us: he simply begins with the moment he and the woman encounter each other. For his purposes, that's all the audience needs to know at first, and details of his physical appearance that explain the woman's response come later, after he tells us about the encounter. Had he given us those details at the outset, the narrative wouldn't have been nearly so effective. In a way, Staples lets the story sneak up on us, as the woman apparently felt he had on her.

Other times you'll need to provide more background information, as an MIT professor does when she uses an anecdote to introduce an essay about young children's experiences with electronic toys. First the writer tells us a little about *Merlin*, the computer tic-tac-toe game that the children in her anecdote play with. As you'll see, the anecdote would be hard to follow without the introduction:

Among the first generation of computational objects was Merlin, which challenged children to games of tic-tac-toe. For children who had only played games with human opponents, reaction to this object was intense. For example, while Merlin followed an optimal strategy for winning tic-tac-toe most of the time, it was programmed to make a slip every once in a while. So when children discovered strategies that allowed them to win and then tried these strategies a second time, they usually would not work. The machine gave the impression of not being "dumb enough" to let down its defenses twice. Robert, seven, playing with his friends on the beach, watched his friend Craig perform the "winning trick," but when he tried it, Merlin did not slip up and the game ended in a draw. Robert, confused and frustrated, threw Merlin into the sand and said, "Cheater. I hope your brains break." He was overheard by Craig and Greg, aged six and eight, who salvaged the by-now very sandy toy and took it upon themselves to set Robert straight. "Merlin doesn't know if it cheats," says Craig. "It doesn't know if you break it, Robert. It's not alive." Greg adds, "It's smart enough to make the right kinds of noises. But it doesn't really know if it loses. And when it cheats, it don't even know it's cheating." Jenny, six, interrupts with disdain: "Greg, to cheat you have to know you are cheating. Knowing is part of cheating."

—Sherry Turkle, "Cuddling Up to Cyborg Babies"

Opening and Closing with Narratives

340–48 Narratives are often useful as **BEGINNINGS** to essays and other kinds of writing. Everyone likes a good story, so an interesting or pithy narrative can be a good way to get your audience's attention. In the following introductory paragraph, a historian tells a gruesome but gripping story to attract our attention to a subject that might not otherwise merit our interest—bubonic plague:

In October 1347, two months after the fall of Calais, Genoese trading ships put into the harbor of Messina in Sicily with dead and dying men at the oars. The ships had come from the Black Sea port of Caffa (now Feodosiya) in the Crimea, where the Genoese maintained a trading post. The diseased sailors showed strange black swellings about the size of an egg or an apple in the armpits and groin. The swellings oozed blood and pus and were followed by spreading boils and black blotches on the skin from internal bleeding. The sick suffered severe pain and died quickly, within five days of the first symptoms. As the disease spread, other symptoms of continuous fever and spitting of blood appeared instead of the swellings or buboes. These victims coughed and sweated heavily and died even more quickly, within three days or less, sometimes in twenty-four hours. In both types everything that issued from the body—breath, sweat, blood from the buboes and lungs, bloody urine, and blood-blackened excrement—smelled foul. Depression and despair accompanied the physical symptoms, and before the end "death is seen seated on the face."

—Barbara Tuchman,
"This Is the End of the World: The Black Death"

Imagine how different the preceding paragraph would be if it weren't in the form of a narrative. Imagine, for example, that Tuchman had begun by defining bubonic plague. Would that have gotten your interest? The piece was written for a general audience. How might it have been different if it had been written for scientists? Would they need (or appreciate) the story told here?

Narrative can be a good way of **ENDING** a text, too, by winding up a discussion with an illustration of the main point. Here, for instance, is a concluding paragraph from an essay on American values and Las Vegas weddings:

348–52

I sat next to one . . . wedding party in a Strip restaurant the last time I was in Las Vegas. The marriage had just taken place; the bride still wore her dress, the mother her corsage. A bored waiter poured out a few swallows of pink champagne ("on the house") for everyone but the bride, who was too young to be served. "You'll need something with more kick than that," the bride's father said with heavy jocularity to his new son-in-law; the ritual jokes about the wedding night had a certain Panglossian character, since the bride was clearly several months pregnant. Another round of pink champagne, this time not on the house, and the bride began to cry. "It was just as nice," she sobbed, "as I hoped and dreamed it would be."

—Joan Didion, "Marrying Absurd"

No doubt Didion makes her points about American values clearly and cogently in the essay. But concluding with this story lets us *see* (and hear) what she is saying about Las Vegas wedding chapels, which sell "'niceness,' the facsimile of proper ritual, to children who do not know how else to find it, how to make the arrangements, how to do it 'right.'"

Considering the Rhetorical Situation

As a writer or speaker, it's important to think about the message you want to articulate, the audience you want to reach, and the larger context you are writing in.

73–74

Access Chapter 30 in the ebook for a video on narration in supporting sentences.

PURPOSE — Your purpose will affect the way you use narrative. For example, in an essay about seat belt laws, you might tell about the painful rehabilitation of a teenager who wasn't wearing a seat belt and was injured in an accident in order to show readers why seat belt use is mandatory in all but one state.

75–78

AUDIENCE — Whom do you want to reach, and do you have an anecdote or other narrative that will help them understand your topic or persuade them that your argument has merit?

79–84

GENRE — Does your genre require you to include narrative? A personal narrative about an important event might be primarily a story, whereas a reflection about an event might focus more on the significance of the event than on what happened.

85–87

STANCE — What is your stance, and do you have any stories that would help you convey that stance? A funny story, for example, can help create a humorous stance.

88–90

MEDIA / DESIGN — In a print or spoken text, you will likely be limited to brief narratives, perhaps illustrated with photos or other visuals. In an electronic text, you might have the option of linking to full-length narratives or videos available on the web.

If you need more help

321
317–18

Glossary

See also the **PROCESSES** chapters if you are assigned to write a narrative essay and need help with drafting, revising, and so on. Two special kinds of narratives are **LAB REPORTS** (which use narrative to describe the steps in an experiment from beginning to end) and **RÉSUMÉS** (which essentially tell the story of the work we've done, at school and on the job). Go to digital.wwnorton.com/fieldguide7h for chapters on these topics.

46 Taking Essay Exams

Essay exams present writers with special challenges. You must write quickly, on a topic presented to you on the spot, to show your instructor what you know about a specific body of information. This chapter offers advice on how to take essay exams.

Considering the Rhetorical Situation

Even in the special circumstance of an essay exam, it's important to consider the message you want to articulate, the audience you need to address, and the context of the course content.

PURPOSE	In an essay exam, your purpose is to show that you have mastered certain material and that you can analyze and apply it in an essay. You may need to make an argument or simply convey information on a topic.	■ 73–74
AUDIENCE	Will your course instructor be reading your exam, or will a teaching assistant? Sometimes standardized tests are read by groups of trained readers. What specific criteria will your audience use to evaluate your writing?	■ 75–78
GENRE	Does the essay question specify or suggest a certain genre? In a literature course, you may need to write a compelling literary analysis of a passage. In a history course, you may need to write an argument for the significance of a key historical event. In an economics course, you may need to contrast the economies of the North and South before the Civil War. If the essay question doesn't specify a genre, look for keywords such as "argue," "evaluate," or "explain," which point to a certain genre.	■ 79–84
STANCE	In an essay exam, the most appropriate stance is usually unemotional, thoughtful, and critical.	■ 85–87

88–90 ■

MEDIA/DESIGN If you're taking a test online, write your answers in a word processor, edit there, and then paste them into the exam. If you're handwriting on lined paper or in an exam booklet, write as legibly as you can.

Analyzing Essay Questions

Essay questions usually include key verbs that specify the kind of writing you'll need to do—*argue* a position, *compare* two texts, and so on. Here are some of the most common kinds of writing you'll be asked to do on an essay exam:

114–45 ▲

- *Analyze.* Break an idea, theory, text, or event into its parts and examine them. For example, a world history exam might ask you to **ANALYZE** European imperialism's effect on Africa in the late nineteenth century and discuss how Africans responded.

- *Apply.* Consider how an idea or concept might work out in practice. For instance, a film studies exam might ask you to apply the concept of auteurism—a theory of film that sees the director as the primary creator, whose body of work reflects a distinct personal style—to two films by Ava DuVernay. An economics exam might ask you to apply the concept of opportunity costs to a certain supplied scenario.

399–416 ◆

- *Argue/prove/justify.* Offer reasons and evidence to support a position. A philosophy exam, for example, might ask you to **ARGUE** whether or not all stereotypes contain a "kernel of truth" and whether believing a stereotype is ever justified.

417–21 ◆

- *Classify.* Group something into categories. For example, a marketing exam might ask you to **CLASSIFY** shoppers in categories based on their purchasing behavior, motives, attitudes, or lifestyle patterns.

422–28 ◆

- *Compare/contrast.* Explore the similarities and/or differences between two or more things. An economics exam, for example, might ask you to **COMPARE** the effectiveness of patents and tax incentives in encouraging technological advances.

114–45 ▲
210–19

- *Critique.* **ANALYZE** and **EVALUATE** a text or argument, considering its strengths and weaknesses. For instance, an evolutionary biology exam might ask you to critique John Maynard Smith's assertion that "scientific theories say nothing about what is right but only about what is possible" in the context of the theory of evolution.

- *Define.* Explain what a word or phrase means. An art history exam, for example, might ask you to **DEFINE** negative space and discuss the way various artists use it in their work.

◆ 429–38

- *Describe.* Tell about the important characteristics or features of something. For example, a sociology exam might ask you to **DESCRIBE** Erving Goffman's theory of the presentation of self in ordinary life, focusing on roles, props, and setting.

◆ 439–46

- *Evaluate.* Determine something's significance or value. A drama exam, for example, might ask you to **EVALUATE** the setting, lighting, and costumes in a filmed production of *Macbeth*.

▲ 210–19

- *Explain.* Provide reasons and examples to clarify an idea, argument, or event. For instance, a rhetoric exam might ask you to explain the structure of the African American sermon and discuss its use in writings of Frederick Douglass and Martin Luther King Jr.

- *Summarize/review.* Give the major points of a text or idea. A political science exam, for example, might ask you to **SUMMARIZE** Hannah Arendt's notion of "the banality of evil" and its relation to authoritarianism.

● 529

- *Trace.* Explain a sequence of ideas or order of events. For instance, a geography exam might ask you to trace the patterns of international migration since 1970 and discuss how these patterns differ from those of the period between 1870 and World War I.

Some Guidelines for Taking Essay Exams

Before the exam

- *Read over* your class notes and course texts strategically, **ANNOTATING** them to keep track of details you'll want to remember.

✳ 15–18

- *Collaborate* by forming a study group to help one another master the course content.

- *Review* key ideas, events, terms, and themes. Look for common themes and **CONNECTIONS** in lecture notes, class discussions, and any readings—they'll lead you to important ideas.

● 515–18

- *Ask* your instructor about the form the exam will take: how long it will be, what kind of questions will be on it, how it will be evaluated, and so on. Working with a study group, write questions you think your instructor might ask and then answer the questions together.

- *Warm up* just before the exam by **FREEWRITING** for 10 minutes or so to gather your thoughts.

During the exam

- *Scan the questions* to determine how much each part of the test counts and how much time you should spend on it. For example, if one essay is worth 50 points and two others are worth 25 points each, you'll want to spend half your time on the 50-point question.

- *Read over* the entire test before answering any questions. Start with the question you feel most confident answering, which may or may not be the first question on the test.

- *Don't panic.* Sometimes when students first read an essay question, their minds go blank, but after a few moments they start to recall the information they need.

- *Plan.* Although you won't have much time for revising or editing, you still need to plan and allow yourself time to make some last-minute changes before turning in the exam. So apportion your time. For a three-question essay test in a two-hour test period, you might divide your time like this:

Total Exam Time—120 minutes
Generating ideas—20 minutes (6–7 minutes per question)
Drafting—85 minutes (45 for the 50-point question,
                          20 for each 25-point question)
Revising, editing, proofreading—15 minutes

Knowing that you have built in time at the end of the exam period can help you remain calm as you write, because you can use that time to fill in gaps or reconsider answers you feel unsure about.

- *Jot down the main ideas* you need to cover in answering the question on scratch paper or on the cover of your exam book, numbering those ideas in the order you think makes sense—and you have an outline for your essay. If you're worried about time, plan to write the most important parts of your answers early on. If you don't complete your answer, refer your instructor to your outline to show where you were headed.

- *Turn the essay question into your introduction,* like this:

    Question: How did the outcomes of World War II differ from those of World War I?

Introduction: The outcomes of World War II differed from those of World War I in three major ways: World War II affected more of the world and its people than World War I did, distinctions between citizens and soldiers were eroded, and the war's brutality made it impossible for Europe to continue to claim cultural superiority over other cultures.

- *State your thesis explicitly,* provide **REASONS** and **EVIDENCE** to support your thesis, and use **TRANSITIONS** to move logically from one idea to the next. Restate your main point in your conclusion. You don't want to give what one professor calls a "garbage truck answer," dumping everything you know into your answer and expecting the instructor to sort it all out.

402

402–9

355–56

- *Write on every other line* and only on one side of each page so that you'll have room to make additions or corrections. If you're typing on a computer, be sure to double-space.

- *If you have time left, go over your exam,* looking for ideas that need elaboration as well as for grammatical and punctuation errors.

After the exam. Your instructor may not return your exam or may not provide comments on it. So consider asking for a conference to go over your work so you can learn what you did well and where you need to improve—important knowledge to take with you into your next exam.

Part 7
Doing Research

We do research all the time, for many different reasons. We search the web for information about a new computer, ask friends about the best place to get coffee, try on several pairs of jeans before deciding which ones to buy. You have no doubt done your share of library research before now, and you probably have visited a number of schools' websites before deciding which college you wanted to attend. Research, in other words, is something you do every day. The following chapters offer advice on the kinds of research you'll need to do for your academic work and, in particular, for research projects.

Doing Research

* ✳ academic literacies
* ■ rhetorical situations
* ▲ genres
* ⬡ fields
* ⁙ processes
* ● research
* ◆ strategies
* ● media / design
* ★ handbook

47 Getting a Start on Research

When you need to do research, it's sometimes tempting to jump in and start looking for information right away. However, doing research is complex and time-consuming. Research-based writing projects usually require you to follow several steps. You need to come up with a topic (or to analyze the requirements of an assigned topic) and come up with a research question to guide your research efforts. Once you do some serious, focused research to find the information you need, you'll be ready to turn your research question into a tentative thesis and sketch out a rough outline. After doing whatever additional research you need to fill in your outline, you'll write a draft—and get some response to that draft. You may then need to do even more research before revising. Once you revise, you'll need to edit and proofread. In other words, there's a lot to do. You need a schedule.

Establishing a Schedule and Getting Started

A good way to start a research project is by creating a timeline for getting all this work done, perhaps using the form on the next page. Once you have a schedule, you can get started. The sections that follow offer advice on considering your rhetorical situation, coming up with a topic, and doing preliminary research; developing a research question, a tentative thesis, and a rough outline; and creating a working bibliography and keeping track of your sources. The chapters that follow offer guidelines for **FINDING SOURCES**, **EVALUATING SOURCES**, and **SYNTHESIZING IDEAS**.

482–503
504–14
515–20

Scheduling a Research Project

	Complete by:
Analyze your rhetorical situation.	_____
Choose a possible topic or analyze the assignment.	_____
Plan a research strategy, and do preliminary research.	_____
Come up with a research question.	_____
Submit a proposal or abstract.	_____
Schedule interviews and other field research.	_____
Find and evaluate sources.	_____
Read sources, and take notes.	_____
Do any field research.	_____
Come up with a tentative thesis and outline.	_____
Write a draft.	_____
Get response.	_____
Do any additional research.	_____
Revise.	_____
Prepare a list of works cited.	_____
Edit.	_____
Proofread the final draft.	_____
Submit the final draft: your deadline.	_____

You may find it useful to start with your deadline—when the final project is due—and work backward from there, so you'll know how much time you have and can estimate how much time you'll need to do each task.

Considering the Rhetorical Situation

As with any writing task, you need to start by considering your purpose, your audience, and the rest of your rhetorical situation:

73–74 ■ **PURPOSE**   Is this project part of an assignment—and if so, does it specify any one purpose? If not, what is your broad purpose? To inform? argue? analyze? A combination?

75–78 ■ **AUDIENCE**   To whom are you writing? What does your audience likely know about your topic, and is there any background information you'll need to provide? What opinions or attitudes do your readers likely hold? What kinds of evidence will they find persuasive? How do you want them to respond to your writing?

GENRE	Are you writing to report on something? to compose a profile? to make a proposal? an argument? What are the requirements of your genre in terms of the number and kind of sources you must use?	79–84
STANCE	What is your attitude toward your topic? What accounts for your attitude? How do you want to come across? As curious? critical? positive? something else?	85–87
MEDIA/DESIGN	What medium or media will you use? Print? Spoken? Electronic? Will you need to create any charts, photographs, video, presentation software slides, or other visuals?	88–90

Coming Up with a Topic

If you need to choose a topic, consider your interests as they relate to the course for which you're writing. What do you want to learn about? What do you have questions about? What topics from the course have you found intriguing? What community, national, or global issues do you care about? Once you've thought of a potential topic, use the questions in Chapter 27, **WRITING AS INQUIRY**, to explore it and find an angle on it that you can write about—and want to. 325–28

If your topic is assigned, make sure you understand exactly what it asks you to do. Read the assignment carefully, looking for keywords: Does it ask you to **ANALYZE**, **COMPARE**, **EVALUATE**, **SUMMARIZE**, or **ARGUE**? If the assignment offers broad guidelines but allows you to choose within them, identify the requirements and the range of possible topics, and define your topic within those constraints. 114–45
422–28
210–19
523
399–416

For example, in an American history course, your instructor might ask you to discuss social effects of the Civil War. Potential but broad topics might include poverty among Confederate soldiers or former slaveholders, the migration of members of those groups to Mexico or Northern cities, the establishment of independent African American churches, or the spread of the Ku Klux Klan—to name only a few of the possibilities.

Think about what you know about your topic. Chances are you already know something about your topic, and articulating that knowledge can help you see possible ways to focus the topic or come up with potential sources of information. **FREEWRITING**, **LISTING**, **CLUSTERING**, and **LOOPING** are all 329
330
330–31
331

good ways of tapping your knowledge of your topic. Consider where you might find information about it: Have you read about it in a textbook? heard stories about it on the news? visited websites focused on it? Do you know anyone who knows about this topic?

Narrow the topic. As you consider possible topics, look for ways to narrow your topic's focus to make it specific enough to discuss in depth. For example:

> **Too general:** fracking

> **Still too general:** fracking and the environment

> **Better:** the potential environmental effects of extracting natural gas through the process of hydraulic fracturing, or fracking

If you limit your topic, you can address it with specific information that you'll be more easily able to find and manage. In addition, a limited topic will be more likely to interest your audience than a broad topic that forces you to use abstract, general statements. For example, it's much harder to write well about "the environment" than it is to address a topic that explores a single environmental issue.

Consulting with Librarians and Doing Preliminary Research

Consulting with a reference librarian at your school and doing some preliminary research in the library can save you time in the long run. Reference librarians can direct you to the best scholarly sources for your topic and help you focus the topic by determining appropriate search terms and **KEYWORDS** —significant words that appear in the title, abstract, or text of potential sources and that you can use to search for information on your topic in library catalogs, in databases, and on the web. These librarians can also help you choose the most appropriate reference works, sources that provide general overviews of the scholarship in a field. General internet searches can be time-consuming, as they often result in thousands of possible sites—too many to weed out efficiently, either by revising your search terms or by going through the sites themselves, many of which are unreliable. Library databases, in contrast, include only sources that already have been selected by experts, and searches in them usually present manageable numbers of results.

485–90

Reading a *Wikipedia* entry on your topic can help you understand background information, come up with new keywords to search, and discover related topics. A list of references—often with hyperlinks—at the bottom of each entry can lead to potential sources. Search tools like *Google* and *Google Scholar*—and AI tools like *ChatGPT*—can also be helpful in providing an initial overview of your topic and the key concepts or issues related to it. See pages 490–92 for advice on using these and other online search tools.

Coming Up with a Research Question

Once you've surveyed the territory of your topic, you'll likely find that your understanding of it has become broader and deeper. You may find that your interests have changed and your research has led to surprises and additional research. That's okay: as a result of exploring avenues you hadn't anticipated, you may well come up with a better topic than the one you'd started with. At some point, though, you need to develop a research question—a specific question that you will then work to answer through your research.

To write a research question, review your analysis of the **RHETORICAL SITUATION** to remind yourself of any time constraints or length considerations. Generate a list of questions beginning with "what," "when," "where," "who," "how," "why," "would," "could," and "should." Here, for example, are some questions about the tentative topic "the potential environmental effects of extracting natural gas through the process of hydraulic fracturing, or fracking":

■ 71

What are the environmental effects of fracking?

When was fracking introduced as a way to produce natural gas?

Where is fracking done, and *how* does this affect the surrounding people and environment?

Who will benefit from increased fracking?

How is fracking done, and *how much* energy does the process use?

Why do some environmental groups oppose fracking?

Would other methods of extracting natural gas be safer?

Could fracking cause earthquakes?

Should fracking be expanded, regulated, or banned?

Select one question from your list that you find interesting and that suits your rhetorical situation. Use the question to guide your research.

Drafting a Tentative Thesis

342–44

Once your research has led you to a possible answer to your research question, try formulating that answer as a tentative **THESIS**. You need not be committed to the thesis; in fact, you shouldn't be. The object of your research should be to learn about your topic, not to find information that simply supports what you already think you believe. Your tentative thesis may (and probably will) change as you learn more about your subject, consider the many points of view on it, and reconsider your topic and, perhaps, your goal: what you originally planned to be an argument for considering other points of view may become a call to action. However tentative, a thesis allows you to move forward by clarifying your purpose for doing research. Here are some tentative thesis statements on the topic of fracking:

> Fracking is a likely cause of earthquakes in otherwise seismically stable regions of the country.

> The federal government should strictly regulate the production of natural gas by fracking.

> Fracking can greatly increase our supplies of natural gas, but other methods of producing energy should still be pursued.

325–28

Glossary

As with a research question, a tentative thesis should guide your research efforts—but you should be ready to revise it as you learn still more about your topic. Research should be a process of **INQUIRY** in which you approach your topic with an open mind, ready to learn and possibly change. If you hold too tightly to a tentative thesis, you risk focusing only on evidence that supports your own view—a tendency called **CONFIRMATION BIAS** that can make your writing biased and unconvincing.

Creating a Rough Outline

335–37

After you've created a tentative thesis, write out a rough **OUTLINE** for your research project. This outline can be a simple list of topics you want to explore, something that will help you structure your research efforts and organize your notes and other materials. As you read your sources, you can use the outline to keep track of what you need to find and where the information you do find fits into your argument. Then you'll be able to see if you've covered all the ideas you intended to explore—or whether you need to rethink the categories on your outline.

Keeping a Working Bibliography

A working bibliography is a record of all the sources you consult. You should keep such a record so that you can find sources easily when you need them and then cite any that you actually use. Your library likely offers tools to store source information you find in its databases and catalog, and software such as *Zotero* or *EasyBib* can also help you save, manage, and cite your sources. You may find it helpful to print out bibliographical data you find useful or to keep your working bibliography on index cards or in a notebook. However you decide to compile your working bibliography, include all the information you'll need later to document any sources you use; follow the **DOCUMENTATION** style you'll use when you write so that you won't need to go back to your sources to find the information. Some databases make this step easy by preparing rough-draft citations in several styles that you can copy, paste, and edit.

538–41

On the next page is most of the basic information you'll want to include for each source in your working bibliography. Go to digital.wwnorton.com/fieldguide7h for templates you can use to keep track of this information.

Keeping Track of Your Sources

- *Staple together photocopies and printouts.* It's easy for individual pages to get shuffled or lost on a desk or in a backpack. Keep a stapler handy, and fasten pages together as soon as you copy them or print them out.

- *Bookmark web sources,* or save them using a free bookmark management tool available through several library databases. For database sources, use the *DOI* or *stable URL*, *permalink*, or *document URL* (the terms used by databases vary)—not the URL in the "Address" or "Location" box in your browser, which will expire after you end your online session.

- *Label everything.* Label your copies with the source's author and title.

- *Highlight sections you plan to use.* When you sit down to draft, your goal will be to find what you need quickly, so as soon as you decide you might use a source, highlight the paragraphs or sentences that you think you'll use. If your instructor wants copies of your sources to see how you used them, you've got them ready. If you're using PDF copies or websites, you can highlight or add notes using an online annotation tool like *Hypothesis* or *Diigo*.

Information for a Working Bibliography

FOR A BOOK
Library call number
Author(s) or editor(s)
Title and subtitle
Publication information: city, publisher, year of publication
Other information: edition, volume number, translator, and so on
If your source is an essay in a collection, include its author, title, and page numbers.

FOR A SOURCE FROM A DATABASE
Publication information for the source, as listed above
Name of database
DOI (digital object identifier) or URL of original source, such as the periodical in which an article was published
Stable URL or permalink for database
Date you accessed source

FOR AN ARTICLE IN A PRINT PERIODICAL
Author(s)
Title and subtitle
Name of periodical
Volume number, issue number, date
Page numbers

FOR A WEB SOURCE
URL
Author(s) or editor(s) if available
Name of site
Sponsor of site
Date site was first posted or last updated
Date you accessed site
If the source is an article or book reprinted on the web, include its title, the title and publication information of the periodical or book, where it was first published, and any page numbers.

- *Use your rough outline to keep track of what you've got.* In the margin of each highlighted section, write the number or letter of the outline division to which the section corresponds. (It's a good idea to write it in the same place consistently so you can flip through a stack of copies and easily see what you've got.) Alternatively, attach sticky notes to each copy, using a different color for each main heading in your outline.

- *Store all your research material in one place.* If you prefer to work digitally, create computer folders and subfolders that correspond to your rough outline. Or use web apps like *PowerNotes* or *Scrible* to collect, annotate, and organize your sources. If you prefer to work with paper, use an accordion file folder or a box. Having your material in one place will make writing a draft easier—and will serve you well if you're required to create a portfolio that includes your research notes, copies of sources, and drafts.

- *Use a reference manager.* Web-based reference or citation management software allows you to create and organize a personal database of resources. You can import references from databases to a personal account, organize them, and draft citations in various formats. *End-Note*, *Mendeley*, and *Zotero* are three such systems; check with your librarian to see what system your library supports, or search online, as several of them are available for free. Be aware, though, that the citations generated are often inaccurate and need to be checked carefully for content and format. So treat them as rough drafts, and plan to edit them.

If you need more help

See the guidelines on **FINDING SOURCES** once you're ready to move on to in-depth research and those on **EVALUATING SOURCES** for help thinking critically about the sources you find.

482–503
504–14

48 Finding Sources

To analyze media coverage of the 2024 Democratic National Convention, you examine news stories and blogs published at the time. To write an essay interpreting a poem by Maya Angelou, you study the poem and read several critical interpretations in literary journals. To write a report on career opportunities in psychology, you interview a graduate of your university who is working in a counseling center. In each of these cases, you go beyond your own knowledge to consult additional sources of information. Depending on your topic, then, you'll need to choose from many sources for your research—from reference works, books, periodicals, and websites to surveys, interviews, and other kinds of field research that you yourself conduct.

This chapter offers guidelines for locating a range of sources—print and online, general and specialized, published and firsthand. Keep in mind that as you do research, finding and **EVALUATING SOURCES** are two activities that usually take place simultaneously. So this chapter and the next one go hand in hand.

504–14

Kinds of Sources

Primary and secondary sources.   Your research will likely lead you to both primary and secondary sources. *Primary sources* include historical documents, literary works, eyewitness accounts, field reports, diaries, letters, and lab studies, as well as any original research you do through interviews, observation, experiments, or surveys. *Secondary sources* include scholarly books and articles, reviews, biographies, textbooks, and other works that interpret or discuss primary sources. Novels and films are primary sources; articles interpreting them are secondary sources. The Declaration of Independence is a primary historical document; a historian's description of the events surrounding the Declaration's writing is secondary. A published report of scientific findings is primary; a critique of that report is secondary.

Whether a work is considered primary or secondary sometimes depends on your topic and purpose. If you're analyzing a poem, a critic's article interpreting the poem is a secondary source—but if you're investigating that critic's work, the article would be a primary source for your own study and interpretation.

Secondary sources are often useful because they can help you understand and evaluate primary source material. Whenever possible, however, you should find and use primary sources, because secondary sources can distort or misrepresent the information in primary sources. For example, a seemingly reputable secondary source describing the 1948 presidential election asserted that the *New York Times* ran a headline reading, "Thomas E. Dewey's Election as President Is a Foregone Conclusion." But the actual article was titled "Talk Is Now Turning to the Dewey Cabinet," and it began by noting "[*the*] *popular view that* Gov. Thomas E. Dewey's election as President is a foregone conclusion." Here the secondary source not only got the headline wrong but also distorted the source's intended meaning by leaving out an important phrase. Your research should be as accurate and reliable as possible; using primary sources whenever you can helps ensure that it is.

Scholarly and popular sources. Scholarly sources are written by academic experts or scholars in a particular discipline and are *peer-reviewed*— evaluated by other experts in the same discipline for their factual accuracy and lack of bias. They are also written largely *for* experts in a discipline, as a means of sharing research, insights, and in-depth analysis with one another; that's why they must meet high standards of accuracy and objectivity and adhere to the discipline's accepted research methods, including its style for documenting sources. Scholarly articles are usually published in academic journals; scholarly books may be published by university presses or by other academically focused publishers.

Popular sources include just about all other online and print publications, from websites to magazines to books written for nonspecialists. These sources generally explain or provide opinion on current events or topics of general interest; when they discuss scholarly research, they tend to simplify the concepts and facts, providing definitions, narratives, and examples to make them understandable to nonspecialist audiences. They are often written by journalists or other professional writers who may specialize in a particular area but who report or comment on the scholarship of others rather than doing any themselves. Their most important difference from scholarly sources is that popular sources are not reviewed by other experts in the field being discussed, although editors or fact-checkers review the writing before it's published.

That said, the distinction can be blurry: many scholars write books for a general readership that are informed by those authors' own scholarship, and many writers of popular sources have extensive expertise in the subject. Even if it's not a requirement, citing scholarly sources often contributes to your own authority as a writer, demonstrating that you are familiar with important research and scholarship and that your own writing is informed by it.

In most of your college courses, you'll be expected to rely primarily on scholarly sources rather than popular ones. However, if you're writing about a very current topic or need to provide background information on a topic, a mix of scholarly and popular sources may be appropriate. To see how scholarly and popular sources differ in appearance, look at the Documentation Map for scholarly journals (p. 563) and at the illustrations on pages 486–87. Here's a guide to determining whether a potential source is scholarly:

IDENTIFYING SCHOLARLY SOURCES: WHAT TO LOOK FOR

- *The author:* Look for the author's credentials, including affiliations with academic or other research-oriented institutions. Make sure the author has expertise on the topic being discussed; an English professor may have academic credentials but not be an expert on the environment, while a journalist may have studied environmental issues for years and know a great deal.

- *The publisher:* Look for academic journals, university presses, and professional organizations such as the Modern Language Association or the American Psychological Association; popular sources are published in general-interest publications such as the *Atlantic* or *Slate* or trade publishers such as Penguin Random House or HarperCollins.

- *Peer review.* Look for a list of reviewers at the front of the journal or on the journal's or publisher's website. If you don't find one, the source is probably not peer-reviewed.

- *Source citations.* Look for a detailed list of works cited or references at the end of the source and citations either parenthetically within the text or in footnotes or endnotes. (Popular sources may include a reference list but seldom cite sources within the text, except in signal phrases.)

- *Language and content.* Look for abstracts (one-paragraph summaries of the contents) at the beginning of articles and for technical or specialized language and concepts that readers are assumed to be familiar with.

- *Other clues.* Look for little or no advertising on websites or within the journal; for a plain design with few or no illustrations, especially in print sources; and for listing in academic databases when you limit your search to *academic*, *peer-reviewed*, or *scholarly sources*.

Searching Effectively Using Keywords

Whether you're searching for books, articles in periodicals, or other material available on the web, chances are you'll conduct most of your search online. Most materials produced since the 1980s and most library catalogs are online, and most periodical articles can be found by searching electronic indexes and databases. In each case, you can search for authors, titles, or subjects.

To search online, you'll need to come up with keywords. Keywords are significant words that stand for an idea or concept. The key to searching efficiently is to use keywords and combinations of them that will focus your searches on the information you need — but not too much of it. Often you'll start out with one general keyword that will yield far too many results; then you'll need to switch to more specific terms or combinations (*homeopathy* instead of *medicine*, or *secondary education Japan* instead of *education Japan*).

Other times your keyword search won't yield enough sources; then you'll need to use broader terms or combinations (*education Japan* instead of *secondary education Japan*) or substitute synonyms (*home remedy* instead of *folk medicine*). Sometimes you'll need to learn terms used in academic disciplines or earlier in history for things you know by other names, such as *myocardial infarction* rather than *heart attack* or *Great War* instead of *World War I*. Or look through the sources that turn up in response to other terms to see what keywords you might use in subsequent searches. Searching requires flexibility, in the words you use and the methods you try.

Finding keywords using word clouds. One way to find keywords to help you narrow and focus your topic is to create a word cloud, a visual representation of words used in a text; the more often a word is used, the larger it looks in the word cloud. Several websites, including *Tagxedo* and *TagCrowd*, let you create word clouds. Examining a word cloud created from an article in a reference work may help you see what terms are used to discuss your topic — and may help you see new possible ways to narrow it. Here, for example, is a word cloud derived from an article in *Scientific American* discussing fracking. Many of the terms — "fracking," "water," "gas," "wells," "drilling" — are just what

Scholarly Source

Published in
an academic
journal.

J Res Pers. Author manuscript; available in PMC 2011 Aug 1.

Published in final edited form as:

J Res Pers. 2010 Aug 1; 44(4): 478–484.

doi: 10.1016/j.jrp.2010.06.001

PMCID: PMC2918908

NIHMSID: NIHMS218233

PMID: 20711512

Sounds like a Narcissist: Behavioral Manifestations of Narcissism in Everyday Life

Nicholas S. Holtzman, Simine Vazire, and Matthias R. Mehl

▶ Author information ▶ Copyright and License information   PMC Disclaimer

Includes an
abstract.

Abstract   Go to: ▶

Little is known about narcissists' everyday behavior. The goal of this study was to describe how narcissism is manifested in everyday life. Using the Electronically Activated Recorder (EAR), we obtained naturalistic behavior from participants' everyday lives. The results suggest that the defining characteristics of narcissism that have been established from questionnaire and laboratory-based studies are borne out in narcissists' day-to-day behaviors. Narcissists do indeed behave in more extraverted and less agreeable ways than non-narcissists, skip class more (among narcissists high in exploitativeness/entitlement only), and use more sexual language. Furthermore, we found that the link between narcissism and disagreeable behavior is strengthened when controlling for self-esteem, thus extending prior questionnaire-based findings (Paulhus, Robins, Trzesniewski, & Tracy, 2004) to observed, real-world behavior.

Cites academic
research using
a consistent
documentation
style.

Lists keywords.

Keywords: narcissism, behavior, personality traits, sexual behavior, language use

Describes research
methods; includes
numerical data as
appropriate.

The Single Item Self-Esteem scale

This single item measure is a reliable and valid measure of self-esteem (Robins, Hendin, & Trzesniewski, 2001). The item is "I see myself as someone who has high self-esteem." The item was measured on a 7-point Likert-type scale, from "strongly disagree" to "strongly agree".

Contributor Information   Go to: ▶

Nicholas S. Holtzman, Washington University in St. Louis.

Simine Vazire, Washington University in St. Louis.

Matthias R. Mehl, University of Arizona.

Authors have
academic
credentials.

Includes complete
list of references.

References   Go to: ▶

1. Back MD, Schmukle SC, Egloff B. Why are narcissists so charming at first sight? Decoding the narcissism-popularity link at zero acquaintance. *Journal of Personality and Social Psychology*. 2010;98:132–145. [PubMed] [Google Scholar]

2. Baumeister RF, Vohs KD, Funder DC. Psychology as the science of self-reports and finger movements: Whatever happened to actual behavior? *Perspectives on Psychological Science*. 2007;2:396–403. [PubMed] [Google Scholar]

Popular Source

Published in general-interest magazine or website. This article is from Business Insider.

HEALTH

3 types of narcissism and how they affect behavior, according to mental-health experts

Julia Naftulin   Jul 16, 2022, 8:00 AM EDT   ↱ Share   ⊓ Save

Catchy, provocative title; no abstract.

Author not an academic or other subject-matter expert.

When someone refers to a narcissist, they may conjure up images of an always-dramatic and attention-seeking ex, or a manipulative former friend or parent. But not every narcissist looks, thinks, and acts in the same way.

Links provided to sources and more information, but no works-cited page.

While most people fall on the narcissistic spectrum to some degree, some have full-blown narcissistic personality disorder, where their sense of self-importance and tendency to be hyper-critical impacts all or most of their relationships. An estimated 6% of the population is diagnosed with narcissistic personality disorder, or NPD.

In addition to NPD, a mental-health diagnosis only trained professionals can give, experts have pinpointed two other distinct types of narcissism, grandiose narcissism and vulnerable narcissism.

People who fall into these categories have "a failure of a healthy sense of self" that leads to an over-inflated sense of self-importance, Dr. Elizabeth G. Loran, assistant professor of medical psychology at Columbia University Medical Center in New York City, told Health.com. Within each category, however, how they exhibit their sense of entitlement, obsession with self, and need for adoration may differ.

Academic experts cited but not documented.

you'd expect. However, some terms—"USGS," "DiGiulio," "coalfired"—may be unfamiliar and lead to additional possibilities for research. For instance, "DiGiulio" is the last name of an expert on fracking whose publications might be worth examining, while "USGS" is an acronym for the United States Geological Survey, a scientific government agency.

61–69

Finding keywords using AI.   Another strategy for finding keywords is to consult a **GENERATIVE AI** tool like *ChatGPT*, *Claude*, or others for help. Such tools can draw on their vast training data to quickly suggest keyword combinations related to your topic. If you've already established your research question, you can type it into the AI tool, and the tool will look for connections among your main ideas to generate keywords you might use. The image below, for example, shows an interaction a student had with *ChatGPT* about keywords for their research question on how fracking affects people living in the surrounding area.

Fracking Impact Research: Keywords

February 29, 2024

Anonymous
I want to research the question of how fracking affects the people who live near fracking sites. What keywords can I use to find sources on this topic?

ChatGPT
Researching the impact of fracking on nearby residents involves exploring a range of topics, from environmental and health effects to economic and social implications. Here are some suggested keywords and phrases that you can use to find sources on this topic:

1. **Fracking health effects** - To find studies or reports on how fracking may affect the health of people living nearby.

2. **Water contamination and fracking** - For research on how fracking may affect water sources in the surrounding areas.

3. **Air quality near fracking sites** - To explore the impact of fracking on air pollution and its potential health risks.

4. **Noise pollution from fracking** - To investigate the impact of noise generated by fracking operations on local residents.

5. **Economic impact of fracking on communities** - To understand the economic benefits and drawbacks for communities near fracking sites.

6. **Fracking and property values** - For information on how proximity to fracking sites affects property values and residential satisfaction.

7. **Social impacts of fracking** - To explore studies on how fracking operations affect the social fabric and quality of life in nearby communities.

Finding keywords using databases. Once you've begun searching for and finding possible sources, you can expand your list of possible keywords by skimming the "detailed record" or "metadata" page for any scholarly articles you find, where full bibliographic information on the source may be found. A search for *fracking* resulted in this source:

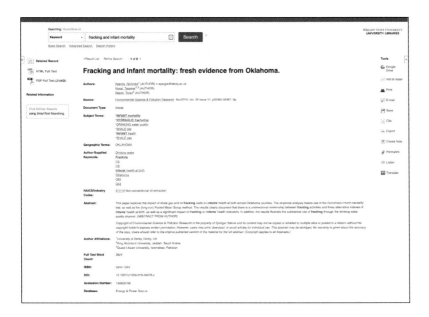

Note the list of author-supplied keywords, which offers options for narrowing and focusing your topic. Each keyword is a link, so simply clicking on it will produce a new list of sources. Also look for "permalink," which will allow you to find the source again quickly.

Advanced keyword searching. Most search sites have "advanced search" options that will help you focus your research. Some allow you to ask questions in conversational language: *What did Thomas Jefferson write about slavery?* Others allow you to focus your search by using specific words or symbols. Here are some of the most common ones:

- Type quotation marks around words to search for an exact phrase — "Thomas Jefferson."
- Type AND to specify that more than one keyword must appear in sources: Jefferson AND Adams. Some search engines require a plus sign instead: +Jefferson +Adams.

- Type OR if you're looking for sources that include any of several terms: Jefferson OR Adams OR Madison.

- Type NOT to find sources *without* a certain word: Jefferson NOT Adams. Some search engines call for a minus sign (actually, a hyphen) instead: +Jefferson –Adams.

- Type an asterisk to search for words in different form. For example, teach* will yield sources containing "teacher"/"teaching."

In addition, look for features that allow you to filter in order to limit results to a specific date range; only full-text articles (articles that are available in full online); and, in library databases, only scholarly, peer-reviewed sites.

If a search turns up too many sources, be more specific (*homeopathy* instead of *medicine*). If your original keywords don't generate good results, try synonyms (*home remedy* instead of *folk medicine*). Keep in mind that searching requires flexibility, both in the words you use and in the methods you try. And remember that the first items in a results list are not necessarily the best; scan what appears beyond page 1 of your results. Exercise "click restraint" by scanning through many items in the results and choosing only the ones that look most promising for your needs. Open each potential source in its own separate tab for evaluation.

Searching Using Popular Sites and Search Engines

When we need to find something out, most of us begin with *Google* or *Wikipedia*. If you aren't familiar with your research topic, these sites provide general information and a variety of perspectives. However, using general search engines can present challenges: it's easy to be overwhelmed by the number of sources, and determining what's trustworthy can be difficult. So you'll want to rely primarily on your library's resources to find accurate, up-to-date, scholarly sources; but the following sites can still serve as helpful starting points.

Wikipedia.　An open, online reference, *Wikipedia* often serves as a starting point for preliminary research. Reading a *Wikipedia* entry on a topic can help you understand background information, come up with new **KEYWORDS** to search, and discover related topics. A list of references— often hyperlinked—at the bottom of each entry can lead to potential sources. Be sure to check information you find on *Wikipedia* for accuracy, since entries can be written or edited by anyone.

485–90

Google, Google Scholar, **and other free search tools.**　To search *Google*, use simple and specific **KEYWORDS**. Googling "fracking environmental

485–90

effects" will turn up more focused results than googling "what is fracking." Scan the list of results and open sources that look promising in a new tab instead of stopping to read the first result that catches your eye. Be sure to look beyond the first page of results; higher placement doesn't always mean most relevant to your topic.

Google Scholar limits your search results to scholarly literature such as researched articles, theses, books, abstracts, and court opinions. Do a keyword search in *Google Scholar*, and scan the results to get an initial idea of the scholarly authors, publications, and databases publishing on your topic. You can sort results by publication date—a good way to check if there's recent research. Some articles and books in *Google Scholar* are full-text, but many are behind paywalls so must be accessed through your campus library.

Here are several more tools for searching online, outside of the library, to get started:

- *Keyword search engines.* Search engines use algorithms to tailor results to you, so search engines—and the results they show you—are not all the same. Compare results from *Google, Microsoft Edge, DuckDuckGo,* and other search sites to get more varied results.

- *Nonlibrary, academic searches.* In addition to *Google Scholar,* for peer-reviewed academic writing in many disciplines, try *Microsoft Academic* or *BASE. Science.gov* offers results from more than fifteen US federal agencies, and *CORE* collects open-access research papers.

- *Social media searches. Google Social Search, Social Searcher,* and *Talkwalker* let you search social media platforms. Use **HASHTAGS** (#) or *Tagboard,* a hashtag-based search engine, to search the contents of posts.

- *AI searches.* Some **GENERATIVE AI** tools can connect to the internet to find sources that may be relevant to your topic. *Copilot* and *Perplexity,* for example, will scour the web for sources and provide brief summaries of their contents, along with links to the sources themselves. You can also try using an AI-powered platform designed specifically for academic research, like *Consensus,* which finds scholarly articles only. *Consensus, Copilot, Perplexity,* and similar tools use "conversational searching," so typing in your full research question typically yields the most helpful results.

Image, video, and audio platforms. *Google Images* and *TinEye* allow you to search for images by keyword or by uploading an image. *Google Video Search* lets you search for videos by keyword, and *YouTube's* Search function

Glossary

61–69

allows you to find videos by relevance, upload date, view count, or rating. *Audioburst Search* provides results from podcast and radio segments.

News sites. Sites for newspapers, magazines, and radio and TV stations provide both up-to-the-minute information and also archives of older stories online. Through news-aggregating sites like *Google News* and *Apple News* you can sort through worldwide news from a wide range of sources. *Google News Archive* has news archives extending back to the 1700s. Beware that **MISINFORMATION** and lies are spread most often as news, so **FACT-CHECKING** sources that *appear* to be news is essential.

Glossary

506–11

Government sites. Many government agencies and departments maintain websites where you can find government reports, statistics, legislative information, and other resources. *USA.gov* offers resources from the US government.

Digital archives. You can find primary sources from the past, including drawings, maps, recordings, speeches, and historic documents, at sites maintained by the National Archives, the Library of Congress, the New York Public Library, and others.

Although many websites provide authoritative information, content found online varies greatly in stability and reliability: what you see on a site today may be different (or gone) tomorrow, so save copies of all pages you use. In addition, many reference and news sites are behind paywalls, their content unavailable unless you pay a fee or subscribe. If you find that a source you need is behind a paywall, check to see if it's available through your library or through interlibrary loan.

Searching in Academic Libraries

College and university libraries typically offer several ways to search their holdings. Their websites may look very different from one another, but most include search boxes like this one, from the Wright State University Libraries:

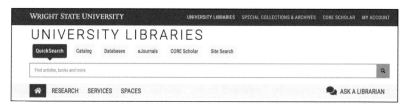

A search box allows you to look through all the library's holdings at once, an option that may be a good way to get started. You may already know, though, that you need to focus your search on one type of source, such as scholarly articles, or search using a particular method. In that case, it's best to use a more advanced search box like this one:

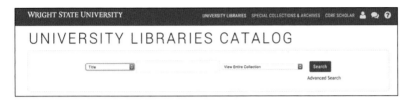

This box lets you shape and limit your search in several ways: the drop-down menu on the left lets you choose to search by title, keyword, author, or several other identifiers; the drop-down menu on the right lets you choose to search the library's entire collection, journals, books, media, or even materials in a specific location, such as course reserves or archives; and Advanced Search gives even more options. When in doubt, take advantage of Ask a Librarian services, which may include texting, chat, email, and phone conversations with reference librarians, when you need help but aren't working in the library.

Reference Works

The reference section of your school's library is the place to find encyclopedias, dictionaries, atlases, almanacs, bibliographies, and other reference works in print. Many of these sources are also online and can be accessed from any computer that is connected to the internet. Others are available only in the library. Remember, though, that whether in print or online, reference works are only a starting point, a place where you can get an overview of your topic.

General reference works.   Consult encyclopedias for general background information on a subject, dictionaries for definitions of words, atlases for maps and geographic data, and almanacs for statistics and other data on current events. These are some works you might consult:

The New Encyclopaedia Britannica

The Columbia Encyclopedia

Webster's Third New International Dictionary

Oxford English Dictionary

National Geographic Atlas of the World
Statistical Abstract of the United States
The World Almanac and Book of Facts

Specialized reference works. You can also go to specialized reference works, which provide in-depth information on a single field or topic. These may also include authoritative bibliographies, leading you to more specific works. A reference librarian can refer you to specialized encyclopedias in particular fields, but good places to start are online collections of many topic-specific reference works that offer overviews of a topic, place it in a larger context, and sometimes provide links to potential academic sources. Collections that are available through libraries include the following:

CQ Researcher offers in-depth reports on topics in education, health, the environment, criminal justice, international affairs, technology, the economy, and social trends. Each report gives an overview of a particular topic, outlines of the differing positions on it, and a bibliography of resources on it.

Gale eBooks offers thousands of full-text specialized encyclopedias, almanacs, articles, and ebooks.

Oxford Reference contains hundreds of dictionaries, encyclopedias, and other reference works on a wide variety of subjects, as well as timelines with links to each item mentioned on each timeline.

Sage Knowledge includes many encyclopedias and handbooks on topics in the social sciences.

Bibliographies. Bibliographies provide an overview of what has been published on a topic, listing published works along with the information you'll need to find each work. Some are annotated with brief summaries of each work's contents. You'll find bibliographies at the end of scholarly articles and books, and you can also find book-length bibliographies, both in the reference section of your library and online. Check with a reference librarian for bibliographies on your research topic.

Books / Searching the Library Catalog

The library catalog is your primary source for finding books. Almost all library catalogs are computerized and can be accessed through the library's website. You can search by author, title, subject, or keyword. The image that follows shows the result of a keyword search for material on looted art in Nazi

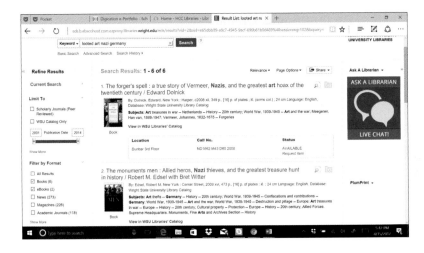

Germany. This search of the library's catalog revealed six items—print books and ebooks—on the topic; to access information on each one, the researcher must simply click on the title or thumbnail image. The image below shows detailed information for one source: bibliographic data about author, title, and publication; related subject headings (which may lead to other useful materials in the library)—and more. Library catalogs also supply a call number, which identifies the book's location on the library's shelves.

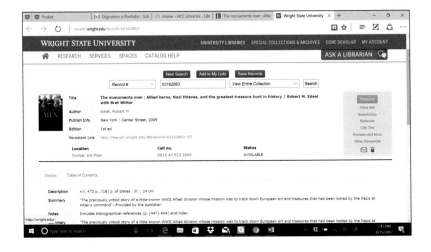

Ebooks / Finding Books Online

Many books in the library catalog are available online. Some may be downloaded to a tablet or mobile device. In addition, thousands of classic works that are in the public domain—no longer protected by copyright—may be read online. *Bartleby*, *Google Books*, *Open Library*, and *Project Gutenberg* are four collections of public-domain works. Here are some other sources of ebooks:

HathiTrust Digital Library offers access to millions of ebooks, about a third of them in the public domain, contributed by university libraries.

Internet Archive includes millions of ebooks as well as audio, video, music, software, images, and the Wayback Machine, which archives historical webpages.

Gale eBooks, Oxford Reference, and *Sage Knowledge* all contain large ebook collections.

Periodicals / Searching Indexes and Databases

To find journal, magazine, and newspaper articles, you will need to search periodical indexes and databases. Indexes provide listings of articles organized by topics; many databases provide the full texts. Some indexes are in print and can be found in the reference section of the library; most are online. Some databases are available for free; most of the more authoritative ones, however, are available only by subscription and so must be accessed through a library.

Many databases now include not only scholarly articles but also dissertations, theses, book chapters, book reviews, and conference proceedings. Dissertations and theses are formal works of scholarship done as requirements for graduate degrees; book reviews offer critical evaluations of scholarly and popular books; and conference proceedings are papers presented, usually orally, at scholarly meetings.

When you access a source through a database, the URL or link address is different each time you log in, so if you want to return to a source, look for a *stable URL, permalink,* or *DOI* option and choose it to copy and paste into your list of sources.

General indexes and databases. A reference librarian can help you determine which databases will be most helpful for your needs, but here are some useful ones:

Academic Search Complete, Academic Search Premier, Academic Search Elite, and *Academic Search Ultimate* are multidisciplinary indexes and databases containing the full text of articles in thousands of journals and indexing of even more, with abstracts of their articles.

Gale Academic OneFile offers millions of full-text articles in a broad spectrum of disciplines and on a wide variety of topics from thousands of scholarly and popular periodicals, including the *New York Times.*

JSTOR archives scanned copies of entire publication runs of scholarly journals in many disciplines, but it may not include current issues of the journals.

ProQuest Central provides access to full-text articles from thousands of books, scholarly journals, conference papers, magazines, newspapers, blogs, podcasts, and websites and a large collection of dissertations and theses.

Single-subject indexes and databases.   The following are just a sample of what's available; check with a reference librarian for indexes and databases in the subject you're researching.

America: History and Life indexes scholarly literature on the history and culture of the United States and Canada.

APA PsycINFO indexes scholarly literature in a number of disciplines relating to the behavioral and social sciences.

BIOSIS Previews provides abstracts and indexes for thousands of sources on a wide variety of biological and medical topics.

ERIC is the US Department of Education's Educational Resource Information Center database. It includes hundreds of journal titles as well as conference papers, technical reports, and other resources on education.

Historical Abstracts includes abstracts of articles on the history of the world, excluding the United States and Canada, since 1450.

Humanities International Index contains bibliographic references to thousands of journals dealing with the humanities.

MLA International Bibliography indexes scholarly articles on modern languages, literature, folklore, and linguistics.

PubMed includes millions of citations for biomedical literature, many with links to full-text content.

Print indexes.   You may need to consult print indexes to find articles published before the 1980s. Here are four useful ones:

General Science Index (print, 1978–; online, 1984–)

Humanities Index (print, 1974–; online, 1984–)

The New York Times Index (print and online, 1851–)

The Readers' Guide to Periodical Literature (print, 1900–; online, 1983–)

Images, Sound, and More

Your library likely subscribes to various databases that allow you to find and download video, audio, and image files. Here is a sampling:

AP Images provides access to photographs taken for the Associated Press, the cooperative agency of thousands of newspapers and radio and television stations worldwide.

ArtStor provides images in the arts, architecture, humanities, and sciences.

The Borror Laboratory of Bioacoustics database includes digitized recordings of the sounds of over 45,000 species of animals.

Dance Online: Dance in Video offers hundreds of videos of dance productions and documentaries on dance.

Music Online: Smithsonian Global Sound for Libraries is a "virtual encyclopedia of the world's musical and aural traditions."

Naxos Music Library contains thousands of classical, jazz, and world music recordings, as well as libretti and synopses of hundreds of operas and other background information.

Theatre in Video provides videos of hundreds of performances of plays and film documentaries.

Doing Field Research

Sometimes you'll need to do your own research, to go beyond the information you find in published sources and gather data by doing field research. Three kinds of field research you might want to consider are interviews, observations, and questionnaires.

Interviewing experts. Some kinds of writing—a profile of a living person, for instance—almost require that you conduct an interview. And sometimes you may just need to find information that you haven't been able to find in published sources. To get firsthand information on the experience of serving as a soldier in Afghanistan, you might interview your uncle who served a tour of duty there; to find current research on pesticide residues in food, you might need to interview a toxicologist. Whatever your goal, you can conduct interviews in person, through *Zoom*, by telephone, through email, or by mail. In general, you will want to use interviews to find information you can't find elsewhere. Some advice on planning and conducting an interview follows.

BEFORE THE INTERVIEW

1. Once you identify someone you want to interview, email or phone to ask the person, stating your **PURPOSE** for the interview and what you hope to learn.

73–74

2. Once you've set up an appointment, send a note or email confirming the time and place. If you wish to record the interview, be sure to ask for permission to do so. If you plan to conduct the interview by mail or email, state when you will send your questions.

3. Write out questions. Plan questions that invite extended response and supporting details: "What accounts for the recent spike in gasoline prices?" forces an explanation, whereas "Is the recent spike in gas prices a direct result of global politics?" is likely to elicit only a yes or a no.

AT THE INTERVIEW

4. Record the full name of the person you interview, along with the date, time, and place of the interview; you'll need this information to cite and document the interview accurately.

5. Take notes, even if you are recording the interview.

6. Keep track of time: don't take more than you agreed to beforehand unless both of you agree to keep talking. End by thanking your subject and offering to provide a copy of your final product.

AFTER THE INTERVIEW

7. Flesh out your notes with details as soon as possible after the interview, while you still remember them. What did you learn? What surprised you? Summarize both the interviewee's words and your impressions.

8. Make sure you've reproduced quotations from the interview accurately and fairly. Avoid editing quotations in ways that distort the speaker's intended meaning.

9. Be sure to send a thank-you note or email.

Observation.   Some writing projects are based on information you get by observing something. For a sociology report, you may observe how students behave in large lectures. For an education course, you may observe one child's progress as a writer over a period of time. The following advice can help you conduct observations.

BEFORE OBSERVING

73–74

1. Think about your research **PURPOSE**: What are you looking for? What do you expect to find? How will your presence as an observer affect what you observe? What do you plan to do with what you find?

2. If necessary, set up an appointment. You may need to ask permission of the people you wish to observe and of your school as well. (Check with your instructor about your school's policy in this area.) Be honest and open about your goals and intentions; college students doing research assignments are often welcomed where others may not be.

WHILE OBSERVING

3. If you're taking notes on paper, you may want to divide each page down the middle vertically and write only on the left side of the page, reserving the right side for information you will fill in later. If you're using a laptop, you can set up two columns or a split screen.

4. Note descriptive details about the setting. What do you see? What do you hear? Do you smell anything? Get down details about color, shape, size, sound, and so on. Consider photographing or making a sketch of what you see.

439–46 ◆

5. Who is there, and what are they doing? **DESCRIBE** what they look like, and make notes about what they say. Note any significant demographic details—about gender, race, occupation, age, dress, and so on.

6. What is happening? Who's doing what? What's being said? Make note of these kinds of **NARRATIVE** details.

◆ 457–65

AFTER OBSERVING

7. As soon as possible after you complete your observations, use the right side of your notes to fill in gaps and include additional details.

8. **ANALYZE** your notes, looking for patterns. Did some things appear or happen more than once? Did anything stand out? surprise or puzzle you? What did you learn?

▲ 114–45

Questionnaires and surveys. Various kinds of questionnaires and surveys can provide information or opinions from a large number of people. For a political science course, you might conduct a survey to ask students who they plan to vote for. Or, for a marketing course, you might distribute a questionnaire asking what they think about an advertising campaign. The advice in this section will help you create useful questionnaires and surveys.

Define your goal. The goal of a questionnaire or survey should be limited and focused, so that every question will contribute to your research question. Also, people are more likely to respond to a brief, focused survey.

Define your sample. A survey gets responses from a representative sample of the whole group. The answers to these questions will help you define that sample:

1. Who should answer the questions? The people you contact should represent the whole population. For example, if you want to survey undergraduate students at your school, your sample should reflect your school's enrollment in terms of gender, year, major, age, ethnicity, and so forth as closely as possible.

2. How many people make up a representative sample? In general, the larger your sample, the more the answers will reflect those of the whole group. But if your population is small—200 students in a history course, for example—your sample must include a large percentage of that group.

Decide on a medium. Will you ask the questions face-to-face? over the phone? on a website such as *SurveyMonkey*? by mail? by email? Face-to-face questions work best for simple surveys or for gathering impersonal information. You're more likely to get responses to more personal questions with printed or online questionnaires, which should be neat and easy to read. Phone interviews may require well-thought-out scripts that anticipate possible answers and make it easy to record these answers.

Design good questions.   The way you ask questions will determine the usefulness of the answers you get, so take care to write questions that are clear and unambiguous. Here are some typical question types:

MULTIPLE-CHOICE
What is your current age?

_____ 15–20   _____ 21–25   _____ 26–30   _____ 31–35   _____ Other

RATING SCALE
How would you rate the service at the campus bookstore?

_____ Excellent   _____ Good   _____ Fair   _____ Poor

AGREEMENT SCALE
How much do you agree with the following statements?

	Strongly Agree	Agree	Disagree	Strongly Disagree
The bookstore has sufficient numbers of textbooks available.	❏	❏	❏	❏

	Strongly Agree	Agree	Disagree	Strongly Disagree
Staff at the bookstore are knowledgeable.	❏	❏	❏	❏
Staff at the bookstore are courteous.	❏	❏	❏	❏

OPEN-ENDED
How often do you visit the campus bookstore?

How can the campus bookstore improve its service?

Include all potential alternatives when phrasing questions to avoid biasing the answers. And make sure each question addresses only one issue—for example, "Bookstore staff are knowledgeable and courteous" could lead to the response "knowledgeable, agree; courteous, disagree."

When arranging questions, place easier ones at the beginning and harder ones near the end (but if the questions seem to fall into a different natural order, follow it). Make sure each question asks for information you will need—if a question isn't absolutely necessary, omit it.

Include an introduction. Start by stating your survey's purpose and how the results will be used. It's also a good idea to offer an estimate of the time needed to complete the questions. Remind participants of your deadline.

Test the survey or questionnaire. Make sure your questions elicit the kinds of answers you need by asking three or four people who are part of your target population to answer them. They can help you find unclear instructions, questions that aren't clear or that lack sufficient alternatives, or other problems that you should correct to make sure your results are useful. But if you change the questionnaire as a result of their responses, don't include their answers in your total.

If you need more help

See **EVALUATING SOURCES** for help determining their usefulness. See also Chapter 51 for help **TAKING NOTES** on your sources.

504–14
521–22

49 Evaluating Sources

Searching the *Health Source* database for information on the incidence of meningitis among college students, you find thirty-four articles. A *Google* search on the same topic produces over 19 million hits. How do you decide which sources to read? This chapter presents advice on evaluating sources—first to determine whether a source might be useful for your purposes and is worth looking at more closely, and then to read with a critical eye the ones you choose.

Considering Whether a Source Might Be Useful

As you consider potential sources—sources you've found online or from library resources—keep your **PURPOSE** in mind. Are you trying to persuade readers to believe or do something? If so, look for sources representing various positions. Are you reporting on a topic? If so, you'll likely need sources that are factual or informative. Consider your **AUDIENCE**. What kinds of sources will they find persuasive? If you're writing for readers in a particular field, what counts as **EVIDENCE** in that field? Following are some questions that can help you judge whether a possible source you've found deserves your time and attention—but remember to consider most or all of the questions rather than relying on a single criterion:

73–74

75–78

402–9

- *Is it relevant?* How well does the source relate to your purpose? What would it add to your work? To see what it covers, look at the title and at any introductory material (such as a preface or an abstract).

- *Is it reliable?* Is it scholarly? peer-reviewed? published in a reputable journal or magazine, or by a reputable publisher? Did you find it in a library database? on the web? Evaluating web-based texts may require more work than using results from library databases. Whatever kind of search you do, skim the results quickly to evaluate their reliability—and use the techniques that follow to fact-check them. You might also check the *Media Bias/Fact Check* website, which ranks news organizations on their political slant and factual reporting.

- *What are the author's credentials?* How is the author qualified to write on the subject? Has the author written other works on this subject? Are they known for a particular position on it? As an expert? a scholar? a journalist? Will your audience find the author credible? If the credentials aren't stated, do a search to see what reliable sources say about the author.

- *What is the* **STANCE**? Does the source explain various points of view or advocate only one perspective? Does its title suggest a certain slant? If it's online, check to see whether it includes links to other sites—and if so, what their perspectives are. You'll want to consult sources with various viewpoints and understand the bias of each source you use.

  ■ 85–87

- *Who is the publisher or sponsor?* If it's a book, what kind of company published it; if an article, what kind of periodical did it appear in? Books published by university presses and articles in scholarly journals are reviewed by experts before they're published. Many books and articles written for the general public also undergo careful fact-checking, but some do not—and they may lack the kind of in-depth discussion that is useful for research.

- *At what level is it written?* Can you understand the material? Texts written for a general audience might be easier to understand but not authoritative enough for academic work. Scholarly texts will be more authoritative but may be hard to comprehend.

- *How current is it?* Check to see when books and articles were published and when websites were last updated. (If a site lists no date, see if links to other sites still work; if not, the site is probably too dated to use.) A recent publication date or update, however, doesn't necessarily mean that a potential source is good—some topics require current information; others call for older sources.

- *Is it cited in other works?* If so, you can probably assume that some other writers regard it as trustworthy.

- *Does it include other useful information?* Is there a bibliography that might lead you to other sources? How current or authoritative are the sources it cites?

- *Is it available?* If it's a book and your school's library doesn't have it, can you get it through interlibrary loan? If it's online and there's a paywall, can your library get you access?

Fact-Checking Popular Sources Online

Scholarly books are edited; scholarly articles are reviewed by experts; established news sources employ fact-checkers to verify information. But many websites and social media sites aren't checked by anyone. As a result, when you're using *Google* and other nonlibrary resources online to get started, you may find misleading information, data, images, and videos.

Sometimes such misleading information takes the form of satires, such as Jonathan Swift's "A Modest Proposal," stories in the *Onion*, or episodes of *The Daily Show*. Such satires offer humorous exaggerations to expose and criticize people and governments. Other misleading or false news stories are malicious, created usually for political ends. World War II Nazi propaganda and more recent fraudulent stories such as "Pope Francis Endorses Donald Trump," a false story that went viral on *Facebook*, are intended to mislead readers. Further complicating things, some politicians and other public figures have taken to calling news reports with which they disagree "fake news"—even though the stories reported are verifiably true and the news outlets are considered trustworthy.

Although false news has been around at least since the invention of the printing press, the internet and social media have led to a huge increase in false news stories, seriously challenging and muddying "real" news. Each false story can rapidly multiply over sites such as *Facebook, TikTok,* and *X* and through email. As a reader and researcher, you need to be able to determine whether a potential news source is false. As a writer, you risk harming your credibility if you cite a false news story as evidence. To conduct sound research—and to use good information to form our own ideas—we need to be able to determine what is true, what is false, and what is trying to manipulate us when reading popular online sources. Professional fact-checkers, people who investigate the truthfulness of assertions made in published work, use the following methods to evaluate their accuracy.

Fact-checkers begin not by immediately reading something they find online that looks relevant, but by first moving *outside* the source—opening new tabs in the same browser—to search and see what other reliable sites say about it. Only after they've done some research to confirm a source's accuracy do they read the source itself. When you find something online that looks relevant, first stop and ask yourself if you know the website publishing the source and have reason to trust it. If not, take the following steps to assess the source before reading any further:

400–401 ◆

- *Look up the main* CLAIMS. Copy and paste the title or a few key words of the article, essay, or post into *Google* or another browser to see if a reliable fact-checking site—*Snopes, FactCheck, Politifact, Allsides,* or *Media Bias / Fact Check*—has already evaluated it. If several reputable sources report the same information, it's probably true. If the information appears in only one source—even if many other people are quoting it—it's worth taking more steps to check whether it's reliable and even-handed enough for your academic writing.

- *Investigate the author's expertise and* **STANCE**. Use *Wikipedia, Google News,* or *Google Scholar* to see if the author is an expert on the topic they're weighing in on. Some signs that the author has expertise include holding an academic position in a relevant field, having published other pieces in reputable sources on the same topic, or having considerable experience in the area being written about. If you can't find any evidence of an author's expertise on the topic, the source may still be useful to you, but don't depend on the information as authoritative. Also, the author's affiliations—the groups they're members of or the places they've published—can help you determine the author's stance.

    ■ 85–87

- *Check out who runs the site.* Don't rely on the site's About page alone. Instead, google the organization's name in quotation marks and add keywords like "who sponsors" or "funding." What do other reputable sites say about the publisher or sponsoring organization? Take note of information on controversy or a specific agenda attached to the organization. Do reliable sources say the organization has a good reputation? a lot of members? a long history? Those are all good signs the publication is trustworthy.

- *Check the date of the story and dates within the story.* Sometimes old stories resurface as "news." They aren't any truer now than they were then.

- *Take stock, and use your judgment.* Consider your **PURPOSE** and what you've found about the source's main claims, author, and publisher. Does the source seem accurate and trustworthy, given what you know about the world and how it works? Do the claims seem designed to generate a strong emotional response, especially anger or fear, rather than appeal to logic or sound evidence? If taking these steps shows you that a source has a strong **STANCE** or bias, that doesn't automatically mean you should discard it, but it does mean you should keep that stance in mind as you work with the source.

    ■ 73–74

    ■ 85–87

If even just one of these steps reveals troubling information, it's best to move on to find a different, more solidly reliable source. As you use these fact-checking moves, don't just click on the first item in a list of search results. Instead, scan the results to get a broad sense of what others are saying, and choose the most trustworthy ones to read.

The graphics on the following pages show good examples of how fact-checking a popular source found on the web works.

Fact-checking photos and video. Visual media—especially images and videos posted online—can also be manipulated to present misleading information. Hoax photos are images taken out of context or doctored in order to deceive using *Photoshop* or another photo manipulation program. For example, this misleading image of presidential candidate John Kerry and antiwar activist and actor Jane Fonda was widely distributed during the 2004 election campaign:

The image was created by combining two photos taken more than a year apart on two different occasions and was used to discredit Kerry's patriotism despite his service in Vietnam.

However, doctoring sometimes isn't even needed: the camera lenses used or the camera's position can lead to very different views. For example, during the coronavirus pandemic, the photo on the left purported to show people ignoring social distancing guidance to stay at least six feet apart on a beach in Florida:

The photo on the right, though, shows that the beachgoers were in fact maintaining a safe distance from one another.

To identify the source of most photographs, you can do a reverse image search using these tools:

- *Google Image.* Click on the small camera icon to the right of the search box, and paste in the image's web address. The results will show other uses of the image as well as similar images.

- *TinEye.* Upload the image or enter its URL in the search box to get a list of other places where the image has appeared online.

Hoax videos are altered or presented in misleading ways. The *Washington Post* identifies three ways hoax videos are made:

- *Missing context.* The video itself hasn't been altered, but it is misrepresented in order to mislead the viewer—using an incorrect date, location, or summary. Or it's a brief clip from a longer video taking an event out of context.

- *Deceptive editing.* Portions of the video have been edited out and the remaining parts spliced together to create a misleading narrative. Or videos shot on two different occasions have been spliced together to create a single false narrative.

- *Malicious transformation.* The video itself has been altered to deceive the viewer, or artificial intelligence has been used to create fake images and audio.

In addition, videos may simply present lies as factual information. For example, during the coronavirus pandemic, online videos included false statements including "The pharmaceutical companies have a cure but won't sell it," "Coronavirus is caused by 5G mobile phone network signals," and "The coronavirus is being used for worldwide population control." Some of these videos are viewed by millions of people, so the popularity of a video may not reflect its accuracy or truthfulness, either.

To evaluate the accuracy of videos, type a brief summary of the video into *Google* to see if fact-checking sites like *Snopes* have reported on it. Also, do your own analysis: Does anything in the video seem doctored? Are the events depicted believable or unlikely? Is the language used inflammatory or demeaning? If the video appears on several websites, do its details change from site to site? Use *Youtube DataViewer*, available at citizen evidence.amnestyusa.org, to see where else a *YouTube* video has been posted, and do a reverse image search on stills from a video.

Fact-Checking Popular Sources

Once you've got a source to fact-check, begin by looking outside the site itself following the steps below.

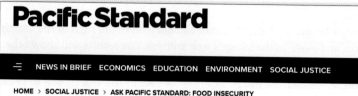

Pacific Standard

NEWS IN BRIEF   ECONOMICS   EDUCATION   ENVIRONMENT   SOCIAL JUSTICE

HOME > SOCIAL JUSTICE > ASK PACIFIC STANDARD: FOOD INSECURITY

COLLEGE STUDENTS ARE GOING HUNGRY

A new report finds that around half of all college students fear running out of food before having the money to buy more.

Look Up the Claim

Other reliable news organizations report similar claims from various sources.

Google   college students going hungry

All   News   Images   Videos   Shopping   More   Settings   Tools

About 43,700,000 results (0.78 seconds)

Tuition or Dinner? Nearly Half of College Students Surveyed in a
https://www.nytimes.com › nyregion › hunger-college-food-insecurity
May 2, 2019 - ... Half of **College Students** Surveyed in a New Report Are **Going Hungry** ... A health sciences student at Stony Brook University on Long Island ...

Millions of College Students Are Going Hungry - The Atlantic
https://www.theatlantic.com › archive › 2019/01 › college-student-hunger ▾
Jan 9, 2019 - As the costs of **college** have climbed, some **students** have gone **hungry**. When they've voiced frustration, they've often been ridiculed: "Ramen ...

Check Out the Website

Wikipedia says the site began in 2008 and closed in 2019. Be skeptical of a new site or one that no longer exists.

A New York Times article confirms the site was funded by a well-established academic publisher and won two awards for quality, so it appears trustworthy.

Google   pacific standard funding who is behind

All   News   Images   Videos   Maps   More   Settings   Tools

About 82,900,000 results (0.63 seconds)

Pacific Standard - Wikipedia
https://en.wikipedia.org › wiki › Pacific_Standard ▾
It continues to get most of its **funding** from Sage Publications, with much smaller amounts from subscription, newsstand, and website revenue.

Closing of Pacific Standard and Topic Shows Perils of ...
https://www.nytimes.com › 2019/08/17 › business › media › pacific-standar...
Aug 17, 2019 - **Pacific Standard** and Topic, a pair of award-winning publications that stood ... academic publishing company Sage Publications, withdrew its **funding**. ... How the Man **Behind** 'The Crown' Made the Monarchy Relevant Again.

Investigate the Author

The author has published several more pieces on the same site.

The author's bio from his book publisher appears at the bottom of the first search results page.

Opening the author's academic webpage shows he's a professor at Texas State University, teaching courses in American history and writing about the history of eating habits.

An *Amazon* page shows the author published a book on food and eating. So he appears credible on this topic.

Reading Sources with a Critical Eye

Approach your sources with an open mind, but consider their arguments with a critical eye. Pay attention to what they say, to the reasons and evidence they offer to support what they say, and to whether they address viewpoints other than their own. Assume that each author is responding to some other argument. Ask some of these questions of each of your sources:

170–96

- *What* **ARGUMENTS** *does the author make?* Does the author present several different positions or argue for a particular position? What arguments is the author responding to?

402
402–9
526–28

- *How persuasive do you find the argument to be?* What **REASONS** and **EVIDENCE** does the author provide to support their positions? Are there citations or links—and if so, are they **CREDIBLE**? Is any evidence presented without citations? Are any of the author's assumptions questionable? How thoroughly does the author consider alternative arguments?

85–87

- *What is the author's* **STANCE**? Does it seem objective, or does the content or language reveal a particular bias? Are opposing views considered and treated fairly? Do the headlines and text try to elicit an emotional reaction?

- *Do you recognize ideas you've run across in other sources?* Does the source leave out any information or perspective that other sources include—or does it include any that they leave out?

75–78
73–74

- *What can you tell about the intended* **AUDIENCE** *and* **PURPOSE**? Are you a member of the audience for which the source was written—and if not, does that affect the way you interpret what you read? Is the main purpose to inform readers about a topic or to argue a certain point?

Access the ebook for a video on evaluating sources.

Glossary

- *Does this source support or challenge your own position—or does it do both?* Does it support your thesis? Does it support a different argument altogether? Does it represent a position you need to address? Don't reject a source just because it challenges your views; work to understand the various perspectives or positions taken on your topic to avoid **CONFIRMATION BIAS**, which is our tendency to believe things that match what we already believe and to discount information that doesn't. Be wary of assuming a story or article is trustworthy just because you agree with the author—you need to step back and make sure your own beliefs aren't clouding your judgment.

Comparing Sources

You may find that two or more of your sources present similar information or arguments. How do you decide which one to use? Compare them, using these questions as a guide:

- *Which source is most current?* Generally, a more recent source is better than an older one, because the newer source includes information or data that is more up to date—and may include (or refute) the information in the earlier source. Be aware, though, that in some fields, such as literary criticism, decades-old sources may still be important.

- *Which argument is more persuasive?* Examine the **CLAIMS**, **REASONS**, and **EVIDENCE** presented in each source. Which source's argument is most logical? Which one has the best supporting reasons and evidence? Which one best **ACKNOWLEDGES**, **ACCOMMODATES**, or **REFUTES** opposing arguments?

◆ 400–401
402
402–9
◆ 411–13

- *Which author or authors are most authoritative?* An expert in the subject is more authoritative than, say, a journalist writing on the subject. An article published in a scholarly journal is more authoritative than one published in a general-circulation magazine or website. The journalist's article may be easier to read and more interesting, but you're best off looking for the best information—not the best read.

- *Which source has the most appropriate* **STANCE**? In general, look for sources that strive for objectivity, rather than a particular bias. Also, be aware that we all tend to favor information that agrees with our views—and that may lead us to choose sources we agree with rather than sources that present all sides of an issue.

■ 85–87

- *Which source best fits your needs?* All other things being equal, the best source to choose is the one that will give you the information you need, support the argument you're making, and perhaps provide useful quotations to add to your writing. The best source will show that you've done appropriate research and will enhance your own credibility as a thinker, reader, researcher, and writer.

Fact-Checking AI Output

If you use **GENERATIVE AI** tools as part of your research process, be sure to take a questioning, skeptical approach to the output you receive. A large

✳ 61–69

language model (LLM) like *ChatGPT* doesn't retrieve information in the way a search engine or database does. Instead, the LLM generates a response based on patterns learned from the billions of words it was trained on. So the response may or may not be reliable—which means you have to check it for inaccuracies, biases, and misinformation.

You can use the same fact-checking and critical-reading strategies mentioned earlier in this chapter to evaluate the veracity of AI output. Consult reputable sources like encyclopedias, scholarly articles, news outlets, and official websites to cross-reference any facts, statistics, or claims an AI tool gives you. If the AI tool cites sources in its response to you, search online to verify that the sources exist—and use the tips on pages 506–11 to make sure the sources are trustworthy. Then read the sources carefully to determine whether the bot accurately represents their content. Even when you use AI tools that provide direct links to online sources, you'll still need to read them with a critical eye.

If you need more help

521–32
533–37

See Chapter 51, **QUOTING, PARAPHRASING, AND SUMMARIZING**, for help in taking notes on your sources and deciding how to use them in your writing. See also Chapter 52, **ACKNOWLEDGING SOURCES, AVOIDING PLAGIARISM**, for advice on giving credit to the sources you use.

50 Synthesizing Ideas

To **ANALYZE** a collection of poetry, you show how the poet uses similar images in three different poems to explore a recurring concept. To solve a crime, a detective studies several eyewitness accounts to figure out who did it. To trace the history of photojournalism, a professor **COMPARES** the uses of photography during the Civil War and during the Vietnam War. These are all cases where someone synthesizes—brings together material from two or more sources in order to generate new information or to support a new perspective. When you do research, you need to go beyond what your sources say; you need to use what they say to inspire and support what you want to say. This chapter focuses on how to synthesize ideas you find in other sources as the basis for your ideas.

114–45

422–28

Reading for Patterns and Connections

Your task as a writer is to find as much information as you can on your topic—and then to sift through all that you have found to determine and support what you yourself will write. In other words, you'll need to synthesize ideas and information from the sources you've consulted to figure out first what arguments *you* want to make and then to provide support for those arguments.

When you synthesize, you group similar bits of information together, looking for patterns, themes, or trends. As an example, take a look at the following excerpt from a 2023 report published in *KFF*, an online health policy newsletter, "The Implications of COVID-19 for Mental Health and Substance Abuse." In the second paragraph alone, the authors synthesize information from five different sources to show a relationship between losing one's job and being anxious or depressed, and that the pandemic made things worse. The sources' titles are in the boxes, and the information used is underlined.

PREVALENCE OF MENTAL ILLNESS AND SUBSTANCE USE DURING THE PANDEMIC
Anxiety and Depression

The pandemic was associated with a high prevalence of anxiety and depression symptoms in adults. Research suggests that these symptoms increased during the pandemic, but the extent of this increase is unclear. Throughout the pandemic, symptoms of anxiety and depression have been more pronounced among several populations.

For example, individuals experiencing household job loss were more likely than their counterparts to report symptoms of anxiety and/or depression (53% vs. 30%) in February 2023. Job loss and unemployment—which have long been associated with adverse mental health outcomes—increased substantially early on in the pandemic.

"KFF Analysis of US Census Bureau, Household Pulse Survey, 2023"

"Unemployment Impairs Mental Health: Meta-Analyses"

"Economic Suicides in the Great Recession in Europe and North America"

"How Job Loss Can Lead to Drug Use"

"Unemployment Rate (Seasonally Adjusted)"

This synthesis brings together information from sources that discuss several different ideas: the role of unemployment in fostering anxiety, depression, and declining mental health; the role of job loss in drug use; how bad economic times lead more people to kill themselves; and how the COVID-19 pandemic affected unemployment rates. Rather than simply summarizing or quoting from each source, the authors show how the main ideas of each source come together to form a new whole:

- Unemployment increased during the pandemic.
- People who lost their jobs during the pandemic said they became anxious or depressed.
- Research shows that unemployment can lead to impaired mental health and drug use.
- Economic bad times lead to increased suicide rates.
- Conclusion: "Throughout the pandemic, symptoms of anxiety and depression have been more pronounced among several populations," including people who lost their jobs.

To achieve the synthesis shown here, the authors most likely spent considerable time reading their sources and identifying patterns and connections among them. Here are some tips for doing the same with the sources you use:

- Read all your sources with an open mind. Withhold judgment, even of sources that seem wrong-headed or implausible. Don't jump to conclusions.

- Take notes, and write a brief **SUMMARY** of each source to help you see relationships, patterns, and connections among your sources. Take notes on your own thoughts, too.

529

- Pay attention to your first reactions. You'll likely have many ideas to work with, but your first thoughts can often lead somewhere that you'll find interesting. Try **FREEWRITING**, **CLUSTERING**, or **LISTING** to see where they lead. How do these thoughts and ideas relate to your topic? Where might they fit into your rough **OUTLINE**?

329
330–31
330
335–37

- Try to think creatively, and pay attention to thoughts that flicker at the edge of your consciousness, as they may well be productive.

- Be playful. Good ideas sometimes come when we let our guard down or take ideas to extremes just to see where they lead.

Ask yourself these questions about your sources:

- What sources make the strongest arguments? What makes them so strong?

- Do some arguments crop up in several sources?

- Which arguments do you agree with? disagree with? Of those you disagree with, which ones seem strong enough that you need to **ACKNOWLEDGE** them in your text?

411

- Are there any disagreements among your sources?

- Are there any themes you see in more than one source?

- Are any data—facts, statistics, examples—or experts cited in more than one source?

- Do several of your sources use the same terms? Do they use the terms similarly, or do they use them in different ways?

- What have you learned about the topic? How have your sources affected your thinking on the topic? Do you need to adjust your **THESIS**? If so, how?

342–44

- Have you discovered new questions you need to investigate?

- Keep in mind your **RHETORICAL SITUATION**—have you found the information you need that will achieve your purpose, appeal to your audience, and suit your genre and medium?

71

What is likely to emerge from this questioning is a combination of big ideas, including new ways of understanding your topic and insights into recent scholarship about it, and smaller ones, such as how two sources agree with each other but not completely and how the information in one source supports or undercuts the argument of another. These ideas and insights will become the basis for your own ideas and for what *you* have to say about the topic.

Synthesizing Ideas Using Notes

You may find that identifying connections among your sources is easier if you examine them together rather than reading them one by one. For example, taking notes on note cards and then laying the cards out on a desk or table (or on the floor) lets you see passages that seem related. Doing the same with photocopies or printouts of your sources can help you identify similarities as well.

In doing research for an essay arguing that the sale of assault weapons should be banned, you might find several sources that address the scope of US citizens' right to bear arms. On the next page are notes taken on three such sources: Joe Klein, a journalist writing for *Time*; Antonin Scalia, a former US Supreme Court justice, quoted in an online news article; and Drew Westen, a professor of psychology writing in a blog sponsored by the *New York Times*. Though the writers hold very different views, juxtaposing these notes and highlighting certain passages show a common thread running through the sources. In this example, all three sources might be used to support the thesis that restrictions on the owning of weapons—but not an outright ban—are both constitutional and necessary.

Synthesizing Information to Support Your Own Ideas

147–69 ▲

If you're doing research to write a **REPORT**, your own ideas will be communicated primarily through which information you decide to include from the sources you cite and how you organize that information. If

114–45 ▲

you're writing a **TEXTUAL ANALYSIS**, your synthesis may focus on the themes, techniques, or other patterns you find. If you're writing a research-

170–96 ▲

based **ARGUMENT**, in contrast, your synthesis of sources must support the position you take in that argument. No matter what your genre, the challenge is to synthesize information from your research to develop ideas about your topic and then to support those ideas.

Source 1

Limits of gun ownership

Although the U.S. Constitution includes the right to bear arms, that right is not absolute. "No American has the right to own a stealth bomber or a nuclear weapon. Armor-piercing bullets are forbidden. The question is where you draw a reasonable bright line."
— Klein, "How the Gun Won" — quote

Source 4

Limits of gun ownership

Supreme Court Justice Antonin M. Scalia has noted that when the Constitution was written and ratified, some weapons were barred. So limitations could be put on owning some weapons, as long as the limits are consistent with those in force in 1789.
— Scalia, quoted in Woods — paraphrase

Source 3

Limits of gun ownership

Westen's "message consulting" research has shown that Americans are ambivalent about guns but react very positively to a statement of principle that includes both the right to own guns and restrictions on their ownership, such as prohibiting large ammunition clips and requiring all gun purchasers to undergo background checks for criminal behavior or mental illness.
— Westen — paraphrase

Entering the Conversation

As you read and think about your topic, you will come to an understanding of the concepts, interpretations, and controversies relating to the topic—and you'll become aware that there's a larger conversation going on. When you begin to find connections among your sources, you'll begin to see your own place in that conversation, to discover your own ideas and your own stance on the topic. This is the exciting part of a research project, for when you write out your own ideas on the topic, you will find yourself entering that conversation. Remember that your **STANCE** as an author needs to be clear: simply stringing together the words and ideas of others isn't enough. You need to show readers how your source materials relate to one another and to your thesis.

85–87 ■

If you need more help

521–32 ●
533–37

See Chapter 51, **QUOTING, PARAPHRASING, AND SUMMARIZING**, for help in integrating source materials into your own text. See also Chapter 52 on **ACKNOWLEDGING SOURCES, AVOIDING PLAGIARISM** for advice on giving credit to the sources you cite.

51 Quoting, Paraphrasing, and Summarizing

In an oral presentation about the rhetoric of Abraham Lincoln, you quote a memorable line from the Gettysburg Address. For an essay on the Tet Offensive in the Vietnam War, you paraphrase arguments made by several commentators and summarize some key debates about that war. When you work with the ideas and words of others, you need to clearly distinguish those ideas and words from your own and give credit to their authors. This chapter will help you with the specifics of quoting, paraphrasing, and summarizing source materials that you use in your writing.

Taking Notes

When you find material you think will be useful, take careful notes. How do you determine how much to record? You need to write down enough information so that when you refer to it later, you will be reminded of its main points and have a precise record of where it comes from.

- *Use a computer file, note cards, or a notebook,* labeling each entry with the information that will enable you to keep track of where it comes from—author, title, and the pages or the URL (or DOI, the digital object identifier). You needn't write down full bibliographic information (you can abbreviate the author's name and title) since you'll include that information in your **WORKING BIBLIOGRAPHY**. 479–81

- *Take notes in your own words, and use your own sentence patterns.* If you make a note that is a detailed **PARAPHRASE**, label it as such so that you'll know to provide appropriate **DOCUMENTATION** if you use it. 526–28
538–41

- *If you find wording that you'd like to quote,* be sure to enclose it in quotation marks to distinguish your source's words from your own. Double-check your notes to be sure any quoted material is accurately quoted—and that you haven't accidentally **PLAGIARIZED** your sources. 536–67

- *Label each note with a number to identify the source and a subject heading* to relate the note to a subject, supporting point, or other element in your essay. Doing this will help you to sort your notes easily and match them up with your rough outline. Restrict each note to a single subject.

Here are a few examples of one writer's notes on a source discussing synthetic dyes, bladder cancer, and the use of animals to determine what causes cancers. Each note includes a subject heading and brief source information and identifies whether the source is quoted or paraphrased.

Source 3

Synthetic dyes

The first synthetic dye was mauve, invented in 1854 and derived from coal. Like other coal-derived dyes, it contained aromatic amines.
Steingraber, "Pesticides," 976 — paraphrase

Source 3

Synthetic dyes & cancer

Bladder cancer was common among textile workers who used dyes. Steingraber: "By the beginning of the twentieth century, bladder cancer rates among this group of workers had skyrocketed."
Steingraber, "Pesticides," 976 — paraphrase and quote

Source 3

Synthetic dyes & cancer

In 1938, Wilhelm Hueper exposed dogs to aromatic amines and showed that the chemical caused bladder cancer.
Steingraber, "Pesticides," 976 — paraphrase

Deciding Whether to Quote, Paraphrase, or Summarize

When it comes time to **DRAFT**, you'll need to decide *how* to use any source you want to include—in other words, whether to quote, paraphrase, or summarize it. You might follow this rule of thumb: **QUOTE** texts when the wording is worth repeating or makes a point so well that no rewording will do it justice, when you want to cite the exact words of a known authority on your topic, when an authority's opinions challenge or disagree with those of others, or when the source is one you want to emphasize. **PARAPHRASE** sources that are not worth quoting but contain details you need to include. **SUMMARIZE** longer passages whose main points are important but whose details are not. Whatever your choice, you'll need to introduce any words or ideas that aren't your own with a **SIGNAL PHRASE** in order to clearly distinguish what your sources say from what *you* have to say.

358–60
523–26
526–28
529
529–32

Quoting

Quoting a source is a way of weaving someone else's exact words into your text. You need to reproduce the source exactly, though you can modify it to omit unnecessary details (with **ELLIPSES**) or to make it fit smoothly into your text (with **BRACKETS**). You also need to distinguish quoted material from your own by enclosing short quotations in quotation marks, setting off longer quotes as a block, and using appropriate **SIGNAL PHRASES**.

HB-93–94
HB-93
529–32

Incorporate short quotations into your text, enclosed in quotation marks. If you are following **MLA STYLE**, short quotations are defined as four typed lines or fewer; if using **APA STYLE**, as below, short means fewer than forty words.

MLA 580–81
APA 624

> Gerald Graff (2003) has argued that colleges make the intellectual life seem more opaque than it needs to be, leaving many students with "the misconception that the life of the mind is a secret society for which only an elite few qualify" (p. 1).

If you are quoting three lines or fewer of poetry, run them in with your text, enclosed in quotation marks. Separate lines with slashes, leaving one space on each side of the slashes.

▶ Access the ebook for a video on introducing and explaining quotations.

> Emma Lazarus almost speaks for the Statue of Liberty with the words inscribed on its pedestal: "Give me your tired, your poor, / Your huddled masses yearning to breathe free, / The wretched refuse of your teeming shore" (lines 10–12).

Set off long quotations block style.   If you are using MLA style, set off quotations of five or more typed lines by indenting the quote one-half inch from the left margin. If you are using APA style, indent quotations of forty or more words one-half inch (or five to seven spaces) from the left margin. In either case, do not use quotation marks, and put any parenthetical documentation *after* any end punctuation.

> Nonprofit organizations such as Oxfam and Habitat for Humanity rely on visual representations of the poor. What better way to get our attention, asks rhetorician Diana George:
>
>> In a culture saturated by the image, how else do we convince Americans that—despite the prosperity they see all around them—there is real need out there? The solution for most nonprofits has been to show the despair. To do that they must represent poverty as something that can be seen and easily recognized. Fallen-down shacks and trashed-out public housing, broken windows, dilapidated porches, barefoot kids with stringy hair, emaciated old women and men staring out at the camera with empty eyes. (210)

If you are quoting four or more lines of poetry, they need to be set off block style in the same way.

Indicate any omissions with ellipses.   You may sometimes delete words from a quotation that are unnecessary for your point. Insert three ellipsis marks (leaving a space before the first and after the last one) to indicate the deletion. If you omit a sentence or more in the middle of a quotation, put a period before the three ellipsis dots. Be careful not to distort the source's meaning, however.

> Faigley points out that Gore's "Information Superhighway" metaphor "associated the economic prosperity of the 1950s and . . . 1960s facilitated by new highways with the potential for vast . . . commerce to be conducted over the Internet" (253).

> According to Welch, "Television is more acoustic than visual. . . . One can turn one's gaze away from the television, but one cannot turn one's ears from it without leaving the area where the monitor leaks its aural signals into every corner" (102).

Indicate additions or changes with brackets.   Sometimes you'll need to change or add words in a quotation—to make the quotation fit grammatically within your sentence, for example, or to add a comment. In the following example, the writer changes the passage "one of our goals" to clarify the meaning of "our."

> Writing about the dwindling attention among some composition scholars to the actual teaching of writing, Susan Miller notes that "few discussions of writing pedagogy take it for granted that one of [writing teachers'] goals is to teach how to write" (480).

Here's an example of brackets used to add explanatory words to a quotation:

> Barbosa observes that Buarque's lyrics have long included "many a metaphor of *saudades* [yearning] so characteristic of *fado* music" (207).

Use punctuation correctly with quotations. When incorporating a quotation into your text, be sure to think about the end punctuation in the quoted material and also about any punctuation you need to add when inserting the quote into your own sentence.

Periods and commas. Put periods or commas *inside* closing quotation marks, except when you have parenthetical documentation at the end, in which case you put the period or comma after the parentheses.

> "Country music," Tichi says, "is a crucial and vital part of the American identity" (23).

After long quotations set off block style with no quotation marks, however, the period goes *before* the documentation, as in the example on page 524.

Question marks and exclamation points. These go *inside* closing quotation marks if they are part of the quoted material but *outside* when they are not. If there's parenthetical documentation at the end of the quotation, any punctuation that's part of your sentence comes after it.

> Speaking at a Fourth of July celebration in 1852, Frederick Douglass asked, "What have I, or those I represent, to do with your national independence?" (35).

> Who can argue with W. Charisse Goodman's observation that media images persuade women that "thinness equals happiness and fulfillment" (53)?

Colons and semicolons. These always go *outside* closing quotation marks.

It's hard to argue with W. Charisse Goodman's observation that media images persuade women that "thinness equals happiness and fulfillment"; nevertheless, American women today are more overweight than ever (53).

Paraphrasing

When you paraphrase, you restate information from a source in your own words, using your own sentence structures. Paraphrase when the source material is important but the original wording is not. Because it includes all the main points of the source, a paraphrase is usually about the same length as the original.

Here is a paragraph about synthetic dyes and cancer, followed by two paraphrases of it that demonstrate some of the challenges of paraphrasing:

ORIGINAL SOURCE

In 1938, in a series of now-classic experiments, exposure to synthetic dyes derived from coal and belonging to a class of chemicals called aromatic amines was shown to cause bladder cancer in dogs. These results helped explain why bladder cancers had become so prevalent among dyestuffs workers. With the invention of mauve in 1854, synthetic dyes began replacing natural plant-based dyes in the coloring of cloth and leather. By the beginning of the twentieth century, bladder cancer rates among this group of workers had skyrocketed, and the dog experiments helped unravel this mystery. The International Labor Organization did not wait for the results of these animal tests, however, and in 1921 declared certain aromatic amines to be human carcinogens. Decades later, these dogs provided a lead in understanding why tire-industry workers, as well as machinists and metalworkers, also began falling victim to bladder cancer: aromatic amines had been added to rubbers and cutting oils to serve as accelerants and antirust agents.

—Sandra Steingraber, "Pesticides, Animals, and Humans"

The following paraphrase borrows too much of the language of the original or changes it only slightly, as the highlighted words and phrases show:

UNACCEPTABLE PARAPHRASE: WORDING TOO CLOSE

Now-classic experiments in 1938 showed that when dogs were exposed to aromatic amines, chemicals used in synthetic dyes derived from coal, they developed bladder cancer. Similar cancers were prevalent among dyestuffs workers, and these experiments helped to explain why. Mauve, a synthetic dye, was invented in 1854, after which cloth and leather manufacturers replaced most of the natural plant-based dyes with synthetic dyes. By the early twentieth century, this group of workers had skyrocketing rates of bladder cancer, a mystery the dog experiments helped to unravel. As early as 1921, though, before the test results proved the connection, the International Labor Organization had labeled certain aromatic amines carcinogenic. Even so, decades later many metalworkers, machinists, and tire-industry workers began developing bladder cancer. The animal tests helped researchers understand that rubbers and cutting oils contained aromatic amines as accelerants and antirust agents (Steingraber 976).

The next paraphrase uses original language but follows the sentence structure of Steingraber's text too closely:

UNACCEPTABLE PARAPHRASE: SENTENCE STRUCTURE TOO CLOSE

In 1938, several pathbreaking experiments showed that being exposed to synthetic dyes that are made from coal and belong to a type of chemicals called aromatic amines caused dogs to get bladder cancer. These results helped researchers identify why cancers of the bladder had become so common among textile workers who worked with dyes. With the development of mauve in 1854, synthetic dyes began to be used instead of dyes based on plants in the dyeing of leather and cloth. By the end of the nineteenth century, rates of bladder cancer among these workers had increased dramatically, and the experiments using dogs helped clear up this oddity. The International Labor Organization anticipated the results of these tests on animals, though, and in 1921 labeled some aromatic amines carcinogenic. Years later these experiments with dogs helped researchers explain why workers in the tire industry, as well as metalworkers and machinists, also started dying of bladder cancer: aromatic amines had been put into rubbers and cutting oils as rust inhibitors and accelerants (Steingraber 976).

Patchwriting, a third form of unacceptable paraphrase, combines the other two. Composition researcher Rebecca Moore Howard defines it as "copying from a source text and then deleting some words, altering grammatical structures, or plugging in one-for-one synonym-substitutes." Here is a patchwrite of the first two sentences of the original source: (The source's exact words are shaded in yellow; paraphrases are in blue.)

PATCHWRITE

Scientists have known for a long time that chemicals in the environ-ment can cause cancer. For example, in 1938, in a series of important experiments, being exposed to synthetic dyes made out of coal and belonging to a kind of chemicals called aromatic amines was shown to cause dogs to develop bladder cancer. These experiments explain why this type of cancer had become so common among workers who handled dyes.

Here is an acceptable paraphrase of the entire passage:

ACCEPTABLE PARAPHRASE

Biologist Sandra Steingraber explains that pathbreaking experiments in 1938 demonstrated that dogs exposed to aromatic amines (chemi-cals used in coal-based synthetic dyes) developed cancers of the blad-der that were similar to cancers common among dyers in the textile industry. After mauve, the first synthetic dye, was invented in 1854, leather and cloth manufacturers replaced most natural dyes made from plants with synthetic dyes, and by the early 1900s textile work-ers had very high rates of bladder cancer. The experiments with dogs proved the connection, but years before, in 1921, the International Labor Organization had labeled some aromatic amines carcinogenic. Even so, years later many metalworkers, machinists, and workers in the tire industry started to develop unusually high rates of bladder cancer. The experiments with dogs helped researchers understand that the cancers were caused by aromatic amines used in cutting oils to inhibit rust and in rubbers to speed up the manufacturing process (976).

SOME GUIDELINES FOR PARAPHRASING

- *Use your own words and sentence structure.* It's acceptable to use some words from the original; but as much as possible, the phrasing and sentence structures should be your own.

529–32

- *Introduce paraphrased text with* **SIGNAL PHRASES**.

- *Put in quotation marks any of the source's original phrasing that you use.*

- *Indicate the source.* Although the wording may be yours, the ideas and information come from another source; be sure to name the author,

MLA 545–80
APA 597–623
536–37

and include **DOCUMENTATION** to avoid the possibility of **PLAGIARISM**.

Summarizing

A summary states the main ideas in a source concisely and in your own words. Unlike a paraphrase, a summary does *not* present all the details, and it is generally as brief as possible. Summaries may boil down an entire book or essay into a single sentence, or they may take a paragraph or more to present the main ideas. Here, for example, is a one-sentence summary of the Steingraber paragraph:

> Steingraber explains that experiments with dogs demonstrated that aromatic amines, chemicals used in synthetic dyes, cutting oils, and rubber, cause bladder cancer (976).

In the context of an essay, the summary might take this form:

> Medical researchers have long relied on experiments using animals to expand understanding of the causes of disease. For example, biologist and ecologist Sandra Steingraber notes that in the second half of the nineteenth century, the rate of bladder cancer soared among textile workers. According to Steingraber, experiments with dogs demonstrated that synthetic chemicals in dyes used to color the textiles caused the cancer (976).

SOME GUIDELINES FOR SUMMARIZING

- *Include only the main ideas; leave out the details.* A summary should include just enough information to give the reader the gist of the original. It is always much shorter than the original, sometimes even as brief as one sentence.

- *Use your own words.* If you quote phrasing from the original, enclose the phrase in quotation marks.

- *Indicate the source.* Although the wording may be yours, the ideas and information come from another source. Name the author, either in a signal phrase or in parentheses, and include an appropriate **IN-TEXT CITATION** to avoid the possibility of **PLAGIARISM**.

● MLA 545–80
APA 597–623
536–37

Introducing Source Materials Using Signal Phrases

You need to introduce quotations, paraphrases, and summaries clearly, usually letting readers know who the author is—and, if need be, something about their credentials. Consider this sentence:

▶ Access the ebook for a video on using signal phrases.

> Professor and textbook author Elaine Tyler May argues that many high school history books are too bland to interest young readers (531).

The beginning ("Professor and textbook author Elaine Tyler May argues") functions as a *signal phrase*, telling readers who is making the assertion and why she has the authority to speak on the topic—and making clear that everything between the signal phrase and the parenthetical citation comes from that source. Since the signal phrase names the author, the parenthetical citation includes only the page number; had the author not been identified in the signal phrase, she would have been named in the parentheses:

> Even some textbook authors believe that many high school history books are too bland to interest young readers (May 531).

MLA and APA have different conventions for constructing signal phrases. In MLA, the language you use in a signal phrase can be neutral—like "X says"/"Y thinks"/"according to Z." Or it can suggest something about the **STANCE** —the source's or your own. The example above referring to the textbook author uses the verb "argues," suggesting that what she says is open to dispute (or that the writer believes it is). How would it change your understanding if the signal verb were "observes"/"suggests"?

In addition to the names of sources' authors, signal phrases often give readers information about institutional affiliations and positions authors have, their academic or professional specialties, and any other information that lets readers judge the credibility of the sources. You should craft each signal phrase you use so as to highlight the credentials of the author. Here are some examples:

> A study done by Keenan Johnson, professor of psychology at Duke University, showed that . . .

The signal phrase identifies the source's author, his professional position, and his university affiliation, emphasizing his title.

> Science writer Isaac McDougal argues that . . .

This phrase acknowledges that the source's author may not have scholarly credentials but is a published writer; it's a useful construction if the source doesn't provide much information about the writer.

85–87

Writing in *Psychology Today*, Amanda Chao-Fitz notes that . . .

This is the sort of signal phrase to use if you have no information on the author; you establish credibility on the basis of the publication in which the source appears.

If you're writing using APA style, signal phrases are typically briefer, giving only the author's last name and the date of publication:

According to Benzinger (2010), . . .
Quartucci (2011) observed that . . .

Signal verbs. The verbs used in signal phrases do more than simply introduce a quote, paraphrase, or reference; they also provide information on the author's intended meaning and give your reader a clue as to how the source should be read. They also can give your writing variety and interest.

SOME COMMON SIGNAL VERBS

acknowledge	comment	dispute	point out
admit	conclude	emphasize	reason
advise	concur	grant	reject
agree	confirm	illustrate	report
argue	contend	imply	respond
assert	declare	insist	state
believe	deny	note	suggest
charge	disagree	observe	think
claim			

Verb tenses. MLA and APA also have different conventions regarding the tenses of verbs in signal phrases. MLA requires present-tense verbs ("writes," "asserts," " notes") in signal phrases to introduce a work you are quoting, paraphrasing, or summarizing.

In *Poor Richard's Almanack*, Benjamin Franklin <u>notes</u>, "He that cannot obey, cannot command" (739).

If, however, you are referring to the act of writing or saying something rather than simply quoting someone's words, you might not use the present tense. The writer of the following sentence focuses on the year in which the source was written—therefore, the verb is necessarily in the past tense:

Back in 1941, Kenneth Burke <u>wrote</u> that "the ethical values of work are in its application of the competitive equipment to cooperative ends" (316).

If you are following APA style, use the past tense to introduce sources composed in the past. If you are referring to a past action that didn't occur at a specific time or that continues into the present, you should use the present perfect.

Dowdall et al. (2020) <u>observed</u> that women attending women's colleges are less likely to engage in binge drinking than are women who attend coeducational colleges (p. 713).

Many researchers <u>have studied</u> drinking habits on college campuses.

APA requires the present tense, however, to discuss the results of an experiment or to explain conclusions that are generally agreed on.

The findings of this study <u>suggest</u> that excessive drinking has serious consequences for college students and their institutions.

The authors of numerous studies <u>agree</u> that smoking and drinking among adolescents are associated with lower academic achievement.

If you need more help

See Chapter 52 for help **ACKNOWLEDGING SOURCES** and giving credit to the sources you use. See also the **SAMPLE RESEARCH PAPERS** to see how sources are cited in MLA and APA styles. And see Chapter 3 if you're writing a **SUMMARY/RESPONSE** essay.

533–37 ●
MLA 585–94
APA 626–33
29–40 ✳

52 Acknowledging Sources, Avoiding Plagiarism

Whenever you do research-based writing, you find yourself entering a conversation—reading what many others have had to say about your topic, figuring out what you yourself think, and then putting what you think in writing—"putting in your oar," as the rhetorician Kenneth Burke once wrote. As a writer, you need to *acknowledge* any words and ideas that come from others—to give credit where credit is due, to recognize the various authorities and many perspectives you have considered, to show readers where they can find your sources, and to situate your own arguments in the ongoing conversation. Using other people's words and ideas without acknowledgment is *plagiarism*, a serious academic and ethical offense. This chapter will show you how to acknowledge the materials you use and avoid plagiarism.

Access the ebook for a video on understanding plagiarism.

Acknowledging Sources

When you insert in your text information that you've obtained from others, your readers need to know where your source's words or ideas begin and end. Therefore, you should usually introduce a source by naming the author in a **SIGNAL PHRASE** and then provide brief **DOCUMENTATION** of the specific material from the source in a parenthetical reference following the material. (Sometimes you can put the author's name in the parenthetical reference as well.) You need only brief documentation of the source here, since your readers will find full bibliographic information about it in your list of **WORKS CITED** or **REFERENCES**.

529–32
MLA 545–80
APA 597–623

MLA 552–80
APA 603–23

Sources that need acknowledgment. You almost always need to acknowledge any information that you get from a specific source. Material you should acknowledge includes the following:

* *Direct quotations.* Unless they are well known (see p. 536 for some examples), any quotations from another source must be enclosed in quotation

marks, cited with brief bibliographic information in parentheses, and usually introduced with a signal phrase that tells who wrote or said it and provides necessary contextual information, as in the following sentence:

In a dissenting opinion on the issue of racial preferences in college admissions, Supreme Court justice Ruth Bader Ginsburg argues, "The stain of generations of racial oppression is still visible in our society, and the determination to hasten its removal remains vital" (*Gratz v. Bollinger*).

- *Arguable statements and information that may not be common knowledge.* If you state something about which there is disagreement or for which arguments can be made, cite the source of your statement. If in doubt about whether you need to give the source of an assertion, provide it. As part of an essay on "fake news" programs, for example, you might make the following assertion:

The satire of *The Daily Show* complements the conservative bias of Fox News, since both have abandoned the stance of objectivity maintained by mainstream news sources, contends Michael Hoyt, executive editor of the *Columbia Journalism Review* (43).

Others might argue with the contention that the Fox News Channel offers biased reports of the news, so the source of this assertion needs to be acknowledged. In the same essay, you might present information that should be cited because it's not widely known, as in this example:

According to a report by the Pew Research Center, 25 percent of Americans got information about the 2016 presidential campaign from comedy shows like *The Late Show with Stephen Colbert* and *Saturday Night Live* (2).

- *The opinions and assertions of others.* When you present the ideas, opinions, and assertions of others, cite the source. You may have rewritten the concept in your own words, but the ideas were generated by someone else and must be acknowledged, as they are here:

David Boonin, writing in the *Journal of Social Philosophy*, asserts that, logically, laws banning marriage between people of different races are not discriminatory since everyone of each race is affected equally by them. Laws banning same-sex unions are discriminatory, however, since they apply only to people with a certain sexual orientation (256).

- *Photographs, visual images, or video.* If you didn't create a photo, image, or video yourself, cite the source. If possible, use the original source, not a version that appears in another source, to ensure that the version you're using hasn't been altered.

- *Any information that you didn't generate yourself.* If you didn't do the research or compile the data yourself, cite your source. This goes for interviews, statistics, graphs, charts, visuals, photographs—anything you use that you didn't create. If you create a chart using data from another source, you need to cite that source.

- *Collaboration with and help from other people—and from AI.* In many of your courses and in work situations, you'll be called on to work with others. You may get help with your writing at your school's writing center or from fellow students in your writing courses. With your instructor's permission, you might also get help from **GENERATIVE AI** tools during parts of your writing and researching process. Acknowledging such collaboration or assistance, in a brief informational note, is a way of giving credit—and saying thank you. See guidelines for writing notes in the **MLA** and **APA** sections of this book.

61–69

MLA 552
APA 602

Sources that don't need acknowledgment.   Widely available information and common knowledge do not require acknowledgment. What constitutes common knowledge may not be clear, however. When in doubt, provide a citation, or ask your instructor whether the information needs to be cited. You generally do not need to cite the following:

- *Information that most readers are likely to know.* You don't need to acknowledge information that is widely known or commonly accepted as fact. For example, in a literary analysis, you wouldn't cite a source saying that Harriet Beecher Stowe wrote *Uncle Tom's Cabin*; you can assume your readers already know that. However, you should cite the source from which you got the information that the book was first published in installments in a magazine and then, with revisions, in book form, because that information isn't common knowledge. As you do research in areas you're not familiar with, be aware that what constitutes common knowledge isn't always clear; the history of the novel's publication would be known to Stowe scholars and would likely need no acknowledgment in an essay written for them. In this case, too, if you aren't sure whether to acknowledge information, it's best to do so.

- *Information and documents that are widely available.* If a piece of information appears in several sources or reference works or if a document has been published widely, you needn't cite a source for it. For example, the date when astronauts Neil Armstrong and Buzz Aldrin landed a spacecraft on the moon can be found in any number of reference works. Similarly, the Declaration of Independence and the Gettysburg Address are reprinted in thousands of sources, so the ones where you found them need no citation.

- *Well-known quotations.* These include such famous quotations as Lady Macbeth's "Out, damned spot!" and John F. Kennedy's "Ask not what your country can do for you; ask what you can do for your country." Be sure, however, that the quotation is correct. Winston Churchill is said to have told a class of schoolchildren, "Never, ever, ever, ever, ever, ever, ever give up. Never give up. Never give up. Never give up." His actual words, however, are much different and begin "Never give in."

- *Material that you created or gathered yourself.* You need not cite photographs that you took, graphs that you composed based on your own findings, or data from an experiment or survey that you conducted—though you should make sure readers know that the work is yours.

A good rule of thumb: *when in doubt, cite your source.* You're unlikely to be criticized for citing too much—but you may invite charges of plagiarism by citing too little.

Avoiding Plagiarism

In North America, authors' words and ideas are considered to belong to them, so using others' words or ideas without acknowledging the source is considered to be a serious offense called plagiarism. In fact, plagiarism is often committed unintentionally—as when a writer paraphrases someone else's ideas in language that is too close to the original. It is essential, therefore, to know what constitutes plagiarism: (1) using another writer's words or ideas without acknowledging the source, (2) using another writer's exact words without quotation marks, and (3) paraphrasing or summarizing someone else's ideas using language or sentence structures that are too close to theirs.

521–22

To avoid plagiarizing, take careful **NOTES** as you do your research, clearly labeling as quotations any words you quote directly and being careful to use your own phrasing and sentence structures in paraphrases and summaries. Be sure you know what source material you must **DOCU-MENT**, and give credit to your sources, both in the text and in a list of **REF-ERENCES** or **WORKS CITED**.

538–41
APA 603–23
MLA 552–80

Be aware that it's easy to plagiarize inadvertently when working with online sources, such as full-text articles, that you've downloaded or cut and pasted into your notes. Keep careful track of these materials, since saving copies of your sources is so easy. Later, be sure to check your draft against the original sources to make sure your quotations are accurately worded—and take care, too, to include quotation marks and document the source correctly. Copying online material right into a document you are writing and forgetting to put quotation marks around it or to document it (or both) is all too easy to do. You must acknowledge information you find on the web just as you must acknowledge all other source materials.

Similar advice applies when your instructor allows you to integrate **GENERATIVE AI** into your writing and researching process: always acknowledge your AI use. That means documenting—both in text and in a references list or works cited page—any AI-generated material that you incorporate into your writing. But it also means adhering to instructor or school policies for disclosing other types of AI use—like getting help from AI with brainstorming, creating an outline, revising, and so on. Your instructor might, for example, ask you to write a formal note acknowledging your AI use or ask you to share the transcript of your AI interaction. Doing so can be an important part of illustrating your academic **HONESTY**. You can find examples of AI **ACKNOWLEDGMENT STATEMENTS** in the **MLA** and **APA** chapters of this book.

61–69

4
68
MLA 551
APA 602

Finally, it's important to recognize that plagiarism and other forms of dishonesty have consequences. Scholars' work will be discredited if it too closely resembles another's. Journalists who are found to have plagiarized lose their jobs, and students routinely fail courses or are dismissed from their school when they are caught cheating—all too often by submitting as their own essays that they have purchased from online "research" sites or essays generated by AI. If you're having trouble completing an assignment, seek assistance. Talk with your instructor; or if your school has a writing center, go there for advice on all aspects of your writing, including acknowledging sources and avoiding plagiarism.

53 Documentation

Access the ebook for a video on understanding in-text documentation.

In everyday life, we are generally aware of our sources: "I read it on Kareem Abdul-Jabbar's *Substack*." "Amber told me it's your birthday." "If you don't believe me, ask Mom." Saying how we know what we know and where we got our information is part of establishing our credibility and persuading others to take what we say seriously.

The goal of a research project is to study a topic, combining what we learn from sources with our own thinking and then composing a written text. When we write up the results of a research project, we cite the sources we use, usually by quoting, paraphrasing, or summarizing, and we acknowledge those sources, telling readers where the ideas came from. The information we give about sources is called documentation, and we provide it not only to establish our credibility as researchers and writers but also so that our readers, if they wish to, can find the sources themselves.

Understanding Documentation Styles

The Norton Field Guide covers the documentation styles of the Modern Language Association (MLA) and the American Psychological Association (APA). MLA style is used chiefly in the humanities; APA is used in the social sciences, sciences, education, and nursing. Both are two-part systems, consisting of (1) brief in-text parenthetical documentation for quotations, paraphrases, or summaries and (2) more-detailed documentation in a list of sources at the end of the text. MLA and APA require that the end-of-text documentation provide the following basic information about each source you cite:

- author, editor, or creator of the source
- title of source (and of publication or site where it appears)
- version or edition of source
- name of publisher
- date of publication
- retrieval information (for online sources)

TITLE　　　　　AUTHOR　　　　　PUBLICATION

MLA and APA are by no means the only documentation styles. Many other publishers and organizations have their own style, among them the University of Chicago Press and the Council of Science Editors. We focus on MLA and APA here because those are styles that college students are often required to use. On the following page are examples of how the two parts—the brief parenthetical documentation in your text and the more detailed information at the end—correspond in each of these systems.

The examples here and throughout this book are color-coded to help you see the crucial parts of each citation: tan for author and editor, yellow for titles, and blue for publication information: name of publisher, date of publication, page number(s), DOI or URL, and so on.

As the examples of in-text documentation show, in either MLA or APA style you should name the author either in a signal phrase or in parentheses following the source information. But there are several differences between the two styles in the details of the documentation. In MLA, the author's first and last names are used in a signal phrase at first mention; in APA, only the last name is used. In APA, the abbreviation "p." is used with the page number; in MLA, there is no abbreviation before a page number. Finally, in APA the date of publication always appears just after the author's name.

Comparing the MLA and APA styles of listing works cited or references also reveals some differences: MLA includes an author's first name while APA gives only initials; MLA puts the date near the end while APA places it right after the author's name; MLA capitalizes most of the words in a book's title and subtitle while APA capitalizes only the first words and proper nouns and proper adjectives in each.

MLA Style

IN-TEXT DOCUMENTATION

As Lester Faigley puts it, "The world has become a bazaar from which to shop for an individual 'lifestyle'" (12).

As one observer suggests, "The world has become a bazaar from which to shop for an individual 'lifestyle'" (Faigley 12).

WORKS-CITED DOCUMENTATION

Faigley, Lester. *Fragments of Rationality: Postmodernity and the Subject of Composition.* U of Pittsburgh P, 1992.

APA Style

IN-TEXT DOCUMENTATION

As Faigley (1992) suggested, "The world has become a bazaar from which to shop for an individual 'lifestyle'" (p. 12).

As one observer has noted, "The world has become a bazaar from which to shop for an individual 'lifestyle'" (Faigley, 1992, p. 12).

REFERENCE-LIST DOCUMENTATION

Faigley, L. (1992). *Fragments of rationality: Postmodernity and the subject of composition.* University of Pittsburgh Press.

Some of these differences are related to the nature of the academic fields in which the two styles are used. In humanities disciplines, the authorship of a text is emphasized, so both first and last names are included in MLA documentation. Scholarship in those fields may be several years old but still current, so the publication date doesn't appear in the in-text citation. In APA style, as in many documentation styles used in the sciences, education, and engineering, emphasis is placed on the date of publication because in these fields, more recent research is usually preferred over older studies. However, although the elements are arranged differently, both MLA and APA—and other documentation styles as well—require similar information about author, title, and publication.

Documenting Sources through Hyperlinks

Depending on your rhetorical situation and your instructor's preferences, another possibility for documenting sources is to link to them from within your text, as in this example:

> In their 2024 analysis of teachers' use of *TikTok*, Carpenter and colleagues found that 48% of survey respondents reported using *TikTok* to get teaching ideas and resources.

Here, the phrase "2024 analysis of teachers' use of *TikTok*" indicates a hyperlink, which readers can click to access the article written by Carpenter and colleagues.

Of course, you'll need to consider your writing context before deciding whether to document your sources through hyperlinks. Does your assignment allow for such documentation? Are all or most of your sources available online? Are you writing in a digital medium—and will your readers access your work digitally? If the answers to these questions are yes, then using hyperlinks can be a sensible choice. Your readers will have direct access to your sources, allowing them to verify your claims and evidence, understand the larger conversations you're contributing to, or learn more about your topic without having to search for your sources manually.

To create a hyperlink to a source in most word-processing programs, you can follow these steps:

1. Highlight the words you want to turn into a link.

2. Right-click and select "Hyperlink," "Insert link," or similar term.

3. Copy and paste the URL for your source.

4. Click "OK," "Apply," or similar term.

5. Test the hyperlink in your document to make sure it works.

Here are some tips for documenting sources through hyperlinks:

- *Think carefully about how you word the clickable text.* Choose words that are specific and informative, giving readers a sense of what the source is about, who wrote it, or where it appeared. For example, instead of using the vague "as this article suggests," use "as Smith's study of athletes' graduation rates suggests." A good guideline: assume that some readers won't click on your link—and make sure that your words alone give them some information about your source.

- *As much as possible, link directly to your source.* For example, link to a specific webpage you're citing—and not to the site's homepage.

- *Remember to paraphrase, summarize, quote, and comment on your source.* A hyperlink doesn't substitute for specific references to the words or ideas in your source—nor does a hyperlink substitute for your own analysis or explanation of a source. You'll still want to help readers understand how the source relates to the points you're making in your essay.

- *Consider including a traditional list of references or works cited at the end of your document.* Your readers may prefer to read a printed copy of your text, and the traditional end-of-text information will help them understand what kinds of sources you're drawing on, who wrote them, and when and where they were published. Plus, if your links become obsolete, your readers will still know what sources you used.

- *Check your assignment guidelines.* Your instructor may have specific requirements for documenting sources through hyperlinks.

54 MLA Style

MLA style calls for (1) brief in-text documentation and (2) complete bibliographic information in a list of works cited at the end of your text. The models and examples in this guide draw on the ninth edition of the *MLA Handbook*, published by the Modern Language Association of America in 2021. For additional information, or if you're citing a source that isn't covered in this guide, visit style.mla.org.

A DIRECTORY TO MLA STYLE

Throughout this chapter, you'll find color-coded templates and examples to help you see how writers include source information in their texts and in their lists of works cited: tan for author, editor, translator, and other contributors; yellow for titles; blue for publication information—date of publication, page number(s), DOIs, and other location information.

IN-TEXT DOCUMENTATION

Whenever you **QUOTE**, **PARAPHRASE**, or **SUMMARIZE** a source in your writing, you need to provide brief documentation that tells readers what you took from the source and where in the source you found that information. This brief documentation also refers readers to the full entry in your works-cited list, so begin with whatever comes first there: the author, the title, or a description of the source.

521–32

You can mention the author or title either in a signal phrase—"Toni Morrison writes," "In *Beowulf*," "According to the article 'Every Patient's Nightmare'"—or in parentheses—(Morrison). If relevant, include pages or other details about where you found the information in the parenthetical reference: (Morrison 67).

Shorten any lengthy titles or descriptions in parentheses by including the first noun with any preceding adjectives and omitting any initial articles (*Norton Field Guide* for *The Norton Field Guide to Writing*). If the title doesn't start with a noun, use the first phrase or clause (*How to Be* for *How to Be an Antiracist*). Use the full title if it's short.

The first two examples below show basic in-text documentation of a work by one author. Variations on those examples follow. The examples illustrate the MLA style of using quotation marks around titles of short works and italicizing titles of long works.

1. AUTHOR NAMED IN A SIGNAL PHRASE

If you mention the author in a **SIGNAL PHRASE**, put only the page number(s) in parentheses. Do not write "page" or "p." The first time you mention the author, use their first and last names. You can usually omit any middle initials.

529–32

David McCullough describes John Adams's hands as those of someone
used to manual labor (18).

In subsequent references to the author, use their last name only. You can
also use a pronoun (use singular "they" if you don't know the author's
pronouns) or another term, like "the author."

2. AUTHOR NAMED IN PARENTHESES

If you do not mention the author in a signal phrase, put the author's last
name in parentheses along with any page number(s). Do not use punctuation between the name and the page number(s).

Adams is said to have had "the hands of a man accustomed to
pruning his own trees, cutting his own hay, and splitting his own
firewood" (McCullough 18).

Whether you use a signal phrase and parentheses or parentheses only,
try to put the parenthetical documentation at the end of the sentence
or as close as possible to the material you've cited—without awkwardly
interrupting the sentence. When the parenthetical reference comes at
the end of the sentence, the period follows it.

3. TWO OR MORE WORKS BY THE SAME AUTHOR

If you cite multiple works by one author, include the title of the work you
are citing either in the signal phrase or in parentheses.

Robert Kaplan insists that understanding power in the Near East requires
"Western leaders who know when to intervene, and do so without
illusions" (*Eastward to Tartary* 330).

Put a comma between author and title if both are in the parentheses.

Understanding power in the Near East requires "Western leaders who
know when to intervene, and do so without illusions" (Kaplan, *Eastward
to Tartary* 330).

4. AUTHORS WITH THE SAME LAST NAME

Give each author's first and last names in any signal phrase, or add the
author's first initial in the parenthetical reference.

TITLE   AUTHOR   PUBLICATION

"Imaginative" applies not only to modern literature but also to writing of all periods, whereas "magical" is often used in writing about Arthurian romances (A. Wilson 25).

5. TWO OR MORE AUTHORS

For a work with two authors, name both. If you first mention them in a signal phrase, give their first and last names.

Lori Carlson and Cynthia Ventura's stated goal is to introduce Julio Cortázar, Marjorie Agosín, and other Latin American writers to an audience of English-speaking adolescents (v).

For a work by three or more authors that you mention in a signal phrase, you can either name them all or name the first author followed by "and others" or "and colleagues." If you mention them in a parenthetical reference, name the first author followed by "et al."

Phyllis Anderson and colleagues describe British literature thematically (A54–A67).

One survey of British literature breaks the contents into thematic groupings (Anderson et al. A54–A67).

6. ORGANIZATION OR GOVERNMENT AS AUTHOR

In a signal phrase, use the full name of the organization: American Academy of Arts and Sciences. In parentheses, use the shortest noun phrase, omitting any initial articles: American Academy.

The US government can be direct when it wants to be. For example, it sternly warns, "If you are overpaid, we will recover any payments not due you" (Social Security Administration 12).

7. AUTHOR UNKNOWN

If you don't know the author, use the work's title in a signal phrase or in a parenthetical reference.

A powerful editorial in *The New York Times* asserts that healthy liver donor Mike Hurewitz died because of "frightening" faulty postoperative care ("Every Patient's Nightmare").

8. LITERARY WORKS

When referring to common literary works that are available in many different editions, give the page numbers from the edition you are using, followed by information that will let readers of any edition locate the text you are citing.

NOVELS AND PROSE PLAYS. Give the page number followed by a semicolon and any chapter, section, or act numbers, separated by commas.

> In *Pride and Prejudice,* Mrs. Bennet shows no warmth toward Jane when she returns from Netherfield (Austen 105; ch. 12).

VERSE PLAYS. Give act, scene, and line numbers, separated with periods.

> Shakespeare continues the vision theme when Macbeth says, "Thou hast no speculation in those eyes / Which thou dost glare with" (*Macbeth* 3.3.96–97).

POEMS. Give the part and the line numbers, separated by periods. If a poem has only line numbers, use the word "line" or "lines" in the first reference; after that, give only numbers.

> Walt Whitman sets up not only opposing adjectives but also opposing nouns in "Song of Myself" when he says, "I am of old and young, of the foolish as much as the wise, / . . . a child as well as a man" (16.330–32).

> One description of the mere in *Beowulf* is "not a pleasant place" (line 1372). Later, it is labeled "the awful place" (1378).

9. WORK IN AN ANTHOLOGY

Name the author(s) of the work, not the editor of the anthology.

> "It is the teapots that truly shock," according to Cynthia Ozick in her essay on teapots as metaphor (70).

> In *In Short: A Collection of Creative Nonfiction,* readers will find both an essay on Scottish tea (Hiestand) and a piece on teapots as metaphors (Ozick).

TITLE   AUTHOR   PUBLICATION

10. ENCYCLOPEDIA OR DICTIONARY

Acknowledge an entry in an encyclopedia or dictionary by giving the author's name, if available. For an entry without an author, give the entry's title.

> According to *Funk and Wagnall's New World Encyclopedia,* early in his career, most of Kubrick's income came from "hustling chess games in Washington Square Park" ("Kubrick, Stanley").

11. LEGAL DOCUMENTS

For legal cases, give whatever comes first in the works-cited entry. If you're citing a government document in parentheses and multiple entries in your works-cited list start with the same government author, give as much of the name as you need to differentiate the sources.

> In 2015, for the first time, all states were required to license and recognize the marriages of same-sex couples (United States, Supreme Court).

12. SACRED TEXT

When citing a sacred text such as the Bible or the Qur'an for the first time, give the title of the edition as well as the book, chapter, and verse (or their equivalent), separated by periods. MLA recommends abbreviating the names of the books of the Bible in parenthetical references. Later citations from the same edition do not have to repeat its title.

> The wording from *The New English Bible* follows: "In the beginning of creation, when God made heaven and earth, the earth was without form and void . . ." (Gen. 1.1–2).

13. MULTIVOLUME WORK

If you cite more than one volume of a multivolume work, each time you cite one of the volumes, give the volume *and* the page number(s) in parentheses, separated by a colon and a space.

> Carl Sandburg concludes with the following sentence about those paying last respects to Lincoln: "All day long and through the night the unbroken line moved, the home town having its farewell" (4: 413).

If you cite an entire volume of a multivolume work in parentheses, give the author's last name followed by a comma and "vol." before the volume number: (Sandburg, vol. 4). If your works-cited list includes only a single volume of a multivolume work, give just the page number in parentheses: (413).

14. TWO OR MORE WORKS CITED TOGETHER

If you're citing two or more works closely together, you will sometimes need to provide a parenthetical reference for each one.

> Dennis Baron describes singular "they" as "the missing word that's been hiding in plain sight" (182), while Benjamin Dreyer believes that "singular 'they' is not the wave of the future; it's the wave of the present" (93).

If you are citing multiple sources for the same idea in parentheses, separate the references with a semicolon.

> Many critics have examined great works of literature from a cultural perspective (Tanner 7; Smith viii).

15. SOURCE QUOTED IN ANOTHER SOURCE

When you are quoting text that you found quoted in another source, use the abbreviation "qtd. in" in the parenthetical reference.

> Charlotte Brontë wrote to G. H. Lewes, "Why do you like Miss Austen so very much? I am puzzled on that point" (qtd. in Tanner 7).

16. WORK WITHOUT PAGE NUMBERS

For works without page or part numbers, including many online sources, no number is needed in a parenthetical reference.

> Studies show that music training helps children to be better at multitasking later in life ("Hearing the Music").

If you mention the author in a signal phrase, or if you mention the title of a work with no author, no parenthetical reference is needed.

> Arthur Brooks argues that a switch to fully remote work would have a negative effect on mental and physical health.

If the source has chapter, paragraph, or section numbers, use them with the abbreviations "ch.," "par.," or "sec.": ("Hearing the Music," par. 2). Don't count lines or paragraphs on your own if they aren't numbered in the source. For an ebook, use chapter numbers. For an audio or video recording, give the hours, minutes, and seconds (separated by colons) as shown on the player: (00:05:21–31).

17. AN ENTIRE WORK OR A ONE-PAGE ARTICLE

If you cite an entire work rather than a part of it, or if you cite a single-page article, there's no need to include page numbers.

Throughout life, John Adams strove to succeed (McCullough).

18. GENERATIVE AI

The results of generative AI are not considered to have an author and don't have titles; instead, identify the source by using the first phrase or clause of your prompt. Use the whole prompt if it's short.

A light bulb, also known as an incandescent bulb, works "on the principle of incandescence" ("Explain how a light bulb works")

NOTES

Sometimes you may need to give information that doesn't fit into the text itself—to thank people who helped you, to acknowledge the use of AI in your writing process, to provide additional details, to refer readers to other sources, or to add comments about sources. Such information can be given in a footnote (at the bottom of the page) or an endnote (on a separate page with the heading "Notes" or "Endnotes" just before your works-cited list). Put a superscript number at the appropriate point in your text, signaling to readers to look for the note with the corresponding number. If you have multiple notes, number them consecutively throughout your paper.

TEXT WITH SUPERSCRIPT
World (and Word) Building: A Gamer's Literacy[1]

NOTE
[1] I want to thank those who gave me feedback on a draft of this literacy narrative, including my teacher Vincent Yu and my classmates Karima and Luke. I also want to acknowledge the use of *ChatGPT* to brainstorm ideas early in my writing process. *ChatGPT* helped me develop the idea of sharing an anecdote about the storytelling skills I learned from playing *Dungeons & Dragons*. I've included my initial prompt and full *ChatGPT* conversation history in an appendix.

LIST OF WORKS CITED

A works-cited list provides full bibliographic information for every source cited in your text. See page 583 for guidelines on formatting this list and page 594 for a sample works-cited list.

Core Elements

MLA style provides a list of core elements for documenting sources in a works-cited list. Not all sources will include each of these elements; include as much information as is available for any title you cite. For guidance about specific sources you need to document, see the templates and examples on pages 556–80, but here are some general guidelines for how to treat each of the core elements.

CORE ELEMENTS FOR ENTRIES IN A WORKS-CITED LIST

- Author
- Title of the source
- Title of any "container," a larger work in which the source is found—an anthology, a website, a journal or magazine, a database, a streaming service like *Netflix*, or a learning management system, among others
- Editor, translator, director, or other contributors
- Version
- Number of volume and issue, episode and season
- Publisher
- Date of publication
- Location of the source: page numbers, DOI, permalink, URL, etc.

The above order is the general order MLA recommends, but there will be exceptions. To document a translated essay that you found in an anthology, for instance, you'd identify the translator after the title of the essay rather than after that of the anthology. You may sometimes need additional elements as well, either at the end of an entry or in the middle—for instance, a label to indicate that your source is a map, or an original year of publication. Remember that your goal is to tell readers what sources you've consulted and where they can find them. Providing this information is one way you can engage with readers—and enable them to join in the conversation with you and your sources.

TITLE   AUTHOR   PUBLICATION

AUTHORS AND CONTRIBUTORS

- An author can be any kind of creator—a writer, a musician, an artist, and so on.

- If there is one author, put the last name first, followed by a comma and the first name: Morrison, Toni.

- If there are two authors, list the first author last name first and the second one first name first: Lunsford, Andrea, and Lisa Ede. Put their names in the order given in the work. For three or more authors, give the first author's name followed by "et al.": Greenblatt, Stephen, et al.

- Include any middle names or initials: Toklas, Alice B.

- If the author is a group or organization, use the full name, omitting any initial article: United Nations.

- If an author uses a handle that is significantly different from their name, include the handle in square brackets after the name: Ocasio-Cortez, Alexandria [@AOC].

- If there's no known author, start the entry with the title.

- If there's an editor but no author, put the editor's name in the author position and specify their role: Lunsford, Andrea, editor.

- If you're citing someone in addition to an author—an editor, translator, director, or other contributors—specify their role. If there are multiple contributors, put the one whose work you wish to highlight before the title, and list any others you want to mention after the title. If you don't want to highlight one particular contributor, start with the title and include any contributors after the title. For contributors named before the title, specify their role after the name: Fincher, David, director. For those named after the title, specify their role first: Directed by David Fincher.

TITLES

- Include any subtitles, and capitalize all the words except for articles ("a," "an," "the"), prepositions ("to," "at," "from," and so on), and coordinating conjunctions ("and," "but," "for," "or," "nor," "so," "yet")—unless they are the first or last word of a title or subtitle.

- Italicize the titles of books, periodicals, websites, and other long works: *Pride and Prejudice, Wired.*

- Put quotation marks around the titles of articles and other short works: "Letter from Birmingham Jail."

- To document a source that has no title, describe it without italics or quotation marks: Letter to the author, Photograph of a tree. For a short, untitled email, text message, social media post, or poem, you may want to include the text itself instead: Dickinson, Emily. "Immortal is an ample word." *American Poems*, www.americanpoems.com/poets /emilydickinson/immortal-is-an-ample-word.

VERSIONS

- If you cite a source that's available in more than one version, specify the one you consulted in your works-cited entry. Write ordinal numbers with numerals, and abbreviate "edition": 2nd ed. Write out names of specific versions, and capitalize following a period or if the name is a proper noun: King James Version, unabridged version, director's cut.

NUMBERS

- If you cite a book that's published in multiple volumes, indicate the volume number. Abbreviate "volume," and write the number as a numeral: vol. 2.

- Indicate volume and issue numbers (if any) of journals, abbreviating both "volume" and "number": vol. 123, no. 4.

- If you cite a TV show or podcast episode, indicate the season and episode numbers: season 1, episode 4.

PUBLISHERS

- Write publishers', studios', and networks' names in full, but omit initial articles and business words like "Inc." or "Company."

- For academic presses, use "U" for "University" and "P" for "Press": Princeton UP, U of California P. Spell out "Press" if the name doesn't include "University": MIT Press.

- Many publishers use "&" in their name: Simon & Schuster. MLA says to use "and" instead: Simon and Schuster.

- If the publisher is a division of an organization, list the organization and any divisions from largest to smallest: Stanford U, Center for the Study of Language and Information, Metaphysics Research Lab.

DATES

- Whether to give just the year or to include the month and day depends on the source. In general, give the full date that you find there. If the date is unknown, simply omit it.

- Abbreviate the months except for May, June, and July: Jan., Feb., Mar., Apr., Aug., Sept., Oct., Nov., Dec.

- For books, give the publication date on the copyright page: 1948. If a book lists more than one date, use the most recent one.

- Periodicals may be published annually, monthly, seasonally, weekly, or daily. Give the full date that you find there: 2019, Apr. 2019, 16 Apr. 2019. Do not capitalize the names of seasons: spring 2021.

- For online sources, use the copyright date or the full publication date that you find there, or a date of revision. If the source does not give a date, use the date of access: Accessed 6 June 2020. Give a date of access as well for online sources you think are likely to change or for websites that have disappeared.

LOCATION

- For most print articles and other short works, give a page number or range of pages: p. 24, pp. 24–35. For articles that are not on consecutive pages, give the first page number with a plus sign: pp. 24+.

- If it's necessary to specify a section of a source, give the section name before the page numbers: Sunday Review sec., p. 3.

- Indicate the location of an online source by giving a DOI if one is available; if not, give a URL—and use a permalink if one is available. MLA notes that URLs are not always reliable, so ask your instructor if you should include them. DOIs should start with "https://doi.org/"—but no need to include "https://" for a URL, unless you want the URL to be a hyperlink.

- For a geographical location, give enough information to identify it: a city (Houston), a city and state (Portland, Maine), or a city and country (Manaus, Brazil).

- For something seen in a museum, archive, or elsewhere, name the institution and its location: Maine Jewish Museum, Portland; Portland Museum of Art, Portland, Maine.

- For performances or other live presentations, name the venue and its location: Mark Taper Forum, Los Angeles.

PUNCTUATION

- Use a period after the author name(s) that start an entry (Morrison, Toni.) and the title of the source you're documenting (*Beloved*.).

- Use a comma between the author's last and first names: Ede, Lisa.

- Some URLs will not fit on one line. MLA does not specify where to break a URL, but we recommend breaking it before a punctuation mark. Do *not* add a hyphen or a space.

- Sometimes you'll need to provide information about more than one work for a single source—for instance, when you cite an article from a periodical that you access through a database. MLA refers to the periodical and database (or any other entity that holds a source) as "containers" and specifies certain punctuation. Use commas between elements within each container, and put a period at the end of each container. For example:

> Semuels, Alana. "The Future Will Be Quiet." *The Atlantic*, Apr. 2016,
>
>   pp. 19–20. *ProQuest*, search.proquest.com/docview
>
>   /1777443553?accountid+42654.

The guidelines that follow will help you document the kinds of sources you're likely to use. The first section shows how to acknowledge authors and other contributors and applies to all kinds of sources—print, online, or others. Later sections show how to treat titles, publication information, location, and access information for many specific kinds of sources. In general, provide as much information as possible for each source—enough to tell readers how to find a source if they wish to access it themselves.

SOURCES NOT COVERED

These guidelines will help you cite a variety of sources, but there may be sources you want to use that aren't mentioned here. If you're citing a source that isn't covered, consult the MLA style blog at style.mla.org, or ask them a question at style.mla.org/ask-a-question.

Authors and Other Contributors

When you name authors and other contributors in your citations, you are crediting them for their work and letting readers know who's in on the conversation. The following guidelines for citing authors and contributors apply to all sources you cite: in print, online, or in some other media.

1. ONE AUTHOR

> Author's Last Name, First Name. *Title.* Publisher, Date.

> Anderson, Chris. *The Long Tail: Why the Future of Business Is Selling Less of More.* Hyperion, 2006.

2. TWO AUTHORS

> 1st Author's Last Name, First Name, and 2nd Author's First and Last Names. *Title.* Publisher, Date.

> Lunsford, Andrea, and Lisa Ede. *Singular Texts/Plural Authors: Perspectives on Collaborative Writing.* Southern Illinois UP, 1990.

3. THREE OR MORE AUTHORS

> 1st Author's Last Name, First Name, et al. *Title.* Publisher, Date.

> Sebranek, Patrick, et al. *Writers INC: A Guide to Writing, Thinking, and Learning.* Write Source, 1990.

4. TWO OR MORE WORKS BY THE SAME AUTHOR

Give the author's name in the first entry, and then use a three-em dash or three hyphens in the author slot for each of the subsequent works, listing them alphabetically by the first word of each title and ignoring any initial articles.

> Author's Last Name, First Name. *Title That Comes First Alphabetically.* Publisher, Date.
> ———. *Title That Comes Next Alphabetically.* Publisher, Date.

> Kaplan, Robert D. *The Coming Anarchy: Shattering the Dreams of the Post Cold War.* Random House, 2000.

> ———. *Eastward to Tartary: Travels in the Balkans, the Middle East, and the Caucasus.* Random House, 2000.

5. AUTHOR AND EDITOR OR TRANSLATOR

> Author's Last Name, First Name. *Title.* Role by First and Last Names, Publisher, Date.

> Austen, Jane. *Emma.* Edited by Stephen M. Parrish, W. W. Norton, 2000.

> Dostoevsky, Fyodor. *Crime and Punishment.* Translated by Richard Pevear and Larissa Volokhonsky, Vintage Books, 1993.

Start with the editor or translator, followed by their role, if you are focusing on that contribution rather than the author's. If there is a translator but no author, start with the title.

> Pevear, Richard, and Larissa Volokhonsky, translators. *Crime and Punishment*. By Fyodor Dostoevsky, Vintage Books, 1993.

> *Beowulf*. Translated by Kevin Crossley-Holland, Macmillan, 1968.

6. NO AUTHOR OR EDITOR

When there's no known author or editor, start with the title.

> *The Turner Collection in the Clore Gallery*. Tate Publications, 1987.

> "Being Invisible Closer to Reality." *The Atlanta Journal-Constitution*, 11 Aug. 2008, p. A3.

7. ORGANIZATION OR GOVERNMENT AS AUTHOR

> Organization Name. *Title*. Publisher, Date.

> Diagram Group. *The Macmillan Visual Desk Reference*. Macmillan, 1993.

For a government publication, give the name that is shown in the source.

> United States, Department of Health and Human Services, National Institute of Mental Health. *Autism Spectrum Disorders*. Government Printing Office, 2004.

When a nongovernment organization is both author and publisher, start with the title and list the organization only as the publisher.

> *Stylebook on Religion 2000: A Reference Guide and Usage Manual*. Catholic News Service, 2002.

If a division of an organization is listed as the author, give the division as the author and the organization as the publisher.

> Center for Workforce Studies. *2005–13: Demographics of the U.S. Psychology Workforce*. American Psychological Association, July 2015.

Articles and Other Short Works

Articles, essays, reviews, and other shorts works are found in journals, magazines, newspapers, other periodicals, and also in books—all of which

TITLE   AUTHOR   PUBLICATION

you may find in print, online, or in a database. For most short works, you'll need to provide information about the author, the titles of both the short work and the longer work where it's found, any page numbers, and various kinds of publication information, all explained below.

8. ARTICLE IN A JOURNAL

PRINT

Author's Last Name, First Name. "Title of Article." *Name of Journal*, Volume, Issue, Date, Pages.

Cooney, Brian C. "Considering *Robinson Crusoe*'s 'Liberty of Conscience' in an Age of Terror." *College English*, vol. 69, no. 3, Jan. 2007, pp. 197–215.

ONLINE

Author's Last Name, First Name. "Title of Article." *Name of Journal*, Volume, Issue, Date, DOI *or* URL.

Schmidt, Desmond. "A Model of Versions and Layers." *Digital Humanities Quarterly*, vol. 13, no. 3, 2019, www.digitalhumanities.org/dhq /vol/13/3/000430/000430.html.

9. ARTICLE IN A MAGAZINE

PRINT

Author's Last Name, First Name. "Title of Article." *Name of Magazine*, Volume (if any), Issue (if any), Date, Pages.

Burt, Tequia. "Legacy of Activism: Concerned Black Students' 50-Year History at Grinnell College." *Grinnell Magazine*, vol. 48, no. 4, summer 2016, pp. 32–38.

ONLINE

Author's Last Name, First Name. "Title of Article." *Name of Magazine*, Volume (if any), Issue (if any), Date, DOI *or* URL.

Brooks, Arthur C. "The Hidden Toll of Remote Work." *The Atlantic*, 1 Apr. 2021, www.theatlantic.com/family/archive/2021/04/zoom -remote-work-loneliness-happiness/618473.

Documentation Map (MLA)
Article in a Print Journal

TITLE OF ARTICLE

Marge Simpson, Blue-Haired Housewife: Defining Domesticity on *The Simpsons*

AUTHOR

JESSAMYN NEUHAUS

MORE THAN TWENTY SEASONS AFTER ITS DEBUT AS A SHORT ON *THE Tracy Ullman Show* in 1989, pundits, politicians, scholars, journalists, and critics continue to discuss and debate the meaning and relevance of *The Simpsons* to American society. For academics and educators, the show offers an especially dense pop culture text, inspiring articles and anthologies examining *The Simpsons* in light of American religious life, the representation of homosexuality in cartoons, and the use of pop culture in the classroom, among many other topics (Dennis; Frank; Henry "The Whole World's Gone Gay"; Hobbs; Kristiansen). Philosophers and literary theorists in particular are intrigued by the quintessentially postmodern self-aware form and content of *The Simpsons* and the questions about identity, spectatorship, and consumer culture it raises (Alberti; Bybee and Overbeck; Glynn; Henry "The Triumph of Popular Culture"; Herron; Hull; Irwin et al.; Ott; Parisi).

Simpsons observers frequently note that this TV show begs one of the fundamental questions in cultural studies: can pop culture ever provide a site of individual or collective resistance or must it always ultimately function in the interests of the capitalist dominant ideology? Is *The Simpsons* a brilliant satire of virtually every cherished American myth about public and private life, offering dissatisfied Americans the opportunity to critically reflect on contemporary issues (Turner 435)? Or is it simply another TV show making money for the Fox Network? Is *The Simpsons* an empty, cynical, even nihilistic view of the world, lulling its viewers into laughing hopelessly at the pointless futility of

NAME OF JOURNAL

VOLUME

ISSUE

PAGES

YEAR

The Journal of Popular Culture, Vol. 43, No. 4, 2010, pp.761-81.
© 2010, Wiley Periodicals, Inc.

558–63
for more
on citing
articles
MLA style

Neuhaus, Jessamyn. "Marge Simpson, Blue-Haired Housewife: Defining Domesticity on *The Simpsons*." *The Journal of Popular Culture*, vol. 43, no. 4, 2010, pp. 761–81.

Documentation Map (MLA)
Article in an Online Magazine

URL

NAME OF MAGAZINE

TITLE OF ARTICLE

AUTHOR

DATE

Segal, Michael. "The Hit Book That Came from Mars." *Nautilus*,
8 Jan. 2015, nautil.us/issue/20/creativity/the-hit-book-that
-came-from-mars.

571–73
for more
on citing
websites
MLA style

10. ARTICLE IN A NEWS PUBLICATION

PRINT

> Author's Last Name, First Name. "Title of Article." *Name*
> *of Publication,* Date, Pages.

> Saulny, Susan, and Jacques Steinberg. "On College Forms, a Question of
> Race Can Perplex." *The New York Times,* 14 June 2011, p. A1.

To document a particular edition of a newspaper, list the edition before the date. If a section name or number is needed to locate the article, put that detail after the date.

> Burns, John F., and Miguel Helft. "Under Pressure, YouTube Withdraws
> Muslim Cleric's Videos." *The New York Times,* late ed., 4 Nov. 2010,
> sec. 1, p. 13.

ONLINE

> Author's Last Name, First Name. "Title of Article." *Name*
> *of Publication,* Date, URL.

> Banerjee, Neela. "Proposed Religion-Based Program for Federal Inmates
> Is Canceled." *The New York Times,* 28 Oct. 2006, www.nytimes
> .com/2006/10/28/us/28prison.html.

11. ARTICLE ACCESSED THROUGH A DATABASE

> Author's Last Name, First Name. "Title of Article." *Name*
> *of Periodical,* Volume, Issue, Date, Pages. *Name of Database,* DOI
> *or* URL.

> Stalter, Sunny. "Subway Ride and Subway System in Hart Crane's 'The
> Tunnel.'" *Journal of Modern Literature,* vol. 33, no. 2, Jan. 2010, pp.
> 70–91. *JSTOR,* https://doi.org/10.2979/jml.2010.33.2.70.

TITLE   AUTHOR   PUBLICATION

Documentation Map (MLA)
Journal Article Accessed through a Database

NAME OF DATABASE

TITLE OF ARTICLE

AUTHOR

PAGES

DATE, VOLUME, ISSUE

NAME OF PERIODICAL

DOI

Neuhaus, Jessamyn. "Marge Simpson, Blue-Haired Housewife:
Defining Domesticity on *The Simpsons*." *Journal of Popular
Culture*, vol. 43, no. 4, Aug. 2010, pp. 761–81. *EBSCOhost*,
https://doi.org/10.1111/j.1540-5931.2010.00769.x.

12. ENTRY IN A REFERENCE WORK

PRINT

> Author's Last Name, First Name (if any). "Title of Entry." *Title
> of Reference Book*, edited by First and Last Names (if any), Edition
> number, Volume (if any), Publisher, Date, Pages.

> Fritz, Jan Marie. "Clinical Sociology." *Encyclopedia of Sociology*, edited
> by Edgar F. Borgatta and Rhonda J. V. Montgomery, 2nd ed., vol. 1,
> Macmillan Reference USA, 2000, pp. 323–29.

> "California." *The New Columbia Encyclopedia*, edited by William H.
> Harris and Judith S. Levey, 4th ed., Columbia UP, 1975, pp. 423–24.

ONLINE

Document online reference works the same as print ones, adding the URL
after the date of publication.

> "Baseball." *The Columbia Electronic Encyclopedia*, edited by Paul Lagassé,
> 6th ed., Columbia UP, 2012, www.infoplease.com/encyclopedia.

13. EDITORIAL OR OP-ED

EDITORIAL

> Editorial Board. "Title." *Name of Periodical*, Date, Page *or* URL.

> Editorial Board. "A New Look for Local News Coverage." *The Lakeville
> Journal*, 13 Feb. 2020, p. A8.

> Editorial Board. "Editorial: Protect Reporters at Protest Scenes." *Los
> Angeles Times*, 11 Mar. 2021, www.latimes.com/opinion/story/2021
> -03-11/reporters-protest-scenes.

OP-ED

> Author's Last Name, First Name. "Title." *Name of Periodical*, Date, Page
> *or* URL.

> Okafor, Kingsley. "Opinion: The First Step to COVID Vaccine Equity Is
> Overall Health Equity." *The Denver Post*, 15 Apr. 2021,
> www.denverpost.com/2021/04/15/covid-vaccine-equity-kaiser.

TITLE   AUTHOR   PUBLICATION

If it's not clear that it's an op-ed, add a label at the end.

> Balf, Todd. "Falling in Love with Swimming." *The New York Times*, 17
> Apr. 2021, p. A21. Op-ed.

14. LETTER TO THE EDITOR

> Author's Last Name, First Name. "Title of Letter (if any)." *Name of*
> *Periodical*, Date, Page *or* URL.

> Pinker, Steven. "Language Arts." *The New Yorker*, 4 June 2012, p. 10.

If the letter has no title, include "Letter" after the author's name.

> Fleischmann, W. B. Letter. *The New York Review of Books*, 1 June 1963,
> www.nybooks.com/articles/1963/06/01/letter-21.

15. REVIEW

PRINT

> Reviewer's Last Name, First Name. "Title of Review." *Name*
> *of Periodical*, Date, Pages.

> Frank, Jeffrey. "Body Count." *The New Yorker*, 30 July 2007, pp. 86–87.

ONLINE

> Reviewer's Last Name, First Name. "Title of Review." *Name of*
> *Periodical*, Date, URL.

> Donadio, Rachel. "Italy's Great, Mysterious Storyteller." *The New York*
> *Review of Books*, 18 Dec. 2014, www.nybooks.com/articles/2014/12
> /18/italys-great-mysterious-storyteller.

If a review has no title, include the title and author of the work being reviewed after the reviewer's name.

> Lohier, Patrick. Review of *Exhalation*, by Ted Chiang. *Harvard Review*
> *Online*, 4 Oct. 2019, www.harvardreview.org/book-review
> /exhalation.

16. COMMENT ON AN ONLINE ARTICLE

> Commenter's Last Name, First Name *or* Username. Comment on "Title of Article." *Name of Periodical,* Date posted, Time posted, URL.

> ZeikJT. Comment on "The Post-Disaster Artist." *Polygon,* 6 May 2020, 4:33 a.m., www.polygon.com/2020/5/5/21246679/josh-trank-capone -interview-fantastic-four-chronicle.

Books and Parts of Books

For most books, you'll need to provide information about the author, the title, the publisher, and the year of publication. If you found the book inside a larger volume, a database, or some other work, be sure to specify that as well.

17. BASIC ENTRIES FOR A BOOK

PRINT

> Author's Last Name, First Name. *Title.* Publisher, Year of publication.

> Watson, Brad. *Miss Jane.* W. W. Norton, 2016.

EBOOK

> Author's Last Name, First Name. *Title.* Ebook ed., Publisher, Year of publication.

> Watson, Brad. *Miss Jane.* Ebook ed., W. W. Norton, 2016.

ON A WEBSITE

> Author's Last Name, First Name. *Title.* Publisher, Year of publication, DOI *or* URL.

> Ball, Cheryl E., and Drew M. Loewe, editors. *Bad Ideas about Writing.* West Virginia U Libraries, 2017, textbooks.lib.wvu.edu/badideas /badideasaboutwriting-book.pdf.

WHEN THE PUBLISHER IS THE AUTHOR

> *Title.* Edition number (if any), Publisher, Year of publication.

> *MLA Handbook.* 9th ed., Modern Language Association of America, 2021.

Documentation Map (MLA)
Print Book

TITLE

YEAR OF PUBLICATION

SUBTITLE

AUTHOR

PUBLISHER

Fontanella-Khan, Amana. *Pink Sari Revolution: A Tale of Women and Power in India.* W. W. Norton, 2013.

566–71 for more on citing books MLA style

18. ANTHOLOGY OR EDITED COLLECTION

Last Name, First Name, editor. *Title.* Publisher, Year of publication.

Kitchen, Judith, and Mary Paumier Jones, editors. *In Short: A Collection of Brief Nonfiction.* W. W. Norton, 1996.

19. WORK IN AN ANTHOLOGY

Author's Last Name, First Name. "Title of Work." *Title of Anthology,* edited by First and Last Names, Publisher, Year of publication, Pages.

Achebe, Chinua. "Uncle Ben's Choice." *The Seagull Reader: Literature,* edited by Joseph Kelly, W. W. Norton, 2005, pp. 23–27.

TWO OR MORE WORKS FROM ONE ANTHOLOGY

Prepare an entry for each selection by author and title, followed by the anthology editors' last names and the pages of the selection. Then include an entry for the anthology itself (see no. 18).

Author's Last Name, First Name. "Title of Work." Anthology Editors' Last Names, Pages.

Hiestand, Emily. "Afternoon Tea." Kitchen and Jones, pp. 65–67.

Ozick, Cynthia. "The Shock of Teapots." Kitchen and Jones, pp. 68–71.

20. MULTIVOLUME WORK

ALL VOLUMES

Author's Last Name, First Name. *Title of Work.* Publisher, Year(s) of publication. Number of vols.

Churchill, Winston. *The Second World War.* Houghton Mifflin, 1948–53. 6 vols.

SINGLE VOLUME

Author's Last Name, First Name. *Title of Work.* Vol. number, Publisher, Year of publication.

Sandburg, Carl. *Abraham Lincoln: The War Years.* Vol. 2, Harcourt, Brace and World, 1939.

TITLE   AUTHOR   PUBLICATION

If the volume has its own title, include it after the author's name, and indicate the volume number and series title after the year.

> Caro, Robert A. *Means of Ascent.* Vintage Books, 1990. Vol. 2 of *The Years of Lyndon Johnson.*

21. BOOK IN A SERIES

> Author's Last Name, First Name. *Title of Book.* Edited by First and Last Names, Publisher, Year of publication. Series Title.

> Walker, Alice. *Everyday Use.* Edited by Barbara T. Christian, Rutgers UP, 1994. Women Writers: Texts and Contexts.

22. GRAPHIC NARRATIVE OR COMIC BOOK

> Author's Last Name, First Name. *Title.* Publisher, Year of publication.

> Barry, Lynda. *One! Hundred! Demons!* Drawn and Quarterly, 2005.

If the work has both an author and an illustrator, start with the one you want to highlight, and label the role of anyone who's not an author.

> Pekar, Harvey. *Bob and Harv's Comics.* Illustrated by R. Crumb, Running Press, 1996.

> Crumb, R., illustrator. *Bob and Harv's Comics.* By Harvey Pekar, Running Press, 1996.

To cite several contributors, you can also start with the title.

> *Secret Invasion.* By Brian Michael Bendis, illustrated by Leinil Yu, inked by Mark Morales, Marvel, 2009.

23. SACRED TEXT

If you cite a specific edition of a religious text, you need to include it in your works-cited list.

> *The New English Bible with the Apocrypha.* Oxford UP, 1971.

> *The Torah: A Modern Commentary.* W. Gunther Plaut, general editor, Union of American Hebrew Congregations, 1981.

24. EDITION OTHER THAN THE FIRST

Author's Last Name, First Name. *Title.* Edition name *or* number, Publisher, Year of publication.

Smart, Ninian. *The World's Religions.* 2nd ed., Cambridge UP, 1998.

25. REPUBLISHED WORK

Author's Last Name, First Name. *Title.* Year of original publication. Current publisher, Year of republication.

Bierce, Ambrose. *Civil War Stories.* 1909. Dover, 1994.

26. FOREWORD, INTRODUCTION, PREFACE, OR AFTERWORD

Part Author's Last Name, First Name. Name of Part. *Title of Book,* by Author's First and Last Names, Publisher, Year of publication, Pages.

Tanner, Tony. Introduction. *Pride and Prejudice,* by Jane Austen, Penguin, 1972, pp. 7–46.

27. PUBLISHED LETTER

Letter Writer's Last Name, First Name. "Title of letter." Day Month Year. *Title of Book,* edited by First and Last Names, Publisher, Year of publication, Pages.

White, E. B. "To Carol Angell." 28 May 1970. *Letters of E. B. White,* edited by Dorothy Lobrano Guth, Harper and Row, 1976, p. 600.

28. PAPER HEARD AT A CONFERENCE

Author's Last Name, First Name. "Title of Paper." Conference, Day Month Year, Location.

Hern, Katie. "Inside an Accelerated Reading and Writing Classroom." Conference on Acceleration in Developmental Education, 15 June 2016, Sheraton Inner Harbor Hotel, Baltimore.

TITLE   AUTHOR   PUBLICATION

29. DISSERTATION

> Author's Last Name, First Name. *Title.* Year. Institution, PhD
>> dissertation. *Name of Database,* URL.

> Simington, Maire Orav. *Chasing the American Dream Post World War II:*
>> *Perspectives from Literature and Advertising.* 2003. Arizona State U,
>> PhD dissertation. *ProQuest,* search.proquest.com/docview/305340098.

For an unpublished dissertation, end with the institution and a description of the work.

> Kim, Loel. *Students Respond to Teacher Comments: A Comparison of*
>> *Online Written and Voice Modalities.* 1998. Carnegie Mellon U, PhD
>> dissertation.

Websites

Many sources are available in multiple media—for example, a print periodical that is also on the web and contained in digital databases—but some are published only on websites. A website can have an author, an editor, or neither. Some sites have a publisher, and some do not. Include whatever information is available. If the publisher and title of the site are essentially the same, omit the name of the publisher.

30. ENTIRE WEBSITE

> Editor's Last Name, First Name, role. *Title of Site.* Publisher, Date, URL.

> Proffitt, Michael, chief editor. *The Oxford English Dictionary.* Oxford UP,
>> 2021, www.oed.com.

PERSONAL WEBSITE

> Author's Last Name, First Name. *Title of Site.* Date, URL.

> Park, Linda Sue. *Linda Sue Park: Author and Educator.* 2021,
>> lindasuepark.com.

Documentation Map (MLA)

Work on a Website

URL

TITLE OF SITE

TITLE OF WORK

DATE

AUTHOR

571–73
for more
on citing
websites
MLA style

McIlwain, John, et al. "Housing in America: Integrating Housing,
Health, and Resilience in a Changing Environment." *Urban
Land Institute*, 28 Aug. 2014, uli.org/report/housing-in
-america-housing-health-resilience.

If the site is likely to change, if it has no date, or if it no longer exists, include a date of access.

> *Archive of Our Own.* Organization for Transformative Works, archiveofourown.org. Accessed 23 Apr. 2021.

31. WORK ON A WEBSITE

> Author's Last Name, First Name (if any). "Title of Work." *Title of Site,* Publisher (if any), Date, URL.

> Cesareo, Kerry. "Moving Closer to Tackling Deforestation at Scale." *World Wildlife Fund,* 20 Oct. 2020, www.worldwildlife.org/blogs /sustainability-works/posts/moving-closer-to-tackling-deforestation -at-scale.

32. BLOG ENTRY

> Author's Last Name, First Name. "Title of Blog Entry." *Title of Blog,* Date, URL.

> Hollmichel, Stefanie. "Bring Up the Bodies." *So Many Books,* 10 Feb. 2014, somanybooksblog.com/2014/02/10/bring-up-the-bodies.

Document a whole blog as you would an entire website (no. 30) and a comment on a blog as you would a comment on an online article (no. 16).

33. WIKI

> "Title of Entry." *Title of Wiki,* Publisher, Date, URL.

> "Pi." *Wikipedia,* Wikimedia Foundation, 28 Aug. 2013, en.wikipedia.org /wiki/Pi.

Personal Communication and Social Media

34. PERSONAL LETTER

> Sender's Last Name, First Name. Letter to the author. Day Month Year.

> Quindlen, Anna. Letter to the author. 11 Apr. 2013.

35. EMAIL OR TEXT MESSAGE

> Sender's Last Name, First Name. Email *or* Text message to First Name
> Last Name *or* to the author. Day Month Year.

> Smith, William. Email to Richard Bullock. 19 Nov. 2013.

> Rombes, Maddy. Text message to Isaac Cohen. 4 May 2021.

> O'Malley, Kit. Text message to the author. 2 June 2020.

You can also include the text of a short email or text message, with a label at the end.

> Rust, Max. "Trip to see the cows tomorrow?" 27 Apr. 2021. Email.

36. POST TO *X, INSTAGRAM,* OR OTHER SOCIAL MEDIA

> Author. "Title." *Title of Site,* Day Month Year, URL.

> Oregon Zoo. "Winter Wildlife Wonderland." *Facebook*, 8 Feb. 2019,
> www.facebook.com/80229441108/videos/2399570506799549.

If there's no title, you can use a concise description or the text of a short post.

> Millman, Debbie. Photos of Roxane Gay. *Instagram*, 18 Feb. 2021, www
> .instagram.com/p/CLcT_EnhnWT.

> President Obama [@POTUS44]. "It's been the honor of my life to serve
> you. You made me a better leader and a better man." *X*, 20 Jan.
> 2017, x.com/POTUS44/status/822445882247413761.

Audio, Visual, and Other Sources

37. ADVERTISEMENT

PRINT

> Description of ad. *Title of Periodical,* Date, Page.

> Advertisement for Grey Goose. *Wine Spectator*, 18 Dec. 2020, p. 22.

VIDEO

"Title." *Title of Site*, uploaded by Company, Date, URL.

"First Visitors." *YouTube*, uploaded by Snickers, 20 Aug. 2020,
www.youtube.com/watch?v=negeco0b1L0.

38. ART

ORIGINAL

Artist's Last Name, First Name. *Title of Art.* Year created, Location.

Van Gogh, Vincent. *The Potato Eaters.* 1885, Van Gogh Museum,
Amsterdam.

IN A BOOK

Artist's Last Name, First Name. *Title of Art.* Year created, Location. *Title of
Book*, by First and Last Names, Publisher, Year of publication, Page.

Van Gogh, Vincent. *The Potato Eaters.* 1885, Scottish National Gallery.
*History of Art: A Survey of the Major Visual Arts from the Dawn of
History to the Present Day*, by H. W. Janson, Prentice Hall / Harry N.
Abrams, 1969, p. 508.

ONLINE

Artist's Last Name, First Name. *Title of Art.* Year created. *Title
of Site*, URL.

Warhol, Andy. *Self-portrait.* 1979. *J. Paul Getty Museum*, www.getty
.edu/art/collection/objects/106971/andy-warhol-self-portrait
-american-1979.

39. CARTOON

PRINT

Author's Last Name, First Name. Cartoon *or* "Title of Cartoon." *Name of
Periodical*, Date, Page.

Mankoff, Robert. Cartoon. *The New Yorker*, 3 May 1993, p. 50.

ONLINE

> Author's Last Name, First Name. Cartoon *or* "Title of Cartoon." *Title of Site*, Date, URL.

> Munroe, Randall. "Up Goer Five." *xkcd*, 12 Nov. 2012, xkcd.com/1133.

40. SUPREME COURT CASE

> United States, Supreme Court. *Name of Case*. Date of decision. *Title of Source Site*, Publisher, URL.

> United States, Supreme Court. *District of Columbia v. Heller*. 26 June 2008. *Legal Information Institute*, Cornell Law School, www.law .cornell.edu/supremecourt/text/07-290.

41. FILM

Name individuals based on the focus of your project—the director, the screenwriter, or someone else.

> *Title of Film*. Role by First and Last Names, Production Company, Date.

> *Breakfast at Tiffany's*. Directed by Blake Edwards, Paramount, 1961.

ONLINE

> *Title of Film*. Role by First and Last Names, Production Company, Date. *Title of Site*, URL.

> *Interstellar*. Directed by Christopher Nolan, Paramount, 2014. *Amazon Prime Video*, www.amazon.com/Interstellar-Matthew-McConaughey /dp/B00TU9UFTS.

If your essay focuses on one contributor, you may put their name before the title.

> Edwards, Blake, director. *Breakfast at Tiffany's*. Paramount, 1961.

42. TV SHOW EPISODE

Name contributors based on the focus of your project—director, creator, actors, or others. If you don't want to highlight anyone in particular, don't include any contributors.

BROADCAST

"Title of Episode." *Title of Program*, role by First and Last Names (if any), season, episode, Production Company, Date.

"The Storm." *Avatar: The Last Airbender*, created by Michael Dante DiMartino and Bryan Konietzko, season 1, episode 12, Nickelodeon Animation Studios, 3 June 2005.

DVD

"Title of Episode." Broadcast Date. *Title of DVD*, role by First and Last Names (if any), season, episode, Production Company, Release Date, disc number. DVD.

"The Storm." 2005. *Avatar: The Last Airbender: The Complete Book 1 Collection*, created by Michael Dante DiMartino and Bryan Konietzko, episode 12, Nickelodeon Animation Studios, 2006, disc 3. DVD.

STREAMING ONLINE

"Title of Episode." *Title of Program*, role by First and Last Names (if any), season, episode, Production Company, Date. *Title of Site*, URL.

"The Storm." *Avatar: The Last Airbender*, season 1, episode 12, Nickelodeon Animation Studios, 2005. *Netflix*, www.netflix.com.

STREAMING ON AN APP

"Title of Episode." *Title of Program*, role by First and Last Names (if any), season, episode, Production Company, Date. *Name of* app.

"The Storm." *Avatar: The Last Airbender*, season 1, episode 12, Nickelodeon Animation Studios, 2005. *Netflix* app.

If you're focusing on a contributor who's relevant specifically to the episode you're citing, include their name after the episode title.

"The Storm." Directed by Lauren MacMullan. *Avatar: The Last Airbender*, season 1, episode 12, Nickelodeon Animation Studios, 3 June 2005.

43. ONLINE VIDEO

"Title of Video." *Title of Site,* uploaded by Uploader's Name, Day Month Year, URL.

"Everything Wrong with *National Treasure* in 13 Minutes or Less." *YouTube,* uploaded by CinemaSins, 21 Aug. 2014, www.youtube .com/watch?v=1ul-_ZWvXTs.

44. PRESENTATION ON *ZOOM* OR OTHER VIRTUAL PLATFORM

Author's Last Name, First Name. "Title." Sponsoring Institution, Day Month Year, online.

Budhathoki, Thir. "Cross-Cultural Perceptions of Literacies in Student Writing." Conference on College Composition and Communication, 9 Apr. 2021, online.

45. INTERVIEW

If it's not clear that it's an interview, add a label at the end. If you are citing a transcript of an interview, indicate that at the end as well.

PUBLISHED

Subject's Last Name, First Name. *"Title of Interview."* Interview by First Name Last Name (if given). *Name of Publication,* Date, Pages *or* URL.

Whitehead, Colson. "Colson Whitehead: By the Book." *The New York Times,* 15 May 2014, www.nytimes.com/2014/05/18/books/review /colson-whitehead-by-the-book.html. Interview.

PERSONAL

Subject's Last Name, First Name. Concise description. Day Month Year.

Bazelon, L. S. Telephone interview with the author. 4 Oct. 2020.

46. MAP

If the title doesn't make clear it's a map, add a label at the end.

Title of Map. Publisher, Date.

Brooklyn. J. B. Beers, 1874. Map.

TITLE   AUTHOR   PUBLICATION

47. MUSICAL SCORE

> Composer's Last Name, First Name. *Title of Composition.* Publisher, Year
> of publication.

> Frank, Gabriela Lena. *Compadrazgo.* G. Schirmer, 2007.

48. ORAL PRESENTATION

> Presenter's Last Name, First Name. "Title of Presentation." Sponsoring
> Institution, Date, Location.

> Cassin, Michael. "Nature in the Raw—The Art of Landscape Painting."
> Berkshire Institute for Lifelong Learning, 24 Mar. 2005, Clark Art
> Institute, Williamstown, Massachusetts.

49. PODCAST

If you accessed a podcast on the web, give the URL.

> "Title of Episode." *Title of Podcast,* hosted by First Name Last
> Name, season, episode, Production Company, Date, URL.

> "DUSTWUN." *Serial,* hosted by Sarah Koenig, season 2, episode 1, WBEZ /
> Serial Productions, 10 Dec. 2015, serialpodcast.org/season-two/1
> /dustwun.

THROUGH AN APP

> "DUSTWUN." *Serial,* hosted by Sarah Koenig, season 2, episode 1, WBEZ /
> Serial Productions, 10 Dec. 2015. *Spotify* app.

50. RADIO PROGRAM

> "Title of Episode." *Title of Program,* hosted by First Name Last
> Name, Station, Day Month Year.

> "In Defense of Ignorance." *This American Life,* hosted by Ira Glass, WBEZ,
> 22 Apr. 2016.

51. SOUND RECORDING

If you accessed a recording on the web, give the URL.

> Artist's Last Name, First Name. "Title of Work." *Title of Album*, Label,
>   Date, URL.

> Beyoncé. "Pray You Catch Me." *Lemonade*, Parkwood Entertainment /
>   Columbia Records, 2016, www.beyonce.com/album/lemonade
>   -visual-album/songs.

THROUGH AN APP

> Simone, Nina. "To Be Young, Gifted and Black." *Black Gold*, RCA Records,
>   1969. *Spotify* app.

ON A CD

> Artist's Last Name, First Name. "Title of Work." *Title of Album*, Label,
>   Date. CD.

> Brown, Greg. "Canned Goods." *The Live One*, Red House, 1995. CD.

52. VIDEO GAME

> *Title of Game.* Version, Distributor, Date of release.

> *Animal Crossing: New Horizons.* Version 1.1.4, Nintendo, 6 Apr. 2020.

53. GENERATIVE AI

At the time of this printing, the *MLA Style Center* website gives brief initial advice on how to cite content generated by AI tools such as *ChatGPT*. See style.mla.org for more information.

> "Prompt fed into AI tool" prompt. *AI Tool,* version, Company, Date,
>   URL.

> "Explain how a light bulb works" prompt. *ChatGPT*, 23 Mar. version,
>   OpenAI, 14 Apr. 2023, chat.openai.com.

If you're citing a creative work, you can use the title and a concise description instead of including the prompt. If there's no title, you can use the first few words of the text.

> "New sneakers, so fresh . . ." haiku about sneakers. *ChatGPT*, 23 Mar.
>   version, OpenAI, 24 Apr. 2023, chat.openai.com.

FORMATTING A RESEARCH PAPER

Name, course, title. MLA does not require a separate title page, unless your paper is a group project. In the upper left-hand corner of your first page, include your name, your instructor's name, the course name and number, and the date. Center the title of your paper on the line after the date; capitalize it as you would a book title. If your paper is a group project, include all that information on a title page instead, listing all the authors.

Page numbers. In the upper right-hand corner of each page, one-half inch below the top of the page, include your last name and the page number. If it's a group project and all the names don't fit, include only the page number. Number pages consecutively throughout your paper.

Font, spacing, margins, and indents. Choose a font that is easy to read (such as Times New Roman) and that provides a clear contrast between regular text and italic text. Set the font size between 11 and 13 points. Double-space the entire paper, including your works-cited list and any notes. Set one-inch margins at the top, bottom, and sides of your text; do not justify your text. The first line of each paragraph should be indented one-half inch from the left margin. End punctuation should be followed by one space.

Headings. Short essays do not generally need headings, but they can be useful in longer works. Use a large, bold font for the first level of heading, and smaller fonts and italics to signal lower-level headings. MLA requires that headings all be flush with the left margin.

First-Level Heading

Second-Level Heading

Third-Level Heading

Long quotations. When quoting more than three lines of poetry, more than four lines of prose, or dialogue between characters in a drama, set off the quotation from the rest of your text, indenting it one-half inch (or five spaces) from the left margin. Do not use quotation marks, and put any parenthetical documentation *after* the final punctuation.

In *Eastward to Tartary*, Robert Kaplan captures ancient and contemporary Antioch for us:

> At the height of its glory in the Roman-Byzantine age, when it had an amphitheater, public baths, aqueducts, and sewage pipes, half a million people lived in Antioch. Today the population is only 125,000. With sour relations between Turkey and Syria, and unstable politics throughout the Middle East, Antioch is now a backwater—seedy and tumbledown, with relatively few tourists. I found it altogether charming. (123)

In the first stanza of Matthew Arnold's "Dover Beach," the exclamations make clear that the speaker is addressing someone who is also present in the scene:

> Come to the window, sweet is the night air!
> Only, from the long line of spray
> Where the sea meets the moon-blanched land,
> Listen! You hear the grating roar
> Of pebbles which the waves draw back, and fling. (lines 6–10)

Be careful to maintain the poet's line breaks. If a line does not fit on one line of your paper, put the extra words on the next line. Indent that line an additional quarter inch (or two spaces). If a citation doesn't fit, put it on the next line, flush with the right margin.

Tables and illustrations. Insert illustrations and tables close to the text that discusses them, and be sure to make clear how they relate to your point. For tables, provide a number (Table 1) and a title on separate lines above the table. Below the table, provide a caption with source information and any notes. Notes should be indicated with lowercase letters. For graphs, photos, and other figures, provide a figure number (Fig. 1) and caption with source information below the figure. Use a lowercase "f" when referring to a figure in your text: (fig. 1). If you give only brief source information, use commas between elements—Zhu Wei, *New Pictures of the Strikingly Bizarre*

#9, print, 2004—and include full source information in your list of works cited. If you give full source information in the caption, don't include the source in your list of works cited. Punctuate as you would in the works-cited list, but don't invert the author's name: Berenice Sydney. *Fast Rhythm.* 1972, Tate Britain, London.

List of works cited. Start your list on a new page, following any notes (see p. 551). Center the title, Works Cited, and double-space the entire list. Begin each entry at the left margin, and indent subsequent lines one-half inch (or five spaces). Alphabetize the list by authors' last names (or by editors' or translators' names, if appropriate). Alphabetize works with no author or editor by title, disregarding "A," "An," and "The." To cite more than one work by a single author, list them as in number 4 on page 557.

SAMPLE RESEARCH PAPER

The following report was written by Jackson Parell for a first-year writing course. It's formatted according to the guidelines of the *MLA Handbook,* 9th edition (2021).

Sample Research Paper, MLA Style

½"

1"

Last name and page number.

Jackson Parell

Professor Hammann

Writing and Rhetoric 1

21 May 2018

Title centered.

Free at Last, Free at Last:

Civil War Memory and Civil Rights Rhetoric

Double-spaced throughout.

When Martin Luther King, Jr., addressed the huge crowd in

Washington, DC, on August 28, 1963, he did so on the steps of

the Lincoln Memorial, in Lincoln's symbolic shadow (Sundquist

146). Using the words and legacy of the Great Emancipator, King

intended to make an appeal to the moral conscience of America

to rid itself of the vestiges of slavery and to realize Lincoln's new

1"

birth of freedom one hundred years after it was first proposed. On

this day, and throughout the Civil War Centennial years (1961–65),

African American leaders, including King, successfully accessed

the language of the Civil War's promise of racial justice to shape

a compelling message for future progress. As historian Robert

Author named in signal phrase, page numbers in parentheses.

Cook writes, "The advent of the Centennial furnished [African

Americans] with powerful leverage in their intensifying efforts to

close the gap between the promise and the reality of American

community life" (96).

However, the rhetoric of the Civil War could only serve as

an appeal for racial equality if Americans commonly understood

its history in the context of social justice and equal rights.

No signal phrase; author and page number in parentheses.

Unfortunately, for many Americans in the 1960s, this was not the

case (Blight 3). Northerners and Southerners alike, looking to mend

1"

1"

Parell 2

sectional strife after the war, were willing to adopt a memory
of reconciliation that focused on the shared honor of battle as
opposed to the racial issues over which those battles were fought.
Civil War valor, bravery, and brotherhood shaped American
wartime memory into a "shared experience"—one that would
remain a potent source of nationalism well into the civil rights
era (Cook 4). "For the majority, especially of white Americans," as
historian David Blight writes, "emancipation in Civil War memory
was still an awkward kind of politeness at best and heresy
at worst. . . . In 1963, the national temper and mythology still
preferred a story of the mutual valor of the Blue and Gray to the
disruptive problem of black and white" (3). Therefore, civil rights
leaders, including King, attempted to remind Americans of the
war's cause and enduring racial legacies. Through pen and podium,
he leveraged that history in a powerful appeal for racial justice one
hundred years after Lee's surrender at Appomattox.

    In October 1961, President John F. Kennedy invited King to
the White House for lunch. The meeting was unofficial—it was
not recorded in the secretary's docket, nor was there any official
business set to be discussed (Branch 27). After lunch, Kennedy
led King on a tour of the residence. Hung outside the door of
Lincoln's bedroom was a copy of the original Emancipation
Proclamation. It gave King the opportunity to bring up, ever so
gently, the issue of civil rights (27). Already, the Montgomery
bus boycotts, the Greensboro sit-ins, and the Freedom Rides had

Embeds signal phrase in the middle of the quotation.

brought racial tensions to the forefront of American culture. King believed he had a solution. "Mr. President," he said, "I would like to see you stand in this room and sign a [second] Emancipation Proclamation outlawing segregation 100 years after Lincoln's. You could base it on the Fourteenth Amendment" (qtd. in Sundquist 34). In the summer of 1962, King and his associates delivered the first copy of this second Proclamation to the White House, bound in leather. This document serves as an important example of the ways in which King reshaped the memory of the Civil War and leveraged its rhetoric to advance claims for equality in civil rights. The proclamation directly engages in the battle between white reconciliationist memory and the memory of racial justice. In it, King pushes back on traditional narratives of mutual valor and bravery by instead placing emphasis on the guarantees of equality embodied in Civil War documents. But before King could make the revisions to Civil War history necessary to frame his plea for racial justice, he needed to provide Kennedy with a compelling reason for doing so. By 1962, racial tensions in the United States had come to a head. Politicians, including Kennedy, wished to deescalate the problem as fast as possible (Branch 52), so in his preamble, King cites increasing racial tensions as well as the Centennial of the Civil War as impetus to dive into the "wellsprings of history" from which the civil rights movement began ("Appeal" 3):

> Mr. President, sometimes there occur moments in the history of our nation when it becomes necessary to pause and reflect

Brackets indicate the quotation has been altered for clarity.

Two works cited within the same sentence.

Uses block format for quotation longer than four lines. Indents $\frac{1}{2}$ inch or five spaces.

Parell   4

upon the heritage of the past in order to determine the most
meaningful course for the present and the future. America
today in the field of race relations is such a moment. We
believe the Centennial of the Emancipation Proclamation is a
particularly important time for all our citizens to rededicate
themselves to those early precepts and principles of equality
before the law. ("Appeal" 1)

Parenthetical documentation follows punctuation in a block quotation.

With his first words, therefore, King encourages the president
to think about Civil War history as a tool for addressing modern
issues.

    After establishing the importance of looking to the past
to resolve the racial tensions of the present, King proposes the
version of Civil War history upon which he believes Kennedy
should reflect. It is a version that promotes the war's promises
of racial equality over the valor and bravery of its veterans.
He references the Gettysburg Address and the Emancipation
Proclamation as the war's defining documents, both of which
place the issue of slavery as the central cause of the Civil War
and uphold concepts of equal justice for all ("Appeal" 1–2). King
engages here with a larger historical movement to remind
Americans of the documents and narratives from their past that
support claims for racial equality. In the 1960s, historians and
researchers alike looked to rewrite Civil War memory in a way
that neither disregarded the importance of slavery as the agent

Includes short title because there's more than one source from that author.

of conflict in the Civil War nor portrayed African Americans as naturally inferior—a people without agency in the struggle for their own freedom (Snyder 1–2, 36). By reshaping the narratives of the past to reflect a nuanced version of the Civil War, these historians attempted to break down the justifications for the racial hierarchy that structured the white status quo.

By reshaping Civil War memory to focus on its promises of equality, King develops a strong appeal for change on the grounds that those promises had not yet been fulfilled. He draws compelling parallels between the past and present, which framed the Civil War as a battle unfinished, one fought today by the civil rights movement:

> The struggle for freedom, Mr. President, of which our Civil War was but a bloody chapter, continues throughout our land today. The courage and heroism of Negro citizens . . . is only further effort to affirm the democratic heritage so painfully won, in part, upon the grassy battlefields of Antietam, Lookout Mountain, and Gettysburg. ("Appeal" 3)

Paragraphs indent ½ inch or five spaces.

The metaphor of a modern Civil War presents Kennedy with the moral imperative to follow in the footsteps of Lincoln, his forebearer, and to help finally end the battle for equality begun one hundred years before. "The time has come, Mr. President, to let those dawn-like rays of freedom, first glimpsed in 1863, fill the heavens with noonday sunlight of complete human decency" ("Appeal" 4). King believed that the present situation demanded more than legisla-

Parell 6

tive action—it demanded from Kennedy an executive order that appealed to the "moral conscience of America" (4).

But Kennedy never responded, and King found his ambivalence very disheartening. Without Kennedy, King felt that the civil rights movement would stall. He needed to re-create the conditions under which a document like the first Emancipation Proclamation came about—to foster the same tensions that brought to light the deep moral flaws of racism and propelled them to a national stage (Ward and Badger 141). Time was running out. The eyes of the world were focused on the civil rights movement, and King intended to capitalize. At midnight on June 1, he called his aides with an urgent message: in August, the civil rights movement would descend on the capital (Branch 53).

Names both authors in a work with two authors.

If King could not convince the president to change the moral conscience of America, he would attempt to do it himself. Two months later, King began to outline the speech that would conclude the ceremonies of the March on Washington. In essence, it reflected the same historical appeal he had made to the president in the Second Emancipation Proclamation. He intended to shift predominant public memory from one that highlighted the mutual sacrifice of the Blue and Gray to one that focused on the Civil War's guarantees of equality. These guarantees served as the grounds on which King would build his argument for modern civil rights progress. Evoking the language of past Republican leaders, including Lincoln, he appealed to the American public to adopt a policy of inclusion, one with a vision for the future that was, in many ways, shaped in stark contrast to America's oppressive past.

On the morning of August 28, the turnout was slim, estimated at 25,000. Soon, however, protesters began arriving in swarms. At Union Station, trains pulled in first from Baltimore, then Georgia, the Carolinas, Maryland, and further north (Hansen 33–35). By the time King took the podium, he spoke before a crowd of nearly 250,000. "Five score years ago," King began, "a great American in whose symbolic shadow we stand today signed the Emancipation Proclamation" ("Dream" 1). This first sentence of King's "Dream" speech refers both to Lincoln's Gettysburg Address and to the Emancipation Proclamation, placing both documents at the forefront of America's Civil War consciousness (Sundquist 145). As in the Second Emancipation Proclamation, King intended to divert the predominant reconciliationist memory of the Civil War to one that memorialized the guarantees of racial justice embodied in the war's documents. Although his remarks on those documents were brief, the broader, more inclusive historical narratives toward which they gesture—those in which slavery is accepted as the cause of the Civil War and African Americans are acknowledged for their strategic contributions to military efforts—gave further justification to uphold the guarantees of equality memorialized in the documents themselves.

These guarantees served as the moral structure of King's national appeal for racial justice. If, as King argues, equality was a right ensured by the course of American history, then segregation was simply a breach of contract between the American government and its African American constituents. He employs the

Includes page range because the information cited spans multiple pages.

Uses past tense ("began") to describe the scene—and present tense ("refers") to describe the text.

Parell   8

metaphor of a "bad check" to explain the chasm between historical promises of racial equality and the realities faced in 1960s culture:

> In a sense we've come to our nation's capital to cash a check. . . . This note was a promise that all men—yes, black men as well as white men—would be guaranteed the unalienable rights of life, liberty and the pursuit of happiness. It is obvious today that America has defaulted on this promissory note insofar as her citizens of color are concerned. ("Dream" 1)

Ellipses indicate that some words are left out.

For a nation that claimed to uphold basic precepts of justice, the "bad check" metaphor was particularly compelling. Americans were posed with a moral imperative to rid themselves of the modern vestiges of slavery or else risk contradicting the principles of equality upon which the nation was founded.

King's powerful appeal to the moral conscience of America was only made possible by shaping a new narrative in Civil War memory that upheld equality as a basic right for all: "Many of our white brothers . . . have come to realize that their freedom is inextricably bound to our freedom" ("Dream" 3). King begins here the process of linking the fulfillment of the civil rights cause to the betterment of the nation as a whole, a process necessary to garner the support of white moderates, partial to their own self-interest and thus indifferent to historical appeals for racial justice.

The incentive for civil rights progress was only strengthened by King's final moments at the podium, from which his speech gains its name. The appeal of King's utopian dream serves as a powerful motive to pursue civil rights equality. He dreams that "sons of former slaves and the sons of former slave-owners will be able to sit down together at the table of brotherhood" ("Dream" 4). He dreams that freedom will ring from "Stone Mountains of Georgia"—where the faces of Confederate generals are etched in rock—to "Lookout Mountain of Tennessee," the site of one of the Civil War's most famous battles (6). In essence, King's dream is that America will finally live up to the principles of freedom espoused at the time of its origin and live out "the true meaning of its creed" (4). Only then, King believes, will the battle for freedom begun at Fort Sumter finally reach its conclusion. King's direct references to the issue of slavery and to the battlegrounds on which the Civil War was fought serve as anchors in history that shape a clearer vision of future progress for all Americans. The moral imperative that King presents to white individuals in order to tender the check of racial justice is thus only made more pressing by the collective will to realize King's dream—a dream rooted in the rhetoric of the Civil War.

Ultimately, therefore, King's "Dream" speech promoted a memory that prioritized the war's promises of equality as opposed to the honor of its many battles. Historian David Blight explains:

> As Lincoln implied in that brief address at Gettysburg, the Civil War necessitated a redefinition of the United States, rooted somehow in the destruction of slavery and the . . . principle of human equality. In the "Dream" speech, King argued the same for his own era: the civil rights movement heralded yet another re-founding in the same principle, one hundred . . . years after Lincoln's promise. (2)

Parell   10

Throughout the Centennial years, civil rights leaders,

including King, waged war not only over modern policies and

ideals, but over historical truth as well. African American activists

pushed back on the predominant Civil War memory of the

1960s, promoting the war's guarantees of equality over those of

reconciliation. Such guarantees became the grounds on which King

and others shaped a compelling appeal for civil rights progress

in the modern era. "Just as abolitionists had sought to exploit the

promises enshrined in the Declaration of Independence," historian

Robert Cook writes, "their intellectual successors had used the

events of the Centennial to raise the conscience of the American

public in the 1960s" (qtd. in Ward and Badger 144). Ultimately,   *Source quoted in*
another source.

therefore, civil rights leaders molded the rhetoric of the Civil War

to inspire a nation to throw off its shackles of oppression and to

breathe new life into the old slave hymn: "Free at last, Free at last,

Great God a-mighty, We are free at last" (King, "Dream" 6).

1"

Works Cited

Heading centered.

The list is alphabetized by authors' last names.

Blight, David W. *American Oracle: The Civil War in the Civil Rights Era.* Belknap Press of Harvard UP, 2013.

Branch, Taylor. "A Second Emancipation." *Washington Monthly,* Jan.–Feb. 2013, pp. 27–52.

Double-spaced.

Cook, Robert. *Troubled Commemoration: The American Civil War Centennial, 1961–1965.* Louisiana State UP, 2011.

Each entry begins at the left margin; subsequent lines are indented ½ inch or five spaces.

Hansen, Drew. *The Dream: Martin Luther King, Jr., and the Speech That Inspired a Nation.* HarperCollins, 2003.

King, Martin Luther, Jr. "An Appeal to the Honorable John F. Kennedy President of the United States." 17 May 1962. *Civil Rights Movement Archive,* www.crmvet.org/info/emancip2.pdf.

Multiple works by a single author are listed alphabetically by title. After first entry, the author's name is replaced with a three-em dash or three hyphens.

——. "I Have a Dream . . . Speech by the Rev. Martin Luther King Jr. at the 'March on Washington.'" 28 Aug. 1963. *National Archives,* www.archives.gov/files/press/exhibits/dream -speech.pdf. Accessed 14 May 2019.

Snyder, Jeffrey Aaron. *Making Black History: The Color Line, Culture, and Race in the Age of Jim Crow.* U of Georgia P, 2018.

Sundquist, Eric. *King's Dream.* Yale UP, 2009.

Every source used is in the Works Cited.

Ward, Brian, and Tony Badger. *The Making of Martin Luther King and the Civil Rights Movement.* Macmillan, 1996.

55 APA Style

American Psychological Association (APA) style calls for (1) brief documentation in parentheses near each in-text citation and (2) complete documentation in a list of references at the end of your text. The models in this chapter draw on the *Publication Manual of the American Psychological Association*, 7th edition (2020). Additional information is available at www.apastyle.org.

A DIRECTORY TO APA STYLE

TITLE   AUTHOR   PUBLICATION

Formatting a Paper   623

Sample Research Paper   625

Throughout this chapter, you'll find models and examples that are color-coded to help you see how writers include source information in their texts and reference lists: tan for author or editor, yellow for title, blue for publication information—publisher, date of publication, page number(s), DOI or URL, and so on.

IN-TEXT DOCUMENTATION

Brief documentation in your text makes clear to your readers precisely what you took from a source. If you are quoting, provide the page number(s) or other information that will help readers find the quotation in the source. You're not required to give the page number(s) with a paraphrase or summary, but you may want to do so if you are citing a long or complex work.

521–32

PARAPHRASES and **SUMMARIES** are more common than **QUOTATIONS** in APA-style projects. As you cite each source, you will need to decide whether to name the author in a signal phrase—"as McCullough (2020) wrote"—or in parentheses—"(McCullough, 2020)." Note that APA requires

529–32

you to use the past tense for verbs in **SIGNAL PHRASES**, or the present perfect if you are referring to a past action that didn't occur at a specific time or that continues into the present: "Moss (2019) argued," "Many authors have argued."

1. AUTHOR NAMED IN A SIGNAL PHRASE

Put the date in parentheses after the author's last name, unless the year is mentioned in the sentence. Put any page number(s) you're including in parentheses after the quotation, paraphrase, or summary. Parenthetical documentation should come *before* the period at the end of the sentence and *after* any quotation marks.

> McCullough (2001) described John Adams as having "the hands of a man accustomed to pruning his own trees, cutting his own hay, and splitting his own firewood" (p. 18).

> In 2001, McCullough noted that John Adams's hands were those of a laborer (p. 18).

> John Adams had "the hands of a man accustomed to pruning his own trees," according to McCullough (2001, p. 18).

If the author is named after a quotation, as in this last example, put the page number(s) after the date within the parentheses.

2. AUTHOR NAMED IN PARENTHESES

If you do not mention an author in a signal phrase, put the name, the year of publication, and any page number(s) in parentheses at the end of the sentence or right after the quotation, paraphrase, or summary.

> John Adams had "the hands of a man accustomed to pruning his own trees, cutting his own hay, and splitting his own firewood" (McCullough, 2001, p. 18).

TITLE   AUTHOR   PUBLICATION

3. AUTHORS WITH THE SAME LAST NAME

If your reference list includes more than one first author with the same last name, include initials in all documentation to distinguish the authors from one another.

Eclecticism is common in modern criticism (J. M. Smith, 1992, p. vii).

4. TWO AUTHORS

Always mention both authors. Use "and" in a signal phrase, but use an ampersand (&) in parentheses.

Carlson and Ventura (1990) wanted to introduce Julio Cortázar, Marjorie Agosín, and other Latin American writers to an audience of English-speaking adolescents (p. v).

According to the Peter Principle, "In a hierarchy, every employee tends to rise to his level of incompetence" (Peter & Hull, 1969, p. 26).

5. THREE OR MORE AUTHORS

When you refer to a work by three or more contributors, name only the first author followed by "et al.," Latin for "and others."

Peilen et al. (1990) supported their claims about corporate corruption with startling anecdotal evidence (p. 75).

6. ORGANIZATION OR GOVERNMENT AS AUTHOR

If an organization name has a familiar abbreviation, give the full name and the abbreviation the first time you cite the source. In subsequent references, use only the abbreviation. If the organization does not have a familiar abbreviation, always use its full name.

FIRST REFERENCE

The American Psychological Association (APA, 2020)

(American Psychological Association [APA], 2020)

SUBSEQUENT REFERENCES

The APA (2020)

(APA, 2020)

7. AUTHOR UNKNOWN

Use the complete title if it's short; if it's long, use the first few words of the title under which the work appears in the reference list. Italicize the title if it's italicized in the reference list; if it isn't italicized there, enclose the title in quotation marks.

> According to Feeding Habits of Rams (2000), a ram's diet often changes from one season to the next (p. 29).

> The article noted that one donor died because of "frightening" postoperative care ("Every Patient's Nightmare," 2007).

8. TWO OR MORE WORKS TOGETHER

If you document multiple works in the same parentheses, place the source information in alphabetical order, separated by semicolons.

> Many researchers have argued that what counts as "literacy" is not necessarily learned at school (Heath, 1983; Moss, 2003).

Multiple authors in a signal phrase can be named in any order.

9. TWO OR MORE WORKS BY ONE AUTHOR IN THE SAME YEAR

If your list of references includes more than one work by the same author published in the same year, order them alphabetically by title, adding lowercase letters ("a," "b," and so on) to the year.

> Kaplan (2000a) described orderly shantytowns in Turkey that did not resemble the other slums he visited.

10. SOURCE QUOTED IN ANOTHER SOURCE

When you cite a source that was quoted in another source, add the words "as cited in." If possible, cite the original source instead.

> Thus, Modern Standard Arabic was expected to serve as the "moral glue" holding the Arab world together (Choueri, 2000, as cited in Walters, 2019, p. 475).

11. WORK WITHOUT PAGE NUMBERS

Instead of page numbers, some works have paragraph numbers, which you should include (preceded by the abbreviation "para.") if you are referring to a specific part of such a source.

> Russell's dismissals from Trinity College at Cambridge and from City College in New York City have been seen as examples of the controversy that marked his life (Irvine, 2006, para. 2).

In sources with neither page nor paragraph numbers, point to a particular part of the source if possible: (Brody, 2020, Introduction, para. 2).

12. AN ENTIRE WORK

You do not need to give a page number if you are directing readers' attention to an entire work.

> Kaplan (2000) considered Turkey and Central Asia explosive.

When you're citing an entire website, give the URL in the text. You do not need to include the website in your reference list. To document a webpage, see number 18 on page 632.

> Beyond providing diagnostic information, the website for the Alzheimer's Association (https://www.alz.org) includes a variety of resources for the families of patients.

13. PERSONAL COMMUNICATIONS

Document emails, telephone conversations, personal interviews, personal letters, messages from nonarchived online discussion sources, and other personal texts as "personal communication," along with the person's initial(s), last name, and the date. You do not need to include such personal communications in your reference list.

> L. Strauss (personal communication, December 6, 2013) told about visiting Yogi Berra when they both lived in Montclair, New Jersey.

14. GENERATIVE AI

The author is the name of the company that created the generative AI tool.

> AI models can be used for predictive modeling, helping researchers anticipate trends, behaviors, or outcomes based on historical data (OpenAI, 2023).

NOTES

You may need to use footnotes to give an explanation or information that doesn't fit into your text or to acknowledge the use of AI in your writing process. To signal a content footnote, place a superscript numeral at the appropriate point in your text. Include this information in a footnote, either at the bottom of that page or on a separate page with the heading "Footnotes" centered and in bold, after your reference list. If you have multiple notes, number them consecutively throughout your text. Here is an example from *In Search of Solutions: A New Direction in Psychotherapy* (2003).

TEXT WITH SUPERSCRIPT

An important part of working with teams and one-way mirrors is taking the consultation break, as at Milan, BFTC, and MRI.[1]

FOOTNOTE

[1]It is crucial to note here that while working within a team is fun, stimulating, and revitalizing, it is not necessary for successful outcomes. Solution-oriented therapy works equally well when working solo.

Here's an example from a student essay:

TEXT WITH SUPERSCRIPT

This essay argues that teacher looping in middle-school grades has multiple benefits for students.[1]

FOOTNOTE

[1]I acknowledge the use of *ChatGPT* in researching my topic and then in writing about it. It helped me get an overview of the concept of belonging in college before starting my research. And then it helped me create an outline for writing my essay. I've included my initial prompts and the full conversation with *ChatGPT* in an appendix.

TITLE   AUTHOR   PUBLICATION

REFERENCE LIST

A reference list provides full bibliographic information for every source cited in your text with the exception of entire websites, common computer software and mobile apps, and personal communications. See pages 624–25 for guidelines on preparing such a list; for a sample reference list, see pages 632–33.

Key Elements for Documenting Sources

To document a source in APA style, you need to provide information about the author, the date, the title of the work you're citing, and the source itself (who published it; volume, issue, and page numbers; any DOI or URL). The following guidelines explain how to handle each of these elements generally, but there will be exceptions. For that reason, you'll want to consult the entries for the specific kinds of sources you're documenting; these entries provide templates showing which details you need to include. Be aware, though, that sometimes the templates will show elements that your source doesn't have; if that's the case, just omit those elements.

AUTHORS

Most entries begin with the author's last name, followed by the first and any middle initials: Smith, Z. for Zadie Smith; Kinder, D. R. for Donald R. Kinder.

- If the author is a group or organization, use its full name: Black Lives Matter, American Historical Association.

- If there is no author, put the title of the work first, followed by the date.

- If the author uses a screen name, first give their real name, followed by the screen name in brackets: Scott, B. [@BostonScott2]. If only the screen name is known, leave off the brackets: AvalonGirl1990.

DATES

Include the date of publication, in parentheses right after the author. Some sources require only the year; others require the year, month, and day; and still others require something else. Consult the entry in this chapter for the specific source you're documenting.

- For a book, use the copyright year, which you'll find on the copyright page. If more than one year is given, use the most recent one.
- For most magazine or newspaper articles, use the full date that appears on the work, usually the year followed by the month and day.
- For a journal article, use the year of the volume.
- For a work on a website, use the date when the work was last updated. If that information is not available, use the date when the work was published.
- If a work has no date, use "n.d." for "no date."
- For online content that is likely to change, include the month, day, and year when you retrieved it. No need to include a retrieval date for materials that are unlikely to change.

TITLES

Capitalize only the first word and any proper nouns and adjectives in the title and subtitle of a work. But sometimes you'll also need to provide the title of a periodical or website where a source was found, and those are treated differently: capitalize all the principal words (excluding articles and prepositions).

- For books, reports, webpages, podcasts, and any other works that stand on their own, italicize the title: *White fragility*, *Radiolab*, *The 9/11 report*. Do not italicize the titles of the sources where you found them, however: NPR, ProQuest.
- For journal articles, book chapters, TV series episodes, and other works that are part of a larger work, do not italicize the title: The snowball effect, Not your average Joe. But do italicize the title of the larger work: *The Atlantic*, *Game of thrones*.
- If a work has no title, include a description in square brackets after the date: [Painting of sheep on a hill].
- If the title of a work you're documenting includes another title, italicize it: *Frog and Toad* and the self. If the title you're documenting is itself in italics, do not italicize the title within it: *Stay, illusion! The* Hamlet *doctrine.*

- For untitled social media posts or comments, include the first twenty words as the title, in italics, followed by a bracketed description: *TIL pigeons can fly up to 700 miles in one day* [Post].

SOURCE INFORMATION

This indicates where the work can be found (in a database or on a website, for example, or in a magazine or on a podcast) and includes information about the publisher; any volume, issue, and page numbers; and, for some sources, a DOI or URL. DOIs and URLs are included in all the templates; if the work you are documenting doesn't have one, just leave it off.

- For a work that stands on its own (a book, a report, a webpage), the source might be the publisher, a database, or a website.

- For a work that's part of a larger work (an article, an episode in a TV series, an essay in a collection), the source might be a magazine, a TV series, or an anthology.

- Give the volume and issue for journals and magazines that include that information. No need to give them for newspapers.

- Include a DOI for any work that has one, whether you accessed the source in print or online. For an online work with no DOI, include a working URL unless the work is from an academic database. You can use a shortDOI (https://shortdoi.org/) or a URL shortened using an online URL shortener, as long as the shorter DOI or URL leads to the correct work. No need to include a URL for a print work with no DOI.

Authors and Other Contributors

Most entries begin with authors—one author, two authors, or twenty-five. And some include editors, translators, or others who've contributed. The following templates show you how to document the various kinds of authors and other contributors.

1. ONE AUTHOR

> Author's Last Name, Initials. (Year of publication). *Title.* Publisher. DOI
> *or* URL

> Lewis, M. (2003). *Moneyball: The art of winning an unfair game.*
> W. W. Norton.

2. TWO AUTHORS

> First Author's Last Name, Initials, & Second Author's Last Name,
> Initials. (Year of publication). *Title.* Publisher. DOI *or* URL

Montefiore, S., & Montefiore, S. S. (2016). *The royal rabbits of London.*
Aladdin.

3. THREE OR MORE AUTHORS

For three to twenty authors, include all names.

> First Author's Last Name, Initials, Next Author's Last Name, Initials, &
> Final Author's Last Name, Initials. (Year of publication).
> *Title.* Publisher. DOI *or* URL

Greig, A., Taylor, J., & MacKay, T. (2013). *Doing research with children:
A practical guide* (3rd ed.). Sage.

For a work by twenty-one or more authors, name the first nineteen authors, followed by three ellipsis points, and end with the final author.

Gao, R., Asano, S. M., Upadhyayula, S., Pisarev, I., Milkie, D. E., Liu, T.-L.,
Singh, V., Graves, A., Huynh, G. H., Zhao, Y., Bogovic, J., Colonell,
J., Ott, C. M., Zugates, C., Tappan, S., Rodriguez, A., Mosaliganti,
K. R., Sheu, S.-H., Pasolli, H. A., . . . Betzig, E. (2019, January 18).
Cortical column and whole-brain imaging with molecular contrast
and nanoscale resolution. *Science, 363*(6424). https://doi.org/10.1126/
science.aau8302

4. TWO OR MORE WORKS BY THE SAME AUTHOR

If the works were published in different years, list them chronologically.

Lewis, B. (1995). *The Middle East: A brief history of the last 2,000 years.*
Scribner.

Lewis, B. (2003). *The crisis of Islam: Holy war and unholy terror.* Modern
Library.

If the works were published in the same year, list them alphabetically by title (ignoring "A," "An," and "The"), adding "a," "b," and so on to the year.

TITLE　　　　　　　AUTHOR　　　　　　PUBLICATION

Kaplan, R. D. (2000a). *The coming anarchy: Shattering the dreams of the post Cold War.* Random House.

Kaplan, R. D. (2000b). *Eastward to Tartary: Travels in the Balkans, the Middle East, and the Caucasus.* Random House.

5. AUTHOR AND EDITOR

If a book has an author and an editor who is credited on the cover, include the editor in parentheses after the title.

Author's Last Name, Initials. (Year of publication). *Title* (Editor's Initials Last Name, Ed.). Publisher. DOI *or* URL (Original work published Year)

Dick, P. F. (2008). *Five novels of the 1960s and 70s* (J. Lethem, Ed.). Library of America. (Original works published 1964–1977)

6. AUTHOR AND TRANSLATOR

Author's Last Name, Initials. (Year of publication). *Title* (Translator's Initials Last Name, Trans.). Publisher. DOI *or* URL (Original work published Year)

Hugo, V. (2008). *Les misérables* (J. Rose, Trans.). Modern Library. (Original work published 1862)

7. EDITOR

Editor's Last Name, Initials (Ed.). (Year of publication). *Title.* Publisher. DOI *or* URL

Jones, D. (Ed.). (2007). *Modern love: 50 true and extraordinary tales of desire, deceit, and devotion.* Three Rivers Press.

8. UNKNOWN OR NO AUTHOR OR EDITOR

Title. (Year of publication). Publisher. DOI *or* URL

Feeding habits of rams. (2000). Land's Point Press.

Clues in salmonella outbreak. (2008, June 21). *The New York Times*, A13.

If the author is listed as "Anonymous," use that as the author's name in the reference list.

9. ORGANIZATION OR GOVERNMENT AS AUTHOR

Sometimes an organization or a government agency is both author and publisher. If so, omit the publisher.

> Organization Name *or* Government Agency. (Year of publication).
> *Title.* DOI *or* URL

> Catholic News Service. (2002). *Stylebook on religion 2000: A reference guide.*

Articles and Other Short Works

Articles, essays, reviews, and other short works are found in periodicals and books—in print, online, or in a database. For most short works, provide information about the author, the date, the titles of both the short work and the longer work, plus any volume and issue numbers, page numbers, and a DOI or URL if there is one.

10. ARTICLE IN A JOURNAL

> Author's Last Name, Initials. (Year). Title of article. *Title of Journal,*
> *volume*(issue), page(s). DOI *or* URL

> Gremer, J. R., Sala, A., & Crone, E. E. (2010). Disappearing plants:
> Why they hide and how they return. *Ecology, 91*(11), 3407–3413.
> https://doi.org/10.1890/09-1864.1

11. ARTICLE IN A MAGAZINE

If a magazine is published weekly, include the year, month, and day. Put any volume number and issue number after the title.

> Author's Last Name, Initials. (Year, Month Day). Title of article.
> *Title of Magazine, volume*(issue), page(s). DOI *or* URL

> Klump, B. (2019, November 22). Of crows and tools. *Science, 366*(6468),
> 965. https://doi.org/10.1126/science.aaz7775

TITLE   AUTHOR   PUBLICATION

Documentation Map (APA)
Article in a Journal with a DOI

TITLE OF JOURNAL

VOLUME AND ISSUE

PAGES

ETHICS & BEHAVIOR, *23*(4), 324–337
Copyright © 2013 Taylor & Francis Group, LLC
ISSN: 1050-8422 print / 1532-7019 online
DOI: 10.1080/10508422.2013.787359

Routledge
Taylor & Francis Group

PUBLISHER

DOI

TITLE OF ARTICLE

Smart Technology and the Moral Life

AUTHOR

Clifton F. Guthrie

Department of Science and Humanities
Husson University

Smart technology is recording and nudging our intuitive and behavioral reactions in ways that are not fully shaped by our conscious ethical reasoning and so are altering our social and moral worlds. Beyond reasons to worry, there are also reasons to embrace this technology for nudging human behavior toward prosocial activity. This article inquires about four ways that smart technology is shaping the individual moral life: the persuasive effect of promptware, our newly evolving experiences of embodiment, our negotiations with privacy, and our experiences of risk and serendipity.

Keywords: persuasive technology, morality, ethics, virtue

PERSUASIVE TECHNOLOGY

For some time, cars have worked to shape our behaviors, beeping to warn us when a door is unlocked or a seat belt unfastened, or giving us fuel efficiency feedback. These straightforward but persuasive sensor systems nudge us toward a repertoire of safe driving behaviors, and we often cannot override them even if we want to. Newer cars include an increasing number of smart technologies that interact with us more intelligently. Some detect the presence of electronic keys and make it impossible for drivers to lock themselves out. Others use sensors to monitor approaching obstacles or lane boundaries and give warnings or even apply the brakes. We are seeing the emergence of street intersections that communicate directly with cars and cars that can communicate with one another (Dean, Fletcher, Porges, & Ulrich, 2012). These are so-called smart technologies because they draw data from the environment and from us, and often make decisions on our behalf. A leading researcher in automated driving noted, "The driver is still in control. But if the driver is not doing the right thing, the technology takes over" (Markoff & Sengupta, 2013).

As cars become smarter they are helping to lead us into what technologists describe as a pervasive, ambient, or calm computing environment. In 1991, Mark Weiser of the Palo Alto Research Center presciently called it "ubiquitous computing" or "ubicomp" in a much-quoted article from *Scientific American*, in which he outlined what has come to be accepted as a standard interpretation of the history of human interaction with computers. This is the age in which computers are increasingly liberated from manual input devices like laptops and cell phones to become an invisible, interactive, computational sensorium. Early examples include motion sensors, smart

Correspondence should be addressed to Clifton F. Guthrie, Department of Science and Humanities, Husson University, 1 College Circle, Bangor, ME 04401. E-mail: cfguthrie@gmail.com

Guthrie, C. F. (2013). Smart technology and the moral life.
Ethics & Behavior, 23(4), 324–337. https://doi.org/10.1080/
10508422.2013.787359

608–12
for more
on citing
articles
APA style

12. ARTICLE IN A NEWSPAPER

If page numbers are consecutive, separate them with an en dash. If not, separate them with a comma.

Author's Last Name, Initials. (Year, Month Day). Title of article.
Title of Newspaper, page(s). URL

Schneider, G. (2005, March 13). Fashion sense on wheels. *The Washington Post*, F1, F6.

13. ARTICLE ON A NEWS WEBSITE

Italicize the titles of articles on CNN and other news websites. Do not italicize the name of the website.

Author's Last Name, Initials. (Year, Month Day). *Title of article.*
Name of Site. URL

Travers, C. (2019, December 3). *Here's why you keep waking up at the same time every night.* HuffPost. https://bit.ly/3drSwAR

14. JOURNAL ARTICLE FROM A DATABASE

Author's Last Name, Initials. (Year). Title of article. *Title of Journal*,
volume(issue), pages. DOI

Simpson, M. (1972). Authoritarianism and education: A comparative approach. *Sociometry, 35*(2), 223–234. https://doi.org/10.2307/2786619

15. EDITORIAL

Editorials can appear in journals, magazines, and newspapers. If the editorial is unsigned, put the title in the author position.

Author's Last Name, Initials. (Year, Month Day). Title of editorial
[Editorial]. *Title of Periodical.* DOI or URL

The Guardian view on local theatres: The shows must go on [Editorial].
(2019, December 6). *The Guardian.* https://bit.ly/2VZHIUg

TITLE   AUTHOR   PUBLICATION

16. REVIEW

Use this general format to document a review that appears in a periodical or on a blog.

> Reviewer's Last Name, Initials. (Year, Month Day). Title of review
> [Review of the work *Title*, by Author's Initials Last Name]. *Title of
> Periodical or Name of Blog.* DOI *or* URL

> Joinson, S. (2017, December 15). Mysteries unfold in a land of minarets
> and magic carpets [Review of the book *The city of brass,* by S. A.
> Chakraborty]. *The New York Times.* https://nyti.ms/2kvwHFP

For a review published on a website that is not associated with a periodical or a blog, italicize the title of the review and do not italicize the website name.

17. COMMENT ON AN ONLINE PERIODICAL ARTICLE OR BLOG POST

> Writer's Last Name, Initials [username]. (Year, Month Day). Text of
> comment up to 20 words [Comment on the article "Title of work"].
> Title of Publication. DOI *or* URL

> PhyllisSpecial. (2020, May 10). How about we go all the way again? It's
> about time . . . [Comment on the article "2020 Eagles schedule:
> Picking wins and losses for all 16 games"]. *The Philadelphia
> Inquirer.* https://rb.gy/iduabz

Link to the comment if possible; if not, include the URL of the article.

18. WEBPAGE

> Author's Last Name, Initials. (Year, Month Day). *Title of work.* Title of
> Site. URL

> Pleasant, B. (n.d.). *Annual bluegrass.* The National Gardening Association.
> https://garden.org/learn/articles/view/2936/

If the author and the website name are the same, use the website name as the author. If the content of the webpage is likely to change and no archived version exists, use "n.d." as the date and include a retrieval date.

> Worldometer. (n.d.). *World population.* Retrieved February 2, 2020, from
> https://www.worldometers.info/world-population/

Documentation Map (APA)
Webpage

URL

TITLE OF SITE

TITLE OF WORK

DATE OF PUBLICATION

AUTHOR

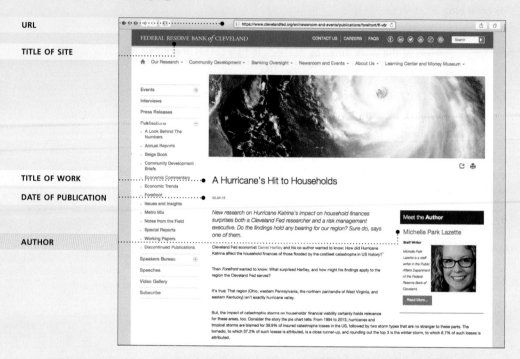

608–12
for more
on citing
webpages
APA style

Lazette, M. P. (2015, February 24). *A hurricane's hit to households.* Federal Reserve Bank of Cleveland. https://www.clevelandfed.org/en/newsroom-and-events/publications/forefront/ff-v6n01/ff-20150224-v6n0107-a-hurricanes-hit-to-households.aspx

TITLE   AUTHOR   PUBLICATION

Books, Parts of Books, and Reports

19. BASIC ENTRY FOR A BOOK

> Author's Last Name, Initials. (Year of publication). *Title.*
>> Publisher. DOI *or* URL

PRINT BOOK

Schwab, V. E. (2018). *Vengeful.* Tor.

EBOOK

Jemisin, N. K. (2017). *The stone sky.* Orbit. https://amzn.com/B01N7EQOFA

AUDIOBOOK

Obama, M. (2018). *Becoming* (M. Obama, Narr.) [Audiobook]. Random
House Audio. http://amzn.com/B07B3JQZCL

Include the word "Audiobook" in brackets and the name of the narrator
only if the format and the narrator are something you've mentioned in
what you've written.

20. EDITION OTHER THAN THE FIRST

> Author's Last Name, Initials. (Year). *Title* (Name *or* number ed.).
>> Publisher. DOI *or* URL

Burch, D. (2008). *Emergency navigation: Find your position and shape
your course at sea even if your instruments fail* (2nd ed.).
International Marine/McGraw-Hill.

21. EDITED COLLECTION OR ANTHOLOGY

> Editor's Last Name, Initials (Ed.). (Year). *Title* (Name *or* number ed., Vol.
> number). Publisher. DOI *or* URL

Gilbert, S. M., & Gubar, S. (Eds.). (2003). *The Norton anthology of literature
by women: The traditions in English* (3rd ed., Vol. 2). W. W. Norton.

Documentation Map (APA)
Book

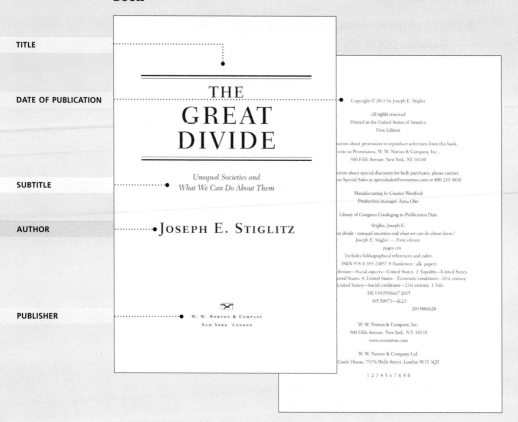

TITLE

DATE OF PUBLICATION

SUBTITLE

AUTHOR

PUBLISHER

THE
GREAT
DIVIDE

*Unequal Societies and
What We Can Do About Them*

JOSEPH E. STIGLITZ

W. W. NORTON & COMPANY
NEW YORK LONDON

Copyright © 2015 by Joseph E. Stiglitz

All rights reserved
Printed in the United States of America
First Edition

...ation about permission to reproduce selections from this book,
...write to Permissions, W. W. Norton & Company, Inc.,
500 Fifth Avenue, New York, NY 10110

...ation about special discounts for bulk purchases, please contact
...on Special Sales at specialsales@wwnorton.com or 800-233-4830

Manufacturing by Courier Westford
Production manager: Anna Oler

Library of Congress Cataloging-in-Publication Data
Stiglitz, Joseph E.
...at divide : unequal societies and what we can do about them /
Joseph E. Stiglitz. — First edition
pages cm
Includes bibliographical references and index.
ISBN 978-0-393-24857-9 (hardcover : alk. paper)
...ibution—Social aspects—United States 2. Equality—United States
...nited States. 4. United States—Economic conditions—21st century.
...United States—Social conditions—21st century. I. Title.
HC110.I5S8667 2015
305.50973—dc23
2015006628

W. W. Norton & Company, Inc.
500 Fifth Avenue, New York, N.Y. 10110
www.wwnorton.com

W. W. Norton & Company Ltd.
...Castle House, 75/76 Wells Street, London W1T 3QT

1 2 3 4 5 6 7 8 9 0

613–17
for more
on citing
books APA
style

Stiglitz, J. E. (2015). *The great divide: Unequal societies and what we
can do about them.* W. W. Norton.

TITLE   AUTHOR   PUBLICATION

22. WORK IN AN EDITED COLLECTION OR ANTHOLOGY

> Author's Last Name, Initials. (Year of edited edition). Title of work. In
> Editor's Initials Last Name (Ed.), *Title of collection* (Name or
> number ed., Vol. number, pp. pages). Publisher. DOI or URL
> (Original work published Year)

> Baldwin, J. (2018). Notes of a native son. In M. Puchner, S. Akbari,
> W. Denecke, B. Fuchs, C. Levine, P. Lewis, & E. Wilson (Eds.), *The
> Norton anthology of world literature* (4th ed., Vol. F, pp. 728–743).
> W. W. Norton. (Original work published 1955)

23. CHAPTER IN AN EDITED BOOK

> Author's Last Name, Initials. (Year). Title of chapter. In Editor's Initials
> Last Name (Ed.), *Title of book* (pp. pages). Publisher. DOI or URL

> Amarnick, S. (2009). Trollope at fuller length: Lord Silverbridge and the
> manuscript of *The duke's children*. In M. Markwick, D. Denenholz
> Morse, & R. Gagnier (Eds.), *The politics of gender in Anthony
> Trollope's novels: New readings for the twenty-first century*
> (pp. 193–206). Routledge.

24. ENTRY IN A REFERENCE WORK (DICTIONARY, THESAURUS, OR ENCYCLOPEDIA)

If the entry has no author, use the name of the publisher as the author. If
the reference work has an editor, include their name after the title of the
entry. If the entry is archived or is not likely to change, use the publication
date and do not include a retrieval date.

> Author's Last Name, Initials. (Year). Title of entry. In Editor's Initials
> Last Name (Ed.), *Title of reference work* (Name or number ed., Vol.
> number, pp. pages). Publisher. URL

> Merriam-Webster. (n.d.). Epoxy. In *Merriam-Webster.com dictionary*.
> Retrieved January 29, 2020, from https://www.merriam-webster.
> com/dictionary/epoxy

25. BOOK IN A LANGUAGE OTHER THAN ENGLISH

Author's Last Name, Initials. (Year). *Title of book* [English translation of title]. Publisher. DOI *or* URL

Ferrante, E. (2011). *L'amica geniale* [My brilliant friend]. Edizione E/O.

26. ONE VOLUME OF A MULTIVOLUME WORK

Author's Last Name, Initials. (Year). *Title of entire work* (Vol. number). Publisher. DOI *or* URL

Spiegelman, A. (1986). *Maus* (Vol. 1). Random House.

If the volume has a separate title, include the volume number and title in italics after the main title.

Ramazani, J., Ellmann, R., & O'Clair, R. (Eds.). (2003). *The Norton anthology of modern and contemporary poetry: Vol. 1. Modern poetry* (3rd ed.). W. W. Norton.

27. RELIGIOUS WORK

Do not include an author for most religious works. If the date of original publication is known, include it at the end.

Title. (Year of publication). Publisher. URL (Original work published Year)

New American Bible. (2002). United States Conference of Catholic Bishops. http://www.vatican.va/archive/ENG0839/_INDEX.HTM (Original work published 1970)

28. REPORT BY A GOVERNMENT AGENCY OR OTHER ORGANIZATION

Author's Last Name, Initials. (Year). Title (Report No. number). Publisher. DOI *or* URL

Centers for Disease Control and Prevention. (2009). *Fourth national report on human exposure to environmental chemicals.* US Department of Health and Human Services. https://www.cdc.gov/exposurereport/pdf/fourthreport.pdf

Include the year, month, and day if the report you're documenting includes that information. Omit the report number if one is not given. If more than one government department is listed as the publisher, list the most specific department as the author and the larger department as the publisher.

29. DISSERTATION

> Author's Last Name, Initials. (Year). Title (Publication No. number) [Doctoral dissertation, Name of School]. Database *or* Archive Name. URL

> Solomon, M. (2016). *Social media and self-examination: The examination of social media use on identity, social comparison, and self-esteem in young female adults* (Publication No. 10188962) [Doctoral dissertation, William James College]. ProQuest Dissertations and Theses Global.

If the dissertation is in a database, do not include a URL. Include a URL if it is published elsewhere online. If it is unpublished, write "Unpublished doctoral dissertation" in brackets, and use the name of the school in place of the database.

30. PAPER OR POSTER PRESENTED AT A CONFERENCE

> Presenter's Last Name, Initials. (Year, Month First Day–Last Day). *Title* [Paper or Poster presentation]. Name of Conference, City, State, Country. URL

> Dolatian, H., & Heinz, J. (2018, May 25–27). *Reduplication and finite-state technology* [Paper presentation]. The 53rd Annual Meeting of the Chicago Linguistic Society, Chicago, IL, United States. http://shorturl.at/msuB2

Audio, Visual, and Other Sources

If you are referring to an entire website, do not include it in your reference list; simply mention the website's name in the body of your paper and include the URL in parentheses. Do not include email, personal communication, or other unarchived discussions in your list of references.

31. *WIKIPEDIA* ENTRY

Wikipedia has archived versions of its pages, so give the date when you accessed the page and the permanent URL of the archived page, which is found by clicking "View history."

> *Title of entry.* (Year, Month Day). In *Wikipedia.* URL

> List of sheep breeds. (2019, September 9). In *Wikipedia.* https://en.wikipedia.
> org/w/index.php?title=List_of_sheep_breeds&oldid=914884262

32. ONLINE FORUM POST

> Author's Last Name, Initials [username]. (Year, Month Day). *Content of
> the post up to 20 words* [Online forum post]. Name of Site. URL

> Hanzus, D. [DanHanzus]. (2019, October 23). *GETCHA DAN HANZUS. ASK
> ME ANYTHING!* [Online forum post]. Reddit. https://bit.ly/38WgmSF

33. BLOG POST

> Author's Last Name, Initials [username]. (Year, Month Day). Title of
> post. Name of Blog. URL

> gcrepps. (2017, March 28). Shania Sanders. *Women@NASA.* https://blogs.
> nasa.gov/womenatnasa/2017/03/28/shania-sanders/

If only the username is known, use it without brackets.

34. ONLINE STREAMING VIDEO

> Uploader's Last Name, Initials [username]. (Year, Month Day). *Title*
> [Video]. Name of Video Platform. URL

> CinemaSins. (2014, August 21). *Everything wrong with* National treasure
> *in 13 minutes or less* [Video]. YouTube. https://www.youtube.com/
> watch?v=1ul-_ZWvXTs

Whoever uploaded the video is considered the author, even if someone else created the content. If only the username is known, use it without brackets.

35. PODCAST

> Host's Last Name, Initials (Host). (First Year–Last Year). *Podcast name* [Audio podcast]. Production Company. URL

> Poor, N., Woods, E., & Thomas, R. (Hosts). (2017–present). *Ear hustle* [Audio podcast]. PRX. https://www.earhustlesq.com/

36. PODCAST EPISODE

> Host's Last Name, Initials (Host). (Year, Month Day). Episode title (No. number) [Audio podcast episode]. In *Podcast name*. Production Company. URL

> Tamposi, E., & Samocki, E. (Hosts). (2020, January 8). The year of the broads [Audio podcast episode]. In *The broadcast podcast*. Podcast One. https://podcastone.com/episode/the-year-of-the-broads

Omit the episode number if one is not given.

37. FILM

> Director's Last Name, Initials (Director). (Year). *Title* [Film]. Production Company. URL

> Jenkins, B. (Director). (2016). *Moonlight* [Film]. A24; Plan B; PASTEL.

> Cuarón, A. (Director). (2016). *Harry Potter and the prisoner of Azkaban* [Film; two-disc special ed. on DVD]. Warner Brothers.

List the director as the author of the film. Indicate how you watched the film only if the format is relevant to what you've written.

38. TELEVISION SERIES

> Executive Producer's Last Name, Initials (Executive Producer). (First Year– Last Year). *Title of series* [TV series]. Production Company. URL

> Iungerich, L., Gonzalez, E., & Haft, J. (Executive Producers). (2018–present). *On my block* [TV series]. Crazy Cat Lady Productions.

Indicate how you watched the TV series (two-disc DVD set, for example) only if the format is relevant to your essay.

39. TELEVISION SERIES EPISODE

> Writer's Last Name, Initials (Writer), & Director's Last Name, Initials (Director). (Year, Month Day). Title of episode (Season number, Episode number) [TV series episode]. In Executive Producer's Initials Last Name (Executive Producer), *Title of series.* Production Company. URL

> Siegal, J. (Writer), Morgan, D. (Writer), & Sackett, M. (Director). (2018, December 6). Janet(s) (Season 3, Episode 10) [TV series episode]. In M. Schur, D. Miner, M. Sackett, & D. Goddard (Executive Producers), *The good place.* Fremulon; 3 Arts Entertainment; Universal Television.

40. MUSIC ALBUM

> Artist's Last Name, Initials. (Year). *Title of album* [Album]. Label. URL

> Jonas Brothers. (2019). *Happiness begins* [Album]. Republic.

41. SONG

> Artist's Last Name, Initials. (Year). Name of song [Song]. On *Title of album.* Label. URL

> Giddens, R. (2015). Waterboy [Song]. On *Tomorrow is my turn.* Nonesuch.

42. *POWERPOINT* SLIDES

> Author's Last Name, Initials. (Year, Month Day). *Title of presentation* [PowerPoint slides]. Publisher. URL

> Pavliscak, P. (2016, February 21). *Finding our happy place in the internet of things* [PowerPoint slides]. Slideshare. https://bit.ly/3aOcfs7

43. RECORDING OF A SPEECH OR WEBINAR

> Author's Last Name, Initials. (Year, Month Day *or* Year). *Title* [Speech
>   audio recording or Webinar]. Publisher. URL

> Kennedy, J. F. (1961, January 20). *Inaugural address* [Speech audio
>   recording]. American Rhetoric. https://bit.ly/339Gc3e

For a speech, include the year, month, and day. For a webinar, include
only the year.

44. PHOTOGRAPH

> Photographer's Last Name, Initials. (Year). *Title of photograph*
>   [Photograph]. Name of Site. URL

> Kudacki, P. (2013). [Photograph of Benedict Cumberbatch]. Time.
>   http://content.time.com/time/covers/asia/0,16641,20131028,00.html

Use this format to document a photograph that is not in a museum or
on a museum website. For a photograph with no title, include a description of the photograph in brackets after the date.

45. MAP

> Mapmaker's Last Name, Initials. (Year). *Title of map* [Map].
>   Publisher. URL

> Daniels, M. (2018). *Human terrain: Visualizing the world's population, in
>   3D* [Map]. The Pudding. https://pudding.cool/2018/10/city_3d/

46. SOCIAL MEDIA POSTS

If only the username is known, do not use brackets. List any audiovi-
sual content (e.g., videos, images, or links) in brackets. Replicate emoji or
include a bracketed description. Follow the spelling and capitalization of
the post.

> Author's Last Name, Initials [@username]. (Year, Month Day).
>   *Content of post up to 20 words* [Description of any audiovisual
>   content] [Type of post]. Platform. URL

X POST

Baron, D. [@DrGrammar]. (2021, March 12). *Got vaxxed and now I'm coming to you in 5g.* [Image attached] [Post]. X. https://bit.ly/3sxEELx

INSTAGRAM PHOTOGRAPH OR VIDEO

Jamil, J. [@jameelajamilofficial]. (2018, July 18). *Happy Birthday to our leader. I steal all my acting faces from you.* @kristenanniebell [Face with smile and sunglasses emoji] [Photograph]. Instagram. https://www.instagram.com/p/BlYX5F9FuGL/

FACEBOOK POST

Raptor Resource Project. (2020, May 8). *Happy Fri-yay, everyone! We'll keep the news short and sweet: today Decorah eaglets D34 and D35 turn 33 days* [Images attached]. Facebook. https://bit.ly/3icwFzN

47. DATA SET

Author's Last Name, Initials. (Year). *Title of data set* (Version number) [Data set]. Publisher. DOI *or* URL

Pew Research Center. (2019). *Core trends survey* [Data set]. https://www.pewresearch.org/internet/dataset/core-trends-survey/

Omit the version number if one is not given. If the publisher is the author, no need to list it twice; omit the publisher.

48. SUPREME COURT CASE

Name of Case, volume U.S. pages (Year). URL

Plessy v. Ferguson, 163 U.S. 537 (1896). https://www.oyez.org/cases/1850-1900/163us537

Obergefell v. Hodges, 576 U.S. ___ (2015). https://www.oyez.org/cases/2014/14-556

The source for most Supreme Court cases is the *United States Reports*, which is abbreviated "U.S." in the reference list entry. If the case does not yet have a page number, use three underscores instead. Italicize the name of the court case in any in-text citations, but do not italicize it in the reference list entry.

49. GENERATIVE AI

The author is the name of the company that created the generative AI tool.

Author. (Date). *Name of tool* (Version of tool) [Description]. URL

OpenAI. (2023). *ChatGPT* (Mar 14 version) [Large language model]. https://chat.openai.com/chat

Sources Not Covered by APA

To document a source for which APA does not provide guidelines, look at models similar to the source you have cited. Give any information readers will need in order to find the source themselves—author; date of publication; title; and information about the source itself (including who published it; volume, issue, and page numbers; and a DOI or URL). You might want to check your reference note to be sure it will lead others to your source.

FORMATTING A PAPER

Title page. APA generally requires a title page. The page number should go in the upper right-hand corner. Center the full title of the paper in bold in the top half of the page. Center your name, the name of your department and school, the course number and name, the instructor's name, and the due date on separate lines below the title. Leave one line between the title and your name.

Page numbers. Place the page number in the upper right-hand corner. Number pages consecutively throughout.

Fonts, spacing, margins, and indents. Use a legible font that will be accessible to everyone, either a serif font (such as Times New Roman or Bookman) or a sans serif font (such as Calibri or Verdana). Use a sans serif font within figure images. Double-space the entire paper, including any notes and your list of references; the only exception is footnotes at the bottom of a page, which should be single-spaced, and text within tables and images, the spacing of which will vary. Leave one-inch margins at the top, bottom, and sides of your text; do not justify the text. The first line of each paragraph should be indented one-half inch (or five to seven spaces) from the left margin. APA recommends using one space after end-of-sentence punctuation.

Headings. Though they are not required in APA style, headings can help readers follow your text. The first level of heading should be bold and centered; the second level of heading should be bold and flush with the left margin; the third level should be bold, italicized, and flush left. Capitalize all headings as you would any other title within the text.

First-Level Heading

Second-Level Heading

Third-Level Heading

Glossary

Abstract. An **ABSTRACT** is a concise summary of your paper that introduces readers to your topic and main points. Most scholarly journals require an abstract; an abstract is not typically required for student papers, so check your instructor's preference. Put your abstract on the second page, with the word "Abstract" centered and in bold at the top. Unless your instructor specifies a length, limit your abstract to 250 words or fewer.

Long quotations. Indent quotations of forty or more words one-half inch (or five to seven spaces) from the left margin. Do not use quotation marks, and place the page number(s) or documentation information in parentheses *after* the end punctuation. If there are multiple paragraphs in the quotation, indent the first line of each subsequent paragraph another one-half inch.

> Kaplan (2000) captured ancient and contemporary Antioch:
>
> > At the height of its glory in the Roman-Byzantine age, when it had an amphitheater, public baths, aqueducts, and sewage pipes, half a million people lived in Antioch. Today the population is only 125,000. With sour relations between Turkey and Syria, and unstable politics throughout the Middle East, Antioch is now a backwater—seedy and tumbledown, with relatively few tourists. (p. 123)
>
> Antioch's decline serves as a reminder that the fortunes of cities can change drastically over time.

List of references. Start your list on a new page after the text but before any notes. Title the page "References," centered and in bold, and double-space the entire list. Each entry should begin at the left margin, and subsequent lines should be indented one-half inch (or five to seven spaces). Alphabetize the list by authors' last names (or by editors' names, if appropriate).

Alphabetize works that have no author or editor by title, disregarding "A," "An," and "The." Be sure every source listed is cited in the text; do not include sources that you consulted but did not cite.

Tables and figures. Above each table or figure (charts, diagrams, graphs, photos, and so on), provide the word "Table" or "Figure" and a number, flush left and in bold (e.g., **Table 1**). On the following line, give a descriptive title, flush left and italicized. Below the table or figure, include a note with any necessary explanation and source information. Number tables and figures separately, and be sure to discuss them in your text so that readers know how they relate.

Table 1

Hours of Instruction Delivered per Week

	American classrooms	Japanese classrooms	Chinese classrooms
First grade			
Language arts	10.5	8.7	10.4
Mathematics	2.7	5.8	4.0
Fifth grade			
Language arts	7.9	8.0	11.1
Mathematics	3.4	7.8	11.7

Note. Adapted from *Peeking Out from under the Blinders: Some Factors We Shouldn't Forget in Studying Writing* (Occasional Paper No. 25), by J. R. Hayes, 1991, National Center for the Study of Writing and Literacy (https://archive.nwp.org/cs/public/print/resource/720). Copyright 1991 by the Office of Educational Research and Improvement.

SAMPLE RESEARCH PAPER

The following sample pages are from "The Benefits of Prison Nursery Programs," a paper written by Analisa Johnson for a first-year writing course. It is formatted according to the guidelines of the *Publication Manual of the American Psychological Association*, 7th edition (2020). While APA guidelines are used widely in linguistics and the social sciences, exact requirements may vary from discipline to discipline and course to course. If you're unsure about what your instructor wants, ask for clarification.

Title bold and centered.

The Benefits of Prison Nursery Programs

Author's name, school name and department, course number and name, instructor's name, and due date.

Analisa Johnson

Writing Program, Boston University

WR 150: Burning Questions: Human Expression

Samantha Myers

May 1, 2017

2

Abstract

The rising population of women in prisons has resulted in the births of some 2,000 babies per year to women behind bars. Female prisoners suffer from a number of inadequacies in their health care, but changes in birthing practices and the provision of nursery programs in prisons could yield important benefits. Currently, nine states offer such programs, and research conducted in these states has shown a number of positive effects. Fully 86.3% of women who have come through these programs remain in their communities after 3 years. Likewise, preschool performance of their children shows better emotional / behavioral adjustment than that of children who have been sent to foster care. Finally, estimates show that the annual costs of such programs are approximately 40% less than those of foster care.

Keywords: birthing practices, correctional, foster care, health care, incarceration, nursery program, prenatal care, preschool, prison, recidivism, sentencing project, shackles

Heading bold and centered.

Limited to 250 words or fewer.

"Keywords:" in italics, indented.

Title bold and centered.

Double-spaced throughout.

First-level headings bold and centered.

Paragraphs indented $\frac{1}{2}$ inch or 5–7 spaces.

1"

3

The Benefits of Prison Nursery Programs

Over the past 40 years or so, the United States has seen a steady increase in incarcerated individuals, with 2.2 million people currently in prisons and jails nationwide, according to statistics on prisons and the criminal justice system provided by the Sentencing Project (2017, p. 2). In particular, the number of incarcerated females has risen dramatically, at a rate 50% higher than that of men since the early 1980s. As recently as 2015, there were nearly 112,000 incarcerated women across the nation (Sentencing Project, 2017, p. 4). While there is a plethora of health care issues that women face when locked up, one of the most concerning is that of reproductive health, specifically pregnancy and birth in prison. Roughly 1 in 25 women entering prison or jail is pregnant (Yager, 2015). As a result, the number of babies born behind bars has also grown at an alarming rate.

1" It is estimated that up to 2,000 infants are born to incarcerated mothers 1" each year, only to be taken from them a scant 24 hours after birth and placed either with a family member or, more often, in the foster care system (Sufrin, 2012). Current scholarly sources have proven prison nursery programs—which allow mothers to keep their infants with them while they serve out their sentences—to be a very effective method in dealing with the issue of incarcerated mothers. Despite this fact, there are only nine nursery programs currently operational in America. In order to make prison nursery programs more prevalent, better education is needed for correctional administrators about the effectiveness of nursery programs.

Inadequacies of Prison Health Care for Pregnant Women

When it comes to women's health care in the prison system, there are many inadequate areas, but two that are of great importance are prenatal care and birthing practices.

1"

4

Prenatal Care

Hotelling (2008) discussed the lack of quality health care provided to expectant mothers behind bars. Despite adequate health care being mandated to all inmates through the Eighth Amendment to the Constitution, women still make up a lesser percentage of total incarcerated individuals than men—a fact that is used by correctional staff to justify providing scarcer health care and rehabilitative programs for incarcerated women. In addition, prisons are not subject to any sort of external review of their standards of inmate care, so they are not encouraged to improve health care services. As a result, many incarcerated women face unnecessarily high-risk pregnancies.

Birthing Practices

Another practice that increases the risk of complications in pregnancy in prison is the custom of shackling female inmates during labor, delivery, and postpartum. This practice is both degrading and inhumane and can pose a problem for health care providers in case of an emergency. In an official position statement, the Association of Women's Health, Obstetric and Neonatal Nurses (2011) noted that the unnecessary practice can interfere with the ability of nurses and health care providers to deliver the proper care and treatment (p. 817). Only 18 states in the United States currently ban the shackling of expectant mothers in prison while they give birth (American Civil Liberties Union Foundation, 2012). The remaining 32 states are left to their own devices, in some cases shackling mothers with no regard to the recommendations of nurses and other health care providers.

Prison Nursery Programs

In order to effectively spread awareness of prison nursery programs, it must be clear exactly what they are and how they serve incarcerated

Author named in a signal phrase, publication date in parentheses after the name.

Second-level headings bold and flush with left margin.

5

mothers. Prison nursery programs offer women who become incarcerated while pregnant the option to keep and parent their child while they serve their sentences. Getting into these programs can be a rigorous process; with limited spots available, prospective mothers must have a nonviolent conviction, no record of child abuse, and be roughly within 18 months of completing their sentence—which is the maximum amount of time a child can stay with their mother behind bars (Stein, 2010, p. 11).

Author name in parentheses when no signal phrase is used.

Benefits

When mothers do get into these programs, there are many benefits to be had for both themselves and their children. For starters, mothers are provided with parenting classes, support groups, substance abuse counseling, and complementary day-care services to attend these classes. Many prisons also provide high school and college courses for those mothers who have not yet completed their education (Wertheimer, 2005). Last, vocational programs are also offered, which aid in the job search once the women are released from prison.

Recidivism

As a result of the programs, many of the mothers have been shown to have a reduced recidivism rate. An astounding 86.3% of women exiting a prison nursery program remained in the community 3 years following their release (Goshin et al., 2013, Results section, para. 3). This is a proven positive for both the mothers and their children.

In-text citation of journal article without pagination.

Cost of Prison Nursery Programs

While it may seem as if implementing prison nursery programs across the country would be an expensive endeavor, it is important to consider by comparison the costs of putting children in foster care. On average, the total financial cost for one child to remain in foster care per

6

year in Oregon is about $26,600 (Fixsen, 2011, p. 3). Conversely, based on
an evaluation of Nebraska's prison nursery program, expenses for the
nursery program would be roughly 40% less per year than foster care
expenses would be for the same babies, and even more money would be
saved if the nursery program reduced recidivism (Carlson, 1998, as cited
in Yager, 2015, para. 34). Rapidly increasing the number of prison nursery
programs across the country may result in some extra money spent in
the short run, but it will provide benefits in the long run, both financially
and socially.

Source quoted in another source identified with "as cited in."

Heading bold and centered.

7

References

American Civil Liberties Union Foundation. (2012). *The shackling of pregnant women & girls in U.S. prisons, jails & youth detention centers* [Briefing paper]. https://www.aclu.org/files/assets/anti-shackling_ briefing_paper_stand_alone.pdf

Alphabetized by authors' last names or first word of organization.

Association of Women's Health, Obstetric and Neonatal Nurses. (2011). *Shackling incarcerated pregnant women* [Position statement]. http://www.jognn.org/article/S0884-2175(15)30763-2/pdf

All lines after the first line of each entry indented.

Fixsen, A. (2011). *Children in foster care*. A Family for Every Child. http://www.afamilyforeverychild.org/wp=content/uploads/2018/04/ children_in_foster_care.pdf

Goshin, L. S., Byrne, M. W., & Henninger, A. M. (2013). Recidivism after release from a prison nursery program. *Public Health Nursing, 33*(2), 109–117. https://doi.org/10.1111/phn.12072

Hotelling, B. A. (2008). Perinatal needs of pregnant incarcerated women. *The Journal of Perinatal Education, 17*(2), 37–44. https://doi. org/10.1624/105812408X298372

Sentencing Project. (2017). *Trends in U.S. corrections* [Fact sheet]. http://sentencingproject.org/wp-content/uploads/2016/01/ Trends-in-US-Corrections.pdf

Stein, D. J. (2010, July/August). Babies behind bars: Nurseries for incarcerated mothers and their children. *Children's Voice, 19*(4), 10–13.

Sufrin, C. (2012, July 1). *Incarcerated women and reproductive health care* [Video]. YouTube. https://www.youtube.com/ watch?v=WNx1ntLyI2Q

8

Wertheimer, L. (2005, November 5). *Prenatal care behind bars* [Radio
broadcast]. NPR. http://www.npr.org/templates/story/story.
php?storyId=4990886

Yager, S. (2015, July/August). Prison born. *The Atlantic.* https://www.
theatlantic.com/magazine/archive/2015/07/prison-born/395297/

All sources cited in
the text are listed.

Part 8
Media/Design

Consciously or not, we design all the texts we write, choosing typefaces, setting up text as lists or charts, deciding whether to add headings—and then whether to center them or align them on the left. Sometimes our genre calls for certain design elements—essays begin with titles, letters begin with salutations ("Dear Auntie Em"). Other times we design texts to meet the demands of particular audiences, formatting documentation in MLA or APA or some other style, setting type larger for young children, and so on. And our designs always depend on our medium. A memoir might take the form of an essay in a book, be turned into a bulleted list for a slide presentation, or include links to images or other pages if presented on a website. The chapters in this part offer advice for **CHOOSING MEDIA**; working with **DESIGN**, **IMAGES**, and **SOUND**; and **GIVING PRESENTATIONS**.

Media/Design

✳ academic literacies   ⬢ fields   ◆ strategies   ⬤ media / design
◼ rhetorical situations   ⁘ processes   ⬤ research   ★ handbook
▲ genres

56 Choosing Media

USA Today reports on contract negotiations between automakers and auto-workers with an article that includes a large photo and a colorful graph; the article on the same story on the *New York Times* website includes a video of striking workers. In your economics class, you give a presentation about the issue that includes *Canva* slides.

These examples show how information about the same events can be delivered using three different media: print (*USA Today*), digital (nytimes.com), and spoken (the main medium for your class presentation). They also show how different media offer writers different modes of expressing meaning, ranging from words to images to sounds and hyperlinks. A print text can include written words and still visuals; online, the same text can also incorporate links to moving images and sound as well as to other written materials. A presentation with slides can include both spoken and written words, can incorporate video and audio elements—and can also include print handouts.

In college writing, the choice of medium often isn't up to you: your instructor may require a printed essay or a classroom talk, a website, or some combination of media. Sometimes, though, you'll be the one deciding. Because your medium will play a big part in the way your audience receives and reacts to your message, you'll need to think hard about what media best suit your audience, purpose, and message. This chapter will help you choose media when the choice is yours.

Print

When you have a choice of medium, print has certain advantages over spoken and digital text in that it's more permanent and doesn't depend on audience access to technology. Depending on your own access to technology, you can usually insert photos or other visuals and can present data and other information as graphs or charts. Obviously, though, print documents are more work than digital ones to update or change, and they don't allow for sound, moving images, or links to other materials—unless you include a QR code that takes readers to online material.

Digital

Online writing is everywhere: on course LMSs and class websites; in virtual discussion groups and wikis; in emails, text messages, and social media. And when you're taking an online course, you are, by definition, always using a digital medium. Remember that this medium has advantages as well as limitations and potential pitfalls. You can add audio, video, and links—but your audience may not have the same access to technology that you do. These are just some of the things you'll need to keep in mind when deciding, say, whether to include or link to videos or a site that has restricted access. Also, digital texts that circulate online through blogs, websites, email, or social media can take on a life of their own; other viewers may forward, like, or repost your text to much larger audiences than you originally considered.

Spoken

If you deliver your text orally, as a speech or presentation, you have the opportunity to use your tone of voice, gestures, and physical bearing to establish credibility. But you must write your text so that it's easy to understand when it is heard rather than read. Speaking from memory or from note cards, rather than reading a script or essay, often makes it easier for the audience to follow your talk. The spoken medium can be used alone with a live, face-to-face audience, but it's often combined with print in the form of handouts, or with digital media in the form of presentation software like *PowerPoint* or *Google Slides*, or designed for remote audiences in formats like webcasts, webinars, podcasts, or videoconferencing platforms such as *Zoom*.

Multimedia

It's increasingly likely that you'll be assigned to create a multimedia text, one that includes some combination of print, oral, and digital elements. It's also possible that you'll have occasion to write a multimodal text, one that uses more than one mode of expression: words, images, audio, video, links, and so on. The words "multimedia" and "multimodal" are often used interchangeably, but "multimodal" is the term that's used most often in composition classes, whereas "multimedia" is the one used in other disciplines and in industry. In composition classes, the word generally refers to writing that includes more than just words.

Considering the Rhetorical Situation

PURPOSE   What's your purpose, and what media will best suit that
purpose? A text message or email may be appropriate
for inviting a friend to lunch, but neither would be ideal
for demonstrating to a professor that you understand a
complex historical event; for that, you'd likely write a
report, either in print or online—and you might include
photos, maps, or other such texts to provide visual
context.

73–74

AUDIENCE   What media are your audience likely to expect—and be
able to access? A blog may be a good way to reach people who share your interest in basketball or cupcakes,
but to reach your grandparents you may want to send
them an email message—or a handwritten note in the
mail. Most employers and graduate school admissions
officers require applicants to submit résumés and applications online, but print versions are still useful for job
fairs and in-person interviews.

75–78

GENRE   Does your genre require a particular medium? If you're
giving an oral presentation, you'll often be expected to
include slides. Academic essays are usually formatted to
be printed out, even if they are submitted electronically.
An online essay based on field research might include
audio files of those you've interviewed, but if your essay
were in print, you'd need to quote (or paraphrase or
summarize) what they said.

79–84

STANCE   If you have a choice of media, think about whether a
particular medium will help you convey your stance. A
print document in MLA format, for instance, will make
you seem scholarly and serious. Posting to a social
media site or blogging, however, might work better for a
more informal stance. Presenting data in charts will
sometimes help you establish your credibility as a
knowledgeable researcher.

85–87

Once you decide on the media and modes of expression you're using, you'll
need to design your text to take advantage of their possibilities and to deal
with their limitations. The next chapters will help you do that.

57 Designing Text

You're trying to figure out why a magazine ad you're looking at is so funny, and you realize that the text's font is deliberately intended to make you laugh. An assignment for a research paper in psychology specifies that you are to follow APA format. Your classmates complain that the *PowerPoint* slides you use for a presentation are hard to read because there's not enough contrast between the words and the background. Another student says you include too many words on each slide. Whether you're putting together your résumé, creating a website for your intramural soccer league, or writing an essay for a class, you need to think about how you design what you write.

Considering the Rhetorical Situation

As with all writing tasks, your rhetorical situation should affect the way you design a text. Here are some points to consider:

73–74

PURPOSE
How can you design your text to help achieve your purpose? If you're reporting information, for instance, you may want to present statistical data in a chart or table rather than in the main text to help readers grasp it more quickly. If you're trying to get readers to 646 care about an issue, a photo or **PULL QUOTE** —a brief selection of text "pulled out" and featured in a larger font—might help you do so.

75–78

AUDIENCE
How can you make your design appeal to your intended audience? By using a certain font style or size to make your text look stylish, serious, or easy to read? What kind of headings—big and bold? simple and restrained?—would your readers expect or find helpful? What colors would appeal to them?

79–84

GENRE
Are you writing in a genre that has design conventions, such as an abstract, an annotated bibliography, or a résumé? Do you need to follow a format such as those prescribed in MLA or APA style?

■ 85–87

STANCE   How can your design reflect your attitude toward your audience and subject? Do you need a businesslike font or a playful one? Would tables and graphs help you establish your credibility? How can illustrations help you convey a certain tone?

Some Basic Principles of Design

Be consistent.   To keep readers oriented while reading documents or browsing multiple webpages, any design elements should be used consistently. In a print academic essay, that task may be as simple as using the same font throughout for your main text and using boldface or italics for headings. If you're writing for the web, navigation buttons and other major elements should be in the same place on every page. In a presentation, each slide should use the same background and the same font unless there's a good reason to introduce differences.

Keep it simple.   One of your main design goals should be to help readers see quickly—even intuitively—what's in your text and how to find specific information. Adding headings to help readers see the parts, using consistent colors and fonts to help them recognize key elements, setting off steps in lists, using white space to set off blocks of text or to call attention to certain elements, and (especially) resisting the temptation to fill pages with fancy graphics or unnecessary animations—these are all ways of making your text simple to read.

Aim for balance.   For a page without images, balance can be created through the use of margins, headings, and spacing. In the journal page shown on page 560, notice how using white space around the article title and the author's name, as well as setting both in larger type and the author's name in all capital letters, helps balance them vertically against the large block of text below. The large initial letter of the text also helps balance the mass of smaller type that follows. MLA and APA styles have specific design guidelines for academic research papers that cover these elements. A magazine page might create a sense of balance by using **PULL QUOTES** and illustrations to break up dense vertical columns of text.

● 646

Use color and contrast carefully.   Academic readers usually expect black text on a white background, with perhaps one other color for headings. Presentation slides and webpages are most readable with a plain, light-colored background and dark text that provides contrast. Remember that not everyone can see all colors and that an online text that includes several colors might be printed out and read in black and white; make sure your audience will be able to distinguish any color variations well enough to grasp your meaning. Colored lines on a graph, for example, should be distinguishable even if readers cannot see the colors. Red-green contrasts are especially hard to see and should be avoided.

Use available templates.   Good design takes time, and most of us don't have training as designers. If you're pressed for time or don't feel up to the challenge of designing your own text, take advantage of the many templates available. In *Microsoft Word*, for example, you can customize "styles" to specify the font, including its size and color; single- or double-spacing; paragraph indentations; and several other features that will then automatically apply to your document. Websites that host personal webpages and blogs offer dozens of templates that you can use or modify to suit your needs. And presentation software offers many templates that can simplify creating slides.

Some Elements of Design

Fonts and line spacing.   You can usually choose from among many fonts, and the one you choose will affect how well the audience can read your text and how they will perceive your **TONE**. Times Roman will make a text look businesslike or academic; Comic Sans will make it look playful. For most academic writing, you'll want to use a font size between 10 and 12 points and a serif font (such as Times Roman or Bookman) rather than a sans serif font (such as Arial, Verdana, or Calibri) because serif fonts are generally easier to read. Reserve sans serif for headings and parts of the text that you want to highlight. Decorative fonts (such as *Magneto*, *Amaze*, Chiller, and Jokerman) should be used sparingly and only when they're appropriate for your audience, purpose, and the rest of your **RHETORICAL SITUATION**. If you use more than one font, use each one consistently: one for **HEADINGS**, one for captions, one for the main body of your text. Don't go overboard—you won't often have reason to use more than two or, at most, three fonts in any one text.

Every font has regular, **bold**, and *italic* forms. In general, choose regular for the main text and lower-level headings, bold for major headings, and italic within the main text to indicate titles of books and other long works and, occasionally, to emphasize words or brief phrases. Avoid italicizing or boldfacing entire sentences or paragraphs, especially in academic writing. If you are following **MLA**, **APA**, or some other style format, be sure your use of fonts conforms to its requirements.

86

71

644–45

MLA 581
APA 623

Finally, consider the line spacing of your text. Generally, academic writing is double-spaced, whereas job application letters and **RÉSUMÉS*** are usually single-spaced. Some kinds of **REPORTS** may call for single-spacing; check with your instructor if you're not sure. You'll often need to add extra space to set off parts of a text—items in a list, for instance, or headings.

Glossary
146–69

Layout.   Layout is the way text is arranged on a page. An academic essay, for example, will usually have a title centered at the top, one-inch margins all around, and double-spacing. A text can be presented in paragraphs—or in the form of **LISTS**, **TABLES**, **CHARTS**, **GRAPHS**, and so on. Sometimes you'll need to include other elements as well: headings, images and other graphics, captions, lists of works cited.

643–44
650

Paragraphs.   Dividing text into paragraphs focuses information for readers and helps them process it by dividing it into manageable chunks. If you're writing a story for a print newspaper with narrow columns, for example, you'll divide your text into shorter paragraphs than you would if you were writing an academic essay. In general, indent paragraphs five to seven spaces (one-half inch) when your text is double-spaced; either indent or skip a line between single-spaced paragraphs.

Lists.   Put into list form information that you want to set off and make easily accessible. Number the items in a list when the sequence matters (in instructions, for example); use bullets when the order is not important. Set off lists with an extra line of space above and below, and add extra space between the items if necessary for legibility. Here's an example:

> Darwin's theory of how species change through time derives from three postulates, each of which builds on the previous one:
>
> 1. The ability of a population to expand is infinite, but the ability of any environment to support populations is always finite.
> 2. Organisms within populations vary, and this variation affects the ability of individuals to survive and reproduce.
> 3. The variations are transmitted from parents to offspring.
>
> —Robert Boyd and Joan B. Silk, *How Humans Evolved*

Do not set off text as a list unless there's a good reason to do so, however. Some lists are more appropriately presented in paragraph form, especially when they give information that isn't meant to be referred to more than

---

*See the ebook at digital.wwnorton.com/fieldguide7h for a chapter on Résumés and Job Letters.

once. In the following example, there's no reason to highlight the information by setting it off in a list—and bad news is softened by putting it in paragraph form:

> I regret to inform you that the Scholarship Review Committee did not approve your application for a Board of Rectors scholarship for the following reasons: your grade-point average did not meet the minimum requirements; your major is not among those eligible for consideration; and the required letter of recommendation was not received before the deadline.

Presented as a list, that information would be needlessly emphatic.

Headings.　Headings make the structure of a text easier to follow and help readers find specific information. Some genres require standard headings—announcing an **ABSTRACT**, for example, or a list of **WORKS CITED**. Other times you'll want to use headings to provide an overview of a section of text. You may not need any headings in brief texts, but when you do, you'll probably want to use one level at most, just to announce major topics. Longer texts, information-rich genres such as brochures or detailed **REPORTS**, and websites may require several levels of headings. If you decide to include headings, you will need to decide how to phrase them, what fonts to use, and where to position them.

Glossary

MLA 552–80 ●

146–69 ▲

Phrase headings concisely.　Make your headings succinct and parallel in structure. You might make all the headings nouns **(Mushrooms)**, noun phrases **(Kinds of Mushrooms)**, gerund phrases **(Recognizing Kinds of Mushrooms)**, or questions **(How Do I Identify Mushrooms?)**. Whatever form you decide on, use it consistently for each heading. Sometimes your phrasing will depend on your purpose. If you're simply helping readers find information, use brief phrases:

Head	**Forms of Social Groups among Primates**
Subhead	*Solitary Social Groups*
Subhead	*Monogamous Social Groups*

If you want to address readers directly with the information in your text, consider writing your headings as questions:

How can you identify edible mushrooms?
Where can you find edible mushrooms?
How can you cook edible mushrooms?

Make headings visible. Headings need to be visible, so if you aren't following an academic style like MLA or APA, consider making them larger than the regular text, putting them in **bold** or *italics*, or using underlining—or a different font. For example, you could use a serif font like Times Roman for your main text and a sans serif font like Arial for your headings. On the web, consider making headings a different color from the body text. When you have several levels of headings, use capitalization, bold, and italics to distinguish among the various levels:

First-Level Head

Second-Level Head

Third-level head

APA format requires that each level of heading appear in a specific style: centered bold uppercase and lowercase for the first level, flush-left bold uppercase and lowercase for the second level, and so on.

● APA 624

Position headings appropriately. If you're following APA format, center first-level headings. If you aren't following a prescribed format, you get to decide where to position your headings: centered, flush with the left margin, or even alongside the text in a wide left-hand margin. Position each level of head consistently throughout your text. Generally, online headings are positioned flush left.

White space. Use white space to separate the various parts of a text. In general, use one-inch margins for the text of an essay or report. Unless you're following MLA or APA format, include space above headings, above and below lists, and around photos, graphs, and other visuals. See the two sample research papers in this book for examples of the formats required by **MLA** and **APA**.

● MLA 581–83

APA 623–25

Typographic ornaments. Typographic ornaments are decorative elements like symbols, lines, shapes, or icons that can enhance the appearance of a document and help guide readers through it. Writers sometimes use such ornaments as visual cues to emphasize key pieces of information or to signal a change in focus. Student writer Ryan McClendon, for example, uses short lines centered across the page to let readers know he's moving from one **VIGNETTE** to another in his personal narrative in Chapter 19 of this book.

▲ 109

Other typographic ornaments you might use, depending on your rhetorical situation, include a large capital letter to indicate the start of a new section of text—or a decorative symbol (like this: ≫) to mark the end of a section. In genres like infographics or brochures, you might use icons or shapes to draw readers' eyes to important parts of your text or to represent key ideas or themes in it. You might also use a pull quote to highlight important information. If you use typographic ornaments, use them sparingly and purposefully, keeping your audience's needs in mind.

Use a pull quote to highlight important information.

Evaluating a Design

Does the design suit your PURPOSE? Does the overall look of the design help convey the text's message, support its argument, or present information?

73–74

How well does the design meet the needs of your AUDIENCE? Will the overall appearance of the text appeal to the intended readers? Is the font large enough for them to read? Are there headings to help them find their way through the text? Does the design help readers find the information they need?

75–78

How well does the text meet any GENRE requirements? Can you tell by looking at the text that it is an academic essay, a lab report, a résumé, a blog? Do its fonts, margins, headings, and page layout meet the requirements of **MLA**, **APA**, or whatever style you're using?

79–84

MLA 581–83
APA 623–25

How well does the design reflect your STANCE? Do the page layout and fonts convey the appropriate tone—serious, playful, adventuresome, conservative, or whatever other tone you intended?

85–87

58 Using Visuals, Incorporating Sound

For an art history class, you write an essay comparing two paintings by Willem de Kooning. For a business class, you create a proposal to improve department communication in a small local firm and incorporate diagrams to illustrate the new procedure. For a visual rhetoric class, you take a photograph of yourself and include a two-page analysis of how the picture distills something essential about you. For an engineering class project, you design a model of a bridge and give an in-class presentation explaining the structures and forces involved, which you illustrate with slides. For a psychology assignment, you interview several people who've suffered foreclosures on their homes in recent years about how the experience affected them—and then create an online text weaving together a slideshow of photos of the people outside their former homes, a graph of foreclosure rates, video and audio clips from the interviews, and your own insights.

All these writing tasks require you to incorporate and sometimes to create visuals and sound. Many kinds of visuals can be included in print documents: photos, drawings, diagrams, graphs, charts, and more. And with writing that's delivered online or as a spoken presentation, your choices expand to include audio and video, voice-over narration, and links to other materials.

Visuals and sound aren't always appropriate, however, or even possible—so think carefully before you set out to include them. But they can help you make a point in ways that words alone cannot. Election polling results are easier to see in a bar graph than in a paragraph; photos of an event may convey its impact more powerfully than words alone; an audio clip can make a written analysis of an opera easier to understand. This chapter provides some tips for using visuals and incorporating sound in your writing.

Considering the Rhetorical Situation

71 ■

Use visuals and sounds that are appropriate for your audience, purpose, and the rest of your **RHETORICAL SITUATION**. If you're trying to persuade voters in your town to back a proposal on an issue they don't know much about, for example, you might use dramatic pictures just to get their attention. But when it's important to come across as thoughtful and objective, maybe you need a more subdued look—or to make your points with written words alone. A newspaper article on housing prices might include a bar or line graph and also some photos. A report on that topic for an economics class would probably have graphs with no photos; a spoken presentation for a business class might use a dynamic graph that shows prices changing over time and an audio voice-over for pictures of a neighborhood; a community website might have graphs, links to related sites, and a video interview with a home owner.

In your academic writing, especially, be careful that any visuals you use support your main point—and don't just serve to decorate the text. (Therefore, avoid clip art, which is primarily intended as decoration and comes off as unsophisticated and childish.) Images should validate or exemplify what you say elsewhere with written words and add information that words alone can't provide as clearly or easily.

Using Visuals

Photos, drawings, diagrams, videos, tables, pie charts, bar graphs—these are many kinds of visuals you could use. Visuals can offer support, illustration, evidence, and comparison and contrast in your document.

399–416 ◆
457–64
452–56

Photographs. Photos can support an **ARGUMENT**, illustrate **NARRATIVES** and **PROCESSES**, present other points of view, and help readers "place" your information in time and space. You may use photos you take yourself, or you can download photos and other images from the internet—within limits. Most downloadable photos are copyrighted, meaning that you can use them without obtaining permission from the copyright owner only if you're doing so for academic purposes, to fulfill an assignment. If you're going to publish your text, either in print or on the web, you must have permission. You can usually gain permission by emailing the copyright holder, but that often entails a fee, so think carefully about whether you need the image. Consider, too, the file size of digital images; large files can clog readers' email in-boxes, take a long time to display on their screens, or be hard for you to upload in the first place, so

An essay discussing the theme of mother and child might compare this painting from the Italian Renaissance (left) with a modern photograph such as Dorothea Lange's *Migrant Mother* (right).

you may have to compress an image in a zip file or reduce its resolution (which can diminish its sharpness).

AI-generated images.   With your instructor's permission, you might use AI tools like *DALL-E* or *Midjourney* to generate illustrations, digital paintings, photorealistic art, and other types of images based on prompts you provide. In using such tools, try to describe in detail the kind of image you want—the subject matter, the style (cartoon? futuristic?), the tone (serious? playful?)—and then refine your instructions after the bot generates its initial output. You may need to go through several rounds of prompting and regenerating to get an image that works for your context.

As with all AI use, you'll want to **EVALUATE** the output for inaccuracies and biases. Are there details in the image that need to be cross-referenced with authoritative sources? Does anything in the image seem implausible? Are there stereotypical or insensitive depictions of groups or cultures? Does the image exclude certain people? Ask others to review the image, and then revise it if needed. And remember to be transparent about your use of AI in creating the image: check with your instructor about whether to cite the AI tool, write an AI **ACKNOWLEDGMENT STATEMENT**, or do something else.

67–68

68

Videos. If you're writing online, you can include video clips for readers to play. If you're using a video already available online, such as on *YouTube*, you can show the opening image with an arrow for readers to click on to start the video, or you can simply copy the video's URL and paste it into your text as a **LINK**. In either case, be sure to introduce the video in your text with a **SIGNAL PHRASE**. As with any other source, be sure to provide an in-text citation and full documentation.

657
529–32

If you want to include a video you made yourself, you can edit it using such programs as *iMovie* or *Shotcut*. Once you're ready to insert it into your online document, the easiest way is to first upload it to *YouTube*, choosing the Private setting so only those you authorize may view it, and then create a link in your document.

Graphs, charts, and tables. Statistical and other numerical information is often best presented in graphs, charts, and tables. If you can't find the right one for your purpose, you can create your own, as long as it's based on sound data from reliable sources. To do so, you can use various spreadsheet programs such as *Excel* or online chart and graph generators such as *Plotly* or *Venngage*. You can also prompt an AI tool like *ChatGPT* to create charts, graphs, and tables based on data you enter.

641
641

In any case, remember to follow basic design principles: be **CONSISTENT**, label all parts clearly, and **KEEP THE DESIGN SIMPLE** so readers can focus on the information and not be distracted by a needlessly complex design. In particular, use color and contrast wisely to emphasize what's most significant. Choose **COLORS** that are easy to distinguish from one another—and that remain so if the graph or chart is printed out in black and white. (Using distinct gradations of color from light to dark will show well in black and white.) Some common kinds of graphs, charts, and tables are shown on the next pages.

641–42

Diagrams, maps, flowcharts, and timelines. Information about place and time is often presented in diagrams, maps, flowcharts, and timelines. If you're using one of these visuals from the web or elsewhere, be sure to **DOCUMENT** it. Otherwise you can create one of these yourself using online tools like *Canva* or the Shape and Chart tabs in your word processing program. Make diagrams and maps as simple as possible for the point you're emphasizing. Unnecessarily complex maps can be more of a distraction than a help. For timelines, make sure the scale accurately depicts the passage of time you're writing about and avoids gaps and bunches.

538–41

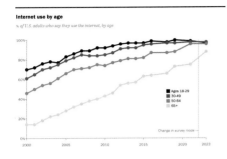

Internet use by age
% of U.S. adults who say they use the internet, by age

Ages 18-29
30-49
50-64
65+

Change in survey mode

Where The Gender Pay Gap Is Widest
% difference in full-time earnings between men/women in selected OECD nations*

South Korea: 36.7%
Japan: 25.7%
Chile: 21.1%
Canada: 18.2%
United States: 18.1%
United Kingdom: 16.8%
Germany: 15.5%
Australia: 14.3%
Spain: 11.5%
France: 9.9%
Italy: 5.6%
Greece: 4.5%

* As a % of the earnings of men. 2016 or latest available year
@StatistaCharts Source: OECD

Forbes statista

Costly walk down the aisle

According to The Wedding Report, the average cost of a wedding in the U.S. is about $25,300. Here's a breakdown of spending:

Venue, catering and rentals: $11,230

Beauty and spa $124

Gifts and favors $641

Invitations $817

Entertainment $1,230

Flowers and decorations $1,510

Planner/consultant $1,540

Attire and accessories $1,610

Photography and video $2,670

Jewelry $3,920

Source: The Wedding Report
Graphic: Dallas Morning News
© 2014 MCT

Poll: What is your top issue this November?

PBS NEWS HOUR

	Inflation	Preserving Democracy	Abortion	Immigration	Crime	Health care
DEMOCRATS	17%	42%	22%	4%	6%	10%
REPUBLICANS	54%	15%	4%	14%	8%	3%
INDEPENDENTS	40%	23%	14%	7%	8%	7%

Line graphs are a good way of showing changes in data over time. Each line here represents the percentage of US adults in a particular age group who use the internet. Plotting the lines together allows readers to compare the data at different points in time. Be sure to label the *x* and *y* axes, and limit the number of lines to avoid confusion.

Bar graphs are useful for comparing quantitative data, measurements of how much or how many. The bars can be horizontal or vertical. This graph compares the gap between men's and women's pay in twelve countries. Some software offers 3-D and other special effects, but simple graphs are often easier to read.

Pie charts can be used to show how a whole is divided into parts or how parts of a whole relate to one another. This pie chart shows the average cost of weddings by expense category. The segments in a pie should always add up to 100 percent, and each segment should be clearly labeled.

Tables are useful for displaying numerical information concisely, especially when several items are being compared. This table shows the results of a poll of Americans on their election-year concerns. Presenting information in columns and rows permits readers to find data and identify relationships among them.

Diagrams and flowcharts are ways of showing relationships and processes. This diagram shows how hardcover books are made. Flowcharts can be made using widely available templates; diagrams, in contrast, can range from simple drawings to works of art. Some simple flowcharts may be found in the genres chapters.

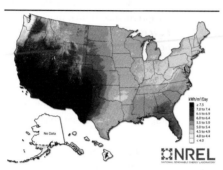

Maps show physical locations. This map shows the annual average direct solar resources for each of the US states. Maps can be drawn to scale or purposefully out of scale to emphasize a point.

395–98 ◆

Timelines show change over time. These are useful to demonstrate **CAUSE** and **EFFECT** relationships or evolution. This timeline depicts how the American party system evolved from 1788 to 1968. Timelines can be drawn horizontally or vertically.

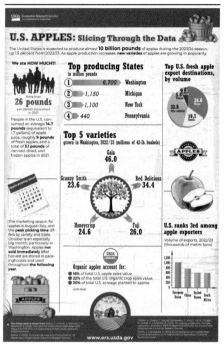

Infographics are eye-catching visual representations of information that help simplify a complicated subject. Infographics typically include an engaging title; a design that reflects the content being displayed; a balance of charts, graphs, and other elements; readable fonts; and the sources of your information. Several websites offer templates to help you design and execute infographics, including *Piktochart*, *Infogram*, and several others.

SOME TIPS FOR USING VISUALS

- Position images as close as possible to the discussion to which they relate. In *Microsoft Word*, simply position your cursor where you want to insert an image; click the appropriate type of visual from the menu on the Insert tab; choose the appropriate image from your files; and click Insert. You may then need to adjust the way the text flows or wraps around the image: in the Layout tab, choose the appropriate option in Wrap Text.

- In academic writing, number all images, using separate sequences of numbers for figures (photos, graphs, diagrams, video clips, and drawings) and tables: Fig. 1, Fig. 2; Table 1, Table 2. Follow style guidelines (e.g., **MLA** or **APA**) for where to place the figure or table number and caption.

  MLA 582–83
  APA 625

- Explain in your written text whatever information you present in an image—don't expect it to speak for itself. Refer to the image before it appears, identifying it and summarizing its point. For example: "As Table 1 shows, Italy's economic growth rate has been declining for thirty years."

- Provide a title or caption for each image to identify it and explain its significance for your text. For example: "Table 1: Italy's Economic Growth Rate, 1990–2020."

- Label the parts of visuals clearly to ensure that your audience will understand what they show. For example, label each section of a pie chart to show what it represents.

Glossary

- Provide **ALTERNATIVE TEXT** (alt text) for visuals you include in a digital text. Alt text briefly describes a visual's content or meaning so that people using screen readers understand what the visual conveys. When writing alt text, think about the purpose the visual serves within your document—and then tailor your description of the visual accordingly. For example, if you're using a photo of a city landmark in a report on the city's history, your alt text would likely identify the landmark and its historical significance. But if you're using the same photo in a proposal to repair the landmark, your alt text might focus on the landmark's crumbling facade and faded lettering. Some word-processing programs auto-generate alt text for visuals, but you'll still want to review the description to ensure it fits your context. If you use a visual that's purely decorative, you don't need to provide alt text.

Glossary

- Provide captions or **TRANSCRIPTS** for videos you create that include sound. If you upload your video to *YouTube*, the platform will auto-generate captions—but be sure to edit them for accuracy.

- Cite the source of any images you don't create yourself. You need not document visuals you create, based on data from your own experimental or field research; but if you use data from a source to create a graph or chart, **CITE THE SOURCE** of the data.

533–36

538–41

- In general, you may use visuals created by someone else in your academic writing as long as you include full **DOCUMENTATION**. If you post your writing online, however, you must first obtain permission from the copyright owner and include permission information—for example: "Photo courtesy of Victoria and Albert Museum, London." Copyright holders will often tell you how they want the permission sentence to read.

Incorporating Sound

Audio can serve useful purposes for writers—like helping to evoke emotions, support an assertion, explain a concept, or bring a scene to life. You might incorporate audio into an online text or spoken presentation, or you might create an entirely audio-based project, like a podcast or audio essay. Here are some forms of audio you could use:

Voice.   When your audience hears your own or others' spoken words, they often connect emotionally with you or your topic. For a **PERSONAL NARRATIVE**, you might embed a recording of you reading your story aloud, adapting your pacing or tone to the events in the narrative and helping your readers feel "present" in it. For a **PROFILE** of a person, you might share snippets of a recorded interview with your subject, letting readers hear your subject's particular way of speaking or sense the emotions behind their words. For an **ARGUMENT** or **REPORT**, you might include short audio clips that provide anecdotes or expert testimony to support a claim or illustrate a point.

▲ 234–45

▲ 246–56

▲ 170–96
146–69

Music.   Music can enhance a text, creating a mood and giving your audience hints about how to interpret the meaning of your words and images. In some texts, like audio essays and podcasts, music serves a more functional role—by indicating a transition between segments, for example, or establishing a theme or "identity" for the piece as a whole. (Think about how you immediately identify your favorite podcast by its intro music.) You can create your own music with an AI tool like *Suno* or search for music online at sites like *Free Music Archive*.

Ambient sounds.   Ambient sounds are the sounds that occur in the background—passing traffic, birdsong, crowd noise at sports events, the clinking of forks and spoons at restaurants. Such sounds can provide your audience a sense of immediacy, of being part of the scene or event you're describing. If you're writing a **PROFILE**, you could record the ambient sounds of the place, event, or person you're profiling and incorporate those sounds into your text. If you're writing a **PERSONAL NARRATIVE**, you could search for relevant ambient sounds online at sites like *Freesound*.

▲ 246–56

▲ 234–45

Sound effects.   Sound effects are distinct sounds—the slamming of a door, the ding of an incoming text message, a thunderclap—that represent a specific action, object, or event. They're often used for dramatic effect, like emphasizing a key point or an important action. You can create and record sound effects yourself or search for them online at sites like *Freesound* and *ZapSplat*.

Silence. Silence can serve as a kind of punctuation, drawing attention, for example, to an especially important or profound quote from someone. Or silence can serve as a transition signaling a move from one topic to another. You can use editing tools like *Audacity* to add a few seconds of silence at appropriate points in an audio recording.

SOME TIPS FOR USING SOUNDS

- If you want to create or edit audio yourself, spend some time experimenting with tools like *GarageBand* or *Audacity*. Search online for basic tutorials to help you get started.

- If you're making a podcast, prepare by writing a script using conversational language, and include questions for any guests who participate. Think about music you might use to "brand" your podcast—and about any other types of sound that might serve as transitions between segments.

- If you're planning to record yourself reading a literacy narrative or something else you've already written, mark up the text with notes to remind yourself where to slow down, speed up, or add emphasis as you read aloud.

Glossary

- Include **TRANSCRIPTS** for any audio files you use. A transcript provides a written record of the spoken content in an audio—and may include notes describing music and other nonspoken sounds. Transcripts are useful for people with hearing impairments and for anyone who prefers to read rather than listen. To create a transcript, you can use free online transcription tools like *Otter* or use the speech-to-text tools available in some word processing programs. Either way, you'll want to review the transcript for accuracy.

MLA 545–51
APA 597–601
538–41

- Provide an **IN-TEXT CITATION** and full **DOCUMENTATION** for any sound material you don't create yourself. If you use clips from online sources like *Freesound* in audio files you create, you should document those sources.

- Consider how you'll share audio files you create yourself. You could upload them to *Google Drive* and share them via a link, use a cloud service like *Podbean*, or talk with your instructor about other options, including those available in your LMS.

Adding Links

If you're writing an online text in which you want to include images, video, or sound material available on the web, it's often easier and more effective to create links to them within the text than to embed them. Rather than provide the URL for the link, use relevant words to make it easier for a reader to decide to click on the link. (See pp. 541–42 for more information on this process.) Such links enable readers to see the materials' original context and to explore it if they wish. Be selective in the number of links you include: too many links can dilute a text.

SOME TIPS FOR CREATING LINKS

- Indicate links with underlining and color (most often blue), and introduce them with a **SIGNAL PHRASE**.

- Don't include your own punctuation in a link. For example, if you add a link at the end of a sentence, don't include the period as part of the link.

- Try to avoid having a link open in a new browser window. Readers expect links to open in the same window.

● 529–32

Editing Visuals and Sounds Carefully and Ethically

You may want to edit a photograph, cropping to show only part of it or using *Photoshop* or similar programs to enhance the colors or otherwise alter it. Similarly, you may want to edit a video, podcast, or other audio file to shorten it or remove irrelevant parts. If you are considering making a change of this kind, however, take care not to do so in a way that misrepresents the content. If you alter a photo, be sure the image still represents the subject accurately; if you alter a recording of a speech or interview, be sure the edited version maintains the speaker's intent. Whenever you alter an image, a video, or a sound recording, tell your readers how you have changed it.

The same goes for editing charts and graphs. Changing the scale on a bar graph, for example, can change the effect of the comparison, making the quantities being compared seem very similar or very different, as shown in the two bar graphs of identical data in Figures 1 and 2 on the next page.

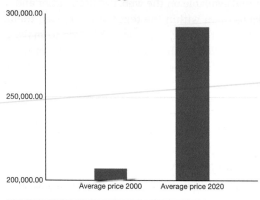

Figure 1. Average housing prices in the United States, 2000–2020 (exaggerated).

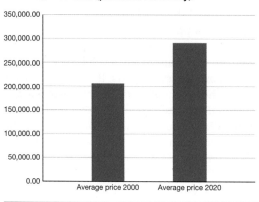

Figure 2. Average housing prices in the United States, 2000–2020 (presented accurately).

Both charts show the increase in average housing costs in the United States between 2000 and 2020. However, by making the baseline in Figure 1 $200,000 instead of zero, the increase appears to be far greater than it was in reality. Just as you shouldn't edit a quotation or a photograph in a way that might misrepresent its meaning, you should not present statistical data in a way that could mislead readers.

59 Giving Presentations

In a marketing class, you give a formal presentation that includes slides and handouts as part of a research project on developing brand loyalty to clothing labels among college students. As a candidate for student government, you deliver several speeches to various campus groups that are simultaneously broadcast over the web. At a good friend's wedding, after you make a toast to the married couple, another friend who couldn't attend in person toasts them remotely using *Zoom*; a third guest records both toasts on his cell phone and uploads them to *Facebook*.

Whether or not you include digital and print media, whenever you are called on to give a spoken presentation, you need to make your points clear and memorable. This chapter offers guidelines to help you prepare and deliver effective presentations. We'll start with two good examples.

GRETA THUNBERG

Our House Is Still on Fire

Greta Thunberg is a climate activist from Sweden. She gave this speech to world leaders at the World Economic Forum in Davos, Switzerland, in 2020. At the time she had just turned seventeen.

> One year ago I came to Davos and told you that our house is on fire. I said I wanted you to panic. I've been warned that telling people to panic about the climate crisis is a very dangerous thing to do. But don't worry. It's fine. Trust me, I've done this before, and I can assure you it doesn't lead to anything.
>
> And for the record, when we children tell you to panic, we're not telling you to go on like before.
>
> We're not telling you to rely on technologies that don't even exist today at scale and that science says perhaps never will. We are not telling you to keep talking about reaching "net-zero emissions" or "carbon neutrality" by cheating and fiddling around with numbers.
>
> We're not telling you to "offset your emissions" by just paying someone else to plant trees in places like Africa while at the same time forests like the Amazon are being slaughtered at an infinitely higher rate.

Planting trees is good, of course, but it's nowhere near enough of what is needed, and it cannot replace real mitigation and rewilding nature. 5

And let's be clear: We don't need a "low-carbon economy." We don't need to "lower emissions." Our emissions have to stop if we are to have a chance to stay below the 1.5-degree target. And until we have the technologies that at scale can put our emissions to minus then we must forget about net zero—we need real zero.

Because distant net zero emission targets will mean absolutely nothing if we just continue to ignore the carbon dioxide budget that applies for today, not distant future dates. If high emissions continue like now even for a few years, that remaining budget will soon be completely used up.

The fact that the U.S.A. is leaving the Paris accord seemed to outrage and worry everyone, and it should.

But the fact that we are all about to fail the commitments you signed up for in the Paris Agreement doesn't seem to bother the people in power even the least.

Any plan or policy of yours that doesn't include radical emission 10 cuts at the source starting today is completely insufficient for meeting the 1.5- or well-below-2-degree commitments of the Paris Agreement.

And again—this is not about right or left. We couldn't care less about your party politics.

From a sustainability perspective, the right, the left, as well as the center, have all failed. No political ideology or economic structure has been able to tackle the climate and environmental emergency and create a cohesive and sustainable world. Because that world, in case you haven't noticed, is currently on fire.

You say children shouldn't worry. You say: "Just leave this to us. We will fix this, we promise we won't let you down. Don't be so pessimistic."

And then nothing. Silence. Or something worse than silence: empty words and promises which give the impression that sufficient action is being taken.

All the solutions are obviously not available within today's societies. 15 Nor do we have the time to wait for new technological solutions to become available to start drastically reducing our emissions.

So, of course, the transition isn't going to be easy. It will be hard. And unless we start facing this now together, with all cards on the table, we won't be able to solve this in time.

In the days running up to the 50th anniversary of the World Economic Forum, I joined a group of climate activists demanding that you, the world's most powerful and influential business and political leaders, begin to take the action needed.

We demand, at this year's World Economic Forum, participants from all companies, banks, institutions, and governments:

Immediately halt all investments in fossil fuel exploration and extraction.

Immediately end all fossil fuel subsidies.   20

And immediately and completely divest from fossil fuels.

We don't want these things done by 2050 or 2030 or even 2021, we want this done now.

It may seem like we are asking for a lot. And you will of course say that we are naive. But this is just the very minimum amount of effort that is needed to start the rapid sustainable transition.

So either you do this or you're going to have to explain to your children why you are giving up on the 1.5-degree target.

Giving up without even trying.   25

Well I'm here to tell you that unlike you, my generation will not give up without a fight.

The facts are clear, but they are still too uncomfortable for you to address.

You just leave it, because you just think it's too depressing and people will give up. But people will not give up. You are the ones who are giving up.

Last week, I met with Polish coal miners who lost their jobs because their mine was closed. And even they had not given up. On the contrary, they seem to understand the fact that we need to change more than you do.

I wonder, what will you tell your children was the reason to fail   30
and leave them facing a climate chaos that you knowingly brought upon them? That it seemed so bad for the economy that we decided to resign the idea of securing future living conditions without even trying?

Our house is still on fire. Your inaction is fueling the flames by the hour. And we are telling you to act as if you loved your children above all else. Thank you.

Thunberg's speech presents a forceful argument on the need for radical action to reduce the causes of climate change. She tries, however, to surprise her audience by feigning cynical resignation: her argument "doesn't lead to anything"; her audience of the world's most powerful people will do nothing; and she invites them to pretend, "to act as if [they] loved [their] children above all else," while letting the world burn. She anticipates and answers various objections to her demands using clear, simple language while acknowledging that "the transition [away from fossil fuels] isn't going to be easy." She uses the phrase "Our house is on fire" as an effective frame, stating it in her opening and echoing it in other parts of her speech.

ABRAHAM LINCOLN
Gettysburg Address

Given by the sixteenth president of the United States, at the dedication of the Gettysburg battlefield as a memorial to those who died in the Civil War, this is one of the most famous speeches ever delivered in the United States.

Four score and seven years ago our fathers brought forth on this continent, a new nation, conceived in Liberty, and dedicated to the proposition that all men are created equal.

Now we are engaged in a great civil war, testing whether that nation, or any nation so conceived and so dedicated, can long endure. We are met on a great battle-field of that war. We have come to dedicate a portion of that field, as a final resting place for those who here gave their lives that that nation might live. It is altogether fitting and proper that we should do this.

But, in a larger sense, we can not dedicate—we can not consecrate—we can not hallow—this ground. The brave men, living and dead, who struggled here, have consecrated it, far above our poor power to add or detract. The world will little note, nor long remember what we say here, but it can never forget what they did here. It is for us the living, rather, to be dedicated here to the unfinished work which they who fought here have thus far so nobly advanced. It is rather for us to be here dedicated to the great task remaining before us—that from these honored dead we take increased devotion to that cause for which they gave the last full measure of devotion—that we here highly resolve that these dead shall not have died in vain—that this nation, under God, shall have a new birth of freedom—and that government of the people, by the people, for the people, shall not perish from the earth.

You won't likely be called on to deliver such an address, but the techniques Lincoln used—brevity, rhythm, recurring themes—are ones you can use in your own spoken texts.

Key Features / Spoken Presentations

A clear structure. Spoken texts need to be clearly organized so that your audience can follow what you're saying. The **BEGINNING** needs to engage their interest, make clear what you will be talking about, and perhaps forecast the central parts of your talk. The main part of the text should focus

340–48

on a few main points—only as many as your listeners can be expected to absorb and retain. (Remember, they can't go back to reread!) The **ENDING** is especially important: it should leave your audience with something to remember, think about, or do. Thunberg ends as she begins, asserting that "our house is still on fire." Lincoln ends with a dramatic resolution: "that government of the people, by the people, for the people, shall not perish from the earth."

348–52

Signpost language to keep your audience on track.   You may need to provide cues—signposts—to help listeners follow your text, especially **TRANSITIONS** that lead them from one point to the next. Sometimes you'll also want to stop and **SUMMARIZE** a complex point to help your audience keep track of your ideas and follow your development of them.

355–56

529

A tone to suit the occasion.   Lincoln spoke at a serious, formal event, the dedication of a national cemetery, and his address is formal and even solemn. Thunberg's speech is also serious in tone, but it's possible to hear in it traces of sarcasm, anger, and frustration as well. In a presentation to a panel of professors, you probably would want to take an academic tone, avoiding too much slang and speaking in complete sentences. If you had occasion to speak on the very same topic to a neighborhood group, however, you would likely want to speak more casually.

Repetition and parallel structure.   Even if you're never called on to deliver a Gettysburg Address, you will find that repetition and parallel structure can lend power to a presentation, making it easier to follow— and more likely to be remembered. "We can not dedicate—we can not consecrate—we can not hallow": the repetition of "we can not" and the parallel forms of the three verbs are one reason these words stay with us more than 150 years after they were written and delivered. These are structures any writer can use. The repetition of "We're not telling you …" in paragraphs 2–4 of Thunberg's speech gives emphasis to what she *is* telling her audience: that half measures aren't enough.

Slides and other media.   Depending on the way you deliver your presenta- tion, you will often want or need to use other media—*PowerPoint, Keynote,* or other presentation slides, video and audio clips, handouts, flip charts, whiteboards, and so on—to present certain information and to highlight key points.

Considering the Rhetorical Situation

As with any writing, you need to consider your rhetorical situation when preparing a presentation:

73–74 **PURPOSE**

Consider what your primary purpose is. To inform? persuade? entertain? evoke another kind of emotional response?

75–78 **AUDIENCE**

Think about whom you'll be addressing and how well you know them. Will they be interested, or will you need to get them interested? Are they likely to be friendly? How can you get and maintain their attention, and how can you establish common ground with them? How much will they know about your subject—will you need to provide background or define any terms?

79–84 **GENRE**

The genre of your text will affect the way you structure and present it. If you're making an argument, for instance, you'll need to consider counterarguments— and, depending on the way you're giving the presentation, perhaps to allow for questions and comments from members of the audience who hold other opinions. If you're giving a report, you may have reasons to prepare handouts with detailed information you don't have time to cover in your spoken text, or links to online documents or websites.

85–87 **STANCE**

Consider the attitude you want to express. Is it serious? thoughtful? passionate? well informed? humorous? something else? Choose your words and any other elements of your presentation accordingly. Whatever your attitude, your presentation will be received better by your listeners if they perceive you as comfortable and sincere.

A BRIEF GUIDE TO WRITING PRESENTATIONS

Whether you're giving a poster presentation at a conference or an oral report in class, what you say will differ in important ways from what you might write for others to read. Here are some tips for composing an effective presentation.

Budget your time. A five-minute presentation calls for about two and a half double-spaced pages of writing, or about 600 words, and ten minutes means only four or five pages, or about 1,000–1,250 words. Your introduction and conclusion should each take about one-tenth of the total time available; time for questions (if the format allows for them) should take about one-fifth; and the body of the talk, the rest. In a ten-minute presentation, then, allot one minute for your introduction, one minute for your conclusion, and two minutes for questions, leaving six minutes for the body of your talk.

Organize and draft your presentation. Readers can go back and reread if they don't understand or remember something the first time through a text. Listeners can't. Therefore, it's important that you structure your presentation so that your audience can follow your text—and remember what you say.

- *Craft an introduction* that engages your audience's interest and tells them what to expect. Depending on your rhetorical situation, you may want to **BEGIN** with humor, with an anecdote, or with something that reminds them of the occasion for your talk or helps them see the reason for it. In any case, you always need to summarize your main points, provide any needed background information, and outline how you'll proceed.

  340–48

- *In the body of your presentation,* present your main points in more detail and support them with **REASONS** and **EVIDENCE**. As you draft, you may well find that you have more material than you can present in the time available, so you'll need to choose the most important points to focus on and leave out the rest.

  402
  402–9

- *Let your readers know you're concluding* (but try to avoid saying "in conclusion"), and then use your remaining time to restate your main points and to explain why they're important. End by saying "thank you" and offering to answer questions or take comments if the format allows for them.

Consider whether to use visuals. You may want or need to include some visuals to help listeners follow what you're saying. Especially when you're presenting complex information, it helps to let them see it as well as hear it. Remember, though, that visuals should be a means of conveying information, not mere decoration.

DECIDING ON THE APPROPRIATE VISUALS

- *Slides* are useful for listing main points and for projecting illustrations, tables, and graphs.

- *Videos, animations, and sounds* can add additional information to your presentations.

- *Flip charts, whiteboards, or chalkboards* allow you to create visuals as you speak or to keep track of comments from your audience.

- *Posters* sometimes serve as the main part of a presentation, providing a summary of your points. You then offer only a brief introduction and answer any questions. You should be prepared to answer questions from any portion of your poster.

- *Handouts* can provide additional information, lists of works cited, or copies of any slides you show.

- *A QR code* on your slides—or on a handout—can give your audience access to your slides and additional resources.

What visual tools (if any) you decide to use is partly determined by how your presentation will be delivered. Will you be speaking to a crowd or a class, delivering your presentation through a podcast, or creating an interactive presentation for a web conference? Make sure that any necessary equipment and programs are available—and that they work. If at all possible, check out any equipment in the place where you'll deliver your presentation before you go live. If you bring your own equipment for a live presentation, make sure you can connect to the internet if you need to and that electrical outlets are in reach of your power cords. Also, make sure that your visuals can be seen. You may have to rearrange the furniture or the screen to make sure everyone can see.

And finally, have a backup plan. Computers fail; projector bulbs burn out; marking pens run dry. Whatever your plan is, have an alternative in case any problems occur.

Presentation software. *PowerPoint, Keynote,* and other presentation software can include images, video, and sound in addition to displaying written text. They are most useful for linear presentations that move audiences along one slide at a time. Cloud-based programs like *Prezi* also allow you to

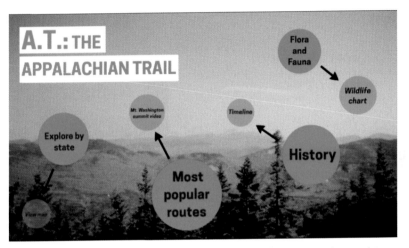

This *Prezi* presentation rotates, includes audio and video, and zooms in and out to let viewers take a closer look.

arrange words or slides in various designs, group related content together, and zoom in and out. Here are some tips for writing and designing slides:

- *Use* **LISTS** *or images, not paragraphs.* Use slides to emphasize your main points, not to reproduce your talk onscreen: keep your audience's attention focused on what you're saying. A list of brief points, presented one by one, reinforces your words. An image can provide additional information that your audience can take in quickly.

  643–44

- *Make your text easy for your audience to read.* **FONTS** should be at least 18 points, and larger than that for headings. Projected slides are easier to read in sans serif fonts like Arial, Helvetica, and Tahoma than in serif fonts like Times New Roman. And avoid using all capital letters, which can be hard to read.

  642–43

- *Choose colors carefully.* Your text and any illustrations must contrast with the background. Dark content on a light background is easier to read than the reverse. And remember that not everyone sees all colors; be sure your audience doesn't need to be able to see particular colors or contrasts in order to get your meaning. Red-green and blue-yellow contrasts are especially hard for some people to see and should be avoided.

Truman
- Conducted whistle-stop campaign
- Made hundreds of speeches
- Spoke energetically
- Connected personally with voters
- Focused on key states

Truman's Whistle-Stop Campaign

Two *PowerPoint* slides on the US presidential election of 1948. The slide on the left outlines the main points; the one on the right shows a map of Truman's whistle-stop campaign, providing a graphic illustration of the miles he traveled as he campaigned to be president.

- *Use bells and whistles sparingly, if at all.* Presentation software offers lots of decorative backgrounds, letters that fade in and out or dance across the screen, and sound effects. These features can be more distracting than helpful; use them only if they help make your point.

- *Mark your text.* In your notes or prepared text, mark each place where you need to click a mouse to call up the next slide.

Handouts. When you want to give your audience information they can refer to later—reproductions of your visuals, bibliographic information about your sources, printouts of your slides—do so in the form of handouts. Refer to the handouts in your presentation, but unless they include material your audience needs to consult before or as you talk, wait until you are finished to distribute them so as not to distract listeners. Clearly label everything you give out, including your name and the date and title of the presentation. You might even upload your handouts to a blog or website and give its URL, share them through a QR code, or provide your email address and invite interested audience members to request your handouts.

Delivering a Presentation

The success of a presentation often hinges on how it's delivered. As you work on your spoken texts, bear in mind the following points:

Practice. Practice, practice, and then practice some more. The better you know your talk, the more confident you will be, and your audience will respond positively to that confidence. If you're reading a prepared text, try to write it as if you were talking. Then practice by recording it as you read it; listen for spots that sound as if you're reading, and work on your delivery to sound more relaxed. As you practice, pay attention to keeping within your time limit. If possible, rehearse your talk with a small group of friends to test their response and to get used to speaking in front of an audience.

Speak clearly. When you're giving a spoken presentation, your first goal is to be understood by your audience. If listeners miss important words or phrases because you don't pronounce them distinctly, your talk will not succeed. Make sure, too, that your pace matches your audience's needs. Often you'll need to speak more slowly than usual to explain complex material (or to compensate for nerves); sometimes you may need to speed up to keep your audience's attention. In general, though, strive for a consistent pace throughout, one that ensures you don't have to rush at the end.

Pause for emphasis. In writing, you have white space and punctuation to show readers where an idea or discussion ends. When speaking, you need to pause to signal the end of a thought, to give listeners a moment to consider something you've said, or to get them ready for a surprising or amusing statement.

Stand up (or sit up) straight, and look at your audience. If you're in the same physical space as your audience, try to look at your audience for at least 75 percent of your speaking time, establishing eye contact with as many listeners as possible, moving your gaze around the room, then moving on to someone else (though not too rapidly). And if you stand or sit up straight, you'll project the sense that you have confidence in what you're saying. If you appear to believe in your words, others will, too. If you're speaking via an online forum like *Zoom*, alternate between looking directly into the camera and at your audience members onscreen. Also, make sure the camera is positioned at your eye level, so you aren't looking down at it (and showing your viewers the ceiling behind you!).

Use gestures for emphasis. If you're not used to speaking in front of a group, you may let your nervousness show by holding yourself stiffly, elbows tucked in. To overcome some of that nervousness, take some deep breaths, try to relax, and move your arms and the rest of your body as you would if you were talking to a friend. If you gesture a lot, keep doing what comes naturally. If you rarely gesture, don't try to invent new and unnatural hand movements. Watch politicians on C-SPAN to see how people who speak on a regular basis use gestures as part of their overall delivery.

Part 9

Handbook

"Pfft, English, who needs that? I'm never going to England."
So says the illustrious Homer Simpson on an early episode
called "The Way We Was." Maybe Homer can ignore the
conventions of English grammar and usage, but that's not the
case for the rest of us. If we want the world to take seriously
what we think and say, we need to pay attention to our
grammar and language. We need to edit our **SENTENCES**
so they're clear, choose our **LANGUAGE** carefully, and
use **PUNCTUATION** purposefully. This handbook provides
guidelines to help you edit what you write.

Handbook

* academic literacies   ● fields   ◆ strategies   ● media / design
■ rhetorical situations   ∴ processes   ● research   ★ handbook
▲ genres

S Sentences

S-1 ELEMENTS OF A SENTENCE

In casual situations, we often use a kind of shorthand, because we know our audience will fill in the gaps. When we say "Coffee?" to dinner guests, they know we mean, "Would you like some coffee?" When we text "7 @ Starbucks?" to a friend, it's understood that we're asking, "Should we meet at 7:00 at Starbucks?" In more formal writing or speaking situations, though, our audience may not share the same context; to be sure we're understood, we usually need to present our ideas in complete sentences. This chapter reviews the parts of a sentence.

S-1a Subjects and Predicates

Glossary

HB-25–31

HB-10–21

A sentence contains a subject and a predicate. The subject, which usually includes a **NOUN** or **PRONOUN**, names the topic of the sentence; the predicate, which always includes a **VERB**, says what the subject is or does.

▶ Birds fly.

▶ Birds are feathered vertebrates.

Sometimes the subject and the predicate contain only one word. Usually, however, both contain more than one word.

▶ Birds of many kinds fly south in the fall.

▶ Flying in a V formation is characteristic of geese.

▶ One of the flock leads the others.

A sentence may contain more than one subject or verb.

▶ Birds and butterflies fly south in the fall.

▶ Birds fly south in the fall and return north in the spring.

At times, the subject comes after the verb.

▶ Here comes the sun.

▶ In the attic were old photographs and toys.

Expressing subjects explicitly

English requires an explicit subject in every **CLAUSE**, even if all the clauses in a sentence are about the same subject.

★ HB-5

                                it

▶ Although the dinner cost too much, ˄ impressed my guests.

The only exception is commands, in which the subject is understood to be "you."

▶ Drink plenty of water on hot days.

In informal conversation, speakers sometimes emphasize a noun subject by repeating it as a pronoun: My friend Jing she changed her name to Jane. In academic writing, though, don't repeat a subject this way.

▶ The visiting students ~~they~~ were detained at the airport.

Sentences beginning with "there" or "it." In some cases where the subject comes after the verb, an **EXPLETIVE**—"there" or "it"—is required before the verb.

Glossary

        There is

▶ ~~Is~~ a problem with the Wi-Fi today.
   ˄

        It is

▶ ~~Is~~ both instructive and rewarding to work with young children.
   ˄

You can often rephrase the sentence to avoid using the expletive.

        Working with young children

▶ ~~It~~ is both instructive and rewarding, ~~to work with young children.~~
   ˄   ˄

S-1b Clauses

A clause is a group of words containing a subject and a predicate. An independent clause can function alone as a sentence: Birds fly. A subordinate clause begins with a **SUBORDINATING WORD** such as "because," "as," or "which" and cannot stand alone as a sentence: because birds fly. (See p. HB-7 for a list of common subordinating words.)

★ HB-7

   ┌— INDEPENDENT CLAUSE —┐ ┌———— SUBORDINATE CLAUSE ————┐

▶ My yard is now quiet because most of the birds flew south.

   ┌———SUBORDINATE CLAUSE———┐ ┌——— INDEPENDENT CLAUSE ———┐

▶ Although they travel really far, the birds always find their way back.

S-1c Phrases

A phrase is a word group that makes sense but lacks a subject, a verb, or both and thus cannot stand alone as a sentence. Some common ones are prepositional, appositive, participial, gerund, and infinitive phrases.

HB-48–50

A prepositional phrase starts with a **PREPOSITION** such as "at," "from," "of," "with," or "in" and usually ends with a noun or pronoun: at school, from home, with them. It usually functions as an **ADJECTIVE** or **ADVERB**.

HB-52–55
HB-52–55

▶ *During Diwali*, the neighbors *on my street* decorate their houses *with lights*.

An appositive phrase follows and gives additional information about a noun or pronoun. It functions as a noun.

▶ We all know that computers and their spawn, *the smartphone and cellphone,* have created a very different world from several decades ago.

—Alina Tugend,
"Multitasking Can Make You Lose . . . Um . . . Focus"

Glossary

A participial phrase contains the **PRESENT PARTICIPLE** or **PAST PARTICIPLE** of a verb plus any **OBJECTS**, **MODIFIERS**, and **COMPLEMENTS**. It functions as an adjective.

▶ *Brimming with optimism,* I headed over to the neighborhood watering hole and waited.

—Hal Niedzviecki, "Facebook in a Crowd"

▶ A study from Princeton *issued at the same time as the Duke study* showed that women in the sciences reported less satisfaction in their jobs and less of a sense of belonging than their male counterparts.

—Anna Quindlen, "Still Needing the F Word"

A gerund phrase includes the -*ing* form of a verb plus any objects, modifiers, and complements. It functions as a noun.

▶ *Asking for candy on Halloween* was called trick-or-treating, but *asking for candy on November first* was called begging.

—David Sedaris, "Us and Them"

An infinitive phrase includes an infinitive ("to" plus the base form of a verb: to read, to write) and any objects, modifiers, and complements. It functions as a noun, an adjective, or an adverb.

▶ The plan *to add more bike parking racks* requires the dean's approval.

▶ The point of encouraging bike use is *to reduce auto congestion on campus.*

S-2 SENTENCE FRAGMENTS

Sentence fragments often show up in advertising: "Got milk?" "Good to the last drop." "Not bad for something that tastes good too." We use them in informal speech and text messages as well. In other kinds of writing, though, some readers consider fragments too informal, and in many academic writing situations, it's better to avoid them altogether. This chapter helps you identify and edit out fragments.

S-2a Identifying Fragments

A sentence fragment is a group of words that is capitalized and punctuated as a sentence but is not a sentence. A sentence needs at least one **INDEPENDENT CLAUSE**, which contains a **SUBJECT** and a **VERB** and does not start with a **SUBORDINATING WORD**.

★ HB-5
HB-4–5
HB-10–21
HB-7

NO SUBJECT   The catcher batted fifth. Fouled out, ending the inning.
Who fouled out?

NO VERB   The first two batters walked. Aaron Judge again.
What did Judge do again?

SUBORDINATING   Although the Yankees loaded the bases.
WORD   *There is a subject ("Yankees") and a verb ("loaded"), but "although" is a subordinating word. What happened after the Yankees loaded the bases?*

SOME SUBORDINATING WORDS

after	because	so that	until	which
although	before	that	when	while
as	if	though	where	who
as if	since	unless	whether	why

S-2b Editing Fragments

Since some readers regard fragments as errors, it's generally better to write complete sentences. Here are four ways to make fragments into sentences.

Add a subject

▶ The catcher batted fifth. ~~Fouled out,~~ He fouled out, ending the inning.

Add a verb

▶ The first two batters walked. Aaron Judge walked again.

HB-15 ★

Sometimes a fragment contains a verb form, such as a present participle or past participle, that cannot function as the main verb of a sentence. In these cases, you can either substitute an appropriate verb form or add a **HELPING VERB**.

▶ As the game went on, the fans started to lose interest. The pitcher's
arm ~~weakening,~~ *weakened,* and the fielders ~~making~~ *made* a number of errors.

▶ The media influence the election process. Political commercials *are* appearing on television more frequently than in years past.

Remove the subordinating word

▶ I'm thinking about moving to a large city. ~~Because~~ I dislike the lack of privacy in my country town of three thousand residents.

Attach the fragment to a nearby sentence

▶ Some candidates spread nasty stories, *about* ~~About~~ their opponents.

▶ These negative stories can deal with many topics, *such* ~~Such~~ as marital infidelity, sources of campaign funds, and drug use.

▶ Put off by negative campaigning, *some* ~~Some~~ people decide not to vote at all.

Note that using a semicolon to attach a fragment to a nearby sentence isn't a good solution. See P–2 for tips on using semicolons.

S-2c Intentional Fragments

Writers sometimes use fragments intentionally.

FOR EMPHASIS
Throughout my elementary and middle school years, I was a strong student, always on the honor roll. I never had a GPA below 3.0. I was smart, and I knew it. *That is, until I got the results of the proficiency test.*

—Shannon Nichols, "'Proficiency'"

TO BE INFORMAL
The SAT writing test predicts how successful a student will be in college. *Since when?*

TO LIST SEVERAL EXAMPLES
The small details stand out. *The bathrooms with green stalls and mirrors with painted Ducks slugging conference foes. The extra-large furniture tested to withstand 500 pounds. The elevators decorated with famous plays in Oregon football history, the actual plays, drawn up in Xs and Os by a coach. The room for professional scouts to watch footage of Oregon players. The ticker running sports scores.*

—Greg Bishop, "Oregon Embraces 'University of Nike' Image"

Though fragments are common in informal contexts, they are often considered errors in academic writing.

>> Go to **InQuizitive for Writers** for an interactive activity on sentence fragments, and practice your skills before applying them in your writing.

S-3 COMMA SPLICES, FUSED SENTENCES

You'll sometimes see a comma splice in ads or literary works: "He dropped the bucket, the paint spilled on his feet." Or the comma may be omitted, forming a fused sentence: "He dropped the bucket the paint spilled on his feet." A comma splice or a fused sentence is generally regarded as an error in academic writing. This chapter shows how to recognize comma splices and fused sentences and edit them out of your writing.

S-3a Identifying Comma Splices and Fused Sentences

A comma splice occurs when two or more **INDEPENDENT CLAUSES** follow one another with only a comma between them.

⭐ HB-5

COMMA SPLICE   T. S. Eliot is best known for his poetry, he also wrote several plays.

A fused sentence occurs when two or more independent clauses follow one another with no punctuation in between.

FUSED SENTENCE   The school board debated the issue for three days they were unable to reach an agreement.

S-3b Editing Comma Splices and Fused Sentences

There are several ways to edit out comma splices and fused sentences.

Make the clauses two sentences

▶ T. S. Eliot is best known for his poetry/. ~~he~~ He also wrote several plays.

Use a comma and a COORDINATING CONJUNCTION

⭐ HB-33–34

▶ The school board debated the issue for three days, but they were unable to reach an agreement.

Use a semicolon

If the relationship between the two clauses is clear without a coordinating conjunction, you can simply join them with a semicolon.

▶ Psychologists study individuals' behavior/; sociologists focus on group-level dynamics.

355–56

When clauses are linked by a **TRANSITION** such as "therefore" or "as a result," the transition needs to be preceded by a semicolon and should generally be followed by a comma.

▶ The hill towns experienced heavy spring and summer rain/; therefore, the fall foliage fell far short of expectations.

Recast one clause as a subordinate clause

HB-7

Add a **SUBORDINATING WORD** to clarify the relationship between the two clauses.

▶ ~~Initial~~ Although initial critical responses to *The Waste Land* were mixed, the poem has been extensively anthologized, read, and written about.

S-3c Intentional Comma Splices

Writers sometimes use only a comma between clauses that are very brief or closely parallel in structure, as in proverbs like "Marry in haste, repent at leisure." In academic writing, though, such sentences may be seen as mistakes.

》 Go to **InQuizitive for Writers** for interactive activities on comma splices and fused (run-on) sentences, and practice your skills before applying them in your writing.

S-4 VERBS

Verbs are the engines of sentences, giving energy, action, and life to writing. "I googled it" is much more vivid than "I found it on the internet"—and the difference is the verb. Sometimes, however, our use of verbs can obscure our meaning, as when a politician avoids taking responsibility by saying, "Mistakes were made." Our choice of verbs shapes our writing in important ways, and this chapter reviews ways of using verbs appropriately and effectively.

S-4a Verb Tenses

To express time, English verbs have three simple tenses—present, past, and future. In addition, each of these verb tenses has perfect and progressive forms that indicate more complex time frames. The present perfect, for example, can be used to indicate an action that began in the past but is continuing into the present. The lists that follow show each of these tenses for the regular verb "talk" and the irregular verb "write."

Simple tenses

PRESENT	PAST	FUTURE
I talk	I talked	I will talk
I write	I wrote	I will write

Use the simple present to indicate actions that take place in the present or that occur habitually. Use the simple past to indicate actions that were completed in the past. Use the simple future to indicate actions that will take place in the future.

▶ Most wealthy industrialized countries *operate* national health-insurance systems.

▶ In 2010, Congress *approved* the Affordable Care Act.

▶ Prohibiting English *will do* for the language what Prohibition *did* for liquor.
　　　　—Dennis Baron, "Don't Make English Official—Ban It Instead"

Use the present tense to express a scientific fact or a general truth even when the rest of the sentence is in the past tense.

▶ The security study showed that taxis and planes are the top places
　where people ~~lost~~ *lose* their phones.

In general, use the present tense to write about literature.

▶ In the first book of the series, Rowling *introduces* us to eleven-year-old Harry Potter; in the seventh and final volume, Harry *enters* full adulthood.

In **APA** style, use the past tense or the present perfect to report on research and the present tense to give your own insights into or conclusions about the results.

● APA 595–633

▶ The bulk of the data collected in this study *validated* the research of Neal Miller; the subjects *appeared* to undergo operant conditioning of their smooth muscles in order to relax their frontalis muscles and increase their skin temperatures. Subjects 3 and 6 each *failed* to do this in one session; subject 7 *failed* to do this several times. This finding *is* difficult to explain precisely.
　　　　—Sarah Thomas, "The Effect of Biofeedback Training on Muscle Tension and Skin Temperature"

Perfect tenses

PRESENT PERFECT	PAST PERFECT	FUTURE PERFECT
I have talked	I had talked	I will have talked
I have written	I had written	I will have written

Use the present perfect to indicate actions that took place at unspecified times in the past or that began in the past and continue into the present (or have relevance in the present).

▶ Many teachers and parents *have resisted* the increasing pressure for more standardized testing of students.

Use the past perfect for an action that was completed before another past action began.

▶ By the time I was born, the Gulf War ^had^ already ended.

The war ended before the writer was born.

Use the future perfect to indicate actions that will be completed at a specific time in the future.

▶ By this time next year, you *will have graduated.*

Progressive tenses

PRESENT PROGRESSIVE	PAST PROGRESSIVE	FUTURE PROGRESSIVE
I am talking	I was talking	I will be talking
I am writing	I was writing	I will be writing

PRESENT PERFECT PROGRESSIVE	PAST PERFECT PROGRESSIVE	FUTURE PERFECT PROGRESSIVE
I have been talking	I had been talking	I will have been talking
I have been writing	I had been writing	I will have been writing

Use progressive tenses to indicate continuing action.

▶ The Cavs *are having* a great year, but the Bucks *are leading* the league.

▶ We *were watching* TV when the doorbell rang.

▶ During the World Cup, soccer fans around the world *will be watching* on TV or online.

▶ Willa joined the robotics club when she was ten, and she *has been building* robots ever since.

S-4b Verb Forms

There are four forms of a verb: the base form, the past, the past participle, and the present participle. Samples of each appear in the lists that follow. All the various tenses are generated with these four forms.

The past tense and past participle of all regular verbs are formed by adding -ed or -d to the base form (talked, lived). Irregular verbs are not as predictable; see the list of some common ones below. The present participle consists of the base form plus -ing (talking, living).

BASE FORM　On Thursdays, we *visit* a museum.

PAST TENSE　Last week, we *visited* the Museum of Modern Art.

PAST PARTICIPLE　I have also *visited* the Metropolitan Museum, but I've not yet *been* to the Cloisters.

PRESENT PARTICIPLE　We will be *visiting* the Cooper-Hewitt Museum tomorrow to see the cutlery exhibit.

Some common irregular verbs

BASE FORM	PAST TENSE	PAST PARTICIPLE	PRESENT PARTICIPLE
be	was/were	been	being
bring	brought	brought	bringing
choose	chose	chosen	choosing
come	came	come	coming
do	did	done	doing
eat	ate	eaten	eating
find	found	found	finding
fly	flew	flown	flying
give	gave	given	giving
go	went	gone	going
hang (suspend)	hung	hung	hanging
have	had	had	having
know	knew	known	knowing
make	made	made	making
prove	proved	proved, proven	proving
rise	rose	risen	rising
set	set	set	setting
sit	sat	sat	sitting
teach	taught	taught	teaching
write	wrote	written	writing

It's easy to get confused about when to use the past tense and when to use a past participle. One simple guideline is to use the past tense if there is no helping verb and to use a past participle if there is one.

▶ For vacation last summer, my family ~~gone~~ *went* to Door County.

▶ After a week at the beach, we had ~~ate~~ *eaten* a lot of seafood.

Gerunds and infinitives

A gerund is a verb form ending in *-ing* that functions as a noun: hopping, skipping, jumping.

▶ Although many people like *driving*, some prefer *walking*.

An infinitive is a verb form made up of "to" plus the base form of a verb: to hop, to skip, to jump.

▶ Although many people like *to drive*, some prefer *to walk*.

Often, infinitives express intentions or desires and gerunds express plain facts.

▶ We planned *to visit* Hollywood, and we also wanted ~~seeing~~ ^to see^ the Grand Canyon.

▶ Unfortunately, we ran out of time, so we postponed ~~to see~~ ^seeing^ the Grand Canyon.

However, there are many exceptions to this pattern, so you may need to consult a dictionary in order to make the appropriate choice.

Some verbs—"begin," "continue," "like," "prefer," and a few others—can be followed by either a gerund or an infinitive with little if any difference in meaning. But with several verbs—"forget," "remember," "stop," and a few others—the choice of an infinitive or a gerund changes the meaning.

▶ I stopped *to eat* lunch.

In other words, I took a break so that I could eat lunch.

▶ I stopped *eating* lunch.

In other words, I no longer ate lunch.

HB-48–50 ★
HB-19–20

Always use a gerund after a **PREPOSITION** or a **PHRASAL VERB**.

▶ The water is too cold for ~~to swim.~~ ^swimming.^

▶ We ended up ~~to spend~~ ^spending^ our whole trip in San Francisco.

≫ Go to **InQuizitive for Writers** for an interactive activity on verb tense and verb form errors, and practice your skills before applying them in your writing.

S-4c Helping Verbs

HB-15–17 ★
HB-10–14
HB-15

"Do," "have," "be," and **MODALS** such as "can" and "may" all function as helping verbs that are used with **MAIN VERBS** to form certain **TENSES** and **MOODS**. "Do," "have," and "be" change form to indicate different tenses; modals do not.

★ HB-17–19

FORMS OF "DO"	do, does, did
FORMS OF "HAVE"	have, has, had
FORMS OF "BE"	be, am, is, are, was, were, been
MODALS	can, could, may, might, must, ought to, shall, should, will, would

"Do," "does," and "did" require the base form of the main verb.

▶ That professor *did take* class participation into account when calculating grades.

▶ Sometimes even the most creative cooks *do* not *like* to modify a recipe.

"Have," "has," and "had" require the past participle of the main verb.

▶ I *have joined* the First Gen club to meet other first-generation students on campus.

▶ When all the visitors *had gone*, the security guards locked the building for the night.

Forms of "be" are used with a present participle to express a continuing action or with a past participle to express the **PASSIVE VOICE**.

★ HB-17

CONTINUING ACTION

▶ The university *is considering* a change in its policy on legacy admissions.

▶ The chef *was reviewing* the week's menu as she filled out the order for the seafood supplier.

PASSIVE VOICE

▶ Six classes per semester *is considered* a heavy course load.

▶ Years ago, vegetables *were chopped* by hand in restaurant kitchens, but now most cooks use electric food processors.

Modals

"Can," "could," "may," "might," "must," "ought to," "shall," "should," "will," and "would": these are modals, a kind of helping verb used with the base form of a **MAIN VERB** to express whether an action is likely, possible, permitted, or various other conditions. Modals don't take the third-person *-s* or the *-ed* or *-ing* endings that ordinary verbs do.

★ HB-10–14

Likelihood will, could, ought to, may, might

▶ The Mavericks *will* win tomorrow. [*very certain*]

▶ The Nuggets *could* defeat the Nets. [*somewhat certain*]

▶ It *ought to* be a very close series between the Clippers and the Sixers. [*moderately certain*]

▶ The Cavaliers *may* win their game tonight. [*less certain*]

▶ The Knicks *might* make the playoffs someday. [*much less certain*]

Assumption must

▶ The dog just started barking; he *must* hear our guests arriving.

Expectation should, ought to

▶ Two large onions *should* be enough for this recipe.

▶ The potatoes *ought to* be ready in twenty minutes.

Ability can, could

▶ Mick Jagger *can* still put on quite a performance, but years ago he *could* sing and throw himself around the stage more dramatically.
How much longer *will* he *be able to* keep rocking?

Necessity or obligation must, should, ought to

▶ Travelers *must* have a passport for foreign travel.

▶ We *should* leave early tomorrow because of the holiday traffic.

▶ You *ought to* get to the airport at least two hours before your scheduled departure.

Permission and requests may, can, could, would, will

▶ People traveling with small children *may* board the plane first.

▶ The hotel's check-in time is 4:00 p.m., but travelers *can* often check in earlier.

▶ *Would* someone help me put my suitcase in the overhead rack?

▶ *Will* you please turn off your phone?

Advice should, ought to

▶ You *should* never text while driving.

▶ You *ought to* be careful about using Wi-Fi networks in public places.

Intention will, shall

▶ Aunt Najwa *will* prepare her famous *atayef* for Eid.

▶ We *shall* overcome.

S-4d Active and Passive Voice

Verbs can sometimes be active or passive. In the active voice, the subject performs the action of the verb (Ja'han solved the problem). In the passive voice, the subject receives the action (the problem was solved by Ja'han).

ACTIVE   One year ago, almost to the day, I *asked* my hairdresser to cut off 16 inches of my hair.
—Suleika Jaouad, "Finding My Cancer Style"

PASSIVE   As a teenager I *was instructed* on how to behave as a proper señorita.
—Judith Ortiz Cofer, "The Myth of the Latin Woman"

Active verbs tend to be more direct and easier to understand, but the passive voice can be useful when you specifically want to emphasize the recipient of the action.

▶ In a sense, little girls *are urged* to please adults with a kind of coquettishness, while boys *are enjoined* to behave like monkeys toward each other.

—Paul Theroux, "Being a Man"

The passive voice is also appropriate in scientific writing when you want to emphasize the research itself, not the researchers.

▶ The treatment order was random for each subject, and it *was reversed* for his or her second treatment.
—Sarah Thomas, "The Effect of Biofeedback Training on Muscle Tension and Skin Temperature"

S-4e Mood

English verbs have three moods: indicative, imperative, and subjunctive. The indicative is used to state facts, opinions, or questions.

▶ Habitat for Humanity *has built* twelve houses in the region this year.

▶ What other volunteer opportunities *does* Habitat *offer*?

The imperative is used to give commands or directions.

▶ *Sit* up straight, and *do* your work.

The subjunctive is used to indicate unlikely or hypothetical conditions or to express wishes, requests, or requirements.

▶ We would be happier if we *had* less pressure at work.

▶ My mother wishes my brother *were* more responsible with his money.

▶ Most colleges require that each applicant *write* an essay.

The subjunctive has two types—one that is the same form as the past tense and one that is the same as the base form.

Conditional sentences

The subjunctive is used most often in conditional sentences, ones that include a clause beginning with "if" or another word that states a condition. Use the indicative in the "if" clause to show that you are confident the condition is possible; use the subjunctive to show that it's doubtful or impossible.

If it's a fact or a possibility. When there's no doubt that the condition in the "if" clause is true or possible, use the indicative in both clauses.

▶ If an earthquake *strikes* that region, forecasters *expect* a tsunami.

▶ A century ago, if a hurricane *struck*, residents *had* very little warning.

▶ If you *go* to the very last car in the train, you *will find* an empty seat.

If it's unlikely, impossible, or hypothetical. When the condition in the "if" clause is not likely or possible, use the subjunctive (same as the past form) in the "if" clause and "would" (or "could" or "might") + the base form of a verb in the other clause. For "be," use "were" in the "if" clause, not "was."

▶ If I *won* the lottery, I *could pay off* my student loans.

▶ If Shirley Chisholm *were* alive, she *would* likely express disappointment that no woman has yet been elected US president.

Because the subjunctive can sound rather formal, it's often not used in informal contexts. In formal and most academic writing, however, it's best to do so.

INFORMAL I *wish* I *was* in Paris.

ACADEMIC In *The Three Sisters,* Masha *wishes* she *were living* in Moscow.

When the "if" clause is about an event in the past that never happened, use the past perfect in the "if" clause and "would have" (or "could have" or "might have") + a past participle in the other clause.

▶ If the police officer *had separated* the witnesses, their evidence *would have been* admissible in court.

Requests, recommendations, and demands

In "that" clauses following verbs such as "ask," "insist," or "suggest," use the subjunctive to express a request, a recommendation, or a demand. Use the base form of the verb in the "that" clause.

▶ I recommended that Rivka *take* a class to get her pilot's license.

▶ The coach will insist that you *be* in uniform on game day.

S-4f Phrasal Verbs

"Act up." "Back down." "Carry on." These are all phrasal verbs, composed of more than one word—usually a verb and a preposition. You know what "act" means. You know what "up" means. If English is not your primary language, however, you may need to check a dictionary to find out that "act up" means to "misbehave." With phrasal verbs, knowing the meaning of each part does not always help you to know what the phrasal verb itself means.

Phrasal verbs can be divided into two categories, separable and inseparable. With separable verbs, the parts can be separated by an **OBJECT**; with inseparable ones, the parts can never be separated.

Glossary

SEPARABLE	I used to *look up* words in a dictionary; now I *look* them *up* on my phone.
INSEPARABLE	Didi has decided to *run for* mayor next year.

With separable phrasal verbs, you have a choice: you can put the object between the parts, or after the complete phrasal verb.

▶ With a hurricane forming nearby, NASA *called off* tomorrow's lunar launch.

▶ Darn! They *called* the launch *off*?

When the object is a long phrase, however, it almost always follows the complete verb.

▶ NASA engineers called the launch of the lunar mission scheduled for tomorrow ~~off~~. (off inserted after "called")

The personal pronouns "me," "you," "him," "her," "it," "us," and "them" are almost always placed between the parts.

▶ The launch was scheduled for yesterday, but NASA called off ~~it~~ ^it^ because of the weather.

Some phrasal verbs never take an object—for example, "come over" (meaning to "visit") and "catch on" (meaning to "become popular").

▶ Why don't you *come over* and see us sometime?

▶ Even the developers of *Snapchat* were astonished by how quickly it *caught on.*

With some phrasal verbs, the meaning changes depending on whether or not there is an object. To "look something up," for instance, means to "find information"; without an object, to "look up" means to "get better."

▶ When in doubt, *look up* phrasal verbs in a dictionary.

▶ The sun's out and the roses are in bloom; things are *looking up!*

Go to **digital.wwnorton.com/links-fieldguide7h** for links to some helpful resources on phrasal verbs.

Some common phrasal verbs

SEPARABLE

back up means to "support": Dodson's hypothesis is well stated, but the data do not back it up.

break down means to "divide into smaller parts": Their analysis might be clearer if it broke the data down state by state.

carry out means to "fulfill" or "complete": We plan to carry out a survey on what the students in our dorm are reading.

find out means to "learn" or "get information": Some parents decide not to find out the sex before their baby is born because they want to be surprised.

point out means to "call attention to": The lizards blended in with the leaves so well that they were hard to see until the guide pointed them out.

INSEPARABLE

call for means to "require" or "deserve": Our current economic situation calls for bold and innovative thinking.

get over means to "recover": Grandma always insisted that the best way to get over a cold was to eat chicken soup.

look into means to "investigate": GAO investigators are looking into allegations of fraud by some college recruiters.

settle on means to "decide on" or "choose": We considered Elizabeth, Margaret, Jane, and many other names for our baby, but finally we settled on Susanna.

touch on means to "mention briefly": The *Wall Street Journal* article focused on productivity and barely touched on issues of worker safety.

DO NOT TAKE AN OBJECT

come about means to "happen" or "occur": How did the dispute come about in the first place?

get by means to "survive" or "manage," usually with few resources: Many retired workers can't get by on just their pensions; they have to find part-time work as well.

give in means to "yield" or "agree": After much discussion, members of the union voted not to give in to management's demands for a reduction in benefits.

show up means to "arrive": Did everyone show up for the rehearsal?

take off means to "leave the ground": The JetBlue flight took off an hour late because of thunderstorms in the Midwest. It also means to "make great progress": Sales of *Where the Crawdads Sing* took off in 2018, after it was recommended by Reese Witherspoon.

S-5 SUBJECT-VERB AGREEMENT

Subjects and verbs should agree: if the subject is in the third-person singular, the verb should be in the third-person singular—"Dinner is on the table." Yet sometimes context affects subject-verb agreement, as when we say that "macaroni and cheese *make* a great combination" but that "macaroni and cheese is our family's favorite comfort food." This chapter focuses on subject-verb agreement.

S-5a Agreement in Number and Person

Subjects and verbs should agree with each other in number (singular or plural) and person (first, second, or third). To make a present-tense verb agree with a third-person singular subject, add -s or -es to the base form.

▶ A 1922 *ad* for Resinol soap *urges* women to "make that dream come true" by using Resinol.   —Doug Lantry, "'Stay Sweet as You Are'"

To make a present-tense verb agree with any other subject, simply use the base form without any ending.

▶ *I make* toast in the morning while *we drink* our coffee.

▶ *Drunk drivers cause* thousands of preventable deaths each year

"Be" and "have" have irregular forms (shown on p. HB-13) and so do not follow the -s/-es rule.

▶ The test of all knowledge *is* experiment.

—Richard Feynman, "Atoms in Motion"

▶ The scientist *has* a lot of experience with ignorance and doubt and uncertainty, and this experience *is* of great importance.

—Richard Feynman, "The Value of Science"

In questions, a helping verb is often necessary. The subject, which generally goes between the helping verb and the main verb, should agree with the helping verb.

▶ How long *does an air filter last* on average?

▶ *Have the 10 ml pipettes arrived* yet?

S-5b Subjects and Verbs Separated

A verb should agree with its subject, not with another word that falls in between.

▶ In the backyard, the *leaves* of the apple tree *rattle* across the lawn.

—Gary Soto, "The Guardian Angel"

▶ The *price* of soybeans ~~fluctuate~~ fluctuates according to demand.

S-5c Compound Subjects

Two or more subjects joined by "and" are generally plural.

▶ Swiss cheese and shrimp *are* both high in vitamin B12.

However, if the parts of the subject form a single unit, they take a singular verb.

▶ Forty acres and a mule ~~are~~ is what General William T. Sherman promised each freed slave.

If the subjects are joined by "or" or "nor," the verb should agree with the closer subject.

▶ Either you or she ~~are~~ *is* mistaken.

▶ Neither the teacher nor his students ~~was~~ *were* able to solve the equation.

S-5d Subjects That Follow the Verb

English verbs usually follow their subjects. Be sure the verb agrees with the subject even when the subject follows the verb, such as when the sentence begins with "there is" or "there are."

▶ There ~~is~~ *are* too many unresolved problems for the project to begin.

▶ In the middle of the room ~~was~~ *were* a desk and a floor lamp.

S-5e Collective Nouns

Collective nouns such as "group," "team," "audience," or "family" can take singular or plural verbs, depending on whether the noun refers to the group as a single unit or to the individual members of the group.

▶ Our klezmer band ~~perform~~ *performs* for the whole campus every year in March, around Purim.

▶ Gregor's family *keep* reassuring themselves that things will be just fine again.
      —Scott Russell Sanders, "Under the Influence"

   The word "themselves" shows that "family" refers to its individual members.

S-5f "Everyone" and Other Indefinite Pronouns

Most **INDEFINITE PRONOUNS**, such as "anyone," "anything," "each," "either," "everyone," "everything," "neither," "nobody," "no one," "one," "somebody," "someone," and "something," take a singular verb, even if they seem plural or refer to plural nouns.

★ HB-26

▶ Everyone in our dorm *has* already *signed* the petition.

▶ Each of the candidates ~~agree~~ *agrees* with the president.

"Both," "few," "many," "others," and "several" are always plural.

▶ Although there are many great actors working today, few *are* as versatile as Toni Collette.

"All," "any," "enough," "more," "most," "none," and "some" are singular when they refer to a singular noun, but they are plural when they refer to a plural noun.

▶ Don't assume that all the members of a family ~~votes~~ ^vote^ the same way.

▶ Most of the music we heard last night ~~come~~ ^comes^ from the baroque period.

S-5g "Who," "That," "Which"

Glossary

The **RELATIVE PRONOUNS** "who," "that," and "which" take a singular verb when they refer to a singular noun and a plural verb when they refer to a plural noun.

▶ In these songs, Lady Gaga draws on a tradition of camp that *extends* from drag queen cabaret to Broadway and disco.

—Jody Rosen, review of *Born This Way*

▶ Bowman, having nearly been sent to a deep-space death by the malfunctioning machine, is calmly, coldly disconnecting the memory circuits that *control* its artificial brain.

—Nicholas Carr, "Is Google Making Us Stupid?"

"One of the" is always followed by a plural noun, and when the noun is followed by "who" or "that," the verb should be plural.

▶ Jaime is one of the speakers who ~~asks~~ ^ask^ provocative questions.

Several speakers ask provocative questions. Jaime is one. "Who" refers to "speakers," so the verb is plural.

If the phrase begins with "the only one," however, the verb should be singular.

▶ Jaime is the only one of the speakers who ~~ask~~ ^asks^ provocative questions.

Only one speaker asks provocative questions: Jaime. "Who" thus refers to "one," so the verb is singular.

S-5h Words Such as "News" and "Physics"

Words like "news," "athletics," and "physics" seem plural but are usually singular in meaning and take singular verb forms.

▶ The *news* of widespread layoffs *alarms* everyone in the company.

Some of these words, such as "economics," "mathematics," "politics," and "statistics," have plural meanings in some uses and take plural verbs.

▶ For my roommate, mathematics *is* an endlessly stimulating field.

▶ The complex mathematics involved in this proof *are* beyond the scope of this lecture.

S-5i Titles and Words Used as Words

Titles and words that are discussed as words are singular.

▶ *The Royal Tenenbaums* ~~depict~~ three talented siblings who are loosely based on characters created by J. D. Salinger.

depicts

▶ "Man-caused disasters" ~~are~~ a term favored by some political analysts as a substitute for the term "terrorist attacks."

is

>> Go to **InQuizitive for Writers** for an interactive activity on subject-verb agreement, and practice your skills before applying them in your writing.

S-6 PRONOUNS

We use pronouns to take the place of nouns so that we don't have to write or say the same word or name over and over. Imagine how repetitive our writing would be without pronouns: Little Miss Muffet sat on a tuffet eating Little Miss Muffet's curds and whey. Luckily, we have pronouns, and this chapter demonstrates how to use them clearly.

S-6a Pronoun-Antecedent Agreement

Antecedents are the words that pronouns refer to. A pronoun must agree with its antecedent in gender and number.

IN GENDER   *Grandma* took *her* pie out of the oven.

IN NUMBER   *My grandparents* spent weekends at *their* cabin on White Bear Lake.

Generic nouns

Generic nouns refer to a type or category of person or thing (a farmer, a shower cap). You'll often see or hear a plural pronoun used to refer to a singular generic noun, especially if the noun refers to a type of person. In conversation and increasingly in academic writing as well, this usage is becoming more and more acceptable.

▶ *Every lab technician* should always wear goggles to protect *their* eyes while working with chemicals.

In some contexts, you may want to stay with more traditional usage; in those cases, you can make the noun plural.

▶ ~~Every lab technician~~ should always wear goggles to protect *their* eyes
  Lab technicians
  while working with chemicals.

Indefinite pronouns like "everyone" and "each"

Indefinite pronouns such as "anyone," "each," "everyone," and "someone" are considered singular even if they seem to be plural because they may refer to plural nouns.

▶ All items on that table will have their prices marked down.

▶ Everything on that table will have ~~their~~ price marked down.
  its

Both sentences have the same meaning, and even though "everything" clearly refers to all the things (plural), the word "everything" is considered singular.

As with generic nouns, in conversation and increasingly in writing as well, "they," "them," and "their" are often used to refer to grammatically singular indefinite pronouns that refer to people. See L-10b for more on this usage.

▶ Everyone in the class did their best.

If you want to stay with more traditional usage, you can change the indefinite pronoun to a genuine plural.

▶ ~~Everyone~~ in the class did their best.
  All the students

Collective nouns like "audience" and "team"

Collective nouns such as "audience," "committee," and "team" take a singular pronoun when they refer to the group as a whole and a plural pronoun when they refer to members of the group as individuals.

▶ Our softball team won ~~their~~ *its* first championship ever.

▶ Our softball team threw ~~its~~ *their* gloves in the air in celebration.

The championship belongs to the team as a unit, so the appropriate pronoun is "its." The gloves were thrown in the air by the individual players, so the appropriate pronoun is "their." These two examples are clear, but collective nouns can often be ambiguous. Sometimes, singular and plural pronouns might both be acceptable. In those cases, you can choose whichever one you think works best, as long as you're consistent.

▶ Her family has their reunion in Charlotte every August.

▶ Her family has its reunion in Charlotte every August.

"He," "his," and other masculine pronouns

To avoid **SEXIST LANGUAGE**, use "he," "him," "his," or "himself" only when you know that the antecedent identifies as male.

★ HB-62

▶ When meeting a new doctor, it's useful to bring a list of questions ~~for him~~.

Another possibility is to use "him or her."

▶ Before meeting a new doctor, many people worry about not liking him/ *or her.*

However, not all people identify as either male or female, so this solution doesn't include everyone. Instead, many writers use "they," "them," and "their" to refer to a person whose gender is unknown or not relevant to the context.

▶ Someone in my building is selling ~~his~~ *their* laptop; ~~he~~ *they* put up a sign by the mailboxes.

This usage, known as **SINGULAR "THEY,"** is becoming more and more accepted. It has been endorsed by Merriam-Webster's dictionary and many other major publications. Ask your instructor if it's OK to use it in your class writing. In addition, some people use "they" rather than "he" or "she" when being referred to in the third-person singular. Always refer to people by using the pronouns they designate for themselves.

★ HB-65–67

▶▶ Go to **InQuizitive for Writers** for an interactive activity on pronouns that don't agree with their antecedents, and practice your skills before applying them in your writing.

S-6b Pronoun Reference

A pronoun usually needs a clear antecedent, a specific word to which it refers.

▶ *My grandmother* spent a lot of time reading to me. *She* mostly read
the standards, like *The Little Engine That Could.*

—Richard Bullock, "How I Learned about the Power of Writing"

Ambiguous reference

If there is more than one word that a pronoun could refer to, rewrite the sentence to clarify which one is the antecedent.

▶ After I plugged the printer into the computer, ~~it~~ ^the printer^ sputtered and died.

What sputtered and died—the computer or the printer? The edit makes the reference clear.

Implied reference

If a pronoun does not refer clearly to a specific word, rewrite the sentence to omit the pronoun or insert an antecedent.

Unclear reference of "this," "that," and "which." These three pronouns must refer to specific antecedents.

▶ Ultimately, the Justice Department did not insist on the breakup of
Microsoft, ~~which~~ ^an oversight that^ set the tone for a liberal merger policy.

Indefinite use of "they," "it," and "you." Except in expressions like "it is raining" or "it seems that," "they" and "it" should be used only to refer to people or things that have been specifically mentioned. "You" should be used only to address your reader.

▶ ~~In many~~ ^Many^ European countries ~~they~~ don't allow civilians to carry handguns.

▶ ~~On the~~ ^The^ Weather Channel ~~it~~ said that storms would hit Key West today.

▶ Many doctors argue that age should not be an impediment to
physical exercise ~~if you~~ ^for people who^ have always been active.

Both in conversation and in writing, antecedents are often left unstated if the audience will easily grasp the meaning. For academic writing, however, it's better not to use implied or indefinite antecedents.

>> Go to **InQuizitive for Writers** for an interactive activity on pronouns with unclear reference, and practice your skills before applying them in your writing.

S-6c Pronoun Case

Pronouns change case according to how they function in a sentence. There are three cases: subject, object, and possessive. Pronouns functioning as subjects or subject **COMPLEMENTS** are in the subject case; those functioning as **OBJECTS** are in the object case; those functioning as possessives are in the possessive case.

Glossary

Glossary

SUBJECT	*We* lived in a rented house three blocks from the school.
OBJECT	I went to my room and shut the door behind *me.*
POSSESSIVE	All *my* life chocolate has made me ill.

—David Sedaris, "Us and Them"

SUBJECT	OBJECT	POSSESSIVE
I	me	my / mine
we	us	our / ours
you	you	your / yours
he / she / it	him / her / it	his / her / hers / its
they	them	their / theirs
who / whoever	whom / whomever	whose

In subject complements

Use the subject case for pronouns that follow **LINKING VERBS** such as "be," "seem," "become," and "feel."

Glossary

▶ In fact, Li was not the one who broke the code; it was ~~me.~~ I.

   If "It was I" sounds awkward, revise the sentence further: "I broke it."

In compound structures

When a pronoun is part of a compound subject, it should be in the subject case. When it's part of a compound object, it should be in the object case.

▶ On our vacations, my grandfather and ~~me~~ I went fishing together.

▶ There were never any secrets between ~~he~~ him and ~~I.~~ me.

After "than" or "as"

Often comparisons with "than" or "as" leave some words out. When such comparisons include pronouns, your intended meaning determines the case of the pronoun.

▶ You help Lalo more than *me*.

This sentence means "You help Lalo more than you help me."

▶ You help Lalo more than *I*.

This sentence means "You help Lalo more than I help him."

Before or after infinitives

Glossary

Pronouns that come before or after an **INFINITIVE** are usually in the object case.

▶ The choreographer asked Ravi and ~~I~~ [me] to show ~~she~~ [her] and the troupe our new steps.

Before gerunds

HB-14 ★

Pronouns that come before a **GERUND** are usually in the possessive case.

▶ Savion's fans loved ~~him~~ [his] tap dancing to classical music.

With "who" or "whom"

Glossary

There's strong evidence that "whom" is disappearing from use in both formal and informal contexts, but some instructors may expect you to use it. Use "who" (and "whoever") where you would use "he" or "she," and use "whom" (and "whomever") where you would use "him" or "her." These words appear most often in questions and in **SUBORDINATE CLAUSES**.

In questions. It can be confusing when one of these words begins a question. To figure out which case to use, try answering the question using "she" or "her." If "she" works, use "who"; if "her" works, use "whom."

▶ ~~Who~~ [Whom] do the critics admire most?

They admire <u>her</u>, so change "who" to "whom."

▶ ~~Whom~~ [Who] will begin the discussion on this thorny topic?

<u>She</u> will begin the discussion, so change "whom" to "who."

In subordinate clauses. To figure out whether to use "who" or "whom" in a subordinate clause, you need to determine how it functions in the clause. If it functions as a subject, use "who"; if it functions as an object, use "whom."

>   whomever
> ▶ You may invite ~~whoever~~ you like.
>   ^
> "Whomever" is the object of "you like."

>   whoever
> ▶ I will invite ~~whomever~~ is free that night.
>   ^
> "Whoever" is the subject of "is free that night." The clause "whoever is free that night" is the object of the whole sentence.

When "we" or "us" precedes a noun

If you don't know whether to use "we" or "us" before a noun, choose the pronoun that you would use if the noun were omitted.

> ▶ *We* students object to the recent tuition increases.
> Without "students," you would say "We object," not "Us object."

> ▶ The state is solving its budget shortfall by unfairly charging *us* students.
> Without "students," you would say "unfairly charging us," not "unfairly charging we."

≫ Go to **InQuizitive for Writers** for an interactive activity on pronouns in the wrong case, and practice your skills before applying them in your writing.

S-7 PARALLELISM

"Been there, done that." "Eat, drink, and be merry." "For better or for worse." "Out of sight, out of mind." All these common sayings are parallel in structure, putting related words in the same grammatical form. Parallel structure emphasizes the connection between the elements and can make your writing rhythmic and easy to read. This chapter offers guidelines for maintaining parallelism in your writing.

S-7a In a Series or List

Use the same grammatical form for all items in a series or list—all nouns, all gerunds, all prepositional phrases, and so on.

> ▶ The seven deadly sins—*avarice, sloth, envy, lust, gluttony, pride,* and *wrath*—were all committed Sunday during the twice-annual bake sale at St. Mary's of the Immaculate Conception Church.   *—Onion*

>   playing
> ▶ After fifty years of running, biking, swimming, weight lifting, and tennis to stay in shape, Aunt Dorothy was unhappy to learn she needed knee surgery.

HB-33–34 ★
HB-34

S-7b With Paired Ideas

One way to emphasize the connection between two ideas is to put them in identical grammatical forms. When you connect ideas with "and," "but," or another **COORDINATING CONJUNCTION** or with "either . . . or" or another **CORRELATIVE CONJUNCTION**, use the same grammatical structure for each idea.

▶ Many rural residents are voting on conservation issues and ~~agree~~ to *agreeing* pay higher taxes to keep community land undeveloped.

▶ General Electric paid millions of dollars to dredge the river and ~~for removing~~ *to remove* carcinogens from backyards.

▶ Sweet potatoes are highly nutritious, providing both dietary fiber and ~~as a good source of~~ vitamins A and C.

▶ Information on local cleanup efforts can be obtained not only from the town government but also ~~by going to~~ *at* the public library.

S-7c On Presentation Slides

PowerPoint and other presentation tools present most information in lists. Entries on these lists should be in parallel grammatical form.

During the 1946 presidential race, Truman
- conducted a whistle-stop campaign
- made hundreds of speeches
- spoke energetically
- connected personally with voters

S-7d On a Résumé

Glossary

Entries on a **RÉSUMÉ** should be grammatically and typographically parallel. Each entry in the example that follows has the date on the left; the job title in bold followed by the company on the first line; the city and state on the second line; and the duties performed on the remaining lines, each starting with a verb. Use the past tense if the candidate has left the position; use the present tense if the candidate is still working in the position.

2024–present   **INTERN**, Benedetto, Gartland, and Company
                            Miami, FL
                            Assist in analyzing data for key accounts.
                            Design *PowerPoint* slides and presentations.

2023, summer   **SALES REPRESENTATIVE**, Vector Marketing Corporation
                            Miami, FL
                            Sold high-quality cutlery, developing client base.

2021, summer   **TUTOR**, Grace Church Opportunity Project
Miami, FL
Tutored children in math and reading.

S-7e In Headings

When you add headings to a piece of writing, put them in parallel form—all nouns, all prepositional phrases, and so on. Consider, for example, the following headings in Chapter 52:

Acknowledging Sources
Avoiding Plagiarism

S-7f With All the Necessary Words

Be sure to include all the words necessary to make your meaning clear and your grammar parallel.

▶ Voting gained urgency in cities, ^in^ suburbs, and on farms.

▶ She loved her son more than ^she loved^ her husband.

The original sentence was ambiguous; it could also mean that she loved her son more than her husband did.

▶ A cat's skeleton is more flexible than ^that of^ a dog.

The original sentence compared one animal's skeleton to a whole animal rather than to another animal's skeleton.

S-8 COORDINATION, SUBORDINATION

When we combine two or more ideas in one sentence, we can use coordination to give equal weight to each idea or subordination to give more emphasis to one of the ideas. Assume, for example, that you're writing about your aunt Irene. Aunt Irene made great strawberry jam. She did not win a blue ribbon at the Iowa State Fair.

COORDINATION   Aunt Irene made great strawberry jam, but she did not win a blue ribbon at the Iowa State Fair.

SUBORDINATION   Though Aunt Irene made great strawberry jam, she did not win a blue ribbon at the Iowa State Fair.

S-8a Linking Equal Ideas

To link ideas that you consider equal in importance, use a coordinating conjunction, a pair of correlative conjunctions, or a semicolon.

COORDINATING CONJUNCTIONS

and   but   for   nor   or   so   yet

▶ The line in front of Preservation Hall was very long, *but* a good tenor sax player was wandering up and down the street, *so* I took my place at the end of the line.

—Fred Setterberg, "The Usual Story"

▶ New models of coursework may need to be developed, *and* instructors may need to be hired.

—Megan Hopkins, "Training the Next Teachers for America"

Be careful not to overuse "and." Try to use the coordinating conjunction that best expresses your meaning.

▶ Mosquitoes survived the high-tech zapping devices, ~~and~~ *but* bites were a small price for otherwise pleasant evenings in the country.

CORRELATIVE CONJUNCTIONS

| either . . . or | just as . . . so | neither . . . nor |
| not only . . . but also | whether . . . or | |

▶ *Just as* the summer saw endless rain, *so* the winter brought many snowstorms.

While a semicolon alone can signal equal importance, you might use a **TRANSITION** such as "therefore" or "in fact" to make the relationship between the ideas especially clear.

355–56 ⁝

▶ Snowplows could not get through; trains stopped running.

▶ The 1996 film *Space Jam* stars Bugs Bunny and Michael Jordan, an unlikely pairing; *however,* the two are well matched in heroic status and mythic strengths.

S-8b Emphasizing One Idea over Others

To emphasize one idea over others, put the most important one in an **INDEPENDENT CLAUSE** and the less important ones in **SUBORDINATE CLAUSES** or **PHRASES**.

HB-5 ★
HB-5
HB-6

┌────PHRASE────┐
▶ Wanting to walk to work, LeShawn rented a somewhat expensive apartment downtown.

┌────SUBORDINATE CLAUSE────┐
▶ His monthly expenses were actually lower because he saved so much money in transportation costs.

S-9 SHIFTS

You're watching the news when your brother grabs the remote and changes the channel to a cartoon. The road you're driving on suddenly changes from asphalt to gravel. These shifts are jarring and sometimes disorienting. Similarly, shifts in writing—from one tense to another, for example—can confuse your readers. This chapter explains how to keep your writing consistent in verb tense, point of view, and number.

S-9a Shifts in Tense

Only when you want to emphasize that actions take place at different times should you shift verb **TENSE**.

★ HB-11–12

▶ My plane *will arrive* in Albuquerque two hours after it *leaves* Portland.

    Otherwise, keep tenses consistent.

▶ As the concert ended, several people ~~are~~ ^{were} already on their way up the aisle, causing a distraction.

In writing about literary works, use the present tense. Be careful not to shift to the past tense.

▶ The two fugitives start down the river together, Huck fleeing his abusive father and Jim escaping slavery. As they ~~traveled,~~ ^{travel,} they ~~met~~ ^{meet} with many colorful characters, including the Duke and King, two actors and con artists who involve Huck and Jim in their schemes.

» Go to **InQuizitive for Writers** for an interactive activity on verb tense and verb form errors, and practice your skills before applying them in your writing.

S-9b Shifts in Point of View

Do not shift between first person (I, we), second person (you), and third person (he, she, it, they, one).

▶ When ~~one has~~ ^{you have} a cold, you should stay home to avoid infecting others.

S-9c Shifts in Number

Unnecessary shifts between singular and plural subjects can confuse readers.

▶ Because of late frosts, oranges have risen dramatically in price. But since ~~the orange is~~ ^{oranges are} such a staple, they continue to sell.

L Language

L-1 WELL-CHOSEN WORDS

"Cool." "Sweet." "Excellent." These three words can mean the same thing, but each has a different level of formality. We usually use informal language when we're talking with friends, and we use slang and abbreviations when we send text messages, but we choose words that are more formal for most of our academic and professional writing. Just as we wouldn't wear an old T-shirt to most job interviews, we wouldn't write in a college essay that *Beloved* is "an awesome book." This chapter offers you help in choosing words that are suitable for different audiences and purposes.

L-1a Formal and Informal Words

Whether you use formal or informal language depends on your **PURPOSE** and **AUDIENCE**.

73–74

75–78

FORMAL   Four score and seven years ago our fathers brought forth on this continent, a new nation, conceived in Liberty, and dedicated to the proposition that all men are created equal.
—Abraham Lincoln, Gettysburg Address

INFORMAL   Our family, like most, had its ups and downs.
—Judy Davis, "Ours Was a Dad"

The first, more formal sentence was delivered in 1863 to twenty thousand people, including many officials and prominent citizens. The second, less formal sentence was spoken in 2004 to a small gathering of family and friends at a funeral.

Colloquial language (What's up? No clue) and slang (A-list, S'up?) are not appropriate for formal speech and most academic and professional writing.

> Many   students
> ▶ A̶ ̶l̶o̶t̶ ̶o̶f̶ high school k̶i̶d̶s̶ have so little time for lunch that they end up
>   ^   ^
> eating
> g̶o̶b̶b̶l̶i̶n̶g̶ ̶d̶o̶w̶n̶ ̶t̶h̶e̶i̶r̶ ̶f̶o̶o̶d̶ as they race to class.
> ^

L-1b Pretentious Language

Long or complicated words might seem to lend authority to your writing, but often they make it sound pretentious and stuffy. Use such words sparingly and only when they best capture your meaning and suit your **WRITING CONTEXT**.

71

> After   claimed
> ▶ S̶u̶b̶s̶e̶q̶u̶e̶n̶t̶ ̶t̶o̶ adopting the new system, managers a̶v̶e̶r̶r̶e̶d̶ that their
>   ^   together   better than expected.
> staff worked s̶y̶n̶e̶r̶g̶i̶s̶t̶i̶c̶a̶l̶l̶y̶ ̶i̶n̶ ̶a̶ ̶w̶a̶y̶ ̶t̶h̶a̶t̶ ̶e̶x̶c̶e̶e̶d̶e̶d̶ ̶p̶a̶r̶a̶m̶e̶t̶e̶r̶s̶.
>   ^   ^

L-1c Jargon

Jargon is a specialized vocabulary of a profession, trade, or field and should be used only when you know your audience will understand what you are saying. A lawyer might easily understand the following sentences from a Supreme Court decision, but most readers would not be familiar with legal terms like "res judicata," "facial relief," and "claim preclusion."

▶ Res judicata neither bars petitioners' challenges to the admitting-privileges requirement nor prevents the Court from awarding facial relief. The fact that several petitioners had previously brought the unsuccessful facial challenge in *Abbott* does not mean that claim preclusion, the relevant aspect of res judicata, applies.

—Supreme Court of the United States,
Whole Woman's Health v. Hellerstedt

When you are writing for an audience of nonspecialists, resist the temptation to use overly technical language.

▶ The ~~mini-sternotomy~~ ^{small incision} at the lower end of the ~~sternum resulted in~~ ^{breastbone preserved} her appearance. ~~satisfactory cosmesis.~~

L-1d Clichés

Steer clear of clichés, expressions so familiar that they have become trite (white as snow, the grass is always greener). Editors and writing instructors in the United States (and much of the English-speaking world) prefer fresh and unique combinations of words rather than familiar and possibly overused phrases.

▶ The company needs a recruiter who thinks ~~outside the box.~~ ^{unconventionally.}

▶ After canoeing all day, we all slept ~~like logs.~~ ^{soundly.}

▶ Nita ~~is a team player,~~ ^{collaborates well,} so we hope she will be assigned to the project.

L-2 PRECISE WORDS

"Serena Overpowers Sloane." "Mariano Finishes Off the Sox." In each case, the writer could have simply used the word "beats." But at least to sports fans, these newspaper headlines are a bit more precise and informative as a result of the words chosen. This chapter offers guidelines for editing your own writing to make it as precise as it needs to be.

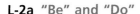

L-2a "Be" and "Do"

Try not to rely too much on "be" or "do." Check your writing to see where you can replace forms of these words with more precise verbs.

▶ David Sedaris's essay "Us and Them" ~~is about~~ *focuses on* his love/hate relationship with his family.

▶ Some doctors no longer believe that ~~doing~~ *solving* crossword puzzles can delay the onset of senility or Alzheimer's disease.

Sometimes using a form of "be" or "do" is the right choice, when, for example, you are describing something or someone.

▶ Most critics agree that *Citizen Kane, Casablanca,* and *The Shawshank Redemption are* some of the finest movies ever made.

L-2b Abstract and Concrete Words

Abstract words refer to general qualities or ideas (truth, beauty), whereas concrete words refer to specific things that can be perceived with our senses (forks, lipstick). You'll often need to use words that are general or abstract, but remember that specific, concrete words can make your writing more precise and more vivid—and can make an abstract concept easier to understand.

▶ In Joan Didion's work, there has always been a fascination with what she once called "the unspeakable peril of the everyday"—the coyotes by the interstate, the snakes in the playpen, the fires and Santa Ana winds of California.
> —Michiko Kakutani, "The End of Life as She Knew It"

The concrete words "coyotes," "snakes," "fires," and "winds" help explain the abstract phrase "peril of the everyday."

L-2c Figurative Language

Figures of speech such as **SIMILES** and **METAPHORS** are words used imaginatively rather than literally. They can help readers understand an abstract point by comparing it to something they are familiar with or can easily imagine.

Glossary

SIMILE The Spice Girls were not the most exacting performers, but they were brassy and buoyant. In the video for "Wannabe," even Posh Spice—forever bedecked in a tiny Gucci dress and strappy heels, rarely smiling in photos—bounds around *like a toddler who has got hold of some chocolate doughnuts.*
> —Amanda Petrusich, "The Boundless Optimism of the Spice Girls"

METAPHOR   And so, before the professor had even finished his little story, *I had become a furnace of rage.*
—Shelby Steele, "On Being Black and Middle Class"

L-3 IDIOMS

"A piece of cake." "Walking on air." "Cute as a button." These are just three of the thousands of English idioms and idiomatic expressions that are used every day. Most idioms are phrases (and sometimes whole sentences) whose meaning cannot be understood by knowing the meanings of the individual words. We use idioms because they give a lot of information in few words and add color and texture to what we say or write. If you're learning English, a well-chosen idiom also demonstrates your fluency in the language. Some idioms appear more often in conversation than in formal writing, but many will be useful to you in your academic work.

L-3a Recognizing Idioms

When you read or hear a phrase that seems totally unrelated to the topic, you have probably encountered an idiom.

▶ Influencing Hollywood is a little *like herding cats.*
—Jane Alexander, *Command Performance*

Cats are notoriously independent and indifferent to following directions; thus a difficult, maybe impossible task is said to be "like herding cats."

▶ As the economy contracts, we Americans are likely to find that we have been living too *high on the hog.*
—*Los Angeles Times*

Ham, ribs, bacon, and other meats that are considered the most tasty and desirable are from the upper parts of the hog. People who live extravagantly or luxuriously are sometimes said to be living "high on the hog."

▶ This internship is not just about class credit. This is about really getting *a leg up* for when you graduate.
—Morgan to Chelsea, *Days of Our Lives*

When a rider is mounting a horse, another person often supports the rider's left leg while the right one swings over the horse's back. Having "a leg up" means you've been given extra help or certain advantages.

▶ I love to see a young girl go out and *grab* the world *by the lapels.*
—Maya Angelou

Grabbing the front of a jacket, or "grabbing someone by the lapels," is a firm and aggressive move that aims to take charge of a situation.

L-3b Understanding Idioms

Idioms may seem peculiar or even nonsensical if you think about their literal meanings, but knowing where they originated can help you figure out what they mean. Many idioms, for example, originate in sports, music, and animal contexts, where their meanings are literal. Used in other contexts, their meanings are similar, if not exactly literal.

▶ When the senator introduced the bill, she thought passage would be a *slam dunk* since public opinion was strongly favorable.

In basketball, a player scores a "slam dunk" by shoving the ball through the basket in a dramatic way. As an idiom, a "slam dunk" refers to a victory gained easily or emphatically.

▶ George Saunders's commencement speech really *struck a chord* with the Syracuse graduates.

A chord is a group of musical notes that harmonize; to "strike a chord" with an audience means to make a connection by bringing up something interesting or relevant to them.

▶ Some members of Congress think that limiting food stamps will get more Americans back to work; I think they're *barking up the wrong tree.*

This idiom refers to a dog in pursuit of an animal that has disappeared into a group of trees; the dog is barking at one tree, but its prey has climbed up another. To "bark up the wrong tree" means to pursue the wrong course of action.

You can sometimes figure out the meaning of an idiom based on its context; but if you're not sure what it means or how to use it properly, look it up online—go to **digital.wwnorton.com/links-fieldguide7h** for links to some helpful sources. The *Cambridge Dictionary of American Idioms* is one useful print source.

L-3c Common Idiomatic Expressions in Academic and Professional Writing

Idiomatic expressions are words that go together like peanut butter and jelly—you often find them together. You've probably encountered expressions such as "with respect to," "insofar as," or "as a matter of fact" in academic or professional writing. Many of these expressions function as **TRANSITIONS**, helping readers follow your reasoning and understand how your ideas relate to one another. You're expected to signal the connections among your ideas explicitly in academic writing, and the following idiomatic expressions can help you do so.

355–56

To shift to a narrower focus

with respect to, with regard to   indicate the precise topic you are addressing: "The global economic situation is much more complicated with respect to certain nations' high levels of debt."

insofar as   sets a limit or scope for a statement: "Despite her short stature, Bates is the team leader insofar as direction and determination are concerned."

in particular   points to something especially true within a generalization: "Cosmetic surgery procedures for men have increased tremendously in the last decade; liposuction and eyelid surgery, in particular, showed dramatic increases."

To give examples

a case in point   frames an example that illustrates a point: "Recent business activity shows a clear trend toward consolidation. The merger of two airlines last year is a case in point."

for instance   indicates an example that illustrates an idea: "Green vegetables are highly nutritious; one serving of kale, for instance, provides the full daily recommended value of vitamins A and C."

To add information

in addition introduces a new but related point: "Locally grown tomatoes are available nearly everywhere; in addition, they are rich in vitamin C."

along the same lines   connects two similar ideas: "Many cities are developing parking meter plans along the same lines as the system in Chicago."

by the same token   signals a point that follows the logic of the previous point: "Insider trading has damaged the reputation of the financial industry in general; by the same token, high-profile embezzlers like Bernie Madoff have eroded the public's confidence in many investment advisers."

as a matter of fact, in fact   signal a statement that explains or contrasts with a previous point: "Wind power is an increasingly common energy source; as a matter of fact, wind energy generation tripled between 2009 and 2019."

To emphasize something

of course   emphasizes a point that is (or should be) obvious: "Fresh foods are preferable to processed foods, of course, but fresh foods are not always available."

in any case, in any event   introduce something that is true regardless of other conditions: "The city has introduced new precautions to ensure the election goes smoothly; the results will be closely scrutinized in any event."

To signal alternatives or conflicting ideas

on the one hand . . . on the other hand   introduces contrasting ideas or conditions: "On the one hand, some critics have loudly rejected reality television; on the other hand, unscripted shows are often received well by the public."

up to a point   signals acceptance of part but not all of an argument or idea: "The senator's statement is correct up to a point, but her conclusions are misguided."

have it both ways   to benefit from two conflicting positions: "Tech companies want to have it both ways, asking the government to be more transparent about its use of user data while not disclosing that they are using these data for their own commercial purposes."

of two minds   signals ambivalence, validates conflicting ideas: "On the question of whether organic food is worth the extra cost, I am of two minds: I like knowing that the food is grown without chemicals, but I'm still skeptical because some studies suggest that the health benefits are questionable."

in contrast   signals a change in direction or a different idea on the same subject: "Large birds such as crows can live for more than ten years; in contrast, tiny hummingbirds generally live less than three years."

on the contrary   signals an opposite idea or opposing position: "Some bankers claim that the proposed mortgage regulations would harm the economy; on the contrary, the new rules would be the most effective means of reinvigorating it."

in fact, as a matter of fact   signal a statement that challenges or refutes a previous statement: "Nicholas Carr suggests that *Google* is making us stupid; in fact, some argue that by giving us access to more information, it's making us better informed."

To summarize or restate something

in brief, in short   introduce a short summary of points already established: "In brief, the accident was caused by a combination of carelessness and high winds."

in other words   signals a restatement or explanation of the preceding idea: "Our opposition to the proposal is firm and unequivocal; in other words, we emphatically decline."

in conclusion, in sum   signal the final statement or section of a text: "In conclusion, the evidence points to a clear and simple solution to the problem."

Sports idioms in business writing.   You'll encounter and use many idioms in business writing, especially ones that come from sports—probably because the competitiveness of the business world makes it easily comparable to sports. Following are some idioms that often come up in business contexts.

a team player someone who acts in the interest of a whole team or group rather than for individual gain: "The best managers are team players, making sure that the credit for a success is shared among everyone who contributed to the effort."

to cover all the bases an expression that comes from baseball, where the fielders must protect all four bases against the other team's runners; as an idiom, it means to be thorough—to deal with all aspects of a situation and consider all possibilities: "Her report was well executed; it covered all the bases and anticipated all possible counterproposals."

across the board a large board at a racetrack displays the names of all the horses in a race; to place an equal bet on every horse is to bet "across the board," so the idiom refers to something affecting all items in a group equally: "Proponents of the new health-care policy insist that it will reduce costs across the board, from doctor visits to medical procedures to prescription medicines."

Considering context. Many idiomatic expressions are quite informal. These can be used effectively in casual conversation or social media, but they are rarely suitable for academic or professional writing. As with all writing, you need to consider your **AUDIENCE** and **PURPOSE** when you use idiomatic expressions.

75–78
73–74

In a conversation with a friend or family member, you might say "let's cut to the chase"; with a business colleague, however, it may be more fitting to suggest that you "get right to the point" or "focus on what's most important."

In a text to a friend, you might say something sounds "like a piece of cake"; with your boss, it would be more suitable to say it sounds "doable" or "easy to do."

On Instagram, you might describe an improv show as "over the top"; in a review for a class, it would be a better choice to say it was "excessive" or "outrageous."

L-4 WORDS OFTEN CONFUSED

When you're tired, do you "lay" down or "lie" down? After dinner, do you eat "desert" or "dessert"? This chapter's dual purpose is to alert you to everyday words that can trip you up and to help you understand the differences between certain words that people tend to confuse.

accept, except "Accept" means "to receive willingly" (accept an award). "Except" as a preposition means "excluding" (all languages except English).

adapt, adopt "Adapt" means "to adjust" (adapt the recipe to be dairy free). "Adopt" means "to take as one's own" (adopt a pet from a shelter).

advice, advise "Advice" means "recommendation" (a lawyer's advice). "Advise" means "to give advice" (We advise you to learn your rights.).

affect, effect "Affect" is usually a verb that means "to produce a change in" (Stress can affect health.). "Effect" is a noun that means "result" (The effects of smoking are well known.). As a verb, it means "to cause" (A mediator works to effect a compromise.).

all right, alright "All right" is the preferred spelling in academic writing.

allusion, illusion "Allusion" means "indirect reference" (an allusion to *Beowulf*). "Illusion" means "false appearance" (an optical illusion).

a lot Always two words, "a lot" means "a large number or amount" or "to a great extent" (a lot of voters; miss her a lot). The phrase is too informal for most academic writing.

among, between Traditionally, "among" is used for three or more items (among the fifty states), while "between" is used with two items (between you and me). In some contexts, however, "between" may be clearer and less awkward (the three-way trade between the Grizzlies, Suns, and Wizards).

amount, number Use "amount" for things you can measure but not count (a large amount of water). Use "number" for things you can count (a number of books).

as, as if, like "Like" introduces a noun or noun phrase (It feels like silk.). To begin a subordinate clause, use "as" or "as if" (Do as I say, not as I do. It seemed as if he had not prepared at all for the briefing.).

bad, badly Use "bad" as an adjective following a linking verb (I feel bad.). Use "badly" as an adverb following an action verb (I play piano badly.).

capital, capitol A "capital" is a city where the government of a state, province, or country is located (Kingston was the first state capital of New York.). A "capitol" is a government building (the dome of the capitol).

cite, sight, site "Cite" means "to give information from a source by quoting, paraphrasing, or summarizing" (cite your sources). "Sight" is the act of seeing or something that is seen (an appalling sight). A "site" is a place (the site of a famous battle).

compose, comprise The parts "compose" the whole (Fifty states compose the Union.). The whole "comprises" the parts (The Union comprises fifty states.).

could of In writing, use "could have" or "could've."

council, counsel "Council" refers to a body of people (the council's vote). "Counsel" means "advice" or "to advise" (her wise counsel; counsel victims of domestic abuse).

criteria, criterion "Criteria" is the plural of "criterion" and takes a plural verb (Certain criteria have been established.).

data "Data," the plural of "datum," technically should take a plural verb (The data arrive from many sources.), but some writers treat it as singular (The data is persuasive.).

desert, dessert "Desert" as a noun means "arid region" (Mojave Desert). As a verb it means "to abandon" (He deserted his post.). "Dessert" is a sweet served toward the end of a meal.

disinterested, uninterested "Disinterested" means "fair" or "unbiased" (a disinterested jury). "Uninterested" means "bored" or "indifferent" (uninterested in election results).

emigrate (from), immigrate (to) "Emigrate" means "to leave one's country" (emigrate from Slovakia). "Immigrate" means "to move to another country" (immigrate to Canada).

etc. The abbreviation "etc." is short for the Latin *et cetera*, "and other things." "Etc." is fine in notes and bibliographies, but avoid using it in your writing in general. Substitute "and so on" if necessary.

everyday, every day "Everyday" is an adjective meaning "ordinary" (After the holidays, we go back to our everyday routine.). "Every day" means "on a daily basis" (Eat three or more servings of fruit every day.).

fewer, less In general, use "fewer" when you refer to things that can be counted (fewer leafblowers). Use "less" when you refer to an amount of something that cannot be counted (less noise).

good, well "Good" is an adjective (a good book; She looks good in that color.). "Well" can be an adjective indicating physical health after a linking verb (She looks well despite her recent surgery.) or an adverb following an action verb (He speaks Spanish well.).

hopefully In academic writing, avoid "hopefully" to mean "it is hoped that"; use it only to mean "with hope" (to make a wish hopefully).

imply, infer "Imply" means "to suggest" (What do you mean to imply?). "Infer" means "to conclude" (We infer that you did not enjoy the trip.).

its, it's "Its" is a possessive pronoun (The movie is rated R because of its language.). "It's" is a contraction of "it is" or "it has" (It's an action film.).

lay, lie "Lay," meaning "to put" or "to place," always takes a direct object (She lays the blanket down.). "Lie," meaning "to recline" or "to be positioned," never takes a direct object (She lies on the blanket.).

lead, led The verb "lead" (rhymes with "bead") means "to guide" (I will lead the way.). "Led" is the past tense and past participle of "lead" (Yesterday I led the way.). The noun "lead" (rhymes with "head") is a type of metal (Use copper pipes instead of lead pipes.).

literally Use "literally" only when you want to stress that you don't mean "figuratively" (While sitting in the grass, he realized that he literally had ants in his pants.).

loose, lose "Loose" means "not fastened securely" or "not fitting tightly" (a pair of loose pants). "Lose" means "to misplace" or "to not win" (lose an earring; lose the race).

man, mankind Use "people," "humans," "humanity," or "humankind" instead.

many, much Use "many" when you refer to things that can be counted (many books). Use "much" to refer to something that cannot be counted (much knowledge).

may of, might of, must of In writing, use "may have," "might have," or "must have."

media "Media," a plural noun, takes a plural verb (Many political scientists believe that the media have a huge effect on voting behavior.). The singular form is "medium" (TV is a popular medium for advertising.).

percent, percentage Use "percent" after a number (80 percent). Use "percentage" after an adjective or article (an impressive percentage; The percentage was impressive.).

principal, principle As a noun, "principal" means "a chief official" or "a sum of money" (in the principal's office; raising the principal for a down payment). As an adjective, it means "most important" (the principal cause of death). "Principle" means "a rule by which one lives" or "a basic truth or doctrine" (against her principles; the principles of life, liberty, and the pursuit of happiness).

raise, rise Meaning "to grow" or "to cause to move upward," "raise" always takes a direct object (He raised his hand.). Meaning "to get up," "rise" never takes a direct object (The sun rises at dawn.).

the reason . . . is because Use "because" or "the reason . . . is (that)," but not both (The reason for the price increase was a poor growing season. Prices increased because of a poor growing season.).

reason why Instead of this redundant phrase, use "the reason" or "the reason that" (Psychologists debate the reasons that some people develop depression and others do not.).

respectfully, respectively "Respectfully" means "in a way that shows respect" (Speak to your elders respectfully.). "Respectively" means "in the order given" (George H. W. Bush and George W. Bush were the forty-first president and the forty-third president, respectively.).

sensual, sensuous "Sensual" suggests sexuality (a sensual caress). "Sensuous" involves pleasing the senses through art, music, and nature (the violin's sensuous solo).

set, sit "Set," meaning "to put" or "to place," takes a direct object (Please set the vase on the table.). "Sit," meaning "to take a seat," does not take a direct object (She sits on the bench.).

should of In writing, use "should have" or "should've."

stationary, stationery "Stationary" means "staying put" (a stationary lab table). "Stationery" means "writing paper" (the college's official stationery).

than, then "Than" is a conjunction used for comparing (She is taller than her mother.). "Then" is an adverb used to indicate a sequence (Finish your work, and then reward yourself.).

that, which Use "that" to add information that is essential for identifying something (The wild horses that live on this island are endangered.). Use "which" to give additional but nonessential information (Abaco Barb horses, which live on an island in the Bahamas, are endangered.).

their, there, they're "Their" signifies possession (their canoe). "There" tells where (Put it there.). "They're" is a contraction of "they are" (They're busy.).

to, too, two "To" is either a preposition that tells direction (Give it to me.) or part of an infinitive (To err is human.). "Too" means "also" or "excessively" (The younger children wanted to help too. It's too cold to sit outside.). "Two" is a number (tea for two).

unique Because "unique" suggests that something is the only one of its kind, avoid adding comparatives or superlatives ("more," "most," "less," "least"), intensifiers (such as "very"), or qualifiers (such as "somewhat").

weather, whether "Weather" refers to atmospheric conditions (dreary weather). "Whether" refers to a choice between options (whether to stay home or go out).

who's, whose "Who's" is a contraction for "who is" or "who has" (Who's the best candidate for the job? Who's already eaten?). "Whose" refers to ownership (Whose keys are these? Tom, whose keys were on the table, had left.).

would of In writing, use "would have" or "would've."

your, you're "Your" signifies possession (your diploma). "You're" is a contraction for "you are" (You're welcome.).

≫ Go to **InQuizitive for Writers** for an interactive activity on words often confused, and practice your skills before applying them in your writing.

L-5 PREPOSITIONS

A great session with your favorite video game. You've finally reached the cave of the dying wise man who will tell you the location of the key that you need. He points a long, bony finger toward a table and struggles to rasp out one word, "jar." You're down to your last life. You only have one chance. Is the key *in* the jar? *under* it? *behind* it? Oh, that one little preposition makes all the difference!

Real life is seldom this dramatic, but accurate prepositions do make a difference. Prepositions are words like "at," "from," "in," and "with" that describe relationships, often in time and space: "at work, in an hour," "with your mom." English has a large number of prepositions compared to other languages, and sometimes it's difficult to choose the right one.

Prepositions are always followed by noun or pronoun **OBJECTS**. (You can't just "write about"; you have to write about something.) Together a preposition and its object form a prepositional phrase. In the following examples, the prepositions are underlined and the prepositional phrases are italicized.

Glossary

▶ This is a book *about writing.*

▶ We're *in the midst of a literacy revolution.* —Andrea Lunsford

▶ Research is formalized curiosity. It is poking and prying *with a purpose.*
                                                    —Zora Neale Hurston

▶ *In the years between 1969 and 1978,* I lived, worked, and played *with the children and their families in Roadville and Trackton.*
                                                    —Shirley Brice Heath

The table and lists that follow summarize the basic differences in the ways to use three common prepositions—"at," "on," and "in."

AT a specific point	●	at home at the gym at noon
ON a line	——	on the avenue on the table on a specific day
IN a shape or enclosure	⬭	in a container in the park in two hours

Prepositions of place

AT   *a specific address or business:* at 33 Parkwood Street, *at* McDonald's
     a public building or unnamed business: at the library, *at* the gym
     a general place: at home, *at* work

ON *a surface:* on the floor, on the grass, on the wall
a street: on Ninth Street, on Western Avenue
an electronic medium: on the radio, on the web
public transportation: on the bus, on an airplane

IN *a container, room, or area:* in the jar, in my office, in the woods
a geographic location: in San Diego, in the Midwest
a printed work: in the newspaper, in Chapter 3

Prepositions of time

AT *a specific time:* at 4:30 p.m., at sunset, at lunchtime

ON *a day of the week:* on Friday
an exact date: on September 12
a holiday: on Thanksgiving, on Veterans Day

IN *a defined time period:* in an hour, in three years
a month, season, or year: in June, in the fall, in 2025
a part of the day: in the morning, in the evening

L-6 UNNECESSARY WORDS

"At this point in time." "Really unique." "In a manner of speaking." Each of these phrases includes words that are unnecessary or says something that could be expressed more concisely. This chapter shows you how to edit your own writing to make every word count.

L-6a "Really," "Very," and Other Empty Words

Intensifiers such as "really" and "very" are used to strengthen what we say. Qualifiers such as "apparently," "possibly," "seem," or "tend to" are a way to soften what we say. It's fine to use words like these when they are necessary. Sometimes, however, they are not. You shouldn't say that something is "very unique," because things either are unique or they're not; there's no need to add the intensifier. And why say that someone is "really smart" when you could say that they are "brilliant"?

▶ Accepted by five colleges, Jackson ~~seems to be facing an apparently very~~ difficult decision.

(edit: replace with "is facing a")

L-6b "There Is," "It Is"

EXPLETIVE constructions like "there is" and "it is" can be useful ways to introduce and emphasize an idea, but sometimes they only add unnecessary words. Eliminating them in such cases can make the sentence more concise and also make its verb stronger.

Glossary

▶ ~~It is necessary for~~ Americans today _{must} to learn to speak more than one language.

▶ ~~There are four~~ ^{Four} large moons and more than thirty small ones ~~that~~ orbit Jupiter.

In certain contexts, however, expletives can be the best choices. Imagine the ending of *The Wizard of Oz* if Dorothy had said "No place is like home" instead of the more emphatic—and sentimental—"There's no place like home."

L-6c Wordy Phrases

Many common phrases use several words when a single word will do. Editing out such wordy phrases will make your writing more concise and easier to read.

WORDY	CONCISE
as far as . . . is concerned	concerning
at the time that	when
at this point in time	now
in spite of the fact that	although, though
in the event that	if
in view of the fact that	because, since

▶ ~~Due to the fact that~~ ^{Because} Professor Lee retired, the animal sciences department now lacks a neurology specialist.

L-6d Redundancies

Eliminate words and phrases that are unnecessary for your meaning.

▶ Painting the house purple ~~in color~~ will make it stand out from the many white houses in town.

▶ Dashing ~~quickly~~ into the street to retrieve the ball, the young girl was almost hit by a car.

▶ Campers should know how much wood is ~~sufficient~~ enough for a fire to burn all night.

L-7 ADJECTIVES AND ADVERBS

Adjectives and adverbs are words that describe other words, adding important information and detail. When Dave Barry writes that the Beatles "were the *coolest* thing you had ever seen" and that "they were *smart*; they were *funny*; they didn't take themselves *seriously*," the adjectives and adverbs (italicized here) make clear why he "wanted *desperately* to be a Beatle." This chapter will help you use adjectives and adverbs in your own writing.

L-7a Choosing between Adjectives and Adverbs

Glossary
HB-25–31 ⭐

Adjectives are words used to modify **NOUNS** and **PRONOUNS**. They usually answer one of these questions: Which? What kind? How many?

▶ *Two* rows of *ancient oak* trees lined the *narrow* driveway.

▶ *Many* years of testing will be needed to determine whether the *newest* theories are *correct*.

▶ If you are craving something *sweet,* have a piece of fruit.

HB-10–21 ⭐

Adverbs are words used to modify **VERBS**, adjectives, and other adverbs. They usually answer one of these questions: How? When? Where? Why? Under what conditions? To what degree? Although many adverbs end in -ly (tentatively, immediately), many do not (now, so, soon, then, very).

▶ Emergency personnel must respond *quickly* when an ambulance arrives.

▶ Environmentalists are *increasingly* worried about Americans' consumption of fossil fuels.

▶ If the governor had known that the news cameras were on, she would not have responded *so angrily*.

"Well" and "good"

Use "well" as an adjective to describe physical health; use "good" to describe emotional health or appearance.

▶ Some herbs can keep you feeling ~~good~~ ^{well} when everyone else has the flu.

▶ Staying healthy can make you feel *good* about yourself.

"Good" should not be used as an adverb; use "well."

▶ Because both Williams sisters play tennis so ~~good,~~ ^{well,} they've frequently competed against each other in major tournaments.

"Bad" and "badly"

Use the adjective "bad" after a **LINKING VERB** to describe an emotional state or feeling. In such cases, the adjective describes the subject.

Glossary

▶ Arguing with your parents can make you feel *bad*.

Use the adverb "badly" to describe an **ACTION VERB**.

Glossary

▶ Arguing with your parents late at night can make you sleep *badly*.

L-7b Using Comparatives and Superlatives

Most adjectives and adverbs have three forms: the positive, the comparative, and the superlative. The comparative is used to compare two things, and the superlative is used to compare three or more things.

COMPARATIVE   Who was the *better* quarterback, Eli Manning or his brother?

SUPERLATIVE   Many Colts fans still consider Peyton Manning the *best* quarterback ever.

The comparative and superlative of most adjectives are formed by adding the endings -er and -est: "slow," "slower," "slowest." Longer adjectives and most adverbs use "more" and "most" (or "less" and "least"): "clearly," "more clearly," "most clearly." If you add -er or -est to an adjective or adverb, do not also use "more" or "most" (or *less* and "least").

▶ The ~~most~~ lowest point in the United States is in Death Valley.

A few adjectives and adverbs have irregular comparatives and superlatives.

	COMPARATIVE	SUPERLATIVE
good, well	better	best
bad, badly	worse	worst
far (distance)	farther	farthest
far (time or amount)	further	furthest
little (amount)	less	least
many, much, some	more	most

L-7c Placing Modifiers Carefully

Place adjectives, adverbs, and other **MODIFIERS** as close as possible to the word or words they modify so that readers clearly understand the connection.

Glossary

▶ The doctor explained advances in cancer treatment to the families of patients. ~~at the seminar.~~   *at the seminar*

The doctor, not the patients, is at the seminar.

> *Before the anesthesiologist arrived, the*
> ~~The~~ surgeons assured the patient that they intended to make only two
> small incisions. ~~before the anesthesiologist arrived.~~

The original sentence suggests that the incisions will be made without anesthesia, surely not the case.

To avoid ambiguity, position limiting modifiers such as "almost," "even," "just," "merely," and "only" next to the word or phrase they modify—and be careful that your meaning is clear. See how the placement of "only" can result in two completely different meanings.

> *only*
> A triple-threat athlete, Martha ~~only~~ played soccer in college.

> *only*
> A triple-threat athlete, Martha ~~only~~ played soccer in college.

Be careful that your placement of "not" doesn't result in a meaning you don't intend.

> *not*
> When I attended college, every student was ~~not~~ using a laptop.

Dangling modifiers

Modifiers are said to be dangling when they do not clearly modify any particular word in the sentence. You can usually fix a dangling modifier by adding a **SUBJECT** that the modifier clearly refers to, either in the rest of the sentence or in the modifier itself.

Glossary

> *the doctor comforted*
> Speaking simply and respectfully, many people ~~felt comforted by the~~
> *with her*
> ~~doctor's~~ presentation.

The doctor was speaking, not the other people.

> *I was*
> While running to catch the bus, the shoulder strap on my bag broke.

Split infinitives

Glossary

When you place a modifier between "to" and the base form of the verb in an **INFINITIVE**, you create a split infinitive: to carefully slice. When a split infinitive is awkward or makes a sentence difficult to follow, put the modifier elsewhere in the sentence.

> *rigorously*
> Professional soccer players are expected to ~~rigorously~~ train every day.

Sometimes, however, a split infinitive is easier to follow.

▶ One famous split infinitive appears in the opening sequence of *Star Trek*: "to boldly go where no man has gone before."

≫ Go to **InQuizitive for Writers** for an interactive activity on misplaced/dangling modifiers, and practice your skills before applying them in your writing.

L-8 ARTICLES

"A," "an," and "the" are articles, words used before a noun to indicate whether something is general or specific. Use "a" or "an" with nouns whose specific identity is not known to your audience: I'm reading a great book. Use "the" with nouns whose specific identity is known to your audience, whether the noun describes something specific: the new book by Colson Whitehead—or is something you've mentioned: Beverly is almost finished writing her book; the book will be published next year. Sometimes no article is needed: Books are now available in print and as ebooks.

L-8a When to Use "A" or "An"

Use "a" or "an" before singular **COUNT NOUNS** referring to something that's not specific or that you're mentioning to your audience for the first time. Count nouns name things that can be counted: one poodle, two poodles. Use "a" before consonant sounds: a tangerine, a university; use "an" before vowel sounds: an orange, an hour.

Glossary

▶ *An apartment* near campus might be rather expensive.
  Any apartment near campus would be expensive, not just a specific one.

▶ I put *a carrot,* some tomatoes, and a little parsley in the salad.
  This carrot is being mentioned for the first time.

Do not use "a" or "an" before a **NONCOUNT NOUN**. Noncount nouns name abstract items (respect, curiosity) and liquids and masses that cannot be measured with numbers (milk, sand, rice).

Glossary

▶ Our team could use *some encouragement* from the coach.

▶ The last thing Portland needs this week is *more rain.*

L-8b When to Use "The"

Use "the" before any nouns whose identity is clear to your audience and before superlatives.

▶ Mando ordered a cheeseburger and french fries and asked for *the burger* to be well done.

The article "the" is used because it refers to a cheeseburger that's already been mentioned: the one that Mando ordered.

▶ His friends had raved about *the fries* at this restaurant.

The specific fries are identified: they are the ones at this restaurant.

▶ His friends were right; these were *the best fries* he'd ever eaten.

"The" is used before a superlative: these were the best fries ever.

Use "the" with most plural proper nouns (the Adirondack Mountains, the Philippines, the Dallas Cowboys) and with singular proper nouns in the following categories.

LARGE BODIES OF WATER   the Arctic Ocean, the Mississippi River

GOVERNMENT BODIES   the US Congress, the Canadian Parliament

HISTORICAL PERIODS   the Renaissance, the Jazz Age

LANDMARKS   the Empire State Building, the Taj Mahal

REGIONS   the East Coast, the Middle East, the Mojave Desert

RELIGIOUS ENTITIES, TEXTS, AND LEADERS   the Roman Catholic Church, the Qur'an, the Dalai Lama

L-8c When No Article Is Needed

No article is needed before noncount nouns (salt, imagination, happiness) and plural count nouns (ideas, puppies) when they refer to something "in general."

▶ *Milk* and *eggs* are on sale this week.

▶ *Information* wants to be free.   —Stewart Brand, *Whole Earth Review*

▶ Be less curious about people and more curious about *ideas.*
                                                            —Marie Curie

Brand and Curie refer to information and ideas in general, not a specific kind of information or specific ideas.

No article is needed with most singular proper nouns: Barack Obama, Lake Titicaca, Yosemite.

L-9 RESPECTFUL AND INCLUSIVE LANGUAGE

"Black." "White." "Hearing." "American." All simple words—ones we know and probably say routinely. But when we use them to refer to people, we need to use them very carefully. That's sometimes easier said than done, because these terms are both important—for their potential to offend or cause harm—and fluid, since the customs and preferences for their use can shift rapidly.

This chapter offers advice for using language that is respectful and inclusive—and that will build common ground with those we wish to reach. It's not intended to give concrete rules about "right" or "wrong" terms; instead, it aims to provide you with information and context about some common words that are used to refer to people so that you can choose the ones most suitable to your own writing situation—and most respectful toward the people you're writing about.

It can be helpful to consider the following questions when deciding whether to use a particular word:

- **Is it** *relevant?* What does the word contribute to your point? For example, if you're talking about a physical therapist's treatment plan for his patients, there would be no reason to mention his sexual orientation, whatever it may be—you would refer to him simply as "the physical therapist," not "the gay physical therapist."

- **Is it** *precise?* Is the word as precise as possible? If you've decided it's relevant to identify someone as Asian, state their country or region of origin. There's a lot of difference, for example, between Cambodia and North Korea.

- **Is it** *respectful?* In other words, do the people you're referring to use it to describe themselves publicly? The most reliable way to know is to ask them. If you can't do that or if you think it would make someone uncomfortable, look on *Instagram, Facebook,* or other sites where they may provide that information. If you can't verify through a reliable source, your best option may be to omit the word.

For some of the terms you'll find in this chapter, there are other, more informal words that are sometimes used between members of a group to refer to themselves. These terms can be deeply offensive, though, when they're used by outsiders. You can probably think of some words that are considered either slurs or reclaimed labels depending on who is using them. If a name or description doesn't apply to you personally, we strongly recommend that you avoid using it when referring to somebody else.

L-9a Avoiding Stereotypes

Stereotypes are generalizations about groups of people and as such can offend because they presume that all members of a group are the same. The writer Geeta Kothari explains how she reacts to a seemingly neutral assumption about Indians: "Indians eat lentils. I understand this as an absolute, a decree from an unidentifiable authority that watches and judges me."

We're all familiar with stereotypes based on sex or race, but stereotypes exist about other characteristics as well: age, body type, education, income, gender identity, occupation, physical ability, political affiliation, region, religion, sexual orientation, and more. Be careful not to make any broad generalizations about any group—even neutral or seemingly positive ones (that Asian students work especially hard, for example, or that Republicans are particularly patriotic).

L-9b Using Person-First and Identity-First Language

Glossary

There are two general approaches to describing someone with a condition or disability: person first and identity first. **PERSON-FIRST** descriptions focus on the individual; some people favor person-first language because it avoids reducing a person to a condition.

► All-night study sessions aren't recommended for ~~epileptics~~, since lack
  of sleep is a common trigger for seizures.

  students with epilepsy

Glossary

IDENTITY-FIRST descriptions focus on the condition—"an amputee," for example, rather than "a person with an amputation." Some people favor identity-first terms because they view the condition as an intrinsic part of their identity.

► I am not a "person with autism." I am an autistic person. —Jim Sinclair

The choice about whether to use person-first or identity-first language comes up often when referring to people with disabilities, but it can come up in other contexts as well. Some common examples follow. Regardless of which approach you take, use the terms and descriptions that the people you're referring to use for themselves.

"experiencing homelessness," "homeless." To avoid a stigmatizing or disparaging description of people who do not have homes, we recommend using person-first language—for example, "students without homes" or "students experiencing homelessness" rather than "homeless students"—unless you know that the people you're referring to use other language. Some people use "unhoused" or "houseless," which recognize that someone who lives in their car, for example, has some kind of a home despite not having fixed housing.

"depressed" / "anxious." The words "depressed" and "anxious" pop up often in casual conversation to mean sad, unhappy, or worried. However, "depression" and "anxiety" are specific terms for mental health conditions that can be serious and debilitating, so avoid using these words to refer to someone who doesn't have a mental health condition. If you are writing about someone who does, we recommend that you use person-first language (unless you know that they prefer identity-first language): "the veteran who has depression" or "the veteran experiencing depression" instead of "the depressed veteran."

"autistic people," "people with autism." "Autistic" is an adjective that refers to someone on the autism spectrum, which is characterized by a range of neurological differences that affect how people process information, engage with their environment, and relate to other people. Many autistic people use identity-first rather than person-first language—"the autistic teacher" rather than "the teacher with autism"—because they experience autism as an intrinsic part of their identity. While the *American Psychological Association's Diagnostic and Statistical Manual*, 5th ed., classifies autism as a disorder, autistic rights activists emphasize that autism is characterized by differences, not deficits.

"deaf," "Deaf" / "hard of hearing." The term "deaf" is used to describe a person who is substantially or completely unable to hear. "Hard of hearing" describes people who can process some sound. Many deaf and hard-of-hearing people communicate using signed languages. There is a robust Deaf culture based on shared languages and experiences; the word "Deaf" (with a capital *D*) is often used to refer to that culture and the people who participate in it. Many deaf people use identity-first language ("the deaf artist") rather than person-first language ("the artist who is deaf"), because deafness is an intrinsic part of their identity. "Hearing impaired" is considered stigmatizing, so avoid using it.

L-9c Using Language That's Precise and Respectful

When it's relevant to specify an aspect of someone's identity, consider which words will be both precise and respectful. These sections define some common terms and provide advice for thinking about how to use them. If you are wondering about a word not listed, consult one of the many freely available inclusive language guides. We recommend languageplease.org.

Race, Ethnicity, Nationality

"African American," "Black." "African American" and "Black" are commonly used to refer to people of African ancestry in the United States. Not all African American people identify as Black (consider some people from Morocco or South Africa); not all Black people are African American (people from the Caribbean or South America, for example); and not all Black people in the United States are Americans (such as the British actor Idris Elba). "Black" is often used to denote a shared cultural and ethnic identity in the United States, and some prefer "Black" because it doesn't presume a specific nationality. Others identify with a specific country or ethnicity—for example, "Haitian American." Never assume someone's race or ethnicity without confirming how they identify. You may see "Negro" or "colored" in old publications, but those words are not used today.

"Black," "black" / "Brown," "brown" / "White," "white." These three broad words are used—each in different ways—to refer to a variety of racial and ethnic categories. "Black" (with a capital *B*) is used by many to recognize the shared history and cultural and ethnic identity of Black people in the United States; capitalizing *B* is in line with English conventions for ethnicities (Cajun, Welsh, for example)—and can be seen to express a measure of respect. Others prefer lowercase *b* to signal the varied and diverse groups "black" encompasses.

"Brown," when referring to people from Latin America, South Asia, or the Middle East, is often used to express solidarity among people of color. It's sometimes capitalized, though others argue against its capitalization (and its use at all), arguing that it's an imprecise word for such a varied group and doesn't convey the same sense of shared history and experience as "Black" does in the United States.

Some capitalize "White" to recognize it as a cultural identity in the United States and to acknowledge that not capitalizing might indicate "white" is the default. One argument against capitalizing "White" is to avoid association with White supremacist and neo-Nazi rhetoric. (See P-8a for more on capitalizing "Black" and "White.")

"Asian" / "Asian American" / "Southeast Asian" / "Pacific Islander" / "AAPI." The continent of Asia is vast, encompassing nearly fifty countries and many more nationalities and ethnicities. "Asian" may refer generally to someone from any of those nations, and "Asian American" recognizes both ancestry and US citizenship. "Southeast Asian" refers to the nationalities and ethnicities in the area that includes Thailand, Laos, Cambodia, Vietnam, Myanmar, Indonesia, Malaysia, the Philippines, and others. People from one of the island nations of the Pacific—Guam, Fiji, and Tonga, among others—are known as Pacific Islanders. When describing an individual, aim to be specific instead of general ("Japanese" instead of "Asian," for example). "AAPI," which stands for "Asian American and Pacific Islanders," is mainly useful in describing large-scale trends or conditions rather than individuals.

"South Asian." "South Asian" refers to people with roots in the nations in and around the Indian subcontinent, including India, Pakistan, Bangladesh, Sri Lanka, Nepal, Bhutan, and others. Afghanistan is also sometimes placed in this group. These nations have diverse populations with numerous ethnic and religious groups. When you're referring to someone whose ethnic or national identity is important to mention, be as specific as possible: Nepalese instead of South Asian, for example.

"Chicano/a/x." Some Americans of Mexican descent use "Chicano," "Chicana," and "Chicanx" to describe their ethnic identity. A large portion of the US Southwest (from California to Texas) was part of Mexico until 1848. People there never immigrated to the United States; they were already here. Chicano/a/x identity reflects Mexican, US, and Indigenous cultures. The terms are specific and are not interchangeable with "Hispanic" or "Latino/a/x."

"Hispanic" / "Latino/a/x." "Hispanic," "Latino," "Latina," and "Latinx" refer to people whose roots are in Spain or Latin America. Broadly, "Hispanic" emphasizes ties to Spain; "Latino," "Latina," and "Latinx" emphasize ties to Latin America—that is, South and Central America, Mexico, and many Caribbean nations, including Cuba, Puerto Rico, and the Dominican Republic. These words are used only in the United States, and they have no "official" definitions. Some people may identify as both Hispanic and Latino/a/x; some may identify as only one or the other. When possible, specify someone's national origin (Honduran, Salvadoran, Mexican, etc.) instead of using these general words.

"Indigenous," "First Nations," "Native American." "Indigenous" refers broadly to the people who first inhabited a place. For Indigenous people in North America, "First Nations" is used in Canada, "Indigenous" is used in Mexico, and both of those terms are used in the United States. "Native American" is still sometimes used in the United States, but it's becoming less common. Don't use the word "Indian" when referring to Indigenous people. When possible, it's best to specify the tribe or population someone belongs to—Miwok, Ojibwe, or Cherokee, for example.

"BIPOC," "people of color." "BIPOC" is an acronym that stands for Black, Indigenous, (and other) people of color. "People of color" and "BIPOC" are used to refer to people who are not White. These terms tend to be used in discussions of social, political, or economic conditions where race is a factor. However, in many cases these terms are too vague and general, lumping together groups that are diverse. Use specific words to identify the groups you're referring to whenever possible.

Gender, Sex, Sexuality

Sexist language is language that stereotypes or ignores women, men, or people of other genders—or that unnecessarily calls attention to someone's gender. You should eliminate such language from your writing. In particular, avoid nouns that include "man" when you're referring to people who may not be men.

INSTEAD OF	USE
man, mankind	humankind, humanity, humans, people
salesman	salesperson, sales rep
fireman	firefighter
congressman	representative, member of Congress
male nurse	nurse
woman truck driver	truck driver

"Latina," "Latino," "Latinx" / "Chicana," "Chicano," "Chicanx." Many Spanish words are masculine or feminine in gender: *tasa* (f "cup"); *vaso* (m "glass"). Masculine gender was once the default and was assumed to include everyone. That's no longer the case, since it excludes women and nonbinary people. The words people use to describe themselves may carry the -o, -a, or -x endings—for example, "My roommates are a Latina drummer and a Chicanx baker." Those who favor -x argue that it is inclusive and deemphasizes gender where it's irrelevant. But many people don't use -x, in part because it breaks Spanish pronunciation rules, but also because it's not widely used by the people it's meant to describe. Some recommend the -e ending ("Latine," "Chicane") as a better gender-neutral option, but it's not yet commonly used in English.

"LGBTQ." The letters in the acronym "LGBTQ" stand for lesbian, gay, bisexual, transgender, and queer. Q can also mean questioning. Variants include the addition of other letters (like IA for intersex and asexual) or a plus sign ("+"). As an umbrella term, "LGBTQ" can be useful in referring to organizations or groups; when writing about an individual, use whatever word that person uses. Make sure the person is comfortable being identified with that word, though, since outing someone may have harmful consequences. Briefly, "lesbian" refers to a woman who is attracted to other women; "gay man" is a man who is attracted to other men. "Gay" can be a general term that refers to anyone who is attracted to a person of the same sex; some lesbians also identify as gay. "Bisexual" refers to someone whose attractions are not limited to a single gender. See the next entry for information about the term "transgender." "Queer" is an ungendered adjective that is used by some people in the LGBTQ community. Others avoid it because historically it has been used as a slur, and it can still be offensive when used by people outside of that community.

"transgender" / "nonbinary" / "cisgender." "Transgender" is an adjective used to refer to someone whose gender identity is not aligned with the sex or gender they were assigned at birth. The word is often shortened to "trans." A trans man is a man who was assigned female at birth; a trans woman is a woman who was assigned male at birth. Unless someone's gender identity is relevant to what you're writing, it needn't be mentioned. Some people identify as "nonbinary" (or "enby"), meaning they are not exclusively female or male. A nonbinary person may have multiple genders or no gender, or they may move fluidly among multiple genders. The adjective "cisgender" (abbreviated "cis") is used to refer to someone whose gender identity aligns with the sex or gender they were assigned at birth.

This information on inclusive and respectful language is ever evolving. Do you have a suggested update or addition? Please let us know at composition@wwnorton.com.

L-10 PRONOUNS AND GENDER

"I like key lime pie." Anyone can make that statement. It may or may not be true, but that first-person pronoun "I" always works, regardless of the gender of the speaker. The same is true for "You are amazing!" That "you" could apply to anyone; the second-person pronouns in English don't indicate gender in any way. Ditto the third-person plural. You could say, "We never saw them play," and the "them" could refer to the Chicago Cubs, the Boston Philharmonic, or the Williams sisters at Wimbledon. Gender wouldn't matter a bit. The only place it matters in English is with third-person singular pronouns: "he," "she," and now, "they." The words are few, but their importance is enormous. This chapter will help you with pronouns and gender in your academic work.

L-10a "He," "She," "They"

Writers once used "he," "him," and other masculine pronouns as a default to refer to people whose sex was unknown to them. Today such usage is not accepted—and it is no way to build common ground. Here are some alternatives.

Replace a singular noun or pronoun with a plural noun

▶ Before ~~anyone~~ travelers can leave the country, ~~he~~ they must have a passport or some other official documentation.

Eliminate the pronoun altogether

▶ Before ~~anyone can leave~~ leaving the country, ~~he~~ a traveler must have a passport or some other official documentation.

Use singular "they"

HB-65–67 ★

Increasingly, **SINGULAR "THEY"** is being used to refer to a person whose gender is unknown or not relevant to the context. This usage is becoming more and more accepted in academic writing; check with your instructor about whether it's acceptable in your writing.

▶ Someone left ~~her~~ their clothes in the washing machine overnight.

Use "he or she"

Some people use "he or she" or other masculine and feminine pronouns joined by "or." However, since not everyone identifies as either a "he" or a "she," this is not the most inclusive option. Also, using it repeatedly may become awkward.

▶ Before anyone can leave the country, he *or she* must have a passport or some other official documentation.

≫ Go to **InQuizitive for Writers** for an interactive activity on pronouns that don't agree with their antecedents, and practice your skills before applying them in your writing.

L-10b Singular "They"

There are two ways to use singular "they": generic and specific. The generic singular "they" has been used for a long time—centuries, really, and even by such prominent authors as Shakespeare and Jane Austen—to refer to someone whose gender is unknown or not relevant to the context. This usage is becoming more and more accepted in academic writing.

▶ Everyone drops their phone sometimes.

The other way of using singular "they" is specific; that is, to refer to *someone* specific. Some people who are nonbinary, trans, gender-nonconforming or who identify as neither exclusively female nor exclusively male designate "they" as their third-person singular pronoun. You've no doubt heard or read some objections to either or both of these applications; it's not easy to change routines or habits, especially language habits. Many of the objections focus on confusion, forgetting that some confusion is already an everyday part of English.

Consider this: a friend asks, "Would you like to come over for dinner on Thursday?" An ordinary and straightforward question, perhaps, but the invitee may be left wondering. Is the invitation meant just for me? Is my spouse included? Kids too? The conversation leading up to the invitation—the context—might make it clear, or it might not. The dual use of the pronoun "you" for both singular and plural reference is something English users take in stride, even though it occasionally causes confusion.

Confusion in conversation can be cleared up easily—we just ask. Writing, however, requires more attention to clarity since readers can't just ask. The two uses of singular "they" present particular challenges for writers, and this section offers some strategies for clearly distinguishing between singular and plural "they" in your academic writing. Context, as always, will do a lot of the work.

Here are a few examples from a March 2020 *Time* magazine article profiling various couples touched by the early circumstances of the COVID-19 pandemic. These examples are describing the couple Rowan and Emily Tekampe:

▶ When Rowan Tekampe found out they may have been exposed to COVID-19, their fever, cough, shortness of breath and body aches suddenly seemed more serious.

A possible interpretation at first glance is that Rowan found out about the exposure of some other people, but the symptoms described here very clearly belong to just one person. A bit later, the article details a painful conversation between Rowan and Emily:

▶ They sat down with their wife Emily . . . and told her she needed to leave the apartment and stay with her dad.

No confusion there. Rowan and Emily are spouses; Rowan's pronoun is "they," and Emily's is "she." Let's look at one more example two paragraphs later:

▶ They've been apart for weeks now, but Emily makes Rowan text her their temperature every hour.

The first instance of "they" in the sentence clearly refers to both spouses. How do we know? We rely on our understanding of the word "apart," which wouldn't make sense applied to one single person. The second instance, the possessive case "their," refers to Rowan's temperature. We are already familiar with Rowan's pronoun from previous context, and we're not surprised that Emily would want frequent updates from Rowan. Another clue is that "temperature" is singular.

Just as we are accustomed to "you" having both a singular and plural application, we will become accustomed in time to the extended applications of "they" in all its forms.

"Themself," "Themselves"

The account of Rowan and Emily doesn't mention this detail, but it could have: Emily would have liked to accompany Rowan to the clinic, but they had to go by themself. "Themself"? Not "themselves"? In fact, at this formative stage in the acceptable use of singular "they," both forms are in use, and logical arguments exist for each option. **MLA**, **APA**, and Chicago accept both forms, as do the *Oxford English Dictionary* and merriam-webster.com. Here are a few examples from other sources:

MLA 542-94
APA 595-633

▶ It's all about letting someone be <u>themself</u>.

—Cambridge Dictionary

▶ There's just something that feels really good about buying your produce from someone who grows it <u>themselves</u>.

—Emily Boyes, *The Hub@TTU,* November 2019

As this book goes to press, the singular form "themself" may be slightly more common, but only time and usage will determine which form will gain more acceptance and become the preferred word. In other words, it's really up to all of us to choose.

L-10c "Ze," "Hir," and Other Coined Pronouns

In addition to singular "they," some people who are nonbinary, trans, or gender-nonconforming or who don't identify as exclusively male or female use coined or invented pronouns, such as "ze" and "hir" and "xe," when being referred to in the third person. Coined pronouns aren't as widely used as singular "they," but there are people who use them, and in fact, such pronouns have been around for centuries. A few of the more common ones are "ze," "hir," "hir"/"hirs" and "xe," "xem," "xyr"/"xyrs," but there are many others.

▶ Jackie brought <u>hir</u> sweater to dinner because <u>ze</u> wanted to eat outside.

L-10d What's Your Pronoun?

"What's your pronoun?" has become a common question. In fact, many people include their pronouns in their email signatures, résumés, and social media profiles. It's a reasonable question to ask of anybody, not just those you think may be trans or nonbinary. Regardless of your personal opinions about others' pronouns, respectful communication requires that we all make every effort to refer to people by the pronouns they indicate for themselves. Are you sometimes unsure which pronoun to use when you refer to someone? You're not alone. When language or grammar rules are uncertain, let courtesy and sensitivity guide you. If you don't know what pronouns someone uses and you're in a situation in which pronouns are relevant, the best thing to do is ask. Keep in mind, though, that not everyone may be comfortable sharing their pronouns or their gender identity. If you feel comfortable sharing your own pronouns, volunteering them can help make others feel at ease. If you don't know a person's pronouns, and you can't or don't think you should ask, best to use singular "they."

L-11 ENGLISHES

"English? Who needs that? I'm never going to England," declares Homer in an early episode of *The Simpsons*. Sorry, Homer. Anyone using this book does need English. In fact, most of us need a variety of Englishes—the academic English we're expected to use at school, the specialized English we use in particular academic and professional fields, and the colloquial English we use in various other communities we belong to.

In fact, you probably speak several other Englishes—and other languages too—in your everyday life, each with its own set of varieties. In academic writing, as in everyday conversation, you may sometimes add a word, phrase, or more from another variety or language. The practices of code switching, or shifting from one language or variety to another, and code meshing, which involves weaving together different languages or varieties, can be powerful tools for adding emphasis, connecting with an audience, or illustrating a point. This chapter offers some guidance in using different varieties of English effectively and appropriately in your academic writing. For example, you can probably say "that doesn't matter to me" in at least half a dozen different ways, but how do you choose which way would work best at any particular moment? In conversation, you make that choice so quickly that you rarely even notice you're doing it. You consider the context of the conversation, the purpose of your statement, and your relationship with the person you're talking with. For academic writing, your decision to mix languages and varieties is made in the same way: thinking about your **PURPOSE** and **AUDIENCE** first.

73–74
75–78

L-11a Edited Academic English

This is the variety used—and expected—in most academic and professional contexts. "Academic" means scholarly, precise, somewhat formal in manner, and suitable for use in college classes and publications. As you'll see in this chapter, other styles may be used in some academic contexts for specific reasons, but the overall tone of academic writing is factual, straightforward, and undramatic. "Edited" means that it is carefully written and polished. And "English"—well, you already know what that is.

L-11b Formal and Informal English

Some of the variation in English comes from levels of formality. Academic writing is usually formal. The tone is serious; information is stated directly. These characteristics display your competence and authority. The most informal language, on the other hand, tends to be found in the ways we talk with our close friends and relatives; those conversations are full of **IDIOMS**, slang, and personal code that's specific to the people talking.

★ HB-40–44

Words with the same basic meaning can convey very different messages when they have different levels of formality—and so the words you choose should always be guided by what's suitable to your **AUDIENCE**, **TOPIC**, and the larger **RHETORICAL SITUATION**.

■ 75–78
∴ 352–53
■ 71

See, for example, two headlines that appeared in two different newspapers after quarterback Andrew Luck announced his retirement from the NFL:

▶ Colts Quarterback Andrew Luck Retires from NFL

—Wall Street Journal

▶ LUCK RUNS OUT: Colts QB Shocks Football World, Retires at 29

—New York Post

The first headline is from the *Wall Street Journal*, a newspaper dedicated to business news, with an audience of corporate and government executives. Its tone is professional and businesslike, and its English is formal. The second is from the *New York Post*, a daily tabloid newspaper known for its sensationalist headlines; its English is informal, going for laughs and making a play on words with Andrew Luck's last name.

In the cartoon below, the adult understands quite well what the child is saying; she's merely suggesting a more formal and polite—and suitable—way to express his judgment of the painting.

"Instead of 'It sucks' you could say, 'It doesn't speak to me.'"

Mixing formal and informal

Occasionally mixing in an informal element—a playful image, an unexpected bit of slang—can enliven formal writing. For example, in a book about the alimentary canal, science writer Mary Roach gives detailed, well-researched descriptions of all aspects of digestion, including the anatomy of the digestive system. Although her topic is serious, she stirs in some irreverent **METAPHORS** and surprising comparisons along the way, as this description of the esophagus shows.

▶ The esophagus is a thin, pink stretchable membrane, a biological bubble gum.

—Mary Roach, *Gulp: Adventures on the Alimentary Canal*

Such everyday imagery makes a potentially dry subject come to life. What's more, the information is easier to remember. Quick: What color is your esophagus? You remembered, didn't you?

L-11c English across Fields

If you've ever listened in on a group of nurses, software engineers, lawyers, or taxi drivers, you probably heard words you didn't understand, jokes you didn't think were funny. All professional fields have their own specialized language.

Restaurant staff, for example, have shorthand for relaying food orders and seating information. In this example from an essay about blue-collar work, UCLA professor Mike Rose describes a restaurant where his mother was a waitress:

▶ *Fry four on two*, my mother would say as she clipped a check onto the metal wheel. Her tables were *deuces, four-tops,* or *six-tops* according to their size; seating areas also were nicknamed. The *racetrack,* for instance, was the fast-turnover front section. Lingo conferred authority and signaled know-how.

—Mike Rose, "Blue-Collar Brilliance"

You might not know what "deuces" or "four-tops" are (or maybe you do), but it's language Rose's mother knew her colleagues would understand. On the one hand, specialized language allows professionals to do their work with greater ease and efficiency; on the other hand, it marks and helps construct a community around a certain field of work.

L-11d English across Regions

Do you ever turn on the subtitles when watching British TV shows? The characters are definitely speaking English, but you may have a hard time understanding them. Every region has its own accent, of course, but there may also be words and expressions that are unfamiliar or mean something different to those who don't live there. In Australia (and parts of Wisconsin), for example, a "bubbler" is a drinking fountain. In India, the "hall" is the part of the house known in the United States as the living room.

In the US South, "y'all" is the way many folks say "you all." Country singer Lainey Wilson, a native of Louisiana, uses "y'all" frequently in her social media, such as in this post the day after winning two Country Music Association awards:

▶ Thank y'all for making my dreams come true right before my eyes.

—Lainey Wilson, @laineywilson, November 10, 2022

In choosing to use "y'all" rather than the more standard "you," Wilson emphasizes her southern heritage and establishes a friendly, down-home tone.

Other regions as well have their own forms of the second person plural. In Chicago and New York you might hear "youse," and in Pittsburgh it's "yinz." Such local language is widely understood in the regions where it is used, though it may sound strange to people from other places. Using regional language in your writing can be a vivid way to evoke a place—and, as in Wilson's, can demonstrate pride in your own regional roots. If you aren't familiar with the regional language of the place you're writing about, though, you should do careful research to be sure you're getting it right.

L-11e Englishes across Cultures and Communities

Some varieties of English are associated with a particular social, ethnic, or other community. Black or African American English is perhaps the best-known of these Englishes. Not all Black people in the United States use it, and those who do may not use it exclusively. Not all its users are Black themselves. All its users, however, follow the conventions and rules that make this variety of English consistent and recognizable.

Linguist Geneva Smitherman has written extensively on this variety of English, often using the language itself to support her points. See how she uses both "academic" English and Black English to establish her authority as an insider and drive home her point with a stylistic punch.

▶ Think of black speech as having two dimensions: language and style. . . . Consider [this example]. Nina Simone sing: "It bees dat way sometime." Here the language aspect is the use of the verb *be* to indicate a recurrent event or habitual condition, rather than a one-time-only occurrence. But the total expression—"It bees dat way sometime"—also reflects Black English style, for the statement suggests a point of view, a way of looking at life, and a method of adapting to life's realities. To live by the philosophy of "It bees dat way sometime" is to come to grips with the changes that life bees puttin us through, and to accept the changes and bad times as a constant, ever-present reality.

—Geneva Smitherman, *Talkin and Testifyin: The Language of Black America*

You'll notice that the use of the verb "be," as Smitherman explains, allows the word to carry a nuanced meaning that is simply absent from other varieties of English. People unfamiliar with that usage or Black English in general may dismiss it as "incorrect"—negative opinions that contribute to the stigma that varieties of English often face. As readers, we would do well to develop flexibility in our judgments about English, a language used by 1.5 billion people all around the world.

Many other communities have developed their own Englishes as well. Ethnic communities often use an English that includes words from another language. Men and women often speak differently, as Deborah Tannen and other linguists have shown. Even young people use an English that might sound very strange coming from a gray-haired elder.

The differences can be subtle but sometimes a single word can make someone sound young, or old, or Texan, or Canadian—and can establish credibility with an audience. See how a simple "FOMO" in the headline of a Bloomberg News article about stock market investing signals a youth-oriented appeal. Bloomberg News is a news agency dedicated to business and financial information—an area more traditionally associated with persons of middle age and up.

▶ FOMO Grows as Investors Scurry to Catch Stock Market Boom

—Bloomberg

FOMO, an acronym for "fear of missing out," is likely very familiar to social media users. The term began to appear on social media in 2004, making it a recent addition to the language. Bloomberg, a relatively new media company that prides itself on "a culture of disruption," made a strategic move in putting "FOMO" in the headline of an article on investment strategies. The acronym is sure to grab some eyeballs of a prized demographic—young investors.

L-11f Mixing Languages and Varieties

As a writer, you can use different varieties of English or different languages for various purposes. If you use Black English or any other variety of English in your daily life and want to include it in your academic work, first consider your **PURPOSE** and **AUDIENCE**. What message are you trying to communicate and how will mixing language varieties contribute to that message? Will it help you connect with your audience? illustrate a point? evoke a specific place, person, or community? draw attention?

■ 73–74
75–78

For example, in a lab report, where precise, straightforward terms are expected so that others can replicate an experiment exactly, you should probably stick with edited academic English—another language variety likely wouldn't be appreciated. When you do mix languages, mark your switches in some way so that your audience can tell what you're doing—for example, by adding a **SIGNAL PHRASE** or using text effects such as italics. You want readers to know that you are making deliberate language choices.

● 529–32

We recognize that it can be risky to use your home language or language variety in your academic writing. Our best advice is to keep your focus on your audience, context, and purpose—just as you do with all your writing, all the time. And while you might be eager to try some of these techniques in your writing, be careful, sensitive, and genuine; cultural appropriation can be offensive and insulting. If a language variety is not part of your everyday life and culture—even if you understand it well and appreciate it enormously—don't try using it in your own writing without the guidance of an insider.

Here are some more suggestions and examples for mixing languages effectively and appropriately.

To evoke a person or represent speech

When you are describing people, you may want to quote their words, to let readers "hear" them talk—and to let them speak for themselves. Some multilingual authors mix their English writing with words or phrases from another language to give readers an authentic sense of someone's words or thoughts. See, for example, how Sandra Cisneros mixes English and Spanish in relating an exchange between her parents as they bicker about a trip to visit relatives. Using two languages in the dialogue adds realism, and the context makes the meaning clear even for readers who don't speak Spanish.

▶ "Zoila, why do you insist on being so stubborn?" Father shouts into the mirror, clouding the glass. "*Ya verás.* You'll see, *vieja*, it'll be fun."

"And stop calling me *vieja*," Mother shouts back. "I hate that word! Your mother's old; I'm not old." —Sandra Cisneros, *Caramelo*

When writing dialogue, you may sometimes want to use nonstandard spelling to mimic dialect or sound, as Flannery O'Connor does with the speech of a young boy questioning an outlaw.

▶ "What you got that gun for?" John Wesley asked. "Whatcha gonna do with that gun?"

—Flannery O'Connor, "A Good Man Is Hard to Find"

If you choose to use a nonstandard spelling to evoke a specific person or manner of speaking, your purpose for doing so should be consistent with your overall purpose, and your intention should be respectful and not derogatory or belittling. Also, make sure that your variant is accurate; will a reader be able to "hear" the pronunciation you've represented? Many nonstandard spellings, such as "gonna" or "c'mon," have been conventionalized, so you should try googling your word to make sure you've got it right.

To evoke a place or an event

In certain settings or situations—sports, auctions, math class—you will hear language you wouldn't hear anywhere else. In some cases, the topics require specialized words. There's no way to talk about golf without mentioning "par" or "putting" or "a hole in one," or to teach math without words like "variable" or "function." In other cases, people tend to use a certain kind of language. Think about the conversations you'd hear in a board meeting, or a sports bar.

Such language can be used to evoke a place or an event, as in this summary of a 2022 NBA game between the San Antonio Spurs and the Milwaukee Bucks.

▶ One of the Spurs' best possessions came midway through the third when Poeltl passed out of the paint to the corner, where rookie Jeremy Sochan instantly whipped the ball to Johnson out on the perimeter. The play ended with [Johnson] burying a 3-pointer.

——Tom Orsborn, *San Antonio Express-News*

The writer can assume that his readers are familiar with the language he uses; in fact, many readers probably watched the game and just read the summary in order to relive it. His use of basketball **JARGON** helps put them back in the action. But for an audience unfamiliar with the game, he'd need to explain terms like "paint" and "burying," ordinary words that have specific meanings in a basketball context.

Glossary

To build common ground with an audience

Language is one good way to establish **CREDIBILITY** and build common ground with readers. For example, in a feature article about how letters to the editor are chosen for publication in the daily newspaper of a city in Minnesota, the writer included the word "uff-da," a purely local touch:

◆ 410–13

▶ [We don't publish] mass-produced letters. There are people in these United States who like to send letters to every newspaper in the country on a weekly basis. Uff-da! These are easy to catch. There are also some lobbying organizations who provide forms for supporters where writers don't actually pen their own thoughts.

—Tim Engstrom, *Albert Lea Tribune*

"Uff-da" is a Norwegian expression that is widely used in the region. It means "wow" or "no kidding" or even "OMG!" depending on the situation. The writer doesn't need it to convey his meaning, but using it demonstrates a sense of local knowledge and pride—and helps build common ground with his readers.

Think carefully, however, before using words from a language or variety of language that you don't speak yourself; you may offend some readers. And if by chance you use words incorrectly, you could even damage your credibility.

P Punctuation/Mechanics

P-1 COMMAS

Commas matter. Consider the title of the best-selling book *Eats, Shoots & Leaves*. The cover shows two pandas, one with a gun in its paw, one whitewashing the comma. Is the book about a panda that dines, then fires a gun and exits? Or about the panda's customary diet? In fact, it's a book about punctuation; the ambiguity of its title illustrates how commas affect meaning. This chapter shows when and where to use commas in your writing.

P-1a To Join Independent Clauses with "And," "But," and Other Coordinating Conjunctions

Put a comma before the **COORDINATING CONJUNCTIONS** "and," "but," "for," "nor," "or," "so," and "yet" when they connect two **INDEPENDENT CLAUSES**. The comma signals that one idea is ending and another is beginning.

★ HB-33–34
HB-5

▶ I do not love Shakespeare, but I still have those books.
—Rick Bragg, *All Over but the Shoutin'*

▶ Most people think the avocado is a vegetable, yet it is actually a fruit.

▶ The blue ribbon went to Reema, and Aiko got the red ribbon.

Without the comma, readers might first think both girls got blue ribbons.

Although some writers omit the comma, especially with short independent clauses, you'll never be wrong to include it.

▶ I was smart, and I knew it. —Shannon Nichols, "'Proficiency'"

No comma is needed between the verbs when a single subject performs two actions.

▶ Many fast-food restaurants now give calorie counts on menus and offer a variety of healthy meal options.

▶ Augustine wrote extensively about his mother, ̸but mentioned his father only briefly.

P-1b To Set Off Introductory Words

Use a comma after an introductory word, **PHRASE**, or **CLAUSE** to mark the end of the introduction and the start of the main part of the sentence.

★ HB-6
HB-5

▶ Typically, a girl has a best friend with whom she sits and talks, frequently telling secrets.
—Deborah Tannen, "Gender in the Classroom"

▶ In terms of wealth rather than income, the top 1 percent control 40 percent.

—Joseph E. Stiglitz, "Of the 1%, by the 1%, for the 1%"

▶ Even ignoring the extreme poles of the economic spectrum, we find enormous class differences in the life-styles among the haves, the have-nots, and the have-littles.

—Gregory Mantsios, "Class in America—2003"

▶ When Miss Emily Grierson died, our whole town went to her funeral.

—William Faulkner, "A Rose for Emily"

Some writers don't use a comma after a short introductory word, phrase, or clause, but it's never wrong to include one.

P-1c To Separate Items in a Series

Use a comma to separate the items in a series. The items may be words, **PHRASES**, or **CLAUSES**.

HB-6 ★
HB-5

▶ I spend a great deal of time thinking about the power of language—the way it can evoke an emotion, a visual image, a complex idea, or a simple truth.

—Amy Tan, "Mother Tongue"

Though some writers leave out the comma between the final two items in a series, this omission can confuse readers. It's never wrong to include the final comma.

▶ Nadia held a large platter of sandwiches—egg salad, peanut butter, ham, and cheese.

Without the last comma, it's not clear whether there are three or four kinds of sandwiches on the platter.

P-1d To Set Off Nonessential Elements

A nonessential (or nonrestrictive) element is one that could be deleted without changing the basic meaning of the sentence; it should be set off with commas. An essential (or restrictive) element is one that is needed to understand the sentence; therefore, it should not be set off with commas.

NONESSENTIAL

▶ Spanish, which is a Romance language, is one of six official languages at the United Nations.

The detail about being a Romance language adds information, but it is not essential to the meaning of the sentence and so is set off with commas.

ESSENTIAL

▶ Navajo is the Athabaskan language that is spoken in the Southwest by the Navajo people.

The detail about where Navajo is spoken is essential: Navajo is not the only Athabaskan language; it is the Athabaskan language that is spoken in the Southwest.

Note that the meaning of a sentence can change depending on whether or not an element is set off with commas.

▶ My sister, Trinh, just auditioned for Cirque du Soleil.

The writer has only one sister.

▶ My sister Trinh just auditioned for Cirque du Soleil.

The writer has more than one sister; the one named Trinh just auditioned for Cirque du Soleil.

Essential and nonessential elements can be clauses, phrases, or words.

CLAUSES

▶ He always drove Chryslers, which are made in America.

▶ He always drove cars that were made in America.

PHRASES

▶ I fumble in the dark, trying to open the mosquito netting around my bed.

▶ I see my mother clutching my baby sister.

—Chanrithy Him, "When Broken Glass Floats"

WORDS

▶ At 8:59, Flight 175 passenger Brian David Sweeney tried to call his wife, Julie.

▶ At 9:00, Lee Hanson received a second call from his son Peter.

—The 9/11 Commission, "The Hijacking of United 175"

Sweeney had only one wife, so her name provides extra but nonessential information. Hanson presumably had more than one son, so it is essential to specify which son called.

≫ Go to **InQuizitive for Writers** for an interactive activity on omitted commas, and practice your skills before applying them in your writing.

P-1e To Set Off Parenthetical Information

Information that interrupts the flow of a sentence needs to be set off with commas.

▶ Bob's conduct, most of us will immediately respond, was gravely wrong.

—Peter Singer, "The Singer Solution to World Poverty"

▶ With as little as two servings of vegetables a day, it seems to me,
you can improve your eating habits.

P-1f To Set Off Transitional Expressions

355–56

TRANSITIONS such as "thus," "nevertheless," "for example," and "in fact" help connect sentences or parts of sentences. They are usually set off with commas.

▶ The real world, *however*, is run by money.

—Joanna MacKay, "Organ Sales Will Save Lives"

HB-5

When a transition connects two **INDEPENDENT CLAUSES** in the same sentence, it is preceded by a semicolon and is followed by a comma.

▶ There are few among the poor who speak of themselves as lower class; *instead*, they refer to their race, ethnic group, or geographic location.

—Gregory Mantsios, "Class in America—2003"

P-1g To Set Off Direct Quotations

Use commas to set off quoted words from the speaker or source.

▶ Pa shouts back, "I just want to know where the gunfire is coming from."

—Chanrithy Him, "When Broken Glass Floats"

▶ "You put a slick and a con man together," she said, "and you have predatory lenders."
—Peter Boyer, "Eviction: The Day They Came for Addie Polk's House"

▶ "Death and life are in the power of the tongue," says the proverb.

P-1h To Set Off Direct Address, "Yes" or "No," Interjections, and Tag Questions

DIRECT ADDRESS "Well, Virginia, I'm glad we cleared that up."

"YES" OR "NO" No, you cannot replace the battery on your iPhone.

INTERJECTION Oh, a PS5. Is it worth the hype?

TAG QUESTION That wasn't so hard, was it?

P-1i With Addresses, Place Names, and Dates

▶ Send contributions to Human Rights Campaign, 1640 Rhode Island Ave., Washington, DC 20036.

▶ Athens, Georgia, is famous for its thriving music scene.

▶ Amelia Earhart disappeared over the Pacific Ocean on July 2, 1937, while trying to make the first round-the-world flight at the equator.

Omit the commas, however, if you invert the date (on 2 July 1937) or if you give only the month and year (in July 1937).

P-1j Checking for Unnecessary Commas

Commas have so many uses that it's easy to add them unnecessarily. Here are some situations when you should not use a comma.

Between a subject and a verb

▶ What the organizers of the 1969 Woodstock concert did not anticipate/was the turnout.

▶ The event's promoters/turned down John Lennon's offer to play with his Plastic Ono Band.

Between a verb and its object or complement

▶ Pollsters wondered/how they had so poorly predicted the winner of the 1948 presidential election.

▶ Virtually every prediction indicated/that Thomas Dewey would defeat Harry Truman.

▶ The *Chicago Tribune*'s famous wrong headline was/an embarrassment to the newspaper.

After a coordinating conjunction

▶ The College Board reported a decline in SAT scores and/attributed the decline to changes in "student test-taking patterns."

▶ The SAT was created to provide an objective measure of academic potential, but/ studies in the 1980s found racial and socioeconomic biases in some test questions.

After "like" or "such as"

▶ Many American-born authors, such as/Henry James, Ezra Pound, and F. Scott Fitzgerald, lived as expatriates in Europe.

After a question mark or an exclamation point

▶ Why would any nation have a monarch in an era of democracy?/you might ask yourself.

▶ "O, be some other name!/" exclaims Juliet.

≫ Go to **InQuizitive for Writers** for an interactive activity on unnecessary commas, and practice your skills before applying them in your writing.

P-2 SEMICOLONS

Semicolons offer one way to connect two closely related thoughts. Look, for example, at Martha Stewart's advice about how to tell if fruit is ripe: "A perfectly ripened fruit exudes a subtle but sweet fragrance from the stem end, appears plump, and has deeply colored skin; avoid those that have wrinkles, bruises, or tan spots." Stewart could have used a period, but the semicolon shows the connection between what to look for and what to avoid when buying peaches or plums.

P-2a Between Independent Clauses

HB-33–34 ★

Closely related independent clauses are most often joined with a comma plus "and" or another **COORDINATING CONJUNCTION**. If the two clauses are closely related and don't need a conjunction to signal the relationship, they may be linked with a semicolon.

▶ The silence deepened; the room chilled.

—Wayson Choy, "The Ten Thousand Things"

▶ The life had not flowed out of her; it had been seized.

—Valerie Steiker, "Our Mother's Face"

A period would work in either of these examples, but the semicolon suggests a stronger connection between the two independent clauses.

355–56 ⁚

Another option is to use a semicolon with a **TRANSITION** that clarifies the relationship between the two independent clauses. Put a comma after the transition.

▶ There are no secret economies that nourish the poor; on the contrary, there are a host of special costs.

—Barbara Ehrenreich,
Nickel and Dimed: On (Not) Getting By in America

P-2b In a Series with Commas

Use semicolons to separate items in a series when one or more of the items contain commas.

▶ There are images of a few students: Erwin Petschaur, a muscular German boy with a strong accent; Dave Sanchez, who was good at math; and Sheila Wilkes, everyone's curly-haired heartthrob.

—Mike Rose, "Potato Chips and Stars"

P-2c Checking for Mistakes with Semicolons

Use a comma, not a semicolon, to set off an introductory clause.

▶ When the sun finally sets⫫, everyone gathers at the lake to watch the fireworks.

Use a colon, not a semicolon, to introduce a list.

▶ Every American high school student should know that the US Constitution contains three sections⫫: preamble, articles, and amendments.

P-3 END PUNCTUATION

"She married him." "She married him?" "She married him!" In each of these three sentences, the words are the same, but the end punctuation completely changes the meaning—from a simple statement to a bemused question to an emphatic exclamation. This chapter will help you use periods, question marks, and exclamation points in your writing.

P-3a Periods

Use a period to end a sentence that makes a statement.

▶ Rose Emily Meraglio came to the United States from southern Italy as a little girl in the early 1920s and settled with her family in Altoona, Pennsylvania.
　　　　　　　　　　　　　　—Mike Rose, "The Working Life of a Waitress"

An indirect question, which reports something that someone else has asked, ends with a period, not a question mark.

▶ Presidential candidates are often asked how they will expand the economy and create jobs⫫.

When a sentence ends with an abbreviation that has its own period, do not add another period.

▶ The Rat Pack included Frank Sinatra and Sammy Davis Jr.⫰

See P-10 for more on periods with abbreviations.

P-3b Question Marks

Use a question mark to end a direct question.

▶ Did I think that because I was a minority student jobs would just come looking for me? What was I thinking?
　　　　　　　　　　　　　　—Richard Rodriguez, "None of This Is Fair"

Use a period rather than a question mark to end an indirect question.

▶ Aunt Vivian often asked what Jesus would do?.

P-3c Exclamation Points

Use an exclamation point to express strong emotion or add emphasis to a statement or command. Exclamation points should be used sparingly, however, or they may undercut your credibility.

▶ "Keith," we shrieked as the car drove away, "Keith, we love you!"
—Susan Jane Gilman, "Mick Jagger Wants Me"

When the words themselves are emotional, an exclamation point is often unnecessary, and a period is sufficient.

▶ It was so close, so low, so huge and fast, so intent on its target that I swear to you, I swear to you, I felt the vengeance and rage emanating from the plane.
—Debra Fontaine, "Witnessing"

P-4 QUOTATION MARKS

"Girls Just Want to Have Fun." "Two thumbs up!" "Frankly, my dear, I don't give a damn." These are just some of the ways that quotation marks are used—to indicate a song title, to cite praise for a movie, to set off dialogue. In college writing, you will use quotation marks frequently to acknowledge when you've repeated others' words. This chapter will show you how to use quotation marks correctly and appropriately.

P-4a Direct Quotations

Use quotation marks to enclose words spoken or written by others.

▶ When the French president once asked [Queen Elizabeth] if she ever got bored, she replied honestly: "Yes but I don't say so."
—Andrew Morton, *The Queen: Her Life*

▶ Newt Gingrich and Jesse Jackson have both pounded nails and raised funds for Habitat for Humanity. This is what Millard Fuller calls the "theology of the hammer."
—Diana George, "Changing the Face of Poverty"

When you introduce quoted words with "he said," "she claimed," or another such **SIGNAL PHRASE**, put a comma after the verb and capitalize the first word of the quote if it's a complete sentence. When you follow a quote with such an expression, use a comma before the closing quotation mark (unless the quote is a question or an exclamation).

▶ When my mother reported that Mr. Tomkey did not believe in television, my father said, "Well, good for him. I don't know that I believe in it either."
    "That's exactly how I feel," my mother said, and then my parents watched the news, and whatever came on after the news.
                                                    —David Sedaris, "Us and Them"

You do not need any punctuation between "that" and a quotation, nor do you need to capitalize the first word of the quote.

▶ We were assigned to write one essay agreeing or disagreeing with George Orwell's statement that/ "the slovenliness of our language makes it easier for us to have foolish thoughts."

In dialogue, insert a new paragraph and a new pair of quotation marks to signal each change of speaker.

▶ "What's this?" the hospital janitor said to me as he stumbled over my right shoe.
    "My shoes," I said.
    "That's not a shoe, brother," he replied, holding it to the light. "That's a brick."
                                            —Henry Louis Gates Jr., "A Giant Step"

See P–8c for help with capitalization in a direct quotation.

P-4b Long Quotations

Long quotations should be set off without quotation marks as **BLOCK QUO-TATIONS**. Each documentation style has distinct guidelines for the length and formatting of block quotations; you'll find more on long quotations in the chapters on **MLA** and **APA**. The following example uses MLA style, which calls for setting off quotations of more than four typed lines of prose by indenting them five spaces (or half an inch) from the left margin. Note that in the following example, the period precedes the parenthetical documentation.

● 524

● MLA 581–82
APA 624

Biographer David McCullough describes Truman's railroad campaign as follows:

No president in history had ever gone so far in quest of support from the people, or with less cause for the effort, to judge by informed opinion. . . . As a test of his skills and judgment as a professional politician, not to say his stamina and disposition at age sixty-four, it would be like no other experience in his long, often difficult career, as he himself understood perfectly. (655)

P-4c Titles of Short Works

Use quotation marks to enclose the titles of articles, chapters, essays, short stories, poems, songs, and episodes of television series. Titles of books, films, newspapers, and other longer works should be in italics (or underlined) rather than enclosed in quotation marks.

▶ In "Unfriendly Skies Are No Match for El Al," Vivienne Walt, a writer for *USA Today,* describes her experience flying with this airline.

—Andy McDonie, "Airport Security: What Price Safety?"

Note that the title of the newspaper is italicized, whereas the newspaper article title takes quotation marks.

▶ With every page of Edgar Allan Poe's story "The Tell-Tale Heart," my own heart beat faster.

▶ Rita Dove's poem "Dawn Revisited" contains vivid images that appeal to the senses of sight, sound, smell, and taste.

P-4d Single Quotation Marks

When you quote a passage that already contains quotation marks, whether they enclose a quotation or a title, change the inner ones to single quotation marks.

▶ Debra Johnson notes that according to Marilyn J. Adams, "effective reading instruction is based on 'direct instruction in phonics, focusing on the orthographic regularities of English.' "

▶ Certain essays are so good (or so popular) that they are included in almost every anthology. *The Norton Reader* notes, "Some essays—Martin Luther King Jr.'s 'Letter from Birmingham Jail' and Jonathan Swift's 'A Modest Proposal,' for example—are constant favorites" (xxiii).

P-4e With Other Punctuation

When other punctuation follows material in quotation marks, it should go inside the closing quotation mark in some cases and outside in others. The following guidelines are those that are conventional in the United States; they differ from those in many other countries.

Commas and periods

Put commas and periods inside closing quotation marks.

▶ "On the newsstand, the cover is acting as a poster, an ad for what's inside," she said. "The loyal reader is looking for what makes the magazine exceptional."

—Katharine Q. Seelye, "Lurid Numbers on Glossy Pages!"

Semicolons and colons

Put semicolons and colons outside closing quotation marks.

▶ No elder stands behind our young to say, "Folks have fought and died for your right to pierce your face, so do it right"; no community exists that can model for a young person the responsible use of the "right"; for the right, even if called self-expression, comes from no source other than desire.

—Stephen L. Carter, "Just Be Nice"

▶ According to James Garbarino, author of *Lost Boys: Why Our Sons Turn Violent and How We Can Save Them*, it makes no sense to talk about violent media as a direct cause of youth violence. Rather, he says, "it depends": Media violence is a risk factor that, working in concert with others, can exacerbate bad behavior.

—Maggie Cutler, "Whodunit—the Media?"

Question marks and exclamation points

Put question marks and exclamation points inside closing quotation marks if they are part of the quotation but outside if they apply to the whole sentence.

▶ Then she began to talk more loudly. "What he want, I come to New York tell him front of his boss, you cheating me?"

—Amy Tan, "Mother Tongue"

▶ How many people know the words to Lizzo's "About Damn Time"?

P-4f With Parenthetical Documentation

When you provide parenthetical **DOCUMENTATION** for a quotation, put the documentation after the closing quotation mark, and put any end punctuation that's part of your sentence after the parentheses.

● 538–41

▶ An avid baseball fan, Tallulah Bankhead once said, "There have been only two geniuses in the world: Willie Mays and Willie Shakespeare" (183).

P-4g Words Discussed as Words

Use quotation marks around a word you are discussing as a word. The same practice applies to phrases and sentences.

▶ In the mayor's speech, you will hear the word "ventilator" eight times.

▶ The phrase "once in a blue moon" refers to something that happens very rarely.

▶ The teacher asked her students to write "All work is my own" at the top of every assignment.

Some writers use italics rather than quotation marks to signal words discussed as words. We recommend quotation marks because they are more legible and accessible than italicized text for many readers. Letters discussed as letters, however, are usually italicized.

▶ Most American dictionaries call for one *t* in the word "benefited."

When referring to a number as a numeral, don't italicize or enclose it in quotation marks.

▶ All computer codes consist of some combination of 0s and 1s.

P-4h Checking for Mistakes with Quotation Marks

Avoid using quotation marks to identify slang or to emphasize a word. Remove the quotation marks, or substitute a better word.

SLANG   Appearing "hip" is important to many parents in New York.

EMPHASIS   The woman explained that she is "only" the manager, not the owner, of the health club.

Do not put quotation marks around indirect quotations, those that do not quote someone's exact words.

▶ Mom always said that "meat that was any good didn't need seasoning."

P-5 APOSTROPHES

"McDonald's: 'I'm lovin' it'" proclaims an ad, demonstrating two common uses of the apostrophe: to show ownership (McDonald's) and to mark missing letters (I'm, lovin'). This chapter offers guidelines on these and other common uses for apostrophes.

P-5a Possessives

In general, use an apostrophe and *s* to make a word possessive: Viola Davis's eyes, someone else's problem, the children's playground.

Singular nouns

To make most singular nouns possessive, add an apostrophe and *s*.

▶ The challenge now will be filling the park's seats.

> —Michael Kimmelman, "A Ballpark Louder Than Its Fans"

▶ In Plato's *Phaedrus*, Socrates bemoaned the development of writing.

> —Nicholas Carr, "Is Google Making Us Stupid?"

▶ Bill Gates's philanthropic efforts focus on health care and education.

If adding an apostrophe and s makes pronunciation awkward, some writers use only an apostrophe with singular nouns that end in -s: Euripides' play, George Saunders' jacket.

Plural nouns

To form the possessive of a plural noun not ending in -s, add an apostrophe and s. For plural nouns that end in -s, add only an apostrophe.

▶ Are women's minds different from men's minds?

—Evelyn Fox Keller, "Women in Science"

▶ The neighbors' complaints about noise led the club owner to install soundproof insulation.

▶ Did you hear that Laurence Strauss is getting married? The reception will be at the Strausses' home.

Personal pronouns

Personal pronouns such as "we," "she," and "you" have their own possessive forms, which never take an apostrophe. See S-6c for a complete list.

▶ The graduates let out a cheer as they tossed *their* hats in the air—and later got a good chuckle when the valedictorian accidentally stepped on *hers*.

"Something," "everyone," and other indefinite pronouns

To form the possessive of an **INDEFINITE PRONOUN**, add an apostrophe and s.

★ HB-23–24

▶ Spaghetti was everyone's favorite lunch.

Joint possession

To show that two or more individuals possess something together, use the possessive form for the last noun only.

▶ Castillo and Medina's book is an introduction to Latinx writers for English-speaking adolescents.

To show individual possession, make each noun possessive.

▶ Jan's and Bo's lung transplants inspired me to quit smoking.

Compound nouns

For nouns made up of more than one word, make the last word possessive.

▶ The surgeon general's report persuaded many people to start flossing.

P-5b Contractions

An apostrophe in a contraction indicates where letters have been omitted.

▶ **I've** learned that sometimes friends and business **don't** mix.

—Iliana Roman, "First Job"

"I've" is a contraction of "I have"; "don't" is a contraction of "do not."

P-5c Plurals

You'll often see apostrophes used to pluralize numbers and abbreviations, and capital letters or words discussed as words when they're in italics: 7's, NGO's, *C's, thank-you's.* Usage has changed, however, and you should leave out the apostrophe in your own writing. To pluralize a lowercase letter, though, you should use an apostrophe for clarity: *a's.* If you use quotation marks for words discussed as words, you shouldn't add an apostrophe for the plural: "thank-yous."

Plural of numbers

▶ The winning hand had three 8**s**.

▶ We never knew that Aunt Beulah won baking contests in the 1950**s**.

Plural of letters

▶ People often forget that there are four *s*'s in "Mississippi."

▶ The admissions officers spoke enthusiastically about the college's no-grades option — and then said we'd need mostly As to get in.

See that letter grades are typically not italicized.

Plural of abbreviations and words discussed as words

▶ How many TV**s** does the average American family have in its home?

▶ The resolution passed when there were more "aye**s**" than "nay**s**."

P-5d Checking for Mistakes with Apostrophes

Do not use an apostrophe in the following situations.

With plural nouns that are not possessive

▶ Both ~~cellist's~~ ^cellists^ played encores.

With "his," "hers," "ours," "yours," and "theirs"

▶ Look at all the lettuce. ~~Our's~~ ^Ours^ is organic. Is ~~your's?~~ ^yours?^

With the possessive "its"

► It's an unusual building; ~~it's~~ *its* style has been described as postmodern,
but it fits beautifully with the Gothic buildings on our campus.

"It's" is a contraction meaning "it is" or "it has"; "its" is the possessive form of "it."

»» Go to **InQuizitive for Writers** for an interactive activity on apostrophe errors, and practice your skills before applying them in your writing.

P-6 OTHER PUNCTUATION

Some carpenters can do their jobs using only a hammer and a saw, but most rely on additional tools. The same is true of writers: you can get along with just a few punctuation marks, but having some others in your toolbox—colons, dashes, parentheses, brackets, ellipses, and slashes—can help you say what you want to more precisely and can help readers follow what you write more easily. This chapter can help you use these other punctuation marks effectively.

P-6a Colons

Colons are used to direct attention to words that follow the colon: an explanation or elaboration, a list, a quotation, and so on.

► What I remember best, strangely enough, are the two things I couldn't understand and over the years grew to hate: grammar lessons and mathematics.
—Mike Rose, "Potato Chips and Stars"

► I sized him up as fast as possible: tight black velvet pants pulled over his boots, black jacket, a red-green-yellow scarf slashed around his neck.
—Susan Jane Gilman, "Mick Jagger Wants Me"

► She also voices some common concerns: "The product should be safe, it should be easily accessible, and it should be low-priced."
—Dara Mayers, "Our Bodies, Our Lives"

► Fifteen years after the release of the Carnegie report, College Board surveys reveal data are no different: test scores still correlate strongly with family income.
—Gregory Mantsios, "Class in America—2003"

Colons are also used after the salutation in a business letter, in ratios, between titles and subtitles, between chapter and verse in biblical references, and between numbers that indicate hours, minutes, and seconds.

▶ Dear President Michaels:

▶ For best results, add water to the powder in a 3:1 ratio.

▶ *The Last Campaign: How Harry Truman Won the 1948 Election*

▶ "And God said, 'Let there be light,' and there was light" (Genesis 1:3).

▶ The morning shuttle departs at 6:52 a.m.

P-6b Dashes

You can create a dash by typing two hyphens (--) with no spaces before or after or by selecting the em dash from the symbol menu of your word-processing program.

Use dashes to set off material you want to emphasize. Unlike colons, dashes can appear not only after an independent clause but also at other points in a sentence. To set off material at the end of a sentence, place a dash before it; to set off material in the middle of the sentence, place a dash before and after the words you want to emphasize.

▶ After that, the roller coaster rises and falls, slowing down and speeding up—all on its own.

> —Cathi Eastman and Becky Burrell, "The Science of Screams"

▶ It did not occur to me—possibly because I am an American—that there could be people anywhere who had never seen a Negro.

> —James Baldwin, "Stranger in the Village"

Dashes are often used to signal a shift in tone or thought.

▶ The best way to keep children home is to make the home atmosphere pleasant—and let the air out of the tires.

> —Dorothy Parker

Keep in mind that dashes are most effective if they are used only when material needs particular emphasis. Too many dashes can interfere with the flow and clarity of your writing.

P-6c Parentheses

Use parentheses to enclose supplemental details and digressions.

▶ When I was a child, attending grade school in Washington, DC, we took classroom time to study manners. Not only the magic words "please" and "thank you" but more complicated etiquette questions, like how to answer the telephone ("Carter residence, Stephen speaking") and how to set the table (we were quizzed on whether knife blades point in or out).
—Stephen L. Carter, "Just Be Nice"

▶ But even companies with a market cap of over $970 billion (Google's parent company, Alphabet) or over $614 billion (Facebook) aren't immune to the punches of potential talent.
—Emma Goldberg, "'Techlash' Hits College Campuses"

▶ To control the appliance, you select a heat mode (like bake, roast, or broil), turn a knob to set the temperature and then wait for the oven to heat up.
—Brian X. Chen, "Gadget of the Year: The Toaster Oven"

P-6d Brackets

Put brackets around words that you insert in a **QUOTATION**.

523–26

▶ As Senator Reid explained, "She [Nancy Pelosi] realizes that you cannot make everyone happy."

If you are quoting a source that contains an error, put the Latin word "sic" in brackets after the error to indicate that the mistake is in the original source.

▶ Warehouse has been around for 30 years and has 263 stores, suggesting a large fan base. The chain sums up its appeal thus: "styley[*sic*], confident, sexy, glamorous, edgy, clean and individual, with it's [*sic*] finger on the fashion pulse."
—Anne Ashworth, "Chain Reaction: Warehouse"

P-6e Ellipses

Ellipses are three spaced dots that indicate an omission or a pause. Use ellipses to show that you have omitted words within a **QUOTATION**. If you omit a complete sentence or more in the middle of a quoted passage, add the three dots after the period.

523–26

ORIGINAL

▶ The Lux ad's visual content, like Resinol's, supports its verbal message. Several demure views of Irene Dunne emphasize her "pearly-smooth skin," the top one framed by a large heart shape. In all the photos, Dunne wears a feathery, feminine collar, giving her a birdlike appearance: she is a bird of paradise or an ornament. At the bottom of the ad, we see a happy Dunne being cuddled and admired by a man.
—Doug Lantry, "'Stay Sweet as You Are'"

▶ The Lux ad's visual content . . . supports its verbal message. Several demure views of Irene Dunne emphasize her "pearly-smooth skin," the top one framed by a large heart shape. . . . At the bottom of the ad, we see a happy Dunne being cuddled and admired by a man.

If you use a quote as a full sentence and the quote doesn't include the end of the original sentence, MLA requires you to add ellipses at the end of the quotation; APA does not. If you use parenthetical documentation after quoted material, place ellipses *before* the parentheses to indicate the deletion of words, but put the end punctuation *after* the parentheses, as in the following example using MLA style.

▶ According to Kathleen Welch, "One can turn one's gaze away from television, but one cannot turn one's ears from it without leaving the area . . ." (102).

P-6f Slashes

When you quote two or three lines of poetry and run them in with the rest of your text, use slashes to show where one line ends and the next begins. Put a space before and after each slash.

▶ In the opening lines of the poem, he warns the reader to "Lift not the painted veil which those who live / Call Life" (lines 1–2).

—Stephanie Huff, "Metaphor and Society in Shelley's 'Sonnet'"

P-7 HYPHENS

If your mother gives you much needed advice, has she given you a great deal of advice that you needed or advice that you needed badly? What about a psychiatry experiment that used thirty five year old subjects? Were there thirty-five subjects who were a year old? thirty subjects who were five years old? or an unspecified number of thirty-five-year-old subjects? Hyphens could clear up the confusion. This chapter provides tips for when to use hyphens and when to omit them.

P-7a Compound Words

Compound words can be two words (ground zero), a hyphenated word (self-esteem), or one word (outsource). Check a dictionary, and if a compound is not there, assume that it is two words.

Compound adjectives

A compound adjective is made up of two or more words. Most compound adjectives take a hyphen before a noun.

▶ a little-known trombonist

▶ a foul-smelling river

Do not use a hyphen to connect an -ly adverb and an adjective.

▶ a carefully executed plan

A compound adjective after a noun is usually easy to read without a hyphen; add a hyphen only if the compound is unclear without it.

▶ The river has become foul smelling in recent years.

Prefixes and suffixes

A hyphen usually isn't needed after a prefix or before a suffix (preschool, antislavery, counterattack, catlike, citywide). However, hyphens are necessary in the following situations.

WITH "GREAT-," "SELF-," "-ELECT"   great-aunt, self-appointed, president-elect

WITH CAPITAL LETTERS   anti-American, post-Soviet literature

WITH NUMBERS   post-9/11, the mid-1960s

TO AVOID DOUBLE AND TRIPLE LETTERS   anti-intellectualism, ball-like

FOR CLARITY   re-cover (cover again) *but* recover (get well)

Numbers

Hyphenate fractions and compound numbers from twenty-one to ninety-nine.

▶ three-quarters of their income

▶ thirty-five subjects

P-7b At the End of a Line

Use a hyphen to divide a multisyllabic word that does not fit on one line. (A one-syllable word is never hyphenated.) Divide words between syllables as shown in a dictionary, after a prefix, or before a suffix. Divide compound words between the parts of the compound, if possible. Do not leave only one letter at the end or the beginning of a line.

op-er-a-tion   knot-ty   main-stream

Dividing internet addresses

Do not insert a hyphen in a URL or DOI that you break at the end of a line. It's standard practice to break URLs or DOIs that won't fit on a line after a double slash or before any other punctuation mark.

P-8 CAPITALIZATION

Capital letters are an important signal, either that a new sentence is beginning or that a specific person, place, or brand is being discussed. Capitalize "Herb," and it's clear that you're referring to a person; write "herb," and readers will know you're writing about a plant or a seasoning. This chapter offers guidelines to help you know what to capitalize and when.

P-8a Proper Nouns and Common Nouns

Capitalize proper nouns, those naming specific people, places, and things. All other nouns are common nouns and should not be capitalized.

PROPER NOUNS	COMMON NOUNS
Sanjay Gupta	a doctor
Senator Duckworth	a senator
Uncle Daniel	my uncle
France	a republic
the Mississippi River	a river
the West Coast	a coast
Christianity	a religion
Allah	a god
the Torah	a sacred text
Central Intelligence Agency	an agency
US Congress	the US government
Kansas State University	a university
Composition 101	a writing course
World War II	a war
July	summer
the Middle Ages	the fourteenth century
Kleenex	tissues

ADJECTIVES derived from proper nouns, especially the names of people and places, are usually capitalized: Shakespearean, Swedish, Chicagoan. There are exceptions to this rule, however, such as "french fries," "roman numeral," and "congressional." Consult a dictionary if you are unsure whether an adjective should be capitalized.

All languages change, and the guidelines for accepted use sprint along to keep up. As we go to press, the capitalization of the names of some social categories is up for debate. Specifically, in the discussion of racism, race, and related topics, most academic and journalistic style guides now call for the capitalization of "Black" when referring to groups, individuals, and cultures or cultural artifacts. With the word "white," however, opinions are more varied. In this book, we capitalize both "Black" and "White," following APA style.

▶ My high school classmates and I were almost all Black and Mexican, but all our teachers were White.

Other style guides and influential sources, such as the *New York Times*, AP, and notable authors are not capitalizing the word "white." The issue is complicated, with arguments from diverse angles, and usage is not likely to be widely settled anytime soon. We suggest that you think, learn, and participate in the discussion yourself. (It's your language too!) For your academic writing, follow the style guide you're using for your course and/ or consult your instructor. Appropriate and respectful usage is your priority; see L-9 for more on respectful and inclusive language.

P-8b Titles before a Person's Name

A professional title is capitalized when it appears immediately before a person's name but not when it appears after a proper noun or alone.

Senator (*or* Sen.) Elizabeth Warren   Elizabeth Warren, the senator

P-8c The First Word of a Sentence

Capitalize the first word of a sentence. The first word of a quoted sentence should be capitalized, but not the first word of a quoted phrase.

▶ Speaking about acting, Clint Eastwood notes, "You can show a lot with a look.... It's punctuation."

▶ Sherry Turkle argues that we're living in "techno-enthusiastic times" and that we're inclined "to celebrate our gadgets."

Glossary

Interrupted quotations

Capitalize the second part of an interrupted quotation only if it begins a new sentence.

▶ "It was just as nice," she sobbed, "as I hoped and dreamed it would be."
—Joan Didion, "Marrying Absurd"

▶ "On the newsstand, the cover is acting as a poster, an ad for what's inside," she said. "The loyal reader is looking for what makes the magazine exceptional."
—Katharine Q. Seelye, "Lurid Numbers on Glossy Pages!"

P-8d Titles and Subtitles

Capitalize the first and last words and all other important words of a title and subtitle. Do not capitalize less important words such as **ARTICLES**, **COORDINATING CONJUNCTIONS**, and **PREPOSITIONS**.

HB-55–56
HB-33–34
HB-48–50

"Give Peace a Chance"
Pride and Prejudice
The Shallows: What the Internet Is Doing to Our Brains

Each documentation style has guidelines for formatting titles in notes and bibliographies. You'll find more on titles and subtitles in the chapters on **MLA** and **APA**.

MLA 542–94
APA 595–633

P-9 ITALICS

Italic type tells us to read words a certain way. Think of the difference between the office and *The Office*, or between time and *Time*. In each case, the italicized version tells us it's a specific television show or magazine. This chapter provides guidelines on using italics in your writing.

P-9a Titles of Long Works

Titles and subtitles of long works should appear in italics. Notable exceptions are sacred writing such as the Qur'an or the Old Testament and historical documents such as the Declaration of Independence.

BOOKS   *War and Peace; The Hobbit; On Earth We're Briefly Gorgeous*

PERIODICALS   *The Atlantic; Teen Vogue; College English*

NEWSPAPERS   *Los Angeles Times*

PLAYS   *Medea; Six Degrees of Separation*

LONG POEMS   *The Odyssey; Paradise Lost*

FILMS AND VIDEOS   *Selma*; *Turning Red*; *The Wizard of Oz*

MUSICAL WORKS OR ALBUMS   *The Four Seasons*; *Rubber Soul*

RADIO AND TV SERIES   *Fresh Air*; *Succession*; *Game of Thrones*

PAINTINGS, SCULPTURES   the *Mona Lisa*; Michelangelo's *David*

DANCES BY A CHOREOGRAPHER   Mark Morris's *Gloria*

SOFTWARE   *Adobe Acrobat XI Standard*

SHIPS, SPACECRAFT   *Queen Mary*; *Challenger*

WEBSITES   *Salon*; *Etsy*; *IMDb*

A short work, such as a short story, an article, an episode of a series, or a song, takes quotation marks.

P-9b Non-English Words

Use italics for an occasional unfamiliar word or phrase in a language other than English. Do not italicize proper nouns.

▶ *Verstehen*, a concept often associated with Max Weber, is the sociologist's attempt to understand human actions from the actor's point of view.

If the word or phrase has become part of everyday English or has an entry in English-language dictionaries, it does not need italics.

▶ An ad hoc committee should be formed to assess the university's use of fossil fuels and ways to incorporate alternative energy sources.

▶ The plot of *Jane Eyre* follows the conventions of a bildungsroman, or a coming-of-age story.

See L-11f for more on mixing languages.

P-9c For Emphasis

You can use italics occasionally to lend emphasis to a word or phrase, but do not overuse them.

▶ It is, perhaps, as much what Shakespeare did *not* write as what he did that seems to indicate something seriously wrong with his marriage.

—Stephen Greenblatt, "Shakespeare on Marriage"

▶ I didn't want to move through my life and not be accountable for recklessness. I wanted to be aware of my Achilles heel. I believed *awareness* was what would release my blessings.

—Viola Davis, *Finding Me: A Memoir*

P-10 ABBREVIATIONS

HBO. USA. JV. DNA. fwiw. DIY. These are some common abbreviations, shortcuts to longer words and phrases. You can use common abbreviations if you are sure your readers will recognize them. If not, spell out the full term with the abbreviation in parentheses the first time it appears. After that, you can use the abbreviation alone.

▶ In a recent press release, officials from the international organization Médecins Sans Frontières (MSF) stressed the need for more effective tuberculosis drugs.

Periods are generally used in abbreviations of personal titles that precede a name and in Latin abbreviations such as "e.g." or "etc." They are not needed for state abbreviations such as "CA," "NY," or "TX," or for most abbreviations made up of initials, like "AP" or "YMCA." In some cases, periods are optional ("BCE" or "B.C.E."). Be sure to use them or omit them consistently. If you're not sure about periods for a particular abbreviation, check a dictionary.

P-10a With Names
Most titles are abbreviated when they come before or after a name.

Mr. Ed Stanford	Ed Stanford Jr.
Dr. Ralph Lopez	Ralph Lopez, MD
Prof. Susan Miller	Susan Miller, PhD
Judge Laquanda Evans	Laquanda Evans, JD

Do not abbreviate job titles that are not attached to a name.

▶ The ~~RN~~ nurse who worked with trauma victims specialized in cardiac care.

P-10b With Numbers
The following abbreviations can be used with numbers.

632 BC ("before Christ")

344 BCE ("before the common era")

AD 800 ("*anno Domini*")

800 CE ("common era")

10:30 a.m. (*or* AM)

7:00 a.m. (*or* AM)

Notice that "BC," "BCE," and "CE" follow the date, while "AD" precedes the date. Remember that the abbreviations in the list cannot be used without a date or time.

▶ By early ~~p.m.,~~ *afternoon,* all prospective subjects for the experiment had checked in.

P-10c In Notes and Documentation

With only a few exceptions, the names of months, days of the week, colleges and universities, cities, states, and countries should not be abbreviated in the body of an essay. But they often are abbreviated in footnotes and bibliographies; follow the rules of whichever documentation system you are using.

The same applies to Latin abbreviations like "ibid.," "op. cit.," and "et al.": while you may use them in notes and documentation, they're not suitable in the body of your text. Use equivalent English expressions (such as "and others" for "et al.") instead.

▶ Being left-handed presents some challenges for writers—~~e.g.,~~ *for example,* it hurts to write in spiral notebooks, and ink smears across the page and the side of your hand.

P-11 NUMBERS

Numbers may be written with numerals (97) or words (ninety-seven). Spell out numbers and fractions that you can write in one or two words (thirteen, thirty-seven, thirty thousand, two-thirds). Use numerals otherwise (578; 5,788). Spell out any number that begins a sentence. Be aware, however, that the conventions for writing numbers vary across disciplines.

MLA recommends spelling out numbers you can write in one or two words (seventy-seven) and using numerals for other numbers (532). Chicago recommends spelling out whole numbers up to one hundred (twenty-five) and any numbers followed by "hundred," "thousand," or "hundred thousand" (fifty-three thousand), but using numerals for specific numbers above one hundred (101).

● MLA 542–94

▶ In a survey of *two hundred* students, *135* said they spent more than two hours each day writing.

In the social sciences, **APA** generally recommends spelling out numbers zero through nine and using numerals for numbers above ten.

● APA 595–633

▶ We conducted *nine* 40-minute interviews of subjects in *three* categories.

In the sciences, CSE recommends using numerals in almost any situation, but spelling out zero and one to avoid confusion with l and O.

▶ The physician recommended *one* dose of *200* mg per day for *8* days.

In most business writing, spell out numbers one through ten and use numerals for all numbers over ten (ten goals, 11 strategies).

▶ We received *35* applications and identified *five* strong candidates, who we'll interview this week.

For very large numbers that include a fraction or decimal, use a combination of numerals and words.

▶ One retailer sold more than *4.5 million* of its basic T-shirts last year.

In addition, numerals are generally used in the following situations.

ADDRESSES   500 Broadway; 107 175th Street

DATES   December 26, 2019; 632 BCE; the 1990s

MONEY IN EXACT AMOUNTS $3.75; $375,000; a deficit of $3.75 trillion

PARTS OF WRITTEN WORKS   volume 2; Chapter 5; page 82; act 3, scene 3

PERCENTAGES   66 percent (*or* 66%)

RATIOS   16:1 (*or* 16 to 1)

STATISTICS   a median age of 32

TIMES OF DAY   6:20 a.m. (*or* AM)

WHOLE NUMBERS WITH DECIMALS OR FRACTIONS   66.7; 66 2/3; 59½

Credits

PHOTOGRAPHS

Chapter 2: p. 15: deisgorelkin/Depositphotos. **Chapter 3: p. 35:** Jerry Carter. **Chapter 12: p. 93:** Kinsey Glanz; **p. 95:** W. W. Norton; **p. 97:** Leslie Erwin; **p. 102:** Ana-Jamileh Kassfy. **Chapter 13: p. 115:** (top) Erica Shires; (bottom) © 2019 CJ ENM Corporation, Barunson E&A. All rights reserved; **pp. 116–19:** © 2019 © 2019 CJ ENM Corporation, Barunson E&A. All rights reserved. **Chapter 12: p. 120:** Courtesy of Danielle Allen. Laura Rose Photography; **p. 124:** Leonardo Cendamo/ Getty Images; **p. 125:** Dylanhatfield/Shutterstock; **p. 135:** DW labs Incorporated/ Shutterstock; **p. 136:** Toles © 2020 The Washington Post. Reprinted with permission of Andrews McMeel Syndication. All rights reserved; **p. 138:** AP Photo/ Jeffrey Phelps; **p. 139:** Courtesy of Ann C. Johns, Ph.D./University of Texas at Austin. **Chapter 14: p. 146:** Renae Tingling; **p. 151:** Courtesy of Frankie Schembri; **p. 152:** Coki10/Shutterstock; **p. 155:** Michaeleen Doucleff; **p. 156:** Jessica Lutz. **Chapter 15: p. 170:** Courtesy of Ben Wildavsky; **p. 171:** Sarah Reingewirtz, Los Angeles Daily News/SCNG; **p. 175:** Karen McQuait; **p. 179:** Sara Krulwich/The New York Times/Redux; **p. 181:** Chet Mehta. **Chapter 16: p. 200:** Photo courtesy of www.donlaurencephotography.com. **Chapter 17: p. 210:** Techspot.com; **p. 211:** Joel Robinson; **p. 212:** Melinda Sue Gordon/© Apple TV/Courtesy Everett Collection. **Chapter 18: p. 220:** Alissa Morris; **p. 222:** (top) dpa picture alliance/ Alamy Stock Photo; (bottom) Krithika Shrinivas. **Chapter 19: p. 234:** Ryan McLendon. **Chapter 20: pp. 246, 247:** Katia Faroun. **Chapter 21: p. 257:** Anthony Behar/Sipa USA/Alamy Live News. **Chapter 22: p. 270:** Keira Hubschman; **p. 272:** Images courtesy of the Utermohlen Estate and GV Art London; **p. 273:** Brial Diehl. **Chapter 23: p. 281:** (top) Todd Jones; (bottom) Photos provided by *Ohio State Alumni Magazine*, published by The Ohio State University Alumni Association (OSUAA). They appear here with the permission of OSUAA, which retains full ownership of the photos; **p. 283:** Courtesy of Rattan Lal. **Chapter 29: p. 333:** Roman Sigaev/Alamy Stock Photo; **p. 334:** (clockwise from top left) jjspring/depositphotos; ffolas/Depositphotos; John D. Ivanko/Alamy Stock Photo; Charlotte Lake/Shutterstock; lifefoto/Shutterstock; celiafoto/Depositphotos; **p. 336:** Trello; **p. 337:** Trello. **Chapter 30: p. 346:** Alvis Upitis/Alamy Stock Photo. **Chapter 36: p. 388:** (top to bottom) Anna Elesina/Shutterstock; Charlie Blacker/ Alamy Stock Photo; Space Oleandr/Alamy Stock Vector. **Chapter 38: p. 407:** © Reagan Louie; **p. 408:** Art of Al Abbazia. **Chapter 39: p. 419:** All photos © New York Apple Association. **Chapter 40: p. 425:** (left) Peter Unger/Getty Images; (right) Patrick T. Fallon/AFP via Getty Images. **Chapter 41: p. 433:** Photo by Swim Ink 2 LLC/Corbis via Getty Images. **Chapter 42: p. 445:** Michigan Economic

TEXT

Glossary/Index

A

"a," "an," HB-55
"a lot," HB-45
abbreviations
    overview, HB-100–101
    periods with, HB-83
    plural forms, HB-90

abstract A writing GENRE that summarizes a book, an article, or a paper, usually in 100–200 words. Authors in some academic fields must provide, at the top of a report submitted for publication, an abstract of its content. The abstract may then appear in a journal of abstracts, such as *Psychological Abstracts*. An *informative abstract* summarizes a complete report; a briefer *descriptive abstract* provides only a brief overview; a *proposal abstract* (also called a TOPIC PROPOSAL) requests permission to conduct research, write on a topic, or present a report at a scholarly conference.

abstract and concrete words, HB-39
academic fields. *See* field of study
academic habits of mind, 41–51
Academic Search Complete, 497
Academic Search Premier, 497
academic searches, nonlibrary, 491

academic writing, 3–10 Writing done in an academic or scholarly context, such as for course assignments. Key Features: honesty • indication of why your topic matters • evidence that you've considered your subject carefully • careful attention to style expectations
    in arts and humanities, 309–10
    in business, 314–15
    in education, 315–16
    in engineering and technology, 316–18
    in health sciences and nursing, 318–19
    rhetorical situation, 307–8
    in science and mathematics, 311–12
    in social sciences, 312–13

"accept," "except," HB-44
accommodating other viewpoints, 49,
    411–12, 513
acknowledging other viewpoints. *See* multiple perspectives, incorporating
acknowledging sources, 533–36

acknowledgment statement, 68, 363, 537, 649 A brief statement in which a writer recognizes the people and resources that supported their writing processes.
    "across the board," HB-44

action verb, 453, HB-53 A VERB that expresses a physical or mental action (jump, consider).

active voice, 373, HB-17 When a VERB is in the active voice, the SUBJECT performs the action: He sent a gift. *See also* passive voice

---

Note: This glossary/index defines key terms and concepts and directs you to pages in the book where you can find specific information on these and other topics. Please note the words set in SMALL CAPITAL LETTERS are themselves defined in the glossary/index.

arguing a position, 170–96 A writing GENRE that uses REASONS and EVIDENCE to support a CLAIM or POSITION and, sometimes, to persuade an AUDIENCE to accept that position. Key Features: clear and arguable position • necessary background information • valid reasons • convincing evidence • appeals to readers' values • trustworthy TONE • careful consideration of other positions

article, HB-55–56 The word "a," "an," or "the," used to indicate that a NOUN is indefinite (<u>a</u> writer, <u>an</u> author) or definite (<u>the</u> author).

and its corresponding parenthetical **DOCUMEN-TATION**, footnote, or endnote provide minimal information about the source; complete bibliographic information appears in a list of **WORKS CITED** or **REFERENCES** at the end of the text.

"cite," "sight," "site," HB-45

claim, 132, 184–85, 399–403 A statement that asserts a belief or position. In an **ARGUMENT**, a claim needs to be stated in a **THESIS** or clearly implied, and requires support by **REASONS** and **EVIDENCE**.

"The Clan of the One-Breasted Women" (Williams), 459
clarity
    assessing own writing, 363–64
    explaining processes, 452
    pronoun, HB-25
    revising for, 369

Clark, Anna, 405
"Class in America—2003" (Mantsios), HB-78, HB-80, HB-91

classifying and dividing, 326, 417–21 A **STRATEGY** that either groups (classifies) numerous individual items into categories by their similarities (for example, classifying cereal, bread, butter, chicken, cheese, cream, eggs, and oil as carbohydrates, proteins, and fats) or breaks (divides) one large category into small categories (for example, dividing food into carbohydrates, proteins, and fats). Classification and/or division can serve as the **ORGANIZING** principle for a whole text.

characteristics
    clear and distinct categories, 419–20
    rhetorical situation, 420–21

cubing and, 332
essay questions on, 466
guidelines
    classifying, 417–18
    dividing, 418

clause A group of words that consists of at least a **SUBJECT** and a **PREDICATE**; a clause may be either **INDEPENDENT** or **SUBORDINATE**. See also independent clause; subordinate clause
    commas with, HB-77–80
    explicit subject in, HB-5
    as sentence element, HB-5

cliché, 374, HB-38 An expression used so frequently that it is no longer fresh: busy as a bee.

clustering, 330–31 A **PROCESS** for **GENERATING IDEAS AND TEXT**, in which a writer visually connects thoughts by jotting them down and drawing lines between related items.

coding, 16 The process of developing and using a system of codes—like stars or other symbols—to track one's thoughts about a text.

coined pronouns, HB-67
Colicchio, Tom, 430

collaboration, 49–50, 535 The **PROCESS** of working with others.

collective noun A **NOUN**—such as "committee," "crowd," "family," "herd," or "team"—that refers to a group.
    pronoun-antecedent agreement, HB-26–27
    subject-verb agreement, HB-23

colloquial language, HB-37

documentation, 538–41 Publication information about the sources cited in a text. The documentation usually appears in an abbreviated form in parentheses at the point of CITATION or in an endnote or a footnote. Complete documentation usually appears as a list of WORKS CITED or REFERENCES at the end of the text. Documentation styles vary by discipline. For example, Modern Language Association (MLA) style requires an author's complete first name if it appears in a source, whereas American Psychological Association (APA) style requires only the initial of an author's first name.

    abbreviations in, HB-101
    in academic writing, 8
    in annotated bibliographies, 201
    in literary analyses, 231
    parenthetical, punctuation with, HB-87
    styles of, 538–40 (*see also* APA style;
        MLA style)
    in summary and response essays, 31

DOI A digital object identifier, a stable number identifying the location of a source accessed through a database.
    APA style, 603, 605, 608
    documenting, 496
    MLA style, 552, 555

dominant impression The overall effect created through specific details when a writer DESCRIBES something.
    description and, 444
    in profiles, 251, 254

"Don't Make English Official—Ban It
    Instead" (Baron), HB-11

Dorsten, E., 311
Doucleff, Michaeleen, 155–59

drafting, 358–60 The PROCESS of putting words on paper or screen. Writers often write several drafts, REVISING each until they achieve their goal or reach a deadline. At that point, they submit a finished final draft.
    writer's block, 359–60
    writing techniques, 358–59

"Dreams from My President" (Powers),
    344–45
Dzubay, Sarah, 344

E

"each"
    pronoun-antecedent agreement, HB-26
    subject-verb agreement, HB-23
Eastman, Cathi, HB-92
EasyBib, 479
ebooks, 496
"Edible Magic" (Schembri), 151–54
edited academic English, HB-68

editing The PROCESS of fine-tuning a text by examining each word, PHRASE, sentence, and paragraph to be sure that the text is correct and precise and says exactly what the writer intends. *See also* proofreading; revision
    paragraphs, 372–73
    sentences, 373–74
    visuals, 657–58
    words, 374–75

education field, writing for, 315–16
effect. *See* cause and effect
"effect," "affect," HB-45

either-or argument, 414 A logical FALLACY, also known as a FALSE DILEMMA, that oversimplifies by suggesting that only two possible POSITIONS exist on a complex issue.

emotional appeal, 413 In ARGUMENT, an appeal to readers' feelings. Emotional appeals should be used carefully in academic writing, where arguments are often expected to emphasize logical reasons and evidence more than emotion.

e-portfolio, 379–80 An electronic collection of writing and other evidence selected by a writer to show their work, including a statement assessing the work and explaining what it demonstrates.

essential element, HB-78–79 A word, PHRASE, or CLAUSE with information that is necessary for understanding the meaning of a sentence: French is the only language <u>that I can speak</u>.

ethical appeal, 410–13 In ARGUMENT, a way a writer establishes credibility with readers, such as by demonstrating knowledge of the topic; pointing out common ground between the writer's values and those of readers; or incorporating the views of others, including opposing views, into the argument.

evaluation, 210–19 A writing GENRE that makes a judgment about something (for example, a source, poem, film, restaurant) based on certain CRITERIA. Key Features: concise description of the subject • clearly defined criteria • knowledgeable discussion of the subject • balanced and fair assessment • well-supported reasons

evidence, 402–9 In ARGUMENT, the data you present to support your REASONS. Such data may include statistics, calculations, examples, ANECDOTES, QUOTATIONS, case studies, or anything else that will convince your reader that your reasons are compelling. Evidence should be sufficient (enough to show that the reasons have merit) and relevant (appropriate to the argument you're making).

H

interjection, HB-80 A word expressing surprise, resignation, agreement, and other emotions. It can be attached to a sentence or stand on its own: <u>Well</u>, if you insist. <u>Ouch!</u>

interpretation, 127, 226, 230, 327 The act of making sense of something or explaining what one thinks it means. Interpretation is the goal of writing a LITERARY ANALYSIS or TEXTUAL ANALYSIS.

irregular verb, HB-12–13, HB-22 A VERB that does not form its past tense and past participle by adding *-ed* or *-d* to the base form (as in "eat," "ate," "eaten").

layout, 643 The way text is arranged on a
page or screen—for example, in paragraphs,
in lists, on charts, with headings.

learning management system (LMS), 56–58 A web-
based educational tool that brings together all
the course information your instructor wants
you to have, along with communication tools,
drop-boxes, and other features.

"The Negro Speaks of Rivers," 222
reading: "Blanco and Hughes: Rivers
    and Identity," 222–25
strategies for, 399, 465
writing guide, 227–32

literature Literary works—including fiction,
poetry, drama, and some nonfiction; also, the
body of written work produced in a given field.

literature review, 206–13, 306 A GENRE of
writing that surveys and synthesizes the
prior research on a TOPIC. In the sciences,
a literature review is a required part of the
introduction to an IMRAD report; in all disciplines, scholars write article-length literature
reviews devoted to specific topics. Key Features: careful, thorough research • accurate,
objective SUMMARIES of the relevant LITERA-
TURE • synthesis of the scholarship • critical
EVALUATION of the literature • a clear focus
    key features, 208–9
    sample review: "Zombie Film
        Scholarship: A Review of the
        Literature," 206–8
    taking stock, 209

"Little Things Can Mean a Lot" (Petroski),
    349–50

logical appeal, 399–409 In ARGUMENT, an
appeal to readers based on the use of logical reasoning and of evidence such as facts,
statistics, statements from authorities on
the subject, and so on.

logical fallacy. See fallacy, logical
logos. See logical appeal

looping, 330 A PROCESS for GENERATING IDEAS
AND TEXT in which a writer writes about a
topic quickly for several minutes and then
reads the results and writes a one-sentence
summary of the most important or interesting idea. The summary becomes the
beginning of another round of writing and
summarizing, and so on, until the writer
finds a tentative focus for writing.

"loose," "lose," HB-47
Los Angeles Times, HB-40
Lowi, Theodore J., 435, 436
"Lurid Numbers on Glossy Pages!" (Seelye),
    HB-86, HB-98

M

MacKay, Joanna, HB-80
main verbs, HB-14–15
Mairs, Nancy, 439–40
"man," "mankind," HB-47, HB-62
Mantsios, Gregory, 406, HB-78, HB-80,
    HB-9
"many"
    vs. "much," HB-47
    subject-verb agreement and, HB-23
mapping ideas, 330–31
maps, 650, 652
"Marrying Absurd" (Didion), 463, HB-98
masculine pronouns, sexist language and,
    HB-27, HB-62
mathematics, academic writing for, 311–12
"The Mathematics of Christmas" (Devlin),
    405–6
"may," HB-14–15
"may of," "might of," "must of," HB-47
Mayers, Dara, HB-91
McAdory, Paul, 440
McDonie, Andy, 347, HB-86

N

noncount noun, HB-55 A word that names something that cannot be counted or made plural: "information," "rice."

nonessential element, 374, HB-78–79 A word, PHRASE, or CLAUSE that gives additional information but that is not necessary for understanding the basic meaning of a sentence: I learned French, <u>which is a Romance language</u>, online. Nonessential elements should be set off by commas.

noun A word that names a person, place, thing, or idea (teacher, Zadie Smith, forest, Amazon River, notebook, democracy).

O

object A word or phrase that follows a PREPO-SITION or that receives the action of a VERB. In the sentence "I handed him the mail on the table," "him" is an indirect object and "mail" is a direct object of the verb "handed"; "table" is an object of the preposition "on."

organizing Arranging parts of a text so that the text as a whole has COHERENCE. The text may use one STRATEGY throughout or may

outlining, 340 A PROCESS for GENERATING IDEAS AND TEXT or for organizing or examining a text. An *informal outline* simply lists ideas and then numbers them in the order that they will appear; a *working outline* distinguishes supporting from main ideas by indenting the former; a *formal outline* is arranged as a series of headings and indented subheadings, each on a separate line, with letters and numerals indicating relative levels of importance.

pathos. *See* emotional appeal

patterns, 133–34, 226

peer-reviewed scholarly sources, 483, 484.
       See also scholarly research sources

"percent," "percentage," HB-47

perfect tenses, HB-12

periodical articles Magazines, newspapers, and journals that are published regularly.
       APA documentation style, 608–12
       finding
              general indexes and databases, 496–97
              print indexes, 498
              single-subject indexes and databases, 497
       MLA documentation style, 558–66

periods, 525, HB-83, HB-86

permalink, 201, 489 A URL that permanently links to a specific web page or blog post.

person
       agreement in, HB-21–22
       shift in, HB-35
personal attack. *See* ad hominem argument

personal narrative, 234–45 A GENRE that focuses on something significant from the writer's past. Key Features: well-told story • vivid details • clear significance
       choosing, 81
       combining genres in, 83
       key features, 240–41
       with other genres, 286
       reading: "The Definition of Love," 234–40
       strategies for, 395, 439, 441, 447, 655
       writing guide, 241–45

person-first language, HB-58 A way of referring to individuals (or groups) with specific characteristics without defining them by those characteristics. "An enslaved person" rather than a "slave." Some people may prefer to be described using IDENTITY-FIRST LANGUAGE; if you don't know their preference, use person-first language.

Peters, Emma, 449–50

Petroski, Henry, 349–50

Petrusich, Amanda, HB-39

photographs, 508–9, 535, 648–49

phrasal verbs, HB-14, HB-19–21

phrase, HB-6, HB-77–78, HB-79 A group of words that lacks a SUBJECT, a VERB, or BOTH.

pie charts, 651

place, prepositions of, HB-49–50

place names, commas with, HB-80

plagiarism, 533–37 The use of another person's words, ideas, or sentence structures without appropriate credit and DOCUMENTA-TION. Plagiarism is a serious breach of ethics.

Plan B 2.0: Rescuing a Planet under Stress and a Civilization in Trouble (Brown), 404, 423

plurals
       apostrophes with, HB-90
       and gendered pronouns, HB-64
podcast
       annotated bibliography, 205
       documenting, APA style, 619
       documenting, MLA style, 579
       evaluation, 219
       exploration, 278–79
       literary analyses, 232
       position papers, 192

proofreading, 375–76 The final **PROCESS** of writing, when a writer checks for correct spelling and punctuation as well as for page order, missing text, and consistent use of **FONTS**. *See also* editing; revision; rewriting

proposal, 257–69 A **GENRE** that argues for a solution to a problem or suggests some action. Key Features: well-defined problem • recommended solution • convincing argument for your solution • responses to anticipated questions • call to action • appropriate **TONE**. *See also* topic proposal

pull quote, 646 A brief excerpt set off within a text in order to highlight certain information. Pull quotes are often set in a different **FONT** or color.

purpose, 73–74 A writer's goal: to explore ideas, to express oneself, to entertain, to demonstrate learning, to inform, to persuade, and so on. Purpose is one element of the RHETORICAL SITUATION.

Q

qualifying word, 401, HB-50 A word such as "frequently," "often," "generally," "sometimes," or "rarely" that limits a CLAIM in some way.

questioning A PROCESS of GENERATING IDEAS AND TEXT about a topic—asking, for example, "What?," "Who?," "When?," "Where?," "How?," and "Why?" or other questions.

response, 372–74 A **PROCESS** of writing in which a reader gives the writer their thoughts about the writer's title, beginning, **THESIS**, support and **DOCUMENTATION**, **ORGANIZING**, **STANCE**, treatment of **AUDIENCE**, achievement of **PURPOSE**, handling of the **GENRE**, ending, and other matters.

résumé A GENRE that summarizes someone's academic and employment history, generally written to submit to potential employers. Key Features: organization that suits goals and experience • succinctness • design that highlights key information. *See* the ebook at digital.wwnorton.com/fieldguide7h for a chapter on Résumés and Job Letters.

> parallelism in, HB-32–33
> reverse chronological order, 458

"Rethinking the Meat-Guzzler" (Bittman), 403

reverse chronological order, 458

reviews of scholarly literature. *See* literature reviews

revision, 367–70 The PROCESS of making substantive changes to a draft so that it contains all the necessary content and presents it in an appropriate organization. During revision, writers generally move from whole-text issues to details with the goals of sharpening their focus and strengthening their position.

rewriting, 370–71 A PROCESS of composing a new draft from another perspective—with a different POINT OF VIEW, AUDIENCE, STANCE, GENRE, or MEDIUM, for example.

rhetorical context, 18

rhetorical situation, 10, 73–90 The CONTEXT in which writing or other communication takes place, including PURPOSE, AUDIENCE, GENRE, STANCE, and MEDIA/DESIGN.

> elements of
> > audience, 75–78

> > genre, 79–84
> > media/design, 88–90, 639, 640–41
> > purpose, 73–74
> > stance, 85–87
> > visuals, 648
> fields of study, 307–8

genres and
> annotated bibliographies, 201–2
> essay exams, 465–66
> evaluations, 216
> explorations, 276–77
> literacy narratives, 105–6
> literary analyses, 227
> memoirs, 242
> portfolios, 377–78
> position papers, 187
> presentations, 664
> profiles, 252
> proposals, 265
> remixes, 287–88
> reports, 162
> research, 474–75
> textual analyses, 128

processes and
> arguments, 409, 415–16
> cause-and-effect analysis, 398
> classification and division, 420–21
> comparison and contrast, 427–28
> definition, 438
> description, 445–46
> dialogue, 450–51
> narration, 464
> process explanation, 454–55

reading across fields of study, 296–97

reflecting on, 384–85

rhetorical reading, 18–19

Richardson, Heather Cox, 341–42

vantage point, 443–44 The physical position from which a writer DESCRIBES something.

verb, HB-10–21 A word that expresses an action (dance, talk) or a state of being (be, seem). A verb is an essential element of a sentence or CLAUSE. Verbs have four forms: base form (smile), past tense (smiled), past participle (smiled), and present participle (smiling). *See also* subject-verb agreement

The Norton Writer's Prize

"I have something to say to the world, and I have taken English 12 in order to say it well." —**W. E. B. Du Bois**

The Norton Writer's Prize recognizes outstanding original nonfiction by undergraduates. All entries are considered for possible publication in Norton texts—in fact, many of the essays that appear in this book were nominated for the prize.

The contest is open to students age 17 and above who are enrolled in an accredited 2- or 4-year college or university. Three cash prizes of $1,000 apiece are awarded annually for coursework submitted during the academic year, one in each of the following three categories:

- Writing by a first-year student in a 2- or 4-year college or university
- Writing by a student in a 2-year college or university
- Writing by a student in a 4-year college or university

Submissions must be between 1,000 and 3,000 words in length. Literacy narratives, literary and other textual analyses, reports, profiles, evaluations, arguments, memoirs, proposals, multimodal pieces, and other forms of original nonfiction will be considered if written by a student age 17 or above in fulfillment of an undergraduate course requirement at an eligible institution. Entries submitted in accordance with the Official Contest Rules will be considered for all applicable prizes, but no more than one prize will be awarded to any single entry.

For full contest rules, eligibility, and instructions on how to enter or nominate students, please visit **wwnorton.com/norton-writers-prize**. For questions, please email us at **composition@wwnorton.com**

A Directory to MLA Style

A Directory to APA Style

Handbook Menu